Statistics

Statistics

A Tool for Understanding Society

Ivy Lee
California State University
Sacramento

Minako Maykovich
California State University
Sacramento

Allyn and Bacon
Boston • London • Toronto • Sydney • Tokyo • Singapore

Senior Editor: Karen Hanson
Vice President, Publisher: Susan Badger
Production Administrator: Marjorie Payne
Editorial Assistant: Sarah Dunbar
Cover Administrator: Linda Knowles
Composition/Prepress Buyer: Linda Cox
Manufacturing Buyer: Megan Cochran
Editorial-Production Service: Raeia Maes
Marketing Manager: Joyce Nilsen

Copyright © 1995 by Allyn and Bacon
A Division of Paramount Publishing
160 Gould Street
Needham Heights, Massachusetts 02194

This book is printed on
recycled, acid-free paper.

Library of Congress Cataloging-in-Publication Data

Lee, Ivy.
    Statistics: a tool for understanding society/Ivy Lee, Minako Maykovich.
        p. cm.
    Includes bibliographical references and index.
    ISBN 0-205-13961-2
    1. Statistics.   I. Maykovich, Minako K.   II. Title
QA276.12.L44 1995
001.4′22′0243—dc20   94-4804
                                                      CIP

Printed in the United States of America

10 9 8 7 6 5 4 3 2 1   99 98 97 96 95 94

To my parents Lee Sai Wing and Pang Choi Mei

Ivy Lee

and

To my parents Kihachiro and Yasuko Kurokawa
and to my husband John J. Maykovich

Minako Maykovich

Brief Contents

Contents

Preface

From years of teaching introductory and graduate statistics courses in the social sciences, we believe students will benefit from a text that adopts an approach that integrates substantive, methodological, and statistical concerns. During the formative stage of the project, we searched for a central theme around which to organize the text. The organization we envisioned would provide students maximum linkage from chapter to chapter so that they would not be left with the impression that the field consists of ever-so-many discrete topics that are beyond their ability to put altogether. Thus we decided to attempt a different approach in this text. Not only would we present statistics within the perspective of doing research in the social sciences, but we would also superimpose a framework on the topics by tying them together through a central character called Anne. Anne is, above all, a researcher in the social science tradition who uses statistics to help her understand the world around her. We realize that this format is unusual. However, there are a number of associated gains. The teaching of techniques becomes grounded on the projects Anne conducts; students have the opportunity to "look over the shoulder" of someone who is doing statistics and acquiring information that they might not otherwise have.

Statistics: A Tool for Understanding Society is written primarily for an undergraduate first course in statistics. It is, however, a multilevel text, since more advanced topics are covered and we focus on the "why" rather than the "how" of statistical analysis. The text is therefore also appropriate for an introductory course at the intermediate level.

Among the important skills that students can gain from a statistics course is the ability to select and then apply the appropriate procedures and, finally, to interpret the results. Consequently, throughout the text we focus on the nature and characteristics of statistical techniques, their underlying assumptions, and their applicability to specific problems to help students develop these skills. Although our approach is both conceptual and analytical, we avoid the use of mathematical terms and explanations whenever possible. In this manner, we attempt to develop a text that is highly readable for students who are not sophisticated in mathematics.

To reinforce the learning from the text, three types of problems and exercises are provided with most chapters: computational problems, Statistical Package for the Social Sciences (SPSS) exercises, and general conceptual problems. The computational problems provide the reader with hands-on experience in using and calculating the formulas. Their main purpose is to help students develop an in-depth understanding of these formulas. However, because these problems are constructed to be solved with a hand calculator alone, they are based on unrealistically simple data with a small number of cases.

A more realistic experience to data analysis may be obtained from the SPSS exercises. These are so called because they can be solved using either the mainframe version of the Statistical Package for the Social Sciences or the personal computer version called SPSS/PC+. The exercises are structured around two real-life data sets. The first is the data set from the 1991 General Social Survey (GSS), an annual public opinion poll conducted on a national sample of approximately 1,500 respondents and covering a wide range of social issues. A sample is taken from this data set to include only 50 variables and 500 cases. To add to the variety of data contained in the GSS, a second data set is provided. This set consists of aggregated data that appear in the county and city data book of the *Statistical Abstract of the United States*, describing the demographic and socioeconomic characteristics of 955 cities with 25,000 or more inhabitants.

The text provides instructions on both SPSS and SPSS/PC+. Students should determine the computer hardware and the SPSS version to which they have access. The mainframe version runs on a wide variety of computers; therefore, before starting to tackle these exercises, students who plan to use this version should also obtain information specific to loading and submitting SPSS programs on their mainframe. Students who do not have access to either version may use other programs such as SAS, BMDP, or MINITAB since the data are written in ASCII.

Finally, the general conceptual problems at the end of each chapter do not require any computation. They are meant to test students' understanding of statistical concepts and techniques, their characteristics, and their appropriateness to solving specific research questions.

Many people have contributed to the writing of this text. In particular, we appreciate the support provided by our colleagues Louise Kanter, Andres Rendon, and Judson Landis of California State University, Sacramento. To our reviewers, Lawrence G. Felice, Baylor University; William Kelly, University of Texas—Austin; Mike Lacy, Colorado State University; Jon Lorence, University of Houston; Ruth Seydlitz, University of New Orleans; and Paul Vogt, State University of New York at Albany, we owe thanks for their many helpful critiques, comments, and suggestions.

We are grateful to the various publishers and authors who have kindly given us permission to reprint some of the tables in Appendix B. We acknowledge the Literary Executor of the late Sir Ronald A. Fisher, F.R.S., Dr. Frank R. Yates, F.R.S., and the Longman Group Ltd., London, for their permission to reprint Tables 3 and 5 from their book *Statistical Tables for Biological, Agricultural and Medical Research* (6th ed., 1974).

Last but not least, we would like to express our sincere thanks to our editor, Karen Hanson, and the entire editorial and production staff at Allyn and Bacon.

I.L.

M.M.

Statistics

$Part$ I

Descriptive Statistics

Chapter 1
Statistics and the Research Process

Chapter 2
Organizing and Presenting Univariate Data

Chapter 3
Describing Univariate Data

Chapter 4
Organizing and Describing Nominal and Ordinal Bivariate Data

Chapter 5
Organizing and Describing Interval Bivariate Data

Chapter 1

Statistics and the Research Process

Statistics is a branch of mathematics that deals with the analysis and interpretation of data collected from the world around us. Like most introductory texts on the subject, this book endeavors to explain the various elementary statistical techniques and their applications. Unlike most introductory texts, however, this book considers statistics from both a mathematical and a research methodological point of view.

Typical social science majors may open this book with trepidation, convinced that they do not like statistics. A statistics course may be a necessary evil to be endured in order to obtain a B.A. or B.S. degree. Once the course is over, the students can forget all about statistics to concentrate on the substantive areas of their disciplines. However, this conception of the role of statistics could not be more erroneous. Statistics is central to the research process, just as the research process lies at the heart of the social sciences. Certainly, if the disciplines are serious about their claims as sciences, then, like every science, they must obtain their answers through research.

While acknowledging the vital role of statistics in research, many social scientists have not impressed on their students a clear linkage between the two. Statistics is often taught as a set of self-contained techniques that stands apart from other substantive concerns in the disciplines. Within this tradition, statistics becomes an end in itself, rather than the indispensable tool that it truly is—a tool that enables social scientists to explore and learn about their world.

This text is written to facilitate the teaching of statistics as an integral part of the research process. Only when the relationship is established between statistics and research and between research and the social sciences can we proceed to discuss in a meaningful manner specific statistical techniques. Throughout the text the aim is to present statistics within the context of the social sciences.

Statistics may be in the foreground, but the social sciences are never far in the background.

Hence, this text will begin with a chapter on the research process. To illustrate the various stages of conducting research, we will draw primarily on an investigation of the homeless by Peter H. Rossi, James D. Wright, Gene A. Fisher, and Georgiana Willis. This project explores a national problem that requires our immediate attention. Its methodology is sound, and the statistics employed are easily comprehended. The results of the investigation are summarized in an article that appeared in *Science* in 1987 [1], and a more detailed account was published in a book by Rossi entitled *Down and Out in America* in 1989 [2].

A careful reading of this chapter is necessary to grasp the process of research and the role of statistics at each stage. Students may not comprehend the statistical aspects of the presentation immediately, but they should not worry, because these ideas are repeated and elaborated on in subsequent chapters. This chapter is meant to serve both as an introduction and an overview, to which students may return as needed to regain a perspective on the research process in which statistics play such a vital role.

1.1 The Research Process

The ultimate goal of science is to arrive at an understanding of the world in which we live. This aim is by no means unique, for it is shared by other human endeavors such as mythology and religion. What is unique about science is how it proposes to achieve this goal. Scientists develop **theories,** abstract ideas that explain how the world works. They then rely on research to confirm or disconfirm these theories. **Research,** therefore, is a systematic activity that scientists engage in to validate abstract ideas using evidence gathered by our senses. Although theories differ, the method of doing research is the same across disciplines as diverse as the social and physical sciences.

Since research is based on observable data, it is an **empirical** venture; that is, the value of scientific ideas is tested by evidence obtained through our senses. Testable ideas are those that can be linked to observable phenomena. Ideas that cannot be tested empirically are put aside into the province of nonscientific concerns.

Second, as a systematic activity, research is governed by an underlying logic that transcends the boundaries of specific disciplines. Its procedures are rationalized into a number of sequential stages. Furthermore, as the researcher attempts to validate his or her ideas through empirical evidence, the process takes place on two different planes: one plane involves the abstract and theoretical, and the other, the concrete and observational. Logic binds together the researcher's operations on these planes by spelling out the implications of the work on one level for the other. Thus research and, therefore, science have both a **logical** and an empirical foundation.

As the defining activity of science, research has the same goal as science: to pursue knowledge. This pursuit can be realized through a full **description** of and, then, a precise **explanation** for the phenomenon of interest. For example, a researcher may first describe the homeless to be predominantly males and then try to explain why men are more likely to be homeless than women. Research, therefore, has the twin functions of description and explanation. These are intertwined goals with most research involving elements of both.

Description constitutes the first step toward acquiring scientific knowledge. One aspect of description involves classifying the world into meaningful categories. To accomplish this, the social scientist first formulates the abstract ideas that she or he has about a phenomenon into clear and precise concepts. "Social class" is such a formulated concept in the social sciences. It divides society into distinct subgroups with different life-styles and life chances. Using this concept, the social scientist may characterize U.S. society as being predominantly middle class.

A classification is most useful when it highlights the interconnections among various classes of phenomena. In showing that that social classes have different values and behaviors, the social scientist establishes an **association** between social class and these traits. The social scientist describes this association when observing, for example, how, with respect to economic issues, members of the middle class are more conservative than members of the lower class.

Thus, in description, the social scientist may focus on one class of phenomenon such as the class structure of a society. Or she or he may delineate the association between two or more classes of phenomena, such as the relationship between middle-class status and economic conservatism. By relating these two concepts, the social scientist takes the first step toward explaining a social attitude such as economic conservatism.

The explanatory goal of science is realized when the researcher moves from the empirical evidence of an association toward establishing a **cause and effect relationship.** The concept of causal relationship is important. For in finding the cause(s) for a phenomenon, the scientist can consider it explained and its dynamics understood. But what is a causal relationship and how can the scientist document its existence? In the preceding example, social class is considered the cause of economic conservatism if it has an impact on an individual's inclination toward economic conservatism. Obviously, the "impact" cannot be observed, only the joint occurrence [3] of social class and economic conservatism. Thus causal linkages cannot be verified on empirical grounds alone. However, on the empirical level the researcher can examine whether the association is genuine or spurious (false). Many people attain middle-class status when reaching a certain age, and by that time they might have also grown conservative. If this is the case, that is, if middle-class status and economic conservatism are a direct result of aging, and not of each other, then the association between the two is spurious. By reconfirming or invalidating the original association under different conditions— in this case by reexamining the effects of social class after eliminating those of age—the scientist has a more or less solid foundation for inferring a causal relationship.

Ultimately, causal links are established in conjunction with systems of abstract ideas called theories. A theory provides a framework to interpret empirical findings and to reconcile seemingly disparate observations. It gives a coherent explanation of a facet of society by answering the questions of why and how in the mind of the scientist and observer. Durkheim, for instance, collected statistics on suicide rates; he then found associations between these rates and diverse factors such as religion and marital status. To explain these associations, he developed a theory of suicide which states that the rate of suicide depends on the level of social integration. Individuals grouped by different religious and marital statuses exhibit varying degrees of integration and therefore different suicide rates [4]. Thus, by establishing a causal link between suicide rates and levels of social integration, the theory explains the associations found between suicide rates and factors such as marital and religious status.

The relationship between theory and research is reciprocal. A theory not only provides a context for making sense out of empirical observations; it also raises new questions for research to answer. Research, on the other hand, is crucial to the effort of theory formulation; it is used to confirm or disconfirm some of the abstract ideas embedded in a theory. This relationship can be seen clearly in the work of Durkheim and other sociologists since his time who have extended the scope of his theory on suicide by extensive research.

1.1.1 Stages of the Research Process

For a more thorough understanding of the research process, each of its six stages should be carefully examined. These stages are:

1. Selection of a topic and review of the literature
2. Formulation of research questions
3. Design of measurement procedures
4. Design of sampling procedures
5. Actual observation and collection of data from the sample
6. Analysis of the data and evaluation of the research questions

How does statistics fit into this overall scheme? Statistics, of course, cannot resolve all research problems. However, if the research involves the observation of a number of cases, then statistics should probably enter into the overall research plan. Except for the selection of topic, statistics plays a crucial role in every stage of the research process. It has implications for how a sample should be selected, how abstract concepts are measured in observable units, how the data are analyzed, and how the obtained information is interpreted to evaluate a researcher's ideas.

The rest of this chapter will be devoted to an elaboration of these stages. Before we proceed, a word of caution is in order. On paper, the division of the research process into stages is tenable; in practice, the steps often overlap. Furthermore, the discussion of the procedures and the strategy involved in each step may be clear-cut when, in actuality, the work is full of compromises. However, without these compromises and ambiguities, the job of the researcher would surely be dull and routine!

1.2 Topic Selection and Literature Review

Social science research begins with a perceived need for more information in an area of interest. A researcher may want to learn more about the problem of drug addiction, the extent of inequalities in our society, or the voting patterns in a community. In these examples, a topic of concern is specified. It may be as broadly defined as the issue of social inequalities or as narrowly focused as the question of support for a specific bill. Rossi, Wright, Fisher, and Willis identified the homeless as their research concern, noting that the plight of these individuals has claimed the attention of social scientists and the nation alike.

Once a problem area is selected, the investigator undertakes a survey of what is known on the subject in order to formulate more precisely what she or he wishes to know. The researcher may talk with leading experts in the field, search for relevant media articles, and/or rely on introspection from personal experience. However, the most fruitful source of information available to a scientist is the accumulated body of research findings and theories in the field. A review of this literature is most likely to yield the insights on which a researcher can build his or her project.

For descriptive research, the review is often a matter of surveying the accumulated knowledge in the area. For explanatory research, the review extends to a search for theories that will help the researcher construct a hypothetical causal scheme to account for the phenomenon under study. In disciplines such as sociology where few theories exist, **theoretical perspectives** may serve the same purpose. According to Skidmore,

> *Perspectives are collections of concepts which are important basically as "sensitizing" agents. They point out important isolated aspects of reality. [5]*

Unlike a theory, a theoretical perspective falls short of providing an internally consistent explanation; it merely suggests important processes to consider when formulating an explanation. Not all social scientists would agree with our definition of a theoretical perspective or of a theory; in fact, these two terms are often used interchangeably.

There are many theoretical perspectives in sociology. We have chosen to focus on three in this text: functionalism, conflict dynamics, and symbolic interactionism. See Box 1.1. Let us consider how these theoretical perspectives could provide guidelines for researching homelessness. A functionalist may consider homelessness as an unintended consequence of urban renewal. More specifically, the

---

Box 1.1   **Theoretical Perspectives in Sociology**

Functionalism

Integrated system: Society is examined as a system of interrelated and interdependent parts.

Key concepts include:
  Function: Every part or structure of the social system contributes to its maintenance.
  Equilibrium: The social system maintains balance and stability even in the face of disturbance.
  Consensus: A central value system shared by everyone holds society together.

Conflict Theory

Change: Society is in a constant process of change based on a cycle of conflict generation and conflict resolution.

Key concepts include:
  Inequality: Societal resources, such as wealth and power, are divided unevenly among various groups.

Conflict: Groups with opposing interests are constantly vying for these scarce resources, resulting in changes in the statuses of these groups and in society.
  Power: Groups in power enforce their preferred social arrangements upon others.

Symbolic Interactionism

Interaction: Society is constructed and interpreted through the face-to-face interaction of individuals.

Key concepts include:
  Symbol: Individuals exchange symbolic cues that have agreed-upon meanings in their interactions.
  Definition of the situation: Interaction is also dependent on individuals' interpretation of a situation according to their own perception of social reality.
  Self: Individuals' perceptions of themselves are formed through their interactions with others.

---

destruction of low-income housing units in downtown areas, their replacement with nondwelling units or with middle-income housing, and the inflation of rental cost in the past decade have led to an unprecedented increase in the homeless population. From the conflict perspective, homelessness may be the result of competition for physical space between two naturally opposing groups, the developers and the marginally housed. Although the two perspectives deal with the same problem, their hypothesized social dynamics are very different. According to the former, urban revitalization that is beneficial to society has produced some unforeseen problems; according to the latter, group struggle for limited space has resulted in a victory for the middle class. Finally, a symbolic interactionist may be interested in studying the dynamics of managing a homeless existence: for instance, how the homeless individual perceives, rationalizes, and incorporates his or her existential condition in dealing with others and self. Not all three perspectives raise questions that are amenable to statistical analysis. Symbolic interactionism, for example, often uses a more qualitative approach to study the dynamics that are specific to a situation.

Sometimes a literature review yields so little information on a subject that the application of a theory or theoretical perspective to the problem is of questionable value. Unable to build on previous work, the researcher must proceed to gain an initial familiarity with the topic. The type of descriptive work conducted under such circumstances is called an **exploratory study.** The work of Rossi and his coauthors is basically exploratory in nature. Their review of the literature revealed little information about the homeless, despite the fact that homelessness is recognized as a serious and growing problem. They did not, therefore, explicitly adopt a particular theoretical perspective in their work.

As part of the review, the researcher identifies the key concepts that will be employed in his or her project. The meanings of the concepts are then clarified through **conceptual definitions.** The investigator may choose to rely on existing conceptual definitions or define his or her own terms. Homelessness, a key concept in the Rossi project, had no agreed-upon definition. Accordingly, the authors formulated a conceptual definition of their own: the homeless were "those who do not have customary and regular access to a conventional dwelling or residence" [6].

Once the investigator arrives at a conceptual definition, she or he proceeds to examine its clarity and utility. The conceptual definition of homelessness was crucial to the Rossi study. For unless they could delineate the homeless population with their definition, the researchers could not begin to collect and analyze data and/or specify the precise dimensions of the problem. In examining their formulation, they found that their initial conceptualization was inadequate to comprehend a complex phenomenon, a rather common occurrence in research. Their initial definition treated homelessness as an all-or-none phenomenon and did not take into account the ambiguous cases. These were the marginally housed, for example, people who were too poor to rent and lived with a relative or friend or in a van.

Instead of revising their definition to allow for a more precise classification of these cases, the researchers chose to circumvent the ambiguities by limiting its application to the "literally homeless" [7]. This group could be easily identified and was likely to be the target for social welfare policy goals. Decisions to restrict the scope of the research are often based on such practical considerations as these. Limiting the scope of an investigation has the added advantage of permitting a more precise statement of the research questions. This narrowing of focus to manageable proportions is an often repeated process as the project progresses.

Exercises

1. Select a research problem on campus, such as students' attitudes toward tuition increase.
   a. Apply three theoretical perspectives to explain the attitudes.
   b. What aspects of the issue would each perspective focus on for research?

1.3 Formulation of Research Questions

A review of the literature helps the scientist formulate the research problem in the form of a **research question** (or questions). The research question states what the researcher wants to learn from the project and therefore determines its boundaries. Although Rossi and his coauthors did not phrase their problem as such, we have abstracted the following research questions from their article:

1. How many homeless people were there in Chicago on a daily and on an annual basis?
2. What were the characteristics of the homeless?

Sometimes, in posing a question, the researcher goes further and develops a tentative answer for it known as a **hypothesis.** Hypotheses are seldom found in exploratory and descriptive studies, because the researcher's main intent is to find an answer rather than to hazard one. Therefore, as expected, the Rossi study provided no tentative solutions to the questions. However, for the sake of illustration, we have developed a plausible hypothesis with regard to the first question:

The homeless constitute one-tenth of the population in poverty in Chicago.

Once the research question is formulated, it guides the investigation by first establishing the appropriate **units** for observation and analysis. These units, also known as **cases,** are entities about which the researcher gathers information. They range from individuals, objects, and events to groups and geographical areas. The units in the Rossi study were individuals and, more specifically, homeless individuals in Chicago.

The researcher next considers how the research question can be resolved through empirical evidence. This involves translating the abstract concepts of the study into empirically observable phenomena called **indicators.** The conversion is accomplished through an **operational definition** of the abstract concept. As an example, let us consider how the Rossi study operationally defined "homelessness." The researchers first identified two subgroups to be included under the term of the "literal homeless": those who spend the night in shelters for the homeless and those who spend the night on the street in "nondwelling unit places" [8]. They further narrowed the scope of the study to the city of Chicago. Together with specified procedures to count the homeless, which will be discussed under sampling designs in Section 1.5, the researchers provided a complete operational definition of the literal homeless. This definition tied the abstract notion of homelessness to specific, observable indicators, such as spending the night in shelters or on the streets. With their definition, the researchers could now identify the homeless in Chicago, the units of analysis for their study.

Often the indicators of interest are observable characteristics that vary from one unit of analysis to the next. Hence the term **variable** is used to refer to these indicators. For example, homelessness in the Rossi study was a variable and an individual in Chicago could be in one of two states: literally homeless or not. If everyone was on the streets in Chicago, then homelessness would not be a variable but a **constant** characteristic.

In analyzing the relevant variables, the researcher may arrive at an answer to his or her research question. Whether a simple or complex statistical analysis is needed depends on the research question itself. It is in this sense that the question guides the investigation and determines its scope. To answer their first question, Rossi and his co-workers needed a distribution of homelessness, that is, a classification of Chicago residents into those who were literally homeless and those who were not and a count, especially, of the former group.

In response to the second question, the Rossi study proposed to describe the homeless group by gender, ethnicity, age, length of poverty, and so on. Homelessness was no longer a variable with reference to this second question but a constant. However, the traits of the homeless, such as age, source of income, and length of homelessness, were variables since they varied from one homeless person to another. The process of taking one characteristic at a time and obtaining information about it is called **univariate analysis.**

While the two research questions delineated the **descriptive** or fact-finding mission of the project, the researchers were also interested in charting a course for further studies. In their section "An Interpretation of Homelessness," they wrote,

> *First, literal homelessness typically results from extreme poverty in housing markets with an inadequate supply of low-cost housing, especially for single persons. . . . The homeless are therefore best seen as the long-term very poor who cannot be taken care of by friends and family . . . and who have been unable, for a variety of reasons, to establish households of their own. . . . All of these factors—chronic extreme poverty, lack of support or rejection by family and friends, difficulty in establishing their own households—are in turn likely to be connected to their disabilities. [9]*

The paragraph can be taken as a hypothesis to account for homelessness and can be diagrammed as in Figure 1.1.

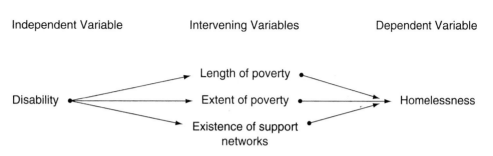

FIGURE 1.1   **Variables in Explaining Homelessness**

Had Rossi and his coauthors tested this hypothesis, their study would have been **explanatory** as well as descriptive. For the hypothesis implied an explanation of homelessness through establishing a causal link between one or more variables and homelessness. To test such a hypothesis, univariate analysis would no longer suffice, and a more complex type of analysis would be needed. The analysis may be **bivariate,** which takes into account two variables at a time, or **multivariate,** which takes into account more than two variables at a time.

Although the distinction is unnecessary in univariate analysis, it is often useful to differentiate the statuses of the variables included in a bivariate or multivariate analysis. In Figure 1.1, the variable homelessness, which the researchers sought to explain (or predict), is known as the **dependent variable.** Disability is the **independent variable**—the variable viewed as having a direct and/or indirect impact on the dependent variable. In this case, the effect of the independent on the dependent variable is indirect, because it is channeled through **intervening variables** such as length and extent of poverty and the existence of a support network.

If disability were not brought into the explanatory scheme, these intervening variables would be considered independent variables. Thus the status of a variable is fluid, not fixed, depending on how the researcher dissects social reality. A dependent variable, the variable to be explained in one study, may become an independent variable, the variable that does the explaining, in another study. In addition, in narrowing the focus of a study, the researcher may deliberately leave out some independent or intervening variables that have a weaker impact on the dependent variable. For the purpose of the study, they are considered inessential to its explanatory scheme and are put into a residual category known as **extraneous variables.**

Note that the explanatory scheme proposed by the Rossi study in Figure 1.1 is not the only one possible, given the variables. For example, it is equally logical to propose the chain of events involving the same variables as shown in Figure 1.2. A hypothesis, therefore, represents a tentative and not necessarily a final answer to a research problem.

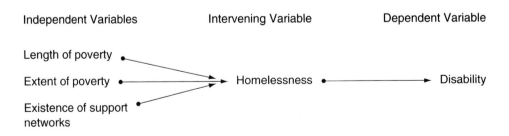

FIGURE 1.2   Another Causal Model Based on the Same Variables

Exercises

2. Restate the research questions in Exercise 1 into research hypotheses.

3. Then identify the independent and dependent variables in these hypotheses. What are some of the intervening and extraneous variables?

4. Select some question that has been puzzling you in your social life. Outline a research project that will help you resolve it.

5. Interpret the social phenomenon in Exercise 4 from the functionalist, conflict, and interactionist perspectives.

6. Restate the research question in Exercise 4 in terms of a research hypothesis.

7. Identify the independent, dependent, and intervening variables, if any, in your project.

1.4 Measurement of Variables

Having provided operational definitions of the relevant concepts, the researcher moves on to the problem of measuring the variables. **Measurement** is the process through which units are classified into categories according to their properties, and numbers or symbols are assigned to these units for analysis. Thus the variable of marital status may be measured by such symbols as "married" and "not married," and the degree of physical disability of the homeless may be measured by such numbers as 1, 2, 3, 4, and 5. Such a *set* of numbers or symbols representing the empirical properties of the units is called a **scale.** For example, in measuring the state of mental health of the homeless, the Rossi study used the individual's length of stay in a mental hospital as an indicator. Here the scale refers to the range of numbers representing the days the homeless individuals could possibly stay in the hospital. The *individual number* or symbol is called a **datum** or **score.** A score in this case refers to the number of days a particular homeless individual stayed in the hospital. These data or scores are the raw materials that statistical procedures analyze. Therefore, statistical considerations figure prominently in the measurement procedures of a research project.

Different traits and different ways of measuring these traits result in data that carry different amounts of information. Consider the variable "length of stay in the hospital." Measured in terms of categories such as "long" versus "short," it would convey much less information than if it were measured in terms of actual days. Such a difference in the amount of information conveyed constitutes what is known as the **measurement level.**

There are four levels of measurement: nominal, ordinal, interval, and ratio. Each level conveys a different amount of information. The information is cumulative in nature, with a higher level containing the information of the lower level and more. Thus the term *levels* of measurement applies.

Statistical techniques vary according to the amounts of information they require of the data. To select the appropriate statistical techniques for analysis, the researcher should know the measurement level of the data. Conversely, if the researcher proposes to use a particular statistical procedure, she or he should ensure that the data meet the measurement requirements of the technique.

1.4.1 Nominal Measurement

The lowest level of measurement is the nominal scale; as such it conveys the least information. A nominal variable contains a minimum of two **categories,** each denoting a particular *attribute* or *state* of a variable. An example of a nominal variable is the gender of the homeless. This variable has two states, male and female. To measure gender means to classify the homeless in the two categories of males and females. Individuals who are similar with respect to an attribute are sorted into the same category, whereas those who are different are sorted into different categories. Thus the information conveyed in nominal measurement pertains to the equivalence or nonequivalence of units.

Other examples of nominal variables used in the study of the homeless are marital status and ethnicity. All these variables are inherently nominal since there can be no question of the amounts involved. Therefore, some social scientists refer to this level as qualitative measurement and to nominal variables as **categorical variables.**

Although there is no rule regarding the number of categories to use for a nominal variable, there are two rules with respect to the construction of these categories. The categories should be mutually exclusive and exhaustive. When the classification scheme is **mutually exclusive,** a case can be sorted into one and only one category. When it is **exhaustive,** every case can be and is sorted into one category, and no case is left unclassified.

The particular procedure of assigning numbers or symbols to represent the categories of a variable is known as **coding.** Nominal categories are sometimes coded in letters, such as "M" for males and "F" for females. When numbers are assigned, a key to the numbers is usually given. For example, the key may read "1 = married," "2 = separated," and so on. Because they are representations of the categories of a nominal variable, these numbers have the same property as the categories. All that is indicated by these numbers is equivalence or nonequivalence, and not quantity or amount. Thus, to assume that "2" is larger than "1" would be erroneous in this case. The assignment of numbers to particular categories is arbitrary; a "4" could represent "married" as well as a "1" or "2." The number chosen to denote a particular category is unimportant for there is no inherent order or magnitude to the categories.

1.4.2 Ordinal Measurement

The categories of an ordinal variable are sometimes referred to as **ranks.** As the term implies, there is an inherent order to these categories because they represent different amounts of a trait. However, although their order is known, the *exact* amounts of the trait measured by these categories are not determined. The health status of the homeless, an ordinal variable from the Rossi study, can be used to illustrate this point. The homeless were assigned to one of four health statuses: excellent, good, fair, and poor. Using these categories, a researcher knows that, if a homeless person is rated as excellent, this individual is healthier than one rated as good. But the question of exactly how much healthier cannot be answered. Nor can the researcher maintain that the difference in health status between excellent and good is the same as the difference between good and fair. Compared to the nominal scale, which establishes only equivalence and nonequivalence among the cases, the ordinal scale adds another piece of information, their rank order. Since an ordinal scale contains indications of relative magnitude, that is, a greater than or less than in the amounts measured, social scientists sometimes refer to the measurement on this and higher levels as quantitative measurement.

Two other examples of ordinal variables in the Rossi study are the prevalence of episodic homelessness and the self-report of potential suicide.

Prevalence of episodic homelessness [10]

Homeless continuously from 1980 through 1985
Homeless more than once during the previous 5 years
Homeless once, for more than a year
Homeless once, for less than a year

Self-report of potential suicide [11]

Has thought about suicide in the past few weeks
Has actually attempted suicide once or more often

The categories of prevalence are arranged from high to low, with the continuously homeless being worse off than those who are homeless more than once during the past 5 years; the latter in turn are more prone to homelessness than those who experience homelessness for the first time. The variable of suicidal self-report may appear to be nominal, but on closer inspection the first category indicates less potential for suicide than the second category. Therefore, the variable is ordinal, with categories denoting different levels of a depressive mental state, not the presence or absence of an attribute.

Ordinal data can be coded in letters or numbers. When numbers are used, they are assigned so as to represent the rank order of the categories. Their assignment is no longer arbitrary as in the nominal scale. For instance, if a 1 is used to represent "homeless once, for less than a year," then a number greater than 1, such as 2, should be used for "homeless once, for more than a year," and a 3 for "homeless more than once," and finally a 4 for "continuously homeless." At the ordinal level, these numbers can be compared as ranks, so that "4 is greater than 3" and "2 is less than 3"; but they are not open to the arithmetic operations of addition, subtraction, multiplication, or division. For example, a computation such as 1 + 2 = 3 with the scores of the prevalence of homelessness scale would be meaningless. The sum of 1, representing homeless once for less than a year, and 2, representing homeless once for more than a year, does not amount to 3, representing homeless more than once during the previous 5 years.

1.4.3 Interval Measurement

An interval scale makes use of a commonly agreed upon unit for measurement. For example, a degree in Celsius or Fahrenheit is such an agreed-upon unit of measurement. Each unit must measure the same amount of a property every time: 1 degree of increase or decrease in Celsius measures a constant amount of change in temperature. The measurement is expressed in terms of quantities of these units called **values:** 100, 0, 2 degrees, and so on, are values on a Celsius scale. Because standard units are used in interval measurement, the additional information on the exact amount of difference between two cases is known through adding or subtracting the values of an interval scale. Thus, by comparing the 40 degrees of today to the 35 degrees of yesterday, we can conclude that today is 5 degrees warmer: 40 – 35 = 5 or 35 + 5 = 40.

The operations of multiplication and division, however, should not be performed on these values, because an interval scale does not have an absolute or nonarbitrary zero point. For example, 40 degrees Celsius is not twice the heat of 20 degrees. Zero degrees Fahrenheit or Celsius is an arbitrary point because it is not the point at which there is no temperature. As a matter of fact, zero degrees Celsius corresponds to 32 degrees Fahrenheit, while zero degrees in Fahrenheit corresponds to –18 degrees in Celsius.

Many traits of interest to the social scientists are not, however, measured in standard units. For example, there are no equally distanced units for intelligence, prestige, or alienation. Thus far social scientists have encountered limited success in constructing interval scales for measuring such traits, although there are continuing efforts to do so. It is unclear at this point whether the inability stems from technical difficulties involved in developing the right tools for measurement or in the intrinsic nature of the attributes to be measured.

1.4.4 Ratio Measurement

A ratio scale has all the properties of an interval scale plus an absolute zero point. The **absolute zero point** is the point or location at which there is an absence of the property being measured. The Kelvin scale is a ratio scale for measuring temperature. Zero kelvins is the point at which there is no temperature, that is, no molecular motion. With an absolute zero point, the additional mathematical operations of multiplication and division may appropriately be performed on the data. For example, a person with $100,000 has twice as much money as someone with $50,000, and 5 kelvins indicates half the amount of heat as 10 kelvins.

To clarify the difference between an interval and a ratio scale, consider Figure 1.3. The first pair of lines is measured on the interval level, whereas the second

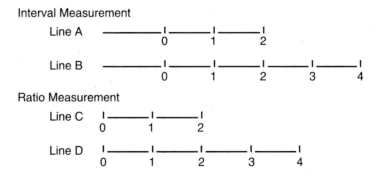

FIGURE 1.3 **Diagram Illustrating Interval and Ratio Measurement**

pair is measured on the ratio level. Because measurement of lines A and B did not begin where the lines start (the absolute zero point), it would be correct to maintain that line B is two (4 − 2 = 2) units longer than line A, but not twice (4/2 = 2) as long. However, since the 0's are nonarbitrary in lines C and D, being placed at the starting points of these lines, line D is not only 2 units longer but twice as long as line C.

Ratio scales in the social sciences are often obtained by counting; the number of people in a family and the number of weeks since last employment are typical examples. Frequently, when the unit of analysis is a group, the frequency count is divided by a base number to produce a standardized measure. The base number in the number of homeless per 100,000 people in the United States is 100,000. Rossi and his coauthors used a number of ratio scales in their work: the number of homeless per night, the cash income of the homeless, the length of time currently homeless, and so on.

Table 1.1 summarizes the information conveyed by the different levels of measurement.

Although in theory, there is a distinction between an interval and a ratio scale, in practice, very few scales in the social sciences are truly interval without being ratio at the same time. With most measurements, if standardized units can be developed, then the absolute zero point can also be located. The temperature

TABLE 1.1 Information Conveyed by Different Levels of Measurement

Information Conveyed	Levels of Measurement			
	Nominal	Ordinal	Interval	Ratio
Equivalence/nonequivalence	×	×	×	×
Rank order		×	×	×
Standard units			×	×
Absolute zero point				×

scales of Fahrenheit and Celsius are truly interval, but income, weight, and time are on the ratio level. As far as statistical techniques are concerned, the distinction between the interval and ratio scale is not as important as the distinction between nominal and ordinal or ordinal and interval. For these reasons, we have combined the interval and ratio scales into a single level and will refer to this combined level as *interval* throughout this text.

1.4.5 Possible versus Actual Measurement Levels

Some traits, such as gender, marital status, and potential for suicide, can be measured only on particular levels. However, the measurement of other characteristics, such as the length of stay in a mental hospital (time), can be carried out on different levels. We may choose to rank the individual as having a "long" or "short" stay, or we may discuss the stay in terms of actual numbers of days. Thus the highest level of measurement possible for a variable and the actual measurement level used may be different. When the values or ranks of a higher-level variable are grouped into discrete categories, this variable, like a nominal variable, is sometimes referred to as a *categorical variable.*

Ultimately, using the variable's operational definition, the researcher determines how and on which level a variable is to be measured. However, whenever there is a choice, it is best to measure a variable at its highest possible level for the following reasons. First, more powerful techniques are available for higher levels of measurement, which permit the researcher to extract more information from the data. Second, the researcher can always ignore the extra information the data carry, but cannot recover information lost through using a lower level of measurement.

1.4.6 Discrete and Continuous Variables

Another important property of data that has implications for their organization and analysis is the continuous or discrete nature of the variable under observation. A variable is continuous if it is capable of taking on any value within its range of possible values. To use a visual analogy, if the values of a continuous variable are compared to a running line, there would be no gaps or breaks in this line. The duration of homelessness is an example of a continuous variable. For any two given homeless individuals who are ever so slightly different in the duration of their being homeless, say a difference of 485 to 486 hours, there is a third person whose duration of homelessness falls in between the two, say at 485.3 hours. Other examples include the degrees of social integration, of deterioration of low-income housing, and of disability. *Realize, however, that we are speaking here of theoretical possibilities rather than of actual measurement.* In practice, fineness of discrimination among varying durations of homelessness depends on the precision of the measurement tools, which may consist of a rather imprecise questionnaire and shelter records.

A discrete variable, on the other hand, can assume only a finite or a countable number of different values. Using the same visual analogy, the values of a discrete variable can be likened to a series of dots along the path of a running line. The gaps between the dots denote values that cannot possibly happen. An example of a discrete variable is the number of homeless in shelters. There can be no fraction of a person to be counted. Other examples include the number of social visits, of friends, and of low-income housing units.

The distinction of discrete and continuous variables intersects that of the different levels of measurement. Although all qualitative measurements are discrete, all quantitative measurements are not necessarily continuous. Attitudes are often assumed to be continuous even when their measurement is ordinal and imprecise. On the other hand, many of the interval or ratio scales used in the social sciences that involve counting are discrete. The distinction should be kept in mind, because it is an additional dimension on which statistical procedures are differentiated. In some texts, this distinction is considered more important as a criterion for selecting a statistical procedure, although in this text it is treated as a secondary consideration.

1.4.7 Matching Statistical Techniques with Data Measurement

Statistical techniques can be applied to *any* set of numbers, whether they be nominal, ordinal or interval, discrete or continuous. The crucial question is whether manipulation of these numbers will yield insights into the true nature of the phenomenon under study. This, in turn, depends on whether the researcher has selected the appropriate statistical techniques.

In developing these techniques, mathematicians assume that the data with which they work carry a certain amount or type of information. As pointed out previously, the more information contained in the data, the more information is obtainable through the analysis. Not only are the techniques that require more information more powerful, but, generally, more of these techniques are available. Statistical techniques, then, can be classified primarily on the basis of the level of information they require of the data. Secondarily, they may be differentiated on the basis of whether they require a continuous quantitative variable.

Therefore, for the researcher to select an appropriate technique, she or he must match the technique to the level of data measurement. Otherwise, if the data contain more information than required, there will be unused information. Although this does not represent an error, it is, nevertheless, a waste and therefore inadvisable. If, however, a powerful technique were used on data that do not meet its requirements, then an error would be made and the results might be meaningless and uninterpretable. In addition, the researcher should be aware that some statistical techniques are not based on the level of measurement per se, but require instead that the variables be continuous in nature.

Exercises

8. Find a newspaper report of an investigation.

   a. What are the major concepts in the report?
   b. How are they operationalized?
   c. What are the levels of measurement of the variables used?

9. Operationally define the following concepts and develop indicators to measure them.

   a. Prejudice
   b. Social integration
   c. Mental health
   d. Homelessness
   e. Disability
   f. Alcoholism

10. Develop nominal, ordinal, and interval measurements for the following concepts:

    a. Education
    b. Intelligence
    c. Temperature

11. Indicate the level of measurement for the following variables:

    a. Income   1: $18,000 and under
                 2: $18,001–$30,000
                 3: $30,001–$50,000
                 4: $50,001–$100,000
                 5: $100,001 and over
    b Liberalism   1: Extremely liberal
                    2: Liberal
                    3: Conservative
                    4: Extremely conservative
    c. Prevalence of homelessness as measured by the number of days homeless during the past 12 months
    d. Social class

12. List examples of discrete and continuous variables.

1.5 Sampling Procedures

The scientist is usually not interested in the particulars of a few cases, but in generalizations, that is, characterizations that are true of a whole set of units. Thus the Rossi study sought conclusions not about some homeless individuals, but about all the homeless in Chicago. The set of units or cases that the researcher may potentially study, such as the homeless in Chicago, is known as the **population.** Although the researcher's interest centers around the entire population, for various reasons it is frequently impossible to observe all of it.

Imagine Rossi and his co-workers canvassing every street of Chicago all night long to enumerate the homeless. The sheer size of the homeless population, small as it may be compared to other populations, would mean a staggering amount of work, even if a simple count rather than a description of the population is involved. Other factors that figure prominently in the researcher's calculations are the time and the cost of completing the project. In the Rossi study, for an exhaustive enumeration, a great number of interviewers must be sent out each night, the cost of which would be prohibitive. In addition, the longer the study takes, the more likely it is that the process of observation will influence the results, producing what social scientists refer to as the **Hawthorne effect.** For example, news of the study may arouse enough interest in the city for concerned officials to implement temporary measures to reduce the population of homeless. The homeless, knowing that such a study is under way, may try to make themselves more or less accessible to the researchers. These two factors would contribute to increase or decrease the homeless population for the duration of the study. Finally, and seemingly paradoxically, a study involving the whole population may result in less accuracy than one involving a carefully chosen subset of the population. Not only is it nearly impossible to locate and interview the whole population, but the quality and the precision of the data collected may actually be worse. To illustrate, studies comparing census data collected every 10 years of the whole population of the United States with data collected from a limited number of households every month have shown the latter to be more accurate in various respects [12].

For the preceding reasons, a researcher usually selects a subset of units from the population, called a **sample,** for actual observation. The process whereby the actual selection of units is carried out is known as **sampling.** After sampling, observing, and measuring the units, with the help of statistical techniques, the researcher may make a **statistical inference.** That is, she or he attempts to generalize or to infer the characteristics of the population from observations made on the sample. As can be expected, statistical considerations enter into devising a sampling plan. If the researcher anticipates making a statistical inference, then she or he should select the type of sample that will provide the foundation for doing so.

1.5.1 Population and Sampling Frame

The task of sampling involves a number of steps. The first is to identify the population to which the researcher wants to generalize his or her results. The population of the Rossi study was the literal homeless in the city of Chicago in the years in which the study was conducted. By confining their population to the literal homeless, the researchers avoided the problem of including the marginally housed, who could not be easily identified. Thus the identification of the population should be made with sampling accessibility in mind.

The researcher next provides an operational definition of the population when she or he constructs a **sampling frame.** The sampling frame consists of the set of cases from which the actual sample is drawn and should therefore include the whole population. To ensure the latter, the sampling frame could give a complete listing of all cases. For example, if we were to sample the students of a particular university, the registrar's list could serve as a sampling frame by providing us with the names of all the students enrolled at the university. If, however, such a list of the homeless were available for Chicago, the problem of sampling as well as part of the reason for the Rossi study would no longer exist. At any rate, a list is not always readily available; neither is listing the only approach to constructing a sampling frame.

An alternative method is to identify a criterion or criteria that define who (or what) belongs to the sampling frame. Like listing, this method ensures the inclusion of the whole population in the sampling frame. Rossi and his coauthors employed this alternative, specifying the criteria for determining the homeless as a person who "was a resident of a shelter for homeless persons or was encountered in our block searches and found not to rent or own a conventional housing unit or was not a member of a household renting or owning a conventional housing unit" [13]. There are two sampling subframes or strata in this description: one consists of 22 homeless shelters in the fall and 27 shelters in the winter, and the other consists of 19,409 census blocks within the city of Chicago.

Ideally, the population and the sampling frame should coincide, for when they diverge generalizations drawn from the sample apply to the units in the sampling frame rather than to the population. However, in practice, it is very difficult to create a sampling frame that includes all relevant cases in the population. To capture the cases excluded in the count that came from their samples, the Rossi study provided an estimate of the homeless population based on additional sources, such as detoxification centers and facilities for the chronically mentally ill. Although Rossi and his co-workers conscientiously combed through a number of these sources, there was still the possibility of missing some members of the homeless population. As this example shows, there is ultimately no accepted standard method for evaluating any discrepancy that may occur between the population and the sampling frame.

1.5.2 Probability Sampling: Simple Random Sample

Since the sample provides the information on which the population characteristics are estimated, the researcher takes great care in selecting a sample that will adequately represent the population. She or he devises a plan called a **sampling design** to determine, primarily, how the units should be selected and, secondarily, how many to select. There are two basic types of sampling plans: **probabilistic** and **nonprobabilistic** designs. In probability sampling, every case in the population has a *known* chance or probability of being selected. In nonprobability sampling, the probability of any case being selected in *unknown*.

Probability samples provide a solid foundation for the researcher to infer population characteristics from sample data. In more advanced texts, statistical inference from samples for which the cases have a *known* but *unequal chance* of selection is discussed. *In an introductory text such as ours, the procedures presented for making statistical inference are based on the assumption that a simple random sample has been drawn.* A **simple random sample** is a probability sample in which all combinations of the same number of cases, that is, all samples of the same size, are equally likely. This book will use the term *random sample* to refer to a simple random sample. Two basic requirements for making statistical inference are incorporated into the (simple) random sample design: (1) **random selection** and (2) **independent selection.** Any procedure that guarantees that each case has an equal and therefore a known chance of being selected is *random*. The principle of independence is met when the selection of one case does not make the inclusion of another more or less likely.

Let us see how a random sample can be drawn to satisfy these two principles. Imagine for a moment that a population of literal homeless exists, consisting of six individuals represented by the letters A, B, C, D, E, and F. The employment history of the six individuals for the past week is given next in terms of the number of days employed in the past 7 days:

Individual	A	B	C	D	E	F
Days employed	2	2	1	0	0	1

Suppose a random sample of 2 is to be drawn from a sampling frame consisting of these six letters. How should the researcher proceed?

Random samples can be generated from a sampling frame using a computer program. Another common method is to use a computer-generated table of random numbers to draw the sample. With either method, it is possible to select the same individual more than once. We refer to this particular aspect of sampling as sampling **with replacement.** The term indicates that after a case is selected it is "put back" in the sampling frame so that it is available for the succeeding draw. Sampling with replacement is equivalent to having an infinite population from which an unlimited number of samples can be taken. In actual practice, most social scientists sample **without replacement.** This procedure involves withdrawing a case from the sampling frame after its inclusion into a sample so that the same case cannot be selected twice. Alternatively, if the case is not actually withdrawn, when selected again, it will not be included twice. That selecting a case in one draw precludes its being selected again technically violates the requirement of independent selection. However, when the population is large, as is often the case, sampling without replacement represents a minor infraction of this principle.

Recall that the researcher selects a random sample to provide a basis for making inferences about the population itself. Suppose our random sample of 2 is chosen to estimate a population characteristic, the average or mean workdays of the six homeless individuals. At this point, it is necessary to make a distinction between sample and population characteristics. Any sample characteristic, such as the mean, is known as a **statistic.** A statistic is often used to estimate a **parame-**

ter, its corresponding characteristic in the population. The mean of the population, that is, the *parameter* in our example, is calculated as follows:

$$\frac{2.0 + 2.0 + 1.0 + .0 + .0 + 1.0}{6.0} = 1.0$$

The mean of the sample, that is the *statistic,* is obtained similarly by summing the workdays of the two individuals included in the sample and dividing the sum by 2.0. Very clearly, the estimate of the population mean given by the sample mean depends on who is included in the sample.

To figure out the estimates obtainable from a sample of 2, imagine samples of 2 being taken *repeatedly* and with replacement. With the six homeless individuals available for each draw, Table 1.2 shows that 36 distinct samples can be drawn, each represented by a cell of the table. Again, each of these 36 samples is equally likely if the procedure of random sampling is adopted. Each cell within the table contains a *statistic,* that is, the mean number of workdays in each sample.

From Table 1.2, we can see that samples drawn randomly from the same population will yield varying estimates of the population parameter. While the population parameter remains constant, in this case 1.0, the possible estimates of this parameter based on sample means range from .0 to 2.0, depending on which sample is selected. The difference between a statistic and its corresponding parameter represents what is known as a **sampling error.** For example, sample 1 in Table 1.2 contains a sampling error of 1.0, which is calculated from the difference between its mean and the mean of the population: (2.0 − 1.0). The portion of the sampling error that occurs specifically as a result of random sampling is referred to as a **random sampling error.** The sample is representative of the population to the extent that the sampling error is minimal.

So far we have shown that even if the procedure of random sampling is followed, there is still no guarantee that the sample statistic will yield the same value as the population parameter. *What, then, is the advantage of having a random sample? Although random sampling errors may result, it is possible to calculate the probabilities of obtaining certain sample estimates and, therefore, the probability of making incorrect estimates.*

TABLE 1.2 Thirty-six Samples with Their Mean Number of Workdays

Second Case Selected	First Case Selected					
	A	B	C	D	E	F
	(2)	(2)	(1)	(0)	(0)	(1)
A (2)	2.0	2.0	1.5	1.0	1.0	1.5
B (2)	2.0	2.0	1.5	1.0	1.0	1.5
C (1)	1.5	1.5	1.0	.5	.5	1.0
D (0)	1.0	1.0	.5	.0	.5	.5
E (0)	1.0	1.0	.5	.0	.0	.5
F (1)	1.5	1.5	1.0	.5	.5	1.5

The calculation of these probabilities is made possible through the use of a sampling distribution. A **sampling distribution** gives all the possible values of a statistic, such as the sample mean, and their probabilities of occurrence based on random sampling. When the statistics within Table 1.2 are grouped in terms of their values and the number of samples showing the same value are counted, the results are as shown in columns 1 and 2 of Table 1.3. Column 1 gives the possible sample means, while column 2 gives the frequency of occurrence of a sample mean with repeated sampling. The probability of a sample mean can be calculated from this latter column. For example, the probability of obtaining a sample mean of .0 is $\frac{3}{36}$ or .083, while the probability of obtaining a sample mean of 2.0 is $\frac{4}{36}$ or .111. These probabilities are given in column 3 of Table 1.3. Column 3 and column 1 comprise the sampling distribution of mean workdays for the population of the six homeless.

Since most of the sample estimates (.0, .5, 1.5, and 2.0) are different from the population value (1.0), the sampling distribution could also be viewed as a distribution of sampling errors. A distinctive pattern emerges when the sampling distribution in Table 1.3 is examined closely. The values of sample statistics are clustered around the true population value of 1.0, with their probabilities of occurrence dwindling as they depart from 1.0. Furthermore, based on the sampling distribution of sample means, we can calculate the risks of making an incorrect estimate of the population mean with a random sample of 2. From Table 1.3, the probability of making a correct estimate is higher (.306) than the probabilities of obtaining any of the other incorrect estimates (.250, .111, or .083).

To summarize, sampling is convenient and sometimes necessary. Samples, however, usually contain sampling errors, so when a sample statistic is used to estimate the population parameter, the estimate may not be accurate. The use of a random sample enables the researcher to calculate the risk of making an incorrect conclusion about the population.

We have deliberately simplified a number of elements in our illustration of random sampling. First, the population in our illustration is so small that little advantage is gained through sampling, but this will seldom be the case in actual research. Second, we skirted the problem of constructing the sampling frame, which is usually an arduous task full of compromises. Third, although basic sampling theory involves the notion of sampling with replacement, in actual

TABLE 1.3 Sampling Distribution of Mean Workdays

Estimates of Mean Workdays	Number of Samples with the Estimate	Probability of Obtaining the Sample
.0	3	.083
.5	9	.250
1.0	11	.306
1.5	9	.250
2.0	4	.111
Total	36	1.000

research, social scientists commonly sample without replacement. In a large population the two methods will produce only a negligible difference; in a small population, however, a correction factor should be employed when sampling without replacement. Fourth, the value of the parameter is known in our example, whereas in practice it is usually unknown. When it is unknown, we do not know whether a particular sample contains sampling error or how large the error is. Finally, although simple random sampling provides the foundation for statistical inference, it is not the most common design used in research.

Three other basic probability designs are systematic, stratified, and cluster sampling. They involve selecting cases with a known but not necessarily equal chance of inclusion. In fact, the Rossi study employed a multistage sampling procedure, incorporating elements of all three designs. Since these designs are not central to our discussion, they will not be presented here. Readers who are interested will find discussions of these designs in Kalton [14] and Kish [15].

1.5.3 Nonprobability Sampling

Nonprobability sampling refers to a process of selecting cases based on the researcher's judgment or the availability of the units, not on chance. Nonprobability samples do not provide a sound basis for making inferences about the population because they are likely to contain **bias.** Bias occurs when there is *systematic as opposed to random sampling error.* Recall from the previous section that a sampling error refers to a discrepancy between the sample statistic and its population parameter. This sampling error can be decomposed into two parts:

$$\text{sampling error} = \text{bias} + \text{random sampling error}$$

When the sample is randomly chosen, bias is eliminated so that the sampling error consists of only random sampling error. Random sampling error can be estimated, as we have shown in Section 1.5.2. Usually, it can also be reduced by increasing the sample size, although it cannot be eliminated.

On the other hand, a nonprobability sample will most likely contain bias. This bias cannot be controlled or estimated, because a sampling distribution may not be derivable with such a sampling design. It is simply an unknown, so when estimating the parameter from the statistic, the researcher cannot assess how accurate the estimation is. Suppose a researcher wishes to estimate the income of the homeless and waits around the neighborhood liquor store until she or he encounters and interviews a few homeless persons. Those who are interviewed constitute a nonprobability sample; only certain homeless would be found in the neighborhood where the search is conducted. It is very probable that this sample includes a large number of alcoholics, whereas their proportion in the population may be much lower. Discrepancies between the sample and the population are difficult to estimate because of the bias introduced into the sample.

If the researcher is not concerned with generalizing beyond the sample data, as is usually the case in exploratory studies, she or he need not adopt probability sampling, especially when it may be much easier to do nonprobability sampling. For example, to explore the behavior patterns of the alcoholic homeless, the best location to do the research may be at a street corner liquor store frequented by *typical* alcoholics. Thus, in certain situations, nonprobability sampling may be appropriate. At the very least, data from nonprobability sampling can give the researcher insight into the research problem.

Exercises

13. Time and money permitting, is it always better to survey an entire population than a sample? Why or why not?

14. Why is a probability sample better than a nonprobability sample?

15. What is sampling error?

16. Flip a coin 10 times and count the number of heads. Ask everyone in the class to do the same. Tally the frequency of the number of heads obtained by each person in class. Then construct a sampling distribution with the results. Based on this distribution, what is the most likely estimate of the number of heads obtained in 10 flips?

1.6 Data Collection and Analysis

Guided by the research question(s), the researcher gathers relevant data from the sample and proceeds to analyze them in the following manner. The sample data are first examined and then described to arrive at conclusions about the sample. The researcher may conclude the research at this point, if the project is exploratory. More often, based on the sample information, the investigator makes certain inferences about the population; these inferences are then used to evaluate the hypothesis or hypotheses and research question(s). If the hypothesis is deduced from a theory, a confirmation or rejection of the hypothesis may lead to either a confirmation or modification of the theory. Finally, the implications of the data for the current state of knowledge in the area are examined. This feedback may lead to a perceived need for more information, and the research cycle begins anew. The practical value of statistics is evident at this final stage of the research process—it is the instrument through which answers are obtained to questions formulated at the beginning of the cycle. As such, it gives meaning and coherence to the earlier stages of activity.

As a result of this two-step approach to data analysis, first the description of the sample, and then the inference about the population, the field of statistics is traditionally divided into two branches: descriptive and inferential. **Descriptive statistics** deals with organizing and summarizing sample data. The data may be organized in the form of a table similar to Table 1.3, or they may be charted with some graphic techniques. Tabular and graphic methods of data organization are presented in Chapter 2.

After the data are organized, the researcher proceeds to capture salient features of the sample data in measures known as *statistics*. There is a wide variety of these statistics; each summarizes some but not every important aspect of the data. From among these statistics, the researcher chooses the appropriate one(s) for his or her purpose. In this selection, the researcher is guided by the level of data measurement, as well as other considerations. She or he must decide which aspects of the sample data to describe and communicate. This involves knowing in detail the properties and functions of each statistic. For example, two of the statistics computed in the Rossi study to summarize the number of months since the last steady job for the homeless are the mean and the mode. The mean of 54.9 tells us that, on the average, a homeless person has been out of work for 54.9 months. The mode of 120.0, on the other hand, indicates that the greatest number of homeless persons were out of steady work for 120.0 months [16]. Second, because the analysis of the sample is a prelude to forming conclusions about the population, the selection of a particular statistic is also guided by what it reveals about its corresponding population parameter. Some statistics give good estimates, whereas others provide biased or less reliable estimates of population parameters.

Descriptive statistics can be further subdivided according to the number of variables involved in the analysis. Univariate analysis, discussed in Chapter 3, is employed primarily to provide a description of the sample data and a foundation for more complex analysis. When Rossi and his coauthors were examining sources of income, the period since the last steady job, marital status, and the like, for the homeless, they were engaged in univariate analysis. The demographic and other traits of the homeless were described one by one, and in the end a composite picture emerged. In the following paragraph, the authors give a demographic profile of the typical homeless in Chicago:

> *Being homeless is predominantly a male condition; . . . Blacks and native Americans constituted considerably more than their proportionate share of the homeless. . . . Although the average age of the homeless, 40 years, was not far from that of the general adult population, there were proportionately fewer of the very young (under 25) and the old (over 65). Nor were the homeless very different from the general population in educational attainment, the typical homeless person being a high school graduate. [17]*

Bivariate analysis, presented in Chapters 4 and 5, describes the association found between two variables in the sample. Since associations are possible indications of causal relationships, bivariate analysis constitutes the first step toward establishing this type of relationship between the variables. Rossi and his coworkers did not perform any bivariate analysis in their study. However, had they pursued the explanation of homelessness discussed in Section 1.3, they would have been dealing with bivariate analysis. They would have examined the nature and the degree of association between the dependent variable, homelessness, and each of the other variables: disability, length and extent of poverty, and supportive network.

To further the search for causal relationships, the researcher identifies and includes in the analysis the variables that may have produced a spurious relationship between the two original variables. Other independent or intervening variables may also be brought into the analysis for a more complete explanation of the dependent variable(s). As more variables are added, the analysis becomes multivariate. For example, if Rossi and his coworkers had performed a multivariate analysis, the effects of disability and length and extent of poverty on homelessness could have been considered *simultaneously*. The techniques of multivariate analysis are more numerous and varied than those of bivariate analysis. Only some of these approaches are discussed in Chapters 14 and 15.

The goal of research usually involves more than a mere description of the sample. Often the researcher wants to know whether his or her sample findings are applicable to the population as a whole. **Inferential statistics** permits the researcher (1) to generalize the results obtained from the sample to the population and (2) to estimate the risk involved in making such inferences. The notion of risk or uncertainty is embodied in the concept of probability and is dealt with in Chapter 6.

Sample statistics used to estimate the population parameters have been shown to vary from sample to sample in Section 1.5.2. The average of all sample estimates yields the true value of the population parameter, but most researchers are in no position to sample more than once. More likely than not, the sample selected contains sampling error. To take into account sampling errors when inferring from samples to populations, the researcher employs sampling distributions, a topic covered in Chapter 7.

Inferential statistics can be subdivided according to two objectives: to estimate population parameters and to test hypotheses. **Estimation** is called for when the researcher has a question to which she or he cannot provide even a tentative answer. The question that the Rossi study raised, "How many homeless are there in Chicago on a daily and on an annual basis?" is such an example. Generally, the estimation takes the form of an **interval** or a range of values within which the true population value is expected to lie. After taking separate counts of the street and the shelter homeless, Rossi and his coauthors constructed intervals around the sample statistics. For instance, the nightly figure for the winter of 1986 was projected to be between 1745 and 2295, which amounted to approximately .07% of the Chicago population [18]. By using an interval such as this, 1745 to 2295, the researchers were able to say that they were 95% confident that the interval would include the true daily average number of homeless. Estimation is discussed in Chapter 10.

In **hypothesis testing**, the researcher evaluates hypotheses, that is, tentative answers stated in response to the research questions. The testing is accomplished mostly through ruling out alternative answers and explanations. The logic and the elements of this indirect method of verification are elaborated on in Chapter 8. More commonly used procedures for hypothesis testing are covered in Chapters 9, 11, 12, and 13.

At the conclusion of the research process, the researcher makes specific conclusions with regard to his or her research questions and hypotheses, and may also reflect on the significance of the findings for a theory or theoretical perspective. Rossi and his coworkers did not explicitly adopt one of the three major sociological perspectives in their work. However, once they had compiled a profile of the homeless, they appeared to lean more toward the conflict perspective in their speculation on the causes and consequences of homelessness. Finally, the researcher may also indicate possible avenues to pursue for future research. Rossi and his coauthors concluded their article by suggesting an interpretation of homelessness and directions for further studies.

Exercises

17. Is the distinction between descriptive and inferential statistics the same as the distinction between descriptive and explanatory research?

18. Is multivariate analysis always explanatory?

19. How does a researcher generalize research findings to a population?

20. In the Rossi study, if a strong association is found between physical disability and homelessness, can the researchers conclude that disability is the cause of homelessness? Explain.

21. What variables might render the association between disability and homelessness spurious?

1.7 Organization of This Text

The process of research has been reviewed, relying primarily on the Rossi project for illustrations. The various steps and the important elements in some of the steps are summarized in Figure 1.4. As the reader may gather from this review, there is much more to statistics than formulas and numbers. How the research questions are posed, the concepts measured, and the data collected have a direct impact on the type of statistical analysis that is adopted. Consequently, throughout this text we will present statistical concepts and techniques as part of an integrated research process.

For this purpose we have created a fictitious researcher named Anne. Anne is a social scientist from a foreign country who is interested in and wants to learn as much as possible about the United States. To this end, she has obtained a position as a visiting research associate in a social research institute affiliated with a public university on the West Coast. Knowing very little about the United States, she approaches this society with insatiable curiosity and innumerable questions. In an attempt to obtain some answers to her questions, she collects data and analyzes them. As her residence in this country lengthens, Anne's questions proceed from the simple to the complex. Not being satisfied with information on particular sample groups and individuals, Anne desires to gener-

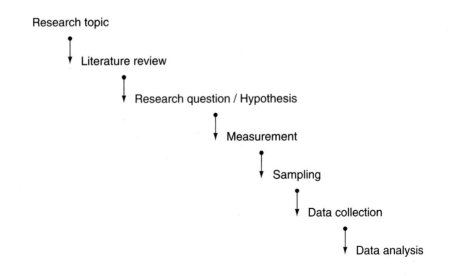

FIGURE 1.4   Stages of the Research Process

alize her understanding to U.S. society as a whole. Thus the progression of Anne's research parallels the development of statistical topics in this text.

Part I of this text focuses on descriptive statistics, reflecting Anne's initial desire for information concerning this country. Within this part, the chapters are organized along the dimension of the number of variables included in the analysis. Initially, Anne's descriptive questions can be answered with univariate analyses; then her more complex questions involve bivariate analyses. Part II deals with inferential statistics, paralleling Anne's desire to generalize her sample findings. Again, the chapters generally progress from simple to more complex analyses, which include more variables as well as samples. Within these two parts, the chapters are roughly divided into sections according to the level of data measurement. Although descriptive techniques are considered apart from inferential procedures up to this point, in actuality the two are very much intertwined in data analysis. Therefore, in Part III, descriptive and inferential multivariate procedures are integrated in the discussions to give a more realistic portrayal of the work in which Anne engages to understand some of the more complex social processes. Overall, statistical techniques are presented within the context of one large research project initiated by a stranger in an attempt to understand this country. This approach will illustrate the role of statistics in research and its applications and utility.

To relieve the tedium of calculation and to provide a more realistic experience of data analysis, the text includes instructions and exercises on a computer program called SPSS. SPSS stands for Statistical Package for the Social Sciences. It originated as a set of prewritten procedures for the mainframe computer. With the invention of and the evolution in microcomputers, the mainframe SPSS has been adapted for use in personal computers, resulting in a version called SPSS/PC+. Since the languages of the two versions are similar, instructions for both packages are incorporated into the text, interspersed in units called SPSS SESSION. The computer exercises are structured around two data sets contained in a diskette that comes with this text. Students who have access to other prewritten programs such as SAS or MINITAB, rather than SPSS, may with slight modifications use these data sets for computer analysis. Although instructions on SAS and MINI-TAB are not included in this text, instruction manuals for their use, written by the authors, are available [19, 20].

In conclusion, this text presents the elements essential to the conduct of research. By integrating statistics with social science and methodological concerns and by introducing the basics of a widely used computer program, the text prepares the student to deal with the exigencies and challenges of being a social researcher.

References

1. Rossi, P. H., Wright, J. D., Fisher, G. A., and Willis, G. (1987). The Urban Homeless: Estimating Composition and Size, *Science* 235:1336–1342.
2. Rossi, P. H. (1989). *Down and Out in America.* Chicago: University of Chicago Press.
3. Hume, D. (1955). *An Inquiry Concerning Human Understanding.* New York: Bobbs Merrill.
4. Durkheim, E. (1950). *Suicide.* Ed. and trans. George Simpson. Glencoe, Ill.: Free Press.
5. Skidmore, W. (1975). *Theoretical Thinking in Sociology.* New York: Cambridge University Press, p. 65.
6. Rossi et al., op. cit., p. 1336.
7. Ibid.
8. Ibid.
9. Ibid., p. 1340.
10. Ibid., p. 96.
11. Ibid., p. 151.
12. Sudman, S. (1976). *Applied Sampling.* New York: Academic Press.
13. Rossi et al., op. cit., p. 1337.
14. Kalton, Graham (1983). *Introduction to Survey Sampling.* Beverly Hills, Calif.: Sage.
15. Kish, Leslie (1965). *Survey Sampling.* New York: Wiley.
16. Rossi et al., op. cit., p. 1337.
17. Ibid., p. 1340.
18. Ibid.
19. Lee, I., and Maykovich, M. (1991). *SAS Manual for Prentice Hall Statistics.* Englewood Cliffs, N.J.: Prentice Hall.
20. Lee, I., and Maykovich, M. (1991). *MINITAB Manual for Prentice Hall Statistics.* Englewood Cliffs, N.J.: Prentice Hall.

$$C \ h \ a \ p \ t \ e \ r \quad 2$$

Organizing and Presenting Univariate Data

New Statistical Topics

Frequency distribution   Percentage and proportion distributions
Cumulative distribution   Grouped frequency distribution
Pie and bar charts   Histogram and polygon
Stem-and-leaf diagram   Line graph

2.1 Overview

Research often begins with a question or questions. The type of question posed by a researcher like Anne, who knows very little about her topic, is usually descriptive rather than explanatory in nature. Before explaining *why* people behave in a certain way, the researcher should describe *how* people do behave. A **descriptive** project, then, simply seeks to depict a particular aspect of the social world.

Anne begins her inquiry by asking descriptive questions that provide a solid foundation for her later work. Overall, she attempts to determine who lives in this country. On a more specific level, she seeks demographic data on the population, data that pertain to its ethnic and political identification and its age and class structure.

To Anne, the question of who lives here also requires an examination of whether the United States is still a land of immigrants. The image of the United States as a melting pot made such an indelible impression on her in her student days that it has remained with her all these years since. She now has the opportunity to investigate to what extent immigration has been taking place, who the recent immigrants are, and whether U.S. citizens presently welcome them with open arms.

Since Anne is not oriented to the folkways in the United States, she feels hesitant about embarking on firsthand data collection. Being a resourceful social scientist, she explores secondary sources of information. Secondary data refer to existing data collected by other researchers for their own projects. The variety of such data is almost limitless. If the data are adaptable to her research objectives, Anne can save considerable time, money, and energy. To her relief, she finds that the Social Research Institute of University X carries an abundance of secondary data, rendering firsthand data collection almost unnecessary. There are data gathered by the federal and local government bureaus, by national opinion pollsters as well as by the Institute itself.

Except for those collected by the Census Bureau, most of these data sets are gathered from random national samples. As explained in Chapter 1, to study the whole population is both unnecessary and impractical when a carefully selected random sample will suffice. Besides, at this exploratory stage of her work, Anne is concerned primarily with the descriptive analysis of available sample data, and not with the extension of the analysis to the population at large.

As a start, Anne organizes and displays her data so as to render the information more readily assimilable. This chapter examines various tabular and graphic methods of organizing univariate data. Since numerous techniques are available, the selection of a format depends on the purpose of the study, the level of measurement, and the continuous or discrete nature of the variable. Although statistical procedures are presented here as being specific to each level of data measurement, with some loss of information methods appropriate for lower-level data can also be used on higher-level data. However, using a higher-level technique on lower-level data represents a technical error and may result in misrepresentation of the data.

2.2 Tabular Organization of Data

The information collected from a sample that has not been subjected to statistical manipulation is referred to as **raw data.** The total collection of observations of the sample is known as a **data set** or **data base.** In univariate analysis, one variable at a time is extracted from this data set for examination. The examination usually begins with a listing of all the cases of a variable. In this form, without further manipulation, we still have raw data. Suppose Anne wants to display the ages of a sample of respondents. For the sake of simplicity, only the first eight respondents from a full data set are processed and shown in Table 2.1(a). The list would not reveal much information, especially if the sample is large. It would not indicate, for example, whether there are more older than younger people. Organization is necessary if Anne is to gain more information from a perusal of the data.

One way to organize the data is by **sorting.** In sorting, cases that have the same value or label are grouped together. When the observations are numerical, they are arranged in descending order from the highest to the lowest value or in

TABLE 2.1 Distribution of Age from Raw Data

(a) Listing		(b) Array	(c) Frequency Distribution		
Case	Age	Age	Age	(Tally)	Frequency
1	29	2	2	(/)	1
2	15	15	15	(///)	3
3	45	15	23	(//)	2
4	2	15	29	(/)	1
5	23	23	45	(/)	1
6	15	23	..	..	.
7	15	29	..	..	.
8	23	45			
.	..	..			
.	..	..			

ascending order from the lowest to the highest value. Otherwise, the labels may be organized alphabetically. Much more information can be gathered from reading a sorted list, called an **array.** The array in Table 2.1(b), for example, shows the youngest age, the oldest age, and the ages in between.

Taking the organization a step further, Anne can tally the **frequency, or the number of cases per category.** Then a **frequency distribution** or a **table** can be constructed as in Table 2.1(c). A frequency distribution gives a listing of all the categories or values of a variable and the number of times each category or value is observed in the sample. Now the variation in ages is much more easily discernible than before.

2.3 Tables for Nominal Data

2.3.1 Frequency Distribution

Research Questions
Anne plans to organize most of her data in the form of frequency distributions. With these distributions, she can examine whether U.S. residents are ethnically, religiously, and politically diverse. Given the high divorce rate in the United States, Anne is also curious as to the predominant family form. Do children come mostly from two-parent or from single-parent families? Family form and ethnic, religious, and political identification are measured at the **nominal level.** They represent qualitative characteristics of the respondents, with categories that indicate the presence or absence of an attribute. The categories, however, do not have an inherent order, nor do they represent magnitude or amount.

The Data and Their Interpretation
Anne locates a data set from Department XXX in the data banks of the Research Institute that has the most recent information on the ethnic composition of a random sample of U.S. residents. Since the raw data are already entered into the

computer, Anne need only instruct SPSS to generate a frequency distribution. The procedure to do so is described in the SPSS SESSION following Section 2.5. From the data base of Department XXX, the computer produces a table of the ethnic composition of the sample as shown in Table 2.2.

With such a table, Anne can see at a glance how many whites, blacks, Hispanics, and other ethnic groups there are in the sample. Of the 4,551 cases in the sample, 3,720 are whites. Blacks constitute the largest minority, totaling 456, while Native Americans comprise one of the smallest groups, consisting of 27. The overall impression conveyed by Table 2.2 is that the sample is ethnically diverse. It should be noted that, although the sample size is fairly large in this survey, nevertheless, to generalize the findings beyond the sample to the population of the United States, Anne must use inferential statistics. For now, however, she is content with examining and describing sample data.

Construction of a Frequency Distribution

Table 2.2 consists of a number of elements essential to reading and understanding the table. It is identified by a title that describes its contents; these are the variable, the sample, and the time the data were collected. Under the title are two columns. The first is comprised of categories of the variable, which are mutually exclusive and exhaustive. **Mutually exclusive** categories do not overlap. Thus the respondents in Table 2.2 are classifiable into one and only one ethnic group. The categories are **exhaustive when all respondents can be classified into a category and no respondent is left unclassified.** The category "Other" in Table 2.2 makes the classification exhaustive by including all the respondents who do not belong to any of the specified groups. The second column gives the tallies or counts per category, symbolized by f. The total or N is obtained by adding all the frequencies under this column.

At the bottom of the table are notes and references. These document the source of the data and give additional information about the data or the analysis whenever necessary. Although the source of Table 2.2 is shown, the reference is unnecessary because the data set is fictitious. *Since we will be using mostly fictitious*

TABLE 2.2 Ethnic Groups in the United States, 1990

Ethnic Groups	Frequency (f)
White	3,720
Black	456
Hispanic	285
Asian American	57
Native American	27
Others	6
Total (N)	4,551

Source: U.S. Department of XXX, 1991.

data, the following convention will be followed in the remainder of the text in referencing tables and data. If the data set is derived from an actual study, it will be noted at the bottom of the table; otherwise, when the source is not given, the data are fictitious.

2.3.2 Relative Frequency Distribution: The Proportion Distribution

Research Question

Anne finds herself comparing the frequencies of different categories as she reads Table 2.2. Although the table gives her a good grasp of the *absolute* number in each ethnic group, she prefers to know the size of each group *relative* to the total sample. Therefore, for the next computer run she decides to generate a **relative frequency distribution** of the religious preferences of U.S. residents, which will show the relative size of each religious group. Given the freedom of religion and the varied ethnic origins, will there be a great diversity in religious preferences?

The Data and Their Interpretation

A single frequency count, by itself, is difficult to interpret, but when compared to other figures, it often takes on significance. The comparison can be carried out through (1) subtracting one number from another and/or (2) dividing one number by another. The latter method yields a **ratio.** As 30 Protestants are a *sizable* subgroup within a sample of 40, but a *small* subgroup within a sample of 1,000, a frequency can be compared to N to indicate its relative size. A **proportion** provides such a comparison by giving the ratio of a frequency to N:

$$P_i = \frac{f_i}{N} \tag{2.1}$$

where P_i refers to the proportion of the *i*th category,
  f_i refers to the frequency of the *i*th category, and
  N refers to sample size.

A **proportion distribution,** on the other hand, gives a listing of proportions corresponding to all the categories of a variable, thus showing their relative sizes.

The letter *i* in Formula 2.1 is known as a **subscript.** Subscripts denote the position of scores, frequencies, proportions, and so on, in an array. Since they are used throughout the text, it is important to have a good grasp of their usage early on. See Box 2.1 for conventions on subscripting.

Table 2.3 shows survey data collected by the National Opinion Research Center (NORC) in the form of a relative frequency distribution of proportions. Reading the table, Anne learns that Protestants comprise almost two-thirds of the sample and Catholics, approximately one-fourth. The rest of the religious groups sum to slightly over one-tenth of the sample. In comparing the proportions within this table, Anne can easily see the relative size of each group.

The category of Protestants is so large that only by giving a detailed breakdown into denominations does the full range of religious affiliation become

Box 2.1   Subscripting an Array

An array is an ordered sequence of elements, frequently of scores. To designate the position of a score in the array, a subscript is used. If X refers to a set of scores, then X_1 refers to the first score, X_2 refers to the second score, and so on, while X_N refers to the last score in an array of size N as follows:

$$X_1 \quad X_2 \quad X_3 \quad X_4 \quad X_5 \quad \dots \quad X_N$$
$$2 \quad \ 2 \quad \ 6 \quad \ 7 \quad \ 7 \quad \dots \quad 12$$

The *position* of a score should not be confused with its *value*. The subscript 3 in X_3 refers to the third score, which has a value of 6.

To designate the position of *any* score rather than the position of a *particular* score in the array, a letter subscript such as i or j is used. The letter subscripts i and j can take on the values of 1 through N, the maximum length of the array. Subscripts are also used with statistical measures such as frequencies, proportions, and percentages. For example, if f refers to an array of frequencies in a table, then f_i refers to the frequency in the ith category of the frequency distribution.

apparent. The different denominations of Protestantism are listed in descending order based on the group size. Summing all the proportions of the different denominations results in .637, the proportion of the Protestants as a whole. Given Table 2.3, Anne may compare (1) Protestants as a whole or a particular Protestant denomination to another group or (2) Protestant denominations to each other. When different Protestant denominations are taken into account, Anne realizes that religious diversity rather than uniformity appears to be the norm.

Construction of a Proportion Distribution
First, construct a frequency distribution for the variable. Then calculate the proportion, P_i, in each category by taking the frequency in that category and dividing

TABLE 2.3 Religious Identification among U.S. Residents, 1991

Religion	Proportion		Frequency	
Protestant	.637		966	
Baptist		.201		305
Methodist		.090		137
Lutheran		.069		104
Presbyterian		.049		74
Episcopalian		.021		32
All others		.207		314
Catholic	.254		386	
Jewish	.021		32	
Other or no answer	.021		31	
No religious preference	.067		102	
Total	1.000		1,517	

Source: National Opinion Research Center, General Social Surveys, 1991.

it by N. For example, $966/1{,}517 = .637$. When all the proportions are added, they should sum to 1.0:

$$P_1 + P_2 + \cdots + P_N = \frac{f_1 + f_2 + \cdots + f_N}{N} = \frac{N}{N}$$

Thus the sample is considered a single entity (a whole), which is divided into portions. Because the proportion denotes a portion of the whole sample, the closer its value is to 1, the larger the portion. The concept of a proportion is probably best conveyed by a pie chart, which will be discussed later in this chapter.

Sometimes the frequencies are displayed with the proportions, but often they are omitted. In the latter case, the total number of respondents should be presented at the bottom of the table so that the proportions can be converted into frequencies again whenever necessary. To convert a proportion into a frequency, use the following formula:

$$f_i = (N)(P_i) \tag{2.2}$$

For example, in Table 2.3, there are 386 Catholics. The frequency of 386 can be obtained through multiplying 1,517 by .254.

2.3.3 Relative Frequency Distribution: The Percentage Distribution

The relative sizes of particular categories can also be shown by using a **percentage distribution**. A **percentage** is a proportion multiplied by 100:

$$P\%_i = (P_i)(100) = \frac{f_i}{N}100 \tag{2.3}$$

The Data and Their Interpretation
Table 2.4 is a percentage distribution that gives the political party identification of U.S. citizens from the same NORC study tabulated with the aid of SPSS. From Table 2.4, Anne gathers that the United States has primarily a two-party system. Over 87% of the people in the sample identify themselves as either Democrats or Republicans or leaning toward those parties, while only a small minority of people consider themselves strictly as Independents. There are some who have not responded to this item on the questionnaire, and still others who identify themselves as completely outside the mainstream of U.S. politics. However, these constitute small enough groups to be listed in separate categories at the bottom of the table.

It is also interesting to note that, of those who identify themselves as Democrats, approximately 33% feel very strongly about their party identification, while

TABLE 2.4 Political Party Identification among U.S. Citizens, 1991

Party Identification		Percentage
Democrat	45.0	
Strong Democrat		15.0
Not very strong Democrat		21.3
Independent, close to Democrat		8.7
Republican	42.4	
Strong Republican		12.1
Not very strong Republican		19.0
Independent, close to Republican		11.3
Independent	12.6	
Total	100.0	
Number of respondents		1,497
Other parties		14
No response		6
Total of all cases		1,517

Source: National Opinion Research Center, General Social Surveys, 1991.

of those who identify themselves as Republicans, fewer, approximately 29%, feel as strongly about it. These percentages are calculated as follows:

    For Democrats:
        Number of strong Democrats in the sample = (.15)(1,497) = 225
        Number of Democrats in the sample = (.45)(1,497) = 674
        Percentage of strong Democrats within the party = (225/674)(100) = 33%
    For Republicans:
        Percentage of strong Republicans within the party = (181/635)(100) = 29%

To understand why (1) an N of 1,497 as opposed to 1,517 is used in the calculation of the number of strong Democrats, and (2) an N of 674 is used in the calculation of the percentage of strong Democrats within the party, see Box 2.2.

Construction of a Percentage Distribution

Construct a distribution of proportions first according to the instructions given in the previous section. Then multiply each proportion, P_i, by 100; the result is a percentage table. As with proportions, the percentage indicates the relative frequency or size of each category; the only difference is that percentages sum to 100, whereas proportions sum to 1.0.

2.3.4 Comparison of Percentage or Proportion Distributions

The advantage of having a percentage or proportion distribution becomes clear when the researcher must compare two samples. Not only do percentages and

Box 2.2   The Choice of a Base for Calculating Percentages and Proportions

Note that different bases or N's are used for the calculations in Tables 2.3 and 2.4. In Table 2.3, N refers to the number of cases in the sample, whereas in Table 2.4 N equals the number of people who have responded with one of the three major party identifications. The value of N depends primarily on the purpose of the analysis. When "no response" and "other parties" are considered irrelevant, their frequencies are excluded from the base, N, as in Table 2.4. On the other hand, if a distinction between "other" and "no preference" and the rest of the categories is desired, as in Table 2.3, then the frequencies of these categories are included in N. In either case, the inclusion or exclusion of these residual categories should be made clear to the readers. When residual categories are not listed in the main body of the table, they are usually shown at the bottom as in Table 2.4.

The information on the number who gave "no response" is especially important when such missing data are considerable. This may indicate problems with the questionnaire, such as ambiguous wordings or meaningless response categories. Missing values may also imply the respondent's ambivalence toward the issue at hand. In any event, the researcher should be very cautious about the interpretation of the data when the missing responses are numerous.

Finally, in Table 2.4, when the percentage of party loyalists is computed, the number of members in a given party is used as the base rather than the total number of cases in the sample. Thus what serves as the base may also depend on the frame of reference. If the Democrats are treated as a whole among whom a differentiation is to be made, then the number of Democrats and not the number of respondents becomes the base for the calculation.

proportions convey the relative category size within a sample, but they are **standard measures** that can be compared across different samples. For example, Anne is anxious to compare the family forms at two different periods of time because she has heard much about the changes in the U.S. family. To this end, she has extracted some data from the data banks of the Research Institute for the years 1970 and 1989, and constructed percentage tables as shown in Table 2.5.

If Anne compares the frequencies of two-parent families, the number is larger in the sample of 1989 than in the sample of 1970: 4,108 to 3,286. However, she cannot conclude that the two-parent family pattern has become more prevalent in 1989 because the sample for that year is also larger. With a larger sample, the count per category can be expected to be higher.

A percentage, unlike a frequency, represents a *standard measure* that expresses the number of cases out of 100 that would fall into a category, regardless of actual sample size. Thus percentage or proportion distributions are comparable across samples of varying sizes. Table 2.5 indicates, as Anne expected, that the percentage of two-parent families has fallen, while that of one-parent families has risen over the years.

Note that the question of whether any *significant* change has occurred in the percentage of two-parent families in the United States is best answered using inferential statistics. Since samples from the *same* population do not necessarily yield identical results (see Section 1.5.2), the difference between the 1970 and 1989

TABLE 2.5 Family Forms in the United States,
1970 and 1989

Respondents' Family of Orientation	Percentages (frequencies)			
	1970		1989	
Two-parent families	88.9	(3,286)	79.9	(4,108)
Mother only	9.9	(366)	16.2	(833)
Father only	1.2	(45)	3.9	(201)
Total	100.0	(3,697)	100.0	(5,142)

samples may result from sampling error rather than a true difference in the populations. All that Anne can conclude at this point is that the later sample shows a noticeable decline in two-parent families, which *may* reflect a corresponding change in the population.

Exercises

1. Anne finds a survey conducted by the Research Institute in which the respondents were asked their marital status. A tally of the responses follows:

Married	190
Single	88
Divorced	56
Cohabitating	42
Widowed	23
Other	18

   a. Construct a percentage table for these data.
   b. What is the percentage of the nonmarried?
   c. What categories are presumably included in the category of "other"?

2. Community studies conducted in Hawaii and California show ethnic compositions tabulated as follows:

Hawaii		*California*	
Haole (white)	80	White	248
Japanese	96	Black	60
Chinese	77	Hispanic	72
Part Hawaiian	38	Asian	12
Other	29	Other	8

   a. Construct percentage tables for these data.
   b. How could ethnic categories be reclassified so as to make the two sets of data comparable?

3. Take a class survey of the occupations of the students' parents.

   a. Develop an appropriate coding scheme to classify occupations.
   b. Construct frequency, proportion, and percentage tables separately for fathers and mothers.
   c. Interpret the results.

4. A survey based on 582 students reports the following percentage distribution. How many nonwhite students are included in this sample?

White	52%
Black	15
Hispanic	11
Asian	5
Other	17

5. The school census reports that 48% or 3,500 of the incoming freshmen are females. What is the total number of freshmen?

2.4 Tables for Ordinal Data

2.4.1 Frequency, Proportion, and Percentage Distributions

Research Question

All the variables Anne has examined so far are nominal variables. In this section, Anne analyzes **ordinal variables.** Measurement at the ordinal level carries more information than at the nominal level. In addition to equivalence or nonequivalence, the categories of an ordinal variable convey information on the amount, the "more or less" of some property. These categories, sometimes referred to as **ranks,** can be arranged in order of increasing or decreasing magnitude.

The United States is one of the richest and most technologically advanced nations. To retain its lead in technology, the country must have an educated work force. Anne decides to examine the formal educational level of U.S. residents to determine how well educated they are. Education could have been measured on the interval level, using the number of years of schooling as an indicator. However, Anne concludes that the purpose of her research is better served using a less precise scale obtained by collapsing some of the categories of the interval variable. The result is an ordinal variable.

The Data and Their Interpretation

Using the same data set of Department XXX, Anne requests the computer to generate the percentage distribution as shown in Table 2.6. Note that each category in Table 2.6 does not measure an equal amount of education, although the categories are ordered according to magnitude. For instance, the first category consists of 0 to 4 years of education, the second, 5 to 7 years, and so on. The criterion used in combining categories depends on the purpose of the analysis and the nature of the data. In Table 2.6, Anne applies as a criterion the commonly made distinctions of grade school, high school, and college education. In another study, the researcher may be guided by the structure of the data; adjoining categories containing only a few cases may be combined, while a category with too many cases may be subdivided. Thus, exploratory tabulation may be necessary prior to recoding.

From reading Table 2.6, Anne learns that U.S. residents are generally well educated. A sizable minority though, 26.1%, does not finish high school. On the

TABLE 2.6   Educational Level in the
United States of Persons Aged 25 and
Over, 1990

Level of Education	Percentage
0 to 4 years	2.7
5 to 7 years	4.8
8 years	6.4
9 to 11 years	12.2
High school graduate	38.2
Some college	16.3
College graduate or more	19.4
Total ($N = 4,551$)	100.0

other hand, a considerable percentage, 19.4%, completes 4 years of college or more. This leads Anne to speculate that perhaps this is a land of contrasts as well as of diversity. Do the diverse ethnic groups contribute to this variation in educational achievement? Or is another factor, such as age, more important? As this example shows, sometimes finding the answer to one research question leads to more questions.

Construction of a (Relative) Frequency Distribution for Ordinal Data

A frequency, proportion, or percentage distribution can be constructed for ordinal data. The same method used in constructing these distributions for nominal data is applicable here. The same rules apply as well. Categories should be nonoverlapping and exhaustive. The choice of N, or the base, should be decided before the calculation of a proportion or percentage. The base of N, again, may or may not equal the number of cases in the sample depending on what is being analyzed.

To display the data, the categories must be presented in rank order from low to high, or vice versa. This rule obviously does not apply to nominal data, since there is no inherent order among their categories. Instead, the categories of nominal measurement are generally presented in the order of declining frequencies.

2.4.2 Cumulative Distribution

Research Question

Another important aspect of any society is its class structure. The United States, being a rich nation, should have a sizable middle class. As Anne tries to find out more about U.S. class structure, she encounters a problem. What should she use as an indicator of class standing? Contemporary social scientists sometimes measure social class standing through a combination of objective criteria such as income, occupation, and education. Yet Anne believes that she would still be missing a certain element by basing class membership on objective criteria alone, regardless of how many indicators she uses. Certainly, an individual's subjective identification with a class, that is, the belief that he or she belongs to a certain class, is important as well, as it may determine his or her values, attitudes, and behaviors.

The Data and Their Interpretation

Anne locates a study conducted by a sociologist on the subjective identification of class membership, as shown in Table 2.7. In this case, a cumulative percentage as well as a percentage distribution is used to organize the data. A **cumulative distribution** gives the frequency, proportion, or percentage of cases that are at and below (or above) each rank. When frequencies are cumulated, we have a cumulative frequency distribution; when proportions and percentages are cumulated, we have a cumulative relative frequency distribution. The cumulative relative frequency distribution of Table 2.7 indicates that a very small percentage of people place themselves in the lower class. Approximately 37% of the sample identify themselves as members of the working class or below. Over 81% identify their status as being middle class or below, and over 97% consider themselves upper middle class or below. Very few people believe they belong to the upper class. It is also interesting to note from the percentage distribution that approximately the same percentages of people identify themselves as upper and lower classes.

Anne wonders if the number of people identifying themselves as belonging to one or the other class is determined by the categories provided by the researcher. In another study with more or fewer categories, would the results remain fairly stable, or would they be very different? In addition, how different would the class structure appear if objective rather than subjective criteria were applied? According to sociological studies, the two approaches produce some overlap, but some differences as well [1]. Anne defers making a conclusion about class structure in the United States until she gathers more information.

Construction of a Cumulative Frequency Distribution

The construction of a cumulative table is similar to that of other tables. First, construct a frequency (proportion or percentage) distribution. Then include a

TABLE 2.7 Class Identification in the United States, 1990

Social Class	Percentage	Cumulative Percentage
Lower class	2.3	2.3
Working class	34.5	36.8
Middle class	44.3	81.1
Upper middle class	16.7	97.8
Upper class	2.2	100.0
Total ($N = 629$)	100.0	

cumulative frequency column, labeled **cf,** which sums the frequencies from the lowest rank up to and including the specified rank. The cf column may also sum in the opposite direction, from the highest down to the specified rank. Thus the cumulative frequency is the frequency of a particular rank plus the frequencies of *all* the ranks below it (or above it, if adding in the opposite direction). For example, in Table 2.7, the cf at "Working Class" is obtained by summing 2.3 and 34.5, which equals 36.8; the cf at "Middle Class" of 81.1 is the result of adding 2.3, 34.5, and 44.3. The last category of the table has a frequency of *N*, a proportion of 1.0, or a percentage of 100.0, indicating the inclusion of everyone in the addition. The direction of the calculation depends on the purpose of the researcher. In summing the frequencies of all lower ranks up to and including a specified rank, the cf indicates the cases at or below that rank. In adding the frequencies of all higher ranks down to and including a specified rank, it gives the cases at or above that rank.

Cumulative distributions are appropriate only for ordinal- or higher-level data, for which information about the size or rank is conveyed. They are inappropriate for nominal-level data.

Exercises

6. The following are the educational aspirations of a sample of eighth-graders:

High school diploma	40
Some college	32
College graduation and above	28

    a. Construct a cumulative percentage distribution.
    b. Convert Table 2.6 into a cumulative percentage distribution table.
    c. Compare the two and comment on them.

7. Take a class survey to obtain the following information:

    Father's educational level
    Mother's educational level
    Respondent's expected educational level

    a. Classify educational level into meaningful categories.
    b. Construct cumulative percentage distributions.
    c. Compare the three distributions and comment on them.

8. According to a report, a sample is split into two strata: 50% middle class and above and 50% working class and below. Within the upper stratum, one out of five belongs to the upper class, and the rest are middle class. Within the lower stratum two out of five belong to the lower class and the remainder are working class. If the sample contains 550 upper-class subjects, how many middle-class and how many working-class subjects are there?

9. A sample is drawn to include three age groups of 100 each. One out of every three young subjects is included, as compared to one out of four middle-aged and one out of every two seniors. What is the population size?

2.5 Tables for Interval Data

2.5.1 Grouped Frequency Distribution for a Continuous Variable

Research Question

One of the most important aspects of a society is its age distributions according to sex. These distributions both describe the population of today and forecast the population of tomorrow. They suggest birth and death rates and the potential for growth.

Clearly, age is an **interval variable**. (Recall from Chapter 1 that both interval and ratio data are grouped and referred to as interval data.) It is measured in standardized units of years and months, has a recognized starting point, and is continuous in nature. Measurement of continuous interval variables generally results in a large range of values. When these values are organized in a simple frequency distribution, it may become unwieldy and difficult to comprehend. Therefore, in tabulating the age distributions by sex in the United States, Anne elects to generate a grouped frequency distribution. A **grouped frequency distribution** makes it easier to detect patterns in the data.

The Data and Their Interpretation

Anne obtains the following age distributions, one for females and the other for males, from the *Statistical Abstract of the United States, 1991*. Note in Table 2.8(a) and (b) that the values of the variable are grouped into *intervals* of 0 to 4, 5 to 9, and so on. For example, in the interval 0 to 4, five values, 0, 1, 2, 3, and 4, are grouped together. The process of grouping is similar to that of collapsing categories. Except for the last interval in Table 2.8, the rest are of equal width, thus retaining the characteristic of interval data.

Comparing the two age distributions, Anne notices a number of interesting phenomena. First, there are more males than females below the age of 35 in every age interval. However, above the age of 34, the females outnumber the males, the trend becoming more and more pronounced with advancing age. Consequently, she concludes that females have a longer life expectancy than males.

Second, the frequencies around the ages of 25 to 39 are higher than the frequencies in other age categories in both distributions. This reflects a higher than usual birth rate around the mid 1940s to the late 1950s and early 1960s, a period commonly referred to as the baby-boom era. Since then, the birth rate has declined, as shown in the lower frequencies of the younger age groups.

Finally, Anne notes with interest what these distributions predict for the future—a "graying of the United States," which demographers have foretold. With the birth rate remaining low, as these baby-boomers move into middle age, the average age of the U.S. population will continue to increase.

Stated and Real Limits, Interval Width, and Midpoints

Age is a continuous variable that can be measured to the second or fractions of a second; its accuracy is limited only by the measuring instrument. However, in the

TABLE 2.8 Age Distribution of Males and Females in the United States, 1989

(a) Males		(b) Females	
Age Group	*f* (in millions)	Age Group	*f* (in millions)
0–4	9.6	0–4	9.2
5–9	9.3	5–9	8.9
10–14	8.7	10–14	8.3
15–19	9.1	15–19	8.7
20–24	9.5	20–24	9.4
25–29	11.0	25–29	10.9
30–34	11.2	30–34	11.1
35–39	9.8	35–39	10.0
40–44	8.3	40–44	8.6
45–49	6.6	45–49	6.9
50–54	5.5	50–54	5.9
55–59	5.1	55–59	5.6
60–64	5.1	60–64	5.8
65–69	4.6	65–69	5.5
70–74	3.5	70–74	4.5
75–79	2.4	75–79	3.6
80–84	1.3	80–84	2.4
85+	.8	85+	2.2
Total	121.4	Total	127.5

Source: Statistical Abstract of the United States, 1991, p. 12.

social sciences, such precision is seldom necessary. Instead, age may be measured to the closest year. If age is measured to the closest year, then two respondents, one of 20 years and 3 months, and the other of 20 years and 1 month, would both be treated as 20 years old. This example illustrates that, while measuring a continuous variable, some sort of grouping is involved and, through grouping, a limit is imposed on the precision of the data.

In constructing a grouped frequency distribution, these principles of grouping and measurement precision are incorporated into the distribution. The intervals of a grouped distribution have a stated lower and upper limit to indicate the range of values they cover. For example, the interval 0 to 4 has a **stated lower limit** of 0 and a **stated upper limit** of 4. **Stated limits** reflect the same level of precision that is found in the measurement of the raw data. If age has been measured to the tenth of a year, then the limits would be stated to the tenth of a year, such as 0.0 to 4.9 and 5.0 to 9.9. From the stated limits in Table 2.8(a) and (b), it is clear that the respondents' ages are measured to the closest year. Note from these tables that a gap exists between the stated lower limit of an interval and the stated upper limit of the one below it. The width of the gap also reflects the accuracy of the measurement. Since measurement is accurate to a year, the gap in

Table 2.8(a) and (b) is 1 year and can be found by subtracting the stated upper limit of an interval from the stated lower limit of the next higher interval. When age is measured to the closest tenth of a year, the gap is .1, the result of subtracting 4.9 from 5.0.

Real limits, on the other hand, reflect the continuous nature of the variable. Theoretically, measurement precision to the second, third, or fourth decimal place is possible with age. To take this theoretical possibility into account, when the real limits are given, they are given with no gaps in between. Real limits are considered to be midway between the stated limits. Thus the real limits of Table 2.8(a) and (b) are –0.5 to 4.5, 4.5 to 9.5, and so on. (The real lower limit of the first interval is specified as –0.5 even when age cannot be less than 0 to retain the same width for this interval as for others.) Although real limits appear to overlap, they should not create a problem for classifying a raw score. For if the stated limits reflect the measurement precision of age to a whole year, the occasion would not arise of having to classify a score that is accurate to fractions of a year, such as 4.5. In other words, given this level of precision, a score of 4 or 5 is possible, but not 4.5, and there should be no ambiguity in placing 4 or 5 into their respective intervals.

Real limits are important because they are used to determine both the width and the midpoint of an interval. The **width** is found by subtracting the real lower limit from the real upper limit. Generally, the interval width is kept constant throughout the distribution, but sometimes an open-ended interval is placed at either or both ends of the distribution. An **open-ended interval** at the lower end of the distribution does not have a stated lower limit, and an open-ended interval at the upper end of the distribution does not have a stated upper limit. Both Table 2.8(a) and (b) have an open-ended interval at the upper end of the distributions.

Each interval also has a **midpoint.** When the original values of the scores are lost or are no longer available after grouping the data, the midpoint is used to represent all the data values within an interval. To determine the midpoint, subtract the real lower limit of an interval from its real upper limit and divide the difference by 2; then add the resulting value to the real lower limit. Thus the midpoint of the interval 5 to 9 is 7.0: $(9.5 - 4.5)/2 + 4.5 = 7.0$.

The concepts of limit, width, and midpoint are equally applicable to an ungrouped frequency distribution of a continuous variable, since the data are treated customarily as if they are grouped. Each value is considered the midpoint of an interval that has a real upper and lower limit. For example, the data values of 1, 2, and 3 are midpoints of intervals ranging from 0.5 to 1.5, 1.5 to 2.5, and 2.5 to 3.5, all having a width of 1.0.

Construction of a Grouped Frequency Distribution
To construct a grouped frequency distribution, such as those in Table 2.8, the number of intervals must first be determined. Keep in mind that a grouped frequency distribution should have sufficient, but no more than sufficient, intervals to highlight the important features of the distribution. Since having too many intervals defeats the purpose of grouping, the maximum number of intervals is frequently set at 20. On the other hand, having too few intervals may obscure the

important characteristics of the data. Therefore, the minimum number of intervals is often set at 10.

Ultimately, the decision regarding the number of intervals depends on the range of values in the data and the intended use of the distribution. For example, a criterion for determining the interval width may be the implication or meaning of the width itself. Had Table 2.8(a) and (b) been constructed for a generational study, age intervals of 10 rather than 5 would be more appropriate.

Once the decision is made with regard to the number of intervals, the width of the interval must be determined. As a rough approximation, subtract the lowest raw score from the highest to calculate the range of the distribution. Then divide the desired number of intervals into this range. Although the result may not be a whole number, it can be rounded to the nearest whole number to give the interval width.

Construct the intervals beginning with the lowest. This interval should include the lowest score, but should not extend too far below it. In the same manner, the highest interval should include the highest score, but should not extend too far above it. In stating the limits of two adjoining intervals, keep in mind that they should have a gap that reflects the same level of accuracy as that found in the measurement of sample data. Open-ended intervals may be used at one or both ends of the distribution.

2.5.2 Grouped Frequency Distribution for a Discrete Variable

The same basic principles apply in constructing a grouped frequency distribution for discrete data as for continuous data. Table 2.9 shows a grouped frequency

TABLE 2.9 Ideal Number of Children for a Sample of U.S. Residents, 1991

Number of Children	Frequencies	
0–1	39	
2–3	758	
4–5	117	
6 or more	9	
Total respondents		923
Other responses		594
Total number of cases		1,517

Source: National Opinion Research Center, General Social Surveys, 1991.

distribution for the discrete variable, the ideal number of children per family. Sometimes, in constructing such a table, the discrete data are treated as if they were continuous to permit statistical manipulations. In such cases, the intervals are assumed to have stated versus real limits, which in Table 2.9 range from −.5 to 1.5, 1.5 to 3.5, and so on.

Exercises

10. Anne takes a random sample of 20 states and finds the divorce rates per 1,000 residents as follows:

> 2.1 3.5 3.2 1.8 2.0 1.4 1.9   3.3 3.3 4.6
> 3.3 2.8 3.9 4.6 6.1 4.9 5.4 24.0 5.4 2.9

a. What are appropriate intervals for grouping the data and why?
b. Using the intervals selected, construct frequency and percentage distributions.

11. Anne takes a random sample of 12 states and finds the percentages of those voting in presidential elections as follows:

> 68.3 61.3 53.3 59.4 45.9 43.2
> 76.2 66.7 37.8 28.1 55.5 66.3

a. What are appropriate intervals for grouping the data and why?
b. Using the intervals selected, construct frequency and percentage distributions.

12. How should a researcher decide on the number of categories to use in grouping data?

13. Critique the following limits for the hourly wage rate:

> 0–5.00
> 0–5.50
> 0–under 5.00

14. The following are the test scores from several classes. Construct grouped frequency and percentage tables. What are the real limits of the intervals?

a. 8 8 9 10 4 2 5 7 7 7 6
b. 98 75 100 85 62 34 80 70 83 72 52
c. 60 62 58 71 65 65 59 63 62 64 60
d. 20.9 63.5 70 81.3 72.4 75.6 99.9 80.3

SPSS Session

All the programs and figures for illustration in this text are based on SPSS/PC+. However, in place of SPSS/PC+, we will use the generic term SPSS in our discussions, unless there is a difference in the commands between the microcomputer and the mainframe version. In such cases, we will specifically denote how the SPSS command is written versus how the SPSS/PC+ command is written.

At this point, students planning to use SPSS should read Sections 1, 2, and 4 of Appendix A, while students planning to use SPSS/PC+ should read Sections 1, 3, and 4 of Appendix A. Our first session on the computer consists of writing the following program to construct tables for a nominal and an ordinal variable.

```
DATA LIST FIXED/SES 1 AGE 3-4.

BEGIN DATA.

3 34

2 21

1 12

....

....

END DATA.

RECODE AGE (0 THRU 4 = 1) (5 THRU 9 = 2) (10 THRU 14 = 3)...

          ...(85 THRU HI = 18).

VALUE LABELS AGE 1  '0-4'  2 '5-9'  3 '10-14'  4 '15-19'... 18 '85+'

          /SES 1  'Lower Class'  2 'Working Class'... 5 'Upper Class'.

MISSING VALUE SES (0).

FREQUENCIES VARIABLES=SES AGE.
```

The DATA LIST command informs the computer of the names assigned to variables and their location and format. The subcommand FIXED refers to the format in which the data are entered. In a fixed format, the codes of a variable are placed in the same column(s) of a data line for each observation. The data consist of two variables, named SES and AGE, per case. Variable names can have a maximum of eight characters. In a fixed format, the location of each variable is specified after the variable name. Thus SES is located in the first and AGE in the third to fourth columns of each data line.

The BEGIN DATA and END DATA commands signal the beginning and ending of data lines. They indicate that the data are entered inline, that is, in between these commands rather than separately from a data file. Since there are 2,543 cases in this data set, not all the data lines are shown. Lines entered but not shown are represented by the symbols "..." in the program.

The RECODE command reclassifies age values into age groups and assigns each group a new value. The name of the variable to be recoded is mentioned first; then each recoding is specified within parentheses. Within the parentheses the original value(s) to be recoded is followed by the equal sign and then the new value. For example, ages 0 to 4 are now grouped and assigned a value of 1. When this command is placed before the FREQUENCIES command, the recoding is executed first. Consequently, FREQUENCIES produces a frequency distribution of the grouped data instead of the original raw data.

The VALUE LABELS command assigns meaningful labels to categories or values of a variable to facilitate the reading of the computer output. Within the command, the variable name is mentioned first and then the value or code, followed by its label in quotes. Thus a label such as 0-4 is attached to the value of 1 in age, 5-9, to the value of 2, and so on, after the recoding. In place of numbers, identifying names are used for each category of SES. To mark the end of the labeling of one variable and to separate it from the beginning of the labeling of another variable, a slash, /, is used. The symbols "..." in both the RECODE and VALUE LABELS commands represent continuing specifications of recoding and value labels that are entered but not shown because they are too long.

The MISSING VALUE command informs the computer that the value of 0 for SES should be considered a missing value. When computing valid percentages, the 0's of SES will not be included into the base. In SPSS/PC+ only one code can be identified as a missing value, whereas in SPSS three codes can be identified as such.

The FREQUENCIES command produces frequency tables, and the VARIABLES subcommand designates the variables for which frequency distributions are to be tabulated.

Only part of the output from the program is shown in SPSS Figure 2.1, consisting of the frequency distribution for SES. A similar frequency distribution produced for AGE is not shown here. Note that SPSS automatically calculates percentages and cumulative percentages for each distribution. In addition, there is a column labeled *Valid Percent*. The *Percent* column computes percentages based on the number of cases in the sample, and the *Valid Percent* column displays the percentages based on the number of valid responses, excluding missing values or cases. When there are no missing values, the two columns of figures are the same.

Value Label	Value	Frequency	Percent	Valid Percent	Cum Percent
Lower class	1.00	59	2.3	2.3	2.3
Working class	2.00	877	34.5	34.6	36.9
Middle class	3.00	1126	44.3	44.4	81.3
Upper middle class	4.00	425	16.7	16.8	98.1
Upper class	5.00	48	1.9	1.9	100.0
	.00	8	.3	Missing	
		-------	-------	-------	
	Total	2543	100.0	100.0	
Valid cases 2535	Missing cases	8			

SPSS FIGURE 2.1   Frequency Distribution of SES

SPSS Exercises

1. Tabulate the ethnicity (ETHNIC) of the GSS respondents.

   a. Construct frequency and percentage tables.
   b. To obtain percentages, what should be used as a base and why?
   c. How should the categories be combined into fewer categories? Construct a percentage table with the collapsed categories.
   d. Interpret the results.

2. Tabulate the working status (WRKSTAT) of the female GSS respondents. If the respondent is male, use his spouse's working status (SPWRKSTA). Then answer the same questions as in Exercise 1.

3. Tabulate the subjective social class (CLASS) of the GSS respondents.

   a. Then construct cumulative frequency and percentage tables.
   b. Interpret the findings.

4. Tabulate the per capita income (INCOME) for cities in the City Data Base.

   a. Find the minimum and the maximum value.
   b. Generate equal-width intervals and construct a frequency distribution.
   c. After examining the table created, generate unequal-width intervals that would give a more meaningful interpretation of the data.
   d. Construct a cumulative percentage distribution.
   e. Interpret the findings.

5. Using the City Data Base, tabulate the discrete variable of city size (POPLATON).

   a. In general, the cities included in this data base have 25,000 or more inhabitants. What would be good intervals to use for classifying city size?
   b. Construct a frequency distribution for the grouped data.
   c. After examining the table created, change the size of the intervals so that they will represent the data more succinctly.
   d. Construct a frequency distribution using the new intervals.
   e. Discuss the findings.

6. Tabulate infant mortality rate (INFANT), a continuous variable.

   a. Construct a frequency distribution of the raw data.
   b. After examining the table created, construct another frequency distribution with equal intervals and interpret the findings.

2.6 Organizing Data in the Form of Graphs

Graphs serve the same functions as tables. Better yet, as the saying goes, "a graph is worth a thousand words," or a thousand numbers as may be the case. Graphs usually have a powerful impact, creating visual images that highlight such important features as the shape and spread of a distribution. Consequently, social scientists find graphs especially useful in exploratory analyses. In constructing and interpreting graphs, the same rules must be followed as for tables. Graphs should organize the data, while being as simple and comprehensible as possible.

2.7 Graphs for Nominal and Ordinal Data

Graphic techniques for ordinal data are very similar to those for nominal data. What is considered appropriate for nominal variables can also be used on discrete ordinal variables. For this reason and because of the scarcity of graphic techniques specific to discrete ordinal variables, the discussion for these two levels is grouped together.

2.7.1 The Pie Chart

Research Question
The United States has always been an immigrant nation. It is still looked on today as a haven for people who seek political and economic freedom. Acutely aware of this image of the country, Anne realizes at the same time that there are other countries, such as Australia, France, and Canada, that have a larger foreign-born population. Is the diversity in ethnicity and religious beliefs that Anne has found in this country being constantly renewed by immigration? Or is it a pattern established through past immigration? Has the United States outlived one of its founding philosophical principles or is it still a nation of immigrants? These are some of the research questions Anne proposes to examine. In initiating an investigation into who the recent immigrants are, Anne decides to employ mostly graphic techniques.

The Pie Chart
Anne obtains the information in columns 1 and 2 of Table 2.10 from the *Statistical Abstract of the United States, 1991*. She summarizes this information graphically with a pie chart.

The **pie chart** is a circle divided into sectors that represent the categories of a variable. The chart creates an immediate impression of the size of the various categories relative to each other and to the whole sample or population. Thus it is an effective method of organizing and presenting nominal data and other data whose values can be recoded as discrete categories.

TABLE 2.10 Immigrants in Thousands by Region of Birth, 1989

Region	f (in thousands)	Proportion	Degrees
Europe	82.9	.076	27
Asia	312.1	.286	103
North America	607.4	.557	201
South America	58.9	.054	19
Other	29.6	.027	10
Total	1,090.9	1.00	360

Source: Statistical Abstract of the United States, 1991, p. 10.

Construction of a Pie Chart

Before constructing a pie chart, compute a proportion for each category as shown in column 3 of Table 2.10. Then draw a 360-degree circle that represents the pie, or the total number of cases, *N*. Next this circle is subdivided into sectors. The size of each sector depends on the degrees of its angle at the center of the circle. The degrees of a sector, in turn, are obtained through multiplying the corresponding proportion by a base of 360:

$$\text{degrees of the sector} = (P_i)(360) = \frac{f_i}{N} 360 \tag{2.4}$$

Thus the size of a sector is ultimately determined by the relative frequency, that is, the proportion or percentage, of that category.

Using Formula 2.4, the proportion of Asian immigrants in Table 2.10, which equals .286, is converted to 103 degrees: (.268)(360). The rest of the proportions are similarly converted to obtain the degrees given in the last column of the table. These degrees are then used for drawing the sectors in Figure 2.1.

Anne is surprised to learn that the largest sector is represented by the *North America* category. However, as used in the *Statistical Abstract of the United States*, this sector includes such diverse countries as Canada, Mexico, the Caribbean islands, and Central America.

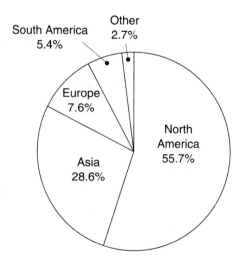

**FIGURE 2.1 Immigrants by
Country of Birth:
United States, 1989**

*Source: Statistical Abstract of the United States,
1991, p. 10.*

2.7.2 The Bar Chart

Research Question

Since too many diverse countries are classified into a region in Table 2.10, Anne decides more information can be obtained by taking a closer look at the immigrants' country of origin. She focuses on countries that have sent a significant number of immigrants to the United States in recent years. This time she uses a bar chart to represent the information in the frequency distribution.

Anne has a specific reason for the choice of a bar chart over a pie chart. She is not presenting data on all immigrants, only on immigrants from selected countries. Because the pie chart creates the impression of a whole, all immigrants in this case, Anne believes that the pie chart may be misleading.

The Bar Chart

A **bar chart** consists of a series of bars, each representing the frequency of a category. The length of a bar is proportional to the number of cases in that category. SPSS Figure 2.2 displays a bar chart constructed by SPSS on the country of origin of recent immigrants. According to the bar chart, Mexico contributes the greatest number of immigrants, followed by El Salvador, and then the Philippines. Of the countries represented in the chart, India sends the fewest immigrants.

Construction of a Bar Chart

Visualize this chart as having two axes, one that extends horizontally, called the *X* axis or the **abscissa,** and the other vertically, called the *Y* axis or the **ordinate.** The information under the two columns of a frequency distribution can be transferred directly onto these two axes. Categories can be arranged along the horizon-

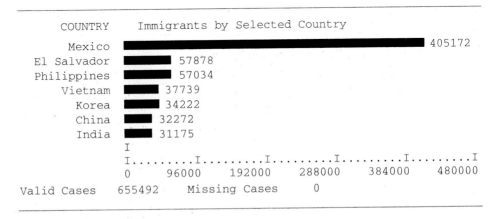

SPSS FIGURE 2.2   Bar Chart of Immigrants by Country of Origin, 1989

tal or vertical axis, while frequencies can be arranged on the other axis. Bars are erected above each category or alongside, if the categories are arranged on the vertical axis. Their height or length is determined by and proportional to the number of cases in each category.

Bar charts are used to represent nominal or categorical data. A glance at the height or length of the bars effectively informs the reader of the relative size of each category. Note that the bars are drawn so that they do not touch and are equally spaced apart. This is done to convey the notion that the categories are discrete, with no inherent order among them.

2.7.3 The Multiple Bar Chart

Research Question
The earliest immigrants who came in search of religious freedom were from western and northern Europe. Obviously, a shift has occurred in the immigration pattern. When did this shift take place?

The Multiple Bar Chart
Whereas the simple bar chart permits Anne to compare the categories of a distribution, the **multiple bar chart** permits her to compare two or more distributions. The multiple bar chart in Figure 2.2 shows the size of immigration by region of origin in 1820 to 1860, 1921 to 1960, and 1961 to 1970 [2].

In the early period of immigration, 95% of the immigrants came from Europe. Even as late as the first half of the twentieth century, Europe contributed 58% of

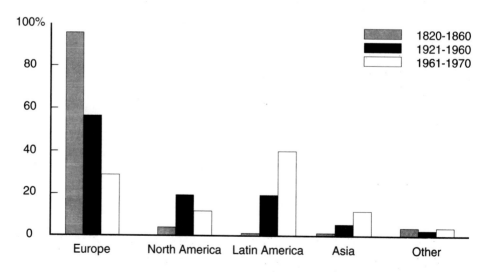

FIGURE 2.2   Percentage of Legal Immigrants to the United States by Region and Time Period

Source: L. F. Bouvier and R. W. Gardner (1986). Immigration to the U.S.: The Unfinished Story. *Population Bulletin*, 41 (2, November). Washington, D.C.: Population Reference Bureau.

the total immigration. A shift began, however, in the decade of the 1960s. By this time, the percentage from Europe had shrunk to 33%, while South America had overtaken Europe. As seen in SPSS Figure 2.2, another shift occurred more recently, with Mexico accounting for 37% of the total immigration.

Construction of a Multiple Bar Chart

The multiple bar chart is constructed in the same manner as the single bar chart with the following exceptions. At each category, a number of bars are drawn without spaces in between. Each bar represents the frequency or the proportion of that category for a particular distribution. Thus, in Figure 2.2, with three time periods or distributions represented in the chart, three bars corresponding to the time periods are erected at each category. These bars are differentiated by shades, colors, or design. A key to identify the time period represented by each bar is given at the upper-right corner of the figure. Although the multiple bars at each category are drawn touching each other, the bars between two regions or categories are still separated by space to denote the discrete nature of the variable.

Exercises

15. Under what circumstance would a pie chart be preferable to a bar chart?

16. a. Use the data in Table 2.2 to construct a pie chart and a bar chart.
    b. Should some categories be collapsed? Why or why not?
    c. Which chart is more effective in summarizing the data?

17. Using the data in Table 2.5, construct two pie charts and a multiple bar chart. Compare their effectiveness.

2.8 Graphs for Interval Data

The graphic techniques introduced in this section are appropriate for interval data. They could, however, be applied to ordinal variables as well, as long as these data are continuous in nature and their values measure approximately the same distances or amounts.

2.8.1 The Histogram

Research Question

What is the attitude of U.S. residents toward immigration? The attitude can be determined partially by what most residents consider as the ideal level of immigration for the country. Anne locates a study in the data banks of the Social Research Institute containing an item that provides some insight into this question. Respondents in this study were asked, "Today immigration accounts for 26% of the nation's population growth. What would you consider an ideal level of immigration in terms of the percentage of population growth?"

The Histogram

The answers, given in terms of percentage increase, are represented by the histogram in Figure 2.3. A **histogram** is another graphic device that employs bars to display the frequencies (or proportions) of values. Note that, although the histogram in Figure 2.3 is constructed for *grouped data*, the graphic technique could also be applied to ungrouped data.

Figure 2.3 shows that most U.S. residents desire to restrict immigration and also to reduce it to a much lower level than the current one. Seventy-seven percent favor restricting immigration to 10% or less of the population growth. Only 8% desire a level higher than the status quo of 26% increase.

Construction of a Histogram

A histogram can be constructed in the same manner as a bar chart to represent how grouped or ungrouped interval values are distributed. There are differences, however, between a histogram and a bar chart. In a histogram, the bars do not have spaces in between, but are contiguous, to indicate the continuous nature of the variable. Each bar represents the frequency of cases within an interval. If the data are ungrouped, bars are erected above the individual values that serve as midpoints of the intervals. The width of the bars are determined by their real limits. Together the area covered by these bars equals N, the total number of cases. When a histogram is used to depict a grouped distribution of proportions, the

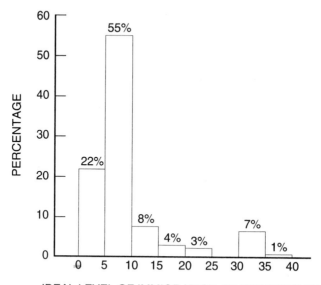

FIGURE 2.3   **Histogram of Ideal Level of Immigration as Percentage of Population Growth, 1989**

total area is set to 1.00. The bars then designate the relative rather than absolute frequencies of the intervals.

In place of a histogram, a continuous sample distribution with a very large *N* or a continuous population distribution may be represented by a smooth curve. Because of the many parallels between a histogram and a smooth curve, a thorough grasp of the former is essential to an understanding of the latter. Box 2.3 points out some of the parallels between the two.

Box 2.3   Histograms and Smooth Curves

Suppose a number of histograms are constructed for a continuous variable, such as the ideal level of immigration expressed in percentages. Imagine also that these histograms are based on samples of increasing size. Now consider what happens to the histograms as *N* increases. With a sample of 10, there will be, at most, 10 different discrete values. To construct a histogram for this sample, the values may have to be grouped into large intervals so that some cases will fall into each interval. With a sample of 1,000, however, these values may be grouped into much smaller intervals, since there are more data values. The larger sample makes it more probable that some cases will be included in each small interval.

Thus, as sample size increases, the width of the intervals decreases. Theoretically, when the sample size becomes very large (given an infinite population), the interval width is decreased to the point where the bars of the histogram are no longer distinguishable from one

another, but instead merge to form a smooth curve. Figure 2.4 shows this gradual convergence to a smooth curve. Because of the similarity between the two, statistics texts often represent large samples and population distributions of both continuous and discrete variables as smooth curves. The area of a smooth curve is conventionally set to 1.00.

Note in Figure 2.4 that the area covered by the bars of the histogram approximates the area covered by the smooth curve. Therefore, in place of particular bars of a histogram, we refer to specific **areas under the curve** for a smooth curve. As the total area under the curve and the proportions of a distribution both sum to 1.00, a specific area under the curve represents the proportion of cases within an interval. The concept that an area under the curve is equivalent to the proportion of cases within an interval or the relative frequency of that interval will be important in later chapters.

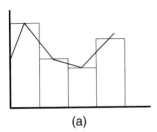 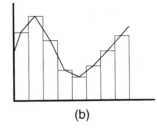 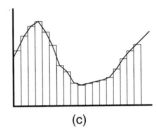

(a)   (b)   (c)

FIGURE 2.4   Histograms with Increasing Sample Size

2.8.2 The Polygon

The data in Figure 2.3 can be represented by another plotting device called a **polygon.** The polygon is generated by connecting the midpoints of each bar in a histogram. Figure 2.5 illustrates the relationship of the polygon to the histogram by superimposing one on the other. Of course, in an actual presentation, one or the other method would suffice.

Construction of a Polygon

The purpose for constructing a frequency or proportion polygon is similar to that of a histogram. The polygon, however, is a step toward approximating the underlying smooth curve and, as such, it imparts the impression of more gradual changes from interval to interval while preserving the general shape of the distribution.

In constructing a polygon, the midpoints rather than the real limits of the intervals are used. A point is plotted above each midpoint at the height corresponding to the frequency, or proportion, of the specified interval. The midpoints are then connected by straight lines. It is customary to close the polygon at either end by extending the line from the first and the last midpoints to locations on the X axis that represent the midpoints of hypothetical adjoining intervals.

The polygon illustrates the **shape** of a distribution more clearly than any of the other graphic devices discussed so far. In both Figures 2.6 and 2.7, the poly-

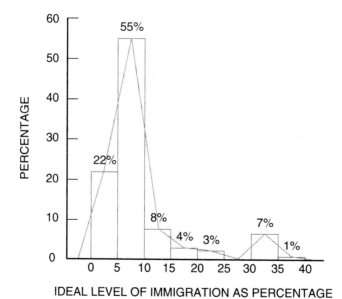

FIGURE 2.5   **Polygon Superimposed over Histogram of Ideal Level of Immigration as Percentage of Population Growth, 1989**

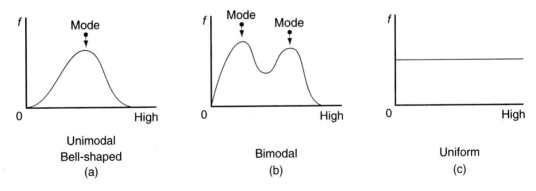

FIGURE 2.6 Shapes of Distributions

gons are smoothed for better visual effect. The distribution may have a **bell shape** as in Figure 2.6(a) or it may be **uniform,** having no peak and being flat with the same height throughout, as in Figure 2.6(c). The peak of the curve in Figure 2.6(a) corresponds to the **mode** of the distribution, the interval with the highest frequency. With one peak, the distribution is said to be **unimodal;** when it has two peaks of approximately the same height, as in Figure 2.6(b), it is **bimodal.**

The portions of the polygon that fall away from the peak are known as the **tails** of the curve. The shape of the distribution can also be characterized through a comparison of these tails. If the tails on both sides of the peak are identical, the distribution is **symmetrical** as in Figure 2.7(a). If one tail is longer than the other, the distribution is **skewed.** Figure 2.7(b) is **positively skewed.** Its right tail is longer, indicating that few sample scores have values much higher than the bulk of the distribution. A distribution with a longer tail to the left of the peak, as in Figure 2.7(c), is **negatively skewed.** It has few data values that are much lower in value than the bulk of the distribution.

For comparison, multiple frequency polygons representing different distributions of the same variable may be superimposed on one another. A multiple frequency polygon serves the same function as a multiple bar chart.

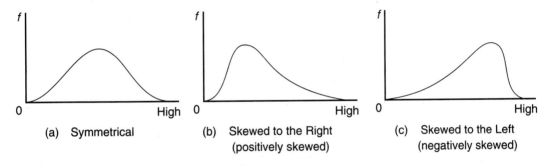

FIGURE 2.7 Symmetry and Skewness

2.8.3 The Stem-and-Leaf Diagram

Research Question

Anne wonders whether college students hold similar attitudes toward immigration as the public. She therefore poses the same question on immigration from the national survey to her class of 47 students at University X. The students are asked to indicate what they consider an ideal level of immigration in terms of the percentage of population growth.

The Stem-and-Leaf Diagram

Other than with a histogram and frequency polygon, interval data can also be represented by a technique called the **stem-and-leaf diagram** [3]. The stem-and-leaf resembles and has the same advantages as a histogram. In addition, it organizes data so as to achieve immediate visual impact without losing information. The stem-and-leaf diagram in Figure 2.8 is constructed from the student data.

Readers can tell at a glance the shape of the distribution in Figure 2.8, its mode or modes, and the amount of dispersion. For example, Anne discerns that the distribution is positively skewed and that the mode is 5%. If the raw data are grouped into the same intervals as those used in Figure 2.3 to facilitate comparison, the modal interval is 5 to 9. **Extreme scores** are segregated from the rest of the distribution. In Figure 2.8 these are 30 and 35. (Extreme scores are discussed in Section 3.7.) At the same time, the entire data set can be reconstructed from the diagram, since it uses the actual value to represent a case. From a line such as "1 . 55567," individual scores of 15, 15, 15, 16, and 17 can be reconstructed. The major drawback to the stem-and-leaf diagram is that large data sets cannot be represented as easily.

From Figure 2.8, Anne concludes that the students in her class hold very similar attitudes toward immigration as do the general population. The stem and leaf has the same mode and similar shape and spread as the histogram in Figure 2.3.

Construction of a Stem-and-Leaf Diagram

To construct a stem-and-leaf diagram, follow these steps:

1. Arrange the observations in an array.
2. Divide each observation into two components, the **stem** and the **leaf.** This is done by deciding how many of the leading digits of a score are to be the stem and how many are to be the leaves. An observation with a value of 132 may be divided in two ways: the stem may consist of the first one or two leading digits, while the leaf may be comprised of the remaining two or one digit. Thus the value of 132 could be represented as stem 1 and leaf 32, or stem 13 and leaf 2. Customarily, however, only one trailing digit is used to represent the leaves, although the stem may be any number of digits.
   a. In Anne's case, since there are, at most, two digits to each score, the leading digit becomes the stem, and the trailing digit, the leaf. For example, the score of 12 has a stem of 1 and a leaf of 2. For single-digit scores in the sample, the stem is 0 and the leaf is the score value. The stem width

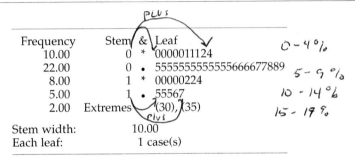

Frequency	Stem	&	Leaf	
10.00	0	*	0000011124	$0-4\%$
22.00	0	.	5555555555555666677889	$5-9\%$
8.00	1	*	00000224	$10-14\%$
5.00	1	.	55567	$15-19\%$
2.00	Extremes		(30), (35)	

Stem width: 10.00
Each leaf: 1 case(s)

FIGURE 2.8   **Stem-and-Leaf Diagram for Desired Level of Immigration**

(referred to at the bottom of the diagram) is 10. If there were three digits to the data values, the stem width would be 100.

3. Write down all the different leading digits from the data set except those of extreme scores in an ascending order *under a column* labeled *Stem.*

4. Under a separate column to the right labeled *Leaf,* write down the trailing digits in ascending order *in a row* next to the corresponding stem. Thus each row represents a stem and each leaf value represents an observation.

5. If there are too many leaves on one stem, the stem may be subdivided into two or more rows. In Figure 2.8 the symbol *, which appears between the stem-and-leaf components, indicates that leaf values 0 through 4 are displayed following this symbol, whereas the symbol • indicates leaf values from 5 to 9 follow on this stem.

6. In a third column labeled *Frequency,* write down the number of cases per stem. This count should correspond to the number of leaves in a row.

7. Extreme values at either end of the distribution are not integrated into the diagram as stems and leaves. Instead, they are listed individually in parentheses, as in Figure 2.8.

Exercises

18. Draw a histogram for the following sample of test scores:

    70 82 43 55 64 90 100 73
    55 95 67 70 82 69   72 89

19. Plot a histogram and a polygon for the age distributions of males and females in Table 2.8. Which plot is more effective?

20. Based on the data in Exercise 18, draw a stem-and-leaf diagram.
    a. Which digits should be used as the stem and which as the leaf? Why?
    b. Compare the stem-and-leaf diagram to the histogram in Exercise 18. Which is more effective?

21. When are the same stem values used more than once in constructing a stem-and-leaf diagram?

2.9 Graph Representing Change

Research Question

Finally, Anne wonders if xenophobia (fear of foreigners) could result when a sizable portion of the U.S. population feels itself beset by unwanted immigrants. Anne reasons that if xenophobia exists it would be directed at specific groups, especially one that has grown rapidly, is physically distinct, and is therefore visible as a target. In looking at her multiple bar chart and her pie chart, Anne identifies the Asians as one such group. How can she tell if xenophobia exists with regard to this group?

Rates as a Standard Measure

Fortunately, Anne locates another study conducted by the institute on xenophobic episodes involving Asian immigrants in a large eastern city. The city has seen a tremendous increase in its Asian population from 1969 to 1987. After settling in the city, the Asians first took over the lowliest of jobs, but since then they have worked their way up to become small entrepreneurs. The institute made a count of the confrontations, harassments, and other incidents involving Asians that were reported on the front page of local newspapers over these 18 years. It then calculated the rates of these incidents per 1,000 Asian immigrants.

In addition to proportions and percentages, **rates** represent another method of standardization. Rates are usually calculated for events that occur within a specified time period. Within that period, the number of *actual* occurrences of an event is compared to the number of *potential* occurrences for standardization. For example, the number of xenophobic incidents may increase over time, but if the number of immigrants settling in the city is also increasing, the potential for such occurrences is much greater. If the absolute number of occurrences is reported, it can be very misleading. Thus, to counterbalance the increasing size of the Asian immigrant population, rates are used in place of the absolute number of incidents.

To calculate these rates, first the number of xenophobic incidents (the number of actual events) is divided by the size of the Asian population within the city (the number of potential events) to control for population size. Then the quotient is multiplied by a factor of 1,000, 10,000, or some such number to avoid small fractional values as follows:

$$\text{rate} = \frac{f_{(\text{actual cases})}}{f_{(\text{potential cases})}} \times 1,000 \tag{2.5}$$

For example, the rate of .1 per thousand in 1969 from Figure 2.9 is calculated by dividing the number of incidents, which is 1, by the number of Asian immigrants, which is 10,000, and then multiplying the quotient by 1,000, as follows: (1/10,000)(1,000). By 1987, the Asian population had doubled and there were 78 incidents that year. The rate per thousand for this year is obtained as follows:

$(78/20,000)(1,000) = 3.9$. Rates can be compared across samples of different sizes. Anne notes from the graph that, even though the population size is controlled, the rate has gone up 39 times in 18 years.

The Line Graph

To track the increase or decrease of such incidents over time, Anne produces the line graph shown in Figure 2.9. A line graph shows the change in frequency, rate, or percentage with respect to a particular variable over a period of time.

The line graph shows that xenophobic incidents climbed sharply in the early 1970s and then leveled off in the middle to late 1980s. A possible explanation for the leveling off is that mutual adjustment and accommodation are taking place between the host society and the immigrant group. Perhaps the slow process of assimilation has begun. Obviously, the data Anne has on hand reflect the experience of only one immigrant group in a city. She must be cautious in extending her conclusion beyond the sample to other groups and their experiences.

Construction of a Line Graph

To draw a line graph, time periods are marked on the X axis starting with a base-line year. Frequencies, rates, or percentages are noted on the Y axis. Each point on the graph represents the rate or frequency at a particular time period. The points are joined by a straight line. No effort is made to connect the graph to the X axis. Compared to the frequency polygon, the line graph is essentially a "floating line." Inspection of this line should give a clear idea of the increase or

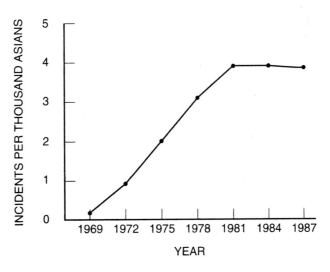

**FIGURE 2.9   Xenophobic Incidents from
1968–1987 in City Y**

decrease over time. Also, any abrupt changes in the slope of the line may be of interest and should be noted.

On the basis of all the data Anne has examined thus far, she concludes that the United States is still very much a nation of immigrants. However, the pattern of immigration has changed since the early nineteenth century. The United States is no longer playing host mainly to European immigrants, but to new immigrants who come mostly from Third World countries with very different histories and cultures. The success of the United States in assimilating these recent groups, while allowing them to retain their own ethnic identity, is very much in question. From Anne's point of view, whether the United States continues to be a nation of immigrants depends on its success in providing a home to these recent immigrant groups.

Exercises

22. Figure 2.10 is a multiple bar chart on men and women in the labor force from 1955 to 1985 in the United States. Convert it into a line graph. Discuss the result.

23. Using the *Statistical Abstract of the United States* in your library, find the family income and the cost of living per family from 1950 to the most recent data available.

    a. Draw line graphs to represent the two variables.
    b. Comment on the graphs.

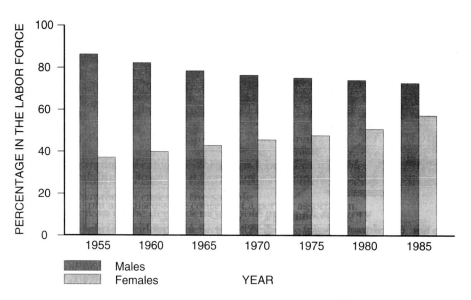

FIGURE 2.10   Percentage in Labor Force by Sex and Year

Source: Statistical Abstract of the United States, 1956–1986.

Summary

Measurement	Tabular Presentation	Graphic Presentation
Nominal	Frequency distribution Proportion distribution Percentage distribution	Pie chart Bar chart Multiple bar chart

Ordinal	Frequency, proportion, and
	  percentage distributions
	Cumulative distribution
		Discrete: pie and bar charts
		Continuous:
		  Histogram
		  Polygon

Interval	Grouped frequency,
	  proportion, percentage and
	  cumulative distributions
		Stem-and-leaf diagram
		Line graph

SPSS Session

SPSS can be used to produce a number of graphic displays, such as the bar chart, the histogram, the stem and leaf, and the line graph. However, it does not plot frequency polygons, nor does it draw pie charts. In the following program, only the command that produces the bar chart is presented. Discussion of the commands for displaying the stem and leaf and the line graph is postponed to later chapters.

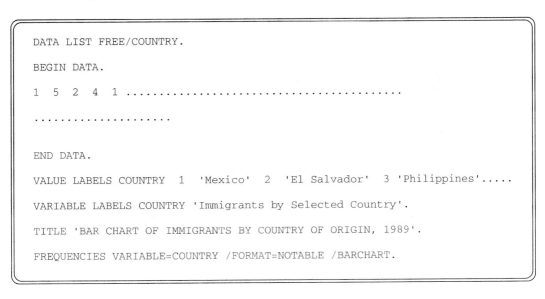

```
DATA LIST FREE/COUNTRY.

BEGIN DATA.

1   5   2   4   1 .........................................

...................

END DATA.

VALUE LABELS COUNTRY   1   'Mexico'   2   'El Salvador'   3 'Philippines'.....

VARIABLE LABELS COUNTRY 'Immigrants by Selected Country'.

TITLE 'BAR CHART OF IMMIGRANTS BY COUNTRY OF ORIGIN, 1989'.

FREQUENCIES VARIABLE=COUNTRY /FORMAT=NOTABLE /BARCHART.
```

In this program, a variable, COUNTRY, is read into the computer through the DATA LIST command. The subcommand FREE indicates that the data are entered in a **free format.** This means that the codes are arranged in the same order as the variables specified in DATA LIST. They are separated by a blank (or comma), but are not found in the same column for each case as in a fixed format. Free format permits the entry of more than one case per line. When there are few variables and many cases, the use of a free format can minimize the number of rows for data entry.

The VARIABLE LABELS command, like the VALUE LABELS command, makes the output more readily understandable by attaching a descriptive label such as 'Immigrants by Selected Country' to the variable, COUNTRY, in the output. The descriptive label follows the variable name in single or double quotes and should be no longer than 60 characters in SPSS/PC+ and 120 characters in SPSS, although some procedures will only print 40 characters.

The TITLE command attaches a descriptive title to every page of the program output until it is replaced by another TITLE command. The title itself is inserted in quotes following the command keyword and can be no longer than 60 characters including blanks.

The FREQUENCIES command requests that tallying be done for the variable, COUNTRY. The subcommand FORMAT NOTABLE, however, suppresses the production of the frequency table for this variable. Instead, the computer produces a bar chart with the BARCHART subcommand. The output of this program was presented previously in SPSS Figure 2.2.

Thus far, only raw data have been entered in the programs. Suppose a frequency distribution already exists, but the reader desires a graphic representation to portray its shape more vividly. In such a case, rather than the raw data, the information from the table can be entered as two variables, as follows:

```
DATA LIST FREE/ IMMIGRAT NUM.

BEGIN DATA.

2.5  66  7.5  165  12.5  24  17.5  12  22.5  9  27.5  0  32.5  21  37.5  3

END DATA.

WEIGHT BY NUM.

VARIABLE LABELS IMMIGRAT 'Level of Immigration As % Pop Growth'.

TITLE 'HISTOGRAM OF DESIRED LEVEL OF IMMIGRATION'.

FREQUENCIES VARIABLES=IMMIGRAT /FORMAT=NOTABLE /HISTOGRAM.
```

The first variable, IMMIGRAT, refers to the level of immigration considered ideal by an individual. As its levels are grouped into intervals, only their midpoints are entered. For example, the code 2.5 represents the midpoint of the interval 0% to 5%, 7.5 represents the midpoint of 5% to 10%, and so on. The second variable, NUM, refers to the number (or frequency) of individuals who gave this level as their response. To convert this frequency distribution into a raw data set, the WEIGHT command is used. With this command, the midpoint of each interval is multiplied by its own frequency. For example, the value of 2.5 is counted 66 times, the value of 7.5, 165 times, and so on. After this conversion, the codes are tallied and a histogram is drawn with the FREQUENCIES command.

The histogram produced by this program is similar to the bar chart drawn by the preceding program and is not shown here. Note that the FREQUENCIES command can be used to produce histograms as well as bar charts, but both graphs cannot be specified under the same command. Therefore, if both types of graphs are desired, two FREQUENCIES commands must be used even if the variables are from the same data set. Although not applicable in this example, the interval width of a histogram can be controlled by the keyword INCREMENT(N), where N is the size of the interval, as follows:

```
FREQUENCIES VARIABLES=Var5 /HISTOGRAM=INCREMENT(4).
```

SPSS Exercises

7. Draw a bar chart for the ethnicity (ETHNIC) of the GSS respondents. How should the categories be combined to produce the most effective graph?

8. Draw a histogram of the per capita income (INCOME) of cities.
    a. Select various intervals by using the keyword INCREMENT(*N*) associated with the subcommand HISTOGRAM.
    b. Which interval width produces the most effective result?

9. Using the crime rates of cities (CRIME), follow the same steps described in Exercise 8.

References

1. Kerbo, H. R. (1991). *Social Stratification and Inequality*. New York: McGraw-Hill.
2. Bouvier, L. F., and Gardner, R. W. (1986). Immigration to the U.S.: The Unfinished Story. *Population Bulletin*, 41 (1, November). Washington, D.C.: Population Reference Bureau.
3. Tukey, J. W. (1977). *Exploratory Data Analysis*. Reading, Mass.: Addison-Wesley.

$$C \ h \ a \ p \ t \ e \ r \quad 3$$

Describing Univariate Data

New Statistical Topics

Mode, median, mean
Variation ratio, range, interquartile range
Variance, standard deviation, average deviation
Coefficient of relative variation, standard scores
Box plot

3.1 Overview

After organizing the raw data, the researcher proceeds to describe the sample. Since the researcher cannot possibly convey all the information the sample distribution contains, she or he must summarize, selectively highlighting the features that best provide a sense of the entire distribution. The researcher's approach is commonsensical; it is no different, for example, than Anne's way of familiarizing herself with U.S. society.

In attempting to understand this society, Anne could either learn about as many individual U.S. residents as possible or she could ascertain how an "average" resident thinks, feels, and acts. Anne believes the first approach to be both impractical and unnecessary, for the second method would provide her with the insight she needs into the society as a whole. Once the profile of the typical group member is developed, Anne can find out how representative it is. The extent to which other members of the population differ from this profile is important. From it Anne can infer how homogeneous or heterogeneous the U.S. population is and how useful the profile may be in predicting its behaviors and attitudes.

Similarly, to describe a sample, the researcher calculates statistical measures that reflect two important features of a distribution: its central tendency and its variability. Measures of central tendency summarize a distribution by its typical or average value. Indexes of variability indicate, through a single number, the extent to which a distribution's observations differ from one another. Together with information on its shape, these measures convey the most distinctive aspects of a distribution.

3.1.1 Social Applications

In the first few months of her sojourn in the United States, Anne experiences culture shock, a feeling of disorientation that results from her entry into an unfamiliar world. For the sake of her studies and for her continuing stay in this country, Anne decides she must learn more about U.S. culture. Culture is a very broad term; it encompasses both material objects and intangible ideas that touch on every aspect of our lives. Being more interested in the latter, Anne elects to study the ideas that will contribute most to her understanding of the people. These are cultural goals, values, and norms. As a result of sharing these ideas, members of a society tend to act alike in similar situations, producing social patterns that render the compilation of the profile of a typical U.S. citizen mean-ingful. In attempting to discover and describe these patterns, Anne makes use of statistical measures of central tendency.

These observed patterns should not, however, obscure the subcultural vari-ations among regions, classes, and ethnic groups in the society. Although major cultural goals, values, and norms structure an individual's behavior, other factors also impinge on it, producing deviations from the norm. Any understanding of the culture involves an appreciation of both the social patterns and their vari-ations. Statistically, the variations can be detected and described through meas-ures of dispersion.

From a methodological perspective, Anne ponders the difficulty of studying norms and values. After all, they are not tangible and, therefore, may not be amenable to empirical investigation. Intangible cultural ideas, however, do manifest themselves through concrete instances of words and behaviors called *indicators* (Section 1.3). By examining these indicators, Anne hopes to clarify the underlying cultural goals, values, and norms of U.S. society. In short, Anne proposes to employ statistical techniques to summarize and describe the central tendency and dispersion of various U.S. attitudes and behaviors.

3.1.2 Statistical Topic: Measures of Central Tendency

To summarize a sample statistically, the researcher often finds a single value that represents what is *typical* or *average* about the distribution. However, the term typical or average is ambiguous and can be conceptualized in various ways. A typical value may be defined as the most frequently observed value. For example, as discussed in Chapter 2, U.S. residents are most likely to be Protestants. There-fore, the typical value for religion is Protestantism. Alternatively, a typical value may be the midpoint that divides the distribution into halves. In describing church attendance, the typical value may be 3, because 50% of the population may attend church three or more times a month, while the other 50% attend less often. Thus, depending on the definition, different averages or **measures of central tendency** could be abstracted from a distribution. The three most commonly used of these measures are the mode, the median, and the mean. Each measure has its own attributes and each differs in how it summarizes the distribution.

The existence of different averages is not surprising. An average is a summary value that is, by necessity, selective, leaving out some features of the distribution while retaining others. Consequently, each average is of limited utility, but each serves as a useful reference point for observing deviations from the typical. Sometimes a researcher will use all three measures to describe a distribution; at other times a researcher will select one from among the three. Later in this chapter, factors that should be taken into account when choosing an average are discussed.

3.1.3 Statistical Topic: Measures of Dispersion

Since a measure of central tendency describes selected features of a distribution, when used alone, it may distort reality. In fact, the very term average implies a single value that represents a number of *unlike* values. Suppose Anne finds that the average age in two U.S. communities is the same, 35. To what extent can she assume that the individuals in these communities have similar ages and perhaps other similar demographic factors? The answer depends on the clustering of ages around the average of 35. Suppose in one community that 35 is arrived at by averaging the ages of mostly young children and seniors, while in the other it is obtained mostly from adults around the ages of 20 to 40. Anne would be making a serious error if, based on the averages, she assumes that age and other demographic factors are alike for the two groups. This example illustrates that representing a group by its average *alone* may be very misleading. Although some groups may have the same average, their patterns of variation may be vastly different.

What is needed, then, is an index of variability to supplement the summary and description of a distribution. These indexes are called **measures of dispersion.** As with measures of central tendency, there are various ways to conceptualize *variability*, thereby giving rise to different measures of dispersion. Nonetheless, these measures yield certain numerical values that have a standard interpretation. A 0 value always means no dispersion, whereas the larger the value is, the more dispersion there is.

3.2 Measures for Nominal Data

Research Questions
Values are abstract ideas that define what is important, desirable, or good in a society. They provide people with broad guidelines for their choices and behav-

iors. For example, in saying that it is good to be respected, but better still to be happy, we are maintaining that happiness is a more important goal than respectability. In a society as large and diverse as the United States, Anne wonders if there are cultural values that are shared by virtually everyone. If so, what are they and how could she document their existence?

If values are shared and if they define acceptable life goals for individuals, then common values would manifest themselves in the shared choice of life goals among individuals. Thus Anne's question can be rephrased as one of life goals: is there a minimal level of agreement among U.S. residents about important life goals? If so, what are these goals and how much agreement or disagreement is there about them?

The Data

In discussing this topic with a colleague one day, Anne is offered some data that her colleague has collected from his introductory sociology class. The students in the class were furnished with a list of 15 goals from which they selected the most important one. Since the course is required of all students, the class represents a cross section of the student body at University X. Anne can use the data to explore what college students consider important and, in the process, obtain some insight as to dominant U.S. values.

Although there were 15 life goals on the original list, 7 were so seldom selected that they are grouped into the residual category of *Other*. Table 3.1 gives the responses from the sociology class.

3.2.1 Describing Central Tendency: The Mode

An Appropriate Statistic

Is there a typical response or are there many typical responses to the inquiry about life goals? To answer the question, Anne needs a measure of central ten-

TABLE 3.1 Most Important Life Goal as Perceived by Students in a Sociology Course, 1989

Goals	f	%
1. To have a happy marriage	198	45.8
2. To have a stable, assured job	87	20.1
3. To receive a high income	51	11.8
4. To maintain good health	42	9.7
5. To rear outstanding children	23	5.3
6. To be respected by friends	11	2.6
7. To have opportunities for creative endeavors	8	1.9
8. To be a good U.S. citizen	2	.5
9. Other	10	2.3
Total	432	100.0

dency. The **mode** is such a measure for a nominal scale. It refers to the category or value that has the highest frequency in a distribution.

Calculation and Interpretation

To obtain the mode, arrange the data in the form of a table and then find the highest frequency within the column of frequencies. Next, trace the frequency back to its corresponding category or value, and that category or value is the mode. The reader should be careful not to confuse the highest frequency with the mode. The mode in Table 3.1 is not 198; it is "To have a happy marriage." No other goal is chosen half as frequently as this. In addition, more than half of the responses are distributed over two goals. From these data, Anne gathers that there are shared values that operate to direct people's choices toward specific goals.

Characteristics and Properties

Suppose Anne were to select a student at random and guess what his or her life goal would be. What would be the best method of prediction? If the prediction is to be evaluated as either correct or incorrect, the best strategy is to predict the mode for every student's response. By guessing the mode, more correct predictions would be obtained than by guessing any other single response. Given the data in Table 3.1, 198 correct guesses would be made with the mode out of a total of 432 cases. Had any other single response been used, the chances of being correct would have been less. Guessing the mode, however, does not necessarily mean that Anne would be more often right than wrong. This would result only if the mode has a relative frequency higher than .5 or 50%. As the best guess for a distribution, the mode provides a typical value that summarizes as well as describes the distribution.

Other than nominal data, the mode can also be employed for data measured at a higher level. However, it is seldom used for quantitative data for a number of reasons. The mode tends to be unstable, changing from sample to sample drawn from the same population. In distributions where the modal frequency is not much higher than other frequencies, the loss of a few cases changes the mode. When the interval widths are changed, the value of the mode may also change. In these and other ways, the mode is often of limited utility, hiding more than revealing the characteristics of a quantitative distribution.

3.2.2 Describing Dispersion: The Variation Ratio

An Appropriate Method

How much agreement or disagreement exists with respect to life goals of college students? Social scientists often enumerate percentages of nonmodal categories to convey the extent of dispersion among the categories. For example, Anne can mention that, other than the mode, the goal that is chosen most often is that of having a stable and assured job; approximately 20% of the sample selected this response. In addition, approximately 87% of the responses are concentrated in four of nine categories. Finally, to summarize the variation in responses by a single value, Anne can compute the **variation ratio,** which gives the proportion of nonmodal responses:

$$\text{variation ratio} = 1 - \frac{f_m}{N} \tag{3.1}$$

where f_m refers to the frequency of the modal category, and
      N refers to the number of cases.

Calculation and Interpretation
In applying this formula to the data in Table 3.1, Anne obtains the following:

$$\text{variation ratio} = 1 - \frac{198}{432} = 1 - .458 = .542$$

According to this measure, although 46% of the respondents desire a happy marriage above all else, 54% have other priorities. From these various indications, Anne concludes that there is a fair amount of disagreement among the students as to their life goals.

Characteristics and Properties
The variation ratio defines heterogeneity as the extent to which the cases in a sample fall outside the mode. It yields a value of 0 when all the cases are concentrated in the mode. Its theoretical upper limit of 1 is approached when the distribution is infinite with no two cases having the same value. Because the variation ratio depends heavily on the value of and the concentration of cases in the mode and the mode is not particularly stable, it provides at best a rough definition and measure of heterogeneity.

In addition to the variation ratio, there are a few other measures of qualitative differences, such as the index of dispersion (D) and the index of qualitative variation (IQV). However, since researchers seldom determine the exact degree of qualitative variation in nominal variables, none of these measures, including the variation ratio, is widely used and reported. Instead, social scientists tend to rely on the more impressionistic method of reporting the percentages of interest in a nominal distribution.

Exercises

A report by Institute Z that has attracted Anne's attention labels contemporary youths as the IDI (I Deserve It) generation based on data that show that they are self-centered and materialistic.

1. The institute's claims are derived partially from the following data:

The most important goal of college education to the IDI generation is:

To enhance knowledge	92
To acquire occupational skills	282
To realize one's potentiality	31
To broaden one's outlook on life	43
To make friends	19
To have fun	20
Other	19

---

   a. Find the mode and calculate the variation ratio for these data.
   b. Interpret the results.

2. Here are more of the data on which the institute based its claim:

Attitude the IDI generation has toward their own cheating in college:

Unethical and never done	39
Unethical but necessary to survive	156
Inevitable because everybody does it	187
A big challenge and lots of fun	80
Other	44

---

   a. Find the mode and calculate the variation ratio for these data.
   b. Interpret the results.

3. Take a class survey to determine the students' goals of college education and their attitude toward cheating.

   a. Find the mode and calculate the variation ratio.
   b. Do the class data replicate the institute's?

3.3 Measures for Ordinal Data

Research Questions

Changing her focus from personal goals to social values, Anne decides to examine freedom, one of the most important values that defines U.S. society. Rightly or wrongly, the United States prides herself on being a land of the free. Yet freedom is a very abstract and elusive concept, which may mean different things when applied to specific issues. For example, the United States was recently embroiled in a controversy over flag burning. The Supreme Court ruled that flag burning is protected under the First Amendment. The ruling, however, has had a mixed reception, prompting some politicians to spearhead an attempt to override it through a constitutional amendment. If the politicians are barometers of their constituents' concerns, then the country's position on freedom of speech may be very different from the Supreme Court's. Through the issue of flag burning, Anne intends to explore how strong a commitment and how much variation in commitment U.S. citizens have toward freedom of speech.

The Data

Because flag burning was an important issue, various pollsters surveyed the public about it. One pollster obtained the fairly typical results shown in Table 3.2 in response to the following statement: "An individual has the right to burn his or her country's flag." The responses are rank ordered in such a way that the higher the commitment is to free speech, the higher the score.

Anne suspects that the university, being a bastion of liberality, may not reflect the opinions of the general public. To find out, she surveys her colleagues at University X with the same question used in the nationwide poll. From a random sample of 24 college professors, she obtains the following responses:

2 3 3 3 3 4 5 5 5 5 5 5 5 5 6 6 6 6 6 6 7 7 7 7

3.3.1 Describing Central Tendency: The Median

An Appropriate Statistic

The data in this case are ordinal. The categories that reveal the intensity of one's feelings toward flag burning imply an underlying order. To describe the typical response given, Anne could use the mode, but it would ignore the information the data carry on intensity. A statistic that makes use of this information is the **median**. The median is a locational measure: it is the score or the point in an *array* above and below which 50% of the cases lie. The median, then, represents the central tendency of a distribution by being its midpoint.

Calculation of the Statistic

To calculate the median, numeric codes are assigned that reflect the underlying order of the categories. If codes are assigned in any order, for example, a 1 for "almost always" and a 2 for "almost never," and so on, then the midpoint of a distribution would be an *arbitrary* rather than a *fixed* point. After coding, the data should be arranged in order. When there are few cases, it is much simpler to use an array. Otherwise, when the sample is large, tabulate the observations into a

TABLE 3.2 Responses to the Question of Whether an Individual Has the Right to Burn His or Her Country's Flag, Based on a National Sample, 1990

Rank/Code	Response	f	cf
7	Always	10	525
6	Almost always	46	515
5	Most of the time	79	469
4	Half of the time	63	390
3	Seldom	91	327
2	Almost never	105	236
1	Never	131	131
	Total	525	

frequency and a cumulative frequency distribution. Two other steps follow. Since the median is a positional measure, determine its *location* first in the array or table. Then determine the *value* of the median.

Finding the Median of an Array.   To find the median of an array, first determine whether N is an odd or an even number. When N is odd, the median is the middle score of the whole distribution. Its *position* is found by the following formula:

$$\text{position of the median} = \frac{N+1}{2}\text{th position}$$

The *value* of the median (mdn) is then determined by the value of the case that occupies the $[(N + 1)/2]$th position:

$$\text{mdn} = X_{[(N+1)/2]} \tag{3.2}$$

For an array such as 1, 1, 2, 3, 4, 4, 5, the median is the fourth case $[(7 + 1)/2]$, which has a value of 3. Using X to represent the observations, Figure 3.1 displays both the position and value of the median in this array.

When N is even, there is no middle score to represent the median. Instead, the median is located midway between two cases. The position of the first of these two cases is found by the following formula:

$$\text{position of the first case} = \frac{N}{2}\text{th position}$$

The second of these cases is simply the one occupying the next higher position, the $[(N/2) + 1]$th position. The value of the median is then determined by taking the average value of these two cases:

$$\text{mdn} = \frac{X_{[N/2]} + X_{[(N/2)+1]}}{2} \tag{3.3}$$

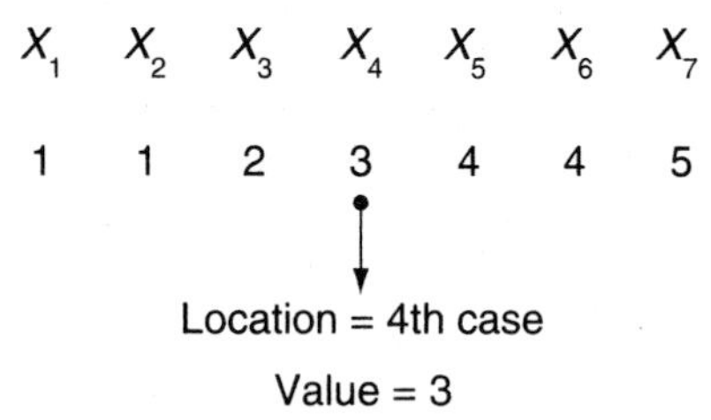

$$X_1 \quad X_2 \quad X_3 \quad X_4 \quad X_5 \quad X_6 \quad X_7$$

$$1 \quad\ 1 \quad\ 2 \quad\ 3 \quad\ 4 \quad\ 4 \quad\ 5$$

Location = 4th case

Value = 3

FIGURE 3.1   Median of an Array Consisting of an Odd Number of Cases

The random sample from the university has an even number of faculty members. To find its median, Anne first finds the positions of the two cases closest to the median. The position of the first case is 12: $N/2 = 24/2$, while the position of the second case is 13: $(N/2) + 1 = (24/2) + 1$. The value of both the twelfth and the thirteenth case is 5, so their average also equals 5: $(5 + 5)/2$. The array in Figure 3.2 represents the data from the university, with the location and value of the median diagrammed. Note that half of the cases, or 12, fall above and half below the median.

Finding the Median of a Table.   The procedure for finding the median of a table is the same as that for an array. In Table 3.2, N is odd. The location of the median can be found by the formula $(N + 1)/2$. According to the formula, the 263rd case $[(525 + 1)/2]$ is the median. To find this case, Anne looks down the column of cumulative frequency, cf, in Table 3.2. The 237th case to the 327th case are all 3's. Since the 263rd case is between the 237th to the 327th case, the median value is 3. See Figure 3.3.

Interpretation of the Data
Thus, as Anne expected, there is a difference between the faculty's and the general public's attitudes toward flag burning. The typical response of the public is 3: an individual is perceived as *seldom* having the right to burn a national flag. This response divides the general public into two equal halves. On the other hand, among faculty members the midpoint is the response code 5, which states that an individual has the right *most of the time* to burn a national flag. Anne concludes that the faculty members are more inclined to endorse the value of freedom of speech.

There is, however, an alternative explanation for the difference between the two groups. Flag burning may present the individual with a dilemma in which she or he must choose between two relevant but, in this case, opposing values of patriotism and freedom of speech. As a result, the lower median value of 3 in the nationwide sample may simply reveal a stronger commitment to patriotism, rather than a lower-level acceptance of freedom of speech.

Because the median and the mode define the *average* or *typical* differently, they need not be of the same rank or value. In the case of the national sample, the

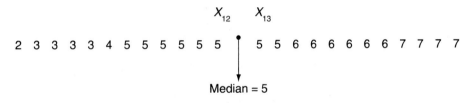

FIGURE 3.2   Median of an Array Consisting of an Even Number of Cases

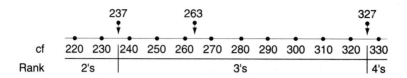

FIGURE 3.3   Location of the Median of Table 3.2

modal rank was 1, or "never." On the other hand, the mode and median may coincide as in the university, where both were "most of the time," or 5.

Characteristics and Properties

The median is a typical response in the sense that it is the midpoint of the distribution. Being the midpoint that partitions the distribution into two equal parts, it is closer to all the scores in the distribution than any other value [1]. From this location of the median we derive the *best guess* interpretation of the statistic. The median represents a best guess of the scores if the prediction is to come as close as possible, on the average, to all the scores in the sample.

In descriptive statistics, the median is a useful measure for a number of reasons. It summarizes the distribution by giving a score most nearly like other scores. It is also a measure of a standard *position* that, when used as a reference point, permits comparison across distributions with different units of measurement. Thus, questions such as the following are meaningful: Is the individual above the median in liberalism as well as in patriotism? Even for higher levels of measurement, the median may provide a simpler and more effective description of a distribution than other measures in many situations.

Related Positional Measures

The median is one of many positional measures known as **quantiles** that give the proportion of scores located above and below a given value. Other quantiles such as **quartiles, deciles,** or **percentiles** divide a distribution into smaller portions. The quartiles partition the distribution into 4 equal parts, the deciles into 10 equal parts, and percentiles into 100 equal parts. The median corresponds to the second quartile, the fifth decile, and the fiftieth percentile of a distribution.

3.3.2 Describing Dispersion: The Range

An Appropriate Statistic

Anne still has to select a measure of dispersion to determine the extent of agreement or disagreement about flag burning. Strictly speaking, there is no measure designed specifically to determine dispersion in ordinal data. The variation ratio can be used, but it does not take into account the quantitative nature of ordinal data. The type of dispersion measures chosen for discussion next determine the distance between two points in a distribution. When the two are the end points of a distribution, the result is the **range.** The range is a simple and extremely rough index of dispersion.

Calculation and Interpretation

To calculate the range, arrange the scores in an array or, in the case of a table, rank order the categories. Then compute the range with the following formula:

$$\text{range} = (H - L) + 1 \qquad\qquad (3.4)$$

where H refers to the highest score or rank and
$\qquad L$ refers to the lowest score or rank of the distribution.

Many texts use the formula $(H - L)$. However, we think it is more consistent with the way the intermediate ranges are calculated to include the first and the last score within the range. The 1 is added for this purpose. In some texts, this is referred to as the inclusive range to differentiate it from the simple range of $(H - L)$.

The range of the university sample is $(7 - 2) + 1 = 6$. The range of the national sample is larger: $(7 - 1) + 1 = 7$. Since there are 7 ranks, the range indicates that the spread of the scores in the university is 1 less than the 7 possible, while on the national level, there is more spread, covering the full range of the ranks.

Characteristics and Properties

As can be seen, the range is not particularly informative. It provides information about the extreme values, but is silent on the pattern of variation between the two extremes. For instance, although the range is similar for the university and national samples, an inspection of their distributions reveals the former to be negatively skewed and the latter to be positively skewed. The bulk of the college professors' scores are spread over the three highest ranks, while close to half of the national scores are concentrated in the two lowest ranks.

The range is particularly ineffective in situations where the respondents are asked to choose from among a predetermined number of categories. A full range of values can usually be expected under the circumstances. On the other hand, if the values are allowed to vary freely, the extreme values may behave erratically. The range may then give the impression of more variability than actually exists in the sample.

3.3.3 Describing Dispersion: The Interquartile Range

An Appropriate Statistic

An alternative to the full range is an intermediate range. Because this type of statistic measures the dispersion from one intermediate location to another, it has the advantage of excluding the extreme and possibly unstable cases. The locations used are generally those of *quantiles,* thus permitting the researcher to leave out the same proportion of cases on either end of the distribution. One such commonly used measure is the **interquartile range** (IQR). This measure determines the distance between the first and third quartiles, thereby excluding the lowest and the highest 25% of the cases from consideration.

Depending on the researcher's needs, fewer cases could be excluded from either end and thus have more covered by the intermediate range. For example, the **interdecile range** covers the spread of the middle 80% of the cases that lie between the first and ninth decile. Essentially, with justification, a researcher can devise his or her own intermediate range to meet the needs of the project.

Calculation and Interpretation

The interquartile range is obtained by taking the difference between the first and third quartile:

$$IQR = Q_3 - Q_1 \tag{3.5}$$

where Q_3 refers to the third quartile, and
$\qquad Q_1$ refers to the first quartile.

To find the *position* of Q_1, multiply N by .25, since 25% of the cases fall below the first quartile. Similarly, multiply N by .75 to find the location of the third quartile. Thus the positions of the quartiles for the university distribution are obtained as follows:

$$\text{position of } Q_1 = (.25)(N) = (.25)(24) \ = \ 6\text{th}$$
$$\text{position of } Q_3 = (.75)(N) = (.75)(24) \ = 18\text{th}$$

When N is evenly divisible by 4, as in this case, the quartiles are located between the position found through multiplying N by .25 or .75 and the next higher position. Thus the Q_1 is midway between the sixth and seventh case and Q_3 is midway between the eighteenth and nineteenth case. Their values are 4.5: [(4 + 5)/2] and 6 [(6 + 6)/2], respectively. The interquartile range is 1.5: (6 – 4.5). See Figure 3.4. Because the median is enclosed within the interquartile range, the IQR can also be interpreted as the variation of 25% of the cases above and 25% of the cases below the median.

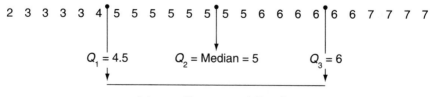

FIGURE 3.4   **Interquartile Range of the Array**

Similarly, the location of the first quartile in the national sample is found by (.25)(525) = 131.25, and the location of the third quartile is found by (.75)(525) = 393.75. When N is *not* evenly divisible by 4, as in this sample, round the fractional value *up* to a whole integer. *This rounding rule applies only to the calculation of the position of these quantiles.* Thus the fractional values 131.25 and 393.75 are rounded up to the 132nd and the 394th case to represent Q_1 and Q_3. From the cf column in Table 3.2, the 132nd case has a rank of 2 and the 394th case has a value of 5. The interquartile range is 3: (5 – 2).

Of a total of seven ranks, the middle 50% of the scores are concentrated in less than two ranks for the university, but are spread over three ranks for the nation. In short, Anne finds that there is substantial agreement within the university that flag burning should be allowed most of the time, whereas within the nation there is more disagreement over the notion that it should seldom be permitted.

Characteristics and Properties

In interpreting intermediate ranges, the possible full range should be mentioned to highlight the relative concentration or spread of the middle cases. An assumption of relatively equal distance between the ranks would help make the interpretation even more meaningful. Otherwise, the spread of cases over a given number of ranks is ambiguous. For if the distance between ranks is variable, the same value of 3 for two IQRs could represent very different distances in one situation, whereas the values of 1.5 and 3 may not represent very different distances in another. In this sense the ranges are not designed specifically for ordinal data and should be used only when the assumption of equal distance among ranks is not seriously violated.

Exercises

4. Compute the median and IQR for the following data:

5 3 9 1 10

5. Given the following age distribution, compute the median and interquartile range.

18 35 18 28 19 23 20 22 21 24

6. Anne is intrigued by the dichotomy of social versus individual responsibility, right versus privilege. From national opinion polls, Anne extracts the following questions that highlight this issue.

Health care is a right not a privilege.	
Strongly agree	98
Agree	163
No opinion	201
Disagree	110
Strongly disagree	43

Please rate on a 7-point scale the following statement, with 1 indicating strong agreement and 7, strong disagreement.

"Immigration is a privilege accorded by the host society rather than the right of individuals who desire it."

1.	80
2.	93
3.	160
4.	170
5.	53
6.	23
7.	11

For these sets of data:

a. Compute the median, the range, and the interquartile range.
b. Interpret the results.

3.4 Measures for Interval Data

Research Questions

Whereas values provide us with general guidelines for behavior, norms refer to specific rules that govern our action. Most norms are derived from values. For example, if it is good to be healthy, then smoking in public should be prohibited because it may endanger the health of others. Based on the value placed on health, a number of communities in California have enacted no-smoking ordinances in public places since Anne's arrival in the United States.

Norms are enforced with sanctions, that is, reward for good behavior and punishment for bad behavior. The application of norms, however, is often variable; whether a norm is upheld depends on the situation, the time, and the individuals involved.

In this section, Anne examines the value of efficiency *in action*. The U.S. worker's sense of efficiency at work is expressed primarily in terms of time. Thus, it is good to be on time, not to waste time, to use the minimal amount of time to accomplish a task, and so on. More specifically, Anne decides to explore the norm of punctuality, which derives from the value we have placed on efficiency. Are U.S. employees typically punctual at work? How much individual variation is allowed in punctuality? Is there a difference in various work settings or is the norm of punctuality equally applicable to all situations?

The Data

Anne chooses two settings in which to collect data: the college and a large factory. With the permission of her department chair at University X, she notes the arrival time of her colleagues to a departmental meeting. Punctuality is measured by the extent of delay in arrival. If a colleague is on time, he or she is given a score of 0. If a colleague is 7 minutes late, a score of 7 is assigned. The following are the scores of 13 members arriving for the departmental meeting:

$$0 \quad 0 \quad 0 \quad 0 \quad 1 \quad 1 \quad 2 \quad 2 \quad 3 \quad 5 \quad 12 \quad 17 \quad 35$$

Anne next obtains the records of a large factory where employees are required to punch in their time when they report to work. She samples 1 out of the last 12 months of records for study. The first two columns of Table 3.3 show the punctuality scores among employees.

3.4.1 Describing Central Tendency: The Mean

An Appropriate Statistic

Time, in this case, is measured on the interval level. The most commonly used measure of central tendency for interval variables is the arithmetic average or the **mean,** symbolized by $\overline{X}$. Whereas the median focuses on the ordinal position of the scores, the mean takes into account the exact magnitude of each score by summing them and then dividing them by the number of cases, N. That is why when $\overline{X}$ is multiplied by N the sum of all the scores in the distribution is obtained. As we will see later, the mean is also the *balance point* of an entire distribution, with the deviations above the mean canceling out the deviations below.

TABLE 3.3 Punctuality Scores of Employees in Factory X, June 1990

X (minutes after 8:00 A.M.)	f	fX
0	256	0
1	123	123
2	221	442
3	301	903
4	89	356
5	72	360
6	25	150
7	6	42
8	2	16
10	4	40
28	1	28
53	1	53
Total	1,101	2,513

Calculation and Interpretation

The formula for calculating the mean of an array or of raw scores is

$$\overline{X} = \frac{\sum\limits_{i=1}^{N} X_i}{N} \tag{3.6}$$

where X_i refers to the individual scores, and
Σ refers to the repeated summation of values.

This formula states that the first through the last scores of a sample are to be summed and then divided by N. See Box 3.1 for an expanded explanation of the summation symbol.

Box 3.1   The Summation Sign

The mathematical operation that is encountered most frequently in statistical computation is repeated summation. Instead of using the + sign repeatedly, a less cumbersome method is to use one symbol that designates the whole process. This is accomplished by using the Greek uppercase letter sigma, Σ. Σ simply means summation.

Items to be summed are specified to the right of Σ. These may be sample scores of a variable, differences of scores, or other values. The scores at which the summation begins and ends are indicated by an index value at the bottom and top of the summation sign, respectively. For example, the following symbols represent instructions to start summing variable X from the first to the last score:

$$\sum_{i=1}^{N} X_i$$

In practice, when summing all the scores, the index values are usually omitted since they are considered to be understood. The following simpler notation is often used:

$$\sum X$$

However, if only some of the scores are to be added, then the index values become a necessary part of the instructions:

$$\sum_{i=2}^{5} X_i$$

The index values of 2 and 5 indicate that summing should start from the second and continue through the fifth case.

If other mathematical operations are specified to the right of the summation sign, they should be performed first before the summation. Operations designated to the left of Σ are performed after the summation. For example,

$$\sum fX$$

means that each X is multiplied by its frequency first before the products are added. On the other hand,

$$N\sum X$$

means that the scores are summed first and then the sum is multiplied by N.

In applying Formula 3.6 to the departmental data, Anne obtains the mean of 6:

$$\overline{X} = \frac{0 + 0 + 0 + 0 + 1 + 1 + 2 + 2 + \cdots + 17 + 35}{13} = \frac{78}{13} = 6$$

Note how convenient the Σ sign is. Imagine how cumbersome it would be if the $+$ sign were used with a large set of scores!

The formula for calculating the mean of data organized in the form of a table is

$$\overline{X} = \frac{\displaystyle\sum_{i=1}^{N} f_i X_i}{N} \tag{3.7}$$

where f_i refers to the frequency of each score, and
$\quad$ X_i refers to the individual scores.

The data for the factory are organized in a frequency table for which Formula 3.7 is applicable. To obtain the mean using this formula:

1. Label the value column of the variable with X and the frequency column with f as shown in Table 3.3.
2. Create an fX column. Numbers under this column are obtained by multiplying each f by its corresponding X in the table. For example, when X is multiplied by f as in the first row of Table 3.3, the result, 0 [(0)(256)], is listed under the fX column. The fX calculation is equivalent to the repeated addition of an X value f times. Thus, adding 256 0's still equals 0, adding 123 1's equals 123, adding 221 2's equals 442, and so on.
3. Sum the fX column to obtain ΣfX of 2,513.
4. Sum the f column to obtain N of 1,101.
5. Divide ΣfX by N to obtain the mean of 2.28: 2,513/1,101.

The mean for the factory is 2.28.

From the calculations, the departmental members are on the average 6.0 minutes late for their meetings, and the factory employees are on the average 2.28 minutes late for work. The means are different, but so are the settings in which the data are gathered. In one case, there is no monitoring device and attendance is not obligatory. Perhaps more importantly, the faculty members are sanctioned for their tardiness in attending meetings only when salary increases or promotions are considered. Thus Anne finds that the norm of punctuality operates differentially, being enforced more vigorously in some circumstances than in others.

Characteristics and Properties
Like the median, the mean is a locational measure that summarizes the distribution by giving its *balance point.* Graphically, it is located at the point at which a

fulcrum can be placed so that a weightless board with uniform weights on it would tilt to neither side, but would remain in balance. See Figure 3.5.

Mathematically, the mean is the point at which

$$\sum(X - \overline{X}) = 0$$

The expression $(X - \overline{X})$ represents a deviation from the mean. Thus this formula states that mean is the point about which the deviations sum to 0. Let us illustrate this with the punctuality scores of the department. The deviation of the first observation 0 from the mean of 6 is calculated as –6: $(0 - 6)$. The deviation of the last score from the mean equals 29: $(35 - 6)$. In Table 3.4, the deviation of each score from the departmental mean is calculated in column 2. Because the positive deviations total +46 and the negative deviations, –46, the sum of the deviations about the mean equals 0 in column 2 of Table 3.4.

The deviations from the mean can be considered as prediction errors when the mean is used to predict the scores of a distribution. With the deviations around the mean summing to zero, the mean is the best guess of the values when the sum of errors is to be kept to 0. The median of 2 does not have this property, as can be seen by summing column 4 of the same table. However, if the signs of the deviations are ignored and the sum of the *absolute deviations* about the median taken, then that sum is at a minimum. Compare this sum of 72 in column 5 of the table to the sum of absolute deviations about the mean, which equals 92 in column 3. Thus the median, as pointed out earlier, is closest on average to each score in the distribution if the direction of the deviation is ignored.

The mean has the additional property that squared deviations about it sum to a minimum value. This is known as the **principle of least squares.**

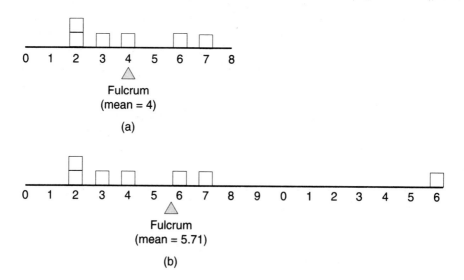

FIGURE 3.5   Mean as a Balance Point

TABLE 3.4 Deviations about the Mean and the Median

X	$(X - \overline{X})$	$\mid X - \overline{X} \mid$	$(X - \text{mdn})$	$\mid X - \text{mdn} \mid$
0	−6	6	−2	2
0	−6	6	−2	2
0	−6	6	−2	2
0	−6	6	−2	2
1	−5	5	−1	1
1	−5	5	−1	1
2	−4	4	0	0
2	−4	4	0	0
3	−3	3	+1	1
5	−1	1	+3	3
12	+6	6	+10	10
17	+11	11	+15	15
35	+29	29	+33	33
Total 78	0	92	52	72

Let us represent the sum of squared deviations as **SS**. Then, according to this principle,

$$\text{SS} = \sum (X - \overline{X})^2 = \text{a minimum value}$$

If a value other than the mean is chosen, the sum of squared deviations about this value will be larger than the sum of squared deviations about the mean. Thus, using the mean to predict the scores in a distribution has the added advantage of yielding a minimum of *squared errors*. We will have occasion to explore the significance of the principle of least squares in later chapters.

The mean, however, is very much influenced by scores that lie far from the center of the distribution. Imagine adding an extreme score of 16 to Figure 3.5(a) as in Figure 3.5(b). The fulcrum would then have to move toward this extreme score, away from other scores, to keep the board in balance. The fact that the mean takes into account the magnitude of every score makes it unduly sensitive to extreme scores that contribute disproportionately to the sum of all scores. The median, on the other hand, considers only the ordinal position of the scores; thus the addition of an extreme score changes the value of the median minimally.

When the distribution is skewed, that is, has extreme scores at one end, different measures of central tendency will yield different values. Generally, in a positively skewed unimodal distribution as in Figure 3.5(b) and 3.6(a),

mean > median

In a negatively skewed distribution, as in Figure 3.6(b),

median > mean

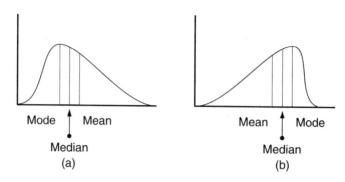

Mode ↑ Mean   Mean ↑ Mode

Median   Median

(a)   (b)

**FIGURE 3.6   Mean, Median, and Mode of a
Positively and a Negatively Skewed
Distribution**

The farther apart the measures are, the more skewed the distribution is in one direction or the other. The reader, however, should not automatically infer that the distribution is symmetrical when the mean nearly equals the median, although a symmetric distribution will always yield the same mean and median. Table 3.3 shows a distribution that is positively skewed, with the bulk of the cases clustering around 0 through 3 and a few extreme scores spreading as far out as 53. Yet the median, 2, of the distribution is very close to the mean, 2.28.

Whether the mean or median should be used to represent a skewed distribution depends partially on the purpose of the research and the nature of the data. If extreme scores are viewed as random deviations, the median will represent the distribution better. On the other hand, when the extreme scores are considered an integral portion of the sample, their values should be taken into account and the mean should be selected as the measure of central tendency.

3.4.2 Describing Dispersion: The Average Deviation, Variance, Standard Deviation, and Coefficient of Relative Variation

Appropriate Statistics

With interval data, the exact distance between two scores can be determined. Given this property of interval data, if a focal point in the distribution can be found, the distances between all the scores and this point can be computed and summed to determine total dispersion in the sample. The focal point should be such that deviations of all scores from it are at a minimum. From our previous discussion, the mean is such a focal point, since it is the balance point of the distribution.

However, as pointed out previously, the algebraic sum of the deviations from the mean always equals 0: $\Sigma(X - \overline{X}) = 0$. Therefore, although taking the sum of deviations about the mean appears to be a good idea, it would not yield a measure of dispersion and alternative approaches are needed. One alternative is to ignore the signs of the individual deviations and compute the sum of the *absolute* deviations about the mean. The total absolute deviation, however, depends on the size of the sample; the larger the sample, the larger is the sum. To eliminate the effect of sample size, this sum can be divided by N to obtain a measure known as the **average deviation.** Although the average deviation can be calculated about the mean, it is normally calculated about the median since the sum of the absolute deviations is smallest from the median (see Table 3.4).

A second alternative is to square each deviation before summing it. This sum will equal 0 when there is no deviation from the mean, but will assume a value greater than 0 when there is any deviation. The sum of squared deviations, SS, also has the desirable quality of being at a minimum when the deviations are measured from the mean. Dividing SS by N yields a measure of the average squared deviation, called the **variance.** The variance gives an average value that reflects the degree of spread in *squared measurement units* per observation. Suppose inches are used as the *original* units of measurement. When deviations are squared to obtain SS, it is equivalent to changing the original linear inches to square inches. The final answer given by the variance is also in square inches or squared measurement units.

The variance therefore does not provide a description of dispersion in the original scale. However, by taking the positive square root of the variance, an index of variability in the original units is obtained called the **standard deviation.** The standard deviation partially undoes the effect of squaring by taking the positive root of the variance. The result is a value that gives a *rough* measure of the average deviation: it equals 0 when there is no deviation and assumes larger values when there is more dispersion.

Calculation and Interpretation

The formula for the average deviation (AD) about the mean is calculated by taking the sum of all the absolute deviations and dividing it by N:

$$AD = \frac{\sum\limits_{i=1}^{N} |X_i - \overline{X}|}{N} \tag{3.8}$$

Based on this formula, the average deviation for the departmental data is calculated as follows:

1. Calculate the absolute deviation of the individual score from the mean, $|X - \overline{X}|$, as in column 5 of Table 3.5.
2. Total this column to obtain the sum of the absolute deviations, $\sum |X - \overline{X}|$, of 92.
3. Divide the sum in step 2 by N to obtain the average deviation of 7.08: 92/13.

TABLE 3.5 Components for the Computation of the Variance, Average, and Standard Deviation

X	$(X - \overline{X})$	$(X - \overline{X})^2$	X^2	$|X - \overline{X}|$	$(X - mdn)$	$|X - mdn|$
0	−6	36	0	6	−2	2
0	−6	36	0	6	−2	2
0	−6	36	0	6	−2	2
0	−6	36	0	6	−2	2
1	−5	25	1	5	−1	1
1	−5	25	1	5	−1	1
2	−4	16	4	4	0	0
2	−4	16	4	4	0	0
3	−3	9	9	3	+1	1
5	−1	1	25	1	+3	3
12	+6	36	144	6	+10	10
17	+11	121	289	11	+15	15
35	+29	841	1,225	29	+33	33
Total 78	0	1,234	1,702	92	52	72

The average deviation, however, is usually calculated around the median since it yields a smaller value:

$$AD = \frac{\sum_{i=1}^{N} |X_i - mdn|}{N} \qquad (3.9)$$

The average deviation around the median for the same set of data is 5.54: 72/13 (from column 7 of Table 3.5). As expected, this value of 5.54 is smaller than the average deviation of 7.08 around the mean. Both values tell Anne how much variation there is from the norm in arrival time to the departmental meeting. On the average, the arrival time differs from the norm of the mean by 7.08 minutes and from the norm of the median by 5.54.

The variance and standard deviation are represented by the symbols s^2 and s. Their formulas are

$$s^2 = \frac{\sum_{i=1}^{N} (X_i - \overline{X})^2}{N} \qquad (3.10)$$

and

$$s = \sqrt{\frac{\sum_{i=1}^{N} (X_i - \overline{X})^2}{N}} \qquad (3.11)$$

According to Formula 3.10, the variance is obtained by first squaring and then summing the deviations from the mean and finally dividing the sum by N. Formula 3.11 shows that the standard deviation is the square root of the variance.

From the third column of Table 3.5, SS = $\Sigma(X_i - \overline{X})^2 = 1,234$ for the departmental punctuality data. Substituting this value and the value of N into Formula 3.10, the variance is computed to be 94.92: $1,234/13$. The standard deviation equals 9.74: $\sqrt{94.92}$.

Formulas 3.10 and 3.11 are known as **definitional formulas,** indicating what the statistics represent. To simplify calculations, a **computational formula,** mathematically derived from the definitional formula, is provided for the variance:

$$s^2 = \frac{\sum_{i=1}^{N} X_i^2}{N} - \left(\frac{\sum_{i=1}^{N} X_i}{N}\right)^2$$

Inserting the values from columns 1 and 4 of Table 3.5 into this formula, the variance and standard deviation are calculated as

$$s^2 = \frac{1,702}{13} - \left(\frac{78}{13}\right)^2 = 94.923$$

$$s = \sqrt{94.923} = 9.743$$

The definitional formula of the variance for a table is

$$s^2 = \frac{\sum_{i=1}^{N} f_i(X_i - \overline{X})^2}{N}$$

Its computational formula is

$$s^2 = \frac{\sum_{i=1}^{N} f_i X_i^2}{N} - \left(\frac{\sum_{i=1}^{N} f_i X_i}{N}\right)^2$$

The elements for calculating the variance and standard deviation of the data in Table 3.3 are given in Table 3.6. Inserting the values from Table 3.6 into Formula 3.14, the variance and standard deviation are calculated as

$$s^2 = \frac{12,255}{1,101} - \left(\frac{2,513}{1,101}\right)^2 = 5.921$$

$$s = \sqrt{5.921} = 2.433$$

TABLE 3.6 Components for the Computation of s^2 and s for Data Organized as a Table

X (minutes after 8:00 A.M.)		f	fX	X^2	fX^2
0		256	0	0	0
1		123	123	1	123
2		221	442	4	884
3		301	903	9	2,709
4		89	356	16	1,424
5		72	360	25	1,800
6		25	150	36	900
7		6	42	49	294
8		2	16	64	128
10		4	40	100	400
28		1	28	784	784
53		1	53	2,809	2,809
	Total	1,101	2,513		12,255

The values of the variance and the standard deviation cannot be interpreted as directly as that of the average deviation. They can nevertheless be used comparatively (1) when the measurement units are the same and (2) when the means of the various samples are similar. The measurement units will be different if punctuality is measured by minutes in one group and by seconds in another. If this is the case, the standard deviation of the second group will naturally be much larger. Also, it would appear perfectly legitimate for Anne to conclude that there is less variation in arrival time to work in the factory versus the department based on their different values for the variance and standard deviation. After all, the units of measurement, minutes after appointed time, are the same and the group sizes are controlled in the calculation. The problem, however, is that the means of the two groups, the department and the factory, are very different (6.00 to 2.28). A deviation of 5 minutes from the norm of a 6-minute delay may not seem extravagant, but when the norm is a 2.28-minute delay, then the deviation of 5 minutes may begin to look extreme.

The amount of variability then, when given alone, is difficult to interpret. To give it added significance, it should be compared with some standard. Since the standard deviation is calculated from the focal point of the mean, it makes sense to standardize the amount of variability by the mean. In so doing, we have a measure of relative variation that can be compared across different samples; it is called the **coefficient of relative variation,** or the **CRV**:

$$\text{CRV} = \frac{s}{\overline{X}} \tag{3.15}$$

Thus, for the department, the CRV is 1.62: 9.74/6.0. The CRV for the factory is 1.07: 2.43/2.28. In both cases, the CRV is larger than 1.0, which means that the standard deviation is larger than the mean. Although an inspection of the standard deviations alone shows that the department has a standard deviation four times that of the factory, when their CRVs are compared, the results show that the two groups do not differ markedly in their *relative* variation.

Characteristics and Properties
The average deviation is the easiest of the measures to interpret. Its value simply means that each score, on the average, differs from either the median or mean by this amount. The variance and standard deviation, on the other hand, are indexes of some sort of average dispersion, but their values are more difficult to interpret. Normally, the value of the variance is not interpreted in *descriptive statistics* since it does not measure deviation on the original scale, but in squared units. The variance, however, is used extensively in inferential statistics. As for the standard deviation, one major use is to find the relative location of a score, a topic that will be explored in Section 3.6. Utilizing both the mean and the standard deviation, the CRV provides a measure of dispersion that can be compared across samples with different units of measurement, means, and standard deviations.

In some statistics texts, the denominator of the formula for variance (and standard deviation) is given as $(N - 1)$ rather than N. Both formulas (with N or $N - 1$) are correct. When the variance is calculated for a purely descriptive purpose, the denominator of N is used. When it is used to estimate the population variance, the numerator is divided by $(N - 1)$ to give a better and unbiased estimate. We will return to this point in Chapter 10. The choice of using one formula over the other depends primarily on the researcher's view of the relative importance of the descriptive versus the inferential role of s^2.

Exercises

7. Compute the mean, median, and mode for the following data. Under what conditions are the three measures the same? Which measure represents the central tendency best?

2 10   2 11   2 13 15 4,000

2 10 12 13 14 14 15

8. Compute the mean, standard deviation, and average deviation of the following data using definitional and computational formulas.

90 85 100 70 92

9. Verify that Equation 3.12 is derived from Equation 3.10.

10. In every society there are age-specific norms for behaviors such as getting married and being able to vote. Anne has observed that such norms in the United States differ considerably not only from those in her country but among different age groups in this country. She extracts the following contrasting data from a national opinion survey:

Appropriate Age for Leaving Parents' Home	Respondents	
	College Students	Parents
18	20	
19	2	
20	40	
21	51	220
22	62	180
23		70
24		60
25	53	90
28	45	
30	50	

For students and parents, separately perform the following tasks:

a. Compute the mean.
b. Compute the average deviation and the standard deviation.
c. Compute the coefficient of relative variation.
d. Interpret the results.

3.5 Measures for Dichotomous Data

Research Questions
Although most norms are derived from values, Anne soon finds that the relationship between the two is very complex and there is no one-to-one correspondence. Besides, there are different types of norms: those codified into laws and buttressed by formal sanctions and those informally enforced. National surveys over the years have shown that a majority of the U.S. population consider homosexuality a form of deviant behavior. The U.S. Supreme Court, in a 1987 decision, upheld the constitutional right of the states to regulate homosexual behavior. With popular opposition to homosexuality running strong, Anne reasons that these sentiments should translate into state laws against such behavior. Do most states in this country have such laws? How much variation is there in the legal treatment of such behavior by the various states?

The Data
The information Anne gathered is presented in Table 3.7.

TABLE 3.7 Sodomy Laws in the Fifty States and the District of Columbia

State Sodomy Laws	f
States that have sodomy laws (including D.C.)	26
States that do not	25
Total	51

3.5.1 *Describing Central Tendency: Proportions as Means*

An Appropriate Statistic

A variable with only two categories is a **dichotomous** variable. With dichotomous data, the best description of central tendency is given by the proportion. The proportion has the same characteristics as the mean and can be considered the mean of a dichotomous variable with one category coded as 0 and the other as 1. See Box 3.2. By the same reasoning, a percentage is the mean of a dichotomous variable with scores of 0 and 100. Demographic rates are also arithmetic averages of variables with values of 0 and 1. However, they are usually weighted or multiplied by a larger numerical base such as 1,000, 10,000, or 100,000 to avoid small fractional values.

Calculation and Interpretation

Proportions are calculated with Formula 2.1. Applying this formula to her data, Anne finds the proportion of states that regulates against homosexual behavior to be

$$P_i = \frac{f_i}{N} = \frac{26}{51} = .51$$

Alternatively, the proportion of states that have no restrictions, Q, equals .49, since $P + Q = 1$. Thus Anne could present her results either in terms of states that have laws or states that do not have laws against homosexual behavior. It depends on which side of the question she would like to focus, although in this specific case it does not make much difference since the two proportions are approximately equal.

BOX 3.2   The Mean and Variance of a Dichotomous Variable

A proportion is the relative frequency of a category or value. If a variable has only two values, X_1 coded as 1 and X_2 coded as 0, then the mean of the variable is simply the proportion of cases with the value of 1, as follows:

$$\overline{X} = \frac{\sum X}{N} = \frac{f_1 X_1 + f_2 X_2}{N} = \frac{f_1(1) + f_2(0)}{N} = \frac{f_1}{N} = P$$

The computational formula of the variance of an interval variable is

$$s^2 = \frac{\sum X^2}{N} - \left(\frac{\sum X}{N}\right)^2$$

With each X being 1 or 0, then each X^2 is also equal to 1 or 0. It follows that $\sum X^2 = \sum X$. Dividing each side of this equation by N, we obtain $\sum X^2/N = \sum X/N$. Since $\sum X/N = P$, $\sum X^2/N = P$. Substituting the P's in the variance formula results in

$$s^2 = P - P^2 = P(1 - P)$$

Let Q represent the proportion of the category coded as 0. With a dichotomous variable, $P + Q = 1$ and therefore $Q = 1 - P$. Substituting Q in the variance formula, we have

$$s^2 = P(1 - P) = (P)(Q)$$

From the data, Anne gathers that, although there may be a strong value against homosexuality, there is no uniform legal stand against such behavior. Even in states where antihomosexuality laws exist, they have seldom led to actual prosecution. Anne speculates that the value is probably expressed through more subtle and informal means, such as disapproval of and discrimination against homosexuals.

3.5.2 Describing Dispersion: The Variance and Standard Deviation of a Dichotomous Variable

An Appropriate Statistic
To determine the extent of variation in the states' legal treatment of homosexual behavior, the appropriate statistics are still the variance and the standard deviation. However, the computational formulas are simplified since the variable has only two categories coded as 0 and 1. See Box 3.2.

Calculation and Interpretation
The formulas for the variance and standard deviation are

$$s^2 = (P)(Q) \tag{3.16}$$

and

$$s = \sqrt{PQ} \tag{3.17}$$

For Anne's data, the variance then is $(.51)(.49) = .249$, while the standard deviation is $\sqrt{.249}$ or $.499$.

Unlike the standard deviation for other types of data, the maximum value of the standard deviation for a proportion can be determined. It is .5, obtained under the condition that P and therefore Q each equal .5. Thus Anne's calculation shows that there is almost maximum variation in the legal treatment of homosexuality among the states.

Exercises

11. Anne finds the following data on court cases involving several issues of norm violation:

Charge	Guilty	Innocent
Euthanasia		
Helping ailing spouse to terminate life	7	18
Public slander		
Publicly slander a racial minority group	23	11
Child support		
Unmarried man not providing for his child	38	18

For each norm:

a. Compute the proportion of guilty versus innocent verdicts.
b. Compute the standard deviation.
c. Interpret the results.

3.6 Standard Scores

Research Questions and Data

Values change over time. The value of work appears to be changing, as people in the U.S. population are living longer but retiring earlier. The work week has also shortened for the average worker, and social scientists expect this trend to continue well into the 21st century. Work has always been an important component in our definition of self-worth; now, however, leisure competes for an equally important place in our hearts.

In partial support of this thesis, Anne finds statistics documenting the changing average retirement age of male workers in the state in which she resides. In 1970, the average retirement age was 63.71, with a standard deviation of 3.32. These figures changed to 60.11 and 4.53 in 1990. Anne wonders how early a retirement age would 60 be in 1970 as compared to 1990? What is the equivalent retirement age in 1970 for a worker who retires at 60 in 1990?

An Appropriate Method

Absolute values are seldom meaningful in and of themselves; instead, they are often compared to a "standard" to convey a sense of meaning and context. One of the major uses of the mean and the standard deviation is to provide that context. To determine the meaning of an *interval* score, such as age, we often find its *relative location* in the distribution. Relative location can be determined through standardizing the deviation from the mean by the standard deviation as follows:

$$z = \frac{X - \overline{X}}{s} \qquad (3.18)$$

The result is a **standard score,** called a **z score,** that gives the distance of X from $\overline{X}$ in standard deviation units. The z-score *value* represents the number of standard deviation units that X is away from the mean. Its *sign* indicates the direction of the deviation, that is, whether it is above or below the mean. For example, a standard score of 0 shows that the score is equal to the mean and does not deviate from it. A standard score of 1 means a distance of one standard deviation *above* the mean, and a standard score of –1.5 represents one and a half standard deviations *below* the mean.

The process of transforming X into z is equivalent to moving various X distributions to the same standard location centered around a mean of 0. Then, whatever its original value, the value of the standard deviation is changed to 1. Thus, in standardization, a new distribution of standard scores is created, with a mean of 0 and a standard deviation of 1.

Calculation and Interpretation

To find out how early a retirement age of 60 is, Anne must determine the relative location of the score 60 within each of the two distributions. For the year 1970, this means transforming 60 into a standard score as follows:

$$z = \frac{X - \overline{X}}{s} = \frac{60 - 63.71}{3.32} = -1.117$$

For the year 1990, the standard score is

$$z = \frac{60 - 60.11}{4.53} = -.024$$

From her calculations, Anne concludes that 60 would indeed be considered an early retirement age in 1970 because that age is approximately 1.12 standard deviations below the typical age of retirement. However, in 1990, it would be in line with the average retirement age because it is only slightly below the mean.

For the second question, Anne must find the value of X in the 1970 distribution that corresponds to an X of 60 in the 1990 distribution. Because 60 standardizes to a z score of –.024 in 1990, Anne is looking for the X in 1970 that standardizes to the same z score of –.024. Again the same standardization formula can be applied; only this time it is used to solve for X rather than z.

$$z = \frac{X - \overline{X}}{s}$$

$$-.024 = \frac{X - 63.71}{3.32}$$

$$X = 63.630$$

A retirement age of 60 in 1990 is equivalent to a retirement age of 63.63 in 1970.

Characteristics and Properties

Standard scores impart an immediate sense of relative standing; in addition, through a theorem formulated by Chebyshev, the proportion of cases that are so many standard deviations from the mean can be found. For example, according to this theorem, regardless of the type of distribution, 25% or fewer of the standard scores will have a value of $|2|$ or more. Conversely, at least 75% of the cases will be included within 2 standard deviations above and below the mean. In a unimodal, symmetrical distribution, at least 89% of the cases will be included between z scores of ±2. Finally, if the sample approximates a type of distribution called the normal distribution, which will be discussed in Chapter 7, then a more precise proportion of cases associated with the relative location of the score can be determined.

Exercises

12. With reference to the punctuality data in Section 3.4, if a person is 5 minutes late, will she or he be considered as a delinquent in the departmental setting and in the factory setting? Why or why not?

13. How much delay in the factory setting is equivalent to a delay of 5 minutes in the departmental setting?

14. Within what range of punctuality do 75% of the departmental members lie? What about in the factory?

SPSS Session

SPSS does not have a command that deals specifically with the *description* of qualitative data; its focus is primarily on continuous quantitative data. Therefore, some of the statistics that are used almost exclusively with nominal and ordinal data are not part of the SPSS package. For example, the package does not have a command or subcommand for calculating the variation ratio. When the median or the percentiles are computed, the values from which they are derived are assumed to be interval. With this in mind, here is a program for obtaining summary statistics from the data on the norm of punctuality.

```
TITLE 'EXPLORATION OF TIME'.

DATA LIST FREE/ TIME NUM.

BEGIN DATA.

0 256    1 123    2  221    3 301    4  89    5  72    6  25

7  6    8  2  10    4    28   1   53   1

END DATA.

WEIGHT BY NUM.

FREQUENCIES VARIABLES=TIME /FORMAT=NOTABLE /STATISTICS=ALL.

DESCRIPTIVES VARIABLES=TIME /STATISTICS=1 5 /OPTIONS 3.

LIST VARIABLES=TIME ZTIME.
```

Two variables are entered in this program representing the information in Table 3.3 of the text. TIME refers to the delay in arrival for work measured in minutes, while NUM refers to the number of employees who are that many minutes late. The WEIGHT command then transforms this frequency distribution into raw data. A tabulation of the raw data is first carried out with the FREQUEN-CIES command, but its output in the form of a table is suppressed with the subcommand FORMAT=NOTABLE. All available descriptive statistics associated with the FREQUENCIES command are requested for this variable through the STATISTICS subcommand and shown in SPSS Figure 3.1.

The output contains more statistics than are discussed in this chapter. The three measures of central tendency are displayed: mean, median, and mode. Measures of dispersion such as the standard deviation (Std Dev), variance, and range are also included in this list. Maximum refers to the highest score and minimum to the lowest score of the distribution, and sum represents $\sum X$.

If the values of the variance and standard deviation are checked against those given in the text, the reader will notice that the values are only very slightly different. Although SPSS uses $(N - 1)$ as the denominator rather than N, the discrepancy is slight when the sample size is large. With smaller samples, the denominator of $(N - 1)$ will produce noticeably larger values for these measures of dispersion.

The DESCRIPTIVES procedure also produces descriptive statistics, such as the mean, the standard deviation, and so on, for quantitative variables. However, it does so without first constructing a frequency distribution for each variable as does the command FREQUENCIES. In addition, z scores can be requested through this procedure. The VARIABLES subcommand specifies the variables for which descriptive statistics are to be calculated. The STATISTICS subcommand requests the calculation and display of various standard descriptive statistics. There is a slight difference in how this subcommand is written in SPSS/PC+ versus SPSS. In SPSS/PC+, the specification of 1 and 5 results in the computation of the mean and the standard deviation, whereas in SPSS the same statistics are obtained with the specification of MEAN and STDDEV. Also, in SPSS/PC+ the OPTIONS subcommand with 3 produces z scores for all variables named after the

```
TIME

Mean           2.282    Std Err       .073    Median       2.000
Mode           3.000    Std Dev      2.434    Variance     5.927
Kurtosis     181.508    S E Kurt      .147    Skewness     9.487
S E Skew        .074    Range       53.000    Minimum       .000
Maximum       53.000    Sum       2513.000

Valid Cases    1101    Missing Cases    0
```

SPSS FIGURE 3.1   Exploration of Time

subcommand VARIABLES and stores them as new variables under names assigned by SPSS/PC+. However, in SPSS the same task is accomplished by using the subcommand SAVE in place of OPTION. Thus the same DESCRIPTIVES command in SPSS would be written as follows:

```
DESCRIPTIVES VARIABLES=TIME /SAVE /STATISTICS=MEAN STDDEV.
```

The newly created *z* scores of a variable have a name assigned to them, beginning with a Z attached to the first seven characters of the original variable name. In this program, the original variable being TIME, its transformed *z* variable is named ZTIME. *The individual z scores, however, are not displayed as part of the output of DESCRIPTIVES.*

To create *z* scores for some but not for all of the variables, insert in parentheses a user-assigned variable name to represent the *z* scores after the original variable name in the VARIABLES subcommand. In this manner, *z* scores are produced only for those variables after which a new name is specified. For both SPSS and SPSS/PC+, the following command illustrates this alternative method of obtaining a *z* score variable, called S_INCOME, from the original variable of INCOME only:

```
DESCRIPTIVES VARIABLES=INCOME (S_INCOME) EDUCAT.
```

To display the newly created *z* scores together with the original raw scores, the LIST command is used. The output from this command is not displayed here because it is very long.

SPSS Exercises

1. Determine the mode and the variation ratio for religious denomination (RELIG) of the GSS respondents.

2. What are the most frequently perceived attitudes about the Bible among the GSS respondents? Do many people view the Bible as the actual word of God or a book of fables (BIBLE)?

3. In the 1988 presidential election, Bush won. In the GSS survey is "Bush" the mode of variable PRES88?

4. In considering different kinds of government in the world today, GSS respondents expressed their feelings toward communism (COMMUN). Compute the median, range, and the interquartile range for their feelings toward communism.

5. GSS asked the respondents to rate on a 7-point scale how often they spend an evening with friends (SOCFREND). Compute the median, range, and IQR for this item and interpret the results.

6. To measure public attitudes toward homosexuality, GSS asked the respondents whether or not they would allow homosexuals to teach at colleges (COLHOMO). Compute the proportion of those who would allow it. What is the variance and standard deviation?

7. GSS also asked if the respondents would favor the death penalty (CAPPUN). What proportion favored capital punishment, and how varied were the responses?

8. Take a 10% sample and compute the mean, standard deviation, variance, and average deviation of serious crime rates (CRIME) among cities. To take a sample from the city data, use the SAMPLE command with the following syntax:

> SAMPLE {sample fraction} or
> SAMPLE {sample size} FROM {data set size}

For example, to draw a 25% sample,

```
SAMPLE .25.
```

To draw a sample of size 100 from a total of 995 cases,

```
SAMPLE 100 FROM 995.
```

9. The city data base provides the number of police officers per 1,000 inhabitants in each city (POLICE). Compute the mean, standard deviation, variance, and average deviation of police protection rates in the sampled cities.

3.7 Graphic Representation of Central Tendency and Dispersion: The Box Plot

Research Questions

So far, Anne has examined various cultural items individually. For a culture to function effectively, these elements should more or less cohere, forming a consistent whole. The consistent interrelation among the various parts of a culture is termed cultural integration. Cultural integration can be subdivided into different types: the integration of cultural goals, of goals with values, of values with behaviors, and so on. Of these, Anne is most interested in normative integration, the agreement between group behaviors and group norms. To investigate normative integration, she takes cities as units of analysis. In a complex and diverse society such as the United States, how much normative integration typically exists among our cities and what is the extent of its variation?

The Data

Multiple indicators are often used in the social sciences to provide a more precise measurement for a rich and complex concept. These multiple indicators are sometimes combined and weighted to form an **index.** Based on the work of R. C. Angell [2], Anne constructs an index of normative integration by combining and equally weighting three different indicators: (1) an inverted crime rate, (2) a welfare effort indicator as measured by the number of grass-roots organizations per 10,000 residents, and (3) voter turnout rate for local issues. It is clear why these three indicators measure conformity to group norms. Crime rate is an inverted measure because the higher the crime rate is the less conformity there is to social norms. The other two indicators determine direct compliance with civic responsibilities.

The constructed index can vary from a low of 0 to a high of 100. The following are the scores for a sample of 48 cities in the United States.

$$
\begin{array}{cccccccccccccccc}
11 & 34 & 36 & 37 & 38 & 38 & 39 & 39 & 39 & 40 & 40 & 40 & 41 & 41 & 42 & 42 \\
43 & 43 & 43 & 43 & 43 & 44 & 45 & 46 & 46 & 46 & 47 & 47 & 48 & 48 & 49 & 49 \\
49 & 49 & 50 & 51 & 52 & 55 & 56 & 56 & 57 & 61 & 66 & 67 & 68 & 69 & 75 & 81
\end{array}
$$

An Appropriate Method

Anne decides to employ a graphic technique to represent the data of this continuous quantitative variable. She chooses the **box plot** because it is more informative than either the histogram or the frequency polygon [3]. In addition to the usual advantages of graphic techniques, the box plot provides a succinct visual representation of the central tendency and dispersion of a distribution. It integrates visual effectiveness with numerical information to give an excellent overview of the data.

Construction of the Box Plot

The box plot in SPSS Figure 3.2 is constructed by SPSS from Anne's data (see the SPSS Session). Note the quadrangle formed by the X and Y axes, which contains the box plot. The values of the variable X are marked on the Y axis. The box within the quandrangle is constructed using the values of the median, Q_1 and Q_3 of the data set. The median is represented by an asterisk (*) or some such distinct symbol. The middle 50% of the cases are represented by a rectangular box around the median such that the lower boundary of the box, sometimes called the **lower hinge,** corresponds to Q_1, and the upper boundary of the box, sometimes called the **upper hinge,** corresponds to Q_3. The length of the box itself equals the interquartile range. For Anne's data, the median is 46, Q_1, 40.5, and Q_3, 51.5. Given these values, the median should lie midway between the two quartiles, but because of the limitations of the printer and computer graphing, Q_2, the median, looks as though it coincides with Q_3.

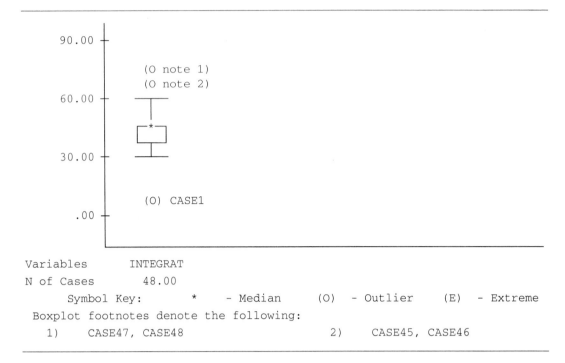

```
Variables        INTEGRAT
N of Cases        48.00
      Symbol Key:          *      - Median      (O)   - Outlier     (E)  - Extreme
  Boxplot footnotes denote the following:
    1)    CASE47, CASE48                        2)    CASE45, CASE46
```

SPSS FIGURE 3.2   Box Plot of Normative Integration of U.S. Cities

Scores that are so extreme that they stand apart from the rest of the distribution are plotted on the graph with different symbols. These extreme scores are classified into two categories:

1. **Outliers,** defined as scores with values between 1.5 to 3 box lengths (1.5 to 3 IQR) away from the hinges or borders of the box
2. **Extreme values,** defined as scores with values more than 3 box lengths away from the hinges of the box

These definitions of extreme scores apply not only to the box plot but also to the stem-and-leaf diagram discussed in Chapter 2.

SPSS uses O to represent outliers and E to represent extreme values as indicated in *Symbol Key* beneath the plot in SPSS Figure 3.2. When two or more outliers or extreme values are in close proximity and cannot be represented individually with a symbol, a footnote is appended to give a clear account of the cases.

The lines that protrude from either end of the box are called **whiskers.** They extend to the lowest or highest value that is not an outlier.

Interpretation of the Box Plot
What could Anne gather from the box plot? First, the interquartile range or box length is short compared to the whole range of the distribution, indicating a

dense concentration of scores in the middle. The median falls somewhere near the middle of the box, so the ranges covered by 25% of the cases above and below the median are approximately the same. The whisker extending from the upper hinge is longer than the whisker from the lower hinge, and there are also more outliers in that direction. In the upper range, cases 45, 46, 47, and 48 with values of 68, 69, 75, and 81 are outliers, and in the lower end, case 1 with a value of 11 is also an outlier. There are no extreme scores. The direction of the longer whisker and most of the outliers indicates that the distribution is positively skewed. An examination of the outliers shows that more cities are extremely well integrated than are extremely poorly integrated. In short, with some exceptions, most cities enjoy similar levels of normative integration.

Characteristics and Properties
The box plot is an informative graphic device. The location, dispersion, and shape of a distribution are conveyed, and the actual summary statistics of central tendency and dispersion can be derived from the plot itself. In addition, details about extreme scores are provided. In comparing distributions of several groups, for which the device is particularly useful, box plots representing the groups can be displayed side by side so that any difference in location and spread can be noted easily.

Exercises

15. **a.** Manually compute the median and the first and third quartiles for the following test scores:

    70 82 43 55 64 90 100 73
    55 95 67 70 82 60   72 89

    b. Compute the box length for a box plot.
    c. Compute the boundaries for whiskers and outliers.
    d. Draw a box plot manually.

16. To explore the concept of normative integration, Anne extracts the following information about 20 schools from the data base at the Research Institute. Schools are rated on 100-point scales according to their (1) academic conformity as measured by GPA and other academic performance measures, (2) behavioral conformity as measured by the crime and drug rates, and (3) social integration as measured by reported grievances concerning minority issues.

Integration Index					Schools					
Academic	82	73	63	77	84	59	63	55	62	54
Behavioral	78	76	52	62	66	42	43	42	51	43
Social	63	75	43	70	73	65	52	61	77	55
Academic	52	43	47	32	49	42	36	23	18	11
Behavioral	50	40	49	40	52	39	35	20	20	23
Social	39	51	51	52	35	61	43	40	50	52

   a. For each index, construct a stem-and-leaf diagram and a box plot.
   b. For each index, compute and then compare the results, and interpret the findings for the mode, median, and mean; the standard deviation; the interquartile range.

SPSS Session

The EXAMINE command provides numerous ways for a researcher to take a careful look at the data before beginning an analysis in earnest. The following program uses this command to produce graphic outputs.

```
TITLE 'BOX PLOT OF NORMATIVE INTEGRATION OF U.S. CITIES'.

DATA LIST FREE/ INTEGRAT.

BEGIN DATA

11 34 36 37 38 38 39 39 39 40 40 40 41 41 42 42 43 43 43 43 43 44 45

46 46 46 47 47 48 48 49 49 49 49 50 51 52 55 56 56 57 61 66 67 68 69

75 81

END DATA.

EXAMINE VARIABLES=INTEGRAT /PLOT=BOXPLOT STEMLEAF.
```

The command begins with the keyword EXAMINE; then the required VARI-ABLES subcommand is given, followed by a list of variables. This subcommand calculates all of the descriptive statistics supplied by FREQUENCIES and more, although the output is not shown here. The optional PLOT subcommand produces various graphic outputs, among which are the box plot displayed in Section 3.7 and the stem-and-leaf diagram discussed in Chapter 2.

SPSS Exercises

   10. Quality of city life can be measured by the per capita income (INCOME), infant mortality (INFANT), and crime rate (CRIME).
   a. Take a 10% random sample of cities.
   b. Draw a box plot for the three variables.
   c. Discuss the findings.

3.8 Selecting Measures of Central Tendency and Dispersion

3.8.1 The Choice of an Average

In our discussion of central tendency, we pointed out that each of the three measures discussed represents a best guess of a distribution. Each provides a value with which to predict the randomly selected scores of a distribution with great success when success is defined and evaluated differently. The mode represents a best guess by being the value that occurs most frequently, the median, by being the value closest to all other values in the distribution, and the mean, by being the balance point of the distribution. When all three measures converge, as in a unimodal and symmetrical distribution, it does not matter which measure is selected to describe the data. However, the selection becomes important when these measures diverge.

The choice is governed by the overriding consideration of the level of data measurement. Selection is irrelevant in the case of nominal data, for which the only appropriate measure is the mode. Starting with ordinal data, the researcher has a choice of the mode or median. Other factors, such as the shape of the distribution or the purpose for which the measure is calculated, must then be taken into account. For instance, the mode is not informative in a uniform or relatively flat distribution. On the other hand, if the distribution is *bimodal* or *trimodal*, the fact that it has two or three modes is usually of interest to the researcher.

The full choice of the mean, median, and mode exists with interval data. For most occasions, the mean is preferable. It tends to vary less from sample to sample, a desirable trait when making inferences about the population. In fact, the mean's properties are so useful that it serves as a logical foundation for other statistical techniques. However, the mean may not adequately describe a skewed distribution, in which it is pulled toward the extreme and away from the bulk of the cases. For a skewed distribution, the median may be more useful and give a value more typical of the distribution. For example, if Anne's primary purpose is to communicate a typical value in Section 3.4.1, she would calculate the median score for tardiness in her department since it serves her purpose much better.

Ultimately, a measure of central tendency may conceal much more than it reveals about the characteristics and shape of the distribution. For this reason, the researcher may consider using all three averages to describe interval variables.

From the opposing view, as a consumer of social research, the reader must be careful in accepting a reported statistic. The selection of a particular statistic may reflect the vested interest of the agency or the individual conducting the research. A politician who is trying to get Congress to pass a flag-burning amendment and a member of the American Civil Liberties Union would probably represent national sentiments on flag burning with measures of central tendency that yield different results.

3.8.2 *The Choice of a Measure of Dispersion*

For a more complete description of a distribution, both its dispersion and central tendency should be given. If measures of central tendency represent various best guesses of a distribution, measures of dispersion indicate the goodness or poorness of these guesses. The more dispersion there is about the central tendency, the less representative the central tendency is of the whole distribution and the less predictive it is of its scores.

The choice of a measure of dispersion, like the selection of an average, is determined to a great extent by the level of measurement in the data. For nominal data, only one possibility has been discussed—the variation ratio. Ordinal data present somewhat of a problem. The variation ratio could be calculated, but it focuses on the concentration or nonconcentration of frequencies and is not sensitive to the ordering of the categories. Range-based statistics presented here measure dispersion as distances between two points of a distribution. However, the concept of distance normally implies interval data. To adopt these measures for ordinal data, the distance must be interpreted as the number of ranks covered by a certain percentage, such as 100%, 80%, or 50%, of the observations.

As usual, with interval data more options are available. The choice of a measure of dispersion depends additionally on the selected measure of central tendency. If the median is chosen, the interquartile range or the average deviation is applicable. The interquartile range is calculated from locational measures or quantiles like the median. The average deviation, on the other hand, has the advantage of accounting for the absolute deviation of every score. The graphic display of the interquartile range in combination with the median and extreme scores is most effectively accomplished by a data exploration technique known as the box plot.

The variance and standard deviation are used with the mean, since both calculate deviations from the mean. Like the mean, the usefulness of these measures extends beyond purely descriptive purposes; they serve as the bases for other inferential techniques. Both, however, have drawbacks. Their interpretations are not straightforward. The variance does not give dispersion in original units of measurements, but rather in squared units, while the standard deviation measures only *roughly* the average deviation of each score.

From the range to the standard deviation, these measures are affected by the magnitude of the data values and the units of measurement. Generally, the larger the data values are the greater the dispersion values. In addition, unless the measurement units are the same, a comparison cannot be instituted among the values yielded by the same measure. With interval data, both of these obstacles to comparison can be surmounted with the coefficient of relative variation. It is a measure of *relative* dispersion, expressing the extent of variation as fractions or multiples of the mean.

If relative dispersion is more readily interpretable, then the relative positions rather than the absolute values of the interval scores in a distribution are also more meaningful. The z-score formula provides a means of computing the relative position of an observation in terms of standard deviation units from the mean.

Summary

Measurement	Central Tendency	Dispersion
Nominal or higher	**Mode**: The most frequently occurring category	**Variation ratio:** $$1 - \frac{f_m}{N}$$
Ordinal or higher	**Median**: The midpoint of the distribution Odd number of cases: $X_{[(N+1)/2]}$ Even number of cases: $(X_{[N/2]} + X_{[(N/2)+1]})/2$	**Range:** $(H - L) + 1$ **Interquartile range:** $$IQR = Q_3 - Q_1$$
Interval	**Mean**: The balance point of the distribution $$\overline{X} = \frac{\sum_{i=1}^{N} X_i}{N}$$	**Variance:** $$s^2 = \frac{\sum_{i=1}^{N} X_i^2}{N} - \left(\frac{\sum_{i=1}^{N} X_i}{N}\right)^2$$ **Standard deviation:** $s = \sqrt{s^2}$ **Average deviation:** $$AD = \frac{\sum_{i=1}^{N} |X_i - mdn|}{N}$$ **Coefficient of relative variation:** $$CRV = \frac{s}{\overline{X}}$$
Dichotomous	**Proportion**: The mean of a dichotomous variable $$P = \frac{f_i}{N}$$ $$Q = 1 - P$$	**Variance:** $s^2 = (P)(Q)$ **Standard deviation:** $s = \sqrt{PQ}$

General Conceptual Problems

1. Discuss the relationships among a proportion, the mean, a rate, and a percentage.

2. Explain how the variation ratio measures the dispersion of a distribution.

3. Explain the concept of the mean as the balance point.

4. Why is the interquartile range not applicable to nominal data?

5. Gender is a dichotomous nominal scale. Is it appropriate to compute the standard deviation for such data?

6. Explain what is meant by the midpoint of the distribution with reference to the median.

7. What are the whiskers and outliers in a box plot?

8. In what context is the median a better measure than the mean?

9. Discuss the advantages and disadvantages of a box plot as compared to a histogram and a frequency polygon.

10. Why is the mode not used frequently for quantitative data?

11. Which measure of central tendency is best used to characterize the following and why? Religious denominations, annual income, degree of patriotism, and gender.

12. Does the value of the mode vary depending on the order in which the data are organized? How about the median and the mean?

13. Explain the principle of least squares.

14. For what type of a distribution is the mean larger than the median?

15. Briefly explain the differences and similarities between the average deviation and the standard deviation.

References

1. Yule, G. U., and Kendall, M. G. (1950). *An Introduction to the Theory of Statistics*. London: Charles Griffin.
2. Angell, R. C. (1942). The Social Integration of Selected American Cities, *American Journal of Sociology*, 47:575–592.
3. Tukey, J. W. (1977). *Exploratory Data Analysis*. Reading, Mass.: Addison-Wesley.

Chapter 4

Organizing and Describing Nominal and Ordinal Bivariate Data

New Statistical Topics

Crosstabulation
Percentage difference
Phi coefficient, contingency coefficient C, Cramer's V, lambda
Gamma, Yule's Q, Somer's d, tau-b

4.1 Overview

To this point, Anne has gathered as much information as she could about U.S. society, with the purpose of increasing her understanding of the social interaction that takes place around her. Although her previous examination of cultural goals, values, and norms has provided her with a *general* framework for interpreting behavior, what *specifically* determines interaction still eludes her. Anne's progress illustrates that the initial aim of social research may be description, but its final goal is the explanation of social phenomena. Toward this end, Anne proposes to observe specific factors that may be associated with social behavior, the phenomenon to be explained. For example, Anne may inquire as to whether an individual behaves differently at home than at work, with a co-worker than with a supervisor. She is interested in what causes individuals to behave differently in different settings.

Thus Anne shifts the focus of her investigation from description to explanation. **Explanatory research** aims at discovering cause-and-effect relationships among social phenomena. As a first step toward this goal, the researcher attempts to establish an **association** or link between two phenomena. In this process, statistics plays an essential role. Not only can statistics help the researcher determine the existence of associations but also if the relationship is meaningful rather than accidental. Furthermore, statistics provides ways of testing if the relationship found in the sample truly exists in the population at large. In this chapter, however, we will confine ourselves to the initial task of **bivariate analysis,** the assessment of an association between two variables in a sample.

As in univariate analysis, bivariate analysis begins with data organization. After the data are organized, the researcher proceeds to a statistical description of the two variables. The description involves summarizing the data with a single value. That value conveys information as to whether an association exists, if so, its strength, and, when applicable, the nature of the relationship. These bivariate descriptive techniques are generally known as **measures of association.**

4.1.1 Social Applications

Social scientists say that people *interact* rather than act. That is, our behaviors are directed toward specific others and take them into account before we act. To explain how an individual takes into account others as well as himself or herself, social scientists turn to the concepts of status and role. A status is a social position that defines who and what we are in relation to specific others. When an individual occupies a status vis-à-vis another, his or her behaviors and responsibilities are broadly defined. For example, the status of a professor implies the existence of students toward whom the professor has certain responsibilities and with whom she or he interacts. We refer to the set of expectations and behaviors appropriate to a particular status as a role.

At the start of a social transaction, the individuals involved attempt to define the situation so as to clarify who the participants are and what is expected of them. The perceived status provides the initial clue to an individual's social identity. As time elapses, the ensuing interaction may also be influenced by such factors as the clarity of social boundaries among the participants and the manner in which the participants present themselves. The pattern of interaction may be fluid in the beginning, but it tends to stabilize as the roles among participants become well defined. Thus our behaviors do not occur in a vacuum; they are influenced by other factors, such as perceived status and impression management. In attempting to link behavior to one or more of these factors, Anne is said to be establishing an association between them. Statistically, the association can be demonstrated through a measure of association.

4.1.2 Statistical Topics

To facilitate the search for an association between two variables, the researcher first organizes the data. The standard data arrangement for nominal variables and ordinal variables with a limited number of ranks is the **bivariate table.** Whereas a univariate table classifies units of analysis by one trait, a bivariate table classifies them by two traits.

Once the bivariate table is completed, the researcher examines it for evidence that an association exists between the variables. Toward this end, one of two criteria is applied. The criterion of **joint occurrence** states that, if the attributes of two nominal variables are observed to occur together regularly, then there is an association between the variables. For example, if doctors are more likely to be males and nurses to be females, we conclude that occupation is associated with gender. For higher levels of measurement, the criterion of **covariation** pertains. If a change in one variable is paralleled by a relatively fixed amount of change in the other variable, the variables are said to covary or vary together. For example, if the intensity of opposition to flag burning increases as the degree of conservatism also increases, then the two variables are associated.

Just as various definitions of the concept of variation result in different measures of dispersion, various methods of documenting joint occurrence and covariation give rise to different *classes* of measures of association. Two such broad classes are the following:

1. Measures based on the departure from **statistical independence.**
2. Measures based on the **proportional reduction in error (PRE)** in prediction.

The concepts of statistical independence and PRE will be fully discussed and examples of these measures will be presented in the following sections.

4.2 Constructing and Determining Association in a Bivariate Percentage Table

Research Question

Every day Anne interacts with strangers of whom she knows very little. What enables her to manage in situations both familiar and unfamiliar, simple and complex (other than her savoir-faire, of course)? Social scientists point out that, consciously or unconsciously, we gather information on an individual, which then forms the basis of our expectations for the ensuing interaction. Some information may originate from first impressions of personal characteristics. More importantly, most of the information is derived from our perception of the other's social identities, that is, their statuses. Among these various statuses, the one that is most influential in shaping any ongoing interaction is the master status.

A research report that Anne finds in her newspaper illustrates this point. Researchers of the project trained white and nonwhite males in the same techniques of negotiation and then sent them to various car dealerships to bargain for a new car. The transactions they made were dichotomized into (1) good deals in which the dealers made under $300 profit and (2) bad deals in which the dealers made profits of $300 or more. The researchers hypothesized that race, being a master status in U.S. society, would have an impact on the expectations of others and, consequently, the negotiations for a car.

The Data

Table 4.1 presents the data from the report. Do the sample data show a connection between race and the type of negotiation that transpired?

4.2.1 Constructing a Contingency Table

It would be difficult to answer this question without first organizing the raw data. Conventionally, the statuses of the two variables are differentiated before the organization. The variable whose distribution the researcher is interested in explaining is the **dependent variable;** it is usually designated with the letter Y. The variable that is presumably linked to and brought in to help explain the dependent variable is the **independent variable;** it is usually denoted with the letter X. In this case, to understand why some individuals make better car deals than others, the researchers examined the race of the individuals involved. Therefore, the type of car deals made is the dependent variable, while race is the independent variable.

To organize the data in the form of a table, the categories of the independent variable are first listed as column headings, while the categories of the dependent variable are displayed as row headings. The resulting two-dimensional table is sometimes referred to as a **crosstabulation** or a **contingency table.** The size of the table is described as $r \times c$ (read r by c), with r referring to the number of rows and c denoting the number of columns. In tabulating Table 4.1, a 2×2 table results, as shown in Table 4.2. By comparison, a univariate distribution forms an $r \times 1$ table, where 1 refers to the single column of frequencies.

Within the body of the table are the **cells,** formed by the combinations or intersections of the categories of the two variables. The cells in Table 4.2 are

TABLE 4.1 Raw Data of Race of Buyer and Type of Transaction

Case No.	Race (X)	Type of Transaction (Y)
1	Nonwhite	Good
2	Nonwhite	Good
3	Nonwhite	Bad
4	Nonwhite	Bad
5	White	Bad
6	White	Good
7	White	Bad
8	Nonwhite	Bad
9	White	Good
10	Nonwhite	Good
11	White	Good
12	White	Good
13	White	Good
14	White	Good

Good = under $300; bad = $300 and more.

TABLE 4.2 Type of Transaction by Race of Buyer

| Type of Transaction (Y) | Race of Buyer (X) | | Row Total |
	Nonwhite	White	
Good	3 (a)	6 (b)	9
Bad	3 (c)	2 (d)	5
Column total	6	8	14

labeled such that *a* refers to nonwhites who made good deals, *b* refers to whites who also made good deals, *c* refers to nonwhites who made bad deals, and *d* refers to whites who made bad deals. The numbers of individuals who fall into each cell are counted and located within the cells as **cell frequencies.** These cell frequencies are usually symbolized by the letter *f*, with the subscripts *i* and *j* designating the row and column number, respectively, as shown in Table 4.3.

To refer to a specific cell frequency, substitute row and column numbers for the subscripts *i* and *j*. For example, f_{11} refers to the frequency in cell *a*, which is formed by the intersection of row 1 and column 1; f_{12} designates the frequency in cell *b*, formed by the intersection of row 1 and column 2. In a 2×2 table, often the letters *a*, *b*, *c*, and *d* are used in place of the symbols f_{11}, f_{12}, and so on.

The row totals are obtained next by summing the frequencies within a row. They are represented by $f_{1.}$ for the first row and $f_{2.}$ for the second row. Note that the distribution of the row totals is the same as the univariate distribution of the row variable, the type of negotiation. Similarly, the column totals are obtained by summing the frequencies within a column. They are designated by $f_{.1}$ and $f_{.2}$, and represent the univariate distribution of the column variable, race. These distributions of column and row totals are known as **marginal distributions** because they are found in the margins of the table. See Table 4.3. Finally, all the cell frequencies are summed to equal $f_{..}$ or *N*, the **grand total.**

4.2.2 Calculating Percentages to Determine Association

When the data are crosstabulated, the researcher examines the bivariate table for evidence of an association between *X* and *Y*. In other words, the researcher asks

TABLE 4.3 Symbols for Cell and Marginal Frequencies and Grand Total

	X_1		X_2		Row Total
Y_1	*a*	f_{11}	*b*	f_{12}	$f_{1.}$
Y_2	*c*	f_{21}	*d*	f_{22}	$f_{2.}$
Column total		$f_{.1}$		$f_{.2}$	*N* $f_{..}$

whether the independent variable has an **effect** on the dependent variable or whether, in this case, the race of the subject affects the type of deal made. *To assess the effect of the independent variable on the dependent variable, the researcher first calculates percentages for the distribution of the dependent variable within each category or rank of the independent variable and then compares these distributions of percentages to determine if they are different.* With the independent variable arranged as the column variable, this means using the column totals as bases (the denominator) to calculate the percentages down a column. The cell percentages then sum to 100% in each column, as shown in Table 4.4.

To understand the logic behind this method of obtaining percentages, Table 4.4 is decomposed into a set of conditional distributions. A **conditional distribution** is a univariate distribution of the dependent variable, given a particular condition or category of the independent variable. Since there are two categories of the independent variable in this case, there are two such distributions. See Table 4.5(a) and (b). If race does have an effect, then sales transactions for whites and nonwhites would differ and the conditional distributions of Y would not be the same for the two groups. Otherwise, the conditional distributions should be the same if no association exists between the variables. To determine which is indeed the case, the researcher *should not* compare the cell frequencies directly, because the total number of observations within each conditional distribution may not be the same. Instead, the conditional distributions are first given in percentages as if each were a univariate distribution and then compared.

Table 4.5 shows that when the buyer's race is nonwhite the type of deal distributes evenly between the *good* and the *bad* categories. In contrast, when the buyer is white, the deals are concentrated in the category of *good*. Thus, by comparing the conditional distributions of Table 4.5, Anne concludes that the race of a buyer is related to the type of car deal he made.

4.2.3 Calculating a Percentage Difference to Determine the Strength of an Association

Once an association is found between the independent and dependent variable, the researcher proceeds to determine the **strength of the relationship.** For nomi-

TABLE 4.4 **Type of Transaction by Race of Buyer: A Table of Percentages**

Type of Transaction (Y)	Race of Buyer (X)		Row Total
	Nonwhite	White	
Good	50%	75%	64.3%
Bad	50%	25%	35.7%
Column total	100%	100%	100%

TABLE 4.5 Two Conditional Distributions of Types of Transactions Based on Race

(a) Nonwhite				(b) White			
Type of Deal		%	*f*	Type of Deal		%	*f*
Good		50	3	Good		75	6
Bad		50	3	Bad		25	2
	Total	100	6		Total	100	8

nal variables, the strength of a relationship is measured by the tendency toward the *joint occurrence* of a category of the independent variable with a specific category of the dependent variable. In our illustration, the question of strength is a question of how much more likely the whites are than nonwhites to strike good bargains.

A rough measure of strength is given by the **percentage difference** computed between the conditional distributions of the percentage table. *To compute this statistic, the percentages are compared and their absolute difference calculated in a direction opposite to that in which the cell percentages are computed.* Therefore, for Table 4.4, the percentage difference is calculated between the two cells of a row. From this table it can be seen that 75% of the car deals made by whites are good, whereas only 50% of the deals made by nonwhites are considered so, resulting in a difference of 25%. Compute the percentage difference for the second row, and the result is the same *absolute* value. Thus, for a 2 × 2 table, one percentage difference suffices to indicate the relationship between the two variables.

The percentage difference shows that the occupant of a higher-ranked master status is 25% more likely to elicit favorable reaction from others than someone whose master status is ranked lower. From this figure, Anne realizes how important race is as a master status in the United States in determining the pattern of social interaction.

4.2.4 No Association and Perfect Association in Percentage Differences

When there is no tendency toward joint occurrence, the percentage difference will compute to 0 to show **no association** between the variables. Any value larger than 0 indicates both the existence of an association and also its strength, with a larger value describing a stronger relationship. The highest possible value is reached when there is 100% difference. In such a case, we say that there is a **perfect association** between the two variables. A perfect association exists when each category of an independent variable is associated with one and only one category of the dependent variable. For example, if all the whites made good deals and all the nonwhites made bad deals, then the percentage difference would be 100% and the association between race and type of negotiation would be perfect.

Exercises

1. Anne suspects that the relationship between sex and success in negotiations varies according to the types of community involved. From a random sample of male and female students who are sent out to negotiate with auto dealers in a small town and in a large cosmopolitan city, she obtains the following information:

Sex and Type of Deal	Small Town	Large City
Male, good deal	7	8
Male, medium deal	4	6
Male, bad deal	3	4
Female, good deal	4	5
Female, medium deal	6	2
Female, bad deal	6	6

The types of deals are classified into three categories rather than the original two: good, medium, and bad. Medium deals refer to those in which the dealers make between $150 and $300 profit. For each type of community, construct a 2×2 table by collapsing categories and then answer the following questions:

a. Identify the independent and dependent variables.
b. Which variable is better used as a column variable?
c. Should the percentages be calculated by column or row?
d. Is there evidence that the variables are related?
e. How can the table be reduced from a 3×2 to a 2×2 without changing the type of relationship between the two variables?
f. Is there a difference between the two communities with respect to the effect of sex on the outcome of negotiation?

2. Anne is annoyed by the fact that students frequently address her as Miss or Mrs., while they refer to a male professor as Professor or Doctor. She asks a sample of professors how they are usually addressed by their students. The data are shown below:

Description			f
Male	Old	addressed as Dr. or Prof.	30
Male	Old	addressed as Mr.	5
Male	Old	addressed with no pattern	10
Male	Young	addressed as Dr. or Prof.	28
Male	Young	addressed as Mr.	10
Female	Old	addressed as Dr. or Prof.	10
Female	Old	addressed as Mrs.	20
Female	Young	addressed as Dr. or Prof.	5
Female	Young	addressed as Mrs. or Miss	26
Female	Young	addressed with no pattern	10

a. How should the titles be collapsed?
b. Construct two 2×2 tables, using sex and age as independent variables and title as the dependent variable.

c. Describe the relation between the professor's sex and age and the way they are addressed by students.

3. Out of 350 respondents, 80% are men, and 40% are rich, and 44% of men are rich.
   a. What percentage of women are rich?
   b. Construct a 2 × 2 table from the information given.
   c. Interpret the results.

SPSS Session

The following program constructs a contingency table for the data in Table 4.1 and calculates column percentages for the table.

```
TITLE 'TYPE OF CAR DEAL BY RACE OF BUYER'.

DATA LIST FREE/ RACE (A) CARDEAL (A).

BEGIN DATA.

nw g nw g nw b nw b w b w g w b nw b w g nw g w g w g w g w g

END DATA.

CROSSTABS TABLES=CARDEAL BY RACE /CELLS=COUNT COLUMN.
```

Although numeric codes are used most of the time, in this example, we bring in two string or alpha variables, that is, variables coded in letters, to show how SPSS handles this type of data. The variables are entered in free format as RACE and CARDEAL. The (A) specified after each variable name in the DATA LIST command indicates that they are in alpha codes. The CROSSTABS command, followed by a TABLES subcommand, produces a crosstabulation of the two variables. The variable named after the subcommand TABLES is the row variable, while the variable named after the keyword BY is the column variable. CROSSTABS provides cell frequencies only, but additional computations are available with the CELLS subcommand. When this subcommand is used, other statistics will take the place of cell frequencies unless the latter are specifically requested through the keyword COUNT. Available computations include column percentages, specified with COLUMN, row percentages, specified with ROW, and percentages using N as the base, specified with TOTAL.

The upper-left corner of the crosstabulation details the contents of the bivariate table as shown in SPSS Figure 4.1. The first value in each cell is the Count or frequency. The second is the Col Pct or column percentage.

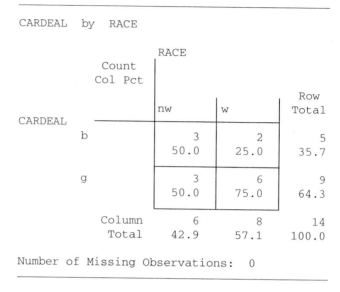

CARDEAL by RACE

SPSS FIGURE 4.1   Type of Car Deal by Race of Buyer

SPSS Exercises

1. Construct a percentage table using RACE and SPKRAC (let racist speak on campus) using the GSS survey. Consider the NAP (not applicable, including no answers) response category as an ambiguous attitude toward the issue. Is there an association between the respondent's race and his or her attitudes toward a racist?

2. Collapse race into whites and nonwhites. Use *allow* and *not allow* categories only for SPKRAC. Construct a 2 × 2 percentage table and compare the results with those from SPSS Exercise 1.

4.3 Measures of Association Based on Statistical Independence

In a 2 × 2 table, the percentage difference can be used for a preliminary and simple assessment of the association between two variables. For larger tables, however, the percentage difference is a rather cumbersome method. An exhaustive comparison of pairs of cells in a larger table will generate numerous percentage differences, yielding information that is less unified and more difficult to interpret.

Therefore, other measures exist to summarize the association with a single value regardless of sample and table sizes. These measures differ in their methods of determining association, but most have certain desirable features in common. Like the percentage difference, they have an upper and lower limit that inform the researcher of both the existence of an association and also the strength of the relationship. The lower limit is set at 0 to indicate no association between the variables. The upper limit is set at 1 to describe a perfect association. Because the concepts of zero and perfect association have different definitions depending on the measure itself, they will be discussed more thoroughly in the context of each measure. The strength of the association between the variables is expressed by values that vary between these limits, with the larger values indicating a stronger relationship.

In this section, one type of measure will be presented that defines the existence and strength of an association as a departure from **statistical independence.** Statistical independence exists when the occurrence of one event, Y, has nothing to do with the occurrence of another event, X. If such is the case, the distribution of the dependent variable Y would not differ under different categories or ranks of the independent variable X. When percentage differences are calculated in a table in which the variables are statistically independent of one another, their values should be 0.

4.3.1 Defining and Calculating Statistical Independence

Let us return to Table 4.2 for an illustration. The row marginals represent the univariate distribution of the dependent variable. They show that there is a total of 64.3% (9/14) good deals and 35.7% (5/14) bad deals. If there is statistical independence, the conditional distributions under the two categories of the independent variable should be the same as the row marginal distribution. In other words, there should be 64.3% good deals and 35.7% bad deals regardless of whether the buyer is white or nonwhite. These percentages are shown in parentheses within the cells of Table 4.6. Thus statistical independence exists in Table 4.6 in which the conditional percentage distributions are identical, yielding a zero percentage difference: 64.3% − 64.3%.

TABLE 4.6 Table of Expectations Based on Table 4.2

Type of Transaction (Y)	Race of Buyer (X)		Row Total
	Nonwhite	White	
Good	3.86 (64.3%)	5.14 (64.3%)	9 (64.3%)
Bad	2.14 (35.7%)	2.86 (35.7%)	5 (35.7%)
Column total	6 (100%)	8 (100%)	14 (100%)

What are the values of the cell frequencies that produce these percentages? The frequency for each of the four cells *a*, *b*, *c*, and *d* is calculated with the following formula:

$$E_{ij} = \frac{(i\text{th row total})(j\text{th column total})}{N}$$

$$= \frac{f_{i.}f_{.j}}{N} \tag{4.1}$$

E_{ij} is called the **expected cell frequency** because it refers to the value of the cell frequency expected under statistical independence. The expected cell frequencies for Table 4.2 are shown in Table 4.6 and are calculated as follows:

$$\text{Cell } a: \quad \frac{(9)(6)}{14} = 3.86$$

$$\text{Cell } b: \quad \frac{(9)(8)}{14} = 5.14$$

$$\text{Cell } c: \quad \frac{(5)(6)}{14} = 2.14$$

$$\text{Cell } d: \quad \frac{(5)(8)}{14} = 2.86$$

Table 4.6 is referred to as a **table of expectations** since it contains the bivariate frequencies expected under the assumption of statistical independence.

4.3.2 Association as Departure from the Table of Expectations

To determine departure from statistical independence, a table of expectations can first be established as a standard so that observed sample data can be compared to it. In our illustration, this means comparing Tables 4.2 and 4.6. The comparison can be made directly because (1) the marginal distributions for the tables of observed and expected values are the same, and (2) the expected frequencies are derived from the observed marginals. In comparing, if the observed frequencies are the same as the expected frequencies, the two variables are not associated. If, however, the observed frequencies are different from the expected frequencies, the two variables are associated. The farther the departure from statistical independence is, the stronger the relationship.

Measures of association based on the principle of statistical independence yield a lower limit of 0 whenever there is no difference between observed and expected frequencies. The upper limit of these measures, however, is problematic in larger than 2 × 2 tables. Some measures can exceed 1, whereas others can never attain 1, depending on the number of rows or columns in the table. Usually, then, these measures have the undesirable characteristic of yielding numerical values that cannot be compared easily across tables of different sizes.

In addition, the exact meaning of values obtained through these measures is difficult to determine. Although a value of .6 indicates a stronger relationship than a value of .3, it does not necessarily mean a relationship twice as strong. Thus these values lend themselves to an approximate rather than a precise interpretation. In the following section, a measure based on statistical independence will be presented.

Exercises

4. Compute the frequencies expected under the assumption of statistical independence between sex and auto deal in Exercise 1.

5. Compute the frequencies expected under the assumption of statistical independence between sex and title in Exercise 2.

6. Repeat Exercise 5, but compute the expected frequencies separately for the two age groups of professors in Exercise 2.

4.4 Phi Coefficient: A Measure Based on Statistical Independence

Research Question
Every interaction begins with an attempt by the participants to define the situation. From the previous example, Anne has seen how the master status of an individual has an impact on this definition, eliciting certain expectations and behaviors from others. However, since the individual is not merely a passive recipient of information, his or her master status also serves to color his or her impressions of the social scene. The same gesture may have different interpretations, and different symbols may have the same meaning to the individual depending on his or her master status. In the following research, Anne investigates how the race of children may have influenced their perception of the role of a police officer.

The Data
Anne collected the data in Table 4.7 as an observer of a third grade class. During one session, the teacher invited a guest speaker to give a presentation to the children about the role of a law enforcement officer. After the guest departed, the children were asked whether they perceived the police as more of a protector of the community or an enforcer of the law. Based on the data, is there an association between the race of the children and their responses?

An Appropriate Statistic
There are various appropriate measures of association Anne can calculate for a 2 × 2 table. One of them is the **phi coefficient,** a commonly used measure based

TABLE 4.7 Responses to the Role of a Police Officer by Race

Responses (Y)		Race (X) Nonwhite	White	Total
Protector of community		22	19	41
Enforcer of law		13	3	16
	Total	35	22	57

on the principle of statistical independence. Phi varies between 0 and 1. The *definitional* formula for phi is

$$\phi = \sqrt{\frac{\chi^2}{N}} \tag{4.2}$$

To use this formula, the chi square, χ^2, must be defined and computed first. It equals

$$\chi^2 = \sum_{j=1}^{c} \sum_{i=1}^{r} \frac{(O_{ij} - E_{ij})^2}{E_{ij}} \tag{4.3}$$

where E_{ij} refers to the expected frequencies,
　　O_{ij} refers to the observed frequencies,
　　r refers to the number of rows, and
　　c refers to the number of columns.

　　The chi-square formula yields a single value that estimates the total *squared* departure of the observed from the expected frequencies under the assumption of statistical independence. If there is no difference between the observed and expected values, the chi-square value will be zero. Otherwise, its value depends on the sample and table size. Note the use of the double summation signs in this formula, which is necessitated by the two subscripts i and j. These double summation signs direct the addition to begin with the set of values denoted by the inner summation sign and then to proceed to the values indicated by the outer summation sign. When applied to a bivariate table, we first take a column and then add up whatever values are computed over the different rows for that column. After having done this for each column, we sum all column values.
　　Since the chi square does not have a standardized upper limit, it is not used directly as a measure of association. Instead, various indexes are derived from the chi square, which have the desirable property of an upper and a lower limit. Phi is one of these chi-square-based measures. In dividing the chi-square value by N, phi essentially discounts the effect of sample size. Then, by taking the square root of the quotient, the coefficient transforms the squared measurement back to the original measurement units. For other measures based on chi square, see Box 4.1.

BOX 4.1   Other Chi-square-based Measures

For a 2×2 table, phi is a widely used measure of association. However, for larger tables, phi can exceed the value of 1, its upper limit being dependent on the size of the table. Therefore, in place of phi, various other measures are used for larger than 2×2 tables; all involve slight modifications of the phi formula. Pearson's **contingency coefficient** C is one such measure and is defined as

$$C = \sqrt{\frac{\chi^2}{\chi^2 + N}} \qquad (4.4)$$

Cramer's V is another of these measures and its formula is

$$V = \sqrt{\frac{\chi^2}{(N)(\text{Min}[r - 1, c - 1])}} \qquad (4.5)$$

where $(\text{Min}[r - 1, c - 1])$ refers to either $(r - 1)$ or $(c - 1)$, whichever is smaller.

Like phi, these measures reduce to 0 when the variables are independent of each other; but when the variables are dependent, they yield values that cannot be interpreted precisely. Unlike phi, the upper limit of C depends on the number of rows and columns in the table. The larger the number is, the higher the limit of C, although it does not reach 1. As a result of not having a standardized upper limit, a comparison of the contingency coefficient cannot be made unless it is between tables of the same size having the same limit. However, for square tables with the same number of rows and columns, the limit of C is

$$\text{Maximum } C = \sqrt{\frac{k - 1}{k}}$$

where k refers to the number of rows or columns in the square table. An upper limit of 1 can be created for these square tables when the obtained value of C is divided by the Maximum C to yield a C'.

Cramer's V, on the other hand, can attain a maximum of 1 in tables of any size. The value generated by Cramer's V is standardized between 0 and 1 regardless of the number of rows or columns. In this respect, Cramer's V is preferable to C.

Calculation and Interpretation
The chi square is calculated as follows:

1. Construct a table of expectations that shows statistical independence between the two variables based on the marginal frequencies of the sample data. Each cell frequency in this table is computed with Formula 4.1, which is repeated here:

$$E_{ij} = \frac{f_i . f_{.j}}{N}$$

   Cell a has the expected value of 25.175: (41)(35)/57; cell b has the expected value of 15.825: (41)(22)/57; cell c contains 9.825: (16)(35)/57; and cell d contains 6.175: (16)(22)/57 expected cases.

2. Arrange these expected frequencies alongside the observed frequencies as in columns 1 and 2 of Table 4.8. Then subtract the expected value from its

TABLE 4.8 Computation of the Phi Coefficient

O_{ij}	E_{ij}	$O_{ij} - E_{ij}$	$(O_{ij} - E_{ij})^2$	$(O_{ij} - E_{ij})^2/E_{ij}$
22	25.175	−3.175	10.081	.400
19	15.825	+3.175	10.081	.637
13	9.825	+3.175	10.081	1.026
3	6.175	−3.175	10.081	1.633
Sum 57	57.000	0.000		3.696

$\phi^2 = 3.696/57 = .065$

$\phi = \sqrt{.065} = .255$

corresponding observed frequency for every cell to determine the departure from statistical independence, as in column 3 of Table 4.8. For example, for cell a, $22 - 25.175 = -3.175$.

3. Square the difference as in column 4 of Table 4.8 to avoid obtaining the algebraic sum of zero in column 3. Again, for cell a, $(-3.175)^2 = 10.081$.

4. Divide each squared difference by its corresponding *expected* cell frequency as in column 5 of Table 4.8. The same amount of squared departure implies a greater difference when the expected frequency is small than when it is large; therefore, the division is necessary. For cell a, $10.081/25.175 = .400$.

5. Add these ratios over all the cells to obtain the χ^2, a single value that represents the degree of association found in the observed table. Table 4.8 shows this sum of column 5 to be 3.696.

To compute phi from the χ^2, divide the latter by N to standardize for sample size. The result is ϕ^2, a value indicating the average squared departure from statistical independence. Finally, to reverse the effect of squaring in step 3, take the *positive* square root of this value to obtain phi:

$$\phi = \sqrt{\frac{3.696}{57}} = .255$$

Formula 4.2 is a definitional formula. It clearly shows the derivation of phi from chi square. Phi, however, can be calculated much more simply from a special *computational* formula for a 2×2 table as follows:

$$\phi = \frac{|bc - ad|}{\sqrt{(a + b)(c + d)(a + c)(b + d)}} \tag{4.6}$$

Using this formula, approximately the same phi value is obtained for Table 4.7:

$$\phi = \frac{|(22)(3) - (19)(13)|}{\sqrt{(41)(16)(35)(22)}} = \frac{181}{\sqrt{505,120}} = .253$$

The phi values are not identical because there are more rounding errors associated with using Formula 4.2.

The phi value of greater than zero shows an association between race and the perception of the role of a police officer. Depending on the researcher, the value of .25 may be interpreted as low to moderate association between the variables. As a summary measure, phi cannot possibly convey all the information about the bivariate table. For a more detailed examination of the results, the researcher often resorts to the additional calculation of percentages. To find out how race specifically affects perception, Anne calculates and examines percentages for Table 4.7. She finds that white children are more likely to define the police as a protector of the community, whereas the nonwhites are more likely to respond to the officer as an enforcer of the law. From various arrest statistics, Anne gathers that, everything being equal, a nonwhite is more likely to be arrested than a white suspect. Such being the case, she is not surprised with her findings.

Characteristics and Properties

Phi equals 0 when there is no association between the variables; it attains unity when there is a perfect association. The meaning of a perfect association is probably best illustrated using models 1 and 2 of Table 4.9. Note that the observations are concentrated in one diagonal of each table, while the other diagonal cells have 0 frequencies.

Models 1 and 2 illustrate a restrictive definition of a perfect association [1], for which a category of X can be associated with one and only one category of Y. In applying model 1 (or 2) to Anne's problem, a phi of 1 is obtained only when all the whites define the officer as a protector and all the nonwhites perceive the police as an enforcer (or vice versa). However, a review of Table 4.7 shows that the marginal distribution of X and Y prevents the total concentration of cell frequencies in a diagonal. Model 3 represents the optimal concentration of cell

TABLE 4.9 Models of Perfect Association and Maximum Association Possible in Phi

(a) Model 1: Perfect Association

	X_1	X_2
Y_1	f_{11}	0
Y_2	0	f_{22}

(b) Model 2: Perfect Association

	X_1	X_2
Y_1	0	f_{12}
Y_2	f_{21}	0

(c) Model 3: Maximum Concentration of Actual Cases in Diagonal

	X_1	X_2
Y_1	35	6
Y_2	0	16

(d) Model 4: Perfect Association

	X_1	X_2
Y_1	35	0
Y_2	0	22

frequencies along the diagonal that could be achieved, given the marginals of Table 4.7. Thus, even if phi has an upper limit of 1 in theory, in practice it depends on the marginal frequencies of the observed table. Only when the marginal frequencies of Table 4.7 are changed such that the number of individuals who gave response Y_1 (or Y_2) is the same as the number of whites, and the number of individuals who gave response Y_2 (or Y_1) is the same as the number of nonwhites, as in model 4, can phi attain unity.

The strength of association is expressed by phi values varying between the lower and upper limits. If a comparison of phi values of .6 and .5 indicates not only that the former is stronger than the latter, but that a 10% difference in strength exists between the two, then we have a more precise interpretation of these values. However, the value can be interpreted precisely only when it is tied to a standard base so that the question of "60% of what?" can be answered. Unfortunately, phi as well as other measures of association derived from χ^2 do not have a standard base from which to interpret their values.

Exercises

7. Do parents have the same expectations of their children as their children have of themselves? Anne asks students in her class and their parents to indicate what GPA levels they hope the students to maintain. The results are shown next.

Desired GPA Level	Parents	Children
A	21	12
C+ to B	9	18

   a. Compute phi using the definitional formula and interpret the result.
   b. Given the marginal distributions, is it possible to attain a perfect association by changing the cell frequencies?

8. Suppose Anne had the following data:

Desired GPA Level	Parents	Children
A	30	12
C+ to B	0	18

Compute phi and discuss the concept of a perfect association.

9. Compute phi for the data in the Section 4.2 example (race and auto deal), and compare it with the percentage difference.

10. With the two age groups combined in Exercise 2, create dichotomous categories of the titles, and compute phi. Do different combinations of categories produce different phi scores?

11. Select one combination of categories of titles in Exercise 2 to produce a dichotomy. Compute phi's for the two age groups separately. Then compare the results to the percentage differences obtained earlier. Interpret the results.

4.5 Measures of Association Based on Predictability

A second class of statistics, known as **proportional reduction in error** or **PRE measures,** employs successful prediction as the criterion for determining a relationship. If two events are associated, the occurrence of one event can be predicted from the occurrence of the other. PRE measures are more widely used by social scientists than measures based on statistical independence and have the distinct advantage of yielding a value that can be interpreted precisely as a proportional reduction in predictive errors.

To illustrate the logic of PRE measures, consider the data in Table 4.10, which Anne collected from students in a class at University X. The students were told to attribute reasons to another student's late submission of a paper. Social scientists have found that we often attribute one of three different causes to behaviors in an attempt to understand them: internal causes, demands of other statuses, or chance factors. Take the example of a student going into a professor's office to explain the late submission of a paper. The student may cite a heavy work load, "I am taking 20 units and working 20 hours this semester" (demands of other statuses), or his or her dog, "My dog ate my paper" (chance factor beyond control). The professor, on the other hand, may charge the student with "lack of motivation" or "pure laziness" (internal causes). Research has shown that the attribution of one or the other cause is not accidental, but may be dependent on such factors as the gender and role of the individual [2].

Anne is interested in verifying whether an individual relies on the same type of attribution when explaining someone else's failure as compared to one's own. She therefore instructed a third of the students in the class to respond as if they were the student; the second third, as if they were a friend; and the last third, as if they were a classmate but not a friend. The written responses of those acting as the student culprit and those acting as his or her friend or classmate are then classified into internal, other status, and chance attributions, as shown in Table 4.10.

4.5.1 Base-line Prediction

To determine whether an association exists, Anne first differentiates between the dependent variable that is to be predicted and the independent variable that is used to predict the dependent variable. Since *attribution* is expected to differ

TABLE 4.10 Type of Attribution by Student Role

| Type of Attribution (Y) | Student Role (X) | | | |
	Self	Friend	Other	Total
Internal causes	2	5	16	23
Demands of other statuses	13	5	6	24
Chance factors	12	17	5	34
Total	27	27	27	81

based on the *role* the student plays, the former is the predicted variable and the latter is the predictor variable.

An inspection of Table 4.10 shows that Anne can predict attribution with some success even without knowing the role the individual plays. Chapter 3 discusses the mode as the best guess for a nominal variable. If Anne were to guess the mode of chance factor as the reason given by every one of the 81 students, she would have made 34 correct predictions and 47 errors. This illustrates that to use predictability as a criterion for association we must first establish a **base line,** or a *minimal level* of predictability. Then only those correct predictions over and above the base-line level are considered as evidence of a relationship.

PRE measures define base-line predictability as the number of correct predictions made of the dependent variable *Y* without reference to the independent variable *X*. The **prediction rules** or the specific strategies involved in the prediction of *Y* without knowledge of *X* vary according to the level of data measurement. For nominal data, the mode of *Y* may be used to predict every *Y* score; for interval data, the mean may be more appropriate. We will label the number of errors made with these prediction rules in base-line prediction as E_1. In Anne's case, E_1 equals 47: (81 − 34).

4.5.2 Prediction of the Dependent Variable Based on the Independent Variable

Next, a rule comparable to the one used in base-line prediction is established for predicting *Y* with knowledge of *X*. Suppose, in the example, the role of a student is known before a prediction is made. Could Anne forecast the type of attribution with more accuracy than in base-line prediction? If there is no association between *X* and *Y*, the knowledge of *X* will not help *improve* the number of correct predictions made of *Y*. That is, the errors resulting from this second prediction rule, labeled as E_2 here, will be the same as in base-line prediction:

$$E_1 = E_2 \quad \text{or} \quad E_1 - E_2 = 0$$

However, if there is an association between the two, there would be an improvement in prediction and a corresponding reduction in errors:

$$E_1 > E_2 \quad \text{or} \quad E_1 - E_2 > 0$$

The extent of improvement, that is, the extent to which *Y* can be accurately predicted from *X* over and above the base-line level, indicates the degree of predictability of *Y* by *X*.

To illustrate, suppose the subject involved is the culprit who turns in the late paper. What type of excuse would most likely be given? The X_1 column, labeled "self," in Table 4.10, indicates that the mode is "demands of other statuses." If Anne guessed this mode for the 27 subjects who played the "self" role, she would have made 13 correct predictions. The 13 represents the modal frequency of *Y* for X_1. On the other hand, the knowledge that the party involved is a friend would change the prediction because "chance factors" are most frequently given (column 2 in Table 4.10). Predicting "chance factors" would yield 17 correct predictions out of 27. Finally, for those playing the role of a classmate, the modal category is "internal." In predicting this mode, Anne would have made 16 correct predictions. The total number of correct predictions, given information on the role, is 46: (13 + 17 + 16); the number of errors, or E_2, is 35: (81 – 46). Anne can claim that there is an association between the two variables because there is an improvement in prediction where $(E_1 – E_2) = (47 – 35) = 12$.

4.5.3 An Index of Proportional Reduction in Error

The magnitude of the improvement, $(E_1 – E_2)$, depends in part on the sample size. Therefore, to standardize for sample size and to provide a meaningful upper limit, the initial amount of error, E_1, is used as a comparison base for the improvement. Thus the generalized formula for a PRE measure has the following form:

$$\text{PRE} = \frac{E_1 - E_2}{E_1} \qquad (4.7)$$

The result is an index whose value can be interpreted precisely as the amount of proportional reduction in predictive errors.

For Anne's data, the proportional improvement in prediction is .255: 12/47. Knowing the role of the student, Anne can improve her prediction of attribution by 25.5%. Had the value been .51 for this index, there would have been *25.5% more* or *twice as much* improvement or reduction in error. Thus PRE values have the full properties of numbers, allowing for a *precise* interpretation.

An inspection of Formula 4.7 shows that when there is no reduction in error the numerator equals 0 and the index reduces to 0. However, a 0 value for a PRE measure is not always equivalent to statistical independence. It is quite possible for statistical dependence to exist, but for some PRE measures to yield a zero value. On the other hand, if statistical independence exists, any PRE measure will yield a zero value.

When there is perfect prediction of Y from X with no resulting error, E_2 equals 0, and Formula 4.7 simplifies to E_1/E_1, or 1. Any intermediate value indicates the existence and strength of a relationship as measured by proportional reduction in error.

Exercises

12. If the race of the dealer is not known in Table 4.2, how should the type of deal be predicted?
    a. How many errors would be made using the strategy chosen above?
    b. If the race of the dealer is known, would the prediction differ?
    c. How many errors would be made, knowing race?
    d. Does knowing race reduce the number of errors made in prediction? Compute a PRE measure for an answer.

13. **a.** In predicting the probability of making a good deal in Exercise 1, what is the base-line prediction?
    b. Does the knowledge of the sex of the negotiator reduce the number of errors made? Compute a PRE measure for an answer.

14. **a.** Does the knowledge of sex reduce the number of errors made in predicting the selection of titles by students in Exercise 2? Compute a PRE measure for an answer.
    b. Compare the results obtained in Exercises 12, 13, and 14. Can generalizations be made regarding the location of modal categories in the conditional distributions and the reduction in errors?

4.6 Lambda: A PRE Measure for Nominal Variables

The PRE measure computed in the previous section is lambda, λ. Lambda is appropriate for nominal data arranged in a 2×2 or larger table. It varies between 0 and 1 regardless of the table size. Lambda has both a **symmetric** and **asymmetric** form. If one of the two variables is specifically designated as the dependent variable, an asymmetric measure would be appropriate. The symbol, λ, is then subscripted, with the subscript of the dependent variable listed before the subscript of the independent variable. Using Y to represent attribution and X, the student's role, Anne has essentially computed λ_{yx} in the preceding section. If the researcher is not interested in the predictability of one variable based on another, but rather in *mutual predictability*, then a symmetric lambda would be appropriate. The symmetric lambda is not subscripted since X and Y are assuming the roles of independent and dependent variables simultaneously.

4.6.1 Asymmetric Lambda: λ_{yx}

Let us first present the computational formula for λ_{yx}, which uses X as the independent or predictor variable and Y as the dependent or predicted variable:

$$\lambda_{yx} = \frac{\sum_{j=1}^{c} fy_j - My}{N - My} \tag{4.8}$$

where fy refers to the modal frequency of Y within each category of X,
  My refers to the modal frequency of the univariate distribution of Y,
  and c refers to the number of categories in X.

To show how Formula 4.8 is used, we will apply it to calculate again the proportional reduction in errors in predicting attribution based on student role in Table 4.10:

1. Identify My, which gives the base-line level of correct predictions. The prediction rule, not knowing X, is to use the mode of Y to predict Y itself. In

predicting the mode of chance factors for every excuse given, the number of correct guesses, *My*, is 34 from this sample of 81.

2. The number of initial errors is $N - My$, or $(81 - 34)$, which equals 47. If there is improvement in prediction, fewer than the 47 original errors should be made. If the improvement is 100%, the 47 original errors would be reduced to 0.

3. Compute Σfy, which yields the number of correct predictions of *Y*, when the information on *X* is given. The prediction rule, knowing *X*, is to predict the modal category of *Y* within each category of *X*. To calculate Σfy, identify and sum the modal frequencies within the conditional distributions of *Y*. The Σfy equals 46: $(13 + 17 + 16)$.

4. Compute the improvement in prediction, $\Sigma fy - My$, which equals 12: $(46 - 34)$.

5. Compute the relative improvement in prediction or proportional reduction in error by taking the ratio of the actual improvement computed in step 4 to the number of initial errors calculated in step 2. The result is lambda. It equals .255: $12/47$.

4.6.2 Asymmetric Lambda: λ_{xy}

The role of *X* and *Y* can be reversed to ask the following question. How much improvement in prediction could Anne obtain by guessing the role of the student while knowing the type of justification he or she made for turning in a paper late? A λ_{xy} can be calculated for the same table with *Y* as the predictor:

$$\lambda_{xy} = \frac{\sum_{i=1}^{r} fx_i - Mx}{N - Mx} \tag{4.9}$$

where *fx* refers to the modal frequency of *X* within each category of *Y*,

Mx refers to the modal frequency of the univariate distribution of *X*, and

r refers to the number of categories in *Y*.

Note that the subscripts of lambda always list the dependent variable first and then the independent variable.

In Table 4.10, $Mx = 27$, and $\Sigma fx = (16 + 13 + 17) = 46$. Therefore,

$$\lambda_{xy} = \frac{46 - 27}{81 - 27} = .352$$

Knowing the type of rationalization given, Anne can improve her prediction of the student's role by 19 out of a possible 54, which equals 35.2%. The two asymmetric lambdas do not necessarily yield the same value as illustrated in this example. In fact, *Y* is a better predictor of *X* than *X* of *Y* since the value of λ_{xy} is higher.

4.6.3 Symmetric Lambda: λ

In addition to the asymmetric lambdas, there is a symmetric lambda with X and Y as both independent and dependent variables. The symmetric lambda is not subscripted and may be viewed as a kind of average of the two asymmetric lambdas:

$$\lambda = \frac{\left(\sum_{j=1}^{c} fy_j + \sum_{i=1}^{r} fx_i \right) - (My + Mx)}{2N - (My + Mx)} \tag{4.10}$$

Applying this formula to Table 4.10, we have

$$\lambda = \frac{(46 + 46) - (34 + 27)}{(2)(81) - (34 + 27)} = .307$$

The value of this lambda indicates the extent of mutual predictability between attribution and student role. It also tells Anne that the strength of the relationship is moderate. However, to obtain a better understanding of the specifics of the relationship, the individual cell percentages should be examined. A single value simply cannot capture all the information contained in the table.

4.6.4 Characteristics and Properties of Lambda

The formulas given in the preceding section for the asymmetric lambdas are computational and are derived from the generalized PRE equation of

$$\lambda_{yx} = \frac{E_1 - E_2}{E_1}$$

The base-line errors as explained previously are calculated from $(N - My)$. This term can be substituted for E_1 in the generalized PRE formula. Predicting Y when X is known yields Σfy, the total number of correct predictions. The errors then equal $(N - \Sigma fy)$, using the second prediction rule. Again, this term can be substituted for E_2 in the generalized formula. With substitution and gathering of the terms in the numerator, the generalized formula becomes

$$\lambda_{yx} = \frac{(N - My) - (N - \sum fy)}{N - My} = \frac{\sum fy - My}{N - My}$$

When asymmetric lambda equals 0, the modal cell frequencies are clustered in a row as in model 1 or in a column as in model 2 of Table 4.11. With these patterns of concentration in cell frequencies, the same mode of the dependent variable, Y or X, is being predicted for every category of the independent variable. The mode is also the same as that of the univariate distribution of the dependent variable. This means that knowing X does not change nor does it improve the prediction of Y; therefore, lambda equals 0.

Having no improvement in predicting Y when X is known does not necessarily mean that there is statistical independence between the two variables. Calculate λ_{yx} for Table 4.7, and a value of zero is obtained. However, an association does exist in this table: the conditional distributions of Y are different for different X's. Although most whites and nonwhites consider the police as protectors of the community, the whites are more likely to do so than nonwhites. Therefore, phi is *not* equal to 0. The relationship between lambda and phi may be stated as follows. When lambda is 0, phi may or may not be 0. When phi is 0, however, lambda will always be 0. Accordingly, when a large number of observations are concentrated in the mode of the dependent variable, resembling the patterns of cell frequency concentration in model 1 or 2 of Table 4.11, lambda may be a poor choice for a measure of association.

The values of the two asymmetric lambdas calculated for the same table may differ, depending on the classification scheme used in the measurement of the independent and dependent variables. Generally, the more precise and refined the coding of the independent variable relative to the dependent variable, that is, the more categories there are in the independent versus the dependent variable, the higher the improvement in prediction.

Finally, lambda reaches unity when there is perfect prediction, with no resulting errors. Its definition of perfect association is as restrictive as that for phi. It can attain unity only when the frequencies are all concentrated in a unique Y_i for each X_j. With such a pattern of cell concentration, all predictions are accurate when Y_i is predicted for every X_j, because all X_j's are Y_i's.

TABLE 4.11 Distribution of Modes When Asymmetric Lambda Equals Zero

(a) Model 1: $\lambda_{yx} = 0$

	X_1	X_2	
Y_1	f_{11}	f_{12}	$f_{1.}$
Y_2	*	*	*
	*	*	N

(b) Model 2: $\lambda_{xy} = 0$

	X_1	X_2	
Y_1	f_{11}	*	*
Y_2	f_{21}	*	*
	$f_{.1}$	*	N

* Refers to nonmodal frequencies.

Exercises

15. Compute lambda for the data in Exercise 1 to determine the effect of community size on auto deal.

16. To determine the extent to which student behavior is based on perceived severity of penalty, Anne conducts the following survey. In response to the question "Will you cheat on an examination if (a) you are absolutely sure that you will not get caught or (b) you are not sure that you will get caught?" Anne obtains the following responses:

	Sure of Not Getting Caught	Not Sure of Getting Caught
Will cheat	20	5
Will not cheat	15	30

a. Compute lambda.
b. Compute phi and the percentage difference.
c. Compare the results obtained by the different measures of association.

17. If the results for Exercise 16 are as follows:

	Sure of Not Getting Caught	Not Sure of Getting Caught
Will cheat	35	5
Will not cheat	0	30

a. Compute lambda.
b. Compute phi and the percentage difference.
c. Discuss the concept of a perfect association in lambda and in phi.

18. If the results for Exercise 16 are as follows:

	Sure of Not Getting Caught	Not Sure of Getting Caught
Will cheat	20	5
Will not cheat	30	15

a. Compute lambda.
b. Compute phi and the percentage difference.
c. Is lambda sensitive to association between two variables under all conditions?

4.7 The Logic of Predicting Order Within Pairs in Ordinal Variables

In this section, PRE measures that take into account the rank ordering of ordinal variables will be presented. There is a wide range in the precision with which ordinal variables are measured. Some may be scaled with fine discrimination, such as the North–Hatt occupational prestige scale, which ranges from 1 to 100.

Others may be coded in a limited number of ranks, such as a 5-point scale of liberalism, which makes only rough distinctions among observations. The manner in which the ordinal variable is scaled determines the prediction strategy on which a PRE measure is built. If a refined rank ordering is used, the actual ranks of the cases may be predicted. If a limited number of ranks are involved, the prediction may be one of comparing the relative ranks of the cases. The measures discussed in this chapter all belong to the latter category; they are based on prediction of the relative order of variables that are roughly quantified. In the next chapter, a measure based on the prediction of actual ranks called Spearman's rho is presented.

The concept of **relative order** involves a comparison of observations rather than an examination of individual cases. More specifically, the strategy common to these measures is to take a *pair of observations* and to predict their order on variable Y based on their order on variable X. Their base-line prediction rule involves predicting the pair's order on Y without knowing their order on X. In the following sections, the common features of these measures are examined first before the specific statistics are introduced.

4.7.1 Types of Ranked Pairs

Let us illustrate the rather unfamiliar idea of predicting relative order with a project Anne is conducting. From E. Goffman's writings, Anne gathers that the presentation of self is an important element that determines ongoing interaction. She further observes from seminars that instruct people how to dress for success that an important part of impression management involves an individual's attire. Based on these ideas, Anne designed an experiment in which students of a class were randomly assigned to be interviewers on six interview teams, labeled A, B, C, D, E, and F. A female collaborator posed as the interviewee, dressed in three distinct styles: (1) informal, (2) formal, and (3) very formal. She presented herself with a prepared speech in exactly the same manner to two different teams in each style of attire. The teams then rated the impression she has made on a scale of (1) unfavorable, (2) favorable, and (3) very favorable. The data are presented in Table 4.12.

TABLE 4.12 Raw Data on Attire and Impression

Interview Team	Formality of Attire (X)		Favorableness of Impression (Y)	
	Rank	Description	Rank	Description
A	3	Very formal	2	Favorable
B	2	Formal	3	Very favorable
C	1	Informal	1	Unfavorable
D	3	Very formal	1	Unfavorable
E	2	Formal	2	Favorable
F	1	Informal	1	Unfavorable

How many pairs of observations can be formed from the six cases, or six interview teams? The total number of pairs of observations, T, with N sample cases is computed as

$$T = \frac{N(N-1)}{2}$$

With six cases, T equals $(6)(5)/2$ or 15 pairs. These 15 pairs are listed under column 1 of Table 4.13; the members of each pair are identified under column 2.

The actual ranks given by each interview team within the pair on attire and on impression are displayed under columns 3 and 5. A comparison of the first with the second rank in column 3 yields the relative rank on attire in column 4. Similarly, the first and second ranks on impression in column 5 are compared to yield the relative rank in column 6. As can be seen from columns 4 and 6, there are three such possible relative rankings:

1. *Higher:* the first rank is higher than the second.
2. *Lower:* the first rank is lower than the second.
3. *Tied:* the first and second ranks are the same.

When the relative ranks of the pairs on both attire and impression in columns 4 and 6 are considered simultaneously, five possible *patterns* or **types of pairs** emerge; these are represented by symbols in column 7 of Table 4.13 and are as follows:

1. **Concordant pairs,** symbolized by N_s. These are pairs ranked in the same order on both attire and impression. Their ranks are either (higher, higher), that is, higher in column 4 and higher in column 6, as in pair 2, or (lower, lower), that is, lower in column 4 and lower in column 6, as in pair 11.

TABLE 4.13 Pairs from Table 4.12: Their Relative Ranks on X and Y and Their Type

Pairs	Teams within Pair	Attire (X)		Impression (Y)		Type of Pair
		Ranks	Comparison	Ranks	Comparison	
1	A,B	3,2	Higher	2,3	Lower	N_d
2	A,C	3,1	Higher	2,1	Higher	N_s
3	A,D	3,3	Tied	2,1	Higher	T_x
4	A,E	3,2	Higher	2,2	Tied	T_y
5	A,F	3,1	Higher	2,1	Higher	N_s
6	B,C	2,1	Higher	3,1	Higher	N_s
7	B,D	2,3	Lower	3,1	Higher	N_d
8	B,E	2,2	Tied	3,2	Higher	T_x
9	B,F	2,1	Higher	3,1	Higher	N_s
10	C,D	1,3	Lower	1,1	Tied	T_y
11	C,E	1,2	Lower	1,2	Lower	N_s
12	C,F	1,1	Tied	1,1	Tied	T_{xy}
13	D,E	3,2	Higher	1,2	Lower	N_d
14	D,F	3,1	Higher	1,1	Tied	T_y
15	E,F	2,1	Higher	2,1	Higher	N_s

2. **Discordant pairs,** symbolized by N_d. These are pairs ranked in the opposite order on attire and impression, such as pair 1 (higher, lower) or pair 7 (lower, higher).
3. Pairs tied on attire, but not tied on impression, symbolized by T_x, such as pair 3 (tied, higher).
4. Pairs tied on impression, but not tied on attire, symbolized by T_y, such as pair 4 (higher, tied).
5. Pairs tied on both attire and impression, symbolized by T_{xy}, such as pair 12 (tied, tied).

The sum of all these different pairs equals the number of unique pairs formed from N cases:

$$T = N_s + N_d + T_x + T_y + T_{xy}$$
$$= 6 + 3 + 2 + 3 + 1$$
$$= 15$$

Earlier in this section a distinction was made between actual and relative rank. The fact that concordance or discordance is based on relative ranks should be clear by this time. For example, in pair 2 of Table 4.13, the actual ranking is 3 to 1 in X (very formal versus informal attire), but 2 to 1 in Y (favorable versus unfavorable impression). The precise ranks within a pair with respect to X and Y need not match, because the objective is not the prediction of actual ranks but of their relative order. Therefore, since A is higher than C on both variables in terms of relative order, the two cases are concordant, that is, ranked in the *same direction* on both X and Y. In the same manner, discordant pairs are formed by comparing relative rather than actual ranks. However, in this case, the ranks are ordered in the *opposite direction* on X and Y.

Figure 4.1 shows the crosstabulation of the raw data in Table 4.12 and the alignment of the concordant, discordant, and tied pairs within the crosstabulation. With X representing attire and Y, impression, carefully note the conventional arrangement of the ranks of X and Y in the table. Going from left to right along the columns, variable X increases in rank; going down the rows, variable Y decreases in rank. As before, the six interview teams are identified by the letters A, B, C, D, E, and F. Find the concordant pairs, such as pair 2 of A and C and pair 11 of C and E in the figure. Observe that one team in each pair is in a cell *above and to the right of the cell below* in which the other team is found. On the other hand, discordant pairs, such as pair 1 of A and B and pair 7 of B and D, are formed by comparing an observation in a lower cell to an observation in a cell *above but to the left* of it. T_x pairs, such as pair 3 of A and D, are derived from a comparison of teams in the same column, but not the same cell. T_y pairs, such as pair 4 of A and E, involve comparison of teams in the same row, but not in the same cell. Finally, T_{xy} pairs, such as pair 12 of C and F, are computed from teams in the same cell. The reader should keep this alignment of the different types of pairs in mind because it will help later in understanding the actual calculation of pairs in a table.

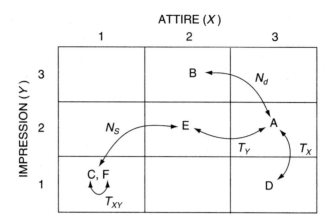

FIGURE 4.1   Crosstabulation of the Data in Table 4.12

4.7.2 Prediction of the Dependent Variable Based on the Independent Variable

Before a PRE measure can be constructed, the strategy of predicting relative order in a pair of cases must be determined. In Table 4.13, excluding the tied pairs T_x, T_y, and T_{xy}, there are nine ranked pairs, out of which six are concordant and three are discordant. Given that there are more concordant than discordant pairs, the best strategy is to predict the same order of ranking in the Y variable as in the X variable. For instance, knowing that the collaborator is more formally dressed in the first than the second interview (information on X), Anne should predict that she also makes a more favorable impression on the first than the second occasion (prediction of Y). Using this prediction rule on all nine pairs would yield six correct predictions and three errors. The three errors here are represented by E_2.

If there were six differently ordered pairs rather than three, the strategy would change to predicting a relative ranking in the Y variable that is different from the relative ranking in the X variable. Following this strategy, if the collaborator is known to be *more* formally dressed in the first interview, then she is predicted to make a *less* favorable impression on that occasion.

When information on X is given, the prediction rule is clear. If there are more N_s pairs than N_d pairs, predict the same order. However, if there are more N_d pairs than N_s pairs, predict a different order.

4.7.3 Base-line Prediction

In addition to determining the predictability of Y based on X, a base-line prediction rule and a base-line level of predictability for Y must be established for comparison. In this case, base-line prediction involves predicting the relative order of Y within a pair without knowledge of X. The situation is equivalent to guessing the outcome of the toss of a fair coin. In coin tossing, the best strategy is to guess head (or tail) every time for all tosses. With such a strategy, the researcher can expect to be correct 50% of the time and also incorrect 50% of the time. In predicting relative order, a parallel strategy is used, which will yield the same result. Select *randomly* a case from the pair and predict that it is higher (or lower) on Y than the other case of the pair. Repeat this process for all pairs for which a prediction is to be made, and the expectation of being correct is 50%. Thus E_1 equals 50%.

Association for this type of PRE measures then means a preponderance of either N_s or N_d pairs. For when there is more of one or the other type of pairs, the success rate will be over 50% in predicting the relative order of Y based on X. The more there are of the N_s or N_d pairs, the stronger is the association.

4.7.4 Predicting Types of Relationship

From the preceding illustration, it can be seen that to establish an association in ordinal variables the *pattern of variation* between X and Y must be taken into account. The pattern of variation gives rise to the concept of *types of relationship.* When there are more concordant than discordant pairs, X and Y are, on the whole, varying in the same direction, and we call that a **positive relationship.** On the other hand, when there are more discordant pairs, X and Y are generally changing in the opposite direction, and we call that a **negative relationship.**

A positive relationship is indicated by a positive sign obtained from the measure of association; a negative relationship is denoted by a negative sign. An example of a positive relationship is that of status and deference: the higher the status of an individual is, the more the others defer to him or her. On the other hand, the relationship between status and punishment is negative: individuals in higher status are less likely to be caught and punished for their deviant acts.

Exercises

19. Anne interviews personnel officers who are in charge of screening job applicants for accountancy and gathers three pieces of information on each candidate: (1) professional competence, (2) sociability assessed by how an applicant presents himself or herself, and (3) personality compatibility with the firm's goals. The results are summarized as follows:

Candidate	Compatibility	Professional Competence	Sociability
1	3	3	3
2	3	2	3
3	1	2	1
4	2	3	2
5	1	2	1
6	1	1	2

To study the relationship between personality compatibility and professional competence, and personality compatibility and sociability:

a. Compute the numbers of concordant pairs, discordant pairs, and tied pairs.
b. What is the prediction strategy, knowing one variable?
c. Using this strategy, how many errors will be made?

4.8 Gamma: A PRE Measure for Ordinal Variables

Research Question

Social interaction is very much conditioned by the existence of intangible boundaries that define the limits of the social self. Even the physical space surrounding an individual is divided by invisible barriers into zones where different types of individuals are permitted and various interactions take place. For example, a zone of intimacy, radiating from the individual to a distance of 18 inches, is reserved for those closest to the individual, whereas a public zone of 12 feet or more from the individual is designated for strangers [3]. Contrary to popular notions, the existence of social boundaries often facilitates social interaction. Anne suspects that the clearer the boundaries are, the less problematic the interaction is among strangers.

The Data

The data come from an experiment conducted by a group of Anne's colleagues to study living arrangements in university dormitories. Each dormitory is three stories high and each room is occupied by two students. The investigators randomly assigned the three floors in each building to different experimental conditions. Within each floor, one of the following conditions exists: (1) rules are clearly established pertaining to house responsibilities and the use of the space in the room, as well as the common areas, (2) some rules are established concerning areas of responsibility, and (3) no rules are established. For Anne's portion of the investigation, roommates were asked to rate the perceived ease of interaction after the first week of sharing the room. The ease of interaction is assessed by the amount of friction experienced and the frequency of joint activities during the week. The data are shown in Table 4.14. Is there an association between the

TABLE 4.14 Ease of Interaction by Clarity of Boundaries

Ease of Interaction (Y)	Clarity of Boundaries (X)			
	Low	Medium	High	Total
High	62	55	146	263
Medium	42	210	71	323
Low	196	35	83	314
Total	300	300	300	900

existence of rules that help define social boundaries and the ability of roommates to interact with ease?

An Appropriate Statistic

Because Anne has two variables that are very roughly quantified, a measure of association based on the prediction of relative order would be appropriate. **Gamma** is one such measure, which varies between 0 and ±1, with the + sign or – sign denoting either a positive or a negative relationship. It is a symmetric measure whose value indicates the amount of reduction in error that results in predicting Y from X, as well as in predicting X from Y. Gamma does not have an asymmetric form and can be used on tables of any size.

Translating the generalized formula for a PRE measure into a formula for gamma results in the following:

$$G = \frac{E_1 - E_2}{E_1} = \frac{.5(N_s + N_d) - \min(N_s, N_d)}{.5(N_s + N_d)} = \frac{(N_s + N_d) - 2\min(N_s, N_d)}{N_s + N_d}$$

where $\min(N_s, N_d)$ refers to either N_s or N_d, whichever is smaller.

Gathering the terms in this formula in such a way that gamma will yield a positive value when $N_s > N_d$ and a negative value when $N_s < N_d$, the following computational formula is obtained:

$$G = \frac{N_s - N_d}{N_s + N_d} \tag{4.11}$$

Calculation and Interpretation

To calculate N_s or N_d for Table 4.14, it is no longer practical to list the individual pairs because they are so numerous. Instead, a starting corner of the bivariate table is located for computing either N_s or N_d. The N_s **corner** is one where the ranks of X and Y agree. There are basically two such N_s corners in each table: the corner in which the lowest rank of X intersects the lowest rank of Y and the opposite diagonal corner where the highest ranks of the variables intersect. In Table 4.14, one N_s corner is represented by the (low, low) cell with its 196 cases. Take an observation from this cell and pair it with any observation from a cell above and to the right of it. A concordant pair is formed in which the observation from the N_s corner cell is lower on both X and Y than the observation in the cell above and to its right (recall Figure 4.1). *Thus, with a table such as Table 4.14, concordant pairs are formed by comparing cells that are above and to the right of the comparison cell.*

The four cells above and to the right of the (low, low) cell are shaded in Figure 4.2(a), and they contain a total of 482 cases: (210 + 71 + 55 + 146). Therefore, 482 pairs can be formed with one case from the comparison (low, low) cell. With 196 cases from this cell, the total number of pairs formed is 94,472: (196)(482).

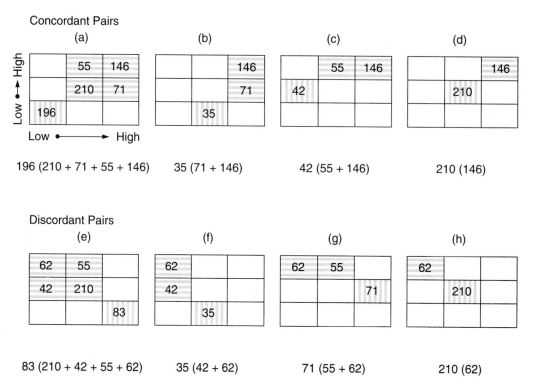

FIGURE 4.2   Calculating Concordant and Discordant Pairs

Other N_s pairs can be formed with other comparison cells in the bottom row. So, proceed to the next cell in this row with its 35 cases [Figure 4.2(b)]. The number of concordant pairs that can be formed from this cell is calculated in the same manner as before: add the cell frequencies above and to the right of the comparison cell and multiply their sum by the cell frequency in the comparison cell. Thus the number of pairs formed by the second comparison cell is 7,595: 35(71 + 146). The last cell in this row does not have any cell that is above and to the right of it. Therefore, no concordant pairs can be formed with this cell.

After the computation is completed for the bottom row, proceed to the middle row of Table 4.14. The first cell in this row has two cells above and to its right [Figure 4.2(c)]. The number of concordant pairs obtained equals 8,442: 42(55 + 146). The second cell in this row has only one cell above and to its right [Figure 4.2(d)]. The number of pairs formed is 30,660: (210)(146). Again, the last cell in this row does not have cells above and to its right and therefore yields 0 concordant pairs.

Concordant pairs cannot be computed from the uppermost row of Table 4.14 because there are no cells above it. Thus the total number of N_s pairs from the table is

$$N_s = 94,472 + 7,595 + 8,442 + 30,660 = 141,169$$

Now locate an appropriate corner to start computing N_d. The N_d **corner** is one where the ranks of X and Y do not agree. There are two N_d corners: one where the highest rank of X intersects the lowest rank of Y and the other where the lowest rank of X intersects the highest rank of Y. Again, these are diagonally opposing corners. We will start computing from the N_d corner at the lower right of Table 4.14. The cell at this corner has a cell frequency of 83. *An observation from this cell forms a discordant pair with an observation from any cell above and to its left.* The observation from the N_d corner cell is higher on X but lower on Y when compared with any observation above and to its left. As seen in Figure 4.2(e), there are four cells above and to the left, containing a total of 369 cases: (210 + 42 + 55 + 62). Since the comparison cell has 83 cases, the number of pairs formed is 30,627: (369)(83). The next cell on the left of the N_d corner cell has 35 cases [Figure 4.2 (f)]. The number of pairs obtained from this comparison is 3,640: 35(42 + 62). The last cell on the bottom row has nothing above and to its left.

The second row yields pairs of 8,307: (71)(55 + 62) and 13,020: (210)(62). See Figure 4.2(g) and (h). Again, no discordant pairs can be calculated from the uppermost row. Therefore, the total number of discordant pairs is

$$N_d = 30{,}627 + 3{,}640 + 8{,}307 + 13{,}020 = 55{,}594$$

Gamma can now be calculated as follows:

$$G = \frac{141{,}169 - 55{,}594}{141{,}169 - 55{,}594} = \frac{85{,}575}{196{,}763} = .435$$

The value and sign of gamma indicate that, when N_s or the same order is predicted in Y as in X for all 196,763 ranked pairs of observations, the proportional reduction in error is .435. Since the measure is symmetric, the proportional reduction in error is the same when using the order in Y to predict the order in X. More generally, Anne concludes that not only is there an association between clarity of boundaries and ease of interaction for the 900 roommates, but also the clearer the boundaries are, the easier it is for them to interact.

Calculation of Tied Pairs

Although gamma does not take ties into account, tied pairs such as those mentioned in Box 4.2 have to be determined for other PRE measures based on relative ranking. To show how tied pairs are calculated, consider Table 4.14 again. Since Y is arranged by row in this table, observations that are in *different cells*, but within the *same row*, are ranked on X, but tied on Y. Start with the first cell in the top row of Table 4.14 to compute the number of T_y pairs in that row. An observation from that cell compared to an observation in another cell of the same row yields ranks that can be ordered on X, but that are tied (high, high) on Y. The number of T_y pairs formed with the first cell in the top row is 12,462: 62(55 + 146). Refer to Figure 4.3(a). With the second cell in the same row, the number of T_y pairs formed

---

Box 4.2   Other Measures Based on the Prediction of Relative Ranks in Pairs

Somer's *d* is an asymmetric measure of association for ordinal variables based on relative ranking. There are two measures of *d*, one with *X* and the other with *Y* as the dependent variable. Like gamma, Somer's *d* is a PRE measure. Unlike gamma, it takes into account in its calculation pairs that are tied with respect to the dependent variable only. For Somer's *d* the fact that a tie has occurred in the dependent variable does not mean that the pair should be excluded from potential prediction. Accordingly, pairs that are tied on the dependent variable only, that is, either the T_y or T_x pairs, are brought into the formulas as follows:

$$d_{yx} = \frac{N_s - N_d}{N_s + N_d + T_y} \quad (4.13)$$

$$d_{xy} = \frac{N_s - N_d}{N_s + N_d + T_x} \quad (4.14)$$

The *d*'s are subscripted, as usual, with the dependent variable first and then the independent variable. Being asymmetric, the two *d*'s do not yield the same value unless the numbers of ties are the same for *X* and *Y*. Their signs, however, should be consistent because the type of relationship remains the same whether *Y* is being predicted from *X*, or vice versa.

Tau-*b* is essentially a symmetric form of Somer's *d* that takes into account the number of ties in *X* as well as in *Y*, but not the number of ties in both variables:

$$\text{tau-}b = \frac{N_s - N_d}{\sqrt{N_s + N_d + T_x}\sqrt{N_s + N_d + T_y}} \quad (4.15)$$

Tau-*b* and the *d*'s are related in the following manner: $\text{tau-}b = \sqrt{d_{yx}d_{xy}}$.

---

is 8,030: (55)(146). See Figure 4.3(b). The pairing between the first and second cells is unnecessary since it has already been completed in the previous step. The last cell on the same row has no successive cell with which to compare; therefore, the total number of T_y pairs from the top row is 20,492: (12,462 + 8,030). Next, move down to the second row to repeat the same process of calculation. The number of T_y pairs from the second row is 26,712: 42(210 + 71) + (210)(71). See Figure 4.3(c) and (d). Finally, from the last row, the number of T_y pairs is 26,033: 196(35 + 83) + (35)(83) [Figure 4.3(e) and(f)]. After computing the number of T_y pairs from the last row, sum all the T_y scores:

$$T_y = 20,492 + 26,712 + 26,033 = 73,237$$

For the computation of T_x, follow the same procedure but proceed by column instead of by row. Again, start with the same cell as in computing T_y. An observation from this cell compared to an observation in another cell of the same *column* yields ranks that are tied (low, low) on *X*, but that can be ordered on *Y*. Thus the comparison of each cell with successive cells down the column will give the total T_x pairs formed per column. In the X_1 column of *low*, the number of pairs formed is 22,988: 62(42 + 196) + (42)(196). See Figure 4.3(g) and (h). The X_2 column gives a total of 20,825 pairs: 55(210 + 35) + (210)(35). Refer to Figure 4.3(i) and (j). The

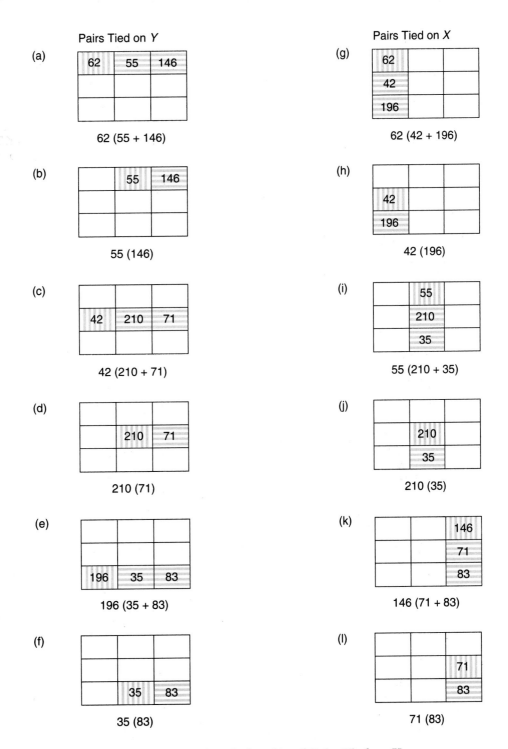

FIGURE 4.3   Calculating Pairs Tied on *Y* and Pairs Tied on *X*

last column yields a total of 28,377 pairs: 146(71 + 83) + (71)(83). See Figure 4.3(k) and (l). Summing all these T_x pairs yields

$$T_x = 22,988 + 20,825 + 28,377 = 72,190$$

Finally, T_{xy} is obtained as follows:

$$T_{xy} = \frac{N(N-1)}{2} - N_s - N_d - T_x - T_y$$
$$= 404,550 - 141,169 - 55,594 - 72,190 - 73,237 = 62,360$$

Characteristics and Properties

Ignoring ties, gamma is concerned only with pairs of observations that can be ranked on both variables. However, as the ties in X, or in Y, or in both X and Y increase, the ranked pairs on which gamma is based decrease with a given sample size. Under such circumstances, gamma may not adequately describe or represent the overall relationship between the two variables. The researcher could antici-pate the problem beforehand by providing a more refined ranking system to measure the variables. This would tend to reduce the number of ties. Otherwise, a different measure of association, such as Somer's d or tau-b, that take ties into account may be preferable. See Box 4.2 for these measures. A comparison of these measures to gamma shows that, as long as ties exist, the value of gamma is always larger than the values of the d's and tau-b.

Gamma has other limitations, which can be illustrated through **Yule's Q,** a simplified gamma for a 2×2 table. The formula for Q is

$$Q = \frac{bc - ad}{bc + ad} \tag{4.12}$$

Yule's Q yields a value of 0 when $N_s = N_d$. Predicting either the same or a different order in this case will produce no better than the 50% base-line prediction level. See model 1 in Table 4.15. Yule's Q attains a −1 or 1 when all the frequencies are concentrated along one or the other diagonal, as seen in models 2 and 3 of Table 4.15. However, it also reaches a maximum value of −1 or 1 whenever one cell in the table is zero. Refer to models 4 and 5. Thus Yule's Q, and therefore gamma, has a less restrictive definition of a perfect association than the measures pre-sented before. If all the ranked pairs are either N_s or N_d, the association is considered perfect and the existence of ties does not affect its value.

These models also illustrate another characteristic of Q and therefore gamma. The same value of Q (gamma) can be produced by different concentrations of cases in the table: both models 3 and 5 in Table 4.15 yield a value of 1. This is possible because of the problem pointed out earlier: ties are not taken into ac-count in the calculation.

TABLE 4.15   Models of No Association and Perfect Association in Yule's *Q*

(a) Model 1: Yule's $Q = 0$

2	4
5	10

(b) Model 2: Yule's $Q = -1$ (c) Model 3: Yule's $Q = 1$

f_{11}	0
0	f_{22}

0	f_{12}
f_{21}	0

(d) Model 4: Yule's $Q = -1$ (e) Model 5: Yule's $Q = 1$

f_{11}	f_{12}
0	f_{22}

f_{11}	f_{12}
f_{21}	0

Exercises

20. The importance of reference groups in determining our attitudes and behavior has been observed by many symbolic interactionists. The following is a crosstabulation of the social class of nonwhites in Los Angeles and the degree of preference for whites as their reference groups:

	Social Class		
Reference Group	Low	Middle	Upper
1 Strongly prefer nonwhites	20	50	10
2 Prefer nonwhites	20	40	15
3 Prefer whites	15	30	20
4 Strongly prefer whites	10	20	8

a. Compute *G*.
b. On how many pairs of cases is the gamma based?
c. What proportion of all possible pairs does this constitute?

21. By combining categories in Exercise 20, create a 2 × 2 table and compute Yule's *Q*.

a. Compute the percentage differences for the original 4 × 3 table and the collapsed 2 × 2 table.

b. Does G or Q describe the bivariate relationship better than the percentage differences? Why or why not?

22. Compute G for the data in Exercise 1 to determine the degree of association between community size and auto deal.

23. Compute G to determine the degree of association between personal compatibility and professional competence for the data in Exercise 19.

24. In a study of personal space, volunteers sit next to another student studying at a table in the library. The distance between the volunteers and the subjects are set at three levels: (1) extremely close, (2) close, and (3) not close. The reactions of the subjects are classified into (1) acceptance of the situation, (2) withdrawal by moving away, and (3) hostility shown toward intruder. The data are summarized as follows:

	Personal Space		
Reaction	Far	Medium	Close
Acceptance	15	7	2
Neutral	2	10	10
Hostility	0	0	5

a. Compute gamma, Somer's d, and tau-b.
b. Compute lambda and Cramer's V.
c. Compare the results and discuss the upper and lower limits of these measurements.

25. For the following data:

	X				X		
	X_1	X_2			X_1	X_2	X_3
Y_1	50	25		Y_1	25	0	0
Y_2	0	25		Y_2	0	0	25
				Y_3	0	50	0

a. Compute various measures of association.
b. Compare the results and discuss the characteristics of these measures.

SPSS Notes

All the statistics introduced in this chapter can be requested from SPSS using the STATISTICS subcommand of the CROSSTABS command. The following is a list of the keywords used to request the statistics:

CHISQ	chi-square	PHI	phi
CC	contingency coefficient	LAMBDA	lambda
BTAU	Kendall's tau-*b*	CTAU	Kendall's tau-*c*
GAMMA	gamma	D	Somer's *d*
ALL	all statistics		

For example, after data entry, the following command will compute gamma and Somer's *d*:

```
CROSSTABS TABLES=INTERACT BY BOUNDARY /STATISTICS GAMMA D.
```

SPSS Exercises

3. Using the GSS survey, crosstabulate SEX and COLHOMO (let homosexual teach at college) and compute the phi coefficient. Interpret the result.

4. Which race (RACE), whites or blacks, favor a law against interracial marriage (RACMAR) among the GSS respondents? Dichotomize and crosstabulate RACE and RACMAR. Compute phi and interpret the results.

5. In SPSS Exercise 4, does it make a big difference in the strength of association if the NAP responses are included in the Yes rather than No category?

6. Examine the relationship between REGION and RACHOME (bring a black home for dinner) among GSS respondents by computing lambda. Should REGION be collapsed into fewer categories? Why or why not?

7. Using GSS data, collapse age (AGE) into three categories of young, middle-aged, and old. Then combine age and sex to create a joint variable. Study the effect of this new variable upon COLHOMO (allow homosexual to teach at college) by computing lambda.

GSS respondents were asked if they like or dislike JAPAN on a 10-point scale (JAPAN). Examine the degree of association between this variable and the following set of variables using various measures of association. Collapse variables first into two categories; then expand into several categories as necessary.

8. Subjective social class (CLASS).

9. Age (AGE).

10. Region (REGION).

4.9 Selecting a Measure of Association

Again, we need to highlight the difference between findings that pertain to a sample and those that apply to a population. In calculating the measures discussed in this chapter, the researcher learns something about the relationship between two variables in a sample. To determine whether sample outcome is indicative of population characteristic, the inferential techniques presented in Chapter 13 must be applied. However, regardless of what a sample has to say about the population, descriptive techniques have a role of their own. They are indispensable in an exploratory or descriptive project for which a nonrandom sample has been selected and the researcher is simply looking for tentative answers. This is the reason they are discussed in a separate chapter, apart from the inferential techniques that test their significance.

For a particular set of data, the researcher is most likely to compute only one measure to determine whether an association exists. In selecting that measure, the researcher should consider the following:

1. Theoretical Issues. Whether a symmetric or an asymmetric measure should be selected and which variable should serve as the dependent variable are issues to be resolved before conducting a bivariate analysis. The choice of a symmetric versus asymmetric measure usually depends on the researcher's interest and theoretical focus. If the theoretical framework specifies a cause-and-effect relationship or if the researcher's aim is to find the better predictor of two variables, an asymmetric measure would be more appropriate. However, if the goal is to assess the relationship between two variables, a symmetric measure would probably be preferable.

2. Measurement Level of the Data. Each statistic requires a specified amount of information from the data; therefore, selecting an appropriate technique means matching the technique to the level of data measurement. A related issue is the degree of precision with which the data are measured. For nominal data, this may mean choosing between a statistic appropriate for 2×2 tables and one appropriate for $r \times c$ tables, where $r > 2$ and/or $c > 2$. For ordinal data that are roughly scaled, a statistic that predicts relative order rather than exact rank would be more appropriate.

3. Characteristics of the Measure. Ideally, measures of association should have the same upper and lower numerical limits so that a standard interpretation can be attached to their values. Some measures do have this characteristic of a standardized lower and upper limit of 0 and |1|. Other measures can attain the value of |1| only under restrictive conditions. Also, some measures do not have a constant upper limit; instead, their upper limit is affected by such factors as sample and table size.

Measures of association should also have a value that can be interpreted precisely and is tied to a comparative base line. PRE measures based on predictability have this desirable characteristic, whereas chi-square-based measures do not. This does not mean that PRE measures are necessarily superior. For example, we have shown how a PRE measure like lambda is not sensitive to association in a table in which the highest cell frequencies are all concentrated in a row or in a column.

To facilitate the selection of an appropriate measure, the major characteristics of each statistic discussed in this chapter are given in the following summaries.

Summary

Measures of Association for Nominal Variables

Measure	Formula	Table Size	Value Range	Symmetry of Relation
Measures Based on Statistical Independence			*Can be used w/ larger tables*	
Phi	$\dfrac{\lvert bc - ad \rvert}{\sqrt{(a + b)(c + d)(a + c)(b + d)}}$	2×2	0 to 1	Symmetric
Contingency Coefficient C	$\sqrt{\dfrac{\chi^2}{\chi^2 + N}}$	$r \times c$	0 to X where $(X < 1.0)$	Symmetric
Cramer's V	$\sqrt{\dfrac{\chi^2}{(N)(\text{Min}[r - 1, c - 1])}}$	$r \times c$	0 to 1	Symmetric
Measures Based on PRE		*any size tables*		
Lambda: λ_{yx}	$\dfrac{\sum\limits_{j=1}^{c} fy_j - My}{N - My}$	$r \times c$	0 to 1	Asymmetric
Lambda: λ	$\dfrac{\left(\sum\limits_{j=1}^{c} fy_j - \sum\limits_{i=1}^{r} fx_i\right) - (My + Mx)}{2N - (My + Mx)}$	$r \times c$	0 to 1	Symmetric

Measures of Association for Ordinal Variables

Measure	Formula	Table Size	Value Range	Symmetry of Relation
Measures Based on PRE				
Gamma (G)	$\dfrac{N_s - N_d}{N_s + N_d}$	$r \times c$	0 to ± 1	Symmetric
Yule's Q	$\dfrac{bc - ad}{bc + ad}$	2×2	0 to ± 1	Symmetric
Somer's d_{yx}	$\dfrac{N_s - N_d}{N_s + N_d + T_y}$	$r \times c$	0 to ± 1	Asymmetric
Tau-b	$\dfrac{N_s - N_d}{\sqrt{N_s + N_d + T_x}\sqrt{N_s + N_d + T_y}}$	$r \times c$	0 to ± 1	Symmetric

General Conceptual Problems

1. Look through the letters to the editor section of a local newspaper and find five statements that imply the need for a coefficient of association. Does each indicate a symmetric or asymmetric relationship?

2. For each illustration, select an appropriate measure of association and give a rationale for the choice.

3. Explain the relationship between statistical independence and proportional reduction in errors. Does PRE = 0 imply statistical independence?

4. Choose pairs of subjects from the cells of the following table to constitute:
   a. Concordant pairs
   b. Disconcordant pairs
   c. Tied pairs (tied on height, on weight, on both).

		Weight	
Height	Light	Medium	Heavy
Tall	a	b	c
Middle	d	e	f
Short	g	h	i

5. Construct a table such that:
   a. lambda = 1, lambda = 0
   b. gamma = 1, gamma = 0 (Yule's $Q = 1$, $Q = 0$)
   c. phi = 1, phi = 0
   d. Somer's $d = 1$, Somer's $d = 0$
   e. tau-$b = 1$, tau-$b = 0$
   f. Contingency coefficient $C = 1$, $C = 0$
   g. Cramer's $V = 1$, $V = 0$

6. Will the value of lambda or gamma change when the order of the columns in a table is reversed?

7. Explain what is meant by base-line prediction and how it is established.

8. Select appropriate statistics to describe the association between the following sets of variables:
   a. Religious affiliation and ethnicity
   b. Religiosity and liberalism
   c. Sex and party affiliation in a two-party system
   d. Occupational prestige and types of school attended with many tied scores
   e. Race and social class in a sample consisting of predominantly whites
   f. Race and class in the South and in the North. Class is divided into five categories in the South and four in the North.

9. Select a contingency table of interest and discuss the logic underlying the following:
   a. Proportional reduction in error
   b. Paired ranking
   c. Statistical independence

10. What characteristics are considered desirable for a coefficient of association?

11. Discuss the similarities and differences among gamma, Yule's *Q*, Somer's *d*, and tau-*b* coefficients.

12. Explain how Yule's *Q* is based on the PRE principle.

13. List the factors that should be considered in interpreting measures of association.

References

1. Loether, H. J., and McTavish, D.J. (1993). *Descriptive and Inferential Statistics: An Introduction*. Boston: Allyn and Bacon.
2. Feldman-Summers, S., and Kiesler, J. (1974). Those Who Are Number Two Try Harder: The Effects of Sex on Attributions of Causality. *Journal of Personality and Social Psychology* 30:845–855.
3. Hall, E. T. (1959). *The Silent Language*. Greenwich, Conn: Fawcett.

Chapter 5

Organizing and Describing Interval Bivariate Data

New Statistical Topics

Scattergram and the regression line
Regression equation and Pearson's r
Coefficient of determination, r^2, and of alienation, K^2
Rank-order correlation
Correlation ratio

5.1 Overview

This chapter focuses primarily on the topic of association between two interval scale variables. Bivariate analysis of interval variables involves two distinct but interrelated aspects: (1) the problem of predicting one variable from another, known as **regression**, and (2) the assessment of **correlation** or association between the variables. Regression and correlation techniques assume a **linear relationship** between the variables. Such a relationship exists when a constant amount of change in one variable is accompanied by a constant amount of change in another variable. As an example, the number of students in a school and the school budget may be linearly related. With the admission of each additional student, the school may receive an additional fixed amount of dollars from the school district for the year.

Before applying regression and correlation procedures, the researcher should determine whether the data are linearly related. To do this, a graphic technique called the scattergram is used, which plots the information on the X and Y variables as data dots. Then a linear prediction rule, called a regression equation, is formulated based on sample data. The evaluation of how well the regression equation fits the actual data gives rise to two measures of association, the correlation coefficient also known as Pearson's r, and the coefficient of determination, r^2.

Two other statistics included in the discussion are based on principles similar to those of the correlation coefficient. Spearman's rho, a rank-order correlation coefficient, is essentially a Pearson's r calculated on ranks rather than on actual values. It can therefore be used on ordinal data. The correlation ratio, on the other hand, determines the association between an interval and a nominal variable by using a prediction rule that does not assume linearity.

5.1.1 Social Applications

In this chapter, our protagonist, Anne, remains concerned with the understanding and predictability of social behavior. She realizes that, in addition to the social statuses of those involved and the dynamics of the interaction situation, the location of the individuals in the stratification system is an important determinant of behavior.

Stratification refers to patterns of inequality in a society that result from individuals being grouped and evaluated according to the access they have to the valuable resources of the society. Wealth, for example, is a valuable asset. When a society is stratified by wealth, individuals with access to this resource are respected and accorded better treatment than those with little or no access. Stratification has a pervasive impact not only on behavior but on every aspect of an individual's life, from values to life chances. Consequently, social scientists consider an individual's or a group's location in this system indispensable to an understanding of that individual or group.

However, before an individual's location in this all-important system is determined, the structure of the system itself bears scrutiny. According to Marx, society is stratified on the basis of one and only one important criterion—the individual's relationship to the means of production in the society. The individual either owns and controls the means of production or works for those who do; everything else in life flows from this important distinction. Weber, on the other hand, contends that social stratification is much more complex in an industrialized society. Three, rather than one, independent dimensions comprise the social hierarchy: wealth, power, and prestige. An individual's rankings on all three dimensions may be consistent, as in the case of a wealthy, powerful, and esteemed judge. Or they may be inconsistent, as in the case of a poor, nonpowerful, but well-respected college professor. The degree of congruence is a matter for empirical investigation since it varies from society to society. Marx's view of stratification is said to be unidimensional, while Weber's is called multidimensional.

Which of these two theorists gives a more accurate description of inequalities in the United States? Anne hopes to clarify this issue through statistical analysis. If stratification is unidimensional, as Marx claimed, there would be a strong association among the various criteria for stratification, and they should perhaps be subsumed under one dimension. If a moderate to low association exists, it would be an indication of a multidimensional system.

5.1.2 Statistical Topics

Central to the understanding of an association between two interval variables is the concept of **covariation**. Recall from Chapter 4 that covariation refers to the tendency of two variables to vary together in a systematic fashion. Before discussing covariation, let us first review the meaning of *variation* in an interval variable. The variation, which is also called deviation, is measured from a focal point: the mean of the distribution: $(X - \overline{X})$ (Chapter 3).

Covariation is derived from the concept of variation. In covariation, we determine the tendency of the deviations of the two variables to vary in either the same or in opposite directions. Mathematically, covariation can be measured by the **cross product**s or the multiplication of the deviations of X and Y from their respective means, as follows:

$$\text{Covariation}(X, Y) = (X - \overline{X})(Y - \overline{Y})$$

For illustration, examine Table 5.1, which gives the number of years of schooling and income of three individuals. Jones is above the mean of schooling by 2 years and above the mean of income by $19,000. Smith, on the other hand, is below the mean both in education and income. The cross products of these variations in the two variables produce both a measure of the amount of covariation and its direction. When a value of X that is above or below its mean is paired with a value of Y that is also above or below its mean, X and Y are varying in the same direction, and their cross product is positive, such as that of Jones and Smith. On the other hand, when a value of X, which is above its mean, is paired with a value of Y that is below its mean, X and Y are varying in opposite directions, and their cross product is negative, as in the case of Adams.

By summing these cross products for the entire sample, $\Sigma(X - \overline{X})(Y - \overline{Y})$, the degree of association between X and Y can also be determined. With N being constant, the larger the *absolute* value of the sum of the cross products is, the

TABLE 5.1 Covariation of Education and Income

Subject	Years of Schooling X	Income (in $1,000) Y	$X - \overline{X}$	$Y - \overline{Y}$	$(X - \overline{X})(Y - \overline{Y})$
Jones	18	62	2	19	38
Smith	13	28	-3	-15	45
Adams	17	39	1	-4	-4
Mean	16	43			
Sum					79

stronger the association of the variables. When the sum is zero, the positive cross products balance the negative ones. In such a case, no linear relationship exists because Y is equally likely to increase or decrease while X increases. It is not surprising, then, that by refining the concept of covariation statistical measures can be derived to determine the linear association between variables and to predict the values of one variable from the values of the other.

5.2 Graphic Organization of Interval Data: The Scattergram

Research Question
Following the footsteps of sociologists who, since Weber's time, have examined more than the dimensions of wealth, power, and prestige, Anne begins her analysis of the stratification system in the United States by looking at the relationship between education and income. How much congruence is there between these dimensions and can they be subsumed under one dimension?

The Data
Anne takes a random sample of eight subjects from a data base at the Research Institute of University X. Their income and educational levels are shown in Table 5.2. Both variables are measured on the interval level, with income coded in thousands of dollars, and education, in number of years of schooling.

An Appropriate Method
An inspection of the raw data shows that there is a tendency for income to vary with education in such a way that as education increases so does income. The statistics Anne plans to use to summarize their association presuppose a linear relationship. Since it is difficult to abstract this information from the raw data, Anne needs a method of organizing the bivariate data to permit a preliminary

TABLE 5.2 Years of Schooling and Income in Thousands for a Sample of Eight

Subject	Education (X) Degree	Education (X) No. of Years	Income (Y) (in $1,000)
Professor	Ph.D.	23	56
Doctor	M.D.	24	125
CPA	MBA	18	100
Secretary	High school	12	25
Clerk	High school	12	28
Plumber	Junior college	14	60
Gas attendant	High school	12	22
Salesperson	College	16	45

assessment of the nature of the relationship. The **scattergram,** sometimes called a **scatterplot,** is such a method. It is a case by case, graphic plot of the bivariate information.

Construction of the Scattergram

Traditionally, the independent variable is plotted along the X axis and the dependent variable, along the Y axis. As Anne's research question does not identify a specific variable as independent, let income be considered as dependent on education. Intervals of education are therefore marked on the X axis and intervals of income are marked on the Y axis to represent the observed values of the variables as in Figure 5.1.

The bivariate information on each case is then plotted as a dot within the quadrangle formed by the axes. The dot is placed at the intersection of the X (education) and Y (income) values in the following manner. Take the first case in Table 5.2 of the professor with 23 years of education and $56,000 of income. Move along the X axis until $X = 23$ is reached; then move up from this point on a path parallel to the Y axis to the height where $Y = 56$. A dot at this point, where X of 23 intersects Y of 56, represents the professor. All eight cases from Table 5.2 are similarly plotted and shown in Figure 5.1.

Interpretation

Now that the data have been organized, the scattergram can be examined for the *nature* of the relationship between education and income. Note that the dots are

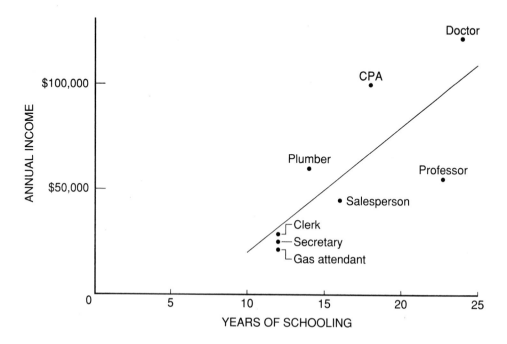

FIGURE 5.1   Scattergram of Education and Income

scattered more or less along the path of a *line* that extends diagonally upward from left to right of the quadrangle. A line is drawn freehand in Figure 5.1 to represent this trend of the scattering of the data dots. This line is referred to as a **regression line.** The fact that a line can be roughly fitted to these dots shows that the relationship is approximately linear. Thus a constant amount of change in one variable, associated with a unit change in the other, translates into a straight line on the graph.

Relationships are not always linear, but may be curvilinear as shown in Figure 5.2(a), where a line would not represent the pattern of scatter. In such a case, the correlation and regression techniques presented in this chapter will not be appropriate for describing the association.

By inspecting the direction of the slope, the type of relationship can be determined. If the regression line extends diagonally upward from the lower left to the upper right of the quadrangle, as in Figure 5.2(b), there is a positive relationship between the two variables. If the line extends from the upper left diagonally downward toward the base line of the X axis as in Figure 5.2(c), the

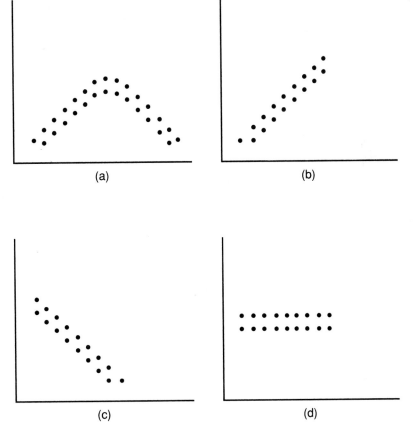

(a)   (b)

(c)   (d)

FIGURE 5.2   Scattergrams

relationship is negative. If there is no relationship between the two variables, the line is flat, having no slope, as in Figure 5.2(d).

The scatter of the data dots around the regression line also yields insight as to the *approximate* degree of association between the two variables. If all the data dots fall exactly on a *sloping* straight line, there is a perfect relationship between *X* and *Y* in which one and only one value of *Y* is associated with each value of *X*. In reality, perfect relationships seldom exist. Instead, for every *X* value, there is usually a range of *Y* values. For instance, in Anne's data set, three different *Y* values are associated with an *X* of 12. Take another example of income for everyone who has graduated with a bachelor's degree. Here, too, there is a range with some earning more than others. This range of *Y* values, associated with a value of *X*, such as 12 or college graduation, is known as the *conditional distribution of Y for X*. (The concept of conditional distribution was discussed in Section 4.2.2. A review of the material may be helpful at this point.) These conditional distributions of *Y* for different values of *X* produce the scattering of data points around the regression line. The more closely the data points cluster around the line, the stronger is the association. In inspecting Figure 5.1, Anne expects to find a fairly strong positive association between education and income.

Exercises

1. Anne expects that occupational advancement is based on merit rather than seniority in the United States. If that is true, salary will not be related linearly to years of work experience. She finds a study of 10 middle- to upper-middle-level managers, with the following data.

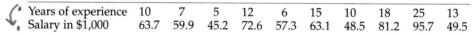

| Years of experience | 10 | 7 | 5 | 12 | 6 | 15 | 10 | 18 | 25 | 13 |
| Salary in $1,000 | 63.7 | 59.9 | 45.2 | 72.6 | 57.3 | 63.1 | 48.5 | 81.2 | 95.7 | 49.5 |

   a. Plot a scattergram.
   b. Do the two variables appear to be related linearly?
   c. Draw a line that best fits the data.

2. Take a class survey of the height and weight of students. Plot a scattergram and draw a line that best fits the data.

3. Give an example in which two variables are nonlinearly related. Draw a scattergram based on fictitious data of these two variables.

5.3 Linear Regression

Research Question
Now that the relationship between education and income has been found to be approximately linear through the scattergram, Anne is ready to proceed with her statistical analysis as planned. Her next question pertains to the predictability of

the two variables. Can a rule be formulated for predicting income from education (or vice versa) so as to give the best prediction possible with a minimal amount of error?

5.3.1 Regression of Y on X

The prediction rules for nominal and ordinal data presented thus far are relatively simple ones that can be stated verbally. For example, the prediction rule in lambda states that the modal value of Y should be predicted within each category of X. The prediction for interval data is much more precise and is calculated from an equation with the following form:

$$Y' = a_{yx} + b_{yx}X \tag{5.1}$$

From this equation, a predicted value of the dependent variable Y is calculated for a value of the independent variable X. These predicted Y values are designated as Y' (read Y prime) to differentiate them from the *observed* Y values. Technically, the prediction rule is said to express the **regression of Y on X** and is therefore called the **regression equation.**

Let us explore how Equation 5.1 can be used. There are three terms in the equation from which Y' is calculated: a, b, and X. The letters a and b are constants and are subscripted to show that Y is being predicted from X. To calculate Y', a and b must be known. Assume for the moment that $a = 15$ and $b = 3$ for a set of hypothetical data. Now if X is 0, then, substituting for a, b, and X, a Y' value of 15 is obtained: $Y' = 15 + 3(0)$. In computing the Y' value for an X value of 1, we obtain a Y' of 18. These two pairs of values, ($X = 0$, $Y'= 15$) and ($X = 1$, $Y'= 18$), can be plotted as two dots on a scattergram. Drawing a straight line through these two points will produce a *regression line* similar to the one in Figure 5.1.

Thus Equation 5.1 is not only a prediction rule, but it is the mathematical expression of a regression line that pairs every value of X with a predicted Y' value. This line can be visualized as a series of dots, each representing a unique combination of X and Y' values. When the observed Y values coincide with the Y' values, the data points of (X, Y) fall on the regression line itself and exact predictions are made. When they differ, the data points are scattered around the line and prediction errors result. The farther the data points are scattered from the regression line, the larger the prediction errors.

Regression Coefficients

The constants a and b are called the **regression coefficients.** Note from the first pairs of (X, Y') values calculated previously that the coefficient a gives the Y' value when X is 0. On the scattergram, a is the **Y intercept,** the point at which the regression line crosses the Y axis. The value of b gives the change in Y' per unit change in X. In our illustration, when X is 0, Y' equals 15; from thereon, when X increases by 1, as from 0 to 1, Y' increases by 3, from 15 to 18. Hence b is an asymmetric measure of the *linear* covariation between X and Y. Graphically, b

represents the **slope** of the regression line. Because the slope is constant, the line is straight.

Criterion of Best Fit: Principle of Least Squares

For purposes of illustration, arbitrary values are assigned to the constants a and b in the preceding example. In practice, these values are mathematically estimated from a set of data based on the criterion of **best fit**. In terms of prediction, the best fit is obtained when errors made in prediction are minimal, that is, when the deviations of the observed Y from the predicted Y' are at a minimum. When such a regression equation is plotted, it results in a line that gives the closest fit to all the data points in a scatterplot.

Recall from Chapter 3 that the mean has a property called least squares in which the sum of the squared deviations about it is minimized. Now, if the regression coefficients a and b are estimated in such a way that the deviations about the regression line are minimized,

$$\sum (Y - Y')^2 = \sum (Y - a - bX)^2 = \text{a minimum}$$

then the regression line would also have the same least-squares property as the mean. This is, in fact, how the regression coefficients are estimated, yielding a regression equation that predicts the mean of the conditional distribution of Y for every value of X. The regression line represents the best fit for the data because, when the conditional means are predicted, the squared errors are at a minimum. Thus, in regression, the criterion of best fit can be expressed mathematically as the principle of least squares.

Since $(Y - Y')$ represents not just a deviation about the mean but an error in prediction as well, the term $\sum (Y - Y')^2$ is known as the **sum of squared errors** or **SSE** for short in regression problems. *The regression line itself is called the least-squares line because it minimizes the sum of squared errors.*

Using the least-squares criterion, the definitional formula of b is derived as follows:

$$b_{yx} = \frac{\text{covariance}(X, Y)}{\text{variance}(X)} = \frac{s_{xy}}{s_x^2} = \frac{\sum_{i=1}^{N} (X_i - \overline{X})(Y_i - \overline{Y})/N}{\sum_{i=1}^{N} (X_i - \overline{X})^2/N} \tag{5.2}$$

Note that the numerator of b is the total covariation of X and Y, standardized (divided) by the sample size. This term is called the **covariance,** or the *mean covariation of X and Y,* and is symbolized by s_{xy}. The covariance is a symmetric measure, but when it is divided by the variance of the independent variable, s_x^2, it becomes the asymmetric measure of covariation, b_{yx}. This b_{yx} determines the change in Y per unit change in X. That using the least-squares criterion yields a measure of covariation is not surprising. Because covariance is measured partially by the variations from the respective means of X and Y, it should retain the property of least squares.

Simplification of the definitional Formula 5.2 yields the following computational formula:

$$b_{yx} = \frac{N\left(\sum\limits_{i=1}^{N} X_i Y_i\right) - \left(\sum\limits_{i=1}^{N} X_i\right)\left(\sum\limits_{i=1}^{N} Y_i\right)}{N\left(\sum\limits_{i=1}^{N} X_i^2\right) - \left(\sum\limits_{i=1}^{N} X_i\right)^2} \tag{5.3}$$

The computational formula for a is

$$a_{yx} = \overline{Y} - b_{yx}\overline{X} \tag{5.4}$$

Calculation of the Regression Line

To calculate the regression equation for education and income, Table 5.3 is set up as follows: columns 1 through 3 are the original data from Table 5.2, columns 4 and 5 give X^2 and Y^2, respectively, and column 6 displays the products of each of the (X, Y) pairs. The remaining columns are used for illustration and calculation in a later section.

Substituting the sums of these values from the table into the formula for b, we have

$$b_{yx} = \frac{N\sum XY - \left(\sum X\right)\left(\sum Y\right)}{N\left(\sum X^2\right) - \left(\sum X\right)^2} = \frac{8(8,548) - (131)(461)}{8(2,313) - (131)^2} = \frac{7,993}{1,343} = 5.952$$

TABLE 5.3 Components for Computation of a, b, and r

Subject	X	Y	X^2	Y^2	XY	Y'	$Y - Y'$	$(Y - Y')^2$
Professor	23	56	529	3,136	1,288	97.057	−41.057	1,685.677
Doctor	24	125	576	15,625	3,000	103.009	21.991	483.604
CPA	18	100	324	10,000	1,800	67.297	32.703	1,069.486
Secretary	12	25	144	625	300	31.585	−6.585	43.362
Clerk	12	28	144	784	336	31.585	−3.585	12.852
Plumber	14	60	196	3,600	840	43.489	16.511	272.613
Gas attendant	12	22	144	484	264	31.585	−9.585	91.872
Salesperson	16	45	256	2,025	720	55.393	−10.393	108.014
Sum	131	461	2,313	36,279	8,548		0.000	3,767.480
Mean	16.375	57.625						

Then a is computed as follows:

$$a_{yx} = 57.625 - 5.952(16.375) = -39.839$$

The regression equation between education and income becomes

$$Y' = -39.839 + 5.952X$$

Plotting of the Regression Line

The predicted values of Y for every observed value of X are calculated from this equation and given under column 7 of Table 5.3. For example, for the first X value of 23, Y' equals

$$Y' = -39.839 + 5.952(23) = 97.057$$

As explained earlier, using any two pairs of (X, Y') values, such as that of the plumber (14, 43.489) and the doctor (24, 103.009), the regression line in Figure 5.3 can be drawn.

Just as a Y' value can be computed for an observed X, we can also obtain a Y' value for an X that is not in the original data base. For instance, Anne can predict the income level for a college dropout with 13 years of education to be

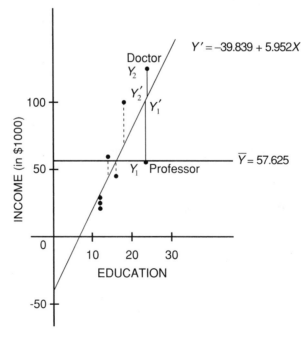

FIGURE 5.3   Regression of Income on Education

$Y' = -39.839 + 5.592(13) = 37.537$. However, if the prediction rule is applied to X values beyond the range of the observed data set, the researcher must be willing to assume that the relationship between X and Y remains linear beyond the range. This assumption is often questionable because extreme values do not necessarily behave in the same manner as the rest of the distribution.

The differences between the observed and the predicted Y values $(Y - Y')$ are computed and displayed under column 8 in Table 5.3. These differences are commonly known as **residuals**. They represent the portion of variation in Y left unexplained by the regression line. Recall that residuals are essentially errors in prediction. For instance, the residual for predicting income based on 24 years of education is 21.991 $(Y - Y' = 125 - 103.009)$, which means that the doctor in Anne's sample is making \$21,991 per year more than would be expected given 24 years of education. This specific prediction error is shown in Figure 5.3 as the *vertical* distance between the regression line and the data point of $(X = 24, Y = 125)$. The professor, on the other hand, is making \$41,057 $(56 - 97.057)$ less than the expected amount. These errors in prediction or deviations from the regression line sum to 0 in column 8 as shown in Table 5.3. In addition, the sum of the squared deviations, the SSE, in column 9 of the same table is at a minimum. That is, the equation just calculated yields the *smallest* SSE of all possible linear prediction rules, satisfying the least-squares criterion. Thus the regression line has the same characteristics as the mean and may be considered a running mean.

Interpretation of the Regression Coefficients a *and* b

The interpretation of a depends on whether the value $X = 0$ is a meaningful value to be found within the range of the linear relationship. If it is, the a of -39.839 means that with no education $(X = 0)$ the individual not only has no income, but must be subsidized in the amount of \$39,839 per year.

A slope of 5.952 means that, for every increase in 1 year of education, the individual would make \$5,952 *more* per year. Compare the professor who had 23 years of education to the doctor who had 24 years of education. Their predicted Y' values are 97.057 and 103.009, respectively, from Table 5.3. As X changes 1 unit from 23 to 24, Y' changes 5.952 units, from 97.057 to 103.009. This increase is *constant* regardless of whether X is changing from 23 to 24 or 13 to 14.

Had b been -5.952, an individual would make \$5,952 *less* with 1 *more* year of education. The regression line would extend from the upper right downward to the lower left of the quadrangle formed by the axes. Therefore the value of b gives the amount of change in the dependent variable per unit change in the independent variable, and its sign signifies whether the relationship between the variables is positive or negative. Because Y changes as a result of a change in X, the variation in Y values is said to be **explained** or **accounted for** by the X values.

The constant b also gives a rough indication of the strength of the association between X and Y, because it equals 0 when there is no association between the two. To clarify this point, we will reexamine the problem of regression, which is a problem of predicting Y from X, or vice versa. If Y is to be predicted more accurately with the knowledge of X, Y must vary with X systematically. From Section 5.1.2, we know that, when X and Y are not covarying, Y is just as likely to increase or decrease with an increment in X, and $\Sigma(X - \overline{X})(Y - \overline{Y}) = 0$. Since this term is the numerator of b (Formula 5.2), b will equal 0 when X and Y are not linearly associated, and the regression equation reduces to $Y' = a$, where $a = \overline{Y}$.

A regression line with a slope of 0 has no slope. This prediction line when graphed is a horizontal line running parallel to the X axis at $\overline{Y}$, as shown in Figure 5.3. Consequently, when there is no association, the best prediction of Y for *any* value of X is the mean of Y.

5.3.2 Regression of X on Y

Given two variables such as education and income, it is as equally logical to predict education from income as income from education. The regression equation with income as the independent or predictor variable is

$$X' = a_{xy} + b_{xy}Y \tag{5.5}$$

This formula expresses the regression of X on Y. Note that the a and b do not have the same values as when Y is regressed on X. X is subscripted first to indicate that it is now the predicted variable; it is followed by Y, the predictor variable. The formulas for b and a are

$$b_{xy} = \frac{N\left(\sum_{i=1}^{N} X_i Y_i\right) - \left(\sum_{i=1}^{N} X_i\right)\left(\sum_{i=1}^{N} Y_i\right)}{N\left(\sum_{i=1}^{N} Y_i^2\right) - \left(\sum_{i=1}^{N} Y_i\right)^2} \tag{5.6}$$

$$a_{xy} = \overline{X} - b_{xy}\overline{Y} \tag{5.7}$$

A comparison of the formulas for the b_{yx} and b_{xy} reveals that their numerators are the same. The difference lies in the denominator, because b_{xy} expresses the ratio of the covariance to the variance of Y.

Calculation and Interpretation

The elements for calculating Formulas 5.6 and 5.7 are found in Table 5.3:

$$b_{xy} = \frac{8(8,548) - (131)(461)}{8(36,279) - (461)^2} = .103$$

$$a_{xy} = 16.375 - .103(57.625) = 10.439$$

The regression equation is

$$X' = 10.439 + .103Y$$

5.3.3 Comparison of b_{yx} and b_{xy}

The value of *b* determines how steep the slope is: the larger the value, the steeper the slope. From Anne's calculations, the slope of the regression of *Y* on *X* is much steeper than the slope of the regression of *X* on *Y*. Since a flat line running parallel to the *X* or *Y* axis at $\overline{Y}$ or $\overline{X}$ indicates no association, the reader may be tempted to conclude that the steeper the slope is the higher the association. However, the larger value of b_{yx} does not indicate better prediction results because the regression coefficients are not standardized for comparison. The magnitude of the coefficient depends on the unit of measurement employed and the standard deviation of one variable relative to that of the other variable. In the current example, the *X* units are years of education, and the *Y* units are thousands of dollars. Suppose for the moment that *Y* is coded in $10,000 rather than $1,000. The value of b_{yx} would become one-tenth of its current value. Similarly, if education is measured in months rather than years, the value of b_{xy} would be greatly inflated. In neither instance has the relationship between the two variables changed. Thus other than the value of 0, which signifies no relationship between the variables, the value of *b* itself is not a good indicator of the strength of the relationship. For this reason, *b* is not used as a *measure of association*, although it does measure the change in the dependent variable relative to the change in the independent variable.

Exercises

4. Anne reasons that, if education is the key to economic success on an individual level, it may serve the same function on a societal level. However, she should not extend the argument without first exploring its validity using group data. Otherwise, Anne would commit the **fallacy of composition** by inferring that an individual property also characterizes the group as a whole. The opposing **ecological fallacy** is committed if the researcher assumes that whatever property characterizes a group also describes its individual members. To avoid the fallacy of composition, Anne takes a random sample of nations and examines the data on educational expenditure and GNP. Could Anne predict higher expenditure on education coded as a percentage of GNP based on the country's GNP, and vice versa?

   Educational expenditure:
   $$6.7 \quad 1.9 \quad 7.2 \quad 5.0 \quad 3.4 \quad 2.0 \quad 5.0 \quad 4.4 \quad 7.3 \quad 2.7$$

   GNP per capita:
   $$18.6 \quad 2.5 \quad 15.6 \quad 19.4 \quad 1.7 \quad 0.6 \quad 11.7 \quad 18.5 \quad 8.7 \quad 0.4$$

5. **a.** Show that the equation of the slope passing through (X_1, Y_1) (X_2, Y_2) can be alternatively written as
   $$b_{yx} = \frac{Y_2 - Y_1}{X_2 - X_1}$$

   b. Find a straight line that passes through (–3, 2) and (5, 6). What is the slope of this line?

6. Using the data from Exercise 1:
   a. Compute the regression coefficients.
   b. Draw the regression line on the scattergram created earlier.
   c. Calculate the expected salary for 10 and 20 years of experience.
   d. Interpret the value of the Y intercept.

7. Statistical data show that, for couples with 0, 1, 2, or 3 children, income (Y) is related to the number of children (X) as follows: $Y = 23,000 + 2,500X$. If a hitherto childless couple has twins, will this increase their income by $5,000?

8. Compute a regression equation for predicting Y from X, given the following data:

$$\overline{X} = 10, \quad \overline{Y} = 20, \quad N = 100, \quad s_{xy} = 20, \quad s_x = 10, \quad s_y = 10$$

9. Using the following data:

$$X:\ 1\ 2\ 3\ 4\ 5$$
$$Y:\ 2\ 3\ 5\ 8\ 9$$

   a. Plot a scattergram, compute the regression equation, and from this equation find the residuals.
   b. Use the following regression coefficients to compute the residuals of the preceding set of data:

$$a = -.4 \quad \text{and} \quad b = 2.3$$
$$a = 2 \quad \text{and} \quad b = 1.5$$

   c. Is the sum of the squared residuals really at a minimum when a and b are determined using Equation 5.1?

10. Suppose the following least-squares line relates the percentage voting for a Democratic candidate (Y) to the percentage having more than high school education (X) in a certain district: $Y' = 30.2 + .1X$.

   a. Is the Y intercept meaningful in this equation? Why or why not?
   b. Would the Y intercept be meaningful if X represents the percentage of registered voters in the district? Why or why not?
   c. Interpret the slope of this equation.

5.4 Correlation: Pearson's r

Research Question

Having confirmed that the more education an individual has, the more income she or he earns, Anne wonders if education and income could be subsumed under one dimension of stratification. To answer this question, Anne needs to determine the degree of association between education and income. The higher the association between the two is, the more grounds Anne has for maintaining that they are different indicators of the same dimension of stratification.

An Appropriate Statistic

From the preceding section, it has been shown that the regression coefficient b gives a rough indication of association. However, not being standardized for different measurement units, it does not have an upper limit. If measurement units for X and Y can somehow be standardized, the regression coefficient of these standardized scores could serve as a measure of association.

Chapter 3 discussed standardizing raw scores into z scores as a way to achieve comparability among observations from different distributions. Through standardization, the original scores are transformed into a z distribution with a mean of 0 and a standard deviation of 1. If the X and Y scores are transformed into their respective z scores and a regression equation is found for these scores, we would have a standardized regression coefficient for measuring association. This standardized regression coefficient, known as **Pearson's r,** also called the **product moment correlation coefficient,** is defined as follows for the regression of Y on X:

$$r_{yx} = \frac{\text{covariance } (Z_x, Z_y)}{\text{variance } (Z_x)} = \frac{\sum (Z_x - \overline{Z}_x)(Z_y - \overline{Z}_y) / N}{\sum (Z_x - \overline{Z}_x)^2 / N}$$

where Z_x and Z_y refer to the standard scores of variable X and variable Y, respectively.

Note that this formula is similar to that of b_{yx}; the only difference is that the X and Y scores are now replaced by the Z_x and Z_y scores. Since the standard deviation and therefore the variance of a z distribution equal 1, the formula simplifies to

$$r_{yx} = \frac{\sum (Z_x - \overline{Z}_x)(Z_y - \overline{Z}_y)}{N} = \text{covariance } (Z_x, Z_y)$$

The regression of Z_x on Z_y produces another standardized slope, r_{xy}, that has the same numerator as r_{yx} but divided by the variance of Z_y, the independent variable. As the variance of the standardized Y distribution also equals 1, the formula becomes

$$r_{xy} = \frac{\text{covariance } (Z_x, Z_y)}{\text{variance } (Z_y)} = \frac{\sum (Z_x - \overline{Z}_x)(Z_y - \overline{Z}_y)}{N} = \text{covariance } (Z_x, Z_y)$$

Thus $r_{yx} = r_{xy} = r$. Subscripts are unnecessary, because the standardized regression coefficient is a *symmetric* measure.

Substituting for Z_x and Z_y in the definitional formula, the following computational formula is obtained:

$$r = \frac{N\left(\sum_{i=1}^{N} X_i Y_i\right) - \left(\sum_{i=1}^{N} X_i\right)\left(\sum_{i=1}^{N} Y_i\right)}{\sqrt{\left[N\sum_{i=1}^{N} X_i^2 - \left(\sum_{i=1}^{N} X_i\right)^2\right]\left[N\sum_{i=1}^{N} Y_i^2 - \left(\sum_{i=1}^{N} Y_i\right)^2\right]}} \tag{5.8}$$

While the numerator of r is the same as those of the two b's, it is divided by the standard deviations of both X and Y. In fact, r is related to the two b's in the following manner:

$$r = \sqrt{b_{yx} b_{xy}}$$

See Box 5.1 for further exploration of the relation between r and the b's.

Pearson's r is a widely used measure of association in the social sciences because it has a number of desirable characteristics. Its value falls between -1 and $+1$, inclusive. When b equals 0, r also equals 0, the value 0 having the standard interpretation of no relationship between X and Y. A positive relationship is indicated by a positive sign, and a negative relationship, by a negative sign. The larger the absolute value of r is, the stronger the degree of linear association. When r equals $+1$ or -1, there is a perfect linear relationship between the two variables, and no prediction error results from using the regression equation.

Calculation

We present a number of formulas for the same statistics throughout this chapter in an effort to clarify the meanings of these statistics. However, to do the calcula-

---

BOX 5.1   Relation of the Correlation to the Regression Coefficient

Because $\overline{Z}_x = \overline{Z}_y = 0$, the definitional formula of r reduces to

$$r = \frac{\sum (Z_x Z_y)}{N}$$

Then substituting $(X - \overline{X})/s_x$ and $(Y - \overline{Y})/s_y$ for Z_x and Z_y, respectively, into the r formula, we have

$$r = \frac{\sum [(X - \overline{X}) / s_x][(Y - \overline{Y}) / s_y]}{N}$$

$$= \frac{\sum (X - \overline{X})(Y - \overline{Y}) / N}{s_x s_y} = \frac{s_{xy}}{s_x s_y}$$

Next multiply r by s_y/s_x:

$$r\left(\frac{s_y}{s_x}\right) = \frac{s_{xy}}{s_x^2}$$

Recalling that $b_{xy} = s_{xy}/s_x^2$, based on the definitional formula of b_{yx}, the relationship between the two b's and r can now be clearly seen as

$$r = b_{xy}\left(\frac{s_y}{s_x}\right) = b_{yx}\left(\frac{s_x}{s_y}\right)$$

As the equation indicates, the value of the correlation coefficient is determined by the slope and the ratio of the standard deviation of the independent to that of the dependent variable. This means that, even in samples where the slopes are the same, the r may take on different values. In addition, depending on the variation of the independent to the dependent variable, a steep slope may yield a small correlation, whereas a relatively flat slope may result in a high correlation.

tions, the reader should use the computational formulas whenever possible. Components for calculating Pearson's r from its computational Formula 5.8 were already given in Table 5.3. From this table, $\sum X = 131$, $\sum Y = 461$, $\sum X^2 = 2{,}313$, $\sum Y^2 = 36{,}279$, and $\sum XY = 8{,}548$. Inserting these values into the formula, an r value of .782 is obtained:

$$ r = \frac{N \sum XY - \left(\sum X \right)\left(\sum Y \right)}{\sqrt{\left[N \sum X^2 - \left(\sum X \right)^2 \right]\left[N \sum Y^2 - \left(\sum Y \right)^2 \right]}} $$

$$ = \frac{8(8{,}548) - (131)(461)}{\sqrt{[8(2{,}313) - (131)^2] \times [8(36{,}279) - (461)^2]}} = \frac{68{,}384 - 60{,}391}{\sqrt{(1{,}343) \times (77{,}711)}} = .782 $$

Interpretation of r as a Measure of Association

Being independent of the specific X and Y units of measurement, r has a standard upper limit of |1|, which means it can be compared across different samples. Because r is not a PRE measure, its value is best interpreted *relative* to its limits or in comparison to the r of another sample. Hays [1] suggests an interesting interpretation of r as "the rate of exchange" between X and Y, in which X, measured in its standard deviation units, is rated against the predicted value of Y, also measured in standard deviation units. According to this concept, the higher the exchange rate is, the stronger the association.

The correlation coefficient of .78 tells Anne that education and income are highly and positively related. Given this value, a strong case can be made that education and income are essentially different aspects of the same dimension of stratification. Anne realizes, however, that unless the value of r is closer to 1 there will always be arguments to the contrary.

5.4.1 Predicting Standardized Scores

Other than being a measure of association, r is also a measure of the standardized regression slope. In place of calculating the covariation between X and Y in original measurement units, r gives the change in standard deviation units of Y per standard deviation unit change in X. Since it is a *symmetric* measure, it also represents the change in X per standard deviation unit change in Y. Sometimes the term **beta weight,** symbolized by b^*, is used to represent the standardized slope in a regression problem, while the symbol r is reserved for problems of correlation. Since $r = b^*$ *in a bivariate regression,* the proliferation of labels for the same statistic can be rather confusing.

A regression equation for standardized scores can be written with r or b^* as the standardized slope. The regression coefficient a in this equation has the same formula as that of Formula 5.4, but with $\bar{Z}_x$, $\bar{Z}_y$ substituted for $\bar{X}$, $\bar{Y}$. With the substitution, the intercept reduces to zero because the means of the standardized distributions of X and Y equal 0:

$$a_{yx} = \overline{Z}_y - r\overline{Z}_x = 0$$

$$a_{xy} = \overline{Z}_x - r\overline{Z}_y = 0$$

The resulting equations for predicting a z score for the dependent variable from the independent variable are

$$Z'_y = rZ_x = b^* Z_x \quad \text{or} \quad Z'_x = rZ_y = b^* Z_y \tag{5.9}$$

To illustrate how r can be used in the prediction of a z score, let us take Anne's data on education and income. The r value of .782 indicates that for one standard unit increase in X there is a corresponding .782 standard unit increase in Y, and vice versa. To predict the standard score of income for the CPA who has a standard score of .35 [(18 – 16.375)/4.580] for education, we substitute Z_x in the regression equation to obtain a Z_y:

$$Z'_y = b^* Z_x = rZ_x = (.782)(.35) = .274$$

The prediction of z scores highlights an interesting phenomenon known as **regression toward the mean.** Given any Z_x, the best linear prediction of Z_y is a score that is closer toward the mean of 0 than Z_x is toward its own mean of 0. For instance, the predictor Z_x of the CPA is .35, while the predicted Z'_y is .27. Clearly, .27 is closer to 0 than is .35. The term *regression* is derived from this characteristic of the equation, which gives as a best guess a Y' score that is closer to $\overline{Y}$ than its predictor X is to $\overline{X}$ *in standard deviation units*. It is interesting to note that regression toward the mean applies to predicted scores only. Misunderstanding often results when the phenomenon is expected to occur in observed scores.

5.5 Coefficient of Determination: r²

Research Question

Although r is a good measure of association for interval scale variables, it is not a PRE measure. Its value can only be interpreted broadly, rather than precisely as a percentage. Therefore, Anne next asks the following questions:

1. How well can she predict income from education, and vice versa, using the regression equations that she has formulated?

2. Can a PRE measure be found based on how well she could predict using these regression equations?

Such a PRE measure would not only describe the association between income and education, it would also indicate precisely the amount of variation in income that can be accounted for by education, and vice versa.

Errors Made in Predicting Y from X

By squaring the product-moment correlation coefficient, Anne obtains the **coefficient of determination,** r^2, a PRE measure. To see why this is the case, let us first review the general form of a PRE measure:

$$PRE = \frac{E_1 - E_2}{E_1}$$

The E_1 represents errors made in the prediction of the dependent variable without knowledge of the independent variable, whereas the E_2 represents errors made with the knowledge of the independent variable. Since the regression line associates a predicted value of Y for every X, in evaluating how well the regression line predicts the value of Y, we can arrive at an estimate of E_2. The variance of the regression line summarizes dispersion about the line and can therefore be used as an index of E_2. It is defined as

$$s_{y.x}^2 = \frac{\sum (Y - Y')^2}{N}$$

Its numerator being the sum of the squared errors, SSE, $s_{y.x}^2$ is often called the *residual variance.* Be careful not to confuse this measure with s_{xy}, the measure of covariance. The residual variance determines the average squared error made per prediction and therefore the precision with which Y is predicted from X. If there is a perfect relationship between X and Y, there will be no errors in prediction, and $s_{y.x}^2$ equals 0. When the residual variance is not 0, X explains some but not all of the variance in Y. The residual variance therefore gives an index of unexplained variance in Y.

Base-line Errors

The E_1, errors made in base-line prediction, still remains to be established. From Chapter 3, we know that the mean is the best guess for an interval variable. Therefore, the mean of the univariate distribution of Y provides a prediction rule comparable to the regression equation, when Y is predicted without the knowledge of X. The index of squared errors, E_1, is obtained through the variance of Y, s_y^2, to which $s_{y.x}^2$ can be compared for improvement.

An Appropriate PRE Measure

In substituting $s_{y.x}^2$ and s_y^2 for E_2 and E_1 in the generalized PRE formula, we arrive at a PRE measure, which is the square of the correlation coefficient r. The definitional formula of r^2 is

$$r_{yx}^2 = \frac{s_y^2 - s_{y.x}^2}{s_y^2} = \frac{\sum_{i=1}^{N}(Y_i - \overline{Y})^2 - \sum_{i=1}^{N}(Y_i - Y_i')^2}{\sum_{i=1}^{N}(Y_i - \overline{Y})^2} \tag{5.10}$$

It is instructive to view the coefficient as an expression of the relationship between various sums of squares obtained when the N's are canceled in the formula. Then it becomes evident that the coefficient is the ratio of the explained sum of squares to the total sum of squares. The explained sum of squares represents the improvement in prediction using the regression line; the total sum of squares refers to the original squared errors in predicting Y from its mean. See Box 5.2 for a more detailed explanation.

The r_{yx}^2 is also a symmetric measure:

$$r_{yx}^2 = r_{xy}^2$$

In other words, the value of r^2 indicates the proportion of variance in Y explained by X, as well as the proportion of variance in X explained by Y. Since the coefficient is symmetric, subscripts are unnecessary and it is simply referred to as r^2.

Conversely, a ratio of the unexplained SS to the total SS, known as the **coefficient of alienation** and symbolized by K^2, can be calculated as

$$K^2 = \frac{s_{y.x}^2}{s_y^2} = 1 - r^2 \tag{5.11}$$

Because r^2 is symmetric, so is the coefficient of alienation. The latter measures the proportion of variance that is not explained by the linear regression equation. The relationship between the two coefficients can be expressed as

$$r^2 + K^2 = 1$$

Box 5.2   Partitioning the Variation

Consider the CPA in Anne's sample, whose income is $100,000. The prediction of yearly income is $57,625, which is the mean of Y when nothing is known about his or her years of education. The original error in prediction is $100,000 - 57,625 = 42,375$. The predicted income changes to $67,297 when his or her educational level is known. The resulting error equals $100,000 - 67,297 = 32,703$. The amount of variation in Y accounted for by the regres-

Continued

Box 5.2 *Continued*

sion equation is represented by the difference between the two errors: $42{,}375 - 32{,}703 = 9{,}672$. These three values of 42,375, 32,703, and 9,672 are interrelated as follows:

$$42{,}375 = 9{,}672 + 32{,}703$$

or

| total error | = | explained variation | + | unexplained or residual error |

Figure 5.4 graphically illustrates this partitioning of the initial error into its two component parts: (1) the distance between the observed score Y and the predicted score Y' on the regression line, which represents the error *unaccounted* for by the regression equation, and (2) the distance between the predicted score Y' and the mean of Y ($\overline{Y}$), which represents the variation *accounted* for by the regression line. Symbolically, the partitioning of the error made in guessing the mean of Y for a value of Y can be represented as

$$(Y - \overline{Y}) = (Y - Y') + (Y' - \overline{Y})$$

However, since the sum of all errors equals zero, the errors are squared to give estimates of E_1 and E_2. Squaring and summing over all cases, we have

$$\sum (Y - \overline{Y})^2 = \sum (Y - Y')^2$$
$$+ 2 \sum (Y - Y')(Y' - \overline{Y}) + \sum (Y' - \overline{Y})^2$$

The middle term of this equation equals zero since $\sum (Y - Y') = 0$. Therefore,

$$\sum (Y - \overline{Y})^2 = \sum (Y - Y')^2 + \sum (Y' - \overline{Y})^2$$

The resulting terms are called sums of squares. $\sum (Y - \overline{Y})^2$ is referred to as the **total sum of squares,** or **TSS** for short. TSS can be decomposed or partitioned into **explained sum of squares** or **SSR,** where R represents the regression, and **unexplained sum of squares** or **SSE.** SSE refers to the familiar $\sum (Y - Y')^2$, which is the sum of squared errors unaccounted for by the regression line; SSR refers to $\sum (Y' - \overline{Y})^2$,

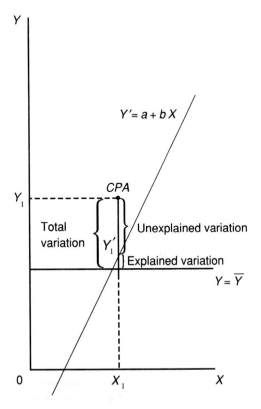

FIGURE 5.4 **Partitioning the Total Variation**

which is the sum of squared errors accounted for by the regression line. Therefore,

$$\text{TSS} = \text{SSR} + \text{SSE}$$

Substituting for $\sum (Y - \overline{Y})^2$ in the r^2 formula of 5.10, it can be seen that the coefficient of determination is the ratio of the explained to the total SS:

$$r^2 = \frac{\left[\sum (Y - Y')^2 + \sum (Y' - \overline{Y})^2 \right] - \sum (Y - Y')^2}{\sum (Y - \overline{Y})^2}$$

$$= \frac{\sum (Y' - \overline{Y})^2}{\sum (Y - \overline{Y})^2} = \frac{\text{SSR (explained SS)}}{\text{TSS (total SS)}}$$

Calculation and Interpretation

Although we have approached the explanation of r and r^2 from two seemingly different angles, mathematically, r^2 is simply the square of r. However, instead of proving this through complicated algebraic manipulation, we will demonstrate it in our computations. First, we will obtain the value of the coefficient of determination by squaring the value of r, as follows:

$$r = .782$$
$$r^2 = .782^2 = .611$$

Using the definitional formula of r^2 (Formula 5.10) and the components for calculation given in Table 5.4, we have

$$r^2 = \frac{\sum (Y - \overline{Y})^2 - \sum (Y - Y')^2}{\sum (Y - \overline{Y})^2} = \frac{9{,}713.90 - 3{,}767.48}{9{,}713.90} = .612$$

Except for a slight rounding error, the value computed with this formula is the same as the value obtained by squaring r.

The coefficient of alienation equals

$$K^2 = 1 - r^2$$
$$= .39$$

Accordingly, 61% of the variance of income is accounted for by education and 61% of the variance of education is accounted for by income. Thirty-nine percent of the original variance in the dependent variable remains unaccounted for by the independent variable. Anne concludes that there is indeed a strong relationship between education and income. However, she defers making a judgment on the dimensionality of the stratification system in the United States. Instead she prefers to continue her investigation into other criteria that stratify U.S. society, hoping that with more research a clearer picture will emerge.

TABLE 5.4 Components for Computation of r^2 with Formula 5.10

Subject	X	Y	$Y - \overline{Y}$	$(Y - \overline{Y})^2$	Y'	$Y - Y'$	$(Y - Y')^2$
Professor	23	56	−1.625	2.64	97.057	−41.057	1,685.677
Doctor	24	125	67.375	4,539.39	103.009	21.991	483.604
CPA	18	100	42.375	1,795.64	67.297	32.703	1,069.486
Secretary	12	25	−32.625	1,064.39	31.585	− 6.585	43.362
Clerk	12	28	−29.625	877.64	31.585	− 3.585	12.852
Plumber	14	60	2.375	5.64	43.489	16.511	272.613
Gas attendant	12	22	−35.625	1,269.14	31.585	− 9.585	91.872
Salesperson	16	45	−12.625	159.39	55.393	−10.393	108.014
Sum	131	461	0.000	9,713.90		0.000	3,767.480
Mean	16.375	57.625					

Characteristics and Features

The coefficient of determination r^2 has most of the desirable features of a measure of association. It attains an upper limit of 1 when there are no errors in prediction. On the other hand, when $b = 0$, the regression equation predicts the mean of Y for every X value, as discussed in Section 5.3.1. This means that the prediction rule with or without knowledge of X is the same, resulting in the same sum of squared errors. Thus $r^2 = 0$ when $b = 0$ where the slope of the regression line is horizontal.

The value of r^2 can be interpreted unambiguously as the proportional reduction in error variance. Being a squared value, however, it can only be positive and therefore does not distinguish between a positive and a negative relationship. Since r is computed before r^2, this information can be obtained directly from r. The point is that, for a more thorough interpretation of the data, both r and r^2 should be computed.

Summary

Linear Correlation and Regression

Linear equation between interval scale variables:

$$Y' = a_{yx} + b_{yx}X$$

where
$$b_{yx} = \frac{N\left(\sum_{i=1}^{N} X_i Y_i\right) - \left(\sum_{i=1}^{N} X_i\right)\left(\sum_{i=1}^{N} Y_i\right)}{N\left(\sum_{i=1}^{N} X_i^2\right) - \left(\sum_{i=1}^{N} X_i\right)^2}$$

$$a_{yx} = \overline{Y} - b_{yx}\overline{X}$$

Pearson's r, a correlation coefficient and standardized slope:

$$r = \frac{N\left(\sum_{i=1}^{N} X_i Y_i\right) - \left(\sum_{i=1}^{N} X_i\right)\left(\sum_{i=1}^{N} Y_i\right)}{\sqrt{\left[N\sum_{i=1}^{N} X_i^2 - \left(\sum_{i=1}^{N} X_i\right)^2\right]\left[N\sum_{i=1}^{N} Y_i^2 - \left(\sum_{i=1}^{N} Y_i\right)^2\right]}}$$

Beta weight, the standardized slope:

$$b^* = r \text{ for bivariate data}$$

Continued

Linear Correlation and Regression *Continued*

Relationships among r, b^*, and b:

$$r = b^* = b_{yx} \frac{s_x}{s_y} = b_{xy} \frac{s_y}{s_x} = \sqrt{b_{yx}b_{xy}}$$

Coefficient of determination, a PRE measure: r^2

Coefficient of alienation: $K^2 = 1 - r^2$

Pearson's r assumes interval measurement and linear relationship:

1. r ranges from 0 to ± 1
2. r is independent of measurement units
3. r^2 is a PRE measure which gives the proportion of variance in Y accounted for by X and vice versa

Exercises

11. In a study of the consequences of stratification, using the states as units of analysis, Anne operationally defines the independent and the dependent variables as follows:

Independent variables: Percent completing college (education)
Per capita income (income)

Dependent variables: Percent of public aid recipients (welfare)
Percent unemployed (unemployed)
Violent crime rate per 100,000 residents (crime)
Infant mortality rate per 1,000 live births (death)
Suicide rate per 100,000 residents (suicide)

State	Education	Income	Welfare	Unemployed	Crime	Death	Suicide
California	26.4	19,929	8.8	6.7	978	8.6	13.7
Florida	19.8	17,647	4.2	5.6	1,109	10.6	16.7
Georgia	18.2	16,053	6.6	5.5	736	12.6	13.4
Illinois	21.1	18,824	6.7	6.0	846	11.3	10.8
Indiana	13.8	15,779	3.6	4.7	406	11.0	11.6
Montana	21.6	14,078	4.6	5.9	116	8.7	18.0
New York	22.8	21,073	7.6	5.1	1,131	10.8	6.7
Texas	21.7	15,702	4.9	6.7	659	9.0	13.4

Using the data:

a. Compute a correlation coefficient using the computational formula.
b. Determine the value of the corresponding beta weight.
c. Discuss the relationship between the regression and correlation coefficients with reference to the data.
d. Compute coefficients of determination and alienation.
e. Compute and compare various beta weights and interpret the results.
f. Compute TSS, SSR, and SSE, and explain verbally what they mean.

12. Illustrate the *regression toward the mean* using data on income and the crime rate from Exercise 11.

13. Fill in the missing blanks for each set of the data:

	b_{yx}	s_x	s_y	s_{xy}	r
a.	0.5	30	70		
b.		100	50	300	
c.		50	50		−.7
d.		200	50		+.9

14. Anne's student assistant confessed that he had mislabeled the variable X as Y and the variable Y as X in computing r. Is it necessary for Anne to recalculate r?

15. Anne's student assistant measured husband's income in thousands of dollars and wife's income in dollars to compute r between the two. Should he have measured both in dollars? Verify the answer using the following data:

Husband	Wife	Husband	Wife
10	5,000	10	5
20	8,000	20	8

16. Anne's assistant computed $s_x = 15$, $s_y = 12$, and $s_{xy} = 200$. Is there a mistake in the computation?

17. Show that $\Sigma(Y - Y')(Y' - \overline{Y}) = 0$.

SPSS Session

Three separate procedure commands are used in the following program to (1) plot the scattergram and (2) compute the correlation coefficient, the regression equation, and related statistics on the education and income data in Table 5.2.

```
DATA LIST FREE / EDUC INCOME.

BEGIN DATA.

23   56   24   125   ...............16   45

END DATA.

PLOT PLOT=INCOME WITH EDUC.

CORRELATION VARIABLES=EDUC WITH INCOME /STATISTICS 1.

REGRESSION VARIABLES=EDUC INCOME /DESCRIPTIVES=MEAN STDDEV

    /DEPENDENT=INCOME /METHOD=ENTER.
```

The PLOT command draws a scatterplot and can also be used for plotting the points of the line graph discussed in Chapter 2. After the subcommand PLOT, specify the variable to be plotted on the *Y* axis first, then the keyword WITH, and finally the variable to be plotted on the *X* axis. The output from this command is not shown here.

The procedure, CORRELATION, computes the correlation coefficients between pairs of variables listed before and after the keyword WITH. Without the keyword WITH, a square matrix of correlations will be displayed. The STATISTICS 1 subcommand in SPSS/PC+ specifies the computation of the mean, standard deviation, and number of cases, excluding missing values. In SPSS, this specification differs slightly:

```
CORRELATION VARIABLES=EDUC WITH INCOME /STATISTICS DESCRIPTIVES.
```

The output from this command is shown in SPSS Figure 5.1. The values of the standard deviations are higher than those given in the text, since SPSS uses (N − 1) rather than N as the denominator. The correlation coefficient of .7824, however, is the same as the text's. The significance level displayed will be discussed in Chapter 13.

The command REGRESSION performs simple or multiple regression analysis, calculating regression coefficients and related statistics. For now, we will examine only the statistics that are discussed in this chapter, postponing the rest to Chapter 15. The command keyword REGRESSION is followed by the VARIABLES subcommand, after which both the independent and dependent variables in the equation are listed. There should be only one VARIABLES subcommand used with the command REGRESSION.

The subcommand DESCRIPTIVES displays descriptive statistics such as mean, MEAN, and standard deviation, STDDEV. *Although not shown here, the specification of CORR after this subcommand will produce a square matrix of correlation*

```
Variables    Cases            Mean           Std Dev

EDUC           8            16.3750          4.8972
INCOME         8            57.6250         37.2518

Correlations:  INCOME

  EDUC         .7824

N of cases:    8            1-tailed Signif:  * - .01   ** - .001

" . " is printed if a coefficient cannot be computed
```

SPSS FIGURE 5.1   Means, Standard Deviations, *N*, and Pearson's *r* of Education and Income

coefficients similar to the one in SPSS Figure 5.1. Note that this subcommand must appear before the subcommand DEPENDENT.

The subcommand DEPENDENT specifies the dependent variable(s) to be used in the analysis. More than one DEPENDENT subcommand may be specified, each of which must be followed by a METHOD subcommand. If more than one dependent variable are listed after a DEPENDENT subcommand, an equation is given for each dependent variable using the same independent variables. In the illustration, only the regression of INCOME on EDUC is requested, but not EDUC on INCOME.

The METHOD subcommand designates a method by which regression coefficients are calculated. The specification ENTER signifies that all the variables named in the VARIABLES subcommand, other than the dependent variable, are entered as independent variables into the equation simultaneously. This subcommand is necessary even if there is only one independent variable.

A portion of the output from the REGRESSION command is shown in SPSS Figure 5.2. The Pearson's *r* is given under "Multiple R," and the coefficient of determination, under "R Squared" in the output. The analysis of variance section provides information pertaining to our discussion on the partitioning of the total sum of squares. The two components of variation, the explained SS, labeled "Regression," and the unexplained SS, labeled "Residual," are presented in the column labeled "Sum of Squares." Summing these two components results in the total SS.

```
               Mean   Std Dev  Label

   EDUC       16.375    4.897
   INCOME     57.625   37.252

   N of Cases =      8

   Multiple R            .78240
   R Square              .61215
   Adjusted R Square     .54751
   Standard Error      25.05820

   Analysis of Variance
                        DF      Sum of Squares    Mean Square
   Regression            1         5946.39324     5946.39324
   Residual              6         3767.48176      627.91363

   F =      9.47008       Signif F =  .0217

   ----------------- Variables in the Equation -----------------

   Variable             B        SE B       Beta        T  Sig T

   EDUC             5.95160    1.93400     .78240     3.077  .0217
   (Constant)     -39.83246   32.88515               -1.211  .2713
```

SPSS FIGURE 5.2 Regressing Income on Education

Unstandardized regression coefficients are shown under the column labeled "B." Specifically, the Y intercept a is shown as the "B" of "Constant," while the slope b is given as the "B" for the independent variable EDUC. Except for rounding errors, these values are the same as those found in Section 5.3.1. Thus the regression equation of income on education is

$$Y' = -39.83 + 5.95X$$

The standardized slope is presented under "Beta," and the value of beta for EDUC is the same as the correlation coefficient "Multiple R" in a bivariate analysis, as pointed out in the text. The standardized regression equation always has a Y intercept of 0 and, therefore, its value is not shown in the output.

SPSS Exercises

For the following sets of variables in the City Database:

1. Educational expenditure (EDUC) and per capita income (INCOME)

2. Percent completing 16 years of schooling (COLLEGE) and per capita income (IN-COME)

3. Unemployment rate (UNEMPLOY) and crime rate (CRIME)

4. Population density (POPDENSE) and crime rate (CRIME)

5. Infant mortality rate (INFANT) and number of hospital beds per 1,000 population (NUMBEDS)

6. Infant mortality rate (INFANT) and percent of professional and technical workers (PROF)

   Perform the following tasks:

   a. Draw a scatterplot.
   b. Regress Y on X.
   c. Regress X on Y.
   d. Examine the default analysis of variance table to find SSR and SSE.
   e. Examine the standardized regression coefficients (BETA).
   f. Interpret the findings.
   g. Compare correlation coefficients obtained by REGRESSION and CORRELATION procedures.

5.6 Rank-order Correlation Coefficient for Ordinal Data: Spearman's Rho

Research Question

Following her investigation of education and income, Anne decides to examine the interrelations between two major dimensions of stratification specified by Weber: prestige and power. Prestige refers to the respect or esteem accorded an individual based on his or her personal qualities or accomplishments. Power is viewed as the ability of an incumbent of a status to affect the behavior of others. In the United States, an individual's occupation is an important source of both power and prestige.

The Data

The Research Institute has drawn a national sample to obtain verbal evaluations of the occupational prestige and power for an exhaustive list of occupations. Respondents are asked to rate these occupations on a scale of 1 to 100. Based on these responses, two scores are calculated and assigned to each occupation, one for power and the other for prestige. Anne then samples 12 occupations from the exhaustive list of occupations. Their scores on power and prestige are shown in Table 5.5.

An Appropriate Statistic

Anne has two options here. Strictly speaking, these scores are ordinal, not interval, in nature. However, when an ordinal variable has a large range of values, these values tend to measure approximately equal amounts. Consequently, Anne can make an assumption that the variables are interval and proceed to apply statistical techniques that are appropriate for interval data. In doing so, she would have more powerful and more numerous techniques at her disposal. Besides, most interval techniques can tolerate some departure from the assumption of interval measurement.

The reader should note that making such an assumption is a rather common occurrence in the social sciences. Frequently, researchers who work with ordinal data assume that they are interval so as to be able to use the more powerful interval techniques. In Anne's case, however, she has a statistic that is comparable to Pearson's r, but that does not require the assumption of interval measurement. This measure, known as **Spearman's rho** or r_s, is obtained from a direct application of the correlation coefficient r to ranks; therefore, it retains most of the

TABLE 5.5 Prestige and Power of Twelve Occupations

Occupation	Prestige	Power
Physician	93	88
Bartender	44	32
Truck driver	54	49
State governor	93	93
Professor	90	70
Farmer	62	79
Air pilot	84	65
Plumber	63	54
Taxi driver	49	30
Shoe shiner	33	23
Banker	88	90
Minister	87	68

characteristics of the latter measure. The r_s statistic is especially appropriate for ordinal data with no or few ties, like those shown in Table 5.5.

Like the correlation coefficient, r_s is symmetric and varies from -1 to $+1$ inclusive. The concept of a linear relationship is inapplicable for ordinal data, but the r_s does measure the general tendency of one variable to vary in the same or opposite direction as the other. The value of Spearman's r_s does not have a PRE interpretation, but when the statistic is squared, a PRE measure is obtained. This r_s^2 determines the extent of reduction in error variance when predicting the *ranks* of Y given the *ranks* of X. The base-line prediction in this case involves predicting the *mean rank* of the dependent variable. The prediction rule in the evaluation of error reduction does not have to be calculated as in Pearson's r. It could be verbally stated as follows:

> *Positive relation:* the prediction of the same rank for the dependent variable as the independent variable.

> *Negative relation:* the prediction of the opposite ranks for the two variables, that is, predicting the highest rank in Y to the lowest rank in X, the second highest to the second lowest, and so on.

Finally, a sample size of 10 or more is required to avoid a large sampling fluctuation of the r_s values.

To compute r_s, X and Y must be ranked or their scores must be converted to ranks in such a manner that there are as many ranks as the number of observations in the sample. The formula for Pearson's r can then be applied directly to these ranks. However, the formula and therefore the calculation can be tremendously simplified because the mean of N ranks without ties equals

$$\overline{R} = \frac{N+1}{2}$$

where R refers to the ranks, $\overline{R}$, the mean of ranks, and N, the number of cases. The sum of squared deviations is given as

$$\sum (R - \overline{R})^2 = \frac{N(N^2 - 1)}{12}$$

Substituting these expressions into the r formula, the **rank-order correlation coefficient** is derived as

$$r_s = 1 - \frac{6 \sum_{i=1}^{N} D_i^2}{N(N^2 - 1)} \tag{5.12}$$

where D_i refers to difference between the X and Y ranks.

Calculation and Interpretation

To calculate r_s for Table 5.5, ranks from 1 to 12 are assigned first to the X and then to the Y scores. Following the customary practice in this text, a rank of 1 is assigned to the lowest score, a rank of 2 to the second lowest, and so on in increments of 1. (Actually, the same result is obtained if a reverse ranking procedure is adopted, that is, the highest score is given a rank of 1, provided the ranking is consistent.) An inspection of Table 5.5 shows that there are two tied scores in X and none in Y. State governors and physicians are rated as having the same amount of prestige. Since the sum of the assigned ranks must equal the sum of the ranks from 1 to 12, the same rank cannot be assigned to both occupations. Instead the mean rank is given to both. The mean rank is found by (1) adding the ranks that would have been assigned to the observations had they not been tied and then (2) dividing the sum by the number of tied observations. State governors and physicians would have occupied ranks 11 and 12. Therefore, the mean of 11.5 [(11 + 12)/2] is assigned to each occupation. The same procedure of using the mean rank applies whether there are two or more tied cases. Ties tend to inflate the value of the coefficient, but it takes a great number of ties to have a significant impact. The X scores are arranged in order, and the assigned X and Y ranks are shown under columns 4 and 5 of Table 5.6.

The difference D between the pair of ranks for each occupation is computed next and given in column 6 of the same table. The sum of the D values yields the expected 0. The D values are then squared in column 7. The sum of these squared values would equal zero if there were a perfect positive relationship between X and Y. A perfect negative relationship would yield a maximum sum of squared differences in such a way that the term $6\Sigma (D^2)/N(N^2 - 1)$ equals 2. If there is no association, this term would be 1.

TABLE 5.6 Components for Computation of the Rank-order Correlation

Occupation	Prestige X	Power Y	Ranks Prestige	Ranks Power	D	D^2
Physician	93	88	11.5	10	1.5	2.25
State governor	93	93	11.5	12	−0.5	0.25
Professor	90	70	10	8	2	4
Banker	88	90	9	11	−2	4
Minister	87	68	8	7	1	1
Air pilot	84	65	7	6	1	1
Plumber	63	54	6	5	1	1
Farmer	62	79	5	9	−4	16
Truck driver	54	49	4	4	0	0
Taxi driver	49	30	3	2	1	1
Bartender	44	32	2	3	−1	1
Shoe shiner	33	23	1	1	0	0
				Total	0	31.50

Substituting values for N and D^2 in the formula, the rank-order correlation coefficient is calculated as

$$r_s = 1 - \frac{6\sum D^2}{N(N^2 - 1)} = 1 - \frac{(6)(31.5)}{12(144 - 1)} = .889$$

Spearman's r_s is interpreted in much the same way as r. An r_s of .89 indicates that the prestige and power dimensions of occupations are highly and positively correlated. Squaring the statistic, an r_s^2 of .79 is obtained. Therefore, the independent variable explains 79% of the variance in the ranks of the dependent variable. Again Anne is impressed with the high correlation between these two supposedly independent dimensions of stratification. She is moving closer to the view that stratification may be more unidimensional than multidimensional in this country.

Summary

Rank-order Correlation

Spearman's rho:

$$r_s = 1 - \frac{6\sum_{i=1}^{N} D_i^2}{N(N^2 - 1)}$$

Spearman's rho assumes ordinal level measurement and few tied ranks.

1. r_s ranges from 0 to ±1.
2. The sample size should be 10 or more.

Exercises

18. A random sample of 11 subjects that Anne has selected shows subjective class identification, conspicuous consumption patterns, and income as follows. Conspicuous consumption is rated on a 10-point scale based on the number and type of cars owned and the amount of money spent for traveling; social class is measured through 7 ranks:

    1: lower lower class   2: lower class
    3: lower middle class   4: middle class
    5: upper middle class   6: lower upper class
    7: upper class

Subject	Subjective Class	Conspicuous Consumption	Income in Thousands
1	4	9	35
2	5	8	48
3	6	7	65
4	3	8	25
5	4	5	55
6	7	9	130
7	5	4	48
8	1	6	18
9	2	6	30
10	3	3	38
11	4	4	40

  a. Compute r_s between (1) subjective class and conspicuous consumption, (2) income and subjective class, and (3) income and conspicuous consumption.

  b. What is the conclusion regarding the relations among objective class (income), subjective class, and symbolic class (conspicuous consumption)?

19. Rank order the data in Table 5.2 and compute r_s. Compare it with the Pearson's r already computed.

20. Anne speculates that the literacy rate, especially of females, is a crucial index of the educational level of a country. She therefore takes a random sample of 12 nations and ranks them on female literacy and GNP per capita. Is there a relation between these two factors?

GNP per capita rank:

     5.0 1.5 11.0 3.0 4.0 9.0 6.0 1.5 12.0 8.0 7.0 10.0

Female literacy rank:

     4.0 1.0 8.5 3.0 6.0 8.5 7.0 2.0 10.5 12.0 5.0 10.5

SPSS Session

Spearman's r_s can be obtained in two ways. It can be specified under the STATISTICS subcommand of the CROSSTABS, discussed in Chapter 4. The following is an alternative to using the CROSSTABS command:

```
DATA LIST FREE/PREST POWER.

BEGIN DATA.

93   88    93 ............33 23

END DATA.

RANK VARIABLES=PREST POWER.

CORRELATION VARIABLES=RPREST RPOWER.
```

```
From       New
variable   variable   Label
--------   --------   -----

PREST      RPREST     RANK of PREST
POWER      RPOWER     RANK of POWER

Correlations:   RPREST      RPOWER

   RPREST      1.0000       .8897**
   RPOWER       .8897**    1.0000

N of cases:    12          1-tailed Signif:  * - .01  ** - .001

 " . " is printed if a coefficient cannot be computed
```

SPSS FIGURE 5.3   Rank-order Correlation of Prestige and Power

The RANK procedure is used to assign ranks to the scores of the two ordinal variables PREST and POWER. It accomplishes this by creating a new variable consisting of ranks for each variable specified after the VARIABLES subcommand. These new variables are then stored under names that begin with "R" followed by the first seven characters of the original variable names. Thus RPREST and RPOWER are created after the execution of the RANK command and contain ranks based on ascending values of the original variables. If ranks are entered directly instead of the values, the RANK command is unnecessary. The CORRELATION command computes Pearson's r on the ranks of the two newly created ordinal variables of RPREST and RPOWER. The result is the Spearman's rank-order correlation coefficient. See SPSS Figure 5.3.

SPSS Exercises

For the following sets of variables in the GSS database, compute r_s and interpret the results.

7. Education (EDUC) and income (RINCOM91)

8. Income (RINCOM91) and subjective class (CLASS)

9. Income (RINCOM91) and occupational prestige (PRESTG80)

10. Education (EDUC) and political views (POLVIEWS)

5.7 Correlation Ratio: η^2

Research Question
In this last section, Anne turns her attention to the ascriptive bases for stratification. Up to this point, she has looked into criteria that measure, more or less, an

individual's achievement. When stratification is based on achievement, the individual's status within the stratification system is not immutable but can be changed, presumably, through his or her efforts. However, society can also stratify individuals according to ascriptive characteristics, that is, characteristics over which an individual has no control. From her observation, Anne gathers that there are two major ascriptive dimensions in U.S. society: race and gender. She further suspects that there is a high correlation between the achieved and ascriptive dimensions of stratification such that the achievement of a member of this society is partially dependent on factors that are beyond the individual's control. To explore whether she has any basis for her hunch, Anne examines the correlation between sex and income.

The Data
Anne takes a random sample of employees in an electronics company in her community. They are all college graduates in their 40's. The salaries (in $1,000) of males and females are displayed next. Is income associated with sex?

Male	65	63	50	45	42	38	46	42	35	22	59	45	38	35
Female	48	43	38	28	25	28	25	22	15	18

An Appropriate Statistic
What Anne needs is a measure of association that determines the strength of association between a *qualitative independent variable* and an *interval dependent variable*. The **correlation ratio,** or **eta squared** (η^2) is such a statistic. Eta squared is a PRE measure based on the accuracy with which the values of the dependent variable can be predicted on the basis of the categories of the independent variable. The logic of η^2 is similar to that of r^2. Whereas r^2 is used to measure linear relationships only, η^2 does not assume linearity. Therefore, not only can η^2 be used as a measure of association between an interval dependent variable and a nominal or ordinal independent variable. It can also be used as a measure of nonlinear relation between two interval variables.

The base-line prediction rule involves guessing the mean of the interval dependent variable for each of its values. The errors associated with the base-line prediction rule, E_1, are determined by the sum of squared deviations from the mean, as in Pearson's r. Thus the term TSS is also applicable here:

$$E_1 = \sum_{i=1}^{N} (Y_i - \overline{Y})^2 = \text{TSS}$$

To determine E_2, the values of the dependent variable are predicted next, with knowledge of the independent variable. When information is given on X, the strategy is to predict the mean of the *conditional distribution* of Y (income) for that category of X (sex). Accordingly, among males the best guess of income is their mean income. The squared errors made in predicting male income are $\sum_{j=1}^{N_1}(Y_j - \overline{Y}_m)^2$, where $\overline{Y}_m$ refers to the mean income of the conditional

distribution of males. Similarly, the mean income of the women is the best prediction for female income. The squared errors made in predicting female income

are $\sum_{j=1}^{N_2}(Y_j - \overline{Y}_f)^2$, where $\overline{Y}_f$ refers to the mean income of women. The total

squared errors, SSE, resulting from the prediction of Y given X, is the sum of these separately computed squared errors. Thus E_2 is computed as

$$E_2 = \sum_{j=1}^{N_1}(Y_j - \overline{Y}_m)^2 + \sum_{j=1}^{N_2}(Y_j - \overline{Y}_f)^2 = SSE$$

The proportional reduction in prediction error is defined as

$$\eta^2 = \frac{E_1 - E_2}{E_1} = \frac{TSS - SSE}{TSS} = \frac{\text{explained variance}}{\text{total variance}}$$

Note the similarity of this definitional formula to that of r^2. Like r^2, the correlation ratio is based on (1) the prediction of the conditional means of Y for every category of X and (2) the partitioning of the total sum of squares into explained and unexplained sums of squares. From the definitional formula, a computational formula is derived:

$$h^2 = \frac{\sum_{j=1}^{k} N_j(\overline{Y}_j - \overline{Y})^2}{\sum_{i=1}^{N}(Y_i - \overline{Y})^2} = \frac{\sum_{j=1}^{k} N_j(\overline{Y}_j - \overline{Y})^2}{\sum_{i=1}^{N} Y_i^2 - \left(\sum_{i=1}^{N} Y_i\right)^2 /N} \qquad (5.13)$$

where k = number of categories of the independent variable
N_j = number of cases in the jth category of the independent variable
N = number of cases in the sample
$\overline{Y}_j$ = mean of the dependent variable in the jth category
$\overline{Y}$ = mean of the dependent variable in the whole sample

Thus η^2 refers to the proportion of variance in Y that is explained by taking the values of X into account. It varies between 0 and +1. Since η^2 can be applied to measure the association between a nominal and an interval variable, the notion of the type of relationship is inapplicable, and the fact that it assumes only positive values is appropriate.

Calculation and Interpretation

The number of cases for the whole sample and for the subgroups, the mean of the whole sample and of the subgroups, $\sum Y$, and $\sum Y^2$ are all shown in Table 5.7. Inserting these numbers into the computational formula yields

$$
\eta^2 = \frac{\sum N_j (\overline{Y}_j - \overline{Y})^2}{\sum Y_i^2 - \left(\sum Y_i\right)^2 / N}
$$

$$
= \frac{14(44.64 - 37.48)^2 + 11(28.36 - 37.48)^2}{39{,}623 - (937)^2 / 25} = \frac{1{,}632.64}{4{,}504.24} = .362
$$

An eta squared of .36 indicates that sex accounts for 36% of the variance in income between males and females in Anne's sample. Although the correlation is not as high as the correlations of income and education, gender still has a substantial impact on earnings. Anne realizes that in the United States women still have not achieved income parity with men. The question is how highly correlated gender is with education and whether some gender effect is channeled through education. The last point could only be clarified through a multivariate analysis.

TABLE 5.7 Components for Computation of Eta Squared

	Male	Y^2	Female	Y^2
	65	4,225	48	2,304
	63	3,969	43	1,849
	50	2,500	38	1,444
	45	2,025	28	784
	42	1,764	25	625
	38	1,444	28	784
	46	2,116	25	625
	42	1,764	22	484
	35	1,225	22	484
	22	484	15	225
	59	3,481	18	324
	45	2,025		
	38	1,444		
	35	1,225		
Sum	625	29,691	312	9,932
N_j	14		11	
$\overline{Y}_j$	44.64		28.36	

$N = 25$ $\sum Y = 625 + 312 = 937$
$\overline{Y} = 37.48$ $\sum Y^2 = 29{,}691 + 9{,}932 = 39{,}623$

Summary

Nonlinear Correlation

Correlation ratio:

$$\eta^2 = \frac{\sum_{j=1}^{k} N_j (\overline{Y}_j - \overline{Y})^2}{\sum_{i=1}^{N} (Y_i - \overline{Y})^2} = \frac{\sum_{j=1}^{k} N_j (\overline{Y}_j - \overline{Y})^2}{\sum_{i=1}^{N} Y_i^2 - \left(\sum_{i=1}^{N} Y_i\right)^2 / N}$$

Eta squared assumes that the dependent variable is interval; the independent variable can be nominal, ordinal, or interval.

Exercises

---

21. Anne suspects that age and income are curvilinearly related in that income reaches a ceiling just before one's retirement age and then declines afterward. She divides her sample into the young (20 to 39), the middle-aged (40 to 64), and the old (65+) and then obtains information on their income. What is the strength of association between age and income?

Subject	Age	Income ($)
1	Young	28,000
2	Middle-aged	40,000
3	Young	35,000
4	Old	45,000
5	Middle-aged	42,000
6	Old	56,000
7	Young	53,000
8	Old	38,000
9	Middle-aged	86,000

22. Under what conditions would r_{yx} be approximately 0 and the correlation ratio 1.00? Create fictitious data to illustrate the situation.

23. Under what conditions would the correlation ratio equal r^2?

SPSS Session

To obtain eta for an interval dependent variable whose values are grouped into intervals, use the CROSSTABS procedure and specify ETA after the STATISTICS subcommand. For an ungrouped dependent variable, use the MEANS procedure as shown in the following:

```
DATA LIST FREE/SEX INCOME.

BEGIN DATA.

1    65    2    48

1    63    2    43

...

END DATA.

MEANS TABLES=INCOME BY SEX /STATISTICS=1.
```

MEANS displays means, standard deviations, and group counts of a dependent variable for groups defined by an independent variable or independent variables. Under the TABLES subcommand, the dependent variable is named first, then the keyword BY, and then the independent variable. In SPSS/PC+, the specification of 1 after the STATISTICS subcommand provides an analysis of variance (see Chapter 12) as well as eta and eta squared. In place of 1, SPSS uses the keyword ANOVA to do the same job:

```
MEANS TABLES=INCOME BY SEX /STATISTICS=ANOVA.
```

SPSS Exercises

Using the City Database, find out if professional and technical workers tend to congregate in certain regions by computing eta squared as follows:

11. Small-sample data:
    a. Draw a random sample of size 10.
    b. Compute the eta squared between region (STATE) and the percentage of professional technical workers (PROF), using CROSSTABS with the STATISTIC subcommand.

12. Large-sample data:
    a. Draw a random sample of size 100.
    b. Compute the eta squared between region and the percentage of professional workers, using MEANS with the STATISTIC subcommand.

General Conceptual Questions

1. Explain the various uses of a scattergram in regression analysis.

2. When $r = 0.0$ between X and Y, is there no relationship between X and Y?

3. Explain what Pearson's r measures with reference to standardized scores.

4. Differentiate between a regression and a correlation problem.

5. What are some of the conditions under which r reduces to 0?

6. What is the value of r if all the sample scores fall on the same straight line with a negative slope?

7. What is being measured by the coefficient of determination?

8. What distinguishes the least-squares line from any other line that might be used to describe the data?

9. Explain how the concept of conditional means can be applied to Pearson's r and eta squared.

10. Compare the characteristics of r^2 and η^2.

11. Is Spearman's r_s^2 a PRE measure? Why or why not?

12. Does the order of the columns or rows affect the magnitude of eta squared?

13. Is the standardized regression coefficient always preferable to the unstandardized when comparing the strength of association among different sets of variables or among different samples?

References

1. Hays, W. L. (1973). *Statistics for the Social Sciences*, 2nd ed. New York: Holt, Rinehart and Winston.

$$Part \; II$$

Inferential Statistics

$$C\ h\ a\ p\ t\ e\ r\ \ \mathit{6}$$

Probability

New Statistical Topics

Counting outcomes in a sample space
Assigning probabilities
Conditional probability
Joint events and sequences

Permutations and combinations
Probability for mutually
  exclusive and nonmutually
  exclusive events

6.1 Overview

A researcher's ultimate goal is to go beyond his or her sample data to make inferences about the population from which the sample is drawn. In inferring, the researcher is no longer stating facts about the sample, but is making generalizations about the population. An element of uncertainty is involved, because these inferences about the population are based on incomplete evidence provided by the sample. Suppose Anne were to conclude on the basis of a sample of 250 U.S. residents that at least 90% of all U.S. residents have committed a deviant act. Her conclusion is an inference, which may or may not be correct because her information originates from some but not all U.S. residents. With the conclusion being uncertain, the investigator must have a method to estimate the likelihood of making incorrect inferences. The method is supplied by probability theory.

Probability theory originates in games of chance, whose outcomes have varying degrees of uncertainty. Its principles provide ways of assessing the degree of risk an individual takes in betting on a particular outcome. The degree of risk depends on the **probability** or the likelihood of the occurrence of the event. The probability, in turn, assumes a value that lies between 0 and 1 inclusive, representing the various degrees of uncertainty or certainty of occurrence.

The researcher who makes an inference about the population is in a situation similar to the bettor's. Both must make a decision, that is, take a chance on an outcome that is by no means certain. In providing a method for coping with uncertainty for the bettor, probability theory also supplies the theoretical and logical foundation for making statistical inferences. **Inferential statistics,** then, may be viewed as a body of formalized procedures for making inferences about populations based on samples drawn from those populations. To understand inferential statistics, the reader must have a working knowledge of elementary probability theory. For this reason, we will devote this chapter to an exploration of probability theory, its meaning and calculation, and its utility before proceeding to inferential statistics.

6.1.1 Social Applications

Anne finds that thinking and conceptualizing in probabilistic terms are especially fruitful in the area of deviance. Deviance refers partly to behaviors that violate social norms. It is often contrasted with conformity, behaviors that are in accordance with social expectations. If conformity produces the accepted or approved behavioral patterns that are observed in a society, deviance accounts for the deviations from these patterns. The mere fact that individuals behave in ways that are statistically rare, however, does not necessarily mean that they are deviants. Deviant behavior elicits from the group social sanctions and efforts to rehabilitate the individual.

Social scientists have approached the study of deviance with an attempt to enumerate the varieties of behaviors or traits that are considered deviant. Deviance has also been treated as a process. As such, it is best described as the final outcome of a series of events, each of which has a certain probability of occurrence. The final outcome is never completely determined at the outset; instead, at any one point, there may be alternative routes and options that could bring about very different results.

Deviant behaviors can further be classified according to whether they are socially or legally defined as deviant. That deviance is not an inherent property of any act can be clearly seen in the selective criminalization of particular acts. Deviant behaviors that are primarily associated with the lower classes have much higher probabilities of being defined as criminal. As official statistics show, law enforcement is also selective. The probability of being caught for a criminal act is much lower for the upper than lower classes. Ultimately, then, deviance is in the eye of the beholder, a societal creation that is best explained through group structures and processes.

6.1.2 Statistical Topics

Consider the experiment in which Anne assigns a term paper for a class. An exhaustive list of student behaviors in response to the assignment includes (1) the student turns in the paper early, (2) the student turns in the paper on time, (3) the student turns in the paper late with an excuse, (4) the student turns in the paper late without an excuse, (5) the student does not turn in the paper at all but has an excuse, and (6) the student does not turn in the paper and has no excuse. Each behavior listed is known as an **elementary event,** an **outcome** of an experiment or a research situation that can occur in one and only one way and is mutually exclusive of other outcomes. Thus a particular student can respond with one and only one of these behaviors. The list constitutes a **sample space (S)**, the set of all possible outcomes or elementary events associated with the experiment. The sample space of Anne's experiment is symbolically designated as follows:

$$S = \{1, 2, 3, 4, 5, 6\}$$

where the values of 1 through 6 refer to student behaviors as listed.

A **compound event**, or **event** for short, refers to a subset of the sample space consisting of any number of mutually exclusive elementary events. For example, if Anne defines conforming behavior under the situation as either turning in the paper early or on time, then conformity is an event. It consists of two mutually exclusive elementary events, which may be designated as follows: $E = \{1, 2\}$. Depending on Anne's definition, deviance may also be treated as an event consisting of elementary events 4, turning in the paper late, and 6, not turning in the paper at all, both without an excuse.

Another illustration of a sample space is one that is associated with the throw of a die. That a 1 appears uppermost is an *elementary event*, since it can occur in only one way. That an even value appears is not an elementary event, but an *event*, because there are three even values: $E = \{2, 4, 6\}$. Note, however, that an elementary event may be an outcome with more than one component. For example, in the experiment of throwing a die *and* tossing a coin, the outcome of a 3 and a head in combination may be considered an elementary event. Here the sample space consists of 12 elementary events, each with two components: (1) a number from the die and (2) a head or tail from the coin, such that $S = \{1H, 2H, \ldots, 6H, 1T, 2T, \ldots, 6T\}$. *Thus what is considered an elementary event or an event may depend on the experiment or research situation and the experimenter's definition.*

There are two different types of sample spaces: discrete and continuous. The sample spaces described previously contain a finite or *countably* infinite number of outcomes and are called **discrete sample spaces.** A **continuous sample space,** on the other hand, consists of an *uncountably* infinite number of elementary events. The possible height and weight of a population are examples of continuous sample spaces. The distinction between these two types of sample spaces parallels the differentiation made in Chapter 1 between a discrete and continuous variable. In this chapter, the discussion focuses primarily on the properties of a discrete sample space.

Once the elementary events or events of a sample space are defined, the question arises as to what their probabilities are. For example, if Anne wonders how likely a (any) student is to conform, she is attempting to determine the **probability** of an event. The calculation of probabilities for events in discrete sample spaces consists of the following steps, each of which will be elaborated on in succeeding sections:

1. Enumerating and counting the elementary events in the sample space
2. Assigning probabilities to elementary events and events
3. Computing probabilities for various types of events based on the elementary events and other events

6.2 Assigning Probabilities

The probability of an elementary event or event is represented by a value that indicates the likelihood of its occurrence. It is important to emphasize that this value is *assigned* by the researcher based primarily on his or her understanding of the nature and the physical properties of the event. The assignment is facilitated by three axioms that, when taken together, provide a framework to establish the limits of a probability value. Although not used for specific assignments, these three rules do ensure that specific assignments are internally consistent. We will take a look at these axioms first before discussing how specific probability values are assigned.

6.2.1 Establishing a Framework for the Specific Assignment of Probability

Since all assigned probability values must satisfy these axioms, they are assumed to be true of all probabilities and to describe the properties of a probability value. These axioms are as follows:

1. For any event (elementary or compound) A, its probability is a nonnegative value equal to or greater than 0:

$$p(A) \geq 0$$

2. The probability of the sample space, S, is 1:

$$p(S) = 1$$

Since the sample space contains all possible outcomes, its probability of occurrence is certain and equals 1. Taken together, axioms 1 and 2 define the limits of a probability measure. Thus, for any event A, specific probability values may be assigned such that $0 \leq p(A) \leq 1$. When occurrence is certain, $p(A) = 1$; when nonoccurrence is certain, $p(A) = 0$. As the values move away from these two limits, they designate an increasing degree of uncertainty until they converge at .5, which epitomizes uncertainty.

3. When the occurrence of an elementary event or event precludes the occurrence of another, these elementary events or events are mutually exclusive. If A and B are mutually exclusive, such as turning in the paper on time or late, then $p(A$ or $B)$ (read "the probability of A or B") equals the sum of their two separate probabilities. This additive characteristic is then the third basic property of probability:

$$p(A \text{ or } B) = p(A) + p(B) \text{ when } A \text{ and } B \text{ are mutually exclusive}$$

To recapitulate, given any event A:

1. $p(A) \geq 0$.
2. $p(S) = 1$.
3. $p(A$ or $B) = p(A) + p(B)$ when A and B are mutually exclusive.

Exercises

1. What restrictions are placed on assigning the probability $p(X)$ for the occurrence of an event?

2. Are the following valid probabilities for these different and exhaustive sets of values of X?

a.	X	$p(X)$	b.	X	$p(X)$	c.	X	$p(X)$
	1	−.5		−1	.3		0	.20
	2	.2		0	.4		3	.30
	3	.3		1	.5		4	.35
				2	.2		9	.15

6.2.2 Different Methods of Assigning Probability Values

The assignment of specific probability values depends on the meaning given to the concept of probability. Unfortunately, the concept is ambiguous, and there is no single interpretation for it. Consider the following probability statements:

1. The probability of obtaining a head in a flip of a fair coin is .5.
2. The probability that students would cheat when no one is proctoring the examination is .23.
3. Mark affirms that he is 95% sure that his friend John would not cheat whether the proctor is present or not.

Each statement is made based on a different conception of probability.

The first statement represents a classical interpretation of probability, which derives from games of chance. Probability values are deduced from some formal property of the experiment or the nature of the situation. Thus, because there are two possible elementary events in the flip of a coin, the probability of any elementary event is 1 out of 2. The values are assigned without first gathering any empirical evidence; that is, the first statement is assumed to be true without any coin being flipped. These then are called **a priori** probabilities. The probability of obtaining a 6 in the toss of a fair die is 1/6. It is 1/35 for Jane being randomly selected from a pool of 35 subjects to be in Anne's experiments. These are all examples of a priori probabilities.

The assignment of values to a priori probabilities is predicated on certain assumptions. Chief among these is that the elementary events, such as the students available for participation in Anne's experiment or the faces of a die, are considered *identical* for the purpose of the research. They are, therefore, **equiprobable elementary events.** Given this assumption, the probability of A is calculated by counting and then dividing the number of outcomes considered to be *A* by the total number of possible outcomes, as follows:

$$p(A) = \frac{\text{no. of elementary events in } A}{\text{total no. of elementary events in sample space}}$$

$$= \frac{f_A}{N}$$

(6.1)

The second statement is based on what is known as the **relative frequency** interpretation of probability. In this case, the probability of *A* is conceptualized as the relative frequency of occurrence of *A* when the experiment is or could be repeated an unlimited number of times under identical conditions. Suppose Anne leaves the classroom in the midst of proctoring an examination to determine whether or not students would cheat. In her observation of a random group of 70 students, 9 cheated. Each student, in this case, may be considered a **trial** or an experiment that produces either the outcome of cheating or no cheating. Combining the results of these trials, the relative frequency of cheating is .13: 9/70. Theoretically, Anne can continue the experiment an *unlimited* number of times to arrive at the true relative frequency and therefore the probability of cheating. In reality, however, a limited number of trials would be completed, and the number of students who cheated would be counted to yield an *empirical* measure of the relative frequency of cheating. Anne would then use this empirical measure to *estimate* the probability of *A*.

The probability assignment in this second case is also a matter of counting the number of actual occurrences and comparing it to the number of potential occurrences. Formula 6.1 can again be used to assign probability values when the concept is thus interpreted, although its terms have different references. Because the assignment is based on *incomplete evidence*, *N* represents a random sample of trials, while f_A is the actual occurrences of *A* within the sample. Both the first and second methods of assignment satisfy all three axioms discussed in Section 6.2.1.

The third statement refers to a probability value assigned on the basis of an individual's subjective estimate. That Mark is 95% sure John would not cheat is a statement of the *strength* of Mark's belief. This type of assignment is unstable: for the same event, different individuals may have very different estimates. Furthermore, these probabilities are often applied to situations that are not necessarily replicable.

Probability statements are useful only to the extent that they are consistent with reality. Whenever a probability value is assigned, it should be validated against reality. Both the first and second methods of assignment can be tested easily against empirical evidence. The third type of estimate, however, presents a problem: there is no *standard* method of validation for these estimates. Therefore, in this text, we are not concerned with this last and subjective method of assignment.

In the validation process, discrepancies may arise between the empirical findings and the probability statement. When they do occur, they may indicate that certain adopted assumptions or procedures are faulty, leading to an inaccurate estimate. The discrepancies may also result from random errors. These are fluctuations that are due to chance, the existence of which does not invalidate the initial probability estimate. It is to resolve the meaning of these discrepancies that inferential statistics has been devised.

Exercises

3. What does probability mean to you? How are probabilities determined? Can the concept of probability be applied to the study of social phenomena? Why or why not?

6.2.3 Assumption of Equiprobable Elementary Events

From the preceding section, it can be seen that the assumption of equiprobable elementary events in a discrete sample space greatly simplifies the problem of assigning probabilities. Since the concept is so important, the question arises as to whether the assumption holds for a limited number or a variety of situations. Fortunately, the assumption is perfectly reasonable for various occurrences, such as outcomes in games of chance. For example, in drawing one card from a well-shuffled deck, the probability of an ace is the same as the probability of any other card. Or in the toss of a die, the values of 1, 2, 3, 4, 5, or 6 are equally probable.

More importantly, even in the case of events which are not equally probable, as long as the observations constitute a random sample, probabilities can be assigned through counting. For example, although student cheating is less likely than noncheating, Anne estimated the probability of cheating by counting in Section 6.2.2. To understand why Anne proceeded in this manner, we must go back to the definition of a random sample. In random sampling, every sample of the same size drawn from the population has the *same* probability of being selected. Also, every unit of analysis has the *same* probability of being included in the sample. Consequently, the units of analysis in a random sample are equivalent to equally likely elementary events and as such they provide the same basis for assigning probabilities. Thus, in assigning a probability to the occurrence of certain events such as cheating among these equally probable units of students, Anne can simply count and compare the number of students who cheated to the whole sample.

Summary

Probability
If all elementary events are equiprobable in a discrete sample space S of an experiment, the probability of event (compound) A is $$p(A) = \frac{\text{no. of elementary events in } A}{\text{total no. of elementary events in sample space}}$$ $$= \frac{f_A}{N}$$

6.3 Enumeration of a Discrete Sample Space

According to Section 6.2, when the classical or long-range relative frequency interpretation of probability is adopted the assignment of probability values can be reduced partially to *counting* the number of elementary events that comprise a compound event. Therefore, knowing the pertinent counting rules can help solve a probability problem. Before counting can take place, however, the elementary events for a discrete sample space must be specified. For example, Simmons [1] surveyed a random sample of U.S. residents in an attempt to arrive at an exhaustive enumeration of deviant behavior. Based on the responses, he compiled a list of 252 deviant acts and persons, which includes such behaviors as murder and drug abuse and also persons such as "smart-alecky" students and "know-it-all" professors. However, even a long list is not necessarily exhaustive. For if deviance is in the eye of the beholder, there may be as many different definitions as there are members of a society. This does not mean that deviant behavior cannot be enumerated. It merely means that a different approach than that of Simmons's is needed.

6.3.1 Number of Elementary Events and Events

Research Question
Merton [2] developed a theory of deviance based on how individuals respond to an anomic or socially disorganized condition. In this country, great cultural emphasis is placed on achieving success; yet the legitimate means to do so are not always available. This discrepancy between goals and means produces an anomic situation in which the individual lacks clear standards for behavior. For when individuals are faced with this inconsistency, confusion arises as to what the appropriate response should be. What are the *possible* responses to anomie?

Specifying Elementary Events
Merton postulated that there are five possible responses: conformity, innovation, ritualism, retreatism, and rebellion. Thus Merton's theory essentially specifies a

sample space consisting of the five responses, each of which can be considered an elementary event. Symbolically, the sample space is denoted by S and is given as

$$S = \{\text{con (conformity), ino (innovation), rit (ritualism),}$$
$$\text{ret (retreatism), reb (rebellion)}\}$$

The elementary events are enumerated so as to ensure that they are *mutually exclusive* and *exhaustive*. These two characteristics are both present in Merton's sample space. Unlike Simmons's list, these elementary events are derived from a logical combination of the possible responses to the valued goal of success and the use of legitimate means to achieve this goal. Each response is distinct, because it represents a different approach to the anomic situation, and all approaches are considered to yield an exhaustive enumeration.

Specifying Events

Within Merton's scheme of classification, deviant behavior can be viewed as an event E that consists of a combination of the following elementary events: innovation, ritualism, retreatism, and rebellion. Symbolically, we have:

$$E = \{\text{ino, rit, ret, reb}\}$$

Merton later refined his concept of deviant behavior and subdivided it into nonconforming and aberrant behavior [3]. Again, each subdivision can be considered an event consisting of elementary events.

Therefore, with a sample space, various combinations of elementary events can give rise to numerous compound events. Usually, no enumeration is provided for compound events, because their number depends on the particular combinations needed. In addition, different sample spaces may be specified for a given situation. For example, rather than using Merton's typology, the FBI's crime index can be adapted to give a list of the elementary events in response to anomie. The index would provide an alternative sample space for anomic responses.

Exercises

4. Toss a die one time and observe the number appearing on the upper face.
   a. State the sample space.
   b. List the elementary events.
   c. Is "an odd number results" an elementary event?

5. Do the following sets constitute valid sample spaces?
   a. Referring to June 1991 in Sacramento County:

      The thefts, rapes, and misdemeanors committed
      The arrest for a crime and no criminal arrest

b. The students in History 101 during Spring 1990 who:

Never missed a class
Missed 1 to 5 classes
Missed 6 to 10 classes
Missed 11 or more classes

6.3.2 Number of Joint Events

Research Question

In a study of delinquent youths, Cloward and Ohlin [4] extended Merton's theory of adaptive responses to anomie. They pointed out that these responses may originate from a lack of illegitimate as well as legitimate means to achieve success. As an illustration, innovative behaviors such as embezzlement are possible only if the individual occupies a status that puts him or her in control of another's funds. Additionally, Johnson [5] suggested that available but inadequate legitimate means can also act as a stimulus for deviant behavior. For example, the police who believe that their efforts to control crime are largely unsuccessful because of the limitations imposed on their means of fighting crime may resort to illegitimate means to enforce the law. Based on these social scientists' observations, an individual's behavior may be viewed as the product of the availability of the illegitimate as well as the adequacy of the legitimate opportunity structures. If Anne constructs a sample space consisting of these behaviors, how many elementary events comprise the sample space?

Applicable Counting Rule

When a sample space is constructed by taking one element from one sample space and pairing it with any one element from another sample space, the collection of pairs or **joint events** may be considered a new set of the elementary events. Note again that the definition of elementary events depends on the researcher; therefore, it is sometimes appropriate to consider a pair of elementary events taken together as an elementary event itself.

For Anne's purposes, a sample space of behaviors resulting from the availability of both legitimate and illegitimate opportunity structures can be defined as

$$S = L \times I$$

where L refers to the sample space of legitimate opportunity structures and I refers to the sample space of illegitimate opportunity structures.

To enumerate the joint events in this new sample space, the number of elementary events in L and I must be known. Incorporating Johnson's observation into the perspective of Cloward and Ohlin, the legitimate structure is now divided into three elementary events of {available, available but inadequate, and unavailable opportunities}. The illegitimate structure consists of {available, un-available opportunities}. The sample space of joint events is thus listed as

$$S_1 = \begin{cases} \text{(legit available, illegit available)} \\ \text{(legit available, illegit unavailable)} \\ \text{(legit inadequate, illegit available)} \\ \text{(legit inadequate, illegit unavailable)} \\ \text{(legit unavailable, illegit available)} \\ \text{(legit unavailable, illegit unavailable)} \end{cases}$$

Mathematically, the number of elementary events can be calculated as follows. If there are K_1 elementary events in the first sample space and K_2 elementary events in the second sample space, the sample space consisting of their joint events has

$$S = (K_1)(K_2) \quad \text{elementary events} \tag{6.2}$$

In Anne's problem, K_1 equals 3 and K_2 equals 2. The number of different responses is 6: (3)(2), confirming the results obtained from a simple listing.

As another example, imagine betting on an outcome involving the throw of a die combined with the drawing of one card, such as (3, ace of clubs), and so on. There would be 312: (6)(52) possible paired events, each considered an elementary event in this sample space.

Exercises

6. Toss two coins in sequence and observe in what order heads or tails appear. List the elementary events.

7. Toss a coin and then a die. List the elementary events.

8. Researchers on juvenile delinquency have emphasized two factors for delinquency: differential association (associate or not associate with delinquents) and social class origin (lower, middle, or upper class). List the elementary events that comprise the sample space of joint events from these two factors.

9. Four men, two from a minority group, were arrested for theft last week and have received four different types of sentences. List the elementary events based on two factors: (1) minority or dominant status and (2) types of sentences.

6.3.3 The Number of Sequences for N Consecutive Trials

Research Question
Responses to deviant behavior are not invariant; instead they depend on a number of factors. Chambliss [6], having studied two teen-age gangs that he called the

Saints and the Roughnecks, concluded that the community has very different perceptions of their equally delinquent behaviors. Among other factors, community reaction is influenced by who the violators are, their general reputation within the community, and their handling of the specific situation at the moment of discovery. In other words, the final outcome of and reaction to the same deviant behavior are dependent on a series of preceding events. In probability, the particular series of events is called a **sequence** of outcomes. Each sequence, in turn, may be considered an elementary event of a new sample space.

The sample space of different sequences may be generated from the outcome of the same experiment administered N times. For example, in 10 tosses of a coin, each toss is a trial that results in the elementary event of either a head or a tail. However, a particular sequence of heads and tails produced by the 10 trials may also be considered an elementary event.

The sequence may also be generated from a number of different *factors*, as in the case of the Roughnecks and Saints. Each factor, such as the identity or the reputation of the delinquents, is also a trial. If Anne applies the concept of sequence to plot the process of reaction to these delinquents, how many possible sequences are there if (1) community reaction is dependent on three factors that precede it and (2) all three factors involved, including community reaction, have two different outcomes?

Applicable Counting Rule

A counting rule can be applied to sequences; it states that if there are K_1 possible outcomes for the first trial and K_2 possible outcomes for the second trial, then there are

$(K_1)(K_2)$ possible outcomes for the two trials viewed as a sequence

This formula can be further extended to N different trials where the number of sequences equals

$$(K_1)(K_2)(K_3) \ldots (K_N) \tag{6.3}$$

Other counting rules discussed in the following sections are basically a variation of this general principle.

If the number of outcomes for each trial is constant, the general counting rule is modified to

$$(K)(K)(K) \ldots = K^N \tag{6.4}$$

This rule states that if there are K different mutually exclusive and exhaustive events that could occur on each of N trials, the number of sequences that could result from N trials equals K^N.

In Anne's experiment, K equals 2 (possible outcomes) and N equals 4 (three factors affecting community reactions plus community reaction). Therefore, the number of sequences is 2^4 or 16: (2)(2)(2)(2).

An Alternative: The Tree Diagram

An alternative approach to counting sequences is the use of a **tree diagram.** The tree diagram provides both a count and a detailed listing of the outcomes within a sequence. The tree diagram in Figure 6.1 displays the possible sequences upon discovery of a delinquent act based on a simplified version of the Chambliss study. The diagram starts with a designation of the situation (experiment) and then branches to all possible initial outcomes. Since there are only two initial outcomes, there are two branches from the starting point. From each branch, again determine and list the possible outcomes; then continue with the procedure until all factors (trials) are represented in the diagram. Now count the number of

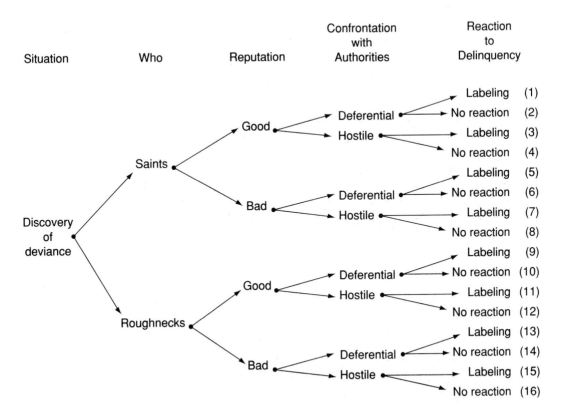

FIGURE 6.1   Tree Diagram of Possible Sequences in the Reaction to Delinquency

end branches. The rightmost column with numbers in brackets gives the tally in Figure 6.1. In this case, there are 16 possible sequences; each is considered an elementary event.

In place of the tree diagram, a simple listing can also be used to display the four-trial sequences:

$$
S = \left\{
\begin{array}{l}
(\text{Saint, good, deferential, labeling}) \\
\vdots \\
(\text{Roughnecks, good, deferential, labeling}) \\
\vdots \\
(\text{Roughnecks, bad, hostile, no reaction})
\end{array}
\right\}
$$

Exercises

10. A person committing a crime will experience different consequences depending on whether or not she or he is arrested. If arrested, the person may become a hardened criminal or a convert; if not arrested, the person may commit another crime or become a convert. List the possible sequences of elementary events.

11. In tossing a coin three times, what are the possible sequences of heads and tails? Draw a tree diagram to enumerate the sequences.

12. Toss a penny, then a dime, and then a die.
    a. Describe a suitable sample space.
    b. Draw a tree diagram.
    c. Express the following events symbolically:
       A = {two heads and an odd number appear}
       B = {one head and a prime number appear}
       C = {no head appears}

13. A man decides to play roulette at most five times, each time gaining $1 if he wins and losing $1 otherwise. He begins with $1 and will stop playing if he loses all his money or if he is lucky enough to win $3. Draw a tree diagram to show the possible outcomes.

6.3.4 Number of Permutations

Research Question
Suppose Merton's anomie theory is applied to the study of an individual's adaptation to his or her environment. Also assume that the individual attempts one mode of adaptation at a time and then abandons it for another until all possible modes are exhausted. Now, what is of interest to Anne in such a situation is not

the fact that all modes are tried, but the order in which they are attempted. In asking how many different sequences of adaptation modes are distinguishable, Anne is looking for the number of permutations. A **permutation** is a sequence in which the order of appearance of an outcome is important.

Applicable Counting Rule
Using the tree diagram or the listing method, individual sequences can be plotted. Otherwise, the applicable counting rule can be applied that states the following: If there are N possible outcomes for the first trial and for each succeeding trial thereafter, there is progressively one less possible outcome, until only one outcome is left for the last trial, the number of permutations or ordered sequences of N outcomes is $N!$. The symbol $N!$ is read as N factorial and it equals

$$N! = (N)(N - 1)(N - 2) \ldots (1). \tag{6.5}$$

To illustrate, there are five options to start with: con, ino, rit, ret, and reb. Whichever mode is selected for the first trial, four other choices are left for the second trial. After one of the four modes is chosen, three others remain for the third trial, and so forth. Observe that once an outcome occurs it is not repeated again in the permutation. Therefore, for five different modes of adaptation, the number of permutations is 5! or (5)(4)(3)(2)(1) = 120.

6.3.5 Number of Partial Permutations

Research Question
Based on Merton's idea of the possible adaptation modes to an anomic situation, Anne designs the following experiment. Students in an experiment were asked to imagine that they were enrolled in a required general education course in which the professor had announced at the beginning of the semester that only 25% of the class would be awarded a passing grade. The students were given five choices as to what they could do during the semester: (1) They could attend class regularly, take notes, study diligently, and try to pass the course (conformity). (2) They could try to pass the course by convincing a straight A buddy to pass them the answers during the examinations (innovation). (3) They could do everything that is required of them without much hope of passing the course (ritualism). (4) They could stop attending class and take the consequences (retreatism). (5) They could make a formal complaint to the chair of the department in order to force a change in the grading policy of the course (rebellion). This hypothetical situation is anomic by Merton's definition, and the responses are similar to his five modes of adaptation. The students are instructed to indicate their first preferred response and then the second. How many different sequences of two responses could Anne obtain, given the five possible?

Applicable Counting Rule

The situation calls for counting **partial permutations,** the selection and ordering of r outcomes from N possible outcomes, where $r \leq N$. Since there are five (N) modes of adaptation, the first selection can be made in five (N) different ways; following this, the second can be chosen in four ($N-1$) different ways. Thus there are 20: (5)(4) distinct ways of selecting and ordering the two modes out of five options.

The counting rule that yields the value of 20 partial permutations is expressed by the following formula for selecting and ordering r outcomes out of N possible outcomes:

$$N(N-1)(N-2)\ldots(N-r+1) = \frac{N!}{(N-r)!} \tag{6.6}$$

The formula can be explained as follows. For the first selection, N choices are available; for the second, $(N-1)$, and so forth. By the time the rth choice is to be made, $(r-1)$ outcomes have been chosen, so only $[N-(r-1)]$ or $(N-r+1)$ outcomes remain. Therefore, the total number of partial permutations, given that r outcomes are to be chosen and ordered out of a total of N, is $[N(N-1)(N-2) \ldots (N-r+1)]$. In multiplying this formula by $(N-r)!/(N-r)!$, Formula 6.6 is obtained:

$$N(N-1)(N-2)\ldots(N-r+1)\frac{(N-r)!}{(N-r)!} = \frac{N(N-1)(N-2)\ldots(N-r+1)(N-r)!}{(N-r)!}$$

$$= \frac{N!}{(N-r)!}$$

Returning to Anne's example, applying this formula, we have

$$\frac{N!}{(N-r)!} = \frac{5!}{(5-2)!} = \frac{5!}{3!} = \frac{(5)(4)(3)(2)(1)}{(3)(2)(1)} = (5)(4) = 20$$

Exercises

14. How many distinct permutations can be formed from all the letters of each word?
    a. CRIME
    b. NONGUILTY
    c. PSYCHOLOGY

15. In how many ways can a jury of 7 persons arrange themselves:
    a. In a row of 7 chairs?
    b. In a row of 9 chairs?

16. For a jury of 3 men and 2 women:
    a. In how many ways can they sit in a row?
    b. In how many ways can they sit in a row if the men and women are each to sit together?

c. In how many ways can they sit in a row if the women alone must sit together?

17. The police commissioner, detective, and police chief are to be selected from a group of 10 candidates. Count the number of ways the positions may be filled.

6.3.6 *Number of Combinations*

Research Question

Suppose Anne is not interested in the order in which the students select their preferred modes of action, but in the number of ways in which two possible courses of action could be selected out of five choices. In this case, Anne is counting **combinations** rather than partial permutations. Thus, when order is irrelevant and only the composition of the subset of outcomes is considered, we have combinations. How many combinations are possible in Anne's problem?

Applicable Counting Rule

From the preceding section, we know that there are $N!/(N-r)!$ ways of choosing and ordering r outcomes from N possible choices. With this method of counting, if a student selects conformity first and then innovation, while another student prefers to innovate first and then conform, we have a total of two permutations or $2!$. However, if the order is unimportant, there is only one *combination* of (conformity and innovation). Clearly, there are more partial permutations than combinations, and the original number of partial permutations should be reduced by a factor of $r!$. The resulting number combinations when r elements are selected from N outcomes is

$$\binom{N}{r} = \frac{N!}{r!(N-r)!} \tag{6.7}$$

With $N = 5$ and $r = 2$, the number of combinations equals

$$\frac{5!}{2!(5-2)!} = \frac{(5)(4)}{2} = 10$$

It should be noted that since the order of division is irrelevant

$$\binom{N}{N-r} = \frac{N!}{r!(N-r)!} = \binom{N}{r} \tag{6.8}$$

Therefore, the number of combinations of size 2 that could be chosen from a set of five elements is the same as the number of combinations of size 3:

$$\binom{5}{2} = \binom{5}{3}$$

Summary

Counting Rules

Joint event: Number of joint events from two sample spaces with K_1 and K_2 outcomes $= (K_1)(K_2)$

Sequence: Number of sequences in N trials where:

$K_1, K_2, \ldots, K_N$ represent possible outcomes $= (K_1)(K_2) \ldots (K_N)$
K represents the outcomes per trial $= K^N$

Permutation: Number of permutations of N objects:

$$\text{Taken all together} = N!$$
$$\text{Taken } r \text{ at a time} = \frac{N!}{(N-r)!}$$

Combination: Number of combinations of N objects taken r at a time:

$$\binom{N}{r} = \frac{N!}{r!(N-r)!}$$

Exercises

---

18. Using factorial notation, verify the following equality:

$$\binom{N}{r} = \binom{N}{N-r}$$

19. If there are seven modes of adaptation available out of which three are to be selected, how many combinations are possible?

20. Find the number of possible events in a sample space (S) containing 15 elementary events.

21. In how many ways can a crime prevention committee consisting of four whites and three blacks be chosen from eight white and five black candidates?

6.4 Calculating Probabilities

In Section 6.3, counting rules for various types of elementary events in a discrete sample space are presented. If the assumption is made that the N outcomes or units of analysis are equiprobable, probabilities can be assigned such that each outcome or unit of analysis equals $1/N$. Very often, however, the researcher is not interested in the probability of a single outcome, but in the probability of events that consist of a number of outcomes or events. These may include mutually exclusive and nonexclusive events, joint events, and dependent and independent events. To calculate these probabilities, other computational rules are needed.

6.4.1 Probabilities for Mutually Exclusive Events

Research Question

Criminal behavior is deviant behavior that violates the law, rather than some informal norm. Serious violations that are punishable by a year or more in prison are known as felonies. The Federal Bureau of Investigation, in its effort to keep track of criminal offenses, has developed a list of eight felonies for which they gather information. The eight felonies are further subdivided into the two major categories of (1) crimes against the person and (2) crimes against property. Specifically, crimes against the person involve invariably an element of violence or threat of violence. Anne, who has heard much about the rising tide of violence in the United States, decides to explore the basis for this claim. According to the FBI criminal statistics, how likely is the occurrence of a crime against the person versus the occurrence of a crime against property?

The Data

Anne turns to the Uniform Crime Reports published by the FBI for the information. According to the reports, there are four categories of crime against the person: homicide, rape, robbery, and aggravated assault. Their relative frequencies in 1989 are murder = .0015, rape = .0067, robbery = .0406, and aggravated assault = .0667.

An Appropriate Method

A crime against the person is an event consisting of the four elementary events specified previously. Probabilities are assigned to each elementary event based on their relative frequency of occurrence. According to axiom 3 in Section 6.2.1, the probability of a crime against the person is simply the sum of the individual probabilities of homicide, rape, robbery, or aggravated assault. Let E represent a crime against the person. The following then applies:

$$p(E) = p(A \text{ or } B \text{ or } C \text{ or } D) = p(A) + p(B) + p(C) + p(D)$$

where A, B, C, and D refer to homicide, rape, robbery, and aggravated assault.

The **complement** of an event, referred to as E', consists of all other elementary events in a sample space that do not belong to E. According to this definition, an event and its complement are **mutually exclusive.** Since the sum of the probabilities of all elementary events in a sample space equals 1 (axiom 2), the probability of an event and its complement is also 1:

$$p(E) + p(E') = 1 \tag{6.9}$$

Therefore, the probability of a complementary event is equal to 1 minus the probability of the event itself:

$$p(E') = 1 - p(E) \tag{6.10}$$

Calculation and Interpretation

The probability of crimes against the person in 1989 equals

$$p(E) = p(A) + p(B) + p(C) + p(D) = .0015 + .0067 + .0406 + .0667 = .1155$$

In the FBI classification scheme, E' constitutes crimes against property.

$$p(E') = 1 - p(E) = 1 - .1155 = .8845$$

The calculation shows that a crime against property is much more likely to occur than a crime against the person. However, without a comparison basis, such as probabilities from an earlier decade, Anne cannot establish that there is a rising tide of violence in this country. In addition, the initial classification scheme has a serious flaw; the categories can in actuality overlap. The FBI reports only the most serious crime in cases in which the individual has committed more than one crime. Accordingly, a burglary resulting in a death would be reported as homicide only.

Exercises

22. In a single toss of a fair die what is the probability of:
    a. Getting a 3?
    b. Not getting a 2?
    c. Getting an odd number?
    d. Getting either an even number or a 3?

23. In three draws from a well-shuffled deck of cards, what is the probability of getting:
    a. Three queens with replacement (Section 1.5.2)?
    b. Three queens without replacement?
    c. At least one jack with replacement?

24. In Merton's scheme, suppose con is five times as likely as ino, ret, or reb, and rit is twice as likely as ino, ret, or reb.
    a. What are the respective probabilities of the adaptation modes?
    b. What is the probability that con or rit occurs?
    c. What is the probability that deviance (nonconformity) occurs?

6.4.2 Probabilities for Nonmutually Exclusive Events

Research Questions

Anne finds that official criminal statistics such as the FBI's Uniform Crime Reports are generally unsatisfactory as social data for a number of reasons. In addition to the deficiency noted in the preceding section, official statistics greatly underestimate the extent of white-collar and corporate crimes despite their prevalence, as shown by the recent Savings and Loan debacle and incidents of insider trading. Such information is seldom routinely compiled and collected; indeed, many categories of white-collar crimes are not found in official reports. To compound the problem, the public appears relatively indifferent to their occurrence. For example, in a survey conducted by one of Anne's colleagues, respondents were given a list of criminal acts and asked to indicate two that they would consider most important as law-and-order issues. The list consists of various acts that can be subsumed under three main types: (a) crimes against the person, (b) crimes against property, and (c) white-collar and corporate crimes. What is the probability that the first or second response given is a type a act? Similarly, what is the probability of one or the other response being a type b or a type c act?

The Data
The data from the survey can be tabulated as a 3 × 3 table as in Table 6.1.

An Appropriate Method
Each type of response in this problem can be considered an event. Because it is possible for respondents to check off the same types of acts for their two responses, the events are not mutually exclusive. Let E_1 refer to the probability of giving a type a response as the first most important issue, and E_2, the probability of giving a type a response as the second most important issue. For events that are nonmutually exclusive, the following rule applies:

$$p(E_1 \text{ or } E_2) = p(E_1) + p(E_2) - p(E_1 \text{ and } E_2) \tag{6.11}$$

where $p(E_1 \text{ and } E_2)$ refers to the **joint probability**, that is, the probability of the occurrence of both E_1 and E_2. The joint probability, $p(E_1 \text{ and } E_2)$, in this case, refers to the probability of giving the same type of criminal acts in both responses.

Calculation and Interpretation
From Table 6.1, it can be seen that the probability of E_1, a type a response given the first time, is its relative frequency, which equals .585: 69/118. The probability of E_2, a type a response given the second time, is .551: 65/118. Note that both of these probability values include the 54 cases who gave a type a response both times. The 54 cases represent the *joint occurrence* of E_1 and E_2 and are located in

TABLE 6.1 Crosstabulation of First with Second Response to Type of Criminal Acts Considered as Law-and-Order Issues

		First Response			
		Type a	Type b	Type c	Total
Second Response	Type a	54	8	3	65
	Type b	12	23	4	39
	Type c	3	9	2	14
	Total	69	40	9	118

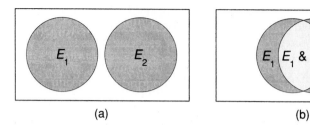

FIGURE 6.2   Venn Diagrams for Joint Events

the *cell* formed by the intersection of E_1 and E_2 in Table 6.1. The probability of the joint occurrence, $p(E_1$ and $E_2)$, equals .458: 54/118. If the probabilities of E_1 and E_2 are simply added to obtain $p(E_1$ or $E_2)$, $p(E_1$ and $E_2)$ calculated from the 54 cases would be counted twice.

Figure 6.2 uses Venn diagrams to illustrate this point. In both figures within Figure 6.2, a rectangular area, which represents the sample of 118, encloses two shaded areas that represent E_1 and E_2. In Figure 6.2(a), the shaded areas of E_1 and E_2 do not overlap. The probability of E_1 or E_2 can be seen clearly as the sum of the two shaded areas. In Figure 6.2(b), they do overlap, creating an area labeled as (E_1 and E_2). The overlapping area indicates that E_1 and E_2 are not mutually exclusive events. A close inspection of this area reveals that it is shaded twice, because E_1 is shaded first to obtain $p(E_1)$ and then E_2 to obtain $p(E_2)$.

Therefore, the jointly shaded area, representing $p(E_1$ and $E_2)$, should be subtracted once from the calculation, as follows:

$$p(E_1 \text{ or } E_2) = .585 + .551 - .458 = .678$$

The probability of (1) a type b response being mentioned first is 40/118 or .339, (2) a type b response being mentioned second is 39/118 or .331, and (3) a type b response being given both times is 23/118 or .195. Therefore, the probability of a type b response given either time is

$$p(E_1 \text{ or } E_2) = .339 + .331 - .195 = .475$$

The probability of giving a type c response the first or second time is equal to

$$p(E_1 \text{ or } E_2) = .076 + .119 - .017 = .178$$

These probability values confirm Anne's suspicion that white-collar and corporate crimes are not what most respondents identified as law-and-order issues.

Exercises

25. Let A, B, and C be events. Formulate an expression that states that:
   a. Exactly one of the three events occurs.
   b. At least two of the events occur.

c. None of the events occurs.

d. *A* or *B*, but not both, occurs.

26. Use a Venn diagram to verify that $p(A) = p[(A \text{ and } B) \text{ or } (A \text{ and } B')]$.

6.4.3 Joint and Conditional Probabilities

Research Question

A related problem with official statistics is that they tend to show a strong connection between crimes and the lower classes, whether one exists or not. This is to be expected because the upper and middle classes have the most power to legislate to their advantage, and the criminal justice system is structured to favor them. Therefore, for various reasons that have little to do with the propensity to commit crimes, lower-class members are much more likely to be caught and become part of the official statistics. However, in studies in which anonymous respondents are asked to identify criminal acts that they have committed, sociologists have repeatedly found no difference in the overall rates among the classes. How much of a class bias is there in the official crime rates? Anne decides to explore this issue by comparing the incidence of theft between official reports and self-reports.

The Data

Anne samples official police statistics in her community. Dichotomizing the data on crimes into theft and nontheft, she determines the relative frequency of theft to be .28. Then she examines the social class of the individuals who have committed the thefts and finds that of those who fall into this category 78% are from the lower class. In applying the same criteria for social class on census data, she concludes that 35% of the people in this country belong to the lower class.

From among the published national social surveys, Anne selects one that has information on the self-reporting of crimes and that can be used for comparison with official statistics. She again dichotomizes the data to obtain Table 6.2.

An Appropriate Method

Let E_1 designate the occurrence of theft, and E_2, the occurrence of lower class. Anne wants to find the probability of a lower-class individual who has committed theft from the two sources for comparison. Therefore, she should calculate $p(E_1$ and $E_2)$, the *joint probability of E_1 and E_2*. Although we have calculated a joint

TABLE 6.2 Crosstabulation of Theft by Social Class

		Lower Class	Middle to Upper Class	Total
Theft		7	34	41
Other criminal acts		105	508	613
	Total	112	542	654

probability in the last section, we have not given a formula for it. The applicable rule for joint probability is

$$p(E_1 \text{ and } E_2) = p(E_1)p(E_2 \mid E_1) = p(E_2)p(E_1 \mid E_2) \qquad (6.12)$$

where $p(E_2 \mid E_1)$ refers to the probability of E_2 given E_1 and
$p(E_1 \mid E_2)$ refers to the probability of E_1 given E_2

The term $p(E_2 \mid E_1)$ within the formula for joint probability is known as the **conditional probability** of E_2. It is used to designate the probability of one event, E_2, given that the other event, E_1, has occurred. The term is so called because the probability of E_2 may change, being *conditional* on whether E_1 has occurred or not. The conditional probability can be calculated with the following formula, which is derived from Formula 6.12:

$$p(E_2 \mid E_1) = \frac{p(E_1 \text{ and } E_2)}{p(E_1)} \qquad (6.13)$$

Alternatively, it can be computed by taking the ratio of elementary events that belong to E_2 to the total number of elementary events in the new sample space consisting of E_1 *only*. Both methods yield the same result.

From the value of the conditional probability, we can deduce whether the events E_1 and E_2 are statistically independent or dependent. If two events are independent, the occurrence of one event has no influence on the occurrence of the other event, and Formula 6.13 becomes

$$p(E_2 \mid E_1) = p(E_2) \qquad (6.14)$$

In other words, statistical independence exists when the probability of E_2 remains the same whether E_1 has occurred or not. In addition, when statistical independence exists, the formula for the joint probability of the two events reduces to

$$p(E_1 \text{ and } E_2) = p(E_1)p(E_2) \qquad (6.15)$$

Using these formulas, Anne can decide whether there is a connection between class and theft in both reports. Probabilities can be calculated to evaluate whether statistical independence exists between two events, and measures of association can also be constructed based on a departure from statistical independence. Thus Formula 6.15 is equivalent to Formula 4.1 for the calculation of the frequencies in a table of expectations. See Box 6.1, which explores the relations among the various measures of probabilities presented thus far.

Calculation and Interpretation

From official statistics, $p(E_1)$, the probability of theft, is .28, while $p(E_2 \mid E_1)$, the probability of lower class given that theft has occurred, is .78. Therefore, the probability of a lower-class person who steals equals

$$p(E_1 \text{ and } E_2) = p(E_1)p(E_2 \mid E_1) = (.28)(.78) = .2184$$

Box 6.1   Using the Bivariate Table to Explore the Calculation of Probabilities

Table 6.3 reproduces Table 6.2 with symbols assigned to the various cell and marginal frequencies in order to explore the computation of and relations among the various types of probabilities.

The probability of theft, $p(E_1)$ in this case, is equal to its relative frequency or $f_1./N$; the probability of other crimes, $p(E_1')$, is equal to $f_2./N$. The sum of the probabilities of these two mutually exclusive events equals 1, as expected: $p(E_1) + p(E_1') = f_1./N + f_2./N = N/N$ (Formula 6.9). Similarly, the probability of lower class, $p(E_2)$, is $f_{.1}/N$, while the probability of upper middle class, $p(E_2')$, is $f_{.2}/N$. The probability of these two events is also equal to 1.

The joint occurrence of lower class and theft is represented by the cell with a frequency of f_{11}. Therefore, its probability, $p(E_1$ and $E_2)$, is f_{11}/N. On the other hand, the joint probability of middle to upper class and theft is f_{12}/N. It can be seen from this that the probability of theft equals the sum of these two joint events, since these joint events are mutually exclusive:

$$p(E_1) = \frac{f_{11}}{N} + \frac{f_{12}}{N} = \frac{f_1.}{N}$$

Furthermore, the probability of nonmutually exclusive events, such as theft *or* lower class, is equal to

$$p(E_1 \text{ or } E_2) = p(E_1) + p(E_2) - p(E_1 \text{ and } E_2)$$

Alternatively, since $p(E_1) = f_{11}/N + f_{12}/N$, $p(E_2) = f_{11}/N + f_{21}/N$, and $p(E_1$ and $E_2) = f_{11}/N$, substituting for these terms gives

$$p(E_1 \text{ or } E_2) = \left(\frac{f_{11}}{N} + \frac{f_{12}}{N}\right) + \left(\frac{f_{11}}{N} + \frac{f_{21}}{N}\right) - \left(\frac{f_{11}}{N}\right)$$

$$= \frac{f_{11}}{N} + \frac{f_{12}}{N} + \frac{f_{21}}{N}$$

TABLE 6.3   Table 6.2 Labeled with Appropriate Symbols

	Lower Class (E_2)	Middle to Upper Class (E_2')	Total
Theft (E_1)	f_{11} (7)	f_{12} (34)	$f_1.$ (41)
Other crimes (E_1')	f_{21} (105)	f_{22} (508)	$f_2.$ (613)
Total	$f_{.1}$ (112)	$f_{.2}$ (542)	N (654)

The conditional probability, $p(E_2 \mid E_1)$, can be calculated as follows:

$$p(E_2 \mid E_1) = \frac{p(E_1 \text{ and } E_2)}{p(E_1)} = \frac{f_{11}/N}{f_1./N} = \frac{f_{11}}{f_1.}$$

As stated, this is equivalent to (1) determining the number of elementary events in E_1 first (it equals $f_1.$) and then (2) counting the number of lower-class individuals, E_2, in E_1 (it equals f_{11}). The ratio of the latter to the former equals $f_{11}/f_1.$. Finally, the joint probability $p(E_1$ and $E_2)$ can also be calculated using conditional probabilities as follows:

$$p(E_1 \text{ and } E_2) = p(E_1)p(E_2 \mid E_1) = \left(\frac{f_1.}{N}\right)\left(\frac{f_{11}}{f_1.}\right)$$

Canceling the marginal frequencies, $f_1.$'s, we obtain

$$p(E_1 \text{ and } E_2) = \frac{f_{11}}{N}$$

Alternatively, $p(E_1$ and $E_2) = p(E_2)p(E_1 \mid E_2)$. Since $p(E_2)$ equals $f_{.1}/N$, while $p(E_1 \mid E_2)$ equals $f_{11}/f_{.1}$, again, canceling the marginal frequencies of $f_{.1}$, the same formula of f_{11}/N is obtained.

From Table 6.2, which contains the data of the self-report survey, the probability of E_1 is .063: 41/654; the probability of (E_1 and E_2) is .011: 7/654. The conditional probability can be calculated from Formula 6.13 as

$$p(E_2 \mid E_1) = \frac{p(E_1 \text{ and } E_2)}{p(E_1)} = \frac{.011}{.063} = .174$$

Alternatively, the conditional probability can be obtained by first counting the outcomes in the new sample space of E_1, which is 41, and then the outcomes of E_2 within this sample space, which equals 7. The ratio of the latter value to the former gives the conditional probability of $p(E_2 \mid E_1)$: 7/41 = .171. Except for rounding errors, the same value is obtained from both methods. Using this value, the joint probability of E_1 and E_2 in the self-report can be verified:

$$p(E_1 \text{ and } E_2) = (.063)(.171) = .011$$

Since the probability of a lower-class person who steals is much higher in the official report than in the survey, a comparison of .218 to .011, Anne speculates that there may indeed be a class bias in official reports. To further explore the notion of a class bias, Anne calculates the joint probability of E_1 and E_2 to assess the independence of class and theft in both reports. If E_1 and E_2 are independent, $p(E_1 \text{ and } E_2) = p(E_1)p(E_2)$ (Formula 6.15).

From police statistics, the probability of theft, $p(E_1)$, equals .28, and from the census, the probability of lower class, $p(E_2)$, equals .35. Therefore, if E_1 and E_2 are independent,

$$p(E_1 \text{ and } E_2) = p(E_1)p(E_2) = (.28)(.35) = .098$$

This value of .098 is not the same as the value of .218 calculated previously for $p(E_1$ and $E_2)$, indicating that the two events are dependent in the police reports. In fact, according to these statistics, the probability of finding a lower-class person who has committed theft is much higher than expected if no association exists between social class and theft: .2184 compared to .0980.

On the other hand, based on the self-report, $p(E_1)$ equals .063, while $p(E_2)$ equals .171: 112/654; therefore, $p(E_1)p(E_2)$ equals .011: (.063)(.171). This value is the same as that calculated for $p(E_1$ and $E_2)$ previously, using Formula 6.12. Thus the two events are independent in the self-report, confirming Anne's hunch that the police report contains a class bias.

Exercises

27. Based on the data in Table 6.2:

   a. What is the probability of getting exactly one middle-to-upper-class criminal and exactly three lower-class criminals in a sample of four when sampling without replacement?

   b. What is the probability of getting at least one middle-to-upper-class thief in a sample of three when sampling with replacement? What is the probability when sampling without replacement?

    c. What is the probability of getting exactly two criminals from each of the four categories based on social class and the type of crime in a sample of eight when sampling without replacement?

    d. What is the probability of getting one middle to upper class thief, one lower-class thief, and one criminal other than a thief in a sample of three when sampling without replacement?

28.   **a.** If $p(A \text{ and } B) = .06$, $p(A) = .2$, and $p(B) = .4$, are A and B mutually exclusive or independent?

    b. If $p(A \text{ and } B) = .09$, $p(A) = .3$, and $p(B) = .5$, are A and B mutually exclusive or independent?

6.4.4 Probabilities for Combinations

Research Question

Through the use of sanctions, society places pressure on the deviant to conform to culturally prescribed norms. Formal sanctions, however, are notoriously ineffective. In the state where Anne resides, approximately 25% of convicts commit another crime within a year after leaving prison. To reduce the recidivism rate, the state recently instituted a program in prison. Anne conducted a pilot study for the state to evaluate its overall success and effectiveness.

The Data

Eleven subjects participated in the pilot study. They were tracked and repeatedly interviewed, and their behavior and life-style were observed over an extended period of time. In addition, their recidivism was noted after 1 year. These are the results: $\{n, n, r, n, n, n, n, r, n, n, n\}$, where n = nonrecidivism and r = recidivism. How likely is Anne to obtain such or better results if the prevention program is ineffective or does not exist?

An Appropriate Method

Let p represent the probability of recidivism and q, the probability of nonrecidivism. With only two possible outcomes, $p + q = 1.0$. Values are assigned to p and q based on the proportion of recidivists in the state before the initiation of the program: $p = .25$ and $q = .75$.

    Because there are 11 subjects in the study, each of whom may become a recidivist or nonrecidivist, Anne is dealing with sequences rather than single outcomes. The order in which recidivism occurs in her 11 subjects is irrelevant and could have happened in various ways, of which the actual sequence given previously is but one. For example, here is another sequence with two recidivists: $\{r, r, n, n, n, n, n, n, n, n, n\}$. Specifically, then, Anne is interested in the probability of a combination: that of obtaining two cases of recidivism out of 11 subjects, *regardless of order*. This involves applying appropriate counting and probability rules.

    In selecting the sample, the 11 subjects are drawn not only randomly but also independently of each other. Therefore, Anne calculates the probability of a particular sequence of *independent outcomes* with Formula 6.15:

$$p(A \text{ and } B \text{ and } C \ldots \text{ and } N) = p(A)p(B)p(C) \ldots p(N)$$

Substituting p's and q's in the formula, we have, for a particular sequence in which r recidivists occur in N subjects, the probability

$$(p)(p)(q)(q)(q)(q)(q)(q)(q)(q)(q) = p^r q^{N-r}$$

However, this is also the probability of any sequence of r out of N subjects regardless of order.

Anne must find the number of combinations next. According to Formula 6.7, there are

$$\binom{N}{r} = \frac{N!}{r!(N-r!)}$$

ways of choosing r recidivists out of N subjects. Combining the counting rule that calculates the number of combinations with the probability of a combination, Anne has the formula for finding the probability of any combination of r successes out of N trials, where the trials are independent of each other:

$$p(r) = \binom{N}{r} p^r q^{N-r} \tag{6.16}$$

Thus Formula 6.16 provides Anne with a way of calculating the probability of obtaining two recidivists out of a sample of 11 exconvicts.

Again, to recapitulate the steps involved in the computation:

1. Assign probability values to p and q.
2. Calculate the number of combinations using the formula $\binom{N}{r}$.
3. Compute the probability per combination using the formula $p^r q^{N-r}$.
4. Multiply the value obtained in step 2 by the value obtained in step 3 to determine the probability of r successes out of N trials.

Calculation and Interpretation

Step 1: Based on the long-range recidivism rate in the state, Anne assigns the following probabilities to each subject (trial): $p = .25$ and therefore $q = .75$.

Step 2: When $r = 2$ and $N = 11$, there are

$$\binom{11}{2} = \frac{11!}{2!9!} = \frac{(11)(10)}{(2)(1)} = 55$$

ways to choose two recidivists out of 11 subjects.

Step 3: The probability of a combination is $(.25^2)(.75^9) = .004692$.

Step 4: Since there are 55 combinations of two successes out of 11, the total probability of all such sequences equals .258060: (55)(.004692). If there is no prevention program or if the program is ineffective, then the probability of having two recidivists out of the 11 exconvicts is .26.

Better results mean that there was 1 or 0 cases of recidivism. The probability of obtaining one case of recidivism out of 11 subjects is .154858: $p(r = 1) = (11)(.25^1)(.75^{10})$. The probability of no recidivism among the 11 subjects is .042235: $p(r = 0) = (1)(.25^0)(.75^{11})$. Because each of the preceding probabilities is mutually exclusive of the other, the probability of obtaining 2, 1, or 0 recidivists equals .455153: $p(r = 2) + p(r = 1) + p(r = 0) = .258060 + .154858 + .042235$.

In using probabilities to help make a decision, the researcher usually calculates the probability of obtaining a set of unlikely results, rather than a single outcome. Without the prevention program, the probability of obtaining two or fewer cases of recidivism is .46. Since it is not unlikely to obtain the sample result of two or fewer recidivists in 11 exconvicts even without the prevention program, the program's effectiveness becomes questionable. Recidivism, however, constitutes only one aspect of Anne's evaluation; whether she will use it as a main indicator of the success of the program depends on the conclusions she derives from her other data.

Summary

Probabilities

Probability for mutually exclusive events:

$$p(E_1 \text{ or } E_2) = p(E_1) + p(E_2)$$

Probability for nonmutually exclusive events:

$$p(E_1 \text{ or } E_2) = p(E_1) + p(E_2) - p(E_1 \text{ and } E_2)$$

Joint probability:

$$p(E_1 \text{ and } E_2) = p(E_1)p(E_2 \mid E_1) = p(E_2)p(E_1 \mid E_2)$$

Conditional probability:

$$p(E_2 \mid E_1) = \frac{p(E_1 \text{ and } E_2)}{p(E_1)}$$

Probability for independent events:

$$p(E_2 \mid E_1) = p(E_2)$$
$$p(E_1 \text{ and } E_2) = p(E_1)p(E_2)$$

Probability for combinations of dichotomous outcomes:

$$p(r) = \binom{N}{r} p^r q^{N-r}$$

Exercises

29. From a well-shuffled deck of cards, choose three. What are the probabilities of obtaining:
    a. Exactly two aces without replacement?
    b. A spade, diamond, and heart (in this order) with replacement?
    c. A spade, diamond, and heart (in any order) with replacement?
    d. A spade, diamond, and heart (in this order) without replacement?
    e. A spade, diamond, and heart (in any order) without replacement?

30. Assume that the probability of winning is .6 in the roulette game in Exercise 13.
    a. What is the expected winning?
    b. What is the probability that there are more than three trials?

31. Eight people witnessed a robbery from a distance. If the suspect is innocent and the probability that a witness will initially falsely identify him is $p_1 = .1$, and upon reexamination is $p_2 = .03$, what is the probability that:
    a. Exactly one person will initially identify him falsely?
    b. At least one will initially do so?
    c. Witness A does so both times?
    d. Witness B does so neither time?
    e. Exactly three witnesses will do so initially and exactly three witnesses will do so later?

6.5 Probabilities for a Continuous Sample Space

So far, we have concentrated only on discrete sample spaces and variables. There are continuous sample spaces, consisting of a noncountably infinite number of elementary events. These elementary events can be compared to the infinite number of points that lie on the length of a line. Since we have presented probabilities using a counting procedure for discrete sample spaces, can probabilities be obtained for events that are noncountably infinite?

The answer is yes, if we consider the probability of a *continuous interval,* which consists of a subset of outcomes rather than a single outcome. Consider a sample space containing the possible ages of a population. Being a continuous variable, age can be measured so precisely that there may be two individuals who are 22.3591 and 22.3592 years old. There may also be a third individual who is in between the first two in age: 22.35915 years old. However, as we measure age more and more precisely, the number of individuals who fall within a progressively smaller age interval becomes smaller and smaller until the probability approaches 0. As we can see from this discussion, the concept of a single outcome is no longer meaningful in the context of a continuous sample space: its probability is 0. That is why we must consider probabilities associated with intervals of outcomes or values, rather than with individual values.

To designate the probability of intervals such as finding someone 23 to 24 years old, with X referring to age, the following method is used:

$$p(23 \leq X \leq 24)$$

The probability of finding someone 23 years old or younger is $p(X \leq 23)$.

Since an interval of outcomes consists of an uncountably infinite number of single outcomes, all of which have 0 probability of occurrence, we cannot compute the probability of an interval through counting. In place of counting, for a continuous sample space, a rule can be specified that assigns probabilities to continuous intervals of outcomes and that satisfies the three axioms stated in Section 6.2.1. The specifics of these types of rules are unimportant here; it is sufficient to know that the pertinent probabilities can be calculated.

In Chapter 7, we will discuss how to calculate the probabilities of continuous variables in the context of a type of distribution called the normal distribution. The probability of an interval of outcomes in this case is equivalent to the *area under the normal curve* between the limits of the interval.

General Conceptual Questions

1. Discuss the use of probability in theory construction.

2. Is it true or false that $p(X) = .5$ is more certain than $p(X) = .1$?

3. How are the probability formulas for $p(A$ and $B)$ and $p(A$ or $B)$ modified when:
   a. A and B are mutually exclusive?
   b. A and B are independent?

4. Identify whether the following is a discrete or continuous variable.
   a. Number of traffic accidents per year
   b. Types of adaptations to goals and means to achieve these goals
   c. Length of stay in a prison
   d. Number of robberies during the last year
   e. Degree of deviance from the norm
   f. Speed of driving in excess of the legal limit

5. If an event A contains three elementary events, E_1, E_2, E_3, how is the $p(A)$ found?

6. Complete each of the following as an equation and then explain verbally.
   a. $p(A$ and B and $C)$
   b. $p(A$ or B or $C)$

7. What is the difference between a partial permutation and a combination of r items selected from N?

8. Can permutations be used to count the number of possible pairs with one person coming from group A and the other from group B? If not, how should they be counted?

9. Criminologists have identified the following five facilitators for crime: differential association with criminals, lower social class background, broken family, personality defects, and lack of social integration. A person associated with any one or more of these factors is predicted to become a criminal. How many different combinations of factors can be identified?

10. Explain briefly the following concepts in your own words:
    a. Elementary event
    b. Event
    c. Compound event
    d. Joint event
    e. Sequential event

References

1. Simmons, J. (1969). *Deviants*. Berkeley, Calif.: Glendessary Press.
2. Merton, R. K. (1938). Social Structure and Anomie, *American Sociological Review* 3:672–682.
3. Merton, R. K. (1976). The Sociology of Social Problems. In R. K. Merton and R. Nisbet (eds.), *Contemporary Social Problems*, 4th ed. New York: Harcourt Brace Jovanovich.
4. Cloward, R. A., and Ohlin, L. E. (1960). *Delinquency and Opportunity: A Theory of Delinquent Gangs*. New York: The Free Press.
5. Johnson, A. G. (1989). *Human Arrangements: An Introduction to Society*, 2nd ed. New York: Harcourt Brace Jovanovich.
6. Chambliss, W. J. (1973). The Saints and the Roughnecks, *Society* 2(November):24–31.

$$Chapter \quad 7$$

Probability and Sampling Distributions

New Statistical Topics

Probability and sampling distributions
Binomial and normal distributions
Expected values
Parameters and statistics
Sampling distribution of means
Central limit theorem

7.1 Overview

Probability theory can be applied to many different situations involving risks and uncertainties. Our main concern here is with the use of its principles to derive **probability distributions.** A probability distribution associates a probability with the occurrence of every possible value or interval of values in a variable according to a mathematical rule. Had Anne computed the probabilities associated with 0 through 11 recidivists out of 11 exconvicts in Chapter 6, she would have had a probability distribution.

Probability distributions play a central role in inference. Consider the process of sampling. From Chapter 1 we learned that different random samples drawn from the same population may yield different outcomes. This variability of sample outcomes, called *sampling error,* is a main obstacle to inferring population characteristics when the researcher has only sample data. However, if we think of the sample outcomes as a variable and its variability as the possible values of the variable, we can apply probability distributions to describe sampling errors.

Probability distributions that describe the variability of sample outcomes are called **sampling distributions.** Whereas a probability distribution associates probabilities with the values of a variable, a sampling distribution provides probabilities of obtaining particular sample outcomes. As the reader will see, sampling distributions are indispensable to the process of statistical inference, for in every inferential procedure discussed later in the text, a sampling distribution is involved. Through the sampling distribution, the researcher estimates the probability of correctly inferring from sample data to population. Without the sampling distribution, the researcher would not know the risk she or he runs in making an inference.

Two probability distributions are introduced in this chapter: one for a discrete and another for a continuous variable. We will consider how these probability distributions are characterized and used to obtain probability estimates and, more importantly, how they can serve as sampling distributions.

7.1.1 Social Applications

According to social scientists, we often create reality by applying labels, terms that categorize or typecast others. These labels may evoke behaviors and situations that might never have occurred without the labeling. For example, the teacher who labels a child a troublemaker may actually call forth more of those troublemaking behaviors in the child.

Labels can be applied intentionally for either constructive or destructive ends. From the proceedings of a heterosexual rape trial, Anne observes how labels can stigmatize the female for circumstances beyond her control. Often, the verdict depends less on whether a rape has actually occurred than on whether the defense has successfully labeled the alleged victim as being the party responsible for eliciting the act.

On the other hand, an experiment by Rosenthal and Jacobson [1] showed how labels can be used to bring about positive results. Teachers in the experiment were told that some of their first and second graders were "academic spurters." Unknown to the teachers, these children were selected randomly and were no brighter than the rest of the class. Yet the positive labeling provided the necessary environment for growth; these children turned in better performances than the class average later in the school year.

Anne intends to explore the power of labeling, using traditional research methods such as participant observation, the survey, and the experiment. In addition, she will apply probability principles to determine how likely certain outcomes are after labels have been applied.

7.1.2 Statistical Topics

To study the verdicts of rape trials, which Anne considers outcomes of a labeling process, she applies the **binomial distribution**. The distribution is so called because it describes a *discrete*, *dichotomous* variable with two possible outcomes. Conventionally, the outcome that is of interest to the researcher is called a **success**, and the other outcome, a **failure**. The variable under consideration is the number of successes or guilty verdicts, r, out of N rape trials. In 10 such trials either by a jury or judge, there are 11 possible r values: from 0 to 10 guilty verdicts. When the 11 r values are each paired with a probability according to a rule, we have a probability distribution of the variable "r successes out of N trials."

The positive power of labeling is explored through a study of improved reading skill after students have been labeled as intelligent. Although it may be measured very crudely, reading skill is a continuous variable. To describe such a continuous variable, Anne uses the **normal distribution.** The normal distribution forms a smooth, unimodal, symmetrical bell-shaped curve. Like the binomial, the mathematical rule that associates probabilities with intervals of values in this distribution is known, permitting probabilities of any particular interval to be assessed.

This chapter revolves around the two distributions, both as probability and as sampling distributions. We will first examine how the binomial is generated by applying probability principles and how the normal distribution is described by its mathematical rule. Since these probability distributions are similar to the empirical univariate distributions we have encountered in Chapter 3, they can be characterized in much the same way through their means and standard deviations or variances. Computation of probabilities for continuous variables will also be introduced within the context of the normal distribution. Finally, we will use these probability distributions in a relatively informal manner as sampling distributions to make inferences about the population.

7.2 Binomial Distribution

7.2.1 Constructing the Binomial Distribution

Research Questions
Anne believes that the power of labeling is demonstrated in the proceedings of heterosexual rape trials. Verdicts that are supposedly dependent on factual evidence are often influenced by the label that the defense attempts to apply to the alleged victim. The victim's character is called into question as evidence that she might have been "asking for it." Consequently, the label, and not the issue of whether a crime has actually taken place, may ultimately decide the verdict.

Anne suspects that juries are especially susceptible to the defense's labeling tactics, whereas judges are more apt to make decisions based on the legal merits of the case. If this is true, convictions are less likely to occur in jury trials. In addition to finding out whether this is the case, Anne would also like to know how much more unlikely these convictions are. In 10 rape trials by a jury for which the number of guilty verdicts ranges from 0 to 10, how likely is each possible outcome? The same question may be asked of 10 rape cases tried by a judge. The results of the two types of trials can then be compared.

The Data
Anne locates a classic study of rape verdicts by Kalven and Zeisel [2] conducted more than two decades ago. The study showed that juries were much less likely

to convict than judges. In comparing simple rape cases, that is, cases in which the victim was threatened with violence but not demonstrably harmed, the researchers found that judges favored conviction 52% of the time, whereas juries handed down guilty verdicts only 7% of the time.

An Appropriate Distribution

Let p represent the probability of conviction and q nonconviction. Based on the Kalven and Zeisel study, Anne assigns the following probabilities to *jury trials*: $p = .07$, and therefore $q = 1 - .07 = .93$. These probabilities are contrasted with those assigned to *trials by a judge*: $p = .52$ and $q = 1 - .52 = .48$.

From Chapter 6 we learned that the formula for finding the probability of any combination of r successes out of N independent trials is

$$p(r) = \binom{N}{r} p^r q^{N-r} \qquad (7.1)$$

Anne, however, is not interested in a specific outcome or combination of r successes so much as all possible outcomes in 10 trials. If she expands Formula 7.1 to find the probabilities of r successes, where r ranges from 0 to N, the result is a <u>binomial probability distribution</u>. Formula 7.1 is therefore the mathematical rule that describes this distribution. The probabilities of the binomial sum to 1.0 like those for elementary events in a sample space.

A closer inspection of Formula 7.1 shows that the values for N, p, and therefore q may vary for different situations. For example, in Anne's case, $p = .07$ for trial by a jury, while $p = .52$ for trial by a judge. Substituting these values into the formula, she would obtain two different binomial distributions. Thus the binomial is really a **family (number) of distributions,** all having the same mathematical rule, but differing in shape and other characteristics.

Calculation and Interpretation

Using Formula 7.1, Anne constructs two distributions that describe the possible outcomes of 10 trials and their probabilities. Table 7.1 displays the probability distribution for trial by jury. The first column of Table 7.1 gives the number of successes (convictions) per 10 trials, and the fourth column lists its associated probability. Together, these two columns comprise the binomial distribution describing jury trials. In summing column 4, we arrive at the total probability for the whole distribution, which equals 1.0 as expected, since every possible combination is encompassed by the distribution. The second column lists the number of combinations for each value of r successes. The distribution of the number of combinations is symmetrical, because

$$\binom{N}{r} = \binom{N}{N-r} = \frac{N!}{r!(N-r)!} \qquad \text{(Formula 6.8)}$$

TABLE 7.1 Binomial Distribution of Jury Verdicts in 10 Trials, Where $p = .07$

r	$\binom{N}{r}$	$p^r p^{N-r}$	$\binom{N}{r}p^r q^{N-r}$
10	1	$(.07)^{10}(.93)^0$	.0000+
9	10	$(.07)^9(.93)^1$	.0000+
8	45	$(.07)^8(.93)^2$	.0000+
7	120	$(.07)^7(.93)^3$	.0000+
6	210	$(.07)^6(.93)^4$	.0000+
5	252	$(.07)^5(.93)^5$	.0003
4	210	$(.07)^4(.93)^6$	.0033
3	120	$(.07)^3(.93)^7$	.0248
2	45	$(.07)^2(.93)^8$	.1234
1	10	$(.07)^1(.93)^9$	.3643
0	1	$(.07)^0(.93)^{10}$	.4839
		Total	1.0000

In other words, the same number of combinations exists for 0 as for 10 successes out of 10 trials, for 1 as for 9 successes out of 10 trials, and so on. Finally, the third column presents the probability for a particular combination.

The probability distribution based on trials by a judge is given in the first and last columns of Table 7.2. This table is arranged similarly to Table 7.1.

The graphic equivalents of Tables 7.1 and 7.2 are given in Figure 7.1(a) and (b). The first histogram is extremely skewed, while the second is almost symmetrical. This shows that when the values of p and q are radically different the distribution is skewed; when the value of q closely approximates the value of p,

TABLE 7.2 Binomial Distribution of the Judge's Verdicts in 10 Trials, Where $p = .52$

r	$\binom{N}{r}$	$p^r p^{N-r}$	$\binom{N}{r}p^r q^{N-r}$
10	1	$(.52)^{10}(.48)^0$	.0014
9	10	$(.52)^9(.48)^1$	.0134
8	45	$(.52)^8(.48)^2$	.0554
7	120	$(.52)^7(.48)^3$	.1364
6	210	$(.52)^6(.48)^4$	.2204
5	252	$(.52)^5(.48)^5$	.2441
4	210	$(.52)^4(.48)^6$	.1878
3	120	$(.52)^3(.48)^7$	.0991
2	45	$(.52)^2(.48)^8$	.0343
1	10	$(.52)^1(.48)^9$	.0070
0	1	$(.52)^0(.48)^{10}$	.0007
		Total	1.0000

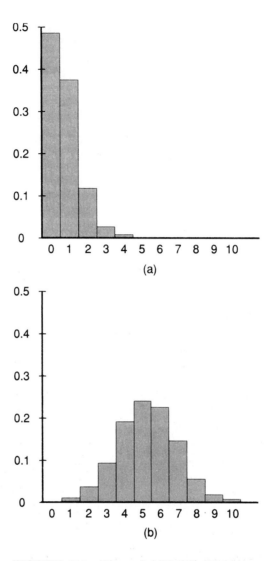

**FIGURE 7.1   Binomial Distributions
Based on $p = .07$ and $p = .52$**

the distribution is relatively symmetrical. The distribution is precisely symmetrical when $p = q$.

Anne compares the two distributions and notes their differences. For example, the probability of getting 5 convictions out of 10 trials is 3 times out of 10,000 in trial by a jury, whereas in trial by a judge it is much more likely, 24 times out of 100. These distributions explain why most accused rapists choose to be tried by a jury rather than by a judge. Their chances of acquittal are significantly higher with a jury.

Exercises

1. Toss a fair coin three times. Find the probability for the following:
   a. Three heads.
   b. Two heads.
   c. One head.
   d. No head.

2. Recalculate the probabilities for Exercise 1 if the coin is unfair and the probability of obtaining a head is .3. Is this distribution symmetrical?

3. The probability of a student cheating is .25 when the temptation arises.
   a. If he encounters such temptations seven times, what is the probability of his cheating at least twice?
   b. How many times must he encounter temptation so that the probability of his cheating at least once is greater than .67?

7.2.2 Characterizing the Binomial Distribution: Expected Values

Research Question and Data
Once a probability distribution is derived, it can be used for various exploratory and research purposes. For example, if Anne were a prosecutor, she might want to know how many convictions she can expect in 10 trials by a jury versus 10 trials by a judge.

An Appropriate Method
Probability distributions can be characterized in much the same way as an empirical frequency distribution: by its central tendency as well as dispersion. The mean of a probability distribution is sometimes called its **expected value**. In this instance, it represents the number of convictions a prosecutor should expect in the long run in every 10 cases being tried by a judge or a jury. The variance of a probability distribution is the expected squared deviation about the expected value. It expresses the expected squared difference between the mean and a particular outcome at any time.

The expected value or **mean of a binomial distribution** of r successes over N trials is

$$E(r) = Np \qquad (7.2)$$

The variance of the binomial distribution is

$$V(r) = Npq \qquad (7.3)$$

Calculation and Interpretation
Based on trials by a jury, the expected (mean) number of convictions per 10 rape trials is $Np = (10)(.07) = .7$. The variance of this binomial distribution is $Npq = (10)(.07)(.93) = .65$. Based on trials by a judge, the expected number of convictions

per 10 trials is 5.2: [(10)(.52)]. The variance is 2.50: [(10)(.52)(.48)]. Thus, for 10 trials, Anne, as the prosecutor, can expect less than 1 conviction if the accused selects trial by a jury, whereas she can expect slightly over 5 convictions if the accused prefers trial by a judge. Although this is what Anne expects, at any particular time, the outcome may be different; in fact, she can expect more variation in the verdicts when the cases are tried by a judge than by a jury: 2.50 to .65.

Summary

Binomial Distribution

Binomial distribution:

$$p(r) = \binom{N}{r} p^r q^{N-r}, \quad \text{for } r = 0, 1, 2, \ldots, \text{ or } N$$

where p refers to the constant probability of success for each trial.

Expected value or mean of the binomial: $E(r) = Np$
Variance of the binomial: $V(r) = Npq$

Exercises

4. The probability is .02 that a child from a broken family will become delinquent. There are 10,000 broken families in Anne's community. Find the expected number and the standard deviation for future delinquent children.

5. Recidivism at a drug rehabilitation center is reported to be .09. The center currently serves 55 addicts. What is the expected number of people who will come back to the center after being released? What is the variance?

6. Let X be a binomially distributed variable with $E(X) = 2$ and $V(X) = 4/3$. What are the values of p and q in this distribution of X?

7.3 Normal Distribution

7.3.1 Normal Approximation to Empirical Data

Research Question
The school district in Anne's area, having heard of the Rosenthal and Jacobson study, decided to try a similar experiment. At the beginning of each school year, first graders evaluated as being below average in reading ability were grouped into separate classes. Teachers who were assigned to these classes were told that the children had greater intellectual potential than other children of their age, but

that neither the children nor their parents were to be told. At the end of the school year, the children were tested again, this time using a standardized reading test for first graders. After three years of experimenting on the incoming first graders, the school district wants the project evaluated before deciding whether or not to continue with it. Anne is given the task of evaluation.

As part of her evaluation, Anne plans to let the school district know what it could expect in terms of the children's reading scores if the experiment continues. This means computing probabilities for certain reading scores. Since reading skill is a continuous variable, to compute the probabilities of reading scores, Anne must find a *probability distribution* that approximates the empirical data.

The Data

The mean reading score of the experimental subjects at the end of the school year is 447.45 and the standard deviation is 100.92. In plotting these scores, Anne discovers that they form a relatively symmetrical and unimodal, mound-shaped histogram. Is there a theoretical distribution of a continuous variable that would provide a good approximation to these data?

An Appropriate Distribution

The normal distribution is a family of smooth, unimodal, symmetrical bell-shaped curves. Although it was first formulated while investigating games of chance, the formulation proves to be highly useful, for it provides a theoretical model that approximates a variety of natural, physical, and social data.

Figure 7.2 illustrates the general form of a normal distribution. Because the distribution is symmetrical, the middle X value under the tallest point of the curve is not only its mode but also its mean and median. From this peak the curve falls in either direction and then gradually levels off, extending indefinitely, but never quite touching the base, to form a bell-shaped curve. The fact that it is a smooth curve indicates that it is the theoretical distribution of a continuous variable; that its tails are unbounded on both ends means that it consists of an infinite number of cases. Imagine folding this curve at its peak, and its tails will coincide since the distribution is symmetrical.

Not every bell-shaped, unimodal, and symmetrical curve is normal, however. A normal distribution is defined by the following mathematical rule:

$$Y = \frac{1}{\sigma\sqrt{2\pi}} e^{-(X-\mu)^2/2\sigma^2} \tag{7.4}$$

where Y = height of the curve for a given value of X
μ (mu) = mean of the distribution of X
σ (sigma) = standard deviation of the distribution of X
π ≈ 3.14159, ratio of the circumference of a circle to its diameter
e ≈ 2.71828, base of Napierian (natural) logarithms

We will not be using this rather formidable looking formula in any computation, but will explore it instead to give the reader a sense of the distribution. Because

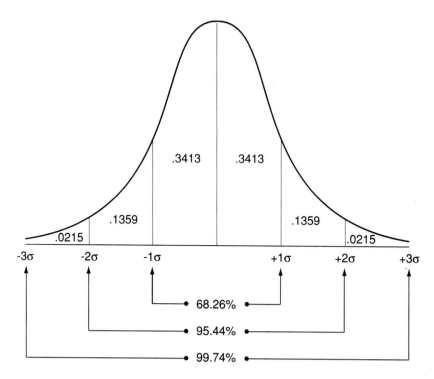

FIGURE 7.2   Normal Distribution

the normal curve is a probability distribution, its mean and standard deviation are represented by Greek rather than Roman letters. Thus, corresponding to $\overline{X}$ in the sample, we have the symbol μ, and equivalent to s in the sample, we have the symbol σ. The μ and σ are referred to as **parameters** to differentiate them from the statistics of a sample.

Since π and e are constants in the equation, the distribution is completely described by its mean and standard deviation. In other words, where a specific normal distribution is located on the X axis is determined by the value of its mean. How flat or peaked it is is determined by the value of its standard deviation. Furthermore, since measurement units vary, a normal curve of height may be drawn in *inches* with a mean of 65 and a standard deviation of 6 inches or in *meters* with a mean of 1.65 meters and a standard deviation of 15.24 centimeters. Thus the normal distribution is a family of curves that is similarly defined by Equation 7.4. They retain the characteristic bell shape, but differ in location, with some being flatter and others being more peaked, as shown in Figure 7.3.

Plotting and Interpretation

In Chapter 2, we noted how a histogram approaches a smooth curve as the sample size increases and the interval width narrows. If the data plotted as a

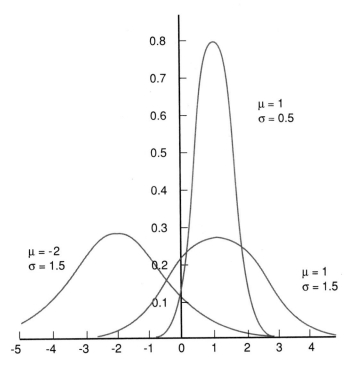

FIGURE 7.3   Family of Normal Curves

histogram are approximately normally distributed, a normal curve superimposed over the histogram should have close correspondence to the histogram. To explore whether this really is the case, Anne draws a histogram of the reading data and, over it, superimposes a normal curve with the following SPSS command:

```
FREQUENCIES VARIABLES=RESP1 /FORMAT=NOTABLE /HISTOGRAM=NORMAL.
```

This command, with its subcommands to suppress the frequency table and to generate the histogram, has been explained in the SPSS Session in Chapter 2. The only new feature is the specification of NORMAL after HISTOGRAM, which produces a superimposed, smooth, normal curve over the histogram, as shown in SPSS Figure 7.1.

In inspecting SPSS Figure 7.1, Anne concludes that her data are approximately normally distributed. That this is the case is not surprising—many attitudes and social and physical traits have been found to fit this normal mold. There are, however, also many exceptions. The distribution of income, for instance, is highly skewed, with a small minority enjoying a great deal of wealth and the have-nots far outnumbering the haves. Obviously, in cases where the normality assumption is untenable, the normal distribution should not be used as a theoretical model.

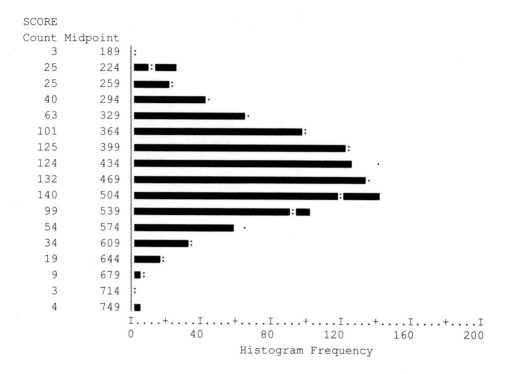

SPSS FIGURE 7.1   Histogram of Reading Scores of the Experimental Group

Exercises

7. Give examples of variables that appear to be normally distributed.

8. Can it be assumed that the following variables are normally distributed?

Suicide rate, accident rate, height, weight
Population growth rate, actual contents of 12-ounce beer cans
Face value of a die when tossed once

7.3.2 Calculating Probabilities Using the Standard Normal Distribution

Research Questions

What is the advantage of having a theoretical curve that approximates the empirical data? The normal distribution has a *fixed area under the curve* included between the mean and distances from the mean as measured by units of the standard deviation. The relationship holds whatever the value of its mean and standard deviation and regardless of the particular measurement unit it employs. Figure 7.2 illustrates this principle. For example, between the mean and 1 standard deviation above the mean, .3413 of the total area of 1.0 is included. As the curve is symmetrical, .3413 of the area is also included between the mean and 1 standard deviation below the mean. In short, more than two-thirds of the area falls within 1 standard deviation of the mean, that is, $\mu \pm 1\sigma$.

As Figure 7.2 shows, .1359 of the area falls between 1 and 2 standard deviations above the mean. Although the distance from the mean to the first standard deviation is the same as that between the first and the second standard deviation (look along the X axis), the area enclosed is different due to the shape of the curve. A total of .4772 (.3413 + .1359) of the area is found between the mean and 2 standard deviations above the mean or between the mean and 2 standard deviations below the mean. Between 2 and 3 standard deviations above or below the mean lies .0215 of the distribution. This means that .4987 (.3413 + .1359 + .0215) of the area falls between the mean and 3 standard deviations above or below the mean. Thus .9974 (.4987 + .4987) of the total area is included between ± 3 standard deviations from the mean. Finally, although only areas associated with 1, 2, and 3 standard deviation units about the mean are shown in Figure 7.2, areas associated with any whole or fractional standard deviation units can be found.

We learned from Box 2.3 that areas under the curve represent relative frequencies, and from Chapter 6, that probabilities are relative frequencies over the long run. Therefore, the area between any two points on the distribution is equivalent to the probability of observing a score that is included in the interval. This being the case, Anne can calculate what the probability is of finding an experimental subject with a reading score of 500 or above. Note that Anne is interested in the probability of an interval rather than an individual value. This is because reading score is a continuous and not a discrete variable.

Because the reading test is standardized for first graders, it has its own distribution for all first graders, who could serve as control for the experimental subjects. The mean and standard deviation of this control distribution are 440 and 100, respectively. What is the probability of finding the same scores of 500 or above in this second distribution? What is the 90th percentile score for both distributions?

An Appropriate Distribution

Since the experimental and control distributions have different values for their means and standard deviations, to find the areas under the two curves, Anne must have either a table appropriate for each distribution or a table that can be used for all normal distributions. Obviously, the latter is the simpler solution. Faced with similar situations, statisticians have compiled a table of areas for a **standard normal distribution** that has a mean of 0 and a standard deviation and variance of 1. To use this table, the researcher must first transform the specific normal distributions into the standard normal distribution.

Recall from Chapter 3 that a formula exists to standardize raw scores to z scores that have a mean of 0 and a standard deviation of 1. The same formula can also be applied to change scores of normal distributions to those of the standard normal distribution. It is given next with changes in notations from those appropriate for use on a sample to those appropriate for use on the normal distribution:

$$z = \frac{X - \overline{X}}{s} = \frac{X - \mu}{\sigma}$$

Table A in Appendix B is a table for the standard normal distribution. It displays areas under the curve that are enclosed between the mean and z scores accurate up to two decimal places. Once the z score is calculated with the formula, Table A can be used to look up associated areas. For instructions on reading this table, see Box 7.1

BOX 7.1   How to Read Table A for Areas under the Normal Curve

Areas under the standard normal curve are obtained by examining Table A in Appendix B. The total area under the curve equals unity, while the table provides areas between the mean and a positive z score. The z value is given to the first decimal place down the row headings of the table. The column headings across the top of the table display the second decimal value of the z score. To find a z score such as 1.91, decompose it into two parts:

1. The row value, containing up to the first decimal place of the score, that is, 1.9
2. The column value, consisting of the difference between the score itself and the row value, that is, 1.91 − 1.9 = .01

Now look down the row headings until the row with the value of 1.9 is found; then look across that row for the column with the value of .01. The value of .4719 at the intersection of this particular row and column represents the area between a z score of 0 and a z score of 1.91 in the standard normal distribution.

The symmetry of the normal curve makes it possible to use a table that gives only areas above the mean for finding areas below the mean. If the area for a negative z score is needed, such as −1.91, the same procedure as before is followed, but the sign is ignored. The area obtained from the table now gives the area from the mean to 1.91 standard deviations below rather than above the mean.

Not only can the area be identified given a z score, but the z score can be found given an area from the same table. To look up a z score for a given area, first examine the body of (within) the table, rather than the row and column headings, for the value of the area. Because the table is not set up to give constant increments of areas, if the exact value of the area cannot be found, use the value that most closely approximates it. Once the exact or approximate value of the area is located, find the intersecting row and column values and add the two to obtain the z score.

The area between the mean of 0 and another z score may not necessarily be the area needed. Instead, the reader may wish to obtain areas above and below a z or areas between two z scores that are not located at the mean. Given the areas in Table A, these problems are easily resolved. Just keep in mind that the total area under the curve is 1.0 and that the mean of 0 divides this symmetrical curve into two equal areas of .5000. In addition, note that areas *cannot* assume negative values, the minimum being 0 or no area. The z scores, however, can be negative, with the negative sign signifying a position below the mean. From experience, we have found that readers grasp this process of finding the appropriate area better when they draw a normal curve and shade the needed area before calculation.

Calculation and Interpretation

To find the area of a score of 500 or above in the experimental distribution, first compute its corresponding z score:

$$z = \frac{X - \mu}{\sigma} = \frac{500 - 447.45}{100.92} = .52$$

From Table A, the area between a z of 0 and a z of .52 is .1985. The area above can be obtained by subtracting the obtained area from .50: .5000 − .1985 = .3015. See Figure 7.4. Since an area is the graphic equivalent of a probability, the probability of obtaining a score of 500 or higher in the experimental distribution is equal to .3015. Although Anne is using the areas under the normal curve to represent probabilities of obtaining certain scores, the areas are also equivalent to the relative frequencies of intervals of values. Therefore, in terms of percentages, approximately 30% of the experimental subjects score at or above 500.

The z score that corresponds to the unstandardized X score of 500 in the control distribution is

$$z = \frac{500 - 440}{100} = .60$$

The area between the mean and a z score of .60 is .2257. The area above 500 is .2743: .5000 − .2257. The probability of finding a first grader with a reading score of 500 or above is higher in the experimental than in the control group: .3015 to .2743.

Chapter 3 discusses how a standard z score informs the reader of the relative position of that score within its distribution. The standard z scores of normal

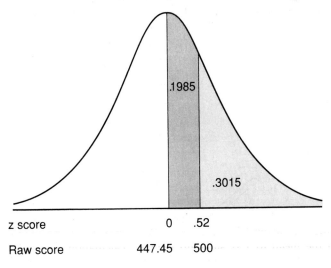

FIGURE 7.4 **Areas between Ordinates**

distributions convey even more information: that of relative positions that have fixed areas above and below it. For example, any raw score from a distribution that is approximately normal and that standardizes to a z score of .52 will have approximately 30% of the distribution above it. In addition, through standardization, raw scores from different normal distributions can be compared. The score of 500 has different meanings in Anne's two distributions: it represents a higher relative score for the control than for the experimental group.

Finally, to find the 90th percentile score for the experimental group, Anne must look for a z score that has .10 of the area above it, or .40 of the area between it and the mean. She first searches the body of Table A for an area of .40 between the mean and the z score. The closest area she can find is .3997. The z score associated with this area has a value of 1.28. Then she substitutes this value into the standardization formula to find the corresponding X score for the experimental group, as follows:

$$1.28 = \frac{X - 447.45}{100.92}$$

$$X = (1.28)(100.92) + 447.45 = 576.63$$

For the control group, the 90th percentile score is

$$X = (1.28)(100) + 440 = 568$$

To be in the 90th percentile of the experimental group, the child must score higher.

Exercises

9. If a variable has a normal distribution with a mean of 10 and a standard deviation of 5, what is the probability that it will take on a value within the following intervals?
   a. 12 to 15
   b. Below 18
   c. Above 7
   d. 5 to 18

10. Find z if the standard normal curve area:
   a. Between 0 and z is .3997.
   b. To the right of z is .01.
   c. To the left of z is .05.
   d. Between −z and +z is .75.
   e. Contains 5% of the total area, evenly divided and situated on the lower and upper tail ends of the curve.

11. A normal distribution has a mean of 72.3. Find its standard deviation if 20% of the area under the curve lies:
   a. To the right of 80.
   b. Between the mean and 75.
   c. Between 62.3 and 82.3.

12. The top and bottom 5% of a national sample of students on an achievement test are selected for special advanced and remedial programs. The national mean for the test is 67 and the standard deviation is 15. Using the same criterion of selection, how many students out of 1,000 at High School X will be included in these programs if this high school has a mean of 72 and a standard deviation of 12?

13. Anne's data on the reading scores are assumed to be distributed normally with a mean of 447.45 and a standard deviation of 100.92. How can she standardize the raw scores to obtain a mean of 500 and a standard deviation of 100?

14. Scores on a questionnaire used for predicting alcoholism range from 0 to 100, with higher values denoting a greater tendency toward alcoholism. When the questionnaire is tested on nonalcoholics, it yields a normal distribution of scores with a mean of 60 and a standard deviation of 10. When it is tested on alcoholics, it also yields a normal distribution with a mean of 80 and a standard deviation of 5. Using this questionnaire on untested subjects, what proportion of the time will a counselor misclassify a nonalcoholic as an alcoholic, and vice versa, if he considers a score of 75 or higher as an indication of potential alcoholism?

SPSS Exercises

Consider the City data base as a study population. Using the following variables:

    Birth rate (BIRTH)
    Death rate (DEATH)
    Infant mortality rate (INFANT)
    Serious crime rate (CRIME)
    Per capita income (INCOME)

1. Draw a histogram and superimpose a normal curve.

2. List the names of the cities and their states whose z scores are above 2.00 and below −2.00.

3. If the population distribution is close to normal, compute the percentile ranks of the cities listed in Exercise 2. Interpret the findings.

4. Take a 10% random sample of a variable whose distribution is approximately normal in the study population. Is the sample distribution close to being normal?

7.4 Three Distributions Involved in Statistical Inference

As Anne changes her focus from description to inference, she must deal with three different distributions. Two of these are the familiar sample and population distributions. They will be reviewed first.

7.4.1 Sample Distribution

Usually, for a research project, the investigator samples once rather than repeatedly and then describes the characteristics of the sample. In the study of the first graders, the sample distribution is the frequency distribution of reading scores among these students. Anne may use the mean reading score of 447.45 to summarize and describe this distribution. In the study of rape trials, the sample distribution is the distribution of guilty and not guilty verdicts in N trials. Anne may describe this dichotomous variable with a proportion, such as .07 conviction.

Statistics such as the mean and the proportion have been used primarily to summarize and describe sample characteristics up to this point. These statistics, however, have another function, that of being **estimators** of corresponding population characteristics. The proportion of convictions in 10 jury trials, for instance, may form the basis for inferring the proportion of convictions in *all* jury trials. In statistical inference, our interest centers on the role of statistics as estimators.

For the purpose of making inferences, the sample that gives rise to these distributions and statistics should be selected randomly. Box 7.2 presents in detail two different methods of drawing a simple random sample.

7.4.2 Population Distribution

The population consists of all the possible cases from which a subset is randomly drawn to be the sample for the study. Thus the population in one of Anne's studies includes all first graders who have, at the start of the experiment, been evaluated as below average in reading ability. The population distribution can be summarized and described in the same manner as the sample. The summary measures are now called **parameters,** and they are symbolized by Greek rather than Roman letters. For example, the mean of the population is μ, the variance is σ^2, and the proportion is π (read as pi). Try not to confuse this π with the π in the formula for the normal distribution.

Whereas the sample statistics are calculated from data, the researcher rarely knows what the parameter values are. Instead, the investigator is confronted with the problem of having to say something about these parameters or about the population distribution as a whole, given only sample evidence. The use of sample information to infer population characteristics poses a problem, however. More likely than not, the sample and therefore any statistic calculated from it contain sampling error. Box 7.2 provides another illustration of how sampling error goes hand in hand with sampling. The μ of the 50 states and the District of Columbia is 35.92. However, using a table of random numbers, a sample with a mean of 35.00 is drawn, and using SPSS, a sample with a mean of 41.10 is obtained. When the researcher has to rely on sample information, the question then becomes how best to make an inference while allowing for these sampling errors. To assist in making this inference, the researcher employs a third distribution, the sampling distribution.

7.4.3 Sampling Distribution

The sampling distribution is a probability distribution of sample outcomes. The sample outcome may be a statistic, such as $\overline{X}$ or P, used in estimating its parameter, or it may be a test statistic. Discussions of sampling distributions of *test*

Box 7.2 Simple Random Sampling

Let us begin with a population distribution consisting of the rates of forcible rapes according to all 50 states and the District of Columbia in the United States in 1989. Data consisting of the ID number (NO), the name of the state (STATE), and the rate of rapes per 100,000 population (RAPE) are entered in the following SPSS program. Note that the (A) that follows STATE in the DATA LIST command indicates that STATE is a string or an alpha variable. Under the procedure FREQUENCIES, the display of a lengthy frequency distribution table is suppressed while a histogram of the data is plotted, over which a normal curve is superimposed. In addition, the mean and standard deviation of these data are computed.

The output from this program of the histogram with its superimposed normal curve is not reproduced here. The graph shows the population distribution to deviate from a normal curve, being positively skewed and having some concentration of cases at the extreme right. The population mean is 35.92 and the standard deviation is 13.98.

There are two simple ways to draw a random sample of 10 states from the population of 50 states and the District of Columbia: by using a table of random numbers and by using SPSS.

I. Using a Random Number Table to Select a Sample

A random sample can be drawn with the help of the random number table included as Table H in Appendix B. To use this table, proceed with the following steps:

1. Attach sequential numbers (from 1 to 51) for identification to all the states and the

```
DATA LIST FREE /NO STATE (A) RAPE.

BEGIN DATA.

 1 ME 19    11 NH 30    21 VT 23    31 MA 32    41 RI 27

 2 CT 28    12 NY 29    22 NJ 32    32 PA 25    42 OH 45

 3 IN 32    13 IL 36    23 MI 71    33 WI 20    43 MN 31

 4 IA 16    14 MO 31    24 ND 12    34 SD 32    44 NE 24

 5 KS 36    15 DE 85    25 MD 38    35 DC 31    45 VA 27

 6 WV 19    16 NC 30    26 SC 46    36 GA 49    46 FL 50

 7 KY 25    17 TN 46    27 AL 31    37 MS 39    47 AR 38

 8 LA 38    18 OK 38    28 TX 47    38 MT 18    48 ID 23

 9 WY 28    19 CO 36    29 NM 46    39 AZ 36    49 UT 29

10 NV 60    20 WA 62    30 OR 47    40 CA 41    50 AK 53    51 HI 45

END DATA.

FREQUENCIES VARIABLES=RAPE /FORMAT=NOTABLE /HISTOGRAM=NORMAL

         /STATISTICS=MEAN STDDEV.
```

Continued

Box 7.2 *Continued*

District of Columbia as in the SPSS program.

2. Within the page of random numbers, select a starting location at random. This could be done by closing your eyes and pointing to a location on the page. Suppose that line 11 of column 5 of the page is selected.

3. Decide on the direction (horizontal, vertical, diagonal) in which numbers are to be read. These numbers represent the ID number of the states. Suppose the numbers are read vertically.

4. The random number shown is five digits long. Since there are only 51 total cases in the population, decide which two digits of the number are to be adopted. Suppose the first 2 of the 5 digits are to be read.

5. Use only those numbers whose value is 51 or below until 10 numbers are selected. These then are the identification numbers for the 10 states to be included in a random sample of size 10. They are as follows:

ID No.	49	48	31	23	42	09	47	13	19	24
State	UT	ID	MA	MI	OH	WY	AR	IL	CO	ND
Rape rate	29	23	32	71	45	28	38	36	36	12

The average rape rate for this sample is 35.00.

II. Using SPSS to Select a Sample

The SAMPLE command draws a random sample from the data currently entered into the computer, using an initial random number called SEED, to generate the succeeding random numbers. The SET command is used to enter or change this initial SEED value. Since SAMPLE is a temporary transformation command, it affects only the procedure that follows it. If two procedures, such as LIST and FREQUENCIES, are to be executed on a sample drawn through a SAMPLE command, the same initial seed value as well as the SAMPLE command must be repeated for each procedure, as follows:

```
SET SEED=5.
SAMPLE 10 FROM 51.
LIST.
SET SEED=5.
SAMPLE 10 FROM 51.
FREQUENCIES VARIABLES=RAPE
/STATISTICS=MEAN STDDEV.
```

Executing these SPSS commands, after initially entering all the data from the 51 states, the following random sample with a mean of 41.10 is obtained.

State	IN	NE	DE	WV	NC	CO	UT	WA	CA	AK
Rate	32	24	85	19	30	36	29	62	41	53

statistics will be deferred to a later chapter. For a more in-depth understanding of sampling distributions than could be obtained from a definition, let us examine two concrete examples next: one of the binomial and the other of the sampling distribution of means.

Exercises

15. Take a random sample of three students from a class and compute the proportion of males.

   a. Based on this information alone, what is the inferred proportion of males in the entire class?

   b. Take another sample of three and find the proportion of males. Repeat this step eight more times.

   c. Assign a value of 1 to males and 0 to females. Then compute the mean and variance of "gender" in (1) each sample distribution, (2) the population distribution, and (3) the sampling distribution of 10 sample means.

7.5 Binomial as a Sampling Distribution

Suppose that Anne were to determine what verdicts were reached in rape trials by jury or by judge in her county based on a sample of 10 court cases; then she would be faced with a problem of inferring from the sample to the population. Anne's sample of 10 verdicts may contain sampling error. For if Anne were to take several random samples of 10 court cases out of all existing county court cases of rape trials and count the number of convictions in each sample, chances are she would obtain slightly different estimates each time. The same applies to flipping a fair coin in exactly the same manner 10 times and then totaling the number of heads each time. Here, too, the results obtained in each 10-flip sequence may be different. Under these circumstances, we say that some chance mechanism is at work, producing a *variability* in the observed sample results. How can such chance results be described?

They can be described by a type of probability distribution known as the *sampling distribution*. Sampling distributions play a vital role in inference because they supply the crucial link between the observed sample results and the inferred population distributions. For instance, the binomials that Anne generated previously in Tables 7.1 and 7.2 are also sampling distributions. As such, they provide information on the probability of obtaining samples with 0 to 10 convictions when:

   1. $p = .52$ for trial by judge, and $p = .07$ for trial by jury in the population.

   2. The 10 jury or judge trials in these samples are selected independently and at random.

If Anne can assume that the probabilities of conviction are true, she can use these distributions to find the probability of obtaining certain sample outcomes. For example, to find the probability of selecting a sample with exactly 3 or 3 or more convictions in 10 trials, Anne first examines the sampling distribution in Table 7.1 of jury trials. The chances of obtaining a sample with 3 convictions in 10 trials is .0248 in this distribution. The probability of selecting a sample with 3 or more convictions is also not very likely: .0284. More specifically, this probability is the sum of the probabilities of obtaining 3, 4, 5, 6, 7, 8, 9, and 10 successes (.0248 + .0033 + .0003). The additive rule of probabilities applies here because these combinations constitute mutually exclusive events.

From Table 7.2, which pertains to trial by judge, Anne notes that the probability of obtaining samples with 3 convictions is much higher: .0991. Also, the probability of obtaining samples with 3 or more convictions is very high: .9580. In place of adding, this last probability could also be calculated as the complement of less than 3 convictions: 1 − (.0343 + .0070 + .0007) (Formula 6.10).

These binomial sampling distributions could also help Anne make a decision in the face of uncertainty. Suppose that Anne has a sample of 10 cases with 4 convictions, but does not know whether this sample is drawn from the population of trial by jury or trial by judge. As long as she has the actual sample outcome, she can evaluate how likely that outcome is to have come from either one or the other population with the probabilities supplied by the sampling distributions.

According to the sampling distribution of trial by jury, the probability of selecting samples with 4 convictions in 10 trials is minuscule: .0033; the probability of selecting samples with 4 or more convictions is still very small: .0036 (.0033 + .0003). In contrast, in the sampling distribution of trial by judge, the probability of selecting samples with 4 convictions is .1878 and of selecting samples with 4 or more convictions is .8589.

Although, strictly speaking, a probability value does no more than account for the likelihood of an event, in so doing it also provides a basis for making a claim. If Anne maintains that this sample comes from a population of trial by jury, she would have to add that she has by chance drawn a very *atypical* sample. However, the sample is not so very atypical if it is selected from a population of trial by judge. The claim that a sample drawn from a population of trial by judge has *4 or more convictions* is even stronger given its higher probability of occurrence. Based on these probabilities, Anne decides the latter assertion is more reasonable. Thus, when going beyond simple probability statements to deciding on a claim, the reasonable claim is the one that makes the sample results more probable. The topic of how to decide whether an inference is reasonable or not based on the sampling distribution will be examined in detail in Chapter 8.

Exercises

16. Using Tables 7.1 and 7.2, compare the probabilities of getting no more than two convictions when tried by a jury and by a judge.

17. Conduct a class experiment in which each student flips a coin 10 times and records the number of heads. Plot the frequencies of students who obtained 0, 1, 2, . . ., 10 heads. Comment on the distribution of the relative frequencies.

18. What is the probability that the number of heads in 10 tosses of a fair coin is equal to or greater than 9 or equal to or less than 1?

19. Find $p(X \geq 9)$ or $p(X \leq 1)$ if the coin is not fair and $p(H) = .6$. Compare the result to the one obtained in Exercise 18.

7.6 Normal Distribution as a Sampling Distribution

For another illustration of the sampling distribution, we turn to the normal curve. Suppose in her second study of the power of labeling that Anne decides to estimate how likely it is for her to obtain a mean reading score of 447.45 *or higher* in the experimental subjects when the population mean is actually 440 and the standard deviation is 100. Anne is concerned because the higher scores of the experimental subjects may be an accidental product of sampling rather than a true difference between the experimental and control groups. In other words, even though the population mean is 440, it is possible to obtain a sample with a mean of 447.45 or higher. However, if it is extremely unlikely that a sample mean this high or higher would be obtained, given the population mean, something other than chance may be operating to produce the difference. That something may very well be the labeling of the children as having great potential, which led to a true difference in reading ability by the end of the school year.

7.6.1 Sampling Distribution of Means

To compute this probability, Anne must derive a sampling distribution of means, in which all possible $\overline{X}_i$ values are plotted against the probability of obtaining these values from a population that has a mean of 440 and a standard deviation of 100. Although this sampling distribution is not empirically obtained, but *theoretically deduced*, let us first see how Anne could *hypothetically* approximate it through repeated sampling. Imagine that Anne takes a sample of N students and calculates their mean reading scores and then takes another sample of N and obtains another $\overline{X}$. Suppose she repeatedly samples until she has a great number of $\overline{X}_i$'s from a great many samples of size N. If she plots these $\overline{X}_i$ values against the *relative frequencies of their occurrences*, she would have a distribution that approximates the **sampling distribution of means.** Since the sample means can theoretically take on any value between two limits, the sampling distribution of means is a probability distribution of a continuous variable.

Let us hasten to add that, in practice, the researcher does not sample repeatedly. There is no reason to approximate this sampling distribution empirically when it could be deduced from the central limit theorem.

7.6.2 Central Limit Theorem

The **central limit theorem** states that, if random samples are drawn repeatedly from a population having a mean of μ and a variance of σ^2, then as sample size increases the sampling distribution of sample means approaches normality with a mean, $\mu_{\overline{X}}$, of μ and a variance, $\sigma^2_{\overline{X}}$, of σ^2/N. According to this theorem, regardless of the nature of the population distribution, the sampling distribution of means is approximately normal given a sufficiently large sample. Of course, if the population distribution is normal to begin with, sample size is unimportant because the sampling distribution of means will be normal. See Box 7.3 for the

---

BOX 7.3   Notations for the Three Distributions

Sampling distributions can be summarized in the same manner as the sample and population distributions. Generally, the summary measures are symbolized by Greek letters to show their nonempirical status and subscripted to differentiate them from population parameters. Specifically, when sample means, $\overline{X}$'s, are examined, the mean of the sampling distribution of means is symbolized by $\mu_{\overline{X}}$ and the variance by $\sigma^2_{\overline{X}}$. The following shows the notations used for these three distributions.

	Sample	Population	Sampling Distribution of Means
A case	X_i	X_i	$\overline{X}_i$
The mean	$\overline{X}$	μ	$\mu_{\overline{X}}$
The variance	s^2	σ^2	$\sigma^2_{\overline{X}}$

---

appropriate notations for the sample, population, and sampling distribution of means.

Thus, given the central limit theorem, Anne can derive her sampling distribution of means without actually sampling repeatedly. If N is sufficiently large, then she should obtain an approximately normal sampling distribution. Alternatively, she could assume that the population distribution is normal if she has a sound basis for so doing, in which case the sampling distribution would also be normal regardless of sample size.

The question still remains as to how large N should be before the normal distribution could be used as an approximation for the true sampling distribution. There is no one answer to this question. Factors affecting the answer include how accurate the estimate must be and how far the population distribution departs from normality. A rather common rule of thumb states that for fairly symmetric (if not bell-shaped) population distributions an N of 30 or larger is large enough to invoke the central limit theorem. If the distribution is skewed, an N of 100 or larger is very often sufficient. Even with relatively small samples, each increase in N adds to the symmetry of the sampling distribution.

Anne has 256 first graders in her sample. Therefore, without making any explicit assumptions about the nature of the population distribution, she deduces on the basis of the central limit theorem that the sampling distribution of means is approximately normal.

7.6.3 Mean and Standard Error of the Sampling Distribution of Means

To employ the sampling distribution of means for inference, its mean, variance, and standard deviation must be known. In fact, these are related to the population parameters of μ and σ^2, without which the sampling distribution cannot be specified. The mean of the sampling distribution of means, $\mu_{\bar{X}}$, is equal to the mean of the population, μ. This makes intuitive sense; for if the mean of the sampling distribution is interpreted as an expected value, then, in drawing repeated random samples and calculating their $\bar{X}$'s, the sample means are *expected* to average to the same value as the population mean. Because μ equals $\mu_{\bar{X}}$, these two symbols are often used interchangeably.

The standard deviation of the sampling distribution is called the **standard error.** In describing the variation around the μ or $\mu_{\bar{X}}$, the standard error essentially measures the extent of sampling errors as indicated by the fluctuation in the value of $\bar{X}$, the sampled statistic. Hence the sampling distribution of means is often referred to as a distribution of sampling errors.

The formula for the variance of the sampling distribution of means is

$$\sigma_{\bar{X}}^2 = \frac{\sigma^2}{N} \tag{7.5}$$

while that of the standard error is

$$\sigma_{\bar{X}} = \frac{\sigma}{\sqrt{N}} \tag{7.6}$$

It can be seen from these formulas that as N increases, the values of the variance and standard error of the sampling distribution decrease. Again, this makes intuitive sense. With larger N's, the samples yield more accurate estimates of the population parameter because their means are more closely clustered around the population mean.

The preceding formulas for $\mu_{\bar{X}}$ and $\sigma_{\bar{X}}$ apply whether the sampling distribution is normal or not and regardless of the sample size. The importance of the central limit theorem lies in its stipulation that as N increases, the sampling distribution of means becomes approximately normal. Since the area under the normal curve between any two points is known, with the central limit theorem the researcher can obtain probability estimates when N is large. By locating the sample mean within the normal sampling distribution, the probability of obtaining this and similar sample means, given a hypothetical μ, can be computed.

Thus, using Formulas 7.5 and 7.6, Anne obtains 39.062 and 6.25 for the variance and the standard error, respectively, for her sampling distribution. With the mean reading score of the experimental subjects equaling 447.45, Anne must find the probability of obtaining a sample that has a mean of 447.45 or *higher* from the population that has a mean of 440. Again, note that the probability of an interval of values rather than a single value is being estimated, a procedure consistent with the treatment of continuous variables.

To obtain this probability, Anne looks for the area that is delimited by the interval of 447.45 or higher in the distribution. She first standardizes the mean score of 447.45 so as to be able to use Table A. Whereas previously an individual score, X, was standardized, now a sample mean, $\overline{X}$, from the sampling distribution is standardized. Therefore, notations in the standardizing formula must be revised as follows:

$$z = \frac{\overline{X} - \mu_{\overline{X}}}{\sigma_{\overline{X}}} = \frac{\overline{X} - \mu}{\sigma/\sqrt{N}} \tag{7.7}$$

Applying this formula to the mean score of 447.45, Anne obtains a standard score of 1.19: $(447.45 - 440)/6.25$. From Table A, the area between this z score and the mean is .3830; the area above it equals .1170. The probability of selecting a sample that has a mean of 447.45 or higher, when the population mean is 440, is unlikely, approximately 12 chances out of 100. Is this an unlikely enough occurrence for Anne to conclude that something else other than chance is operating? Obviously, the decision should not be based on the whims of the individual researcher, but should flow from a guideline that could be applied systematically in similar situations. This guideline, which is an integral part of the inferential procedures, will be discussed in Chapter 8.

7.6.4 Central Role of the Normal Distribution in Inference

Two sampling distributions, the normal and the binomial, have been used to illustrate how certain inferences about μ and the number of successes in the population can be made from sample evidence. In addition to these parameters, there are many others, such as σ^2 and the median, that can be estimated as well. To make any inference, the sampling distribution of the particular sample statistic must be known. This poses a problem for some statistics, because for some the appropriate sampling distributions have yet to be discovered and for others the mathematics involved may be extremely cumbersome. In such cases, instead of deriving the *exact* sampling distribution, statisticians have resorted to finding a distribution with known properties and using it as an approximation to the true sampling distribution.

The normal distribution is such a distribution. Not only is the mathematical rule that describes the distribution known, but the distribution also provides good approximation to various other sampling distributions. For example, according to the central limit theorem, the normal distribution approximates the exact sampling distribution of means when the sample size is large, regardless of the shape of the population distribution. More importantly, many other sampling distributions of discrete as well as continuous variables become approximately normal with increasing sample size.

The binomial, a discrete probability distribution, converges to a normal distribution when N approaches infinity. As the number of trials (N) grows larger and larger, the binomial conforms more and more closely to a normal distribution. This means that in place of using the binomial distribution, which is cumbersome to compute when N is large, the normal distribution can be employed to determine the desired probabilities. Exactly how large N must be to use the normal approximation depends on how close the value of p is to .5, where p, in this case, represents the smaller of the two binomial probabilities. With a value close to .5, if $N \geq 20$ and $Np \geq 5$, the normal distribution provides a good approximation.

Corollaries of the central limit theorem also state that the sampling distributions of the difference between two sample means or proportions, that is, $(\overline{X}_1 - \overline{X}_2)$ or $(P_1 - P_2)$, have sampling distributions that are approximately normal for large N's. Without further enumeration, suffice it to say that, because it provides a good approximation to many other probability distributions, the normal distribution serves as the sampling distribution for many inferential procedures to be discussed later in this text.

7.7 Assumptions Made in Deriving Sampling Distributions

Once the sampling distribution for a particular procedure is identified, other information is needed to specify it completely. Generally, the information comes from three main sources: the population, the sampling procedure, and the sample size. To return to the binomial distribution for illustration, the value of p must be known to specify the distribution. Based on Kalven and Zeisel's work, the p's are set to .07 and .52 in jury trials and trials by a judge, respectively. The same applies to the sampling distribution of means. The population mean μ and its variance σ^2 must be known to specify it. In addition, for both illustrations the information is necessary that a random sample of size N is drawn from the population. From these sources of information the binomial or the normal sampling distribution is derived.

When we delve into the nature of the information regarding the population, we realize that it is not necessarily factual but may be based on assumptions. Some or all of the values of the population parameters may be hypothetical. For example, for the binomial, the value of p is *assumed* to be .52 (or .07) based on the relative occurrence of convictions in a large number of past trials. For the sampling distribution of means, the sample is assumed to have been selected from a population that has a μ of 440 and a σ of 100. By making these assumptions, the researcher simplifies the derivation process.

As for the sampling procedure, a routine *assumption* is made that a simple random sample is drawn. It should be noted again that the assumption of a simple random sample (equiprobable cases or units of analysis) is not necessary as long as the probability of selection is known. However, this assumption greatly simplifies the derivation of the sampling distribution and is the assumption made throughout this text.

The assumptions about the population influence the sample space of possible sample outcomes, whereas the assumption of random sampling provides a probability structure for the occurrences of the various sample values. Although these two types of assumptions are necessary for the specification of the sampling distribution, they do not have the same *logical status*. The assumption of sampling procedures is accepted as necessary, whereas some of the assumptions about the population are tested against sample evidence.

In conclusion, two classes of assumptions are necessary to deduce the sampling distribution in statistical inference: those to be tested and those accepted or assumed to be true in order to proceed with the testing. The first class of assumptions about the population is called **statistical hypotheses.** The latter group of assumptions constitutes what is known as the **test model** of a statistical procedure. This group may consist of assumptions about sampling procedures and, depending on the particular inferential procedure, of additional assumptions about the population such as its normality and/or about the level of data measurement. For there to be a valid test of the statistical hypothesis, these conditions in the model must be met. In other words, the conclusion of any testing is warranted only if an appropriate statistical model is used. The result of a test is meaningful insofar as the researcher is relatively certain of the assumptions made in the model.

Exercises

20. Refer to Exercise 17. Verify the central limit theorem using the data gathered.

21. National algebra test scores are reported to be normally distributed with a mean of 67 and a standard deviation of 24. A random sample of 100 students at University X has a mean of 65. How likely is it to obtain a sample with a mean of 65 or lower if the population mean is indeed 67?

SPSS Session

One advantage of using SPSS is that we can simulate the process of repeatedly drawing samples of the same size, thereby approximating the sampling distribution of means. To illustrate, we will draw samples of size 10 repeatedly 50 times from the population distribution of the 50 states and the District of Columbia in Box 7.2. For each sample drawn, the DESCRIPTIVES procedure, with 1 (SPSS/PC+) or MEAN (SPSS) specified after the STATISTICS subcommand, computes its mean. To produce 50 samples, the following set of commands must be executed 50 times:

```
SAMPLE 10 FROM 51.

DESCRIPTIVES VARIABLES=RAPE /STATISTICS=1.
```

Although there are several ways of approaching the problem, the simplest is to copy the commands 50 times using an editor.

The resulting 50 sample means are entered as XRAPE into a new program as shown next. Then, using the FREQUENCIES command, a histogram is drawn with the normal distribution superimposed, and the mean and standard error of the sampling distribution are computed.

```
DATA LIST FREE/XRAPE.

BEGIN DATA.

41.1   42.1   34.1   40.6   35.4   30.9   38.8   37.1   42.8   35.8

42.1   38.8   37.5   31.8   35.2   38.6   35.4   34.9   41.5   30.5

43.0   37.1   37.4   39.6   31.8   42.8   34.0   31.1   36.4   32.1

36.4   42.6   38.8   38.0   39.8   36.6   35.4   40.7   28.1   44.0

33.4   39.1   32.2   39.0   39.7   42.2   31.7   37.8   32.1   39.3

END DATA.

FREQUENCIES VARIABLES=XRAPE /FORMAT=NOTABLE

     /HISTOGRAM=NORMAL /STATISTICS=MEAN STDDEV.
```

The sampling distribution, which is not reproduced here, is not a normal curve, because the population is not normal and the sample size is small. The mean of the sampling distribution is 37.14 as compared to the population mean of 35.92. The standard error of this sampling distribution is 3.964 as compared to 4.42, the value that would be obtained if the true σ of 13.98 is used in the computation. This empirical approximation to the true probability distribution is probably not as close as it could be because of the small number of samples taken. The reader could try taking 100 samples of 10 to obtain a better approximation.

SPSS Exercises

5. Simulate the central limit theorem using the crime rate (CRIME) in the City data base. Consider the 500-city data as a study population.
    a. Run DESCRIPTIVES to compute the mean and standard deviation.
    b. Plot a histogram for 500 cities. Decide if it is distributed normally by superimposing a normal curve.
    c. Take 50 samples of size 4. For each sample, draw a histogram with a normal curve superimposed. Compute the mean and standard deviation.
    d. Repeat steps b and c for samples of sizes 10, 30, 50, and 100.
    e. As the sample size increases, does the distribution of the sample means approach normality? Do the $\mu_{\bar{X}}$ and $\sigma_{\bar{X}}$ approach μ and $\sigma/\sqrt{N}$?

General Conceptual Problems

1. In what way is the normal distribution useful in statistical analysis?

2. Give examples of social problems that can be described by the binomial distribution.

3. What are the properties of a binomial experiment?

4. Under what conditions can the normal distribution be used to approximate binomial probabilities?

5. Does the central limit theorem specify:
   a. How large N should be?
   b. That the mean of the sampling distribution of sample means is the same as the population mean?
   c. That the binomial approaches the normal distribution when N is large?
   d. That the sampling distribution approaches the normal for sufficiently large N?

6. Explain the following statement: "The sampling distribution is not an empirical distribution."

7. What is the role of the sampling distribution of a statistic in statistical inference?

8. Explain the two types of assumptions used in statistical inference: the test model and statistical hypothesis.

9. Can any type of distribution be standardized into a standard normal distribution?

10. Can a sample of scores be assumed to be normally distributed if it is drawn from a standardized test whose scores are normally distributed?

11. What is the relationship between the sample size and the variability of the sampling distribution of sample means?

References

1. Rosenthal, R., and Jacobson, L. (1968). Teacher Expectations for the Disadvantaged, *Scientific American*, 218(April):19–23.

2. Kalven, H., Jr., and Zeisel, H. (1966). *The American Jury*. Boston: Little, Brown.

Chapter *8*

Illustrating the Logic of Statistical Inference with One-sample Tests

New Statistical Topics

Null and alternative hypotheses	Type I and Type II errors
Rejection region and significance level	Power of a test
	Parametric and nonparametric tests
One- and two-tailed tests	One-sample z test
Critical value	

8.1 Overview

Anne began her venture by looking at sample data. These sample data are meaningful in and of themselves, but they are also significant for the bearing they have on two separate issues: those of theory development and statistical inference.

Taken together, the discrete facts Anne gathered from the various projects are like pieces of a puzzle. At some point in her analyses, she must bring some coherence to the gathered information. There are two basic ways in which Anne can proceed: (1) by constructing a theory or theories from the empirical data or (2) by finding an existing theory or theories that can be superimposed on the information. Either method will yield a framework for linking and unifying the empirical findings and for interpreting and explaining the observations.

On a different but related level, sample data are useful indicators of the characteristics of the population. As such, Anne can use them to make inferences about the population from which the sample is drawn. In inferring, she is seldom completely sure of her conclusions because of the existence of sampling errors. However, Anne can use a body of formalized procedures called inferential statistics to help her make decisions about population characteristics based on sample data.

This chapter interrelates the two issues of theory development and statistical inference to present a detailed account of the logical foundation of the latter. Although the individual statistical procedures differ, the underlying logic for making an inference is the same. Statistical inference is integrated within the framework of theory development and research to give the reader an overall view of the role of inferential statistics in the social sciences.

8.1.1 Social Applications

Social scientists subscribe to the belief that the conclusions arrived at through research are not merely collections of facts. An important part of a social scientist's effort is directed at formulating a set (or sets) of abstract ideas that not only link and unify these observations, but extend beyond them to explain a particular facet of society. As the reader may recall, the set of abstract ideas is called a *theory*.

An intimate interplay exists between theory and facts. From observations arises a theory. In explaining and interpreting existing findings, the theory becomes a device for predicting future events as well. The utility of a theory is tested when new ideas, derived from the theory, are either corroborated or contradicted by facts.

From the discussion, it can be seen that the social scientist's effort to develop a theory has two interrelated aspects: theory formulation and theory verification. The interplay between theory and facts is seen most clearly in the two basic research strategies that complement these two aspects of theory development. According to Francis Bacon in *Novum Organum* [1], one strategy starts with "the senses and particulars" to arrive at "the most general axioms." It is an inductive process by which the scientist formulates abstract theories from concrete observations. This, suggests Bacon, is the preferable, although largely untried, method at his time. The other strategy is one of theory verification, developed most explicitly by Popper [2]. It dictates the formulation of theories first, from which less abstract statements are then derived and tested by facts. Unlike the former approach, this involves deductive as well as inductive reasoning.

Reynolds [3] captures the relation of these research strategies to theory development with two descriptive phrases: "research-then-theory" and "theory-then-research." He further points out that these strategies reflect different assumptions about the relation between the social world and scientific knowledge. Without going into the assumptions, it is important to note that these are complementary approaches rather than opposing strategies. Both are employed in the social sciences; both have their more or less parallel approaches in inferential statistics.

8.1.2 Statistical Topics

Regardless of which strategy the researcher adopts, she or he starts with a random sample and then infers population characteristics from the sample information. In making this inference, the researcher normally employs statistics to estimate parameters, as pointed out in Chapter 7. There are two basic ways of employing a statistic as an estimator. In the first instance, the researcher has no notion of the population distribution, and the sample distribution is used to gain some insight about it. This task is known as point or interval estimation. Point or interval estimation can be fruitfully employed within the research-then-theory tradition to help formulate theories. This topic will be discussed at length in Chapter 10.

In the second instance, the researcher formulates a hypothesis about a population parameter. The sample estimator is then used to confirm or disconfirm the hypothesis. This task is known as **hypothesis testing.** Hypothesis testing is employed within the theory-then-research strategy to help verify existing theories. Statistical procedures for testing may be subdivided into two types. There are the parametric tests, so called because they involve assumptions about population distributions and parameters, and the nonparametric tests, which do not entail the same assumptions. This chapter discusses hypothesis testing as a major step within the context of theory verification.

8.2 Theory Verification

Very briefly, theory verification begins with deriving a concrete hypothesis from a theory and then subjecting the hypothesis to empirical verification. If the hypothesis is supported by data, the theory itself is considered partially validated. The researcher then proceeds to test other hypotheses derived from the same theory. If, however, the hypothesis is not supported by data, the adequacy of the theory and/or the data collection method are questioned and changes are made accordingly for further testing.

8.2.1 Hypothetico-deductive Method

Four major steps comprise the theory-then-research approach. These four steps have also been known as the **hypothetico-deductive** method [4] of theory validation. As an illustration of this method, we will use one of Anne's research projects, conducted to explore the labeling theory of deviance.

The first step of this method involves formulating a **proposition** to be tested. As used here, the term proposition refers to a statement, usually one of relationship between or among abstract concepts. From Chapter 1, we know that, although the proposition could have originated from a number of sources, the most fruitful of these sources is a theory. Let us examine how Anne derives a proposition from the labeling theory for testing. According to this theory, being a deviant is a matter of being so labeled, and the outcome of the labeling process is by no means certain. Anne arranges some of the propositions in the theory in a logical order as follows:

Since the deviant label represents a social stigma, it is to be resisted.
To resist the label, one must have resources at one's disposal.
Those who have power have more resources at their disposal.

From these, Anne deduces another proposition, which states that those who have power are less likely to be labeled.

Usually, the proposition derived from a theory is too abstract to be tested directly. Therefore, in the second step of the hypothetico-deductive method, empirical consequences, stated in the form of a *research hypothesis*, are derived from the proposition. In applying the proposition to the concrete situation of a criminal trial, and with additional assumptions made, Anne obtains a testable research hypothesis. The additional assumptions are that a court trial represents a labeling process and that the middle-class status carries more power than the nonmiddle-class status. Here middle class is operationalized to include the very small percentage of population from the upper class as well. The deduced research hypothesis states that the proportion of convictions after arrest for the middle class is lower than the overall proportion of convictions after arrest in Anne's county.

In the third step, data are gathered to test the research hypothesis. Using an index of social-class status based primarily on address, Anne searches through and dichotomizes the court records into those pertaining to the middle class and those that do not. With the help of a computer, she takes a random sample of the middle-class cases and computes the proportion of convictions in her sample. She then compares this sample proportion to the proportion for the whole county. Seldom would the data provide clear-cut, conclusive evidence for confirming or disconfirming the research hypothesis. Usually, the researcher must employ statistical procedures to help make a decision. Thus statistical inference constitutes a major component of the third step.

Finally, based on the data or the results obtained from the application of statistical procedures, the researcher reaches a conclusion. The research hypothesis is either confirmed or disconfirmed in the fourth step of the hypothetico-deductive method. Observe that we have not used the terms "proven true or false." Instead, we say that the hypothesis is confirmed or disconfirmed, meaning that it is more or less credible, probably true or false. Why?

8.2.2 Logic of Confirmation versus Disconfirmation

By arranging and diagramming the hypothetico-deductive method as an argument, we can examine the validity of its underlying logic more carefully. In simplified form, the following argument is made in confirmation:

> 1. If P, then E
> 2. E is true
> _____
> 3. Therefore P is true

where P represents the proposition, and E, its empirical consequences or the deduced research hypothesis.

This argument, as diagrammed, is invalid because the conclusion that P is true does not *necessarily follow* from statements 1 and 2. For even if E is true, there could be a number of rival hypotheses that could explain the outcome: the juries may be predominantly middle class and sympathetic to their own members only, the prosecutors are too overworked to prosecute effectively, the alleged middle-class offenders are innocent, and so on. Any of these conditions, other than P, could lead to E. In other words, if an argument assumes the form diagrammed previously, there is no way that P could be proved to be true.

In contrast, in disconfirmation, the following simplified argument is made:

1. If P, then E
2. E is false
---
3. Therefore P is false

This argument, as diagrammed, is valid because, if the premises are true, the conclusion is guaranteed.

The foregoing, however, oversimplifies the logic of confirmation and disconfirmation to permit a comparison of the two forms of argument. In reality, there are inherent problems with both forms. Part of the difficulty arises from the probabilistic rather than the deterministic nature of the statements in the arguments and the statistical procedures used to bolster them. Additionally, the measurement of the concepts may be problematic and unreliable.

For example, in the first statement of both arguments, assumptions are made to derive the research hypothesis E from the proposition P, as mentioned earlier in the discussion of the second step of the hypothetico-deductive method. Whether these assumptions are tenable depends mainly on where a strong link exists between the abstract concepts in P and their empirical indicators in E. Questions may be raised as to whether middle-class status can be measured accurately from street addresses and whether criminal trials are indeed labeling processes. Thus a more accurate restatement would be as follows: if P is true, E is *probably* true.

In the second statement, the status of E is determined by the way data are collected and analyzed. For example, if the measurement of social class is unreliable, the differentiation of the subjects into the powerful and the powerless would be meaningless. Furthermore, statistical findings based on a sample are merely probabilistic estimates of the population characteristics. Thus the second statement in both arguments would be more accurately rephrased as follows: E is probably true/false. Finally, as the premises of the argument are probabilistic, so is the conclusion.

Despite these shortcomings, disconfirmation of a proposition, based on a valid form of argument, represents a stronger method than confirmation. Consequently, researchers and scientists alike prefer to formulate a proposition in such a way that it could be disconfirmed rather than confirmed. However, because the method of disconfirmation is by no means infallible, a researcher should use the method of confirmation whenever she or he considers it appropriate.

To increase the probability of making a correct decision, the researcher routinely employs safeguards in his or her work. Some of these include the following:

1. Conducting multiple tests of the same proposition with different operational definitions and measurements
2. Disconfirming a plausible rival proposition that may have produced the same empirical consequences

Exercises

1. Apply the functionalist or any other theory to explain why a judge is more likely to convict an alleged male rapist than a jury is.

2. Deduce propositions from the theory in Exercise 1.

3. Represent the theory in hypothetico-deductive form.

4. What are some of the problems involved in trying to confirm or disconfirm the preceding propositions?

8.3 Procedure for Testing Statistical Hypotheses

So far we have discussed the general logic of the theory-then-research approach to theory verification. The statistical underpinning for this strategy is known as hypothesis testing. Hypothesis testing involves using sample evidence to evaluate a hypothesis about the population. It occurs in the third step of the hypothetico-deductive method and entails the following:

1. A pair of statistical hypotheses is formulated from the substantive research hypothesis: the null hypothesis, H_0, which is to be tested directly, and an alternative hypothesis, H_1, which is to be tested indirectly.
2. An appropriate sample statistic (or other sample information) is selected for use in the testing. Usually, a number of alternative tests can be performed for a given *research hypothesis*. Two criteria should be taken into account in the selection of the test: (a) the type of test, that is, whether it is parametric or nonparametric, and (b) the power of the test. The latter is partially a function of the former.
3. Additional assumptions about the population characteristics and/or about sampling procedures are made to permit the specification of the sampling distribution.
4. The sampling distribution of the test statistic in step 2 is specified based on the null hypothesis and assumptions made in step 3.
5. A decision rule is chosen that defines a region or regions of rejection in the sampling distribution. The region of rejection contains sample values that are highly improbable if the null hypothesis is true.

    a. The decision rule is chosen in accordance with the researcher's willingness to accept a certain level of risk. The risk comes in the form of making an error in either rejecting or not rejecting the null hypothesis.

    b. The level of risk determines the size of the region of rejection.

    c. The location of this region in one or both tails of the sampling distribution follows from the alternative hypothesis. If only one region of rejection is specified, the test is one-tailed; otherwise, with two regions of rejection, the test is two-tailed.

6. A random sample is drawn and the test statistic computed.

7. The test statistic is located within the sampling distribution to determine whether it falls within or outside the region of rejection.

8. If the test statistic falls within the region of rejection, the null hypothesis is rejected. Otherwise, it is accepted or judgment about it is suspended.

Although hypothesis testing concludes with step 8, the researcher goes on to determine the implications the statistical test has for the research hypothesis and the abstract theoretical proposition. In effect, the statistical procedure dovetails into step 4 of the hypothetico-deductive method at this point. Figure 8.1 shows the link between the statistical procedure and the general methodology of theory verification. An elaboration and illustrations of the steps involved in hypothesis testing are given in the following sections.

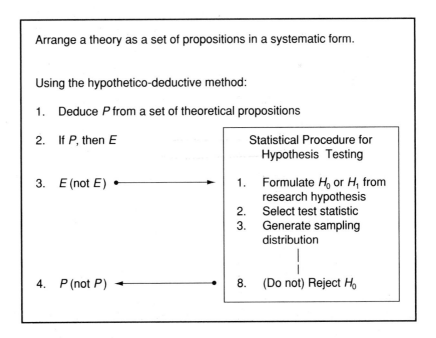

FIGURE 8.1   **Relation of Hypothesis-testing Procedure to the Theory-Then-Research Approach**

8.4 Null and Alternative Hypotheses

Propositions that are deductively derived from theories are seldom directly testable. They employ concepts that are too abstract, having no empirical referents. Even the less abstract research hypotheses must be translated into statistical terms before they can be tested. The **statistical hypotheses** thus generated are assumptions regarding population characteristics (Chapter 7). They may be descriptive statements of the parameter of one or more populations. Or they may assert that population distributions have a certain form. For example, a statistical hypothesis may state that $\mu = 35$ or $\mu_1 = \mu_2$.

As a more in-depth illustration, let us follow Anne's research into the conviction rates of the middle class. In Section 8.2, Anne formulated the following research hypothesis: "the proportion of convictions is lower for the middle class than for the overall population under arrest." She must now convert her research hypothesis into a statistical hypothesis.

In the conversion, the researcher has two main considerations. First, the reasoning for confirmation is weaker than the reasoning for disconfirmation of a hypothesis, as discussed in Section 8.2.2. Therefore, the preferred strategy is to set up a statistical hypothesis that can be rejected in the testing. Second, the parameter from the test hypothesis is used to derive the sampling distribution. Therefore, the test hypothesis should be *specific* rather than *diffuse*.

To understand the difference between specific and diffuse hypotheses, examine the following pair of statements:

Statement 1: The proportion of convictions is lower for the middle class than for the overall population under arrest.

Statement 2: The proportion of convictions is the same for the middle class as for the overall population under arrest.

The second statement yields a statistical hypothesis with an exact parameter value to be tested, whereas the first does not. The parameter value comes from county statistics; in searching through county records, Anne finds the proportion of convictions for all cases to be .50 after arrest.

Given that the overall proportion of convictions is .50, statement 1 is translated as follows: "The proportion of convictions for the middle class after arrest is less than .50." Let π represent the population proportion, that is, the proportion of convictions for all middle-class members who are under arrest. According to this hypothesis, π can assume values ranging from .00 to, but exclusive of, .50. Because the value of π is indeterminate, the first statement yields a diffuse hypothesis. Without an exact value for π in the hypothesis, the sampling distribution cannot be specified.

When the second statement is converted, it reads as follows: "The proportion of convictions for the middle class is .50." The fact that an exact value can be attached to the population parameter π makes the hypothesis a specific one. The value of π is then set to .50 for the derivation of the appropriate sampling distribution.

Therefore, in view of the logic behind testing as well as the ease of testing a specific rather than a diffuse hypothesis, a *pair* of statistical hypotheses is formulated for any testing situation. Of the pair, the **null hypothesis,** symbolized by H_0, is tested directly, whereas the **alternative hypothesis,** symbolized by H_1, is tested indirectly. As the hypothesis to be tested directly, the null hypothesis is formulated with a specific parameter value, in a manner that could be rejected. It usually, although not always, involves a contradiction of the research hypothesis. Statement 2 is an example of the contradiction of statement 1. At the same time, the alternative hypothesis generally affirms the assertion made in the research hypothesis. *In rejecting the null hypothesis, the researcher, in effect, finds support for the alternative hypothesis.*

This procedure of indirect testing is common in the social sciences, in which research hypotheses tend to be diffusely stated. Chambliss may assert that the Saints are not sanctioned for the same acts that the Roughnecks are. However, to test the hypothesis directly, he would have to specify the amount of the differential treatment between the two groups. To affirm directly that there is a correlation between the social class of the criminal and the victim, the researcher must designate the degree of the correlation. Often it is difficult to assign an exact value to the extent of differential treatment or correlation. On the other hand, the denial of any amount of difference is the assertion of no difference. The contradiction of any degree of correlation is the declaration of no correlation. These statements of "no difference" and "no correlation" are more readily testable, because they yield an exact 0 value.

To return to Anne, although her interest centers on statement 1, she concludes that the second statement is much more appropriately used as the test hypothesis H_0, and the first statement, as the alternative hypothesis H_1. As explained, in testing the second statement directly, she is also testing the first indirectly, and in rejecting H_0, she would be supporting H_1.

Strictly speaking, when the alternative hypothesis calls for $\pi < .50$, its logical contradiction is $\pi \geq .50$ and not $\pi = .50$. However, the statement $\pi = .50$ represents the most extreme exact estimate of the range of values in $\pi \geq .50$. If the null hypothesis of $\pi = .50$ can be rejected with a minimum degree of risk, then all other possible null hypotheses of $\pi > .50$ can be also rejected at a lower level of risk. Therefore, in testing an H_0 of $\pi = .50$, Anne is, in effect, simultaneously testing a host of other H_0's with less extreme values or values of greater than .50.

Exercises

5. From reports about ethical standards on campus, a researcher is convinced that 40% or more of the students would cheat on an examination when the students are not being monitored.

   a. Formulate a research hypothesis.
   b. State the null hypotheses both in specific and diffuse forms.

8.5 Interpreting the Sample Outcome in Light of the Sampling Distribution

Frequently, the researcher formulates H_0 with a statistic in mind for the purpose of testing. For example, when Anne states that $\pi = .50$ under H_0, she has, in effect, selected the sample proportion P to test this hypothesis. To proceed with the testing, she next selects a random sample of 96 trial cases from county records to determine P.

8.5.1 Specifying the H_0 Sampling Distribution

Now that Anne has the sample size, she is ready to specify the *sampling distribution of the null hypothesis.* The sampling distribution should be a probability distribution of the sample proportions of a dichotomous variable that has the two categories of conviction and nonconviction. In Chapter 7, the binomial distribution was presented as a sampling distribution of r, the frequency (number) of success, in N trials. However, a probability distribution of r is the same as a probability distribution of P, since proportions are *relative* frequencies:

$$p(r = a \text{ in } N \text{ trials}) = p\left(P = \frac{a}{N} \right)$$

Therefore, the sampling distribution Anne must derive is a binomial. To do this, she needs the following information: the hypothesized π value of .50, the sample size of 96, and the sampling procedure of random and independent selection. On further examination, Anne concludes that generating the binomial distribution with $N = 96$ would be a very cumbersome task. A better alternative is to use the normal approximation to the binomial.

From Chapter 7, we learn that when $N \geq 20$ and $Np \geq 5$, where p refers to the smaller of the two binomial probabilities, the normal distribution provides a good approximation for the binomial. In this case, in place of p we have π, and $N\pi$ is much greater than 5. Furthermore, the sample proportion P being the mean $\overline{X}$ of a dichotomous variable having two values, 0 and 1, the hypothesized population proportion π is equivalent to μ. It follows that, in making an inference about π with a large sample, the normal approximation is actually a sampling distribution of means. The normal sampling distribution of means has the advantage of being easily specifiable. When standardized, its probabilities are completely tabulated and given in Table A in Appendix B.

The normal approximation of the binomial has an expected value or mean that equals the population mean,

$$\mu_P = \pi \tag{8.1}$$

and a standard error of

$$\sigma_P = \sqrt{\frac{\pi(1 - \pi)}{N}} \tag{8.2}$$

Formula 8.2 follows from the fact that, because the variance of the sample proportions s^2 is equal to PQ (Chapter 3), that of the population σ^2 equals $[\pi(1 - \pi)]$. Since the standard error of the sampling distribution of means is $\sigma/\sqrt{N}$, substituting $\sqrt{\pi(1 - \pi)}$ for σ, Formula 8.2 is obtained. Now, obviously, the sample variance, s^2 of PQ, can also be used to estimate the standard error. Frequently, however, statisticians use the π value, because when H_0 is true then $[\pi(1 - \pi)]$ is the true variance, whereas PQ is merely an estimate. On the other hand, when H_0 is untrue, the sample estimate probably provides the better estimate.

8.5.2 Calculating the Test Statistic

With the sampling distribution specified, Anne computes the proportion of convictions in the sample. It equals .38 for the 96 cases. To determine how likely it is to obtain a P of .38 when π equals .50, Anne must standardize P first. Then she could use Table A to find its probability. The z score that corresponds to a P of .38 is

$$z = \frac{\overline{X} - \mu_{\overline{X}}}{\sigma/\sqrt{N}} = \frac{P - \pi}{\sqrt{\pi(1 - \pi)/N}} = \frac{.38 - .50}{\sqrt{(.50)(.50)/96}} = -2.352$$

8.5.3 Locating the Sample Outcome within the H_0 Sampling Distribution

Anne now compares the sample outcome with the outcome expected under the null hypothesis. The z score of -2.35 signifies that the sample mean is *below* expectation or below the mean of the population distribution by 2.35 standard deviation units. By locating this sample outcome in the sampling distribution, Anne will be able to tell how likely or unlikely the departure is of 2.35 or more standard deviation units when H_0 is true and π equals .50.

If the sample statistic not only deviates from the population parameter hypothesized under H_0, but the extent of the deviation is highly unlikely, there are two possible interpretations of this unusual sample data:

1. The null hypothesis is true but the researcher has obtained a very unusual sample by chance.
2. The null hypothesis is untrue.

On the other hand, if there is no discrepancy or a small one between the sample outcome and the hypothesis, it means the sample outcome is highly probable under H_0. In this case, there are three possible interpretations of the result:

1. The null hypothesis is false, but the researcher has obtained an unusual sample.
2. The true parameter value in the alternative hypothesis is close enough to the false value in the null hypothesis to produce the small deviation between the sample outcome and H_0.
3. The null hypothesis is true.

To decide among the possible interpretations, the researcher resorts to a broad guideline. This guideline states that if the obtained sample outcome is highly unlikely, given a hypothesized population parameter, then random sampling variation (sampling error) may not account for the result. Therefore, when such an outcome is obtained, the researcher rejects the null hypothesis in favor of the alternative hypothesis. The interpretation is clear-cut in this case. On the other hand, when the statistic has a high probability of occurrence under H_0, the null hypothesis is not rejected. The interpretation is less clear-cut, and the researcher has the option of deferring judgment on the null hypothesis or concluding that it is true.

8.6 *Critical Value and the Region of Rejection*

In addition to the broad guideline discussed in Section 8.5, the researcher needs a *specific decision rule*. This rule dictates *exactly* how unlikely the departure from expectation must be, before she or he decides to reject the null hypothesis. The **critical value** (or critical values) is the value of a sample outcome that represents the utmost extent of departure tolerable in the testing. It partitions the sample space of possible outcomes into those for which the researcher decides to reject H_0 and those for which she or he decides not to reject H_0. The partitioning is best seen in a graph of the H_0 sampling distribution (Figure 8.2), in which a line is drawn perpendicular to the X axis representing the location of the critical value.

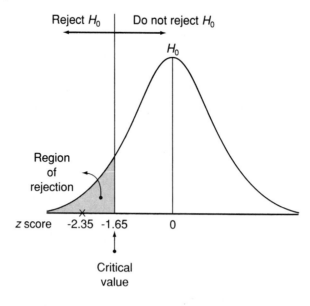

FIGURE 8.2   Critical Value and the Region of Rejection

Sample outcomes as great or greater than the critical value are represented by the shaded tail portion of the sampling distribution lying beyond the critical value. The relative size of this region represents the probability of obtaining such sample outcomes given that H_0 is true. When a sample outcome falls in this region, it departs from expectation (or the mean of the sampling distribution) more than is tolerable, and H_0 is rejected. Sample outcomes falling outside this region will not lead to a rejection of H_0. Hence, this tail portion of the sampling distribution is referred to as the **region of rejection.**

In choosing a critical value associated with a small region of rejection, the researcher maximizes the probability of rejecting H_0 correctly. Accordingly, Anne chooses a rejection region as small as .05. The rationale for selecting the value of .05 will be explained in Section 8.7.3. From Table A in Appendix B, the z score that partitions approximately .45 of the area between the mean and the score itself is −1.65. This then is also the critical value associated with a tail area of .05.

The reader may have a question at this point as to why Anne does not select outcomes that deviate 1.65 standard deviation units or more *above* expectation. Recall that the alternative hypothesis states that the proportion of convictions is less than .50. With a critical value of −1.65, Anne could focus on sample outcomes that could disconfirm H_0 while providing support for H_1 at the same time. If the sample outcome falls in the region of −1.65 or less, she has a basis for arguing that $\pi < .50$ rather than $\pi = .50$ is true.

8.7 Type I and Type II Errors

Since the obtained sample proportion standardizes to −2.35, it falls in the region of rejection. Anne decides to reject the null hypothesis in favor of the alternative hypothesis. She concludes that the proportion of convictions is lower for the middle class with a 5% chance of being wrong.

The sample outcome of −2.35 is marked by an × on the H_0 sampling distribution in Figure 8.2. An inspection of this figure shows that, regardless of how extreme the particular sample outcome may be (and the term "extreme" is used relative to what is expected under the null hypothesis), there is a possibility of its occurrence in the long run. *This means that the possibility of error always exists in rejecting a null hypothesis based on an unusual sample outcome.* At any one point, there is no way of telling whether the mistake has been made. However, in the long run, that is, with random samples of 96 drawn repeatedly, the mistake occurs no more than 5% of the time. The mistake is called a **Type I error,** and it occurs when the researcher rejects a null hypothesis that is true. In terms of Anne's project, a Type I error means deciding that π is not .50 when it is, in fact, .50.

On the other hand, when the researcher obtains a sample statistic that does not fall into the region of rejection, the specific decision rule dictates that the null hypothesis should not be rejected. Here, too, there is a possibility for making what is known as a **Type II error.** A Type II error results when the researcher does

TABLE 8.1 Four Possible Outcomes of a Statistical Test Based on Whether H_0 or H_1 Is True and the Researcher's Decision

	H_0 Is True	H_1 Is True
Reject H_0	Type I error	Correct decision
Do not reject H_0	Correct decision	Type II error

not reject a null hypothesis that is false. It happens if Anne decides that π is .50 when, in fact, it is less than .50.

Depending on whether the null or alternative hypothesis is true and what the researcher's decision is, there are four possible outcomes in hypothesis-testing, as represented in Table 8.1. In reality, of course, only one of the four outcomes applies once the decision is made. For this particular problem, when she decides to reject H_0, Anne runs the risk of making a Type I error.

8.7.1 Determining the Probability of Type I and Type II Errors

The probability of making a Type I error is symbolized by a. It is also variously labeled as the **significance** or a **level**. Being equivalent to the size of the rejection region in Figure 8.2, it is determined by the critical value. Although Anne is in no danger of making a Type II error for this problem, she would like to determine its probability also. The probability of making a Type II error is symbolized by b. *To obtain the exact probability for β, the researcher must derive the sampling distribution of H_1.* To derive the sampling distribution of H_1, Anne must have an exact hypothesized value in H_1. In Anne's H_1, however, the π value is indeterminate, and therefore the sampling distribution cannot be specified.

Suppose, however, that Anne finds a study that argues the true proportion of convictions for the middle class is .33. She could test this specific alternative hypothesis against the null hypothesis of .50. Using Formulas 8.1 and 8.2, she derives the sampling distribution of H_1, which has an expected mean value of .33 and a standard error of .048: $\sqrt{(.33)(.67)/96}$. Figure 8.3(a) graphs the sampling distribution of H_1 in relation to that of H_0. On this graph, a vertical line is again drawn on the sampling distribution of H_0 where the critical value is. This line both divides the H_0 curve into two areas and partitions the H_1 curve into two similar areas.

The area of the H_1 curve to the right of the critical value represents β, the probability of making a Type II error. An obtained sample statistic falling in this area will *not* lead to the rejection of H_0, even though it may belong to the sampling distribution of H_1. By not rejecting the null hypothesis when the sample could have come from the H_1 curve, the researcher runs the risk of making a Type II error. *Thus, whereas the probability of a Type I error is obtained from the sampling distribution of H_0, the probability of a Type II error is calculated from the sampling distribution of H_1.* Again, with any particular decision to retain H_0, we do not know whether an error is made. In the long run, however, its probability equals β.

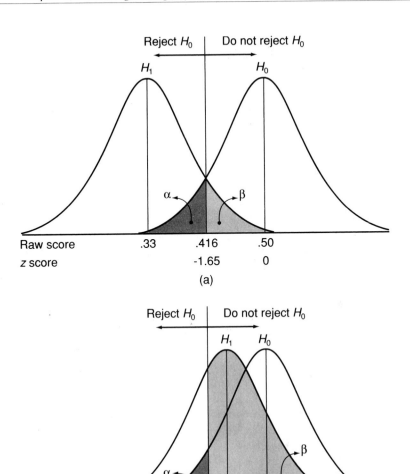

FIGURE 8.3   Type I and II Errors Graphed onto H_0 and H_1 Sampling Distributions with Standardized and Unstandardized Parameter Values

Hypothesis testing, then, is equivalent to deciding from which curve, H_0 or H_1, the obtained sample point could have come. Any sample point, however, could have come from either sampling distribution because of the overlap between the curves. The question is which is more probable, given one or the other sampling distribution. Thus, although the decision is expressed mainly in terms of the null hypothesis, the situation is more accurately described as one involving a choice between the null and the alternative hypothesis.

Now that Anne has the H_1 sampling distribution, she can calculate β. She first changes the critical value of -1.65 to its corresponding raw score in the H_0 sampling distribution, as follows:

$$-1.65 = \frac{P - .50}{\sqrt{(.50)(.50)/96}} \quad \frac{P - .50}{.051}, \qquad P = .416$$

Then she transforms the raw score of .416 into a standardized score in the H_1 sampling distribution:

$$z = \frac{.416 - .33}{.048} = 1.792$$

From Table A in Appendix B, the tail portion of the curve associated with a z of 1.79 is .0367: (.5 − .4633). The probability of making a Type II error is .0367.

In addition to the probabilities of the two types of error, the probability of making a correct decision when either H_0 or H_1 is true can also be determined. If the probability of a Type I error is α, the probability of not rejecting H_0 when it is true is $(1 - \alpha)$, since the probability of either making or not making a correct decision with respect to H_0 is 1. On the graph in Figure 8.3(a), $(1 - \alpha)$ is represented by the area of the H_0 curve lying to the right of the critical value. Similarly, if the probability of a Type II error is β, the probability of deciding in favor of H_1 when it is true is $(1 - \beta)$. This probability is represented by the area of the H_1 curve lying to the left of the critical value. For Anne's problem, $(1 - \alpha)$ equals .95 and $(1 - \beta)$ equals .9633. The four possible outcomes of Anne's hypothesis testing with their respective probabilities and symbols are given in Table 8.2.

In Figure 8.3(b) a hypothetical H_1 sampling distribution is drawn at $\pi = .45$, while the H_0 sampling distribution remains centered at .50. Although the critical value of -1.65 has not been changed, the β area from H_1 is much larger compared to that of Figure 8.3(a). This shows that when the hypothesized parameter in H_1 is closer to that of H_0, .45 as opposed to .33, the probability of making a Type II error is higher, with the Type I error held constant. It also explains why an exact alternative hypothesis is crucial to the calculation of β. The probability of a Type II error changes with the location of the H_1 sampling distribution. The location, however, cannot be determined unless it is given in the alternative hypothesis.

TABLE 8.2 Probabilities of the Four Possible Outcomes Associated with a Critical Value of −1.65

	H_0 Is True	H_1 Is True
Reject H_0	.05 (α)	.9633 $(1 - \beta)$
Do not reject H_0	.95 $(1 - \alpha)$	.0367 (β)

8.7.2 Inverse Relation between Type I and Type II Errors

Now suppose that Anne changes her decision rule to decrease the probability of a Type I error to .01. What is the probability of making a Type II error? Again from Table A, the z score associated with this rejection region of .01 is −2.33. The critical value of −2.33 is transformed into its corresponding raw score of .381 in the H_0 sampling distribution as follows:

$$-2.33 = \frac{P - .50}{.051}, \qquad P = .381$$

Then the raw score of .381 is transformed into a standardized score on the H_1 distribution as follows:

$$z = \frac{.381 - .33}{.048} = 1.063$$

The tail portion of the curve associated with a z of 1.06 is .1446: (.5 − .3554). The probability of making a Type II error increases, from .0367 to .1446, now that the probability of making a Type I error is smaller. Figure 8.4(a) and (b) shows the change of the α level from .05 to .01. These figures confirm the increase of the area in the H_1 curve lying to the right of the critical value. Thus the probability of a Type I error is inversely related to the probability of a Type II error: the smaller the α, the larger the β.

8.7.3 Choosing a Significance or Alpha Level

We can now return to the problem of choosing a critical value after fully considering the nature of Type I and Type II errors. Since Type I and Type II errors are inversely related, finding a critical value that decreases the probability of both types of errors is not possible. The researcher should decide which is the more serious error of the two, based on the consequence of making one versus the other type of error. Then she or he should balance the size of the rejection region against the probability of making a Type II error.

Unfortunately, in the social sciences a researcher can seldom assign a value for an erroneous decision, especially when the decision involves no more than rejecting or accepting a hypothesis and therefore the theory from which it is deduced. In addition, the probability of a Type II error may not even be calculable with a diffuse alternative hypothesis. Therefore, the social scientist frequently falls back on the convention of selecting a small Type I error to ensure that the null hypothesis is not rejected falsely.

Conventional levels of Type I errors are set at .05 or .01. With these α levels, the researcher would make a Type I error no more than 5 or 1 out of 100 times if

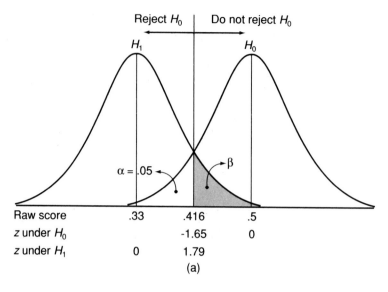

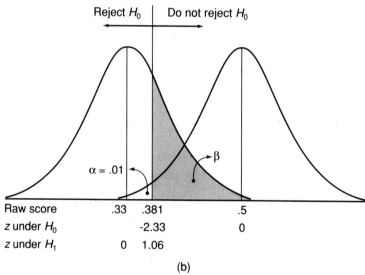

FIGURE 8.4   **Type I and II Errors Associated with Different Significance Levels**

the study is repeated over and over again. However, if a sampling distribution is discrete, such as the binomial, a selected significance level such as .05 or .01 may not convert to possible values of the sample statistic. This is certainly true for the binomials of Tables 7.1 and 7.2. In such cases, critical values are chosen directly, and their corresponding significance levels calculated accordingly.

Exercises

6. Suppose the true proportion of cheating during an unmonitored examination is not .4 but is larger: $\pi = .65$.
   a. Deduce the sampling distributions for both H_0 and H_1 for $N = 50$.
   b. Set the Type I error at .01. What is the associated critical value?
   c. What is the probability for a Type II error?

7. With reference to Exercise 6, discuss the pragmatic implications for minimizing the Type I or Type II error in the context of student disciplining.

8.8 Power of a Test

The value $(1 - \beta)$, which represents the probability of correctly rejecting H_0 when H_1 is true, has special significance. It is referred to as the **power of a test** to discriminate between the pair of H_0 and H_1 hypotheses. Clearly, the researcher wishes to maximize the power so as to reject H_0 when H_1 is true. An examination of the factors that affect the power of a test can help the researcher in this task. These factors are as follows:

1. *Choice of α:* In Figure 8.4(a), when α is .05, β is .0367, and the area corresponding to $(1 - \beta)$ in the H_1 sampling distribution equals .9633. In Figure 8.4(b), when α is .01, β is .1446, and $(1 - \beta)$ equals .8554. Thus, not only does a reduction in Type I error lead to an increase in Type II error, but it also results in a decrease in the power of the test.

2. *Choice of N, the size of the sample:* More specifically, the sample size affects the power by either increasing or decreasing the value of the standard error. The formula for the standard error, $\sqrt{\sigma^2/N}$, shows that, although σ^2 is not subject to manipulation, N is. By increasing N, a smaller value for the standard error is obtained. In reducing the dispersion of the sampling distributions of H_0 and H_1, their overlapping areas are minimized, although their means and locations remain constant. Compare the shaded areas of Figure 8.5(a) and (b), which represent the power of the test when $N = 96$ for (a) and $N = 192$ for (b). This illustrates that by increasing the sample size the researcher achieves a simultaneous decrease in Type I and II errors and an increase in the power of the test. It should be noted that the foregoing statement applies not only to a normal or a binomial, but to most sampling distributions. The researcher has a powerful weapon in the sample size.

3. *Value of the hypothesized parameter in H_0 versus that in H_1:* As shown in Figure 8.3, the closer the value of π in H_1 is to the value of π in H_0, the greater the β and the less the power of the test to detect the true hypothesis given the sample evidence.

Thus far, for a better understanding of Type I and II errors, we have used a specific alternative hypothesis for illustration. We now return to Anne's situation

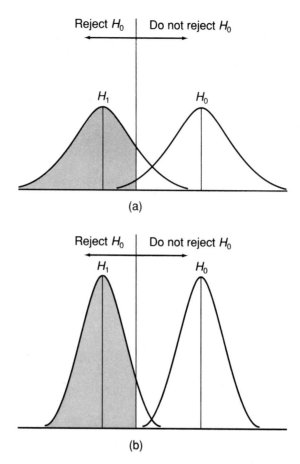

FIGURE 8.5   Power and the Sample Size

of having an H_1 whose value is diffusely specified, a testing situation typical of the social sciences:

$$H_0: \ \pi \ = \ .50$$
$$H_1: \ \pi \ > \ .50$$

In this case, the exact probability of a Type II error, β, cannot be found, because the location of the sampling distribution of H_1 is indeterminate. The latter could be centered anywhere between the range of .00 to, but exclusive of, .50. Since β cannot be determined, $(1 - \beta)$, the power of a statistical test, is also left unspecified with a diffuse H_1. Although the power is unknown, the factors that go toward maximizing it are still the same, and they should be considered in the testing.

Exercises

8. a. Compute different levels of power for testing an H_0 of $\pi = .45$ against an H_1 of $\pi = .65$ with N of 50.

   b. Discuss the relationship between the true value (π) and the power.

9. Compute the power of the test in Exercise 8 for an α of .01 when $N = 200$. Then decrease the sample size to 100 and recompute the power of the test. Discuss the relationship between the sample size and the power of a test.

8.9 One- and Two-tailed Tests

Whereas the significance level determines the critical value, and vice versa, the alternative hypothesis, H_1, dictates the *location* of the rejection region(s) in one or the other tail or in both tails of the sampling distribution of H_0. Consider the following pairs of hypotheses:

$$\text{Pair 1} \quad H_0: \pi = .50$$
$$H_1: \pi > .50$$
$$\text{Pair 2} \quad H_0: \pi = .50$$
$$H_1: \pi < .50$$
$$\text{Pair 3} \quad H_0: \pi = .50$$
$$H_1: \pi \neq .50$$

The null hypothesis remains the same in all three pairs, while the alternative hypotheses differ. The alternative hypotheses of the first two pairs specify direction, but not an exact parameter value, while the third alternative hypothesis is both diffuse and nondirectional. Suppose the researcher has selected an α level of .05 for testing all three pairs of hypotheses. With the first pair, H_1 dictates the location of the rejection region to be in the upper 5% of the tail with a critical value of 1.65, as shown in Figure 8.6(a). With the second pair, the region of rejection is located in the opposite tail, where the critical value is −1.65, as shown in Figure 8.6(b). For both tests, *a critical value* marks the beginning of the region of rejection on a tail, the area of which equals .05. The third pair requires that the value be split in two and located in both tails of the H_0 sampling distribution. There are *two critical values*, +1.96 and −1.96, marking two regions of rejection, each having an area of .025 (.05/2), as in Figure 8.6(c). Consequently, the first two pairs of hypotheses are said to require a **one-tailed test,** whereas the third pair dictates a **two-tailed test.**

Whether a hypothesis is directional or nondirectional depends on the theory from which the hypothesis is deduced and/or on the knowledge of the researcher. If the theory is highly articulated, it may specify a directional test; if it is still in the formative stage, a two-tailed test may be more appropriate. The same applies for the researcher who, having more information on the subject, usually

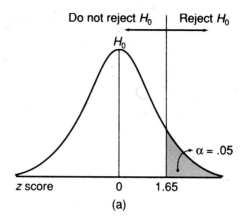

(a)

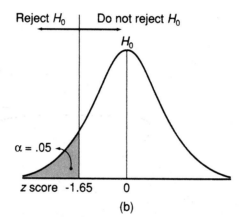

(b)

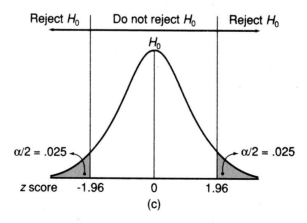

(c)

FIGURE 8.6   One- and Two-tailed Tests

calls for a one-tailed test. One-tailed tests have the advantage of being more powerful than two-tailed tests when the direction of the H_1 is as anticipated.

8.10 Decision Rule for Hypothesis Testing

The decision rule in hypothesis testing can now be articulated in full:

1. In the absence of reasons for deciding otherwise, choose a small α or significance level such as .01 or .05.
2. In conjunction with H_1, demarcate the region of rejection on either one or both tails of the sampling distribution of H_0, and determine the critical value or values associated with such a region or regions of rejection.
3. Locate the sample outcome in the sampling distribution of H_0 and make a decision to reject or not to reject H_0, contingent on where the sample outcome falls in relation to the critical value(s) and the region(s) of rejection.

The result of the statistical test is then couched in terms of rejection or nonrejection of the null hypothesis at a particular significance level. When the null hypothesis is rejected, the sample statistic is said to be **statistically significant** at the predetermined level of .05 or .01. This means that if the study is replicated a great many times the researcher would falsely reject the null hypothesis 5% or 1% of the time. When the researcher fails to reject the null hypothesis, the statistic is said to be not significant at these levels.

As part of the testing, Anne now reviews the assumptions in the *test model* of the binomial to ensure that she has not violated any. Recall that these assumptions do not have the same logical status as the hypotheses; the former are accepted as true so that inferential procedures can be carried out. These assumptions pertain to the sampling procedure: that each case is selected independently and randomly. In addition, another assumption is made that the normal sampling distribution of means can be substituted for the binomial distribution.

Finally, Anne reflects on the implications of the test results for the proposition and therefore the labeling theory. Although the null hypothesis is rejected, the sample outcome is not far from the critical value at the .01 level of significance. Also, Anne is not altogether certain of the validity of measuring power in terms of middle-class status. Consequently, Anne decides to carry out more testing, in other situations and with other operational definitions of power, before lending her support to the selected proposition.

Had Anne chosen the critical value of –3.09 with a significance level of .001, she could not have rejected the null hypothesis. This highlights again the probabilistic nature of any statistical testing and explains Anne's reluctance to support the proposition before more testing. The final decision concerning H_0 cannot be dichotomized as either being correct or incorrect. Instead, the decision is made with a certain level of risk, that of its being incorrect 1 out of 100 times or 1 out of

1,000 times. Therefore, in evaluating statistical inference, the reader should observe not only the substance of the conclusion but, more importantly, its significance level or degree of certainty.

Summary

One-sample Test for a Proportion

Large sample: z test
Null hypothesis: $\pi = a$

$$z = \frac{P - \pi}{\sqrt{\pi(1 - \pi) / N}}$$

Test model:

1. Random selection of sample cases
2. Dichotomous variable
3. $N \geq 20$ and $N\pi \geq 5$, where $\pi \leq (1 - \pi)$
4. Normal approximation of the binomial

Exercises

10. According to the FBI's crime report, the proportion of crimes against the person is .1098 out of all crimes in the early 1990s. Anne suspects that her community is somewhat different in this respect from the national average, but is not sure of the direction of the difference. She takes a random sample of 75 crimes reported and finds that 14 are crimes against the person. Does she have a basis for concluding that her community is different from the national average?

11. A criminologist who is critical of the FBI's report claims that the true proportion of crimes against the person is .15. Compute the power of the test in Exercise 10 against this alternative hypothesis.

12. The proportion of whites among state prison inmates is reported to be .49. If the percentage is in fact representative of the prison population at large, what is the probability that in a sample of 120 prisoners the sample proportion of whites will exceed 55%?

8.11 One-sample z Test of a Mean

The preceding sections of the chapter have detailed what is known as the **test of a proportion** involving one sample. This section presents another one-sample test called the *z* **test of a mean.**

Anne uses the z test to explore the proposition derived from the conflict perspective that the state is an instrument of the powerful that perpetuates existing inequality. Applying this proposition to the operations of the criminal justice system, Anne obtains the research hypothesis that minorities tend to serve longer sentences for the same type of crime. In this study, Anne operationally defines the powerful as those with dominant group status and the powerless as minority group members. A sample of 100 minority members who have been convicted of robbery is selected from county records. Their mean years behind bars is calculated to be 2.3 years and their variance is .38 year. Records show that the mean prison term for all convicted of robbery is 2.1 years with a variance of .32. Does the sample evidence support the research hypothesis?

To answer this question, Anne conducts a z test of means involving the following steps:

Step 1: Formulate a Pair of Hypotheses

Assuming that the prison terms of minorities are of the same length as others convicted of robbery, then

$$H_0: \ \mu = 2.1$$

However, if the minorities serve longer sentences, then

$$H_1: \ \mu > 2.1$$

Step 2: Derive the Sampling Distributions

Since the sample outcome is summarized by $\overline{X}$, Anne must derive a sampling distribution of means. Her sample consists of 100 cases, which is large enough for her to assume that the sampling distribution is approximately normal. Also, from the hypothesized value of μ in H_0, that of σ^2 in the test model, and the sample size, the summary characteristics of the sampling distribution can be determined using the central limit theorem. The mean of this normal approximation is identical to that of the population:

$$\mu_{\overline{X}} = \mu = 2.1$$

This indicates that a sample drawn from the population specified under H_0 is expected to have a mean value of 2.1. Because of the existence of sampling errors, however, the sample mean may depart from expectation. The variance of the sampling distribution gives an index of the expected squared departure, while its square root yields the standard deviation or standard error of the sampling distribution. In this case, the variance equals σ^2/N or .0032 (.32/100) and the standard error, .0565.

The location of the sampling distribution under the alternative hypothesis cannot be determined because H_1 is diffuse. However, testing can proceed without specifying this sampling distribution.

Step 3: Select a Significance Level and Critical Value(s)

Because Anne does not have a guideline to help her evaluate the seriousness of a Type I versus a Type II error, she adopts the conventional .01 significance level. To locate the region(s) of rejection on the appropriate tail(s), Anne examines the alternative hypothesis. According to this hypothesis, a one-tailed test is called for, with the region of rejection located on the upper tail of the H_0 sampling distribution. From Table A, she finds the standard z score that partitions 1% of the tail end of the sampling distribution. It equals 2.33.

   Two points should be noted. It is simple to derive the sampling distribution of H_0 when the central limit theorem is applicable and the normal distribution can be used as an approximation. With the normal distribution the critical values are expressed as z scores.

Step 4: Compute the Sample Statistic and Compare the Result to the Critical Value to Reach a Decision

The obtained sample mean is an unstandardized 2.3 years. The critical value of 2.33, however, is a standardized score. Before the sample mean can be compared to the critical value, it must be standardized:

$$z = \frac{\overline{X} - \mu}{\sigma/\sqrt{N}} = \frac{2.3 - 2.1}{.0565} = 3.539$$

A comparison of 3.54 to the critical value of 2.33 shows that the sample mean lies beyond the critical value in the region of rejection. See Figure 8.7.

   Anne rejects H_0 at the .01 level to conclude that minorities probably serve longer sentences for the same crime. In reaching this conclusion, Anne runs the

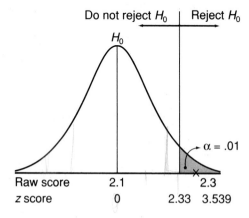

**FIGURE 8.7   One-tailed Test of
a Mean**

risk of making a Type I error 1% of the time. The result of this test reinforces the conclusion reached through the last test. Using different measures of the concept "the powerful," these tests have provided convergent evidence that the less powerful are more likely to be penalized by the criminal justice system.

Summary

> ### One-sample *z* Test for a Mean
>
> Null hypothesis: $\mu = a$
>
> $$z = \frac{\overline{X} - \mu}{\sigma/\sqrt{N}}$$
>
> Test model:
>
> 1. Random sampling
> 2. Interval scale measurement
> 3. Normal population or large N
> 4. Known σ^2

Exercises

13. A researcher who does not support the conflict perspective is sure that minority members have an average sentence length different from but not necessarily higher than the overall average. State the appropriate hypotheses and perform a two-tailed test based on the data in Section 8.11.

do for 3/25

14. The mass media in Anne's state speculate that a new governor will approve an overall law enforcement budget cut of approximately $15 out of every $100. The budget cut is not distributed evenly across counties and budgetary items. The variance is estimated to be $5.5. Taking a random sample of 100 budgetary categories in her county, Anne finds that the average budget reduction is $16 per $100. Is there a significant difference in the budget cut in her county as compared to the statewide average at the .05 level?

15. If an alternative hypothesis proposed by another researcher, of a reduction of $15.5, is in fact true in Exercise 14, what is the probability of a Type II error? What is the power of the test?

16. If the researcher wants to raise the power of the test to .60 in Exercise 15, what probability of a Type I error must be tolerated?

8.12 *Parametric versus Nonparametric Tests*

Before proceeding to Chapter 9, one final distinction should be noted between two different *classes* of tests. It was pointed out in Chapter 7 that to specify a sampling distribution for statistical inference, some assumptions must be made about the population distribution. In hypothesis testing, whether an assumption is made with regard to the *form* of the population distribution gives rise to two broad classes of statistical tests: parametric and nonparametric. **Parametric tests** require, in addition to other conditions in their test model, the assumption that the population distribution has some known form. In this text, the known form refers mostly to a normal distribution. There may be additional requirements for specific parametric procedures, but it is from the assumption made concerning the form of the population distribution that the tests derive their name. For instance, the z test of a mean is a parametric test since it requires that the population distribution be normal or, in cases where this assumption is in doubt, that a large sample be taken.

Nonparametric tests, on the other hand, do not require the assumption of normality or any other form in the population distribution. Nonparametric tests are *distribution-free,* in the sense that their sampling distributions can be specified independently of the nature of the population. In addition, they require a less *stringent* set of conditions for their use. For example, although their models include random sampling, interval measurement is not necessary. Some nonparametric procedures require that the variable tested be continuous in nature, which means they can be applied to ordinal data. Others are constructed specifically for nominal data.

The choice of a parametric versus a nonparametric test revolves around the following factors:

1. *Assumption of normality and/or other applicable characteristics of the population:* If the researcher does not want to make assumptions concerning the form of the population distribution, nonparametric tests are appropriate.

2. *Level of data measurement:* The requirement of interval-level measurement, which goes hand in hand with parametric tests, may be untenable for a great deal of social data. Rather than making an assumption about the level of data measurement, the researcher may prefer to use a nonparametric test.

3. *Power of the test:* Although nonparametric tests require less stringent assumptions, parametric tests are more powerful. However, the power of a test can be increased with a larger sample size, provided that all the assumptions in the test model are met. In fact, sample size is used as a standard to formalize the comparison between the power of two different tests. The term **power efficiency** refers to the power of one test relative to another, expressed in terms of sample size. If a test, A, is said to be 95% as efficient as another, B, it simply means that for A and B to attain the same power A will have to use 100 cases for every 95 cases in B. Therefore, the lower power efficiency of nonparametric tests can be surmounted with the use of larger samples. Often the power efficiency of a nonparametric test is only slightly lower than that of the corresponding parametric test, while the former test may not require the assumptions necessary for many of the latter tests.

In the following chapters, whenever nonparametric tests are introduced, they will be noted as such. Unless otherwise indicated, the procedures are parametric.

8.13 Test Models

Finally, let us turn our attention again to the test model of a statistical procedure. We can fully detail what elements comprise the model now that we have made the distinction between parametric versus nonparametric tests. The test model contains assumptions upon which the statistical test is based. In addition, it has requirements that must be met or are assumed to have been met. A test model then usually involves the following requirements and assumptions:

1. *Level of data measurement:* As with descriptive statistics, each inferential procedure requires a certain level of information in the data. Sometimes, however, a procedure may require a continuous variable, rather than a particular level of measurement.
2. *Characteristics of the population distribution:* For many tests discussed in this text, the population distribution is assumed to be normally distributed.
3. *Sampling procedure:* The tests usually require a random sample or the assumption of one.
4. *Sample size:* Many tests, such as those that rely on the application of the central limit theorem, require a certain minimum sample size.

It is important to keep in mind a particular test model and to attempt to meet all its conditions in the process of testing. Otherwise, if these are violated, the validity of hypothesis testing and the test results become questionable.

General Conceptual Problems

1. What makes statistical inference a scientific endeavor? What distinguishes it from mere guessing?

2. Compare the assumptions that are generally required for parametric and nonparametric tests.

3. What are the functions of a theory?

4. Discuss the relationship between theory and research.

5. Discuss the relationship between Type I and Type II errors.

6. Why would a researcher try to reject the null hypothesis instead of trying to confirm a research hypothesis directly?

7. What effects does the increase in sample size have on Type I and II errors and the power of a test?

8. Compare the logic behind the hypothetico-deductive method and statistical inference. In what respects are they similar or dissimilar?

9. What is the relationship between the alternative hypothesis and the region of rejection?

10. If sample size remains fixed, what happens to Type II error when the probability of Type I error is increased?

11. Explain in your own words the concept of the power of a test.

References

1. Bacon, F. (1863). *The Works of Francis Bacon: Novum Organum,* Vol. 8. Translated by James Spidding et al. Cambridge, England: Riverside Press.

2. Popper, K. R. (1963). *Conjectures and Refutations: The Growth of Scientific Knowledge.* New York: Harper & Row.

3. Reynolds, P. D. (1971). *A Primer in Theory Construction.* Indianapolis, Ind.: Bobbs-Merrill.

4. Salmon, W. (1963). *Logic.* Englewood Cliffs, N.J.: Prentice Hall.

$$C \; h \; a \; p \; t \; e \; r \quad 9$$

More One-sample Tests

New Statistical Topics

One-sample t test

Goodness-of-fit χ^2 test

One-sample test of a variance

Kolmogorov–Smirnov test

9.1 Overview

The logic and procedure of statistical inference, discussed in Chapter 8, will further be applied to one-sample problems in this chapter. One-sample procedures are easily understood and clearly illustrate the principles underlying statistical inference. However, they are not as widely used in the social sciences as procedures involving more than one sample. To conduct a parametric one-sample test, an exact parameter value must be specified in the null hypothesis. Similarly, in nonparametric procedures, a theoretical model of the distribution must be clearly delineated with an appropriate rationale for testing. Exact values or models are difficult to arrive at unless they can be derived from a theory or gathered from past research. Therefore, although they provide a good illustration of the fundamental concepts involved in statistical inference, one-sample tests have less practical utility than the tests discussed in later chapters.

9.1.1 Social Applications

Inferential techniques are employed partially to assist the researcher in developing theories. However, in the social sciences, in place of highly formalized theories, various loosely structured theoretical perspectives are often developed. These perspectives have essentially the same functions as theories in explaining the social world and in sensitizing the social scientist to possible research areas. As a result, they are referred to as theories as well as perspectives. In sociology, for example, three theoretical perspectives give a very different understanding of society, its structure, its maintenance and operation, and its changes through time. These perspectives were first introduced and discussed in Chapter 1.

The functionalist views society as a set of interlocking social systems. A social system, such as a family or the economy, is a network of relations among people or cultural elements organized to meet societal needs and goals. How these systems maintain and adapt themselves becomes a central part of the functionalist's analysis. The operations that contribute to the society's maintenance are referred to as *functions*. Those that interfere with the stability of society are called *dysfunctions*. Complicated and intricate in their operations, most social systems have both functional and dysfunctional aspects.

From the conflict perspective, societies are built on the inequities in the distribution of scarce resources such as wealth and power. Most social arrangements benefit some groups over all others, producing, as a result, conflict among these groups. In examining social processes, the conflict theorist focuses primarily on their potential for generating conflict and the changes brought about through conflict resolution.

While the functionalist and conflict theorist take a holistic view of society, the symbolic interactionist explores society from the perspective of its participants. From this angle, the world "out there" has meaning insofar as it is experienced and interpreted through our daily interaction with others. We interact using symbols; through these symbols, our expectations, shared rules of behavior, and values are conveyed. In this sense, society is continually reaffirmed or changed through our symbolic interactions.

Anne intends to apply all three perspectives to a study of the U.S. political institution in this chapter. Institutions are relatively permanent social systems that exercise great influence over members of a society throughout their lives. The political institution, in particular, defines how power is distributed and used in a society. In viewing this institution through the three perspectives, Anne hopes to derive various research questions that can be resolved through hypothesis testing.

9.1.2 Statistical Topics

Indispensable to the process of hypothesis testing is the sampling distribution of a statistic. The sampling distribution enables the researcher to identify and measure random sampling errors in reaching a conclusion about the hypothesized population. Therefore, as various new inferential procedures are presented, the reader should pay special attention to the sampling distributions involved.

Two new sampling distributions, the *t* and the chi square, will be introduced in this chapter. The *t*, like the normal distribution, is used for making inferences about the mean of a population. It was first formulated by Gosset under the pseudonym of Student. Gosset, employed in a brewery at the turn of the century, was forced to use small samples in his work on the brewing process. He soon discovered that available statistical techniques did not apply as well to small as to large samples. For samples of 10 or less, it makes a great deal of difference whether the sample standard deviation, s, is divided by N or $(N - 1)$. If the denominator of $(N - 1)$ is used, the sampling distribution of means does not have a normal form for small N's. From his research, Gosset articulated the mathematical rule that describes a new probability distribution, the Student's t. The t distribution is especially appropriate when sample sizes are small and the central limit theorem is not applicable.

Although most social scientists discuss inference in terms of central tendency, the description and comparison of the variability of distributions are important as well. In studying variances, the chi-square distribution applies. Like the normal distribution, the chi-square distribution provides a good approximation to many other sampling distributions that are not easily specifiable. In this and other chapters, we will see the chi-square distribution employed in parametric as well as nonparametric procedures. From the chi square, it is a simple step to develop a sampling distribution that involves a comparison of variances, the F distribution. This distribution will be discussed at length in Chapter 12.

Together with the normal distribution, the t, chi-square, and F distributions form the core of the sampling distributions needed for many parametric and nonparametric procedures. Two of them, the z and t, are useful for inferences concerning central tendency, while the other two, the chi square and the F, pertain to analyses of variability. Interestingly, these sampling distributions are all related to one another. In addition, the t, chi-square, and F distributions all require the population from which the sample is drawn to be normal. Thus the normal distribution is important not only because it provides a good approximation to other distributions when N is large, but because it has properties important for the derivation of certain other sampling distributions as well.

9.2 One-sample Test for Interval Data: The t Test

Research Question

The conflict theorist views the state as an instrument of the powerful used to maintain existing social inequality. As an example of how the federal government favors those with above-average income in this country, Anne notes a study conducted by a Wall Street firm and published in the *Washington Post*. According to this article, families with annual incomes of $47,900 or more would benefit by $9.2 billion, whereas families with incomes of less than $47,900 would lose by $8 billion from the 1981 and 1982 tax and budget cuts [1].

Anne wonders whether state governments operate similarly. A number of states in the 1990s face a budget deficit produced by the combined effects of earlier overspending, a recession, and a gradual reduction of federal money. Anne compiles a sampling frame of all states with budgetary problems and randomly selects one to examine how the state government seeks to deal with the crisis. At whose expense would the state propose to balance its budget?

The Data

The proposed budget of the selected state includes items that range from welfare cuts to a tax increase imposed on the well-to-do. Anne decides to focus on the effects of the tax increase only. This increase was to come from, among other sources, a general sales tax and the raising of the marginal tax rate for individuals with incomes of over $200,000. Published sources estimate the tax hikes to cost families of four an average of $164 per year. Through further investigation, Anne recalculates the average as a percentage of the annual family income. She finds that, on the average, a family of four would pay an additional 52 cents per every $100 earned on the tax increase.

From the data banks of the Research Institute, Anne finds a recent survey of the same state conducted by a marketing firm, whose primary interest was to determine consumer habits and patterns. The data base, however, also contains information on the respondents' income. With this information available, Anne further samples within the respondents to obtain 47 families of four with incomes of $25,000 or less a year. The effect of the proposed tax increase for this group is computed to be a mean increase of 54 cents per every $100 earned with a variance of 21 cents.

Anne calculates the tax increase in the form of an increase per $100, rather than as an absolute amount, in order to ascertain whether the poorer families are paying relatively more. In comparing the mean increase per $100 for a *sample* of this group to the hypothesized mean increase for the overall state *population*, Anne finds the sample mean to be higher: 54 as compared to 52 cents. Should this discrepancy be attributed to random sampling error or should it be considered as evidence in support of Anne's research hypothesis?

The Statistical Hypotheses

If the tax burden does not fall disproportionately on a particular group, the amount the group must pay per $100 would be the same as that of the population as a whole. Since the mean increase for the population is 52 cents, the mean increase for the population with income of $25,000 or below should also be the same:

$$H_0: \quad \mu = 52$$

where μ refers to the mean increase for the population with income of $25,000 or below. Observe that the hypothesis is always about some characteristic of the population and not of the sample.

Following the conflict perspective, Anne suspects that the effect of the whole tax package is regressive, placing more of a burden on the lower income groups. If this is true, the mean increase for the lower-income group would be greater than that for the population as a whole. Therefore,

$$H_1: \quad \mu > 52$$

The alternative hypothesis is directional as well as diffuse. It is formulated from Anne's research hypothesis.

An Appropriate Test

Anne is dealing with an interval variable, for which the mean is the best summary statistic. The z test of a mean is certainly an appropriate procedure for the purpose at hand, except that it requires knowledge of σ^2. Anne does not have this information. Indeed, it is unlikely that a researcher would know σ^2, but not μ. Anne may, of course, estimate σ^2 by s^2. However, the sample normally has less variation than the population. Therefore, the sample variance s^2 is a *biased* estimator, generally underestimating the value of its parameter. To correct for the bias, a compensation factor is included in s^2 when it is used to estimate σ^2. This estimator with the correction factor incorporated is symbolized by $\hat{\sigma}^2$ (read sigma hat squared) and is computed as follows:

$$\hat{\sigma}^2 = \frac{N}{N-1} \frac{\sum_{i=1}^{N}(X - \overline{X})^2}{N} = \frac{N}{N-1}(s)^2 \tag{9.1}$$

The symbol $\hat{\ }$ (hat) denotes, here as well as in other measures, the status of being an estimator.

With the use of the estimated variance $\hat{\sigma}^2$, rather than σ^2, the appropriate test is no longer the z but the one-sample t test of a mean. The t test employs a ratio, similar to that of z, to evaluate the discrepancy between the sample mean and the hypothesized parameter value. The standard error of this t ratio, however, is estimated, using $\hat{\sigma}^2$:

$$\hat{\sigma}_{\overline{X}} = \sqrt{\frac{\hat{\sigma}^2}{N}} = \sqrt{\frac{Ns^2}{N-1}\frac{1}{N}} = \frac{s}{\sqrt{N-1}}$$

The formula for this t ratio is

$$t = \frac{\overline{X} - \mu_{\overline{X}}}{\hat{\sigma}_{\overline{X}}} = \frac{\overline{X} - \mu}{s / \sqrt{N-1}} \tag{9.2}$$

The t ratio is called a **test statistic,** for although it is calculated from the sample mean and sample standard deviation, it does not correspond to any particular population characteristic. Based on sample statistics that contain sampling errors, the t test statistic itself changes in value when calculated from different samples drawn from the same population. Thus the t statistic has its own sampling distribution, which, when specified, can be used in testing.

9.2.1 The t Sampling Distribution

The *t* sampling distribution is very difficult to ascertain unless the two statistics used in computing the *t* ratio, $\overline{X}$ and *s*, are statistically independent of each other. However, even with random sampling, the standard deviation would not normally be independent of the sample mean since the former is calculated around the latter. Therefore, in addition to random sampling and interval measurement, the *t* procedure requires another assumption: the population distribution of the variable must be normal, a stipulation that is especially important when the sample size is small. Only with this added assumption can the sample mean and standard deviation be assumed to be independent and the *t* distribution derived. The assumption of a normal population is also required in other inferential procedures in which both the sample mean and the standard deviation are employed in the calculations. Because there are many of these procedures, the assumption is very commonplace.

The *t* distribution is described by a mathematical formula that is not reproduced here as it is inessential to the discussion. Like the standard normal distribution, the *t* is a unimodal and symmetrical, bell-shaped curve with a mean of 0. Unlike the *z*, which is a single, standardized distribution, the *t* is a family of distributions. While retaining the general bell shape, the individual *t* distributions may assume a more peaked or a flatter form, varying according to their **degrees of freedom**. See Box 9.1 for a detailed explanation of the concept of degree of freedom.

The degrees of freedom account for the shape of a *t* distribution because the variance of a *t* distribution is defined in terms of its degrees of freedom. For df > 2, where **df** stands for degrees of freedom, the variance equals df/(df – 2). Therefore, for every value of df, there is a slightly different *t* distribution with different dispersion. The degrees of freedom, in turn, depend on the sample size as pointed out in Box 9.1. For a one-sample test, df equals (*N* – 1).

Figure 9.1 depicts some *t* distributions within this family. In general, these distributions have more variation and are therefore flatter than the *z* distribution.

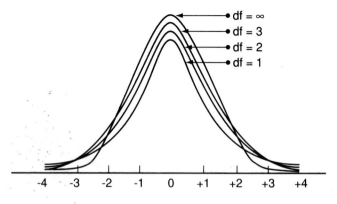

FIGURE 9.1   Family of *t* Distributions

BOX 9.1   Concept of Degrees of Freedom

The concept of degrees of freedom refers to the number of unknown elements in an equation that are allowed to assume different values without changing the relation expressed in the equation. To illustrate, suppose we have the following sum of the three unknown elements of X, Y, and Z such that

$$X + Y + Z = 100$$

Although the sum is predetermined to be 100, any value may be substituted for any two of the elements. That is, two elements are free to vary. However, once the substitution has taken place, the value of the third element is fixed since the three must sum to 100. In fact, the value of Z equals (100 − X − Y). Thus, given three elements that must sum to 100, the number of degrees of freedom is (3 − 1) or 2. This principle for determining the number of degrees of freedom can be generalized to N elements of an equation. The number of degrees of freedom is 1 less than N, the total number of unknown elements. The case can further be extended to a situation involving more than one equation linking unknown elements. In general, then, the number of degrees of freedom is equal to the number of unknown variables less the number of equations necessary to solve them.

In inferential statistics, the concept of degrees of freedom refers primarily to the number of independent comparisons necessary to estimate the variance of the population. When the concept is applied to a specific test, it is tailored to the requirements of the procedure. For example, in a one-sample t test, the number of degrees of freedom is derived from the formula of the sample variance that is used to estimate the population variance. In computing the deviations of the scores about the mean, the sum of the simple deviations is equal to 0, a restriction similar to the one imposed on the sum of the previous X, Y, and Z elements. Assume that the scores are unknown and are free to vary as long as their deviations from the mean sum to zero. With N scores, the number of scores that are free to vary, that is, the number of degrees of freedom for this equation, is (N − 1). Thus the concept of degrees of freedom, when applied to a one-sample test of a mean, assumes a value of (N − 1).

This characteristic can be gathered from the formula of the *t* ratio. As the standard deviation *s* changes from sample to sample with sampling error, the denominator of *t* also varies. The denominator of *z*, on the other hand, is constant, with fixed values of σ and N. Therefore, the same value of $\overline{X}$ in different samples will yield the same *z* score, but not necessarily the same *t* score because the latter vary by the values of *s* as well as $\overline{X}$ in different samples. It follows that there is more variation among the *t* than *z* scores.

More specifically, as the variance in *t* equals df/(df − 2) for df > 2, by substituting different df values into the formula, it can be seen that the smaller the value of df is, the larger the variance and the flatter the shape of the *t* curve. As df becomes very large, the variance approaches 1, and the *t* distribution approximates the standardized normal distribution, which has a variance of 1. When df is infinite, the *t* distribution converges to the standard normal distribution with a mean of 0 and a variance of 1. Thus *t* is related to *z* in two ways: the population distribution must be normal if the *t* distribution is to be used as a sampling distribution, and the *t* distribution itself approaches normality when df is large.

Reading the t Table

In performing a *t* test, we must know which *t* sampling distribution to use. This means knowing the df or the sample size, since df = *N* − 1. Table B in Appendix B gives various points of different *t* distributions. This table is arranged differently from the *z* table. A *t* distribution is represented by each df value in the table. Since df ranges from 1 to 30 and then equals 40, 60, 120, and infinity, the total number of distributions represented is 34: (30 + 4). With more distributions represented, the information given on each distribution is sketchy rather than relatively complete—only certain points of each distribution are displayed.

The information given per *t* distribution is displayed across a row of the table. At the intersection of a row with a column is a *t* score. To find the appropriate column after a row is selected, the researcher must not only choose a significance level, but must also determine whether a one- or two-tailed test is to be conducted. A double heading of α levels is given *per column* of *t* scores, with the top α value for a one-tailed and the second α value for a two-tailed test. Note that the α values for a two-tailed test are always double those of a one-tailed test. For example, under the column where .10 is listed for a one-tailed test, .20 is given for a two-tailed test. This stands to reason, for if .10 of the curve is partitioned on one tail for a region of rejection, a total of .20 would be included in both tails for the two regions of rejection. Consequently, the critical *t* value for a .10 α level of a one-tailed test is also the critical |*t*| value for a .20 α level of a two-tailed test.

To find the critical *t* value for a hypothetical example with *N* = 30, α = .01 in a one-tailed *t* test, first go down the row headings to find a df of 29. Then locate the column headings for a one-tailed test and within these headings find the value of .01. The intersection of the row where df = 29 with this column gives a *t* score of 2.462. If the alternative hypothesis indicates the less-than direction, the critical *t* value is −2.462.

Before leaving the *t* table, the last row of the table should be noted. This row represents a df of infinity. As the *t* distribution converges to the *z* distribution when df is infinite, this row essentially gives the critical values of the *z* test, too. In fact, the table is arranged in such a way that it is probably easier to find the critical values in this row for the *z* test than in Table A. For a simple illustration of the convergence of *t* to *z* scores, follow the column of *t* scores at an α level of .05 for a one-tailed test. Note how the *t* values go from 2.132 for df = 4 and 1.729 for df = 19 to 1.697 for df = 30 and 1.658 for df = 120, and finally to 1.645 when df equals infinity. As the number of degrees of freedom increases, the *t* scores approach the *z* scores in value. Because of this convergence, the *t* ratio can be treated as a *z* score for large *N*. *In fact, many texts use sample size to differentiate between the two types of tests: a large-sample z test and a small-sample t test.*

9.2.2 Calculating and Interpreting the Test Statistic

The particular *t* distribution that Anne needs for her problem has a df of 46 (47 − 1). She next selects a significance level so that the critical value and the region of rejection can be specified. This value should be chosen after carefully weighing the consequences of making either a Type I or Type II error. In this case, however, the seriousness of committing one or the other type of error is difficult to assess. Therefore, Anne chooses the conventional level of .01. This means that the region of rejection is to be no larger than 1% of the area under the sampling curve. In view of the alternative hypothesis, Anne determines this region to be located on the right tail of the sampling distribution. Because there is no row corresponding to a df of 46 in Table B, she uses the row with a df of 40 to obtain the critical value. Note how Anne uses the closest df that is *lower* than the actual df value when the latter is not available. This strategy produces a *conservative* estimate of the critical value, for it results in a larger critical value, which requires a more extreme deviation to reject the null hypothesis. For example, if Anne had used 60 rather than 40 df, she would have a critical *t* of 2.390 instead of a *t* of 2.423.

The selection of an α level and its corresponding critical value completes the specification of the decision rule. This rule states that, should the test statistic yield a *t* score of 2.423 or more, the null hypothesis is rejected in favor of the alternative hypothesis. Otherwise, Anne would defer judgment on or accept the null hypothesis.

Finally, Anne calculates the *t* score using Formula 9.2:

$$t = \frac{54 - 52}{\sqrt{21 / (47 - 1)}} = \frac{2}{.675} = 2.962$$

The Decision

The *t* score of 2.962 falls in the region of rejection beyond the critical value of 2.423. If the mean increase of the population with income of $25,000 or less is really the same as that of the general population, that is, if $\mu = 52$, it is extremely unlikely for Anne to obtain a sample mean increase of 54. The value of 54, however, is not unlikely and, in fact, may be highly likely if the alternative hypothesis ($\mu > 52$) is true. Figure 9.2 shows the probabilities of obtaining the value of 54 from two sampling distributions, one under H_0 and the other under

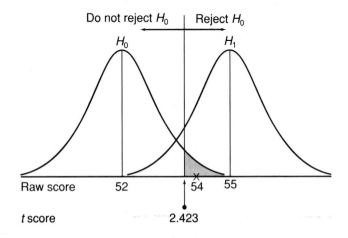

FIGURE 9.2   *t* **Distributions for Testing an H_0 of**
.52 against an H_1 of .55

H_1 for a specific μ value of 55 selected from the range of the diffuse alternative hypothesis. Since both H_1 and H_0 are hypothetical, the one that should be selected as true is the one that is most likely to give rise to a sample mean of 54. Anne therefore concludes that the tax increase in the state places a disproportionate burden on the less well-to-do.

Anne is aware that even with such a large discrepancy between obtained and expected results there is a possibility that she has made an error. That is, the null hypothesis may be correct, and the sample may simply be a very atypical one drawn from the population hypothesized under the null hypothesis. The probability for making such a Type I error is the same or less than the significance level of .01. This means that in replicating the study, when the H_0 is true, Anne would make a Type I error no more than 1 time out of 100 replications. Thus the significance level indicates the probability of obtaining an unlikely sample mean as well as that of making a Type I error.

On the other hand, if there is a serious violation of the test model, the probability of Type I error cannot be specified. Reviewing the t test model, Anne is certain that a random sample has been selected. Yet she is less certain about meeting the requirement of a normal population distribution. Fortunately, this constitutes the less serious of the two possible violations. The assumption of normality can be violated without jeopardizing the conclusion of the t test as long as the sample is sufficiently large. With a moderate sample size of 30 to 50, even relatively severe departures from normality can be tolerated. Thus the t test is said to be **robust** with respect to this requirement.

9.2.3 Large-sample t Test

The conflict perspective draws attention to the growing influence of special-interest groups as election politics become more and more expensive. Prospective candidates cannot hope to win unless they receive substantial contributions from their supporters. The Federal Election Campaign Act severely limits the amount of individual contributions. Special-interest groups, however, are allowed to form political action committees (PACs) that are exempt from the act. By contributing heavily to candidates who champion their causes, PACs often exert undue influence over election politics. Once elected, the politicians are beholden to these PACs whose money helped to elect them.

Anne suspects that the PACs' influence is equally pervasive in state and local election politics. A report on selected states that held elections for their legislative and other local governmental positions in 1990 finds that the candidates received on the average \$35,800 in PAC contributions. Conjecturing that the winners must have received more than the average amount, Anne takes a random sample of 125 winners from a candidate list and calculates the mean PAC contributions among them to be \$39,700, with a standard deviation of \$16,093.

Since Anne anticipates that winners receive more than the average candidate, she formulates the alternative hypothesis as

$$H_1: \quad \mu > 35,800$$

Therefore, the null hypothesis is

$$H_0: \quad \mu = 35{,}800$$

Again, Anne is dealing with an interval variable for which the mean is the best summary statistic. However, since the information on the population variance, σ^2, is not available, the t test is used in place of the z. The t sampling distribution that is appropriate for this test has 124 (125 − 1) degrees of freedom. Because the number of degrees of freedom is large, over 120, the t approximates the z distribution, and the critical value for a z test applies. For a one-tailed z test with an α of .01, the critical value is 2.33.

The t score is computed as

$$t = \frac{39{,}700 - 35{,}800}{16{,}093 \, / \, \sqrt{125 - 1}} = \frac{3{,}900}{1{,}445.262} = 2.698$$

The obtained t score of 2.70, which is larger than the critical value of 2.33, falls in the region of rejection. Anne therefore rejects the null hypothesis to conclude that winners of those elections received more PAC contributions than the average candidates.

This conclusion by no means establishes that there is a direct linkage between the initial campaign contributions of the PACs and the subsequent legislative decisions of these elected officials in the interests of the PACs. It does indicate, however, the potentiality of a linkage. Beyond the possibility of Type I error, Anne is concerned with the implications of her conclusion for the conflict theory. She does not wish to be overzealous in confirming the theory, while losing sight of the limitations of her data. Accordingly, she defers making a judgment on the conflict thesis until additional data are gathered.

9.2.4 Power of a t Test

In general, the same factors that affect the power of a z test apply to a t test. Thus, the power of a t test increases under the following conditions:

1. Sample sizes are larger.
2. The value of σ is small.
3. The true value of the parameter differs from that in the null hypothesis by a substantial amount.
4. A higher probability for Type I error is chosen.

Knowing these relevant factors, the researcher can attempt to increase the power of a t test anytime. We will not, however, discuss the actual calculation of the power of a t test, because it is difficult to do so without a more detailed t table than is given in Appendix B.

Summary

One-sample t Test for Interval Data

Null hypothesis: $\mu = a$

$$t = \frac{\overline{X} - \mu}{s / \sqrt{N - 1}} \qquad \text{with df of } (N - 1)$$

Test model:

1. Random sampling
2. Interval scale
3. Normal population

$H_0 \cdot M \neq \overline{X}$

Exercises

---

1. A random sample of 41 higher-income individuals was asked to estimate the amount of additional tax each must pay given a salary raise of $1,000 a year. The mean increase was calculated to be $182 and the standard deviation, $50. For the same year, the national average increase among all tax payers is reported to be $320.
   a. State H_0 and H_1 to test if the sample reflects the national average.
   b. Test the hypothesis at the .05 level.

2. A random sample of 100 subjects age 50 and above pays an average additional tax of $325 per $1,000 increase in income with a standard deviation of ($65) 65.
   a. Compare this sample to the national average increase in Exercise 1 and state H_0 and H_1.
   b. Test the hypothesis at the .01 level.

3. Increase the sample size in Exercise 2 to 150 and retest the hypothesis with this sample size. Discuss the relationship between the sample size and the significance level.

4. A researcher estimated the average number of hours college students contributed to a governor's election campaign to be no more than 10 a week. His random sample of 61 students averaged 11 hours a week with a standard deviation of 3 hours. Is the researcher's hypothesis confirmed?

5. The 1988 presidential election cost an estimated $400 million, about half of which was spent on TV commercials. From this figure, a researcher estimates that the candidates for state legislative positions also spent half of their PAC contributions of $27,900 for TV commercials. Since she is not sure whether winners spend more or less for TV, she decides to perform a two-tailed test. She finds that a sample of 130 winners reported to have spent an average of $28,400 with a standard deviation of $1000.
   a. State H_0 and H_1 for the study.
   b. Test the hypothesis at the .01 level.

6. Anne estimates the average number of hours college students spent watching the presidential election campaign coverage on TV to be 8 per week. Using a random sample of 150, she sets the critical value to be 9 hours for rejecting H_0, which would result in a Type I error of .01. What is the sample standard deviation?

9.3 One-sample Test for Interval Data: The Chi-square Test of a Variance

Research Question

In contrast to the conflict theorists, the pluralists contend that political power is diffused in this country among various competing interest groups. No one group dominates the political scene; instead, depending on the issue at hand, governmental decisions are influenced by such groups as farmer blocs, labor unions, environmentalists, and ethnic and religious groups. When an issue affects a number of these groups, they compete for the allegiance of the unorganized masses. By aligning themselves with these groups, the average citizens gain some political power.

The pluralists' view has gained much support from the more recent emergence of single-issue special-interest groups. These groups pursue a narrowly defined goal such as abortion, gun control, and the like, to the exclusion of all else, mobilizing their resources only when their interests are at stake. As a result, the public often becomes fragmented, lacking sufficient consensus to form an effective coalition capable of addressing the country's most pressing problems. If these single-issue groups have become more dominant recently, then, Anne reasons, on any particular election the turnout from different communities would vary depending on whose interest is being threatened. Is there more variability in voting turnout in recent elections?

The Data

Anne selects a state in which immigration and migration have not been a major factor and then obtains the official statistics of its voting turnout for a state election 20 years ago. From published precinct figures, she calculates the variance of voting turnout for the whole state, σ^2, to be 32.8%. The most recent election figures are harder to obtain. Therefore, instead of using data on all precincts, Anne takes a sample of 30 precincts whose voting statistics are available immediately and calculates their variance s^2 to be 49.1%.

An Appropriate Test and Its Assumptions

Both the z and t tests would be inappropriate, because Anne's interest does not center on the level so much as the variability of voting turnout. The variability of an interval variable is best summarized by the variance. Therefore, what Anne needs is a test of a single population variance. As will be explained in the section on sampling distribution, the χ^2 (chi square) provides the appropriate test statistic for testing a single variance. The χ^2 test statistic with $(N - 1)$ degrees of freedom is defined as

$$\chi^2_{(N-1)} = \frac{(N - 1)/\hat{\sigma}^2}{\sigma^2} \tag{9.3}$$

It is computed from the sample variance from which $\hat{\sigma}^2$ is obtained and the population variance hypothesized under the null hypothesis. To use the test, Anne must have a random sample of an interval variable whose population distribution is normal. Unlike the t test, which is robust with respect to the assumption of normality in the population, the chi-square test requires a large sample if the normality assumption is violated. Anne is reasonably sure that the normality assumption is tenable in this case; otherwise, she would run the risk of making an error in using the chi-square distribution when she has only a moderate sample size of 30.

The Statistical Hypotheses

If single-issue special-interest groups are not influential in recent politics, the variability in voting turnout would probably not be any different now than 20 years ago. Since the variability, measured in terms of the variance, equals 32.8% 20 years ago, the null hypothesis states that

$$H_0: \quad \sigma^2 = .328$$

where σ^2 represents variability in voting turnout for the most recent election.

If special-interest groups have been especially influential in recent years, there would be more variability:

$$H_1: \quad \sigma^2 > .328$$

9.3.1 Chi-square Sampling Distribution

The χ^2 is a family of distributions, all of which are described by the same mathematical rule, each of which differs according to its degrees of freedom. Like the t distribution, the exact shape of a particular chi-square distribution is determined by these degrees of freedom.

More specifically, the chi-square distribution of df = 1 is extremely skewed, because it is equivalent to distributing a squared standard score, z^2, from a normal distribution. When cases are sampled from a normal population distribution, approximately 68% of the sampled scores fall within one standard deviation of the mean. When standardized and squared, these scores lie between 0 and 1. Approximately 27% of the χ^2 scores lie between 1 and 4 because the square of a z score whose value is between −2 and −1 or +1 and +2 is between 1 and 4. Finally, approximately 5% of the scores are greater than 4 because the square of a z value greater than +2 or less than −2 exceeds 4 (Chapter 7). Thus χ^2 with df = 1 is a positively skewed distribution with only one tail.

A χ^2 distribution with df = 2 is equivalent to a distribution of the sum of two squared standardized scores from a normal distribution. The distribution is slightly less skewed since the probability is smaller that the sum of two squared z's will lie between 0 and 1. A χ^2 distribution with N degrees of freedom is simply a distribution of the sum of N squared standardized scores. Because we are always dealing with z's that are squared, the distribution must take on a range of positive values from 0 to infinity with no negative scores. Because the squared standard scores are summed, with increasing df, the proportion of z^2 scores assuming values of 0 and 1 decreases in the chi-square distribution. This means that when df is small the chi-square distribution is extremely positively skewed, but as df increases, the distributions become less and less skewed. When df reaches infinity (∞), the distribution converges to a normal distribution. Figure 9.3 shows the chi-square distributions for 1, 3, 5, and 8 degrees of freedom. See Box 9.2 for another implication of this additive property of chi squares.

The chi-square distribution is used for making inferences about the population variance because the estimated variance, $\hat{\sigma}^2$, is related to the χ^2 in the following manner:

$$\hat{\sigma}^2 = \frac{\chi^2_{(df)}\sigma^2}{df} \tag{9.4}$$

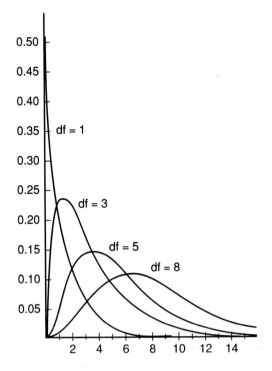

**FIGURE 9.3   Family of Chi-square
Distributions**

Box 9.2   Additivity of the Chi-square Distribution

Observe from our description of the chi-square distributions that a chi square with df = 2 is obtained by adding two chi squares with df = 1. Also, the *sum* of several independent chi-square variables is distributed as a chi square with the degrees of freedom equal to the sum of the degrees of freedom for the original distributions.

$$\chi^2_{(df_1 + df_2)} = \chi^2_{(df_1)} + \chi^2_{(df_2)}$$

This *additive* property of the chi-square distribution is very useful. For if independent chi-squares can be summed, their sum can also be partitioned. By partitioning the chi square into subsets, we can examine which segment of the data contributes most to the total chi square.

The sampling distribution of $\hat{\sigma}^2$ is a chi-square distribution multiplied by σ^2 and divided by its own degrees of freedom. Instead of specifying another sampling distribution of the estimated variance, a chi-square distribution can be used as long as an appropriate test statistic is derived from the relationship. For a one-sample test, in which 1 df is lost in estimating the variance, df equals $(N - 1)$. Therefore, substituting $(N - 1)$ for df and moving the terms to isolate the χ^2, the χ^2 test statistic in Formula 9.3 is derived from Formula 9.4.

Reading the Chi-square Table

Organized in very much the same manner as the *t* table, Table C in Appendix B is also a condensed one, displaying chi-square values for selected probabilities only. Each row with a different df represents a different chi-square distribution. The column headings give the various probabilities and areas partitioned above the χ^2 value listed within the table. To read this table, first select the appropriate row by identifying df. Then move to the appropriate column by choosing the probability corresponding to the α level, when testing the direction of "greater than." At the intersection of the appropriate row and column, the critical χ^2 value is given. Suppose in this problem that Anne wants to test the directional hypothesis of "greater than" at a .05 α level. With an N of 30, she finds the critical value by going to the row where df = 29 first and then moving across the row to the column where the probability level is listed at .05. The critical value given at this intersection is 42.557. Any obtained chi-square value that is greater than 42.557 will lead to a rejection of H_0.

The chi square, unlike the *t* distribution, is not symmetrical, nor does it have values below 0. Therefore, in testing a directional alternative hypothesis of "lower than," the reader must find the α level by finding the column that has the corresponding probability of $(1 - \alpha)$. Had Anne tested a directional hypothesis of "less than," she would be looking at the intersection of the row where df = 29 and the column where $p = .95$: $(1 - .05)$ for the critical value of 17.708. In this case, if the obtained value is *less than* 17.708, then H_0 would be rejected. A two-tailed test

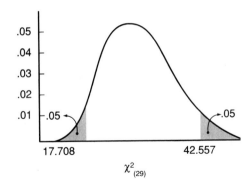

FIGURE 9.4 **Critical Values and Rejection Regions of the Chi-square Distribution**

at the α level of .10 (.05 on each tail) means that Anne would be considering a rejection of H_0 with values lower than 17.708 or higher than 42.557. See Figure 9.4.

9.3.2 Calculating and Interpreting the Test Statistic

With $N = 30$ and $s^2 = .491$, it follows that $\hat{\sigma}^2 = .508$: $(.491)(30)/29$ (Formula 9.1). The value of σ^2, .328, is given in the null hypothesis. Therefore, χ^2 is calculated as

$$\chi^2_{(N-1)} = \frac{(N-1)\,\hat{\sigma}^2}{\sigma^2} = \frac{29(.508)}{.328} = 44.915$$

Since the obtained value of 44.915 is greater than the critical value of 42.557, Anne rejects the null hypothesis at the .05 significance level to conclude that voting turnout is much more variable in the most recent election than 20 years ago. Special-interest groups may have contributed much to this variability. However, Anne is not altogether sure about the validity of the indicator she selected. Is there a more direct measurement of the operations of special-interest groups than variability in voting turnout? Note also that had Anne used an α level of .01 the critical value would have been 49.588 and she would *not* have been able to reject the null hypothesis. This highlights again the probabilistic nature of any statistical testing. For these various reasons, Anne is reluctant to conclude, without more evidence, that the pluralistic model gives a more accurate picture of the distribution of power in the United States than the conflict perspective.

Summary

One-sample Chi-square Test of Variance

Null hypothesis: $\sigma^2 = a$

$$\chi^2_{(N-1)} = \frac{(N-1)\hat{\sigma}^2}{\sigma^2} \qquad \text{with df of } (N-1)$$

Test model:

1. Random sampling
2. Interval scale
3. Normal population

Exercises

7. A presidential candidate claims that he has broad-based support by pointing to the average age of his supporters, which is the same as the national average. Based on the variance in age, Anne argues he is making a false claim. Is the variance in age of 45 supporters, which equals 8.2, significantly different from the variance of the nation, which equals 12.4 years? Does Anne have a point?

8. A researcher suspects that contemporary college students are more diverse in their political interests and activities than college students of the 1960s. A 1960s study reported the students to have a variance of 3.5 in the number of hours per week devoted to political causes, whereas a recent study with a random sample of 30 finds a variance of 4.2. Is the difference significant?

9. The variance in voting rate among college students is reported to be .50 at the national level. In Anne's state, political education was instituted to raise the political consciousness among college students. Anne expects that such an education will not only increase the voting rates across the colleges in her state, but will result in a smaller variance. Her random sample of 20 colleges indicates a variance of .44. Is she correct in her speculation?

10. A random sample of 10 yields $\Sigma X^2 = 125$ and $\Sigma X = 31$. Test the hypothesis $H_0: \sigma^2 = 2.0$ at the .02 level using a two-tailed test.

SPSS Note

Because one-sample testing is not frequently performed in the social sciences, there is no standard command for dealing with one-sample parametric tests in SPSS. The two-sample T-TEST command can be adapted for one-sample testing, but on the whole, it is simpler to calculate the t score for a one-sample test by hand.

9.4 One-sample Test for Ordinal Data: The Kolmogorov–Smirnov Goodness-of-Fit Test

Research Question

If political power is concentrated in the hands of an elite group, as the conflict theorist alleges, then the average citizen has little influence over the country's political agenda. There is some evidence to show that this may be the case even on the local level. For example, the Lynds found Muncie, Indiana, to be dominated politically, economically, and socially by a single family in the 1920s and 1930s [2]. Hunter documented that the 40 or so people who held political power in Atlanta, Georgia, in the 1960s also occupied the top positions in the city's economy [3].

The symbolic interactionist may consider objective data demonstrating the existence of an elite group on a national or local level as secondary. To them, the important question revolves around how people perceive their political position. Their subjective definition of a given situation would influence the way they behave. Do average citizens feel that they have the power over local government decisions?

The Data

Anne locates a national survey based on a random sample of U.S. residents. Among numerous other questions, the subjects were asked to respond to the following: "How much influence do you think you have over local government issues?" The respondents rated their influence on a five-point scale with 1 indicating no power at all and 5 indicating very much power. See Table 9.1.

An Appropriate Test and Its Assumptions

We have thus far concentrated on *parametric* tests, which are generally justified on the basis of certain assumptions made regarding the population distribution and parameters. With this project, however, Anne has an ordinal variable, whose population is unlikely to be normally distributed. Also, the z or t test of a mean is inappropriate, because the median rather than the mean should be used in characterizing ordinal data.

TABLE 9.1 Perception of Power Over Local Politics

	Response	Frequency	Proportion
Very much power . . .	5	6	.080
	4	16	.213
	3	20	.267
	2	22	.293
No power at all . . .	1	11	.147
	Total	75	1.000

Therefore, Anne resorts to a *nonparametric* technique. This type of procedure is used to test hypotheses involving the entire population distribution, rather than a single *narrowly defined* parameter. To say that a parametric test does not deal explicitly with an entire population, however, does not mean that it provides no conclusion with regard to the population (or populations). For if the obtained sample mean comes from a population with a mean different from the hypothesized population mean, then the population distributions cannot be the same.

Chapter 2 shows that, for an ordinal variable whose ranks are arranged in order, cumulative frequencies or proportions can be used to describe the distribution. The **Kolmogorov–Smirnov test,** or K–S test for short, is a nonparametric procedure that compares a sample cumulative distribution to a hypothesized population cumulative distribution. For this reason, the K–S test is known as a **goodness-of-fit test:** it compares the entire distribution of the sample to that of the population to measure the fit between the two. A significant lack of agreement between the two is taken as evidence that the sample did not come from the population specified in the null hypothesis.

More specifically, the K–S test employs the test statistic D to measure the largest absolute difference found between the sample and the population cumulative proportion. D is defined as

$$D = \text{maximum} \, |cp - C\pi| \tag{9.5}$$

where cp refers to the cumulative proportion in the sample and
$C\pi$ refers to the cumulative proportion expected under H_0

The K–S test model requires a variable that is continuous in nature, but permits the variable to be crudely scaled to yield only a few ordered categories. When the measurement is crude, many ties frequently result. Table 9.1 shows that there are 6 cases tied for the rank of 5, 16 cases tied for the rank of 4, and so on. As usual, the assumption of random sampling is required.

The Statistical Hypotheses

If, on the whole, respondents do not perceive they have either great or little power over local politics, Anne reasons that they would be just as likely to choose any of the five responses provided. She would have a *uniform population distribution* for which the frequencies of all five categories are equal: $F_1 = F_2 = F_3 = F_4 = F_5$, where F_i refers to the frequencies in the population. In addition, the cumulative proportion distribution of the population would be such that $C\pi_1 = .2$, $C\pi_2 = .4$, $C\pi_3 = .6$, $C\pi_4 = .8$, and $C\pi_5 = 1.0$. The D that measures the fit between the sample and the population cumulative distribution is expected to be 0 for a sample drawn from this population:

$$H_0: \quad D = 0$$

However, if the respondents lean toward one or the other direction, they would prefer some answers over others. The maximum absolute difference between the population and sample distributions would be significantly greater than 0:

$$H_1: \quad D > 0$$

Because D refers to the maximum *absolute* difference, the alternative hypothesis of $D > 0$ is equivalent to a two-tailed test. With it, Anne tests whether a difference exists between the sample and the population distribution, but not a particular direction of the difference.

The Sampling Distribution of **D**

Due to sampling fluctuations, the test statistic D will not ordinarily be 0, even if the sample comes from the population hypothesized under H_0. Instead there will be a sampling distribution of D when H_0 is true. In fact, the sampling distribution of D is a family of distributions, each dependent on the sample size. Table D in Appendix B, which is organized in a manner similar to that of Table B, gives the critical values of D for various levels of significance and different sample sizes. To read the table, first find the row with the appropriate sample size. Then select the appropriate column according to the desired α level. The value given at the intersection of the row and column is the critical D value. An obtained D that is greater than the critical value leads to a rejection of the null hypothesis at the specified α level. Table D provides critical values of D for sample sizes ranging from 1 to 35. For sample sizes over 35, the formulas to calculate the critical D values for various α levels are given in the bottom row of the table. Specifically, for an α of .05

$$\text{critical } D = \frac{1.36}{\sqrt{N}}$$

Therefore, with a sample of 75, Anne computes the critical value at an α level of .05 to be

$$\text{critical } D = \frac{1.36}{\sqrt{75}} = \frac{1.36}{8.66} = .157$$

Computation of **D**

To calculate D, first cumulate the proportions in the second column of Table 9.1 and list them under a column of observed cumulative proportions as in Table 9.2. Then calculate the expected cumulative distribution under H_0. Because the answers are distributed, theoretically, evenly over five responses, the expected proportion in each response category is .20, while the expected cumulative proportions are as shown in Table 9.2. Once this column of expected cumulative

TABLE 9.2 Observed versus Expected Cumulative
Distribution for the Computation of K–S

Response	Observed	Expected	|Diff|
5	1.000	1.000	.000
4	.920	.800	.120 -> D
3	.707	.600	.107
2	.440	.400	.040
1	.147	.200	.053

proportion is found, take the absolute difference between the observed and expected cumulative proportion as in the last column of the table. An inspection of this column indicates that the maximum absolute difference D is .120.

The Decision
The D value of .120 is less than the critical value calculated earlier of .157. To Anne's surprise, the data may be more consistent with the null hypothesis than with the alternative hypothesis. There is insufficient evidence to indicate that the ordinary citizen feels deprived of his or her power to influence local politics in the United States. The result, however, does not address directly the issue of the existence of the local power elites, nor can Anne infer from it that the average citizen feels that she or he has an impact on state or national politics.

SPSS Note

The NPAR TESTS procedure in SPSS calculates various types of nonparametric tests; included is the one-sample K–S test. However, because of the way SPSS calculates this test, the procedure should not be used unless the sample contains a large number of different values, approximating a continuous distribution. If it is applied to grouped data or to data values having a limited range, such as 1 to 5, with many ties in one or more categories, as in the illustration of Section 9.4, the D value obtained under SPSS could be very different from the D value calculated from the formula described in this text.

Exercises

11. A random sample of blue-collar workers yields the following results:

Perception of Power over Local Politics		Frequency
Very much power	5	5
	4	7
	3	10
	2	12
No power at all	1	13

a. State H_0 and H_1 for the study.
b. Test the hypothesis at the .01 level.

12. Are people satisfied with the government's economic policy? A survey of 46 individuals yields the following results:

Level of Satisfaction		Frequency
Very satisfied	5	7
	4	10
	3	12
	2	9
Very dissatisfied	1	8

a. State H_0 and H_1 for the study.
b. Test the hypothesis.

13. Anne finds a survey on the educational background, measured by the number of years of schooling, of 12 registered Democrats as follows:

$$8 \quad 10 \quad 12 \quad 13 \quad 14 \quad 14 \quad 15 \quad 15 \quad 16 \quad 16 \quad 16 \quad 17$$

Using the K–S test, test the hypothesis at an α of .05 that the registered Democrats are distributed evenly in educational attainment.

14. Multiply each of the observed frequencies in Exercise 13 by 10 so that there are 120 Democrats in the sample.

a. Test the hypothesis at the .05 level.
b. Discuss the relationship between the sample size and the significance level.

15. Combine the number of years of schooling in Exercise 13 into the following categories:

   7–8   Junior high school
   9–12   High school
   13–15 Some college
   16–18 College graduate and above

a. State H_0 and H_1 for these data.
b. Test the hypothesis.
c. Discuss the effect of grouping on the significance level.

9.5 One-sample Test for Nominal Data: The Chi-square Goodness-of-Fit Test

Research Question

An important element of the U.S. political institution is the two-party system. A political party is an organization of people with similar views formed for the express purpose of influencing the political process. From the functionalist view, these parties have persisted because they perform important societal functions. Some of these include promoting political pluralism, increasing political involvement, and maintaining political stability.

Yet Anne questions whether in recent elections the two-party system in the United States is becoming dysfunctional. Instead of promoting political pluralism, the parties endorse platforms that are so similar that sometimes it is difficult to distinguish between them. More importantly, in voting for candidates of the two parties, the voters often feel that they are simply choosing between the lesser of two evils. This may in part account for the low voting turnout of U.S. citizens in recent national elections. If voters were given a chance in a survey to voice their dissatisfaction with the candidates of the two major parties, would they do so?

The Data

Fortunately for Anne, this is a year for the election of the governor of the state in which she resides. The field is open for this position because the present governor decides not to run for reelection. Numerous exhaustive polling studies have already been conducted to determine voter preference. The results of these studies, consisting of a total of 2,000 respondents, are tabulated in column 1 of Table 9.3, with all minority-party candidates grouped into one category.

With the help of the Research Institute, Anne conducts her own survey of voter preference based on a random sample of 300. The survey is modeled on the exhaustive polling studies conducted previously, with one exception. In addition to the list of candidates for the Democratic and Republican parties as well as for minority parties, the response of "none of the above candidates" is given. In effect, this additional category allows the respondents to express directly their dissatisfaction with the existing candidates and to indicate their disaffection with this political process.

Column 2 of Table 9.3 shows what Anne obtained from the survey. Is there a difference in the survey results when the respondents are provided the choice of a protest vote?

An Appropriate Test and Its Assumptions

The "choice of candidate" is a nominal variable. For a one-sample test of nominal data, the **goodness-of-fit chi-square test** is appropriate. In later chapters, we will

TABLE 9.3   Voting Preferences Based on Polls and on Anne's Study

Candidates		Poll Data	Anne's Data
Democratic		640	69
Republican		900	105
Other parties		140	24
Don't know or undecided		320	36
None of the above		N/A	66
	Total	2,000	300

discuss chi-square tests of independence. The goodness-of-fit chi square, like other tests in this category, examines the agreement between the sample and the hypothesized population distribution. Since the chi-square test requires no higher level than nominal data, it examines simple cell frequencies and not cumulative proportions, as does the K–S test. Whether the sample frequency distribution agrees with the hypothesized population frequency distribution is then taken as evidence for or against the null hypothesis.

Theoretically, given a discrete population distribution, the exact probability of obtaining a particular sample distribution can be ascertained using probability principles. However, when N is large, the calculation of these exact probabilities becomes extremely cumbersome. In such cases, it is more efficient to find a known sampling distribution that can approximate these probabilities. The following test statistic, which gives a good index of fit between the sample and the distribution expected under H_0, is distributed *approximately* as a χ^2 when N is large, with a df of $(k - 1)$:

$$\chi^2_{(k-1)} = \sum_{i=1}^{k} \frac{(O_i - E_i)^2}{E_i} \tag{9.6}$$

where O_i refers to the observed cell frequency of a category i
  E_i refers to the expected cell frequency of a category i and
  k refers to the number of categories

The observed frequencies in the formula refer to obtained sample frequencies, and the expected frequencies are derived from the theoretical population distribution specified by the null hypothesis. An inspection of the chi-square formula shows its similarity to the chi square given in Chapter 4. The only difference is that one rather than two subscripts is used in Formula 9.6 since Table 9.3 is univariate and therefore unidimensional.

A review of the meaning of this formula is in order. To determine how well the sample distribution fits the theoretical population distribution, a frequency-by-frequency comparison between the two distributions is made. Recall, however, that the sum of these differences turns out to be 0, and therefore it cannot be used as an index of fit or the lack thereof:

$$\sum (O_i - E_i) = 0$$

To circumvent this problem, the deviations are squared. Next, each squared difference is weighted by its own expected frequency so that the same amount of squared deviation may count for more when there are fewer individuals expected in the category. Finally, the weighted, squared differences are summed to yield an overall index of the discrepancy between the sample and the hypothesized population distribution.

The following assumptions are made in the chi-square test model: (1) mutually exclusive and exhaustive categories and (2) random and independent selection of cases. A third requirement that N be large is rather problematic because there is little agreement concerning the appropriate size of a sample. A conservative rule of thumb is to apply the chi square only if each E_i is 5 or larger.

The Statistical Hypotheses

Anne would like to know if her sampled voters show the same pattern of party preference as that observed in the exhaustive polls when her voters are given a chance to express their discontent with the candidates. If voting preference remains constant, the responses of her sample (O_i's) and those of the polls (E_i's) should be the same; χ^2 should yield a 0 value:

$$H_0: \quad O_i = E_i, \quad \text{for all } i\text{'s,} \quad \text{or} \quad \chi^2 = 0$$

However, if people are dissatisfied with the candidates from existing political parties, the sample responses would differ substantially from those of the polls; χ^2 would be significantly greater than 0:

$$H_1: \quad O_i \neq E_i, \quad \text{for some or all } i\text{'s,} \quad \text{or} \quad \chi^2 \neq 0$$

The Sampling Distribution

The chi-square distribution provides an approximation to the exact probabilities when the smallest E_i is equal to or greater than 5. In testing the hypothesis of goodness of fit, the researcher is interested only in the larger χ^2 values that indicate extreme disagreement between the sample and the hypothetical distribution. Therefore, the region of rejection is located only in the upper tail of the chi-square distribution. To find the critical χ^2 value that demarcates this region in Table C, df must first be calculated. As usual, how df is calculated depends on the problem at hand. For a goodness-of-fit χ^2 test, the df is $(k - 1)$, where k equals the number of categories in the variable. This stands to reason because the k differences between the obtained and the expected frequencies must sum to 0. Therefore, $(k - 1)$ of the differences are free to vary, but the last difference is fixed. With four categories in the variable, Anne finds the row where df = 3 in Table C and looks across to find the column where $p = .05$. The critical value given at the intersection is 7.8147 for an α of .05.

Computation of the Chi Square

Table 9.4 shows the components for the calculation of the χ^2. If voters are not disaffected, Anne can expect the same responses in her sample as in the polls. In other words, the poll results are those expected under H_0. Anne, however, cannot

TABLE 9.4 Table for Computation of the Goodness-of-Fit Chi Square for Voting Preferences

Candidates	O	E	$(O - E)$	$(O - E)^2$	$(O - E)^2/E$
Democratic	69	96	−27	729	7.593
Republican	105	135	−30	900	6.666
Other parties	24	21	3	9	.428
None of the above and other answers	102	48	54	2916	60.750
Total	300	300	0		75.437

compare her sample responses directly to those of the polls to see if there is any difference because the N's are not the same. She must first convert the responses of the polls in such a way that they sum to 300 instead of 2,000. For example, since 640 out of 2,000 (32%) were Democrats in the previous studies, if a sample of 300 is taken, 96 (32%) respondents are expected to be Democrats. Expected frequencies calculated in this manner are shown under the column labeled E for expected frequencies in the table.

Anne's sample results are reproduced under the observed frequency column, column "O," of Table 9.4. For the comparison to be valid, the sample should have the same number of categories as the population. Therefore, the extra category of "none of the above" is combined with the residual categories of "don't know" and "undecided" to yield the same number of categories as in the expected distribution. The last column of Table 9.4 gives the weighted, squared deviations; as shown, these sum to 75.437.

The Decision

Since the χ^2 of 75.44 is much greater than the critical value of 7.82, Anne rejects the null hypothesis in favor of the alternative hypothesis at an α of .05. Again, the α level indicates that if H_0 is true the chance of obtaining a chi-square value this large is less than 5 in 100 times. It appears that prospective voters, when given an opportunity to voice their dissatisfaction with the candidate slate, will do so to the detriment of the two major parties. Anne is aware, however, of a possible confounding factor in her conclusion. When comparing the distribution of the sample to that of the hypothesized population, the number and type of categories should be the same for both sample and population distributions. Since Anne has given her respondents the additional choice of "None of the above," to achieve the same number of categories in her sample as in previous surveys, she collapsed this response with that of "Don't know/undecided." The discrepancy between sample and hypothesized population distributions may be due to the artifact of initially having an extra category rather than a true difference. However, this is only a remote possibility considering how great the difference is between the observed and expected distributions.

Summary

One-sample Tests for Goodness of Fit

Ordinal data: K–S test
  Null hypothesis: $D = 0$

$$D = \text{maximum } |cp - C\pi|$$

where cp = cumulative proportion in the sample and
  $C\pi$ = cumulative proportion expected under H_o

Test model:

1. Random sampling
2. Ordinal or higher-level scale
3. Continuous distribution

Nominal data: Chi-square test
  Null hypothesis: $O_i = E_i$ for all i's

$$\chi^2_{(k-1)} = \sum_{i=1}^{k} \frac{(O_i - E_i)^2}{E_i}, \qquad \text{with df of } (k-1)$$

where O_i = observed cell frequency and
  E_i = expected cell frequency

Test model:

1. Random and independent selection of cases
2. Nominal or categorical variable with mutually exclusive and exhaustive categories
3. $E_i \geq 5$ for each i

Exercises

---

16. Decrease the frequency counts in Anne's data in Table 9.4 to 200 and compute χ^2. Discuss the relationship between the sample size and χ^2.

17. Convert Anne's data in the same table to percentages and compute χ^2. Is the result the same as the one obtained using the raw scores? When percentages are used, what adjustment is needed?

18. To find out if people's priorities for government expenditure agree with actual spending, Anne conducts an experiment. She asks a sample of 80 to allocate a total of $1,000 to various government functions. The mean allocation for each function is shown beside the actual expenditure in the following table.

Government Function	Expenditure (in $million)	People's Priorities for Government Spending
National defense	285,400	170
International affairs and foreign aid	9,900	2
Interest on debt	147,900	70
Social Security and Medicare	298,600	300
Income security and welfare	129,600	100
Education	33,700	60
Health and hospital	44,500	80
Environment	15,100	20
Law enforcement	5,000	10
Others (transportation, science, technology, veteran's benefits)	65,700	100
Other (none of the above)		88
Total	1,035,400	1,000

a. State H_0 and H_1 for the study.
b. Is the chi-square test an appropriate procedure for this problem?
c. Should some of the categories be combined? If so, in what way?
d. Test the hypothesis in part (a) using the chi-square test.

19. a. Based on the data in Table 9.1, test the hypothesis of uniform (even) distribution of respondents into five categories using the chi-square test.
    b. Combine existing categories into two groups, (1, 2, 3) and (4, 5), and rerun the chi-square test.
    c. Discuss the relationship between the number of categories and the significance level.

20. Starting from the top of the first column in the random number table, select 50 numbers by column. Test the hypothesis that they are from a normal distribution using a chi-square test.

SPSS Session

The following program requests a chi-square test using the NPAR TESTS command. Within the program, the categories of the nominal variable are entered under CANDIDAT and its frequencies under NUM. When CANDIDAT is weighted by NUM, the observed frequencies in Table 9.4 are obtained. Within the NPAR TESTS command, the CHISQUARE subcommand is specified first, following which the name of the test variable is entered. The minimum and maximum values of this variable can be given within parentheses, allowing the researcher to limit the analysis to a part of the distribution. With no specification, the whole range of values entered for the data will be analyzed. The subcommand EX-

PECTED designates the expected frequency counts derived from the theoretical model of the null hypothesis. In this case, the values entered after this subcommand are those found under the expected frequency column of Table 9.4. Unless expected frequencies are entered with this subcommand, the CHISQUARE procedure assumes equal expected frequencies per category. For this illustration, it would mean 75 cases for each candidate category.

```
DATA LIST FREE/ CANDIDAT NUM.

BEGIN DATA.

1 69 2 105 3 24 4 102

END DATA.

WEIGHT BY NUM.

NPAR TESTS CHISQUARE=CANDIDAT (1,4) /EXPECTED=96 135 21 48.
```

Except for a slight difference, the output is completely consistent with the text and should be self-explanatory. The .000 significance level simply means that the probability of obtaining a chi-square of 75.439 is less than 5 in 10,000.

Chi-square Test

CANDIDAT

Category	Cases Observed	Expected	Residual
1.00	69	96.00	-27.00
2.00	105	135.00	-30.00
3.00	24	21.00	3.00
4.00	102	48.00	54.00
Total	300		

Chi-Square	D.F.	Significance
75.439	3	.000

SPSS FIGURE 9.1   Goodness-of-Fit Chi-square Test

SPSS Exercises

1. Using the chi-square test, compare the GSS data on party identification (PARTYID) with the poll data presented in Table 9.3 in the text. Are they significantly different?

2. GSS asked the respondents if they would vote for a female president (FEPRES) if they considered her to be qualified for the job. Test the hypothesis that voters are split evenly among three positions: Yes, No, and Don't Know.

3. GSS respondents were asked if they thought the government was spending too much, too little, or about the right amount of money on education (NATEDUC). Test the hypothesis that respondents are evenly split among three positions.

General Conceptual Problems

1. Does the sample size affect the chi-square value? How?

2. Is the t distribution more variable than the z distribution? Explain with reference to the formulas for the t and z test statistics.

3. Explain the relationship between the normal and the chi-square distribution.

4. Can the K–S test or the chi-square test be applied to a small sample?

5. Explain how the K–S test compares the sample and population distributions.

6. When does the test statistic $(\overline{X} - \mu)/(\sigma/\sqrt{N})$ have a normal or a t sampling distribution?

7. List the distributions discussed so far, which consist of a family of subdistributions.

8. When H_0 is true, what value does χ^2 approach?

9. Does the K–S test assume a continuous distribution? Could the test be conducted with ties?

10. Does the number of categories affect the critical chi-square value? How?

References

1. Rowan, H. (1982). A Widening Gap between Rich and Poor, *Washington Post*, March 11, p. A29.

2. Lynd, R. S., and Lynd, H. M. (1937). *Middletown in Transition*. New York: Harcourt Brace Jovanovich.

3. Hunter, F. (1963). *Community Power Structure*. Garden City, N.Y.: Doubleday.

$Chapter$ **10**

Point and Interval Estimation

New Statistical Topics

Point estimation	Unbiased, consistent,
Interval estimation	efficient estimators
Confidence interval for a mean	Confidence interval for
Determining sample size	a proportion

10.1 Overview

This chapter may be considered a continuation of Chapter 8. We noted in Chapter 8 that the social scientist, in doing research, has the two-part goal of formulating and then verifying social theories. While discussing theory verification, we did not address the issue of how social scientists initially develop the new ideas that can be used later in constructing a new theory. The *research-then-theory* approach based on inductive logic provides a context for the emergence of these new ideas. We will now examine this strategy of theory formulation and some of the statistical techniques that parallel this approach.

10.1.1 Statistical Topics and Social Applications

In the research-then-theory approach, the researcher begins with the selection of a phenomenon of interest for study. After making measurements on various characteristics of the phenomenon, the researcher analyzes the data with an eye toward discovering *patterns* in them. Theoretical generalizations are formulated to explain these patterns once they are found. These abstract propositions serve as the bases for a new theory from which other propositions are derived to be tested in the theory-then-research cycle. Thus, by treating the two strategies as complementary, rather than as opposing procedures, the researcher benefits the most.

The initial stages of doing research-then-theory can be characterized as exploratory. As such, no particular statistical technique is especially adapted to the task. Instead, the whole body of descriptive statistics can be employed in one way or another to assist the researcher in the task of discovering data patterns. For example, the correlation and regression techniques presented in Chapters 4 and 5 can be used to search for relationships between variables. But whatever the researcher discovers through these techniques pertains to the sample only. It may not exist in the population at large, being more a product of sampling errors. Before too much theoretical importance is attached to sample results, the researcher must ascertain that these observations characterize the population also. For this task, she or he employs a statistical procedure called **estimation.**

In estimation, the researcher does not know, nor does she or he hazard a guess about the value of the population parameter. To gauge this value, a statistic is calculated from the sample. In hypothesis testing, on the other hand, the researcher does have an assumption about the value of the parameter, and a sample is taken to verify or refute this assumption. Other than this initial difference of having or not having a hypothesis, the goal of estimation is the same as that of hypothesis testing: to infer population characteristics from sample data. Estimation is an invaluable tool that aids the social scientists in their task of discovery.

In addition to social scientists, pollsters have also made extensive use of the statistical procedures of estimation, although their objective is primarily informational. In polling, a sample is taken for the explicit purpose of examining the attitudes of the country or a segment of the country. Until fairly recently, public opinion on major social issues had been a matter of guesswork. As late as 1936, the *Literary Digest,* a leading magazine of the time, conducted a huge poll of voting preferences to predict that Alf Landon would win the presidential election in a landslide with 60% of the vote. In fact, Roosevelt won handily. The magazine made the mistake of selecting respondents from telephone directories and automobile registration lists during the Depression era, thus ensuring an overrepresentation of the well-to-do.

In the same year, modern polling techniques were employed by George Gallup to predict a Roosevelt victory based on a poll of a much smaller sample. Gallup, whose aim was to provide frequent reports of public opinion on major political, social, and moral issues, founded the American Institute of Public Opinion, which soon became known as the Gallup Poll. Today, polling is a major industry that employs sophisticated sampling techniques and estimation procedures in much of its work. Polls provide the social scientists with an invaluable source of descriptive information for formulating as well as testing theories. In this chapter, Anne draws on the polls for various insights into the economic, political, and social issues of the day.

10.2 Point Estimation

Estimation begins with the utilization of sample statistics as estimators of their corresponding population parameters. If no other information is utilized for the inference, we have a case of **point estimation**. In point estimation, the value of the sample statistic is taken as the single best estimate of the value of the population parameter. Consider a research example: Anne is interested in characterizing the typical supporters of a third-party candidate running for presidency. She finds in the data banks of University X a random sample of 150 such supporters with information on their educational level. She computes their mean years of education to be 13.82 with a variance of 2.56 years. If she estimates from these figures the average educational level of all supporters to be 13.82 years with a variance of 2.56 years, she would be doing point estimation. The values of $\overline{X}$ and s^2 are used to estimate directly the corresponding values of the parameters μ and σ^2.

For the researcher to have confidence in the point estimate, the sample statistic should be a *good* estimator, which has the following properties:

1. Lack of bias, so that in the long run, it does not under- or overestimate the population parameter
2. Consistency, so that it provides a more precise estimate with a larger sample
3. Relative efficiency, so that its estimates vary less from sample to sample than estimates given by other comparable statistics

In point estimation, then, the researcher's central problem is to select a statistic that has as many of these desirable properties as possible.

10.2.1 Unbiased Estimators

A statistic, *St*, is said to be an *unbiased estimator* if its expected value equals the value of the population parameter:

$$E(St) = \theta$$

where *St* refers to a sample statistic and
θ refers to its corresponding population parameter

The preceding equation states that in the long run, if *St* is averaged over all random samples, its value will equal θ. That is, the mean of the sampling distribution of *St*, an unbiased estimator, is the same as θ.

We have encountered both biased and unbiased estimators in our discussions. For example, we have noted in several of the preceding chapters that the expected value of a sample mean is the population mean:

$$E(\overline{X}) = \mu$$

Therefore, the sample mean is an unbiased estimator of the population mean. In the same manner, the proportion of cases in a sample is an unbiased estimator of the population proportion:

$$E(P) = \pi$$

The sample variance, however, is a *biased* estimator, as discussed in Chapter 9:

$$E(s^2) \neq \sigma^2$$

Whenever the mean of a sample differs from that of the population, the squared deviations of the sample values about the mean will be smaller than the squared deviations about the population mean. Most of the time the sample variance tends to underestimate the variance of the population in such a way that its expected value equals the difference between the population variance and the variance of the sampling distribution of means:

$$E(s^2) = \sigma^2 - \sigma_{\bar{x}}^2$$

Through substitution and manipulation of this equation, it can be shown that the underestimation can be corrected by incorporating the correction factor of $N/(N-1)$ into the calculation to give an unbiased estimate as follows:

$$\hat{\sigma}^2 = \frac{N}{N-1} \frac{\sum (X - \overline{X})^2}{N} = \frac{\sum (X - \overline{X})^2}{N-1}$$

Recall that the denominators of the variance and the standard deviation are given as $N-1$ in some texts (Chapter 3). The reason now becomes clear: in these texts the correction for the underestimation is made early in the descriptive stage. The expected value of $\hat{\sigma}^2$ equals the variance of the population:

$$E(\hat{\sigma}^2) = \sigma^2$$

The standard deviation, on the other hand, is a biased estimator even when the correction factor is incorporated into its formula. Thus

$$E(\hat{\sigma}) = E\left(\sqrt{\frac{\sum (X - \overline{X})^2}{N-1}} \right) \neq \sigma$$

On the average, by incorporating the correction factor the sample standard deviation still underestimates the population standard deviation. For this reason, the variance is used more often than the standard deviation in statistical inference.

10.2.2 Consistent Estimators

A second desirable property of estimators is their consistency. A statistic is a consistent estimator if, as N becomes larger, the variance of the sampling distribution of the statistic becomes smaller. Thus, as N increases, the sample statistic will provide a closer and closer estimate of the population value. When N reaches infinity, the statistic gives an exact estimate of the parameter:

$$E(St - \theta)^2 \to 0, \quad \text{as } N \to \infty$$

The sample mean and variance and the sample proportion are all consistent estimators because they tend to approximate their corresponding parameters better with a larger sample.

10.2.3 Efficient Estimators

A third criterion for selection is the *relative efficiency* of estimators. If a statistic is more efficient, the variance of its sampling distribution is smaller than the variance of the sampling distribution of other comparable statistics for a fixed sample size N. Thus

$$E(St - \theta)^2 = \text{minimum value for } N$$

Since efficiency is relative, it is only through comparing the variance of the sampling distribution of one estimator, St_1, with the variance of the sampling distribution of another estimator, St_2, that we can arrive at an evaluation of their relative efficiency:

$$\frac{\sigma_{st1}^2}{\sigma_{st2}^2} > 1, \quad \text{if } St_2 \text{ is more efficient than } St_1$$

For example, if Anne knew that a population distribution is unimodal and symmetrical, she has the choice of using either $\overline{X}$ or the median as an estimator of its central tendency, since both the population median and mean have the same value: $mdn = \mu$. To decide between the two, Anne should use the criterion of efficiency. For this type of population distribution, the variance of the sampling distribution of means is smaller than that of medians, so

$$\frac{\sigma_{mdn}^2}{\sigma_{\overline{x}}^2} > 1.00$$

Being a more efficient estimator than the median, the mean is more often used in statistical inference when the population is unimodal and symmetrical.

On the other hand, the median may be the more efficient estimator for other types of population distributions. Note, then, that efficiency is not an inherent attribute of the estimator, but is influenced by the population distribution under consideration.

Exercises

1. Survey the class on age. Take a random sample of five students and ask their ages. Repeat this process 10 times. Usually, this will indicate that the sample mean is an unbiased estimator. Is it true for these samples?

2. Is the sample variance in Exercise 1 a biased estimator?

3. Repeat the survey in Exercise 1 by taking 10 random samples of size 20. Compare the sample means and variances to those of Exercise 1. Does this indicate that these statistics are consistent estimators?

4. Using the data gathered for Exercise 1, compute sample medians. Does this indicate that the mean is more efficient than the median as a measure of central tendency?

10.3 Procedure for Interval Estimation

Point estimation does not take into account sampling error, which, in all likelihood, is a part of the sample estimate. Without this provision, the researcher has no idea of how accurate the estimate is. A more meaningful approach is to estimate the amount of sampling error and incorporate it into the point estimate. In so doing, the researcher places a *range of values* around the point estimate to give an **interval estimation** that has a specified and usually high probability of including the population parameter. For example, when Anne states in her study that she is 95% confident that the mean years of education for supporters of a third-party candidate are between 13.57 to 14.07 years, she is doing interval rather than point estimation.

Generally, then, interval estimation consists of the following steps:

1. Compute a statistic to summarize the characteristic of interest in a randomly drawn sample.
2. Specify the appropriate sampling distribution for the statistic and calculate the standard error of this distribution.
3. Use the standard error to determine a range of values, that is, an interval centered about the sample statistic. The width of the interval depends on how confident the researcher wants to be that the parameter would be included in this interval: hence the label **confidence interval.** Traditionally, a 95% or 99% level of confidence is selected, corresponding to the .05 or .01 significance level in hypothesis testing. The range of values then represents an interval that would contain the parameter with either a 95% or 99% probability.

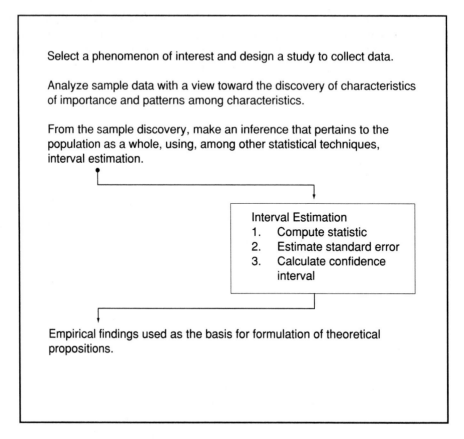

Select a phenomenon of interest and design a study to collect data.

Analyze sample data with a view toward the discovery of characteristics of importance and patterns among characteristics.

From the sample discovery, make an inference that pertains to the population as a whole, using, among other statistical techniques, interval estimation.

Interval Estimation
1.   Compute statistic
2.   Estimate standard error
3.   Calculate confidence
      interval

Empirical findings used as the basis for formulation of theoretical propositions.

**FIGURE 10.1   Relation of Estimation Procedure to the
Research-Then-Theory Approach**

A pollster conducting a survey would stop with step 3. For the social scientist, however, this procedure is an integral part of theory formulation, as seen in Figure 10.1.

10.3.1 Elements of Interval Estimation

Although estimation is presented as a statistical method used in the context of discovery rather than of verification, the procedure itself involves elements very similar to those in hypothesis testing. The assumption of random sampling is, as usual, indispensable. Having a nonrandom sample defeats the purpose of estimation, no matter how large the sample is, as seen with the *Literary Digest* poll of 1936. The appropriate sampling distribution of the statistic must also be specified.

To simplify the derivation process, the researcher often makes assumptions regarding the population, as in hypothesis testing.

The standard error of the sampling distribution also figures prominently in estimation. Because it measures the extent of *variability* in the sample statistic, the standard error is an index of sampling error. By calculating and incorporating an index of sampling error into the point estimate, we can provide an error margin for the point estimate.

10.4 The Logic of Interval Estimation for a Mean

To delineate a profile of the typical supporters of a third-party candidate, Anne takes a sample of 150 supporters and calculates their mean years of education to be 13.82. From this point estimate, she obtains a 95% confidence interval that ranges 13.57 to 14.07 years of education. We will now examine how she arrives at this interval and the logic underlying her method.

Before constructing an interval around the point estimate of 13.82, Anne decides that the estimated interval should have a 95% probability of including the population parameter. The 95% probability also means that Anne is 95% confident that the estimated interval will encompass the parameter μ. Anne next identifies the appropriate sampling distribution for her task to be the sampling distribution of means. According to the central limit theorem, when $N \geq 100$, the sampling distribution of means is approximately normal, regardless of the actual shape of the population. This being the case, roughly two-thirds of the sample means are within 1 *standard error*, and 95% of them are within 1.96 standard errors of the mean of the sampling distribution. Since the mean of the sampling distribution is the same as the mean of the population, $\mu_{\bar{x}} = \mu$, 95% of the sample means are also within 1.96 standard errors of the parameter Anne wishes to estimate. See Box 10.1 for the rationale of using the value of 1.96.

Note that for any particular sample the researcher does not know (1) whether its $\overline{X}$ is one of those that is within 1.96 standard errors of the μ and, if so, (2) whether it is 1.96 standard errors *above* or *below* its μ. Suppose, however, that an interval corresponding to the distance of 1.96 standard errors is placed around the $\overline{X}$, such that

$$\overline{X} \pm 1.96 \, \sigma_{\bar{x}}$$

This interval will include μ if $\overline{X}$ is within ± 1.96 standard errors of the μ. Also, in the long run, if samples are drawn repeatedly and an interval like this is calculated around each sample mean, 95% of the intervals will include the population mean μ. See Figure 10.2 for a graphic illustration of this concept.

Because 95% of the intervals computed with this procedure will include μ, this means the probability that an interval will contain the population mean is .95.

BOX 10.1 **Finding the Standard Error of the Normal Sampling Distribution of the Means to Calculate a Confidence Interval**

When the normal sampling distribution of means is used to find the 95% confidence interval, two z scores are needed to demarcate an area under the normal curve that contain 95% of the total area. Since precision is desired, the interval between the two z scores should be the smallest possible. This is obtained by selecting z scores that partition an area of .025 on *each* tail of the distribution. Note that the z scores for computing a 95% confidence interval are the same as the critical values for a two-tailed test at the .05 level: they are ±1.96. Similarly, for a 99% confidence interval, the critical values of the z distribution for a two-tailed test at the .01 level are used: they are ±2.58.

Note that other intervals could have been constructed for the 95% confidence interval if asymmetrical areas totaling 5% are located on the tails. For example,

$$\overline{X} - 1.75\sigma_{\overline{x}} \le \mu \le \overline{X} + 2.33\sigma_{\overline{x}}$$

also yields a 95% confidence interval, as does the following:

$$\overline{X} - 2.06\sigma_{\overline{x}} \le \mu \le \overline{X} + 1.88\sigma_{\overline{x}}$$

These estimates, however, all yield a wider range of values than that using the z of ±1.96 and are therefore less efficient. Furthermore, the use of the symmetric values has the advantage of yielding an estimate that corresponds to a two-tailed test of the population mean.

The probability of .95 could also be interpreted as the level of confidence the researcher has in the procedure itself: the researcher is 95% certain that a particular interval obtained will contain the parameter. Hence, the 95% **confidence interval for a mean** is

$$95\% \text{ confidence interval} = \overline{X} \pm 1.96\,\sigma_{\overline{x}} \qquad (10.1)$$

Keep in mind that the parameter is a fixed value and that what varies from sample to sample are the sample means and therefore the intervals calculated around them. As these intervals change, they may or may not encompass μ, and their probability of enclosing μ depends on the width of the interval itself. For a 99% confidence interval of a mean, given a large sample size, the following applies:

$$95\% \text{ confidence interval} = \overline{X} \pm 2.58\,\sigma_{\overline{x}} \qquad (10.2)$$

From Formulas 10.1 and 10.2, it can be seen that the higher the confidence level is, the wider the interval. In addition, the expressions $1.96\sigma_{\overline{x}}$ and $2.58\sigma_{\overline{x}}$ are sometimes called the **error margins** because they indicate the extent to which $\overline{X}$ may deviate from μ due to sampling error.

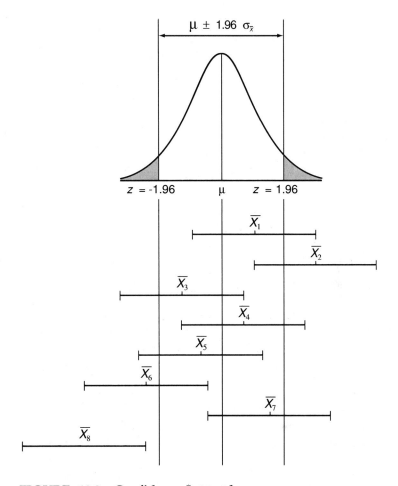

FIGURE 10.2 Confidence Intervals

10.4.1 Calculating and Interpreting Confidence Interval for a Mean

To return to Anne's study, after selecting a 95% confidence level, Anne is ready to compute the standard error. As its formula indicates, the value of the standard error is partly a function of the value of the population variance σ^2. Again, in most research it is highly unlikely that the value of σ^2 is known when the value of μ must be estimated. It is more probable that the researcher employs a point estimate of σ^2 in order to calculate the confidence interval for μ. In such cases the standard error is estimated as

$$\hat{\sigma}_{\bar{x}} = \sqrt{\frac{s^2}{N-1}}$$

When σ^2 must be estimated, strictly speaking, the t and not the z is the appropriate sampling distribution. Anne should examine the t table for critical values of a t distribution with 149 degrees of freedom. However, as pointed out in Chapter 9, the t approximates the z distribution with larger df's and ultimately converges to the z distribution when df equals ∞. Therefore, in practice, a t distribution with df of 100 or more can be treated as the z distribution, with the same critical values as the z.

In Anne's case, with N of 150, the t distribution is approximately normal, so the z scores can be used in place of the exact t scores. Applying the preceding formula to her data, Anne obtains an estimated standard error as follows:

$$\hat{\sigma}_{\bar{x}} = \sqrt{\frac{2.56}{150 - 1}} = .131$$

The 95% confidence interval then equals

$$\overline{X} \pm 1.96\,\hat{\sigma}_{\bar{x}} = 13.82 \pm (1.96)(.13) = 13.82 \pm .25 = [13.57, 14.07]$$

According to her calculations, Anne is 95% confident that the true mean years of education for supporters of a third-party candidate can be found in the interval extending from 13.57 to 14.07 years. In polling terms, the results can also be interpreted to mean that the average educational level of supporters of a third-party candidate is 13.82 years with an error margin of $\pm.25$ years.

Before proceeding to explore further demographic information about these supporters, Anne reviews the procedure and the requirements for calculating a confidence interval for the mean. First, the limits of the interval are computed using z scores that represent the critical values of a two-tailed test of hypothesis. The population variance σ^2 is assumed to be known or must be estimated. The assumptions that make the calculation of the interval possible are the interval measurement of the variable, random sampling, and a normal population distribution or a sufficiently large sample for the central limit theorem to apply.

Had Anne calculated the 99% confidence interval from the same set of data, it would extend from 13.48 to 14.16:

$$\overline{X} \pm 2.58\,\hat{\sigma}_{\bar{x}} = 13.82 \pm 2.58(.13) = 13.82 \pm .34 = [13.48, 14.16]$$

By increasing the confidence level, the risk of error is reduced, but the width of the interval is increased, thus yielding less precision in the estimate.

10.4.2 Comparing Confidence Interval with Hypothesis Testing

The confidence interval can also be thought of as a range of estimates about μ that the researcher obtains from one sample. If any of the estimates within the range of the 95% confidence interval is selected to be the parameter of a null hypothesis in a two-tailed test, the hypothesis could not be rejected at an α of .05 using that sample. In the preceding section, Anne's 95% confidence interval yields a range of μ estimates whose values extend from 13.57 to 14.07. Any two-tailed test of the μ value within this interval of 13.57 to 14.07, for instance a μ of 14.05, would not result in a rejection of H_0 based on her sample.

However, if the value of μ in the null hypothesis is not included in this range of estimates, then, based on the evidence from this particular sample, the hypothesis would be rejected. Had Anne tested an H_0 of $\mu = 13.33$, a value not included within the confidence interval, on the same set of data, H_0 would have been rejected. The reader may wish to verify this by performing a t test with the given sample values in the preceding section. In this sense, calculating a confidence interval is equivalent to conducting a two-tailed test on the range of μ values estimated from a particular sample.

Exercises

5. Based on a random sample of 100 registered Republicans, Anne finds the mean years of military service to be 1.02 with a standard deviation of .025 years. Compute a 95% confidence interval for estimating the average years of military service in this population.

6. Based on other available data, Anne's colleague hypothesizes the average years of military service for the Republicans to be either 1.19 or 1.32.
   a. State H_0 and H_1 of the study.
   b. Test the hypothesis at the .05 level.
   c. Discuss the relationship between interval estimation and hypothesis testing.

7. Using the data for Exercise 5 and assuming that $\overline{X}$ and s remain constant, determine the widths of 95% confidence intervals based on samples of size 20, 50, and 150. Discuss the effect of the sample size on the width of a confidence interval.

8. Based on the same study of 100 registered Republicans, Anne notes that the mean income is $42,000 and the standard deviation is $5,000.
   a. Estimate the mean income using a 99% confidence interval.
   b. Compute 90% and 95% confidence intervals.
   c. Explain the relationship between the width of the interval and the level of confidence given a fixed sample size.

SPSS Exercise

This exercise simulates the construction of confidence intervals using per capita income (INCOME) from the City data set. Follow these steps to complete the exercise:
   a. Compute the mean μ and the standard deviation σ of per capita income for the study population of 500 cities.

b. Take 50 samples of size 121. For each sample, read in the variable INCOME. Then, in SPSS/PC+, obtain the sample mean and the standard error of the mean with the subcommand STATISTICS = 1 2 of the DESCRIPTIVES command:

```
DESCRIPTIVES VARIABLES=INCOME /STATISTICS=1 2.
```

Recall that SPSS uses keywords to specify the statistics:

```
DESCRIPTIVES VARIABLES=INCOME /STATISTICS=MEAN SEMEAN.
```

c. Construct a 99% confidence interval for each sample based on the output from the DESCRIPTIVES command and using the COMPUTE statements as follows:

```
COMPUTE LOW = (enter mean) - 2.58 * (enter standard error).

COMPUTE HIGH = (enter mean) + 2.58 * (enter standard error).
```

d. Determine how many of the 50 intervals contain the population mean of the per capita income with the LIST command. Comment on the findings.

10.5 Determining Sample Size for Estimating a Mean

Research Question

The governor of the state in which Anne lives becomes very concerned with the notion that people in the United States and those in his state especially are living beyond their means. Studies in recent years have continually cited statistics that show the United States to be one of the largest debtor nations with a huge budget deficit and its citizens to be much more interested in consuming than in saving. Compared with the Japanese, who have the highest savings rate of 16%, and the Germans, whose rate exceeds 12%, our savings is at a low of 2% to 3%. Before launching a media blitz to induce his state to save more, the governor needs some pertinent facts and figures. He therefore commissions the Research Institute at University X to conduct a poll to determine how much people in his state save, their attitude toward saving, and the obstacles they perceive to saving more. The governor desires a high degree of confidence in a very precise estimate that is to be within .05% of the true savings rate within the state. Anne is given the task of coordinating the poll. How could she achieve this level of precision in her estimate?

An Appropriate Method

The researcher can target a certain level of precision in interval estimation by taking a certain sample size. Recall from Chapter 8 that the standard error of the sampling distribution of means is determined by two factors: the (estimated) population variance and the sample size. Given the same value for the population variance, the larger the sample size is, the smaller the standard error. By decreasing the standard error, the researcher, in hypothesis testing, increases the power of a test and, in estimation, reduces the width of a confidence interval to obtain a more precise estimate. Because precision is a function of sample size, given a certain level of precision, the sample size necessary for achieving it can be estimated. More specifically, to determine the necessary sample size, Anne must set a confidence level in addition to the desired error margin such that

$$\text{EM} = z_{a/2}\sigma_{\bar{x}} = z_{a/2}\frac{s}{\sqrt{N}} \tag{10.3}$$

where EM refers to the error margin and
$z_{\alpha/2}$ refers to the z values for a 95% or 99% confidence level

Formula 10.3 sets the width of *half* the confidence interval in terms of the required error margin. Once EM is specified in terms of a value such as .05% saving rate, Formula 10.3 can be rearranged to solve for N:

$$N = \left[\frac{(z_{\alpha/2})(\sigma)}{\text{EM}}\right]^2 = \sigma^2\left(\frac{z_{\alpha/2}}{\text{EM}}\right)^2 \tag{10.4}$$

Calculation and Interpretation

The z score for a 99% confidence interval is 2.58, and the error margin in this case is to be no more than .05. As usual, the σ^2 in Formula 10.4 must be estimated. Anne has a number of options. She could use s^2 from the national figures or she could conduct a pilot study to obtain s^2. She could even conservatively guess the highest value possible for σ^2. In any case, the researcher must arrive at an approximate value for σ^2 to solve the equation. Using a variance of .22 and a standard deviation of .47 estimated from a national poll, Anne determines the necessary sample size as follows:

$$N = \left[\frac{(2.58)(.47)}{.05}\right]^2 = 24.252^2 = 588.159$$

A sample of 588 is needed to estimate to within .05% of the true savings rate, whatever it is, with a probability of .99.

Sometimes the researcher might attempt to set the error margin in terms of fractions of the standard deviation of the population σ as follows:

$$EM = k\sigma$$

where k refers to multiples of σ. By so doing, σ is dropped from the formula, making it unnecessary to point estimate this parameter. The formula becomes

$$EM = k\sigma = z_{\alpha/2}\frac{\sigma}{\sqrt{N}}$$

$$\sqrt{N} = \frac{(z_{\alpha/2})(\sigma)}{k\sigma}$$

$$N = \left(\frac{z_{\sigma/2}}{k}\right)^2 \tag{10.5}$$

For example, if Anne does not have the information on the variance from the national poll, she could have set the error margin in terms of fractions of σ. Note, however, that this method still requires some crude notion of σ. Suppose from reading various reports Anne assumes that σ is no higher than .59. She therefore sets EM at .08σ, which would give her an approximate EM value of .05 if σ ≈ .59. Then, substituting .08σ into Equation 10.5, she obtains the sample size estimate of 1,040 as follows:

$$N = \left(\frac{z_{\alpha/2}}{k}\right)^2 = \left(\frac{2.58}{.08}\right)^2 = 1,040.062$$

Regardless of the true value of σ, this larger sample should provide Anne with a smaller interval and EM and therefore a more precise estimate.

Exercises

9. A survey institute reports the mean income of the registered voters in their community to be $20,815 with a standard deviation of $5,000. How large a sample must be taken to be 95% confident that the error margin of his estimate will not exceed $500?

10. A public opinion pollster for a city wishes to estimate the average age of those who would favor a budget increase for crime prevention to within a margin of error of one-tenth of σ at the 95% confidence level. How large a sample is needed?

11. Anne wishes to know the average number of lobbyists sent to Congress from major occupational groups. Considering the 95% confidence interval to be of desirable precision, she takes a random sample of size 100. Assuming a normal population, within how many σ units of μ will the sample estimate fall with a probability of .95?

10.6 Confidence Interval for a Proportion

Research Question

Anne notes that the Republican Party has recently expended much effort to discredit the liberal position on a political spectrum that ranges from radicalism to extreme conservatism. Global labels such as "conservative" and "liberal," however, have been shown to be misleading because they tend to obscure the fact that there are at least two main dimensions in U.S. political attitudes: the individual's position on economic and on social issues. A study by Barone and Ujifusa [1] estimated that 45% of the population is consistently conservative or liberal on both dimensions, but, more importantly, 55% or the majority of the population is liberal on one but conservative on the other dimension. Nonetheless, before the 1992 election, the Republican Party has managed to attach a certain stigma to the liberal position, associating it with the country's social and economic woes. Given this political climate, Anne wonders what proportion of U.S. voters identify themselves as liberal. Instead of including all age groups, Anne decides to concentrate on those between 17 and 18 years old because they would provide a more conclusive indication of the future direction of the country. What percentage of the country's youths between the ages of 17 and 18 identify themselves as liberal now?

The Data

In a poll of 125 high school graduates, Anne finds 38% identified themselves as liberal. The original question contained five response categories: radical, liberal, middle-of-the-road, conservative, and extremely conservative. For the purpose of her study, however, Anne dichotomized the responses into the categories of liberal and nonliberal. The former category consists of the two responses of "radical" and "liberal," while the latter is comprised of all responses other than these two.

An Appropriate Method and Sampling Distribution

This problem requires the calculation of a **confidence interval for a proportion.** For smaller sample sizes, the proportion can be converted to r successes in N trials, and the binomial would be the appropriate sampling distribution to use. However, for larger samples, for which π represents the smaller of the two proportions and $N\pi \geq 5$, the binomial approximates the normal distribution and the z sampling distribution can be applied. With the use of the z distribution, the critical values for the 95% and 99% confidence intervals are the same as those for the mean: ± 1.96 and ± 2.58. The standard error of $\sigma/\sqrt{N}$ is replaced by the following formula:

$$\sqrt{\frac{\pi(1 - \pi)}{N}}$$

The formulas for confidence intervals of proportions are

$$95\% \text{ confidence interval} = P \pm 1.96\sqrt{\frac{\pi(1-\pi)}{N}}$$

$$99\% \text{ confidence interval} = P \pm 2.58\sqrt{\frac{\pi(1-\pi)}{N}}$$

(10.6)

The population proportion π is unknown and must be estimated. Using P as a point estimate of π is acceptable, even without incorporating a correction factor for sampling error, because the sampling error is probably small when the sample size is large. However, if a more conservative approach is desired, the method that yields the largest value possible for the standard error should be adopted. The largest standard error is obtained when $\pi = .5$. Thus, .5 can be substituted into the standard error formula for π whenever a more conservative method is needed. With this conservative method, a wider interval is obtained.

Calculation and Interpretation

The sample proportion P is .38 and there are 125 cases. With P as a point estimate of π, the 95% confidence interval equals

$$.38 \pm 1.96\sqrt{\frac{(.38)(.62)}{125}} = .38 \pm .085 = [.295, .465]$$

The proportion of youths who identify themselves as liberal is 38% with an error margin of $\pm .085\%$. Anne is 95% confident that the true proportion, π, is included within the interval of .295 to .465.

With the second and more conservative method of substituting .5 for π, the interval equals

$$.38 \pm 1.96\sqrt{\frac{(.5)(.5)}{125}} = .38 \pm .088 = [.292, .468]$$

As expected, the second method yields a slightly wider interval. Anne notes that regardless of which method is used the true proportion of those between the ages of 17 and 18 who consider themselves liberal is under 50%, since the π value of .5 is not included in either interval.

Based on her estimations of the demographic characteristics, such as the average education, income, and age of Republicans and Democrats, and also of political attitudes and self-identification, Anne speculates that there may be a declining proportion of youths identifying themselves as Democrats. This, how-ever, is a research question more easily handled with two-sample techniques, which permit the comparison of attitudes at two time periods. With one-sample procedures, all she could do is estimate the proportion of either Democratic or Republican youths, but she could do this with a great deal of precision.

10.7 Determining Sample Size for Estimating a Proportion

Research Question

Although most U.S. citizens would not identify themselves as liberal politically, their stance on some social issues is fairly liberal. As an example, in the General Social Survey, 70% of the general population said that they would vote for a female candidate running for the presidency in 1972, but the percentage had increased to 84% in 1986. Suppose Anne wishes to estimate the current proportion to within 2% of its true value with 95% confidence. How many cases would she need?

An Appropriate Method and Calculation

Determining the sample size for estimating a proportion is easy if Anne takes the most conservative route by assuming that $\pi = .5$. With this assumption, the $\hat{\sigma}^2$ that equals $\pi(1 - \pi)$ assumes the largest value possible. Substituting the appropriate symbols for σ^2 in Formula 10.4, the appropriate formula is obtained:

$$N = \pi(1 - \pi)\left(\frac{z_{\alpha/2}}{\text{EM}}\right)^2 = .25\left(\frac{z_{\alpha/2}}{\text{EM}}\right)^2 \qquad (10.7)$$

With Formula 10.7, Anne estimates that the sample size she needs is 2,401:

$$N = .25\left(\frac{1.96}{.02}\right)^2 = 2,401$$

Exercises

12. **a.** A public opinion pollster wants to estimate with 95% confidence to within .01 the proportion of registered voters favoring a Republican nominee if P is approximately .5. How large a sample should be taken?
    b. Based on her study, Anne estimates the population proportion favoring the Republican nominee to be approximately .4. Does she need a larger sample and why?

13. Based on a random sample of 80 people between the ages of 18 and 24, Anne finds that 39.8% voted in the last presidential election.

    a. Compute a 95% confidence interval for estimating the percentage of voters among the young.
    b. To estimate it to within a 5% voting rate, how large should the sample be?

14. Refer to Exercise 13. The percentage of the same voting-age population voting for president in the last election is officially reported to be 49.9%. Based on Anne's data, test the hypothesis that the official report is correct.

    a. State H_0 and H_1.
    b. Test the hypothesis at the .05 level.
    c. Explain how interval estimation can be used for hypothesis testing.

15. In Anne's study of 120 random respondents, 61% consider that party affiliation of a candidate is a factor in deciding for whom to vote to become members of Congress.

    a. Compute a 99% confidence interval for estimating the proportion of people who regard party as a factor.
    b. To estimate to within a $.1\sigma$ margin of error, how large a sample would be needed?

16. Based on the data in Exercise 15, test the hypothesis that voters are evenly divided as to the importance attached to the political affiliation of a candidate for Congress.

    a. State H_0 and H_1.
    b. Test the hypothesis at the .01 level.
    c. How is this hypothesis testing related to the preceding interval estimation?

17. A sample of 150 university students are interviewed by Anne concerning their tolerance for nonconformity. Anne is 95% confident that a range of 31.2% to 46.8% will enclose the true proportion of those who are willing to have a communist as a college teacher. What is the value of the estimated proportion based on which Anne has arrived at the stated confidence interval?

18. Anne finds a research report stating that .7% of 1,000 respondents randomly sampled favor a tax increase.

    a. Estimate the proportion of the U.S. population that would favor a tax increase using a 95% confidence interval.
    b. Use a conservative estimate in calculating the standard error. Discuss the relationship between the interval width and the value of π used in estimating the standard error.

10.8 Interval Estimation in the Social Sciences

Other than in polling, interval estimation is not as commonly carried out as hypothesis testing in the social sciences. We can only speculate on the reasons as to why this is so. Perhaps the exact hypothesized values in the null hypotheses convey the impression of precision, whereas the intervals constantly remind the researcher of the uncertainty with which she or he is dealing. However, it should be remembered that even in hypothesis testing the researcher deals with ranges of values, although not in as obvious a manner. When the researcher rejects the null hypothesis in favor of the alternative, the latter often does not contain a parameter that has an exact value. When the deviation between a sample outcome and a hypothesized parameter is small, it means that a range of similar values about the exact value stated in the null hypothesis cannot be rejected.

Perhaps social scientists do not resort to estimation as often because the research-then-theory approach within which estimation can be gainfully employed produces meaningful results only when certain conditions are met. According to Reynolds [2], there should be a small number of significant traits or variables accounting for the phenomenon under examination. There should also be a limited number of significant, but obvious patterns to be found in the data. Often neither condition is met. For any new phenomenon under study, there are usually innumerable ways of conceptualizing its properties, resulting in a great many variables to be considered. Causal relationships are difficult to uncover because of the multitude of social forces acting simultaneously on the outcome. The social scientist who goes into an investigation without some preconception of what is important may find the situation confusing rather than illuminating. Regardless of the reasons, since estimation is not often used, we will focus primarily on hypothesis testing in the remainder of this text.

Summary

Point and Interval Estimation

Point estimate: $\overline{X} = \mu$

$(1 - \alpha)100\%$ Confidence interval:

$$\overline{X} \pm z_{\alpha/2} \frac{\sigma}{\sqrt{N}}$$

$$P \pm z_{\alpha/2} \sqrt{\frac{\pi(1 - \pi)}{N}}$$

Determining sample size:

For a mean: $\quad N = \sigma^2 \left(\dfrac{z_{\alpha/2}}{\text{EM}} \right)^2 \quad$ where EM is error margin

For a proportion: $\quad N = .25 \left(\dfrac{z_{\alpha/2}}{\text{EM}} \right)^2$

General Conceptual Problems

1. List the factors essential for determining the sample size.

2. Why is the sample mean a good estimator of the population mean?

3. Can a one-tailed test be conceptualized as part of an interval estimation? Why or why not?

4. How do point and interval estimates differ? How is the precision (goodness) of these estimates measured?

5. Interpret the interval $\overline{X} \pm 1.96 \dfrac{s}{\sqrt{N-1}}$.

References

1. Barone, M., and Ujifusa, G. (1981). *The Almanac of American Politics*. Washington D.C.: Barone and Co.

2. Reynolds, P. D. (1971). *A Primer in Theory Construction*. Indianapolis, Ind.: Bobbs-Merrill.

$$C \; h \; a \; p \; t \; e \; r \quad \mathbf{\mathmit{11}}$$

Inference from Univariate Data: Two Samples

New Statistical Topics

t Test: equal variance model, unequal variance model, paired samples model
z Test: difference of proportions
Mann–Whitney *U* test

11.1 Overview

Social scientists are far more likely in their analyses to compare several social groups than to make inferences about one group. For example, while studying the constituents of the two political parties in Chapter 10, Anne wonders whether there is a declining proportion of youths who identify themselves as Democrats. A research question such as this, which involves a comparison of different time periods, requires two-sample techniques to explore.

There are a number of reasons for the prevalence of multigroup comparisons. First, similarities and differences among groups are of intrinsic interest to social researchers. Second, with one-sample parametric tests, it is necessary to formulate a hypothesis that predicts a specific parameter value, a task requiring much research. With two or more groups, a statement of *comparative value* would suffice. If Anne hypothesizes that the *same* percentage of Republican as Democrat youths identify themselves as liberal, the statement can be tested without having an *exact* value attached to that percentage.

This chapter presents statistical methods for the comparison of two groups. Anne finds these procedures particularly useful in her study of the changing U.S. family. As before, she utilizes the major sociological perspectives to help her derive hypotheses to be tested using two-sample techniques.

11.1.1 Social Applications

Anne begins with a review of the literature to identify the central concerns of the functionalists in this area. A key article by Murdock [1] concluded, after a survey of 250 representative societies in 1949, that the nuclear family is the prevailing family type or the basic unit for more complex familial forms. In explaining its apparent universality, Murdock identified four essential functions the nuclear family performs that contribute to the continuity of society. These are: (1) channeling sexual drives into stable relationships, (2) developing economic cooperation within the family, (3) assuring societal continuation via reproduction, and (4) socializing offspring as members of society.

Since Murdock's classic work, major social changes have taken place in the United States with profound effects on the family. To determine the extent and direction of changes in family structure and functions, Anne performs a number of comparisons: cross-cultural and domestic, for different historical periods, and across different regions and social groups.

The longer Anne resides in the United States, the more she is impressed by the problems that beset the average family. Newspapers and TV are replete with stories of child abuse, spousal abuse, and teen-age drug addiction and pregnancies. These stories make her wonder if the conflict theory is more applicable, since this theory views the family as an ongoing process of conflict generation and resolution. She intends to explore the causes for family conflict by comparing the rates of domestic conflict among subgroups differentiated by such factors as female employment, age at marriage, and courtship period.

11.1.2 Statistical Topics

In two-sample tests, the researcher must address the issue of whether the two samples are independent or dependent. With independent samples, not only should each sample element be selected independently of others within the first sample, but also independently of other elements in the second sample. As a result, the scores in one sample cannot be predicted from the scores of the other.

With dependent or **paired** samples, the selection of a case in the first sample implies the inclusion of a corresponding case in the second sample. Dependent samples are used in test–retest and before-and-after experimental designs to examine changes in the attitudes or behaviors of the same individuals. Dependent samples may also be formed through matching, whereby each subject in the first sample is matched on one or more characteristics with a subject in the second sample. Matched samples may originate from natural pairings, such as husband and wife, mother and child, and twin siblings. Some research designs demand dependent samples, but, in general, matching is not a recommended substitute for random sampling or random selection of experimental and control subjects.

The concept of the number of samples requires some clarification at this point. To select two independent samples, it may appear necessary for the researcher to construct two sampling frames representing two different populations. In practice, this may or may not be the case. More often than not, only one random sample is taken, within which two samples are differentiated, based on the attributes of a dichotomous variable. For example, if Anne divides an original survey sample into two groups of males and females, each group would be an independent random sample in its own right. This follows from the fact that, if every element in the original sample is randomly chosen, the male and female subsamples are also randomly chosen from the male and female populations. Thus every randomly chosen combination of observations within the initial random sample also constitutes a random sample in itself.

Another point for clarification is the data structure in this chapter. On the surface, it appears that the data are univariate in that only one variable is being measured and used in the calculation of the test statistic. In essence, however, two variables are considered simultaneously: the dependent variable that is being measured and the independent variable that is used to differentiate the populations under study. In testing, the researcher examines whether or not any difference exists in the dependent variable within the two subgroups generated by the independent variable. If a significant difference is found between these distributions, which are in effect conditional distributions, it implies the existence of an association between the two variables (Chapter 4). To illustrate, in acknowledging a difference in the birthrates between high- and low-income families, Anne is concluding at the same time that income and birthrates are related. Therefore, all the procedures dealing with two-sample comparisons in this chapter are essentially *implied* tests of association between a nominal or categorical variable and another variable measured at the interval, ordinal, or nominal level.

11.2 Two-sample Test for Interval Data: t Test for Difference of Means—Equal Variance Model

Research Question
One of Anne's central research questions revolves around the strength of the U.S. family as an institution. Since Murdock's classic work in 1949, more and more of the younger generation in the United States are experimenting with alternatives to marriage and the family. On the other hand, few of these social changes have touched any of the Asian societies. In such societies, marriage is still the only respectable option open to youngsters contemplating a stable relationship with the opposite sex. Consequently, Anne hypothesizes that there is a significant difference in the strength of the family between the U.S. and Asian societies. After reviewing a number of operational definitions and taking into consideration the availability and ease of obtaining the information, Anne uses first-time marriage rates to measure family strength.

The Data

Anne draws random samples of 55 U.S. cities and 53 Asian cities. She then searches through secondary sources such as census and related materials to compile the first-time marriage rates per thousand adults, age 18 and above. The results are shown in Table 11.1.

Anne finds that, on the average, the rate of first-time marriages is higher in Asian than U.S. cities in her samples. The difference between the two rates is 11.7 per thousand. Is this sample difference large enough to indicate that a true difference exists in the two populations?

An Appropriate Test and Its Assumptions

Anne has two random samples of cities for which she has taken measurements of their first-time marriage rates. Since marriage rate is measured on the interval level, the two samples can best be described and summarized in terms of their mean marriage rates. When the samples are thus summarized, an appropriate test is the z or t **test for the difference of means**. The z or t test determines whether a difference in the means of two samples indicates a true difference in their populations. The primary difference between these tests is whether the values of the population variances are known. A z test is selected if the *population variances are known*. If the population variances must be estimated, a t test is appropriate.

To conduct a t test, the researcher must assume that the populations are normally distributed. In addition, a choice must be made between two t test models: one involves an assumption of common or equal variances, and the other involves an assumption of unequal variances. Note that the variances could be *equal* or *unequal* without their values being *known*.

The Statistical Hypotheses

Anne's null hypothesis states that there is no difference between the mean rates of first-time marriages in U.S. and in Asian cities. In other words,

$$H_0: \ \mu_1 - \mu_2 = 0$$

where μ_1 represents the mean marriage rate of U.S. cities and
μ_2 represents the mean marriage rate of Asian cities

TABLE 11.1 First-time Marriage Rates per Thousand for a Sample of U.S. and Asian Cities

	U.S. Cities	Asian Cities
Sample size	55	53
Sample mean rate	76.5	88.2
Sample standard deviation	18.0	17.8

The alternative hypothesis is directional, based on Anne's contention that the strength of the family is weaker in the United States:

$$H_1: \quad \mu_1 - \mu_2 < 0$$

See Box 11.1 for variations on the statement of these hypotheses.

BOX 11.1   Different Forms of the Null and Alternative Hypotheses for Testing the Difference of Means

The null hypothesis of the difference of means can be stated in various ways, depending, to a certain extent, on what the researcher knows. Usually, it is formulated in such a way that knowledge of the specific values of the two population means is not required. For example, in

$$H_0: \quad \mu_1 = \mu_2, \text{ which implies that } \mu_1 - \mu_2 = 0$$

the specific values of μ_1 and μ_2 are irrelevant; they could very well be 1 or 100. It is their *comparative value* that is important. In this sense, the null hypothesis of the two-sample test is easier to formulate than that of the one-sample test, because a specific value of μ must be stated for the latter.

The research hypothesis, in most cases, is formulated as the alternative hypothesis. As in the test of a mean, different forms of the alternative hypotheses can be tested with the same null hypothesis. For example, the alternative hypothesis may be nondirectional, specifying that there is a difference between the means of the two populations:

$$H_1: \quad \mu_1 \neq \mu_2, \text{ which implies } \mu_1 - \mu_2 \neq 0$$

For this hypothesis, a two-tailed test is appropriate, evaluating, other than 0, a range of positive and negative values.

With more knowledge on the researcher's part or with more specific derivation from a theory, a direction may be indicated such that

$$H_1: \quad \mu_1 > \mu_2, \text{ which implies } \mu_1 - \mu_2 > 0$$

or

$$H_1: \quad \mu_1 < \mu_2, \text{ which implies } \mu_1 - \mu_2 < 0$$

Both of these hypotheses involve one-tailed tests. In the first instance we are testing a range of positive values and in the second, a range of negative values.

In certain situations, a precise value for the difference may be tested. Suppose we are interested in whether the mean age of marriage for U.S. women is 5 years older than for Asian women; then our null hypothesis becomes

$$H_0: \quad \mu_1 - \mu_2 = 5$$

The alternative hypothesis might be

$$H_1: \quad \mu_1 - \mu_2 \neq 5 \text{ or } \mu_1 - \mu_2 > 5 \text{ or } \mu_1 - \mu_2 < 5$$

To formulate such a specific null hypothesis requires a great deal of knowledge based either on past research or precise deduction from a theory. Usually, social scientists do not have such prior knowledge and are satisfied with a general rather than a specific statement of the comparative values of the two population means as their null hypothesis.

Sampling Distribution of the z Test

If the populations are normally distributed, the sampling distribution of the differences between sample means is also normal. Otherwise, the central limit theorem, which is useful in establishing the sampling distribution for a one-sample z test, must be invoked to derive the sampling distribution of a two-sample z test. According to a corollary of this theorem, if independent random samples of sizes N_1 and N_2 are taken repeatedly and with replacement from two populations with means and variances of μ_1, σ_1^2 and μ_2, σ_2^2, and if the differences between the two sample means $\overline{X}_1$ and $\overline{X}_2$ are computed, these differences distribute approximately normally when N_1 and N_2 are large. This sampling distribution consisting of the differences of sample means, $(\overline{X}_1 - \overline{X}_2)$'s, has a mean of $(\mu_1 - \mu_2)$ and a standard error of $\sqrt{\sigma_1^2/N_1 + \sigma_2^2/N_2}$.

The sampling distribution of the differences between means represents an extension of the sampling distribution of means. As the expected value of $\overline{X}$ is μ, the expected value of $(\overline{X}_1 - \overline{X}_2)$ is $(\mu_1 - \mu_2)$. Under the null hypothesis that $\mu_1 = \mu_2$, any difference found between a pair of sample means is due to sampling fluctuation. In the long run, these differences should distribute normally around a mean difference of 0 when the samples are sufficiently large or when the populations are normal.

The standard error measures the variability of the differences between pairs of sample means, $(\overline{X}_1 - \overline{X}_2)$'s, around a difference of the population means $(\mu_1 - \mu_2)$, of 0. Some intuitive sense may be made of its formula by noting that there are two sources of variation, one from each population. Thus this standard error can be expected to be larger than the standard error of the sampling distribution of means. The value of the standard error of the differences between means is also dependent on the values of σ_1^2 and σ_2^2 and the sample sizes, N_1 and N_2. The smaller the population variances and the larger the sample sizes are, the smaller will be the standard error.

The test statistic used to evaluate the null hypothesis of $\mu_1 - \mu_2 = 0$ is the z score:

$$z = \frac{(\overline{X}_1 - \overline{X}_2) - (\mu_1 - \mu_2)}{\sigma_{\overline{X}_1 - \overline{X}_2}'} = \frac{\overline{X}_1 - \overline{X}_2}{\sqrt{\dfrac{\sigma_1^2}{N_1} + \dfrac{\sigma_2^2}{N_2}}} \tag{11.1}$$

The z formula is basically a formula for standardizing $(\overline{X}_1 - \overline{X}_2)$. The mean of the sampling distribution, $(\mu_1 - \mu_2)$, under the null hypothesis is subtracted from the raw score, $(\overline{X}_1 - \overline{X}_2)$, and then divided by the standard error, $\sigma_{\overline{X}_1 - \overline{X}_2}$. The probability of occurrence of such a z value can be obtained from Table A in Appendix B. Based on a comparison between this obtained z score and a selected z critical value, a decision is made as to whether the null hypothesis should be rejected.

Sampling Distribution of the t Test

To calculate the z test statistic with Formula 11.1, the population variances must be specified. Usually, however, information on the population variances is not available. Instead, the standard error must be estimated from sample information. The correction factor is first applied to each sample variance to generate unbiased estimators of the population variances. Then the standard error is estimated as follows:

$$\hat{\sigma}_{\overline{X}_1 - \overline{X}_2} = \sqrt{\frac{\hat{\sigma}_1^2}{N_1} + \frac{\hat{\sigma}_2^2}{N_2}}$$

where
$$\hat{\sigma}_1^2 = \frac{N_1}{N_1 - 1} s_1^2 \quad \text{and} \quad \hat{\sigma}_2^2 = \frac{N_2}{N_2 - 1} s_2^2$$

With an estimate of the standard error, we have a t test statistic. Under the null hypothesis of $(\mu_1 - \mu_2) = 0$, the t test statistic reduces to

$$t = \frac{(\overline{X}_1 - \overline{X}_2) - (\mu_1 - \mu_2)}{\hat{\sigma}_{\overline{X}_1 - \overline{X}_2}} = \frac{\overline{X}_1 - \overline{X}_2}{\sqrt{\frac{\hat{\sigma}_1^2}{N_1} + \frac{\hat{\sigma}_2^2}{N_2}}}$$

Do not confuse this equation with the one for the one-sample t test despite their resemblance. In this formula, $(\overline{X}_1 - \overline{X}_2)$ is being compared to $(\mu_1 - \mu_2)$ or 0.

There are two different models of the t test: one assumes that the population variances are equal and one does not. The researcher selects a model by making an assumption about the equality or inequality of variances based on past observations, theory, or a combination thereof. Alternatively, she or he can use an F ratio (to be discussed in Chapter 12) to test the null hypothesis that $\sigma_1^2 = \sigma_2^2$. The rejection of this null hypothesis results in the adoption of the model for unequal variances; otherwise, the model for equal variances is adopted. A statistical software package such as SPSS automatically completes an F test and provides t tests for both equal and unequal variances whenever a t test is requested.

When $\sigma_1^2 = \sigma_2^2$ can be assumed, subscripting is unnecessary. Both σ_1^2 and σ_2^2 can be represented by σ^2, the **common variance**. Using the symbol of the common variance, the formula for the estimated standard error can be simplified as

$$\hat{\sigma}_{\overline{X}_1 - \overline{X}_2} = \hat{\sigma} \sqrt{\frac{1}{N_1} + \frac{1}{N_2}}$$

Furthermore, because the population variances are equal, we are in effect estimating the same parameter σ^2. The sample variances can be pooled for this estimation such that:

$$\hat{\sigma} = \sqrt{\frac{N_1 s_1^2 + N_2 s_2^2}{N_1 + N_2 - 2}}$$

Finally, the estimated standard error of the t distribution is calculated by combining the two preceding formulas as follows:

$$\hat{\sigma}_{\bar{X}_1 - \bar{X}_2} = \sqrt{\frac{N_1 s_1^2 + N_2 s_2^2}{N_1 + N_2 - 2}} \sqrt{\frac{N_1 + N_2}{N_1 N_2}} \qquad (11.2)$$

The t test statistic assuming a common population variance becomes

$$t = \frac{\bar{X}_1 - \bar{X}_2}{\sqrt{\frac{N_1 s_1^2 + N_2 s_2^2}{N_1 + N_2 - 2}} \sqrt{\frac{N_1 + N_2}{N_1 N_2}}} \qquad (11.3)$$

This test statistic has a t sampling distribution with $(N_1 + N_2 - 2)$ degrees of freedom. Since $(N_1 - 1)$ and $(N_2 - 1)$ are the degrees of freedom associated with the two independent estimators of σ^2, the estimated variance using pooled information from both samples has $(N_1 - 1) + (N_2 - 1)$ or $(N_1 + N_2 - 2)$ degrees of freedom.

Calculation of the Test Statistic
After inspecting the sample variances, which are very similar, Anne makes an assumption of equal population variances. Her data produce the following results:

1. The estimated standard error:

$$\hat{\sigma}_{\bar{X}_1 - \bar{X}_2} = \sqrt{\frac{(55)18^2 + (53)17.8^2}{55 + 53 - 2}} \sqrt{\frac{55 + 53}{(55)(53)}} = 3.469$$

2. The test statistic: $t = \dfrac{76.5 - 88.2}{3.469} = -3.372$

3. The df: $55 + 53 - 2 = 106$

The Decision
Since the t table does not provide a distribution with df = 106, Anne takes the conservative approach of obtaining the critical value from one with a smaller df, that with a df of 60. At an α of .05 for a one-tailed test with df = 60, the t value necessary to reject the null hypothesis is −1.671 or lower. The obtained t score of −3.372 falls in the region of rejection. Therefore, the null hypothesis is rejected in favor of the alternative hypothesis. The results of the test also imply that there is an association between different cultures and the strength of the nuclear family.

To understand why the null hypothesis is rejected, a review of the logic of hypothesis testing is necessary. When the null hypothesis is true and $\mu_1 = \mu_2$, the difference between two sample means, $(\bar{X}_1 - \bar{X}_2)$, is expected to be 0. However, since sampling errors may occur, values of $(\bar{X}_1 - \bar{X}_2)$ may differ from 0. Although small variations from 0 are likely, large variations are unlikely if the null hypothesis is true. Therefore, if a large deviation from zero is obtained, the assumption that H_0 is true becomes questionable; instead H_1 may be true. For if the alternative hypothesis is true and $\mu_1 - \mu_2 < 0$, then a large deviation from 0 in the negative direction is to be expected.

The question remains as to what constitutes a large deviation from the expected result when the null hypothesis is true. This is decided through selecting a critical t value that is associated with a .05 or .01 significance level. If the deviation represented by the obtained t score is greater than the deviation represented by the critical t value associated with a .05 (or .01) α level, the sample result is highly unlikely. Such a t value occurs only 5 (or 1) out of every 100 times of sampling, given that the null hypothesis is true. Therefore, when Anne obtains a deviation of this magnitude in one sampling, she rejects the null hypothesis and concludes that there is evidence to support the alternative hypothesis.

In the process of making a decision on her hypotheses, Anne reviews the assumptions required in the t-test model to ensure that they have been met. The requirement of interval-level measurement is met in the variable of marriage rate. Also, Anne is confident that she drew independent random samples. The assumption of the normality of populations in her study is dubious because she has no idea as to the distributions of the marital statuses in Asian and U.S. societies. The t test, however, is robust with respect to this requirement. When the sample sizes are fairly large, as in this case, the t test can tolerate some departure from normality. The assumption of equal variances is more important. Anne is sure that she is appropriately using the equal variance model because the sample variances are very similar.

Thus an evaluation shows that Anne has adhered to all the requirements for performing a t test. Although she cannot conclusively prove her research hypothesis, she has a great degree of confidence in its truth.

Summary

Equal Variance Model t Test

Null hypothesis: $\mu_1 - \mu_2 = 0$

Test statistic:

$$t = \frac{\overline{X}_1 - \overline{X}_2}{\sqrt{\dfrac{N_1 s_1^2 + N_2 s_2^2}{N_1 + N_2 - 2}}\sqrt{\dfrac{N_1 + N_2}{N_1 N_2}}}, \qquad \text{where df} = (N_1 + N_2 - 2)$$

Test model:

1. Interval measurement
2. Independent random samples
3. Normal populations with $\sigma_1^2 = \sigma_2^2 = \sigma^2$

Exercises

1. Suspecting that the more urbanized the areas, the higher the divorce rate is, Anne takes random samples of 50 census tracts from Los Angeles and another 50 from Fresno and compares their divorce rates. Is there a significant difference in divorce rates between the two cities?

	Los Angeles	Fresno
Sample size	50	50
Sample mean	14.3	7.8
Sample standard deviation	2.1	2.2

2. Anne gathers information on family size from two random samples of blacks and Hispanics residing in San Jose, California, to test the hypothesis that there is no difference in family size between the two groups. What is her conclusion?

	Blacks	Hispanics
Sample size	100	80
Sample mean	7.0	7.8
Sample standard deviation	1.5	1.4

3. Noticing a wide variation in marriage rates among different occupations, Anne compares the rates of the unmarried per 100 adults among professionals and farmers in Sacramento and its surrounding farming area. Is there a significant difference between the two occupational groups?

	Professionals	Farmers
Sample size	75	75
Sample mean	19	12
Standard deviation	9	8

4. To test the hypothesis that marriage rate has not changed drastically over the years in the United States, Anne obtains first-time marriage rates per 1,000 in 1940 and 1990 as follows. What is her conclusion?

	1940	1990
Sample size	50	60
Sample mean	78.3	55.3
Sample standard deviation	17.3	18.8

11.3 Two-sample Test for Interval Data: t Test for Difference of Means—Unequal Variance Model

Research Question
Now that Anne has evidence to support the hypothesis that there is a relative decline of family strength in the United States, she continues to test auxiliary hypotheses related to the same issue. Note the term "relative strength" of the family is used because marriage is still the prevalent mode in the United States, although it is not as common as in Asian societies or as in the past. According to functionalism, the nuclear family persists because it performs certain necessary functions for society, such as the reproduction and socialization of the young. If the strength of the family has declined, it should be accompanied by a relative loss of these functions. To test whether this is the case, Anne formulates the hypothesis that the average number of children per family is smaller now than before. Because of the rapidity of change in the United States today, she further deduces that the variation in the number of children per family is probably much larger now than in the past.

The Data
For her analysis, Anne takes two independent random samples of 23 and 25 cities from the 1940 and the 1980 U.S. census data. The data include the average number of children per family, as shown in Table 11.2.

An Appropriate Test and Its Assumptions
Anne has exactly the same type of data and samples as in the first illustration. However, based on her reasoning and after inspecting the sample standard deviations, Anne suspects that the assumption of equal variances would not pertain to this problem. What she needs, therefore, is a *t* test that does not assume equal variances in the populations.

The Statistical Hypotheses
The null hypothesis states that there is no difference in the average number of children per family between 1940 and 1980:

$$H_0: \quad \mu_1 - \mu_2 = 0$$

where μ_1 refers to the mean number of children per family in 1940 and
μ_2 refers to the mean number of children per family in 1980

TABLE 11.2 Number of Children per Family in 1940 and 1980

	1940	1980
Sample size	23	25
Sample mean	4.309	2.796
Standard deviation	.614	.990

Rejection of this hypothesis will lend credence to Anne's research hypothesis that families have fewer children nowadays:

$$H_1: \ \mu_1 - \mu_2 > 0$$

The Sampling Distribution

The sampling distribution for the unequal variances model is the same t distribution. However, Anne can no longer pool the sample estimates to obtain the value of a common variance. Because the population variances are unequal, each must be estimated separately with its own sample variance. Estimating σ_1^2/N_1 with $s_1^2/(N_1 - 1)$ and σ_2^2/N_2 with $s_2^2/(N_2 - 1)$, the estimated standard error of the difference of sample means is calculated as follows:

$$\hat{\sigma}_{\overline{X}_1 - \overline{X}_2} = \sqrt{\frac{s_1^2}{N_1 - 1} + \frac{s_2^2}{N_2 - 1}} \tag{11.4}$$

The following t-test statistic is appropriate for the unequal variances assumption:

$$t = \frac{\overline{X}_1 - \overline{X}_2}{\sqrt{\dfrac{s_1^2}{N_1 - 1} + \dfrac{s_2^2}{N_2 - 1}}} \tag{11.5}$$

The number of degrees of freedom for this t test is calculated differently, depending on sample sizes. When sample sizes are large, a combined ($N_1 + N_2$) of 100 or more, or when they are approximately equal, the formula ($N_1 + N_2 - 2$) applies. However, if N_1 is much smaller than N_2, $s_1^2/(N_1 - 1)$ would not be as efficient an estimate of σ_1^2/N_1 as $s_2^2/(N_2 - 1)$ would be of σ_2^2/N_2. Therefore, when one or the other of the preceding conditions is not met, the number of degrees of freedom is calculated with a formula that takes into account the relative efficiency of the two variance estimators:

$$df = \frac{\left(\dfrac{s_1^2}{N_1 - 1} + \dfrac{s_2^2}{N_2 - 1}\right)^2}{\left(\dfrac{s_1^2}{N_1 - 1}\right)^2 \left(\dfrac{1}{N_1 + 1}\right) + \left(\dfrac{s_2^2}{N_2 - 1}\right)^2 \left(\dfrac{1}{N_2 + 1}\right)} - 2 \tag{11.6}$$

Calculation of the t Test by SPSS

To verify that the population variances are indeed different, Anne submits the following SPSS program to compute the t-test statistic for the data in Table 11.2.

SPSS automatically calculates an *F* ratio to test the assumption of equal variances whenever the *t* test is requested.

```
DATA LIST FREE/TIME CHILD.

BEGIN DATA.

1   4.00   2   3.11

1   5.23   2   1.26

1   3.98   2   .37

.  .  .

.  .  .

END DATA.

T-TEST GROUPS=TIME (1,2) /VARIABLES=CHILD.
```

In the program, TIME is the independent variable whose scores of 1 and 2 refer to the periods of 1940 and 1980, respectively. It is also called a *grouping variable*, from whose values the samples are generated. The dependent variable CHILD refers to the number of children per family. To perform a *t* test, two subcommands of the command T-TEST are required: GROUPS and VARIABLES. The GROUPS subcommand designates the grouping variable. The value specification after TIME is optional in this case, since there are only two values of TIME. However, when there are more than two values in the grouping variable, the specification becomes necessary. Otherwise, SPSS will use the default values of 1 and 2. The VARIABLES subcommand specifies the dependent variable CHILD whose means between the two groups are compared.

The output from the program is shown in SPSS Figure 11.1. It includes the *F* ratio to test the equal variances assumption, the *t* scores under the two models of equal and unequal variances, and the degrees of freedom associated with each *t*. Note that the values of sample standard deviations are slightly different from those of the text because of the use of $(N - 1)$ as the denominator.

The *F* ratio of the two variances equals 2.59 with a two-tailed probability of .028. With this probability, Anne can reject the null hypothesis of equal variances at the .05 level; the population variances are probably unequal. She therefore selects the *t*-test output under the "Separate Variance Estimate" to interpret. The *t* value is shown to be 6.15 with a two-tailed probability of less than .0005. This means that Anne can reject the null hypothesis for a one-tailed *t* test at or beyond the .00025 level. Had the probability of *F* been higher than .05, she would have chosen the portion of the *t*-test output under "Pooled Variance Estimate" to interpret.

	Number of Cases	Mean	Standard Deviation	Standard Error
Group 1	23	4.3091	.642	.134
Group 2	25	2.7964	1.032	.206

F Value	2-Tail Prob.	Pooled Variance Estimate			Separate Variance Estimate		
		t Value	Degrees of Freedom	2-Tail Prob.	t Value	Degrees of Freedom	2-Tail Prob.
2.59	.028	6.03	46	.000	6.15	40.58	.000

SPSS FIGURE 11.1   Equal and Unequal Variance Model t Tests

Manual Calculation of the t Test
Calculating the t test by hand, Anne obtains the following:

1. The estimated standard error: $\hat{\sigma}_{\bar{X}_1 - \bar{X}_2} = \sqrt{\dfrac{.614^2}{23-1} + \dfrac{.990^2}{25-1}} = .240$

2. The t-test statistic: $t = \dfrac{4.309 - 2.796}{.240} = 6.304$

Although the sample sizes are not very different, they are not large. Therefore, Anne uses Formula 11.6 to calculate the degrees of freedom for her test:

$$ df = \frac{\left(\dfrac{.614^2}{23-1} + \dfrac{.990^2}{25-1} \right)^2}{\left(\dfrac{.614^2}{23-1} \right)^2 \left(\dfrac{1}{23+1} \right) + \left(\dfrac{.990^2}{25-1} \right)^2 \left(\dfrac{1}{25+1} \right)} - 2 = 42.011 $$

Note that, had Anne calculated the degrees of freedom using $(N_1 + N_2 - 2)$, she would have obtained 46. The two answers are not very different.

The t and df values are slightly different from those obtained from SPSS because of the rounding errors involved in hand calculation. These rounding errors are unimportant because the decision reached is the same. From the t table, the critical value associated with a one-tailed t test at α of .01 with 40 degrees of freedom is 2.423. The computed t score of 6.30 is much greater than this critical value and is therefore significant at beyond the .01 level. Again, this significance level indicates that if the H_0 is true Anne would obtain this type of sample result no oftener than 1 time out of 100 times of repeated sampling. Anne concludes that there is enough evidence to support the alternative hypothesis that family size had declined by 1980.

Note that when the two variances are equal or similar in value the unequal variance model can still be used. The estimate of the standard error in Formula 11.4 is merely less efficient than the estimate provided by Formula 11.2. When the two population variances are not markedly different and sample sizes are similar, results from the two models are very similar. Also, as N_1 and N_2 become large, the two models yield similar t scores and either test statistic is appropriate.

Summary

Unequal Variance Model t Test

Null hypothesis: $\mu_1 - \mu_2 = 0$

Test statistic: $t = \dfrac{\overline{X}_1 - \overline{X}_2}{\sqrt{\dfrac{s_1^2}{N_1 - 1} + \dfrac{s_2^2}{N_2 - 1}}}$

where df $= \dfrac{\left(\dfrac{s_1^2}{N_1 - 1} + \dfrac{s_2^2}{N_2 - 1}\right)^2}{\left(\dfrac{s_1^2}{N_1 - 1}\right)^2\left(\dfrac{1}{N_1 + 1}\right) + \left(\dfrac{s_2^2}{N_2 - 1}\right)^2\left(\dfrac{1}{N_2 + 1}\right)} - 2$

Test model:

1. Interval measurement
2. Independent random samples
3. Normal populations with $\sigma_1^2 \neq \sigma_2^2$

Exercises

---

5. To compare the rates of married women in the work force between 1950 and 1990, Anne selects random samples of 100 cities of approximately the same size for these years. The results are as follows. Is there an increase in female employment over the years?

	1950	1990
Sample size	110	100
Sample mean	5.21	6.63
Sample standard deviation	1.33	.95

6. For the socialization function of the family, Anne uses the following measurement: the number of hours parents spend with children per week for educational and moral guidance. Is there a difference between time spent on this function between 1955 and 1988?

	1955	1988
Sample size	25	60
Sample mean	6.9	3.5
Sample standard deviation	1.8	3.3

7. For the following two sets of data, test H_0 at the .05 level by a one-tailed test and compare the results.

	$\overline{X}_1$	$\overline{X}_2$	s_1	s_2	N_1	N_2
Data set 1	50	53	9	18	26	25
Data set 2	50	53	9	18	260	250

8. Repeat the same tests in Exercise 7 with the following data:

	$\overline{X}_1$	$\overline{X}_2$	s_1	s_2	N_1	N_2
Data set 1	50	54	9	18	26	25
Data set 2	50	54	9	18	260	250

SPSS Exercises

1. Using the City data, answer the following questions. Do family forms vary by the population density of the city? In a larger and more congested city, do we find smaller families more often? Are smaller cities more likely to retain traditional family forms? First, RECODE the population of 500 cities into two groups: cities with above and below the median population densities (POPDENSE). Then take a 20% random sample from the recoded population. Using the *t* test, compare the two groups of cities with respect to the following:

   a. Mean number of persons per household (HOUSESIZ)
   b. Mean percentage of female family householders (FEHOUSE)
   c. Mean percentage of one-person households (SOLO)

2. Are older people more likely to be drawn to the sun-belt cities? First, RECODE the population into two regions (STATE): the sun-belt states (California, Arizona, New Mexico, Texas, Louisiana, Florida, and Hawaii) and the rest. Then take a 20% random sample of the population.

   a. Determine if there is a significant difference in the mean percentage of people over 65 years old (ELDERLY) between the two regions.
   b. Perform the same test using the January temperature (JANTEMP) to classify cities into two groups: severe versus temperate climate.

3. Test the hypothesis that teen-age pregnancy (YGBIRTH) is more prevalent in large cities. RECODE the population into those with more than 50,000 inhabitants (POPLATON) and the rest. Take a 20% random sample of the population. Is there a significant difference in the mean percentage of births to teen-age mothers by city size?

11.4 t *Test for Paired Samples*

Research Question

Functionalists view the family as an integrated social system characterized by a broad consensus on basic values. From this postulate, Anne derives the hypothesis that husbands and wives generally agree on how many children they should have.

The Data

Anne selects 14 couples that are representative of the social classes of her community and interviews husbands and wives separately. The spouses' perceptions of the ideal number of children are shown in Table 11.3. Is there a significant difference between husbands and wives or can Anne conclude that they share the same view?

An Appropriate Test and Its Assumptions

Anne cannot use the *t* test described in the earlier sections to test this hypothesis because the two samples are *not independent*. The husbands and wives in her study constitute matched samples because they are selected as husband–wife pairs and not independently of each other. When two samples do not vary

TABLE 11.3 Ideal Number of Children According to Each Spouse

Couple Number	Number Desired by Husband	Number Desired by Wife	D_i
1	0	4	−4
2	3	2	1
3	4	2	2
4	3	4	−1
5	2	2	0
6	5	3	2
7	1	2	−1
8	3	5	−2
9	4	2	2
10	1	1	0
11	5	5	0
12	3	3	0
13	2	4	−2
14	0	0	0

independently of each other, a *t* test for **paired samples** is appropriate. This *t* test for paired samples is very similar to the one-sample *t* test of means discussed in Chapter 9.

The Statistical Hypotheses

Anne suspects that husbands and wives agree on a very basic issue of their marriage—the number of children they desire to have. Therefore,

$$H_0: \ \mu_D = 0$$

Note that although the null hypothesis is stated verbally in the same manner as in a difference of means test with two independent samples, symbolically, it is formulated differently. μ_D is used instead of $\mu_1 - \mu_2$, where μ_D refers to the mean of the population of *difference scores*. For a more thorough explanation of the notation, see the following section on sampling distribution.

Note also that, unlike the null hypotheses of the two preceding illustrations, this is the research hypothesis for which Anne is attempting to provide empirical support. This illustrates that the research hypothesis may be formulated as the null rather than the alternative hypothesis.

It is possible that husbands and wives do not agree, in which case, functionalism is incorrect in its assumptions. Therefore,

$$H_1: \ \mu_D \neq 0$$

The Sampling Distribution

To understand the sampling distribution, we must identify what constitutes the sample and the population distribution first. In a paired-sample test, if a husband desires to have 3 children while his wife prefers 2, the score for this pair is 1: (3 – 2), not 3 or 2. This difference score of 1 is symbolized by D_i. Because each pair is measured by a difference score, there is, in effect, only one population and one sample of these difference scores. Table 11.3, for example, shows a sample of 14 difference scores drawn from the population of all possible D_i's.

According to the central limit theorem, if large samples of *N* pairs are drawn repeatedly from a population of difference scores (D_i's), with a mean of μ_D and a standard deviation of σ_D, the sampling distribution of mean difference scores, $\overline{D}_i$'s, will be approximately normal. This sampling distribution has a mean of $\mu_{\overline{D}}$, which equals μ_D, and a standard error of $\sigma_{\overline{D}}$, which equals $\sqrt{\sigma_D^2/N}$. Thus the appropriate sampling distribution consists of the means of these difference scores in various samples, $\overline{D}_i$'s, and their associated probabilities.

However, since Anne does not have the information for σ_D, she must estimate it. With an estimated standard error, the appropriate test statistic is the *t* score:

$$t = \frac{\overline{D} - \mu_{\overline{D}}}{\hat{\sigma}_{\overline{D}}}$$

This t test statistic has a t sampling distribution with $(N - 1)$ degrees of freedom. To use the test, an assumption must be made that the population of difference scores is normally distributed. Anne considers this a reasonable assumption for her problem. The assumption becomes less important if the sample is large enough (N of 30 to 50), since the t test is robust with respect to this assumption.

The standard error is estimated from the sample as follows:

$$\hat{\sigma}_D = \sqrt{\frac{\hat{\sigma}_D^2}{N}} = \sqrt{\frac{s_D^2}{N - 1}}$$

Since $\mu_D = 0$ under the null hypothesis, substituting for the estimated standard error, we have the following t-test statistic:

$$t = \frac{\overline{D}}{s_D / \sqrt{N - 1}} \qquad (11.7)$$

The sample mean $\overline{D}$ is calculated as

$$\overline{D} = \frac{\sum\limits_{i=1}^{N} D_i}{N}$$

while the variance is calculated as

$$s_D^2 = \frac{\sum\limits_{i=1}^{N} D_i^2}{N} - \left(\frac{\sum\limits_{i=1}^{N} D_i}{N} \right)^2$$

Calculation of the Test Statistic

Let us see how the t statistic is computed from Anne's data. Note that in Table 11.3 the pairwise differences are already calculated in the last column. Based on these difference scores, Anne obtains the following:

1. Sample mean: $\overline{D} = (-4) + 1 + 2 + (-1) + \cdots /14 = -.214$

2. Sample variance: $s_D^2 = \dfrac{39}{14} - \left(\dfrac{-3}{14} \right)^2 = 2.739$

3. Estimated standard error: $\hat{\sigma}_{\overline{D}} = \sqrt{\dfrac{2.739}{13}} = .459$

4. t-Test statistic: $t = \dfrac{-.214}{.459} = -.466$

The Decision

With the degrees of freedom being 13, the *t* value must be larger than |2.160| on a two-tailed test to reject the null hypothesis at the .05 level. Since the observed data produce a *t* score of –.466, Anne fails to reject the null hypothesis that husbands and wives share the same value. In other words, it is not unlikely for Anne to obtain a mean of –.214 in the sample when the population mean is 0. The data seem to support the functionalist claim for a common value system in the family as far as the desired number of children is concerned. To substantiate this claim completely, multiple testing of different values would be necessary.

Summary

Paired Samples *t* Test

Null hypothesis: $\mu_D = 0$

Test statistic: $t = \dfrac{\overline{D}}{s_D / \sqrt{N-1}}$

where N = number of difference scores or pairs of subjects
   $df = (N-1)$

Test model:

1. Interval measurement
2. Dependent samples: random sampling of pairs
3. Normal distribution of population differences

Exercises

The interview data on the 14 couples collected by Anne contain the following additional information. Test the null hypotheses that husbands and wives share common values in these areas by computing the pairwise difference scores.

9. Ideal number of hours they should spend together for recreation per week.

Husband	8	9	8	10	15	8	12	10	7	8	10	8	10	5
Wife	20	7	5	20	17	16	13	8	14	10	12	9	10	10

10. Ideal percent of income they should save.

Husband	20	30	15	10	5	10	20	25	20	10	15	20	40	10
Wife	20	15	25	20	10	15	20	30	15	10	5	30	10	10

11. Desired frequency of sexual intercourse per week.

| Husband | 5 | 2 | 3 | 4 | 6 | 7 | 3 | 2 | 2 | 3 | 4 | 2 | 3 | 3 |
| Wife | 2 | 3 | 1 | 2 | 2 | 2 | 3 | 3 | 2 | 1 | 2 | 1 | 2 | 3 |

SPSS Session

The following is the program Anne submits for a *t* test for paired samples:

```
DATA LIST FREE/HUSBAND WIFE.

BEGIN DATA.

0 4

3 2

. . .

END DATA.

T-TEST PAIRS=HUSBAND WITH WIFE.
```

The number of children desired by husbands and wives is entered separately under the variables of HUSBAND and WIFE. Each variable, in this case, gives rise to one of the two dependent sample distributions. The *t* test for paired samples is performed by the T-TEST procedure with the subcommand PAIRS. After the PAIRS subcommand, specify the first variable, then the keyword BY, and then the second variable.

According to the SPSS output shown in SPSS Figure 11.2, the mean numbers of children desired by husbands and wives are 2.5714 and 2.7857, respectively.

Variable	Number of Cases	Mean	Standard Deviation	Standard Error
HUSBAND	14	2.5714	1.651	.441
WIFE	14	2.7857	1.477	.395

(Difference) Mean	Standard Deviation	Standard Error	2-Tail Corr.	Prob.	t Value	Degrees of Freedom	2-Tail Prob.
−.2143	1.718	.459	.401	.155	−.47	13	.648

SPSS FIGURE 11.2   Paired Samples *t* Test

The difference between these two means is −.2143, which produces a *t* value of −.47 with the degrees of freedom being 13. A two-tailed probability of .648 does not allow Anne to reject the null hypothesis. SPSS also calculates the correlation coefficient, Pearson's *r*, between the ideal number of children desired by husbands and wives, which equals .401.

SPSS Exercises

4. According to the GSS survey, is there a significant difference between husband's and their wives educational attainment (EDUC, SPEDUC)?

5. Is there a significant difference between husbands and their wives with respect to the number of hours they worked during the previous week (HRS1, SPHRS1)?

11.5 z Test for Difference of Proportions

Research Question
The strength of the family as measured by the first-time marriage rate and its function as measured by desired family size have definitely been changing, as Anne has learned. Such alternatives to marriage as cohabitation and singlehood abound, especially where the social climate is more tolerant of experimentation and among segments of the population that are more open to change. Anne decides to investigate how the level of acceptance of these alternatives varies among different social groups, strata, and regions in the country. More specifically, she reasons that if experimentation with alternatives to traditional familial relationships is going on, it is more likely to be found among the younger generation.

The Data
Anne therefore takes a random sample of 550 college students from University X. She sends the students questionnaires to determine their demographic profiles and their attitudes toward and experience in the previously mentioned topics. Surprisingly, Anne receives close to 90% of the responses. She divides the returned questionnaires into two groups, based on whether the students have been raised in a rural or urban area. The percentages of respondents who have experienced cohabitation in each group are shown in Table 11.4.

An Appropriate Test and Its Assumptions
Although it appears that Anne has sent the questionnaires to one group only, she has, in effect, two independent random samples. As explained in Section 11.1.2, when the initial random sample is partitioned into the rural and urban segments, these segments constitute random samples of the rural and urban student populations at University X.

The variable, cohabitation, is dichotomous. An appropriate summary measure of a dichotomous variable is the proportion. Therefore a **z test for the differ-**

**TABLE 11.4 Cohabitation Experience among
College Students from Rural and Urban Areas**

		Students from:	
Cohabitation		Rural Area	Urban Area
Experienced		12%	25%
Have not experienced		88%	75%
	Total	100%	100%
	N	(196)	(290)

ence of proportions is appropriate here. This test is a special case of the test of difference between two means. As such, it is treated in this section, although it could also be classified under procedures for nominal data.

The Statistical Hypotheses

The null hypothesis that cohabitation has spread equally in rural and urban areas can be expressed as follows:

$$H_0: \ \pi_1 - \pi_2 = 0$$

where π_1 refers to the proportion of students from urban areas who have experienced cohabitation and π_2 represents the proportion of students from rural areas who have experienced cohabitation.

The alternative hypothesis is that cohabitation is not equally accepted. Therefore,

$$H_1: \ \pi_1 - \pi_2 \neq 0$$

The Sampling Distribution

Applying the central limit theorem to the case of proportions, we have the following. When both sample sizes are sufficiently large, the sampling distribution of the difference between proportions will be approximately normal with a mean of $(\pi_1 - \pi_2)$ and a standard error of $\sigma_{\pi_1 - \pi_2}$, where

$$\sigma_{\pi_1 - \pi_2} = \sqrt{\frac{\sigma_1^2}{N_1} + \frac{\sigma_2^2}{N_1}} = \sqrt{\frac{\pi_1(1 - \pi_1)}{N_1} + \frac{\pi_2(1 - \pi_2)}{N_2}}$$

Since the null hypothesis states that $\pi_1 = \pi_2$ and since the variances of both populations are calculated from these equal proportions, where $\sigma_1^2 = \pi_1(1 - \pi_1)$ and $\sigma_2^2 = \pi_2(1 - \pi_2)$, the two population variances must be equal: $\sigma_1^2 = \sigma_2^2 = \sigma^2$. When the variances of the populations are equal, a common variance can be estimated, as in the case of the t test, by pooling the sample variances. By substituting the appropriate symbols into the formula for pooled variances, we have an estimate of $\hat{\sigma}_{\pi_1 - \pi_2}$ as follows:

$$\hat{\sigma}_{\pi_1 - \pi_2} = \sqrt{\hat{\pi}(1 - \hat{\pi})} \sqrt{\frac{N_1 + N_2}{N_1 N_2}} \qquad (11.8)$$

where $\hat{\pi}$ refers to the estimated π.

The population proportion π can, in turn, be estimated from the two sample proportions:

$$\hat{\pi} = \frac{N_1 P_1 + N_2 P_2}{N_1 + N_2} \qquad (11.9)$$

The test statistic is z. Although there is no information on σ^2, the sample sizes are large enough that the distinction between t and z becomes unimportant. Under an H_0 of no difference in the population proportions, z equals

$$z = \frac{(P_1 - P_2) - (\pi_1 - \pi_2)}{\hat{\sigma}_{\pi_1 - \pi_2}} = \frac{(P_1 - P_2)}{\hat{\sigma}_{\pi_1 - \pi_2}} \qquad (11.10)$$

Calculation of the Test Statistic

The total number of students N is 486 instead of 550 because some students did not return the questionnaire. Inserting Anne's data into the formulas, the following results are obtained:

1. Pooled estimate of π: $\hat{\pi} = \dfrac{196(.12) + 290(.25)}{196 + 290} = .197$

2. Pooled estimate of $(1 - \pi)$: $1 - \hat{\pi} = 1 - .197 = .803$

3. Pooled estimate of the standard error:

$$\hat{\sigma}_{\pi_1 - \pi_2} = \sqrt{(.197)(.803)} \sqrt{\frac{196 + 290}{(196)(290)}} = .0367$$

4. z-Test statistic: $z = \dfrac{.25 - .12}{.037} = 3.513$

The Decision

The critical values for a two-tailed z test at the .05 significance level is ± 1.96. With a z value as extreme as 3.51, Anne can reject the null hypothesis at beyond the .05 significance level that cohabitation is equally prevalent among rural and urban college students at her university.

Anne must be especially cautious in reaching this conclusion because the response rate in her survey is not 100%. There is always the possibility that those students who have not returned the questionnaires are systematically different from those who have. Had these students returned the questionnaires, the results and the conclusion might have been different. The problem of less than 100% response rate, however, is not specific to Anne's project, but is common in surveys. If a researcher waits until all questionnaires are returned before making a conclusion, she or he is not likely to reach any conclusion. The strategy is to make a tentative conclusion while acknowledging the possibility of error.

Summary

z Test for Difference of Proportions

Null hypothesis: $\pi_1 - \pi_2 = 0$

Test statistic: $z = \dfrac{(P_1 - P_2)}{\hat{\sigma}_{\pi_1 - \pi_2}}$

where $\hat{\sigma}_{\pi_1 - \pi_2} = \sqrt{\hat{\pi}(1 - \hat{\pi})}\sqrt{\dfrac{N_1 + N_2}{N_1 N_2}}$ and $\hat{\pi} = \dfrac{N_1 P_1 + N_2 P_2}{N_1 + N_2}$

Test model:

1. Measurement level: dichotomy
2. Large independent random samples
3. Assumption of $\sigma_1^2 = \sigma_2^2 = \sigma^2$

Exercises

Anne's surveys of family relations in the 1990s have yielded the following data. Apply the test for the difference of proportions to confirm or disconfirm the null hypothesis that the emerging new family patterns are equally prevalent in urban and rural areas. Is there enough evidence to conclude that these new family styles are here to stay permanently?

	Rural ($N = 100$)	Urban ($N = 150$)
Percentages of respondents:		
12. Who have experienced single parenthood	4%	13%
13. Who approve gay marriage	7%	10%
14. Who plan to stay single throughout their lives	19%	42%

15. According to a research report, 95 out of a sample of 160 people below the age of 30 and 50 out of a sample of 140 people in their 50's have experienced cohabitation.
    a. Perform a test of the difference of proportions.
    b. Would a test of the difference of means be appropriate? Why?
    c. Compare the results.

16. Suppose the alternative hypothesis in Exercise 14 states that the percentage of those planning to stay single is 5% higher in the urban area than in the rural area. If the Type I error is set at .05, what is the probability of Type II error?

11.6 Two-sample Test for Ordinal Data: Mann–Whitney U Test

Research Question

In contrast to functionalism, which treats the family as a more or less integrated system, conflict theory views the family as a constantly changing process in which conflicts are generated and resolved. Taking the conflict perspective, Anne decides to examine family conflict that arises from female employment outside the house. Women who have outside employment may suffer from role conflict of being wife, mother, and employee at the same time. Husbands who expect their wives to play the traditional feminine roles will be frustrated by the situation. Thus Anne hypothesizes that families whose wives have outside employment are more likely to be laden with conflict.

The Data

To test this research hypothesis, Anne obtains data from a family counselor. The counselor initially develops a profile of each family seeking help. As a part of the profile, the counselor evaluates the intensity of conflict between the spouses and assigns a score that ranges from 1 to 10, with 1 being the lowest and 10, the highest score. The working status of the wife is also part of the information contained in this report.

Anne divides the caseload of this counselor into two subgroups: wives who have outside employment and wives who do not. From each subgroup Anne takes a proportionate random sample, which results in a total of eight families as shown in Table 11.5.

11.6.1 Mann–Whitney U Test for Small Samples

An Appropriate Test and Its Assumptions

Conflict is measured on an ordinal level. Since the *t* test requires interval data, it cannot be used unless an assumption is made that the ordinal data are approximately interval. Being unwilling to make such an assumption, Anne decides to use a nonparametric substitute for the *t* test, the **Mann–Whitney U test.** Under

TABLE 11.5 Family Conflict According to Wife's Employment Status

Wife's Employment Status			
No Outside Employment		Outside Employment	
Conflict Score	Rank	Conflict Score	Rank
1	1	3	3
2	2	7	6
5	4	8	7
6	5		
9	8		
$N_2 = 5$	$R_2 = 20$	$N_1 = 3$	$R_1 = 16$

the null hypothesis of this test, two independent random samples are assumed to have been drawn from two populations with the same continuous distribution. The test statistic is then calculated on the *ranks* assigned to the actual scores of the sample observations. Therefore, the required minimal level of data measurement for the Mann–Whitney U is ordinal.

The power efficiency (Chapter 8) of the Mann–Whitney U for large samples is approximately 95% as compared to the t test. Even for small samples, its power efficiency is very high. It is therefore a powerful alternative to the t test when (1) the researcher has interval data, but is unwilling to assume that the population distributions are normal, or the samples are too small to risk a violation of this assumption, or (2) the researcher has ordinal data.

The Statistical Hypotheses

Anne is testing the null hypothesis that there is no difference in the conflict levels between the two types of families. In statistical terms, this means that the conflict scores of the two types of families are drawn from two identical continuous populations. Therefore,

$$H_0: \ p(W > H) = .5 \ \text{ or } \ U = U'$$

where H represents a conflict score from the population of wives without outside employment, W represents a conflict score from the population of wives with outside employment, and $p(W > H)$ refers to the probability that a score from the latter population has value greater than a score from the former population. The U and U' are explained in detail in the sampling distribution section.

The alternative hypothesis is a directional one for which the conflict level is expected to be higher for families whose wives have outside employment:

$$H_1: \ p(W > H) > .5 \ \text{ or } \ U > U'$$

The Sampling Distribution

If the sample scores came from two identical populations, their values should be similar. Suppose pairs of sample scores, W's and H's, are randomly selected, one from each distribution, for comparison. Then, according to the null hypothesis, half of the time the W's are expected to be greater in value than the H's, and the other half of the time the reverse should be true.

To determine if this is the case, combine the scores of both samples as if they form one sample and arrange them in order from the lowest to the highest. Next, assign ranks to the scores: a rank of 1 to the lowest score, a rank of 2 to the second lowest, and so on. Then, taking each score in the smaller sample, count the number of scores in the larger sample that exceed it and have higher rank values. In Anne's case, she would be counting the number of times the scores of housewives (or of the larger sample) exceed the scores of the wives with outside employment (or of the smaller sample) in rank. Let us call the sum of these counts U. The larger sample can also be used as a starting point for tallying the number of scores in the smaller sample that exceed in rank the scores in the larger sample. This second count yields another sum, U'. In Anne's case, U' represents the number of times the scores of wives with outside employment exceed in rank the scores of housewives.

Counting, however, may be cumbersome. Instead of counting, when the sample sizes are larger or if ties occur, use the following formulas to obtain U and U':

$$U = N_1 N_2 + \frac{N_1(N_1 + 1)}{2} - R_1 \tag{11.11}$$

$$U' = N_1 N_2 + \frac{N_2(N_2 + 1)}{2} - R_2 \tag{11.12}$$

where N_1 is conventionally used to designate the smaller of the two samples and N_2, the larger of the two samples, while R_1 and R_2 refer to the sums of the ranks of the two samples. One U can also be obtained from the other using the following formulas:

$$U = N_1 N_2 - U' \quad \text{and} \quad U' = N_1 N_2 - U \tag{11.13}$$

If the null hypothesis is true, then $U = U'$. Furthermore, since the sum of U and U' equals $N_1 N_2$, the total number of possible pairs from both samples, $U = U' = N_1 N_2 / 2$. However, because of sampling error, the values of U and U' may not be the same even though the samples may have come from two identical populations. To test the null hypothesis, select the test statistic U or U', whichever has the smaller value of the two, regardless of the predicted direction in the alternative hypothesis. The smaller U (or U') is also the statistic that is less than $N_1 N_2 / 2$. In testing, the researcher must decide how much U (or U') should deviate from $N_1 N_2 / 2$ before deciding that the two population distributions are different. For this purpose the sampling distribution of U (or U') is needed.

When neither N_1 nor N_2 is larger than 8, the *exact probabilities* of U (or U') under the null hypothesis are calculated for each sampling distribution and given in Table E in Appendix B. Table E consists of a number of tables grouped under the sample size of the larger sample. To use these tables, the values of N_1, N_2, and U (or U', whichever is smaller) must be known in order to look up the probability of U (or U'). The probability given in the table can then be compared to the conventional significance levels of .05 or .01 to make a decision as to whether the null hypothesis should be rejected. *This procedure applies to a one-tailed test for which the alternative hypothesis specifies the direction of greater than or less than. To obtain the probabilities of a two-tailed test, simply double the probability value given in the table.*

When one N is between 9 and 20 and the other between 1 and 20, it is too cumbersome to give the entire sampling distribution of U. Instead, Table F provides *critical values* of U for a one-tailed test at the specified significance levels of .001, .01, .025, and .05, which are equivalent to significant levels for a two-tailed test of .002, .02, .05, and .10. In other words, these are condensed tables in which only probabilities of certain U values are given for each sampling distribution. Unlike the set of tables under Table E, this set of tables under Table F is organized according to the level of significance. Since the smaller U is used, an observed U that is equal to or smaller than the critical U given in the table leads to the rejection of the null hypothesis. For example, for $\alpha = .05$, with direction predicted (one-tailed test), with $N_1 = 12$ and $N_2 = 15$, a U of 55 or *smaller* is needed to attain significance.

Calculation of the Test Statistic

To calculate U for Anne's sample data, first combine the scores of both samples as if they form one sample and arrange them in order from the lowest to the highest score. Then assign them ranks. The resulting ranks are shown under columns 2 and 4 in Table 11.5.

Next, calculate U and U':

$$U = 3(5) + \frac{3(4)}{2} - 16 = 5$$

$$U' = 3(5) + \frac{5(6)}{2} - 20 = 10$$

Since U yields a smaller value, it is used as the test statistic.

The Decision

For Anne's problem, $N_1 = 3$, $N_2 = 5$, and $U = 5$. Since both N's are less than 8, use the first set of tables under Table E. Look up the appropriate table by first selecting the one with $N_2 = 5$. Within this table, look down the column which lists U values until $U = 5$ is reached. Then go across the row of $U = 5$ to its intersection with $N_1 = 3$. The value given is the probability of obtaining a U of 5 or less in a one-tailed test when the null hypothesis is true. Table E shows that $U \leq 5$ has a probability of occurrence of .286 under the null hypothesis with direction as predicted. In conclusion, Anne's data do not lead to a rejection of the null hypothesis at the .05 level. There is no significant difference in conflict level between the families in which wives work outside and families in which wives do not in the counselor's caseload.

11.6.2 Mann–Whitney U for Large Samples

The Data

Fearing that her samples are too small, Anne takes a random sample of five counselors in the clinic and collects a total of 38 cases at random from these counselors. The results are shown in Table 11.6. Anne decides to retest her hypothesis with this new data set. However, she realizes that even with the larger samples her conclusion is limited to the clients of the clinic.

TABLE 11.6 Family Conflict According to Wife's Employment Status

Wife's Employment Status			
No Outside Employment		Outside Employment	
Conflict Score	Rank	Conflict Score	Rank
1	2.5	1	2.5
1	2.5	1	2.5
2	8	2	8
2	8	2	8
2	8	2	8
3	13.5	3	13.5
3	13.5	3	13.5
4	16.5	5	19
4	16.5	6	22.5
5	19	6	22.5
5	19	7	26
6	22.5	8	29
6	22.5	9	33
7	26	9	33
7	26	10	37
8	29	$N_1 = 16$	$R_1 = 286$
8	29		
9	33		
9	33		
9	33		
10	37		
10	37		
$N_2 = 22$	$R_2 = 455$		

The Statistical Hypotheses
The null and alternative hypotheses are the same as before.

The Sampling Distribution
As sample size increases, the sampling distribution of U rapidly approaches the normal distribution. Therefore, instead of finding the exact probability of U as before, the probability can be approximated using the normal distribution. The formulas for the mean and standard error of this sampling distribution are

$$\text{mean} = \frac{N_1 N_2}{2}$$

$$\text{standard error} = \sqrt{\frac{N_1 N_2 (N_1 + N_2 + 1)}{12}}$$

The test statistic, the z score, is computed as follows:

$$z = \frac{U - \dfrac{N_1 N_2}{2}}{\sqrt{\dfrac{N_1 N_2 (N_1 + N_2 + 1)}{12}}} \tag{11.14}$$

Basically, this z formula calculates the extent to which the scores of one sample exceed in rank the scores of another sample when this is expected to occur no more than half of the time. The procedure is analogous to the difference of means test.

The U's for this z test are computed using the same Formulas 11.11 and 11.12. Unlike that of the smaller samples, either U or U' can be substituted for U in the z formula *for a two-tailed test.* By substituting both in turn, the reader will see that the resulting z's have the same *absolute* value, but a different sign, since the normal distribution is symmetrical.

For a one-tailed test, however, the sign of z is important. In this illustration, since H_1 states $p(W > H) > .5$, a comparison of the W's (from the smaller sample) to the H's (from the larger sample) is needed. Therefore, the test statistic U' is appropriate and is substituted into the z formula. Otherwise, if H_1 states a comparison of the H's (from the larger sample) to the W's (from the smaller sample), U is used. The student may want to reread the explanation of the U's in Section 11.6.1 at this point. The probability of greater than (>) .5 in H_1 also indicates that the critical value is located at the right tail of the z curve. At an α level of .05, the critical z value is 1.65.

Calculation of the Test Statistic
Before calculating z, the problem of tied scores must be resolved. Tied observations, in this case, are determined after the two samples are combined. Within this combined distribution, the average of the ranks these scores would have, had they not been tied, is given to each of the tied observations. For example, there

are four 1's in the combined distribution of samples 1 and 2 in Table 11.6. Therefore, an average of these ranks, 2.5 (1 + 2 + 3 + 4/4), is assigned to each observation. All other tied ranks are similarly calculated and assigned in the table.

Using Anne's data, we have the following results:

1. U statistic: $U = (16)(22) + \dfrac{(16)(16+1)}{2} - 286 = 202$

2. U' statistic: $U' = (16)(22) + \dfrac{(22)(22+1)}{2} - 455 = 150$

Note that $(U + U') = N_1 N_2$: 202 + 150 = 352. The test statistic U' should be substituted into the z formula:

$$z = \frac{150 - \dfrac{(16)(22)}{2}}{\sqrt{\dfrac{(16)(22)(16 + 22 + 1)}{12}}} = \frac{-26}{33.823} = -.769$$

The Decision

A z score of $-.77$ shows that the sample outcome is in a direction different from that anticipated in the alternative hypothesis. Thus Anne cannot reject the null hypothesis. In addition, she may have to rethink the whole problem through to determine whether it is possible that more conflict exists in families whose wives do not have outside employment. She realizes, however, that her samples consist of clinic clients only on whom a selection effect may be operating. Families seeking a counselor are likely to experience higher levels of conflict than others whether or not the wives have outside employment. For a better test of her hypothesis, Anne concludes that samples from the general population rather than from counselors should be taken.

Correction for Ties

With the crude measurement used in the preceding example and in much social research, there are many tied scores. The Mann–Whitney test, however, assumes underlying continuity in the distribution of scores. Therefore, when tied scores occur, the value of z is affected. To take into account the effect of ties, the average of the ranks is given to each tied observation in Table 11.6. An additional procedure for the correction of ties can be applied to the standard error of the sampling distribution of U as follows:

$$\text{standard error} = \sqrt{\left(\frac{N_1 N_2}{N(N-1)}\right)\left(\frac{N^3 - N}{12} - \sum_{j=1}^{k} T_j\right)} \qquad (11.15)$$

where k refers to the number of sets of tied scores.

Within this formula $N = N_1 + N_2$, and

$$T = \frac{t^3 - t}{12} \qquad (11.16)$$

where t refers to the number of observations tied for a given rank.

The sum of T, ΣT, is obtained by summing the T scores over all sets of tied observations. With the correction for ties added, Z is computed as follows:

$$z = \frac{U - \dfrac{N_1 N_2}{2}}{\sqrt{\left(\dfrac{N_1 N_2}{N(N-1)}\right)\left(\dfrac{N^3 - N}{12} - \displaystyle\sum_{j=1}^{k} T_j\right)}} \qquad (11.17)$$

Table 11.6 shows the following sets of tied scores:

4 scores of 1   7 scores of 2   4 scores of 3   2 scores of 4   3 scores of 5
4 scores of 6   3 scores of 7   3 scores of 8   5 scores of 9   3 scores of 10

With t's of 4, 7, 4, 2, 3, 4, 3, 3, 5, and 3, ΣT is obtained as follows:

$$\Sigma T = \frac{4^3 - 4}{12} + \frac{7^3 - 7}{12} + \frac{4^3 - 4}{12} + \frac{2^3 - 2}{12} + \frac{3^3 - 3}{12} + \frac{4^3 - 4}{12} + \frac{3^3 - 3}{12} + \frac{3^3 - 3}{12} + \frac{5^3 - 5}{12} + \frac{3^3 - 3}{12}$$
$$= 61.5$$

Thus the z score is calculated as

$$z = \frac{150 - \dfrac{(16)(22)}{2}}{\sqrt{\left(\dfrac{(16)(22)}{38(38-1)}\right)\left(\dfrac{38^3 - 38}{12} - 61.5\right)}} = -.774$$

As observed earlier, the obtained z value is in a direction different than that anticipated by Anne. Correcting for ties does not change the direction but the absolute value of the z score. Note that the absolute value of this second z with ties is only slightly larger than that of the first z, which does not take ties into account ($-.774$ as compared to $-.769$). As this example illustrates, (1) ties have only a negligible effect on z, and (2) the correction factor has a tendency to increase the absolute value of z, making the rejection of the null hypothesis more likely. Therefore, a conservative approach is to correct for ties only if the proportion of ties is very large.

Summary

Mann–Whitney U Test

Null hypothesis: $U = U'$

Test statistics for small samples: U or U', whichever is smaller

$$U = N_1N_2 + \frac{N_1(N_1 + 1)}{2} - R_1, \qquad U' = N_1N_2 + \frac{N_2(N_2 + 1)}{2} - R_2$$

where $N_1 < N_2$

Test statistic for large samples: $z = \dfrac{U - \dfrac{N_1N_2}{2}}{\sqrt{\dfrac{N_1N_2(N_1 + N_2 + 1)}{12}}}$

where N_1, N_2 = numbers of observations in the smaller and larger samples
R_1, R_2 = sums of ranks of smaller and larger sample

Test model:

1. Continuous variable
2. Ordinal measurement level
3. Two independent random samples

Exercises

All variables in the following exercises are scaled from 1 to 10, with 10 representing the highest level of the variable.

17. Using the survey data at her institute, Anne compares the levels of marital satisfaction between those who have been married for less than 3 years and those married for over 10 years. The data are shown next.

3 years	5	9	2	7	8
10 years	6	4	10	3	

   a. Compute U and U'; make corrections for ties if necessary.
   b. Discuss the findings.

18. Suspecting that economic hardship has an effect on family abuse, a researcher compares spousal tension between low-income and middle-income families. Is there a significant difference based on the following data?

| Low-income family | 9 | 8 | 9 | 8 | 7 | 5 | 6 | 9 | 8 | 7 | 6 |
| Middle-income family | 4 | 3 | 4 | 5 | 6 | 7 | 9 | 2 | 3 | 4 | 3 | 5 |

19. Compare the degree of life satisfaction between the married and the unmarried based on the following data. Make corrections for ties.

| Married | 4 | 3 | 5 | 6 | 2 | 9 | 8 | 3 | 4 | 5 | 2 | 4 | 1 | 5 | 3 | 6 | 3 | 4 | 7 | 6 |
| Unmarried | 5 | 6 | 7 | 3 | 2 | 1 | 4 | 9 | 8 | 7 | 4 | 3 | 4 | 3 | 6 | 4 | 7 |

SPSS Session

The following program performs the Mann–Whitney U test for the data in Table 11.6.

```
DATA LIST FREE/CONFLICT SAMPLE.

BEGIN DATA.

2.5    2    2.5    1

2.5    2    2.5    1

. . .

END DATA.

NPAR TESTS M-W=CONFLICT BY SAMPLE (1,2) /STATISTICS=ALL.
```

Either ranks or scores of the dependent variable could be entered after BEGIN DATA to perform the Mann–Whitney test; the results would be the same. In this case, the ranks of the conflict scores are entered as CONFLICT. The independent or grouping variable SAMPLE specifies the sample to which a rank or score belongs. The value 1 refers to the sample of wives who have outside employment, while the value 2 refers to the sample of wives who do not.

The Mann–Whitney test is requested through the M–W subcommand of the NPAR TEST. The specification of the dependent variable (CONFLICT) follows, then the keyword BY, and then the grouping variable (SAMPLE). The values of the grouping variable used to generate the samples are enclosed in parentheses. Again, if no values are specified, the default values of 1 and 2 are assumed. The subcommand STATISTICS with the specification of ALL provides descriptive statistics for the variable CONFLICT to go along with the results of the M–W test.

As shown in SPSS Figure 11.3, the M–W subcommand produces the mean rank for each sample, the Mann–Whitney U statistic, the Wilcoxon W, or the rank sum (R statistic in the text) of the smaller group, the exact significance level of U,

```
- - - - Mann-Whitney U - Wilcoxon Rank Sum W Test

    CONFLICT
 by SAMPLE

    Mean Rank    Cases

       17.88        16   SAMPLE = 1.00
       20.68        22   SAMPLE = 2.00
                    --
                    38   Total

                              EXACT              Corrected for Ties
         U            W       2-tailed P          Z        2-tailed P
       150.0        286.0       .4555          -.7739         .4390
```

SPSS FIGURE 11.3   The Mann–Whitney *U* Test

and the z statistic and its probability after correcting for ties. Note that SPSS uses U to refer to the smaller of the U values and that this smaller U value is substituted into the z formula. Therefore, the z value is always negative in the output, regardless of which direction the researcher is actually testing. According to SPSS Figure 11.3, the z distribution provides a close approximation: its probability is .4390 as opposed to .4555 when the exact probability is calculated. The associated two-tailed probability of a z score of $-.7739$ is .4390, from which the one-tailed probability of .22 is obtained.

SPSS Exercises

6. Despite the improvement of women's status, most occupations held by women are still rated as less prestigious than those occupied by men. Using the GSS data on occupational prestige (PRESTG80), test if there is a significant difference between the sexes.

7. GSS asked respondents for the number of sexual partners they had during the last 12 months. The response categories are grouped to form an ordinal-level variable (SEX-FREQ). Test the hypothesis that there is no difference between males and females (SEX).

11.7 Two-sample Test for Nominal Data: Chi-square Test for r × 2 Table

When the researcher has a nominal dependent variable and two independent random samples differentiated by the categories of a nominal variable, the appropriate test is the nonparametric chi-square procedure. As we saw in Chapter 9, the chi-square test provides a comparison of two frequency distributions, each of which has the same grouping scheme. Whereas in a one-sample test one distribution is theoretical, given under H_0, in a two-sample test, both distributions are empirically obtained, one from each of the two samples. In effect, the two-sample chi-square test is equivalent to a chi-square test of association or independence between two variables in a sample (Chapter 4). The dichotomous independent variable in a test of association becomes the grouping variable that gives rise to the two samples under study in a two-sample test. The dependent variable is equivalent to the measured variable. Regardless of whether the chi square is considered to be a test of association or a two-sample test, an assumption must be made that each observation is selected independently of all others. The sample size must be relatively large such that the expected frequency of any cell is 5 or greater. Because the two-sample chi-square test is no different from the χ^2 test for 3 or more samples, the discussion of this test statistic is deferred until Chapter 12.

11.8 Significance and Sample Size

In Section 11.1 we stated that a significant result for tests discussed in this chapter implies the existence of an association between the dependent or measured variable and the independent variable whose categories define the two populations. It would appear a logical extension to say that the more significant the result is, the stronger the relationship. Unfortunately, there is not necessarily a direct relationship between the two. Without taking into account sample size, the same level of significance does not imply the same degree of association. Only when the sample sizes are the same does a higher level of significance mean a stronger relationship.

To clarify this point, let us review how a t-test statistic is calculated. The difference between two sample means is divided by the estimated standard error to obtain the t statistic. For the same difference between two sample means, the value of the t score depends on the value of the estimated standard error. However, as we know from the preceding chapters, the larger the sample size is, the smaller the estimated standard error. The relationship holds for both multisample and one-sample procedures. Thus, for a given difference in means, the larger the sample size is, the larger the calculated t value and the smaller the probability of obtaining that difference.

It follows that with a larger sample the power of the test is increased, making it easier to reject a false H_0, even if the true value in H_1 differs slightly from the false value in H_0. However, this also means that, if the researcher uses a large enough sample size, a slight departure from independence can yield a significant result. Since very few social phenomena are completely independent of other social phenomena, obtaining a significant result does not necessarily indicate that the researcher has found a relationship between two variables that is worth pursuing.

Thus a significant result should signal the beginning rather than the end of a search for a meaningful relationship. After obtaining a significant result, the researcher's next step may be to determine the exact strength of the association. In short, in evaluating relationships the researcher should use more than the criterion of significance, and finding significant results should be one among many goals of doing research.

General Conceptual Questions

1. Explain how the central limit theorem is applied to testing the difference between means.

2. State the assumptions under which a *t*-test statistic can be used in making inferences about the difference between two population means.

3. When is it appropriate to use a paired-difference analysis rather than an unpaired analysis?

4. State the null and alternative hypotheses that are tested when using the Mann–Whitney *U* test.

5. Explain why a sample taken for a survey can be used to test a difference of means between two samples.

6. A family counselor wishes to investigate whether:
   a. The divorce rate is higher in cities than in small towns.
   b. Children of divorced parents are more self-reliant than other children.
   c. There is a difference in the proportions of married and divorced people who join many organizations.

   For each of these situations:
   a. State the null and alternative hypotheses.
   b. Select an appropriate test statistic.
   c. State the necessary assumptions.

7. What is the number of degrees of freedom for a *t* test of difference of means? How is it derived?

8. In testing for a difference between means, what are the questions that must be answered to find an appropriate test statistic? And what are the available appropriate statistics?

9. When there is a significant difference between sample scores on marital satisfaction between men and women, does it imply that sex determines the level of marital satisfaction?

References

1. Murdock, George. (1949). *Social Structure.*
New York: Macmillan.

$C\ h\ a\ p\ t\ e\ r$ **12**

Inference from Univariate Data: Multisamples

New Statistical Topics

One-way analysis of variance
Kruskal–Wallis test
Chi-square test

12.1 Overview

Parametric procedures to test the difference of means among several groups are called ANOVA, an acronym for analysis of variance. Although the null hypothesis of ANOVA deals explicitly with the equality of means, the inference is drawn through an analysis of the variances among and within the sample groups. This chapter discusses **one-way analysis of variance,** which examines the impact of one nominal or categorical independent variable on an interval dependent variable.

For dependent variables measured on the ordinal level, the nonparametric equivalent of analysis of variance, the **Kruskal–Wallis test,** is presented. This test compares the mean of *ranks* among several groups. When both the dependent and independent variables are categorical or measured on the nominal level, the **chi-square test** for k samples can be employed. This test examines whether or not the groups formed by the independent variable have the same distributions.

12.1.1 Social Applications

Having studied the family as a basic institution in U.S. society, Anne next examines the health care profession as a vital institution. To help her derive hypotheses about health behaviors and about the health care institution, Anne again employs the three major sociological perspectives. The conflict perspective directs Anne's attention to the inequitable distribution of health care in U.S. society. As a scarce resource, health care is distributed less according to need than to the ability to pay. Within this institution, the physician occupies a central role and performs an invaluable function for society as a whole. Therefore, from a functionalist perspective, physicians are not only handsomely compensated but accorded great esteem for their work. Although health and illness are physiological states, being healthy or ill is a social response that is affected by many social factors. Among these are the symbolic elements in doctor–patient relations. From the interactionist perspective, the wonders of medical science may be achieved more readily through a doctor who has good bedside manners rather than one who is only professionally competent.

12.1.2 Statistical Topics

With these various theoretical perspectives in mind, Anne develops research hypotheses to explain health behaviors and health care in U.S. society. Since she plans to examine more than two groups at a time, the t test is inappropriate. With three groups, this procedure would require three pairwise comparisons when comparing a pair of means at a time: $N(N - 1)/2 = 3(2)/2$ (Chapter 6). The three comparisons consist of comparing group 1 to group 2, group 1 to group 3, and finally group 2 to group 3. With five groups, there are 10 comparisons: $5(4)/2$. Not only does the number of comparisons increase rapidly with an increase in the number of samples, but the results of these comparisons can be confusing.

Suppose for the moment that these 10 t tests are independent of each other. With 10 independent tests, the probability of getting at least one significant result by chance when the α level is set at .05 for each test is no longer .05, but much larger:

$$\text{prob (at least one significant result)} = \text{prob (not all nonsignificant results)}$$
$$= [1 - (1 - \alpha)^{10}] = (1 - .95^{10}) = .40$$

Thus the more t tests that are performed, the more likely the researcher is to make the mistake of claiming that a true difference exists when it is merely due to sampling variation.

In reality, when 10 comparisons are made on the same samples, a sample mean is being compared repeatedly to other sample means, and the t tests are no longer independent. Instead, they are dependent and carry overlapping information about the samples. For such dependent tests, the significance levels are difficult to determine. The pairwise t test of means is therefore inappropriate for problems involving more than two groups.

In place of the t test, the analysis of variance or ANOVA can be used. It is a procedure for testing whether or not the means of two or more populations are equal. Assumptions made in this test model include independent random samples drawn from populations that have normal distributions and equal variances. If these assumptions together with the null hypothesis are true, the researcher has several identical populations. Samples drawn from identical populations are equivalent to samples selected from one parent population. This being the case, the variations (1) among the sample means and (2) within each sample can be used as two independent estimates of the same population variance σ^2, as will be shown later. When the null hypothesis holds, these estimates yield similar values; otherwise, their values differ. Through this method of comparing the variance of the means to the average variance of all the samples, more than two means can be evaluated simultaneously and an inference made as to their equality or difference.

12.2 *Two Independent Estimates of the Population Variance*

We will now explore how the two independent estimates of σ^2 are actually derived. Under H_0, together with the assumptions of the test model, repeated sampling from these populations will yield a sampling distribution that is normal with a mean of μ and a variance of σ^2/N. In particular, the estimated variance of the k sample means can be calculated as follows:

$$\hat{\sigma}_{\overline{X}}^2 = \frac{\sum_{j=1}^{k} (\overline{X}_j - \mu_{\overline{X}})^2}{k-1}$$

where k refers to the number of samples. Note that $(k-1)$ is used as the denominator instead of k in order to obtain an unbiased estimate. This $\hat{\sigma}_{\overline{X}}^2$, which measures the deviation of the sample means from the population mean, can be used in estimating the population variance σ^2 when multiplied by N_j, where N_j refers to the individual sample size of the k samples. Since $\hat{\sigma}_{\overline{X}}^2 = \hat{\sigma}^2/N_j$,

$$N_j\hat{\sigma}_{\overline{X}}^2 = \hat{\sigma}^2$$

Because $N_j\hat{\sigma}_{\overline{X}}^2$ provides an estimate of the population variance that is based on the variation among the samples or groups under H_0, we will label this estimate, $N_j\hat{\sigma}_{\overline{X}}^2$, as $\hat{\sigma}_B^2$. The subscript B refers to the *between group variation*. The $\hat{\sigma}_B^2$ based on the variation among the k sample means is unbiased *only* if the population means are in fact equal, that is, H_0 is true. Otherwise, it would be a biased estimate, which yields a value larger than the population variance σ^2. For when H_0 is false and the means of the various populations are not equal, the estimate will include not only sampling variation but the true variation among the sample means as well.

A second estimate of the population variance can be obtained by taking the weighted average of the variances within each sample as follows:

$$\hat{\sigma}_W^2 = \frac{\displaystyle\sum_{j=1}^{k}(N_j)s_j^2}{\displaystyle\sum_{j=1}^{k}(N_j - 1)}$$

This estimate is equivalent to the pooled estimate of the population variance in the equal-variance model t test. Note again that $(N_j - 1)$ instead of (N_j) is used in the denominator to obtain an unbiased estimate.

If $\hat{\sigma}_B^2$ measures the between-group variation, then $\hat{\sigma}_W^2$ determines the *within-group variation*. The subscript W is used accordingly to differentiate the latter estimate from the former. This second estimate is unbiased even if the sample means are very different from one another. Each variance is calculated from the mean of that particular sample and is therefore independent of the variances calculated from other sample means. Together they give an estimate of the common variance assumed in the test model.

Thus there are two ways of estimating the common variance σ^2:

1. An indirect estimate, $\hat{\sigma}_B^2$, called the between-group variation. It is obtained from multiplying $\hat{\sigma}_{\bar{X}}^2$ by N_j. The $\hat{\sigma}_B^2$ is an unbiased estimator only if the population means are equal and therefore H_0 is true.
2. A direct estimate, $\hat{\sigma}_W^2$, called the within-group variation. It is a weighted average of the variances within each sample. This estimate is unbiased even if the population means differ among themselves because of the assumption of equal variances in the test model.

A comparison of these two estimates will indicate whether or not the population means are in fact equal. The comparison is made by calculating the F test statistic, which is the ratio of the estimate based on between-group variation to the estimate based on within-group variation:

$$F = \frac{\hat{\sigma}_B^2}{\hat{\sigma}_W^2}$$

If the null hypothesis is true, both are estimates of the same parameter, and their ratio should approximate unity. If the population means differ, the between-group variation will be larger, and the ratio will be greater than unity.

Although the F ratio is presented here as a test statistic for the ANOVA procedure, it is also used in other contexts to test the equality of variances from two independent samples. For example, the researcher may need to test the equal-variance assumption before selecting a particular t-test model (Chapter 11).

In such cases, the numerator of F represents the larger of the two variance estimates, and its denominator, the smaller of the two estimates. When the F ratio departs from unity, the researcher must find the probability of F. The answer can be obtained through the F sampling distribution, which provides probabilities for all F ratios under H_0, whether H_0 pertains to a test for the equality of variances or to an ANOVA. This distribution is discussed in Section 12.3.1.

12.3 One-way Analysis of Variance

Research Question
As partakers of the U.S. health care system, we may wish to adopt the view that the health care institution is a well-integrated system with equitable availability of health care to all. However, this institution has been called by some "the system without a system." Without centralized planning, the distribution and availability of health care facilities is uneven, leaving some categories of people totally deprived. From the conflict perspective, the distribution is very much governed by the consideration of who can afford health care as opposed to who should have access to it. Extending this line of reasoning to different regions of the country, Anne wonders if health care is also unevenly distributed among different regions. If so, it would be concentrated in the more urbanized and affluent regions.

The Data
To test the hypothesis of uneven distribution, Anne takes a random sample of standard metropolitan areas in four regions and compares the number of physicians per 100,000 population as shown in Table 12.1. The data appear to support Anne's research hypothesis because the number of physicians differs greatly. The more urbanized and affluent metropolitan areas in the East and West have more physicians than areas in the South or Central. Are these differences in Anne's samples large enough to suggest an uneven distribution of physicians?

TABLE 12.1 Number of Physicians in Standard Metropolitan Areas by Region

	East	West	South	Central
	208.8	183.7	93.4	118.7
	190.7	196.7	232.1	154.1
	216.4	178.5	149.4	127.9
	131.7	202.9	144.2	119.1
	186.0	272.4	139.4	93.7
	216.1	212.6	118.5	108.5
	123.9	206.1	182.1	108.2
	212.5	169.7	94.7	139.9
Mean	185.76	202.83	144.23	121.26

Before we proceed further, let us represent the data schematically as shown in Table 12.2. The reader should keep in mind how the various measures are represented symbolically and subscripted because it will help to understand the symbols used in the formulas later.

An Appropriate Test and Its Assumptions

The dependent variable, the number of physicians per standard metropolitan area, is measured on the interval level. The independent variable, region of the country, is a nominal variable with four categories that define four different populations: East, West, South, and Central. From each region an independent random sample is taken. Since Anne is comparing four population means, an appropriate test is ANOVA. Again, although the hypotheses pertain to population means, ANOVA works directly with variances, allowing for comparison of as many different samples as necessary. Specifically, the procedure compares two variances computed from these samples to determine if they could be estimating a common variance.

To use ANOVA, Anne must assume, in addition to random sampling, the populations under study are normally distributed and their variances are equal. Anne is sure the important requirement of random sampling has been met. Based on previous nationwide studies, Anne determines the assumption that the number of physicians per metropolitan area is normally distributed is tenable. When normality of population is assumed, the sample size need not be large; for example, Anne has only eight cases in each of her samples. In addition, since ANOVA is robust with respect to a violation of this assumption, with moderate sample sizes, the F distribution will not be distorted seriously even if the study populations are not quite normal. Furthermore, ANOVA is not particularly sensitive to the violation of the assumption of equal variances as long as the sample sizes are the same or similar. However, to be cautious, Anne requests a test of the equality

TABLE 12.2 Symbolic Representation of Data in ANOVA

Cases	Groups or Treatments				Total
	1	2	. . .	k	
1	X_{11}	X_{12}	. . .	X_{1k}	
2	X_{21}	X_{22}	. . .	X_{2k}	
3	X_{31}	X_{32}	. . .	X_{3k}	
. . .	. . .	. . .		. . .	
N_j	$X_{N_1 1}$	$X_{N_2 2}$		$X_{N_k k}$	
Sum	$\sum\limits_{i=1}^{N_1} X_{i1}$	$\sum\limits_{i=1}^{N_2} X_{i2}$		$\sum\limits_{i=1}^{N_k} X_{ik}$	$\sum\limits_{j=1}^{k}\sum\limits_{i=1}^{N_j} X_{ij}$
Mean	$\overline{X}_1$	$\overline{X}_2$		$\overline{X}_k$	$\overline{X}$
Number of cases	N_1	N_2		N_k	N

of variances at the same time that she submits an SPSS program for the ANOVA. The test results show that the null hypothesis of equal variances cannot be rejected. See the SPSS SESSION.

The Statistical Hypotheses

Anne's null hypothesis states that physicians are evenly distributed among different regions of the country:

$$H_0: \quad \mu_1 = \mu_2 = \mu_3 = \mu_4$$

where μ_1 represents the mean number of physicians in the East, μ_2 represents the mean in the West, μ_3 represents the mean in the South, and μ_4 represents the mean in the Central.

The alternative hypothesis states that physicians are unevenly distributed among different regions of the country:

$$H_1: \quad \mu_i \neq \mu_j, \quad \text{for some } i \text{ and } j$$

The alternative hypothesis in ANOVA never states a direction because the concept is inapplicable when more than two groups are being compared. Analysis of variance always tests whether there is a difference among the groups and not whether a certain group mean is larger or smaller than other group mean(s).

12.3.1 F Ratio and Sampling Distribution

The appropriate sampling distribution is the F distribution. The F is a theoretical continuous distribution of the F ratio, which is defined as

$$F = \frac{\chi_1^2/df_1}{\chi_2^2/df_2} = \frac{\chi_1^2/(N_1 - 1)}{\chi_2^2/(N_2 - 1)}$$

As can be seen from the definition, the chi-square test statistic, used for making inferences about a single population variance, is related to the F ratio. The latter is, in effect, the ratio of two independent chi-square variables, each divided by its own degrees of freedom. From Chapter 9, we know that

$$\hat{\sigma}^2 = \frac{\chi_{df}^2 \sigma^2}{df}$$

Therefore,

$$\frac{\chi^2}{N - 1} = \frac{\hat{\sigma}^2}{\sigma^2}$$

Since the population variances in an F test are assumed to be equal, $\sigma_1^2 = \sigma_2^2$, the F ratio becomes

$$F = \frac{\hat{\sigma}_1^2 / \sigma_1^2}{\hat{\sigma}_2^2 / \sigma_2^2} = \frac{\hat{\sigma}_1^2}{\hat{\sigma}_2^2} \quad \text{or} \quad \frac{\hat{\sigma}_2^2}{\hat{\sigma}_1^2}, \qquad \text{whichever is larger}$$

That is, when independent random samples of size N_1 and N_2 are drawn repeatedly from two normal populations with *equal* variances, the ratio of the two sample estimates ($\hat{\sigma}_1^2$ and $\hat{\sigma}_2^2$) of the true variances (σ_1^2 and σ_2^2) has an F sampling distribution.

Not only is the F related to the chi square, but the t is a special case of the F distribution, being the square root of the F ratio with 1 and $(N-1)$ degrees of freedom:

$$t_{(N-1)}^2 = F_{(1, N-1)}$$

Like the t and chi-square distributions, the F is also a family of distributions, all of which is described by a single mathematical rule. Within the family, the distributions differ depending on two parameters, the degrees of freedom for the estimate in the numerator and the degrees of freedom for the estimate in the denominator. See Figure 12.1 for some of the F distributions in the family.

The F ratio is expected to equal unity when the null hypothesis is true in ANOVA. To determine how much departure from unity is tolerable before the null hypothesis is rejected, the researcher must find the critical F values. They are given in three separate tables under Table G in Appendix B. Each table provides the F values for a different level of significance: .05, .01, and .001. To find the appropriate F distribution once an α level is selected, determine df for the numerator and df for the denominator. Read down the column of row headings to

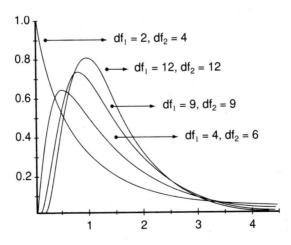

FIGURE 12.1   A Family of F Distributions

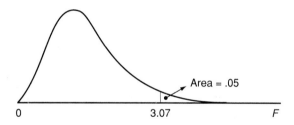

**FIGURE 12.2   Critical Value for the F
Distribution with 8 and 10
Degrees of Freedom**

find df for the denominator, and then read across the row of column headings to find df for the numerator. At the intersection of the appropriate row and column is the critical F value at a given level of significance. For example, for degrees of freedom $df_1 = 8$ and $df_2 = 10$ at the .05 level, the F table gives the critical value of 3.07, which separates 5% of the upper tail end from the rest of the distribution. See Figure 12.2. If the ratio of variance estimates is greater than 3.07, the null hypothesis of equal variances is rejected. The significance level indicates that a value of this magnitude could happen less than 5% of the time when samples are drawn repeatedly from normal populations with equal variances.

12.3.2 Definitional Formulas for the Two Independent Estimates

The definitional formulas for the two independent estimates of the common variance defined in Section 12.2 will be examined next. Because they are derived from the concept of sums of squares first introduced in Chapter 5, an analogy can be drawn between ANOVA and regression techniques. Like the t test, ANOVA is an implied test of the statistical association between a nominal or categorical independent variable, such as the region of the country, and a dependent interval variable, such as the number of physicians per standard metropolitan area. Thus it can be approached alternatively as a problem of improvement in prediction for which the focus is on explaining the variation of the individual scores in the samples. To the extent that region is associated with the number of physicians, knowing the region should improve the prediction of the number of physicians.

Recall in regression analysis that if no information is given about the region (the independent variable) the prediction of the number of physicians would be the mean number of physicians in all regions (the mean of the dependent variable). In other words, for each case, the **grand mean** of 163.52 is predicted, which is obtained as follows when all N_j are equal:

$$\overline{X} = \text{grand mean} = \frac{185.76 + 202.83 + 144.23 + 121.26}{4} = 163.52$$

The variation of an individual score from this grand mean, $(X_{ij} - \overline{X})$, is known as the **total variation** of a score. Recall from Chapter 5 that the total variation can be partitioned into two components.

The first component of the total variation is the *explained variation*. The explained variation equals $(\overline{X}_j - \overline{X})$. It is so called because when information is given on region the group mean $\overline{X}_j$, rather than the grand mean, is used as the prediction of the metropolitan area's score. In short, the explained variation represents the effect of the independent variable, which in Anne's problem refers to the effect of being a member of group (j). For the four groups, we have the following:

> Being in the East has the effect of $(185.76 - 163.52) = 22.24$
> Being in the West has the effect of $(202.83 - 163.52) = 39.31$
> Being in the South has the effect of $(144.23 - 163.52) = -19.29$
> Being in Central has the effect of $(121.26 - 163.52) = -42.26$

In ANOVA, the explained variation is equivalent to the *between-group variation*, which measures the *variation of the group means from the grand mean.*

However, not every metropolitan area in a region has the same number of physicians. The variation of an individual score from its group mean, $(X_{ij} - \overline{X}_j)$, can be viewed as an error in prediction since it is *not explained* by the independent variable. The *unexplained variation* then represents the second component of the total variation. In ANOVA, this second component is called the *within-group variation*. See Figure 12.3.

In Chapter 5 the partitioning of the total variation was represented symbolically as

$$X_{ij} - \overline{X} = X_{ij} + (\overline{X}_j - \overline{X}_j) - \overline{X} = (X_{ij} - \overline{X}_j) + (\overline{X}_j - \overline{X})$$

Also, by squaring the total variation and summing over all cases, the total sum of squares is obtained, which can be partitioned as follows:

$$\sum_{j=1}^{k}\sum_{i=1}^{N_j} (X_{ij} - \overline{X})^2 = \sum_{j=1}^{k}\sum_{i=1}^{N_j} (X_{ij} - \overline{X}_j)^2 + \sum_{j=1}^{k}\sum_{i=1}^{N_j} (\overline{X}_j - \overline{X})^2$$

In ANOVA, different terminologies are used for the same sums of squares. Whereas in regression analysis the sum of squared deviations of the group means from the grand mean is known as the *explained SS*, it is known as the *between sum of squares*, SS_B, in ANOVA:

$$SS_B = \sum_{j}\sum_{i} (\overline{X}_j - \overline{X})^2 = \sum_{j} N_j (\overline{X}_j - \overline{X})^2$$

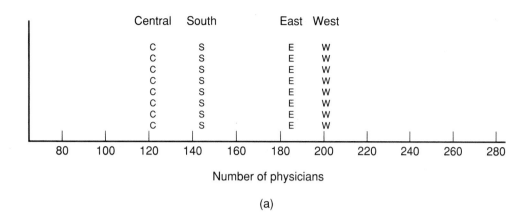

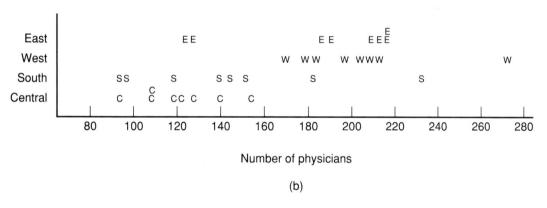

FIGURE 12.3 **Two Types of Variation: (a) Between-group Variation; (b) Within-group Variation**

Whereas in regression analysis the squared deviations of the individual scores from their respective group means are referred to as the *unexplained SS*, it is called the *within sum of squares*, SS_W, in ANOVA:

$$SS_W = \sum_j \sum_i (X_{ij} - \overline{X}_j)^2$$

In actual computation, these two component SS's are used to derive estimates for the common population variance σ^2. Finally, the total sum of squares equals the sum of the within sum of squares and the between sum of squares, or

$$SS_T = SS_W + SS_B$$

More specifically, the estimates are obtained through dividing these component sums of squares by their appropriate degrees of freedom. To obtain these component df's, which are associated with the sums of squares, the total degrees of freedom are partitioned. The total SS has $(N - 1)$ degrees of freedom because 1 degree of freedom is lost in computing the SS about the grand mean. The between SS has $(k - 1)$ degrees of freedom since, once the grand mean and $(k - 1)$ group means are known, the jth group mean is determined automatically. Finally, $(N - k)$ degrees of freedom are associated with the within SS because 1 degree of freedom is lost in each group while computing the variation about the group mean. Therefore, the total degrees of freedom are partitioned as follows:

$$\text{total df (df}_T) = \text{between SS df (df}_B) + \text{within SS df (df}_W)$$

or

$$N - 1 \quad = (k - 1) \quad + (N - k)$$

In dividing the two component SS's by their df's, the two estimates of the common variance are obtained:

$$\text{between-group estimate } = \text{MSS}_B = \frac{\text{SS}_B}{k - 1} = \frac{\sum\limits_{j=1}^{k} N_j(\overline{X}_j - \overline{X})^2}{k - 1} \tag{12.1}$$

$$\text{within-group estimate } = \text{MSS}_W = \frac{\text{SS}_W}{N - k} = \frac{\sum\limits_{j=1}^{k}\sum\limits_{i=1}^{N_j}(X_{ij} - \overline{X}_j)^2}{N - k} \tag{12.2}$$

These estimates are also referred to as the **mean sums of squares (MSS).**

The F-test statistic is a ratio of the between-group estimate MSS_B to the within-group estimate, MSS_W:

$$F = \frac{\text{MSS}_B}{\text{MSS}_W} = \frac{\text{SS}_B/\text{df}_B}{\text{SS}_W/\text{df}_W} \tag{12.3}$$

By comparing the two estimates, the procedure examines whether the effect of the independent variable is significantly larger than or simply equal to the random sampling effect. Finally, because the F ratio is computed to test the equality of means in several populations, when the estimates are radically different, they also indicate that the means of the populations are unequal.

12.3.3 Calculating and Interpreting the Test Statistic

To obtain an F ratio, Anne must calculate SS_B and SS_W first. However, since SS_W is somewhat cumbersome to work out, she will obtain it indirectly as the difference between SS_T and SS_B. The computational formula for SS_T is

$$SS_T = \sum_{j=1}^{k}\sum_{i=1}^{N_j}(X_{ij} - \overline{X})^2 = \sum_{j=1}^{k}\sum_{i=1}^{N_j} X_{ij}^2 - \frac{\left(\sum_{j=1}^{k}\sum_{i=1}^{N_j} X_{ij}\right)^2}{N} \tag{12.4}$$

The two terms within SS_T are calculated as follows:

1. $\displaystyle\sum_{j}\sum_{i} X_{ij}^2 = (208.8)^2 + (190.7)^2 + \cdots + (139.9)^2 = 923{,}605.5$

2. $\displaystyle\frac{\left(\sum_{j}\sum_{i} X_{ij}\right)^2}{N} = \frac{5{,}232.60^2}{32} = 855{,}628.18$

Therefore, $SS_T = 923{,}605.5 - 855{,}628.18 = 67{,}977.32.$
   The computational formula for SS_B is

$$SS_B = \sum_{j=1}^{k} N_j(\overline{X}_j - \overline{X})^2$$

$$= \left[\frac{\left(\sum_{i=1}^{N_1} X_{i1}\right)^2}{N_1} + \frac{\left(\sum_{i=1}^{N_2} X_{i2}\right)^2}{N_2} + \cdots + \frac{\left(\sum_{i=1}^{N_k} X_{ik}\right)^2}{N_k}\right] - \left[\frac{\left(\sum_{j=1}^{k}\sum_{i=1}^{N_j} X_{ij}\right)^2}{N}\right] \tag{12.5}$$

The second term of SS_B is the same as the second term of SS_T and has already been calculated. The first term equals

$$\left[\frac{\left(\sum_{i=1}^{N_1} X_{i1}\right)^2}{N_1} + \frac{\left(\sum_{i=1}^{N_2} X_{i2}\right)^2}{N_2} + \cdots + \frac{\left(\sum_{i=1}^{N_k} X_{ik}\right)^2}{N_k}\right]$$

$$= \frac{(208.8 + \cdots + 212.5)^2}{8} + \cdots + \frac{(118.7 + \cdots + 139.9)^2}{8} = 889{,}209.03$$

Therefore, $SS_B = 889,209.03 - 855,628.18 = 33,580.85$.
Finally,

$$SS_W = SS_T - SS_B \qquad (12.6)$$

Therefore, $SS_W = 67,977.32 - 33,580.85 = 34,396.47$.
The degrees of freedom are

$$df_T = N - 1 = 32 - 1 = 31$$
$$df_B = k - 1 = 4 - 1 = 3$$
$$df_W = N - k = 32 - 4 = 28$$

The two estimates of variances are computed as follows:

$$MSS_B = \frac{33,580.85}{3} = 11,193.62$$
$$MSS_W = \frac{34,396.47}{28} = 1,228.44$$

Therefore,

$$F = \frac{MSS_B}{MSS_W} = \frac{11,193.62}{1,228.44} = 9.11$$

The results are summarized in Table 12.3.

The Decision

Is the F ratio large enough for Anne to reject the null hypothesis? Looking at the F table for the .05 α level, an F with 3 and 28 degrees of freedom, $F_{(3,28)}$, equals 2.95. If her null hypothesis is true and the assumptions in the test model are valid, she would obtain an F value equal to or larger than 2.95 for 5% or less than 5% of the time with repeated sampling. Since her data produced a much larger F value, 9.11, Anne has sufficient evidence to reject the null hypothesis. Although ANOVA does not tell between which regions the differences are found, the sample data suggest that physicians are concentrated in the East and West, the more affluent and urbanized regions.

TABLE 12.3 Computation of Analysis of Variance

	Sum of Squares (SS)	Degrees of Freedom (df)	Estimate of Variance (MSS)	F Ratio
Total	67,977.32	31		
Between	33,580.85	3	11,193.62	
Within	34,396.47	28	1,228.44	9.11

Summary

One-way Analysis of Variance

Null hypothesis: $\mu_1 = \mu_2 = \cdots = \mu_k$

Test statistic: $F = \dfrac{\mathrm{MSS_B}}{\mathrm{MSS_W}} = \dfrac{\mathrm{SS_B}/\mathrm{df_B}}{\mathrm{SS_W}/\mathrm{df_W}}$, where

$$\mathrm{SS_T} = \sum_{j=1}^{k}\sum_{i=1}^{N_j} X_{ij}^2 - \frac{\left(\displaystyle\sum_{j=1}^{k}\sum_{i=1}^{N_j} X_{ij}\right)^2}{N}$$

$$\mathrm{SS_B} = \left[\frac{\left(\displaystyle\sum_{i=1}^{N_1} X_{i1}\right)^2}{N_1} + \frac{\left(\displaystyle\sum_{i=1}^{N_2} X_{i2}\right)^2}{N_2} + \cdots + \frac{\left(\displaystyle\sum_{i=1}^{N_k} X_{ik}\right)^2}{N_k}\right] - \left[\frac{\left(\displaystyle\sum_{j=1}^{k}\sum_{i=1}^{N_j} X_{ij}\right)^2}{N}\right]$$

$$\mathrm{SS_W} = \mathrm{SS_T} - \mathrm{SS_B}$$
$$\mathrm{df_B} = k - 1$$
$$\mathrm{df_W} = N - k$$

Test model:

1. Measurements: Interval dependent variable
   Nominal independent variable
2. Independent random samples
3. Normal populations with $\sigma_1^2 = \sigma_2^2 = \cdots = \sigma_k^2$

Exercises

1. Given the following data, perform one-way analysis of variance as a ratio of the two estimates of the population variance.

A	B	C	D
1	2	1	5
2	4	2	5
3	6	6	5

   a. Compute the estimate of the population variance as a weighted average of the variances within each separate sample.
   b. Compute the estimate of the population variance as the deviation of the sample means about the grand mean.
   c. Compute the F ratio.

2. Decompose the observed scores in Exercise 1 into the base-line effect (the total sum of squares), the effect of the independent variable (the between-group sum of squares), and the sampling error effect (the within-group sum of squares).

3. Find the degrees of freedom and the critical values of F for the following data:
   a. $\alpha = .01$, 6 groups, 30 subjects each
   b. $\alpha = .05$, 7 groups, 20 subjects each
   c. $\alpha = .001$, $N_1 = 5$, $N_2 = 8$, $N_3 = 10$
   d. $\alpha = .01$, $N_1 = 100$, $N_2 = 120$, $N_3 = 150$, $N_4 = 160$

4. Compute the two estimates of the population variance based on the following data. Are they significantly different?

Group:	1	2	3
N	15	15	15
Mean	10	20	30
s	4	3	5

5. Compute the between-group and within-group sums of squares and perform an ANOVA in Exercise 1.

6. Refer to Table 12.1 in the text.
   a. Draw a box plot for the four regions separately.
   b. Compare the medians, dispersions, and means.

SPSS Session

One-way analysis of variance can be performed by either the ANOVA or the ONEWAY command in SPSS. ANOVA handles one or more independent variables. ONEWAY deals with only one independent variable.

```
DATA LIST FREE/REGION DOCTOR.

BEGIN DATA.

1   208.8   2   183.7   3   93.4    4   118.7

1   190.7   2   196.7   3   232.1   4   154.1

1   216.4   2   178.5   3   149.4   4   127.9

.   .   .

END DATA.

ONEWAY VARIABLES=DOCTOR BY REGION (1,4)/STATISTICS=1 3.
```

After the command keyword ONEWAY, the VARIABLES subcommand specifies the dependent variable DOCTOR, that is, the number of physicians, the keyword BY, and then the independent or grouping variable REGION. The minimum and maximum values of the independent variable are specified as 1 and 4 in parentheses. This instructs SPSS to compare the means of REGION among the four groups defined by these values of 1 to 4. In SPSS/PC+, the means and their associated 95% confidence intervals, the standard deviations, and standard errors of the different groups are requested through the specification of 1 in the STATISTICS subcommand. In addition, the specification of 3 under STATISTICS produces three different tests for the equality of variances among the groups. In SPSS, keywords rather than numbers are used after the STATISTICS subcommand, as follows:

```
ONEWAY VARIABLES=DOCTOR BY REGION (1,4)

    /STATISTICS=DESCRIPTIVES HOMOGENEITY.
```

The ONEWAY produces results identical to those in Table 12.3 of the text (see SPSS Figure 12.1). The exact probability associated with the F ratio of 9.11 is given here as .0002. This means that if the H_0 is true it is highly unlikely to obtain an F ratio of 9.11; the probability is 2 out of 10,000 times with repeated sampling.

The specification of 3 (SPSS/PC+) or HOMOGENEITY (SPSS) in the STATISTICS subcommand produces the tests for the homogeneity of variances in SPSS Figure 12.2. The P's of these tests are larger than either .01 or .05. Therefore, the assumption of the equality of variances cannot be rejected.

```
                       Analysis of Variance

                          Sum of        Mean           F      F
         Source     D.F.  Squares       Squares     Ratio  Prob.

Between Groups        3   33580.8412   11193.6137   9.1120  .0002
Within Groups        28   34396.4475    1228.4446
Total                31   67977.2887
```

SPSS FIGURE 12.1   One-way Analysis of Variance

```
Cochrans C = Max. Variance/Sum(Variances) =  .4333, P =  .266 (Approx.)
Bartlett-Box F =                            1.582 , P =  .192
Maximum Variance / Minimum Variance         5.790
```

SPSS FIGURE 12.2   Tests for Homogeneity of Variances among Three or More Groups

SPSS Exercises

Using the City data, answer the following questions. Are there regional differences in the health level of the city dwellers and health care facilities available in the city?

1. RECODE the states (STATE) into several regions according to a criterion of your choice. Take a 20% random sample of the recoded population. Then run one-way analysis of variance to test the null hypothesis of no regional difference with respect to:

   a. Infant mortality rate (INFANT)
   b. The number of hospital beds by 1,000 population (NUMBEDS)
   c. The percentage of the total city government expenditure for health care (HEALTH)

   Do not forget to test for the homogeneity of variances at the same time.

12.4 Multiple Comparison of Means

According to the results of the ANOVA, Anne could reject the null hypothesis that there is no difference in the distribution of physicians among the four regions. Just as in the *t* test, finding that a difference exists among the regions is but a starting point. Anne may want to ascertain specifically which region(s) enjoys a significantly greater concentration of physicians as compared to which other region(s).

When the researcher has specific questions that involve multiple comparisons of means based on the same set of data, she or he has two alternative approaches: an *a priori*, planned comparison, and an a posteriori, post hoc comparison. In *planned comparisons*, individual hypotheses about specific means are formulated *before* actual testing. In place of an overall comparison of all sample means provided by ANOVA, the researcher opts for a number of specific comparisons. These comparisons employ techniques that represent an extension of the *t* test. Unlike the *t* test, however, these tests are formulated in such a manner that the α levels are not affected by the multiple testing, and each test is *independent* of all others. With *k* sample means, it is possible to conduct $(k - 1)$ independent comparisons.

Post hoc comparisons are conducted *after* a significant result has been obtained from an initial ANOVA test. Unlike planned comparisons, post hoc comparisons need not be independent of one another. A number of procedures are available for post hoc comparisons. The Scheffé technique in particular allows all pairwise and nonpairwise comparisons to be made without exceeding the significance level set by the initial ANOVA test. It is less powerful than other alternative tests, but it has the advantage of simplicity and versatility. The Scheffé test may be applied to groups of unequal size and is relatively insensitive to departures from normality and equality of variances. Readers who are interested in this test may wish to consult Scheffé [1] and Neter and Wasserman [2].

12.5 Kruskal–Wallis One-way Analysis of Variance

Research Question

Regardless of the theoretical perspective Anne employs, the physician is seen as having a dominant status in U.S. society. While the conflict theorist focuses on the doctor's financial and political power, the symbolic interactionist observes the media portrayal of a halo effect surrounding the physician's role. Finally, the functionalist provides a rationale for the physician's exalted status in our society. To acquire the necessary skill, the doctor undergoes a long period of training involving a great deal of sacrifice. In addition, the physician is perceived as having technical expertise that few possess, required for the performance of an essential societal task. Therefore, as an inducement for qualified individuals to train for the profession, society must reward the status with money, power, and esteem.

While these theorists attempt to interpret why doctors are influential, Anne has misgivings that patients actually endorse this view nowadays. Recent surveys show a relative decline in the public's confidence in the medical profession. Physicians are no longer seen as single mindedly serving humanity, but rather as promoting their own interests. As an indication of this crisis of confidence, patients are increasingly seeking nontraditional medical approaches and finding them more satisfactory. To test whether the physicians' professional dominance is intact or whether gradual erosion of this position has set in, Anne decides to compare the degree of confidence accorded by patients to medical practitioners and other health care professionals.

The Data

Anne randomly chooses seven patients from various private physicians' and herbalists' offices and chiropractor clinics in her community. These patients are asked to rank the degree of confidence they have in their health practitioners on a 10-point scale. The results are shown in Table 12.4. A higher score indicates a higher degree of confidence shown by the patients. Based on the data, can Anne conclude that physicians are in fact more trusted than herbalists or chiropractors?

TABLE 12.4 Degree of Confidence in Health Practitioners

Physician	Herbalist	Chiropractor
7	10	8
10	5	9
6	6	7
7	6	8
6	7	6
7	7	9
8	8	9

An Appropriate Test and Its Assumptions

The degree of confidence is an ordinal variable; the mean would be an inappropriate statistic to summarize the data. Also, the data do not meet all the requirements needed to conduct an analysis of variance. An appropriate substitute under such circumstances is the nonparametric Kruskal–Wallis test.

The Kruskal–Wallis one-way analysis of variance tests the null hypothesis that samples come from identical populations. It attempts to determine whether any obtained difference in central tendency among the samples is due to sampling fluctuation or genuine population differences. The test assumes that all samples are randomly drawn from their respective populations. In addition to independent selection within each sample, mutual independence among the various samples is assumed. The variable under study, that is, the dependent variable, must have an underlying continuous distribution, although its measurement may be discrete, as in this case. Also, the measurement scale must be at least ordinal.

The Kruskal–Wallis test is not as efficient as the F test. Thus it will require larger sample differences before the null hypothesis can be rejected. The power efficiency varies depending on the sample size. It is lower for smaller samples, but may reach 95% efficiency with larger samples when compared to ANOVA.

The Statistical Hypotheses

Anne's null hypothesis states that there is no difference in the degree of confidence patients have in their doctors versus their herbalists and chiropractors. Since the dependent variable is ordinal, the equality of the central tendencies of the populations is stated in terms of their ranks:

$$H_0: \ M_1 = M_2 = M_3$$

where M_1, M_2, and M_3 refer to the average ranks in the population of doctors, herbalists, and chiropractors, respectively. The alternative hypothesis states that at least one population tends to show a higher degree of confidence than others:

$$H_1: \ \text{not all } M_i\text{'s are equal}$$

The Test Statistic and Its Sampling Distribution

The Kruskal–Wallis procedure works on the *ranks of the scores* and not the scores themselves. To rank the scores, pool all scores from all samples. Then assign ranks in such a manner that if there are N observations the lowest score has the rank of 1 and the highest score has the rank of N. In case of ties, the mean value of the ranks is assigned to each tied observation.

Once the ranks are assigned, they are regrouped into the k different samples. The sum of ranks, R_j, is then computed for each sample. When the assignment of ranks is correctly carried out, the total of the rank sums for all samples, $\sum R_j$, equals $[N(N + 1)]/2$, where N refers to the total number of observations in all samples.

If the null hypothesis is true that the samples are selected from identical populations, the ranks should be randomly distributed among the k different samples. Each R_j is a proportion of the $\sum R_j$, the proportion being determined by the particular sample size, N_j, compared to the total number of observations in all samples, N. For the jth sample, with N_j cases, the expected R_j when all the M_i's are equal in the populations is

$$E(R_j) = \frac{N_j}{N}\left[\frac{N(N + 1)}{2}\right] = \frac{N_j(N + 1)}{2}$$

To the extent that a particular R_j deviates radically from its expected value, the sample results depart from the predicted results under H_0. The total squared departure can be obtained through calculating the variance of all the R_j's from their expectations as follows:

$$\sum_{j=1}^{k}\left(R_j - \frac{N_j(N + 1)}{2}\right)^2$$

If this sum equals 0, H_0 cannot be rejected; if, on the other hand, it is much greater than 0, H_0 can be rejected in favor of H_1. The sampling distribution of this test statistic, however, is not fully specified. Fortunately, a related test statistic can be formulated as follows:

$$H = \frac{12}{N(N + 1)}\sum_{j=1}^{k}\frac{1}{N_j}\left(R_j - \frac{N_j(N + 1)}{2}\right)^2$$

$$= \left(\frac{12}{N(N + 1)}\sum_{j=1}^{k}\frac{R_j^2}{N_j}\right) - 3(N + 1) \qquad (12.7)$$

where N refers to the total number of cases in all samples
    N_j refers to the number of cases in the jth sample
    R_j refers to the sum of ranks for the jth sample and
    k refers to the number of samples

The test statistic H has a chi-square distribution with $(k - 1)$ degrees of freedom if each sample has at least five observations. Basically, H is also a measure of the variance of the rank sums $R_1, R_2, \ldots, R_k$. If the ranks are distributed evenly among the samples, H will be relatively small. If, on the other hand, samples vary greatly from one another, H will be large and the null hypothesis can be rejected. Tables with critical values of H for N of less than 5 are available in other texts, such as Siegel's [3]. For larger N's, the value of H is essentially a chi-square value with $(k - 1)$ degrees of freedom, and therefore the chi-square table can be used.

When there are ties, the value of H is affected. To correct for the effect of ties, H is divided by the following correction factor:

$$\text{correction for ties} = 1 - \frac{\sum_{i=1}^{g} T_i}{N^3 - N} \tag{12.8}$$

where $T = t^3 - t$, while

t refers to the number of tied scores in a set of tied scores and

g refers to the number of sets of tied scores

The H test statistic corrected for ties is

$$\text{corrected } H = \frac{\left(\dfrac{12}{N(N + 1)} \sum_{j=1}^{k} \dfrac{R_j^2}{N_j} \right) - 3(N + 1)}{1 - \left(\sum_{i=1}^{g} T_i / (N^3 - N) \right)} \tag{12.9}$$

Since the correction for ties increases the value of H, the same result is more significant when corrected for ties. Most of the time, however, the effect of the correction is negligible.

Calculation of the Test Statistic

After the data in each sample are sorted in ascending order and assigned overall ranks, the results shown in Table 12.5 are obtained. The sum of ranks for the samples are given as 71.5 (R_1), 63 (R_2), and 96.5 (R_3). Each sample consists of seven observations (N_1, N_2, N_3), totaling 21 cases (N). Thus H is computed as follows:

$$H = \frac{12}{21(21 + 1)} \left(\frac{71.5^2}{7} + \frac{63^2}{7} + \frac{96.5^2}{7} \right) - 3(21 + 1) = 2.250$$

TABLE 12.5 Rank Ordering of the Degree of Confidence in Health Practitioners

Physician		Herbalist		Chiropractor	
Score	Rank	Score	Rank	Score	Rank
6	4	5	1	6	4
6	4	6	4	7	9.5
7	9.5	6	4	8	14.5
7	9.5	7	9.5	8	14.5
7	9.5	7	9.5	9	18
8	14.5	8	14.5	9	18
10	20.5	10	20.5	9	18
R_j	71.5		63.0		96.5

The following ties are observed in Anne's data:

5 ties of score 6; therefore, $t = 5$ and $T = 5^3 - 5 = 120$
6 ties of score 7; therefore, $t = 6$ and $T = 6^3 - 6 = 210$
4 ties of score 8; therefore, $t = 4$ and $T = 4^3 - 4 = 60$
3 ties of score 9; therefore, $t = 3$ and $T = 3^3 - 3 = 24$
2 ties of score 10; therefore, $t = 2$ and $T = 2^3 - 2 = 6$

The correction factor for these ties is calculated as

$$1 - \frac{120 + 210 + 60 + 24 + 6}{21^3 - 21} = .954$$

The *H* statistic with correction for ties is computed as

$$\text{corrected } H = \frac{2.250}{.954} = 2.358$$

The Decision

Since each sample has more than five cases, the chi-square table is used. With 2: ($k - 1 = 3 - 1$) degrees of freedom, a chi square of 5.991 or larger is needed to reject H_0 at the .05 level. Since *H* equals 2.25 and corrected *H* equals 2.36, the null hypothesis that patients hold the same degree of confidence in various health care practitioners cannot be rejected at this level. Patients do not appear to have more confidence in doctors than in other health practitioners, as Anne has suspected.

Summary

Kruskal–Wallis One-way Analysis of Variance

Null hypothesis: $M_1 = M_2 = \cdots = M_k$, or samples are drawn from identical populations

Test statistic with correction for ties:

$$\text{corrected } H = \frac{\left(\dfrac{12}{N(N+1)} \displaystyle\sum_{j=1}^{k} \dfrac{R_j^2}{N_j}\right) - 3(N+1)}{1 - \left(\displaystyle\sum_{i=1}^{g} T_i \,/\, (N^3 - N)\right)} \qquad \text{with df of } (k-1)$$

where k = number of samples

Test model:

1. Measurement level: Ordinal or higher
2. Independent random samples from continuous distributions

Exercises

---

7. Conflict theorists would argue that the medical ascendance comes from the American Medical Association's (AMA's) lobbying power against other vested interest groups. Would various lobbyists perceive that doctors have too much power, too little power, or a fair amount? Anne selects at random five representatives each from the AMA, AFL–CIO, AARP (American Association of Retired Persons), and UFW (United Farm Workers), and asks them to rate doctor's power on a 10-point scale. The score 10 means "too much power" and the score 1 represents "too little power." The results are shown next.

AMA	AFL–CIO	AARP	UFW
5	10	5	9
4	9	6	8
4	8	5	7
6	9	6	8
5	10	7	7

Is there a significant difference in the perception of the physician's power among various interest groups?

SPSS Session

The program to compute the Kruskal–Wallis test is shown next. The dependent variable VALUE refers to the degree of confidence in health practitioners; the independent grouping variable GROUP refers to the three types of health care practice: medical, herbalist, and chiropractic. Being a nonparametric test, the Kruskal–Wallis is requested through the NPAR TESTS command. The K–W subcommand specifies VALUE to be a dependent variable and GROUP to be an independent variable. The values within the parentheses following the independent variable show that there are three groups, 1, 2, and 3, to be compared.

```
DATA LIST FREE/VALUE GROUP.

BEGIN DATA.

7   1   10   2   8   3        10   1    5   2   9   3        6   1   6   2   7   3

7   1    6   2   8   3         6   1    7   2   6   3        7   1   7   2   9   3

8   1    8   2   9   3

END DATA.

NPAR TESTS K-W=VALUE BY GROUP (1,3).
```

SPSS outputs the mean rank instead of the sum of ranks for each group. Thus the mean rank for the doctor's patients is 10.21, that of the herbalist's patients is 9.00, and for the chiropractor's patients it is 13.79 in SPSS Figure 12.3. The chi-square values with and without corrections for ties, 2.3576 and 2.2505, respectively, are the same as those calculated manually in the text. SPSS provides exact significance levels associated with these two chi squares: .3076 and .3246. These significance levels indicate that the sample results are likely to occur, 30 to 32 times out of 100 times with repeated sampling, when the H_0 is true.

SPSS Exercises

2. Among the GSS respondents, is there a significant difference in health status (HEALTH) by subjective social class (CLASS)?

3. Is there a significant difference in the GSS respondents' attitudes toward the government subsidy of medical bills (HELPSICK) according to their social class (CLASS)?

4. Do these attitudes (HELPSICK) vary by the health status of the respondents (HEALTH)?

```
      VALUE
by  GROUP

   Mean Rank      Cases

       10.21          7    GROUP  =    1
        9.00          7    GROUP  =    2
       13.79          7    GROUP  =    3
                     --
                     21    Total

                                            Corrected for Ties
      CASES    Chi-Square   Significance   Chi-Square  Significance
         21       2.2505          .3246       2.3576         .3076
```

SPSS FIGURE 12.3   Kruskal–Wallis One-way Analysis of Variance

12.6 Chi-square Test for k Samples

Research Question

According to symbolic interactionism, the key determinant of social reality is face-to-face interaction rather than objective facts. Thus a patient may recover faster if convinced that he or she is taken care of by a "good doctor." However, what constitutes a "good doctor," and is the image of a "good doctor" invariant in the population or is it based on different symbolic elements?

Anne suspects that the latter is the case. She further hypothesizes that different occupational groups would evaluate the medical profession differently. Therefore, as an independent variable Anne chooses four occupational categories: professional, managerial, service, and other white-collar workers. The dependent variable is their perception of what constitutes a good doctor, which is classified into three categories: doctors who (1) have good bedside manners, (2) have achieved professional recognition, and (3) are white males.

The Data

Having taken random samples from the four occupations, Anne then surveys each group as to which one of the three aspects they consider most important in a "good" doctor. The results are shown in Table 12.6.

An Appropriate Test and Its Assumptions

Anne's dependent and independent variables are both nominal. She finds neither the assumptions of the *F* test nor those of the Kruskal–Wallis test appropriate for her nominal data; she therefore selects the chi-square test. The chi-square test for three or more independent samples is a direct extension of the chi-square test for

TABLE 12.6 Image of a Good Doctor Held by Four Occupational Groups

Good Doctor	Professional	Managerial	Service	Others	Total
Bedside manner	5 (14.09)	34 (33.39)	40 (32.65)	13 (11.87)	92
Professional competence	27 (11.80)	36 (27.94)	10 (27.32)	4 (9.94)	77
White and male	6 (12.11)	20 (28.67)	38 (28.03)	15 (10.19)	79
Total	38	90	88	32	248

two independent samples. Because a test of difference is an implied test of association (Chapter 11), the chi-square test involving two or more independent samples is equivalent to a test of association or independence between two variables in a sample. The data arrangement in Table 12.6 can be viewed either as an $r \times c$ contingency table or as four separate univariate distributions. When considered as a contingency table, the cells in Table 12.6 are formed through the crosstabulation of a category of the measured variable, such as "professional competence," with one of the four samples. Recall the test requires that the samples be selected independently and randomly from the different populations. In addition, the expected frequencies must be five or larger for the chi-square sampling distribution to be used as an approximation.

The Statistical Hypotheses

The research hypothesis can be stated in two ways. There is no difference among occupational groups with respect to their image of a good doctor. Or there is no relationship between occupation and perception of a good doctor. When translated into statistical terms, it states

$$H_0: \quad O_{ij} = E_{ij}, \quad \text{for all cells, or} \quad \chi^2 = 0$$

where E_{ij} represents the expected cell frequencies and O_{ij} represents the observed cell frequencies.

The alternative hypothesis states that there is a difference among occupational groups:

$$H_1: \quad O_{ij} \neq E_{ij}, \quad \text{for some or all cells, or} \quad \chi^2 > 0$$

The Test Statistic and Its Sampling Distribution

To calculate χ^2, the data are treated as if they are arranged in the form of a contingency table. A table of expected frequencies is generated under the null hypothesis of no difference among population distributions or of no association between the variables. From Chapter 4, the formula for calculating expected frequencies is

$$E_{ij} = \frac{f_{i.} f_{.j}}{N}$$

where $f_{i.}$ refers to the appropriate row marginal frequency, and $f_{.j}$ refers to the appropriate column marginal frequency.

The observed frequencies are then compared to the expected. When the null hypothesis is true, the observed frequencies should not deviate radically from the expected. However, if they are very different, the difference may be attributed to the fact that the samples come from different populations (or the variables are associated). A chi-square statistic is used to summarize the total weighted discrepancy between observed and expected frequencies. The formula for the χ^2 statistic, given next, is the same as that given in Chapter 4:

$$\chi^2 = \sum_{j=1}^{c} \sum_{i=1}^{r} \frac{(O_{ij} - E_{ij})^2}{E_{ij}} \tag{12.10}$$

where r equals the number of rows and
  c equals the number of columns

This test statistic has a chi-square distribution with the following number of degrees of freedom:

$$df = (r - 1)(c - 1) \tag{12.11}$$

Calculation of the Test Statistic

Expected values are computed and shown in parentheses in Table 12.6. The chi-square statistic is calculated as follows:

$$\chi^2 = \frac{(5 - 14.09)^2}{14.09} + \frac{(34 - 33.39)^2}{33.39} + \frac{(40 - 32.65)^2}{32.65} + \cdots + \frac{(15 - 10.19)^2}{10.19}$$
$$= 55.5948$$

with degrees of freedom = $(r - 1)(c - 1) = (3 - 1)(4 - 1) = 6$.

The Decision

With 6 degrees of freedom, the critical chi-square value at the .01 significance level is 16.8119. The calculated chi square of 55.5948 far exceeds the critical value. Hence Anne rejects the null hypothesis that there is no difference among occupational groups in their perception of a good doctor.

Summary

Chi-square Test for k Samples

Null hypothesis: $O_{ij} = E_{ij}$ or no difference between two or more populations with respect to cell frequencies.

Test statistic:

$$\chi^2 = \sum_{j=1}^{c} \sum_{i=1}^{r} \frac{(O_{ij} - E_{ij})^2}{E_{ij}}, \qquad \text{with df of } (r-1)(c-1)$$

where O_{ij} = observed number of cases in each cell
  E_{ij} = number of cases expected under H_0 in each cell
  r = number of rows
  c = number of columns

Test model:

1. Measurement level: Nominal
2. Independent random samples where each $E_{ij} \geq 5$

Exercises

8. Is there a significant difference between the classes in interaction patterns in case of disagreement based on the following data?

	Middle Class	Working Class
Physical violence	3	25
Emotional outburst	28	20
Graceful exit	10	11
Mutual accommodation	25	5
Other	15	13

9. Traditionally, doctors do not advertise because of professional ethics rooted in the Hippocratic oath. Recently, however, some doctors and dentists began to appear on TV to advertise their practice, producing a great impact on public opinion and behavior. Anne takes random samples of different occupational groups and determines their attitudes toward doctor's advertising on TV shows as follows.

Attitudes	Doctors	Lawyers	Professors	Businesspersons	Truck Drivers
Unethical	30	20	10	20	22
Unprofessional	44	57	66	32	39
Efficient	7	15	22	19	11
Helpful for patients	6	11	9	13	26

a. Is there a significant difference between the professionals (doctors, lawyers, professors) and nonprofessionals (businesspersons, truck drivers)?
b. Among the professionals, is there a significant difference between occupations?
c. Among the nonprofessionals, is there a significant difference among occupations?
d. Can you demonstrate the additivity of the chi squares based on the preceding analysis?

SPSS Session

The following program computes χ^2 for the data presented in Table 12.6. The data are entered in a contingency table form. The value of the dependent variable IMAGE is entered first, then the value of the independent variable OCCP, and finally the cell frequency count NUM for each combination of IMAGE and OCCP. The command WEIGHT re-creates the raw data from which the contingency table is initially tabulated.

```
DATA LIST FREE/IMAGE OCCP NUM.

BEGIN DATA.

1   1    5   1   2   34   1   3   40   1   4   13

2   1   27   2   2   36   2   3   10   2   4    4

3   1    6   3   2   20   3   3   38   3   4   15

END DATA.

WEIGHT BY NUM.

CROSSTABS TABLES=IMAGE BY OCCP /CELL=COUNT COLUMN EXPECTED

        /STATISTICS=CHISQ.
```

The CROSSTABS command generates a contingency table specified by the TABLES subcommand. Under the CELLS subcommand, the COUNT displays cell frequencies, the COLUMN, column percentages, and the EXPECTED, frequencies expected under the null hypothesis. Finally, the STATISTICS subcommand requests that a χ^2 statistic be calculated.

The table generated by the CROSSTABS command is not reproduced here. However, note that the top value displayed in each cell refers to the observed frequency, the second value shows the frequency expected under the null hypothesis, and the third value gives the column percentage.

SPSS Figure 12.4 shows the chi-square statistics produced by the STATISTICS subcommand. Three different chi squares are calculated. The one that corresponds to that discussed in the text is Pearson's χ^2. Its value of 55.59 is the same

```
        Chi-Square                    Value          DF        Significance
-------------------------         -----------        ----      ------------

Pearson                            55.59464            6          .00000
Likelihood Ratio                   56.93710            6          .00000
Mantel-Haenszel test for            2.18766            1          .13912
    linear association

Minimum Expected Frequency -        9.935
```

SPSS FIGURE 12.4   Chi-square Test of Independence

as that given in the text. With 6 degrees of freedom, the probability of obtaining a χ^2 this large or larger is less than .000005. SPSS also displays the minimum expected frequency so that the researcher knows whether the requirement for the minimum expected frequency of 5 is met.

SPSS Exercises

5. According to the GSS survey, is there a significant difference in the attitudes toward governmental subsidy (HELPSICK) by race (RACE)?

6. Is there a significant difference in the GSS respondents' attitudes toward abortion (ABANY) by religious affiliation (RELIG)?

7. Do GSS respondents' views on abortion (ABANY) vary significantly by their political ideologies (POLVIEWS)?

General Conceptual Questions

1. Explain why a test of means of more than two samples is called analysis of variance.

2. Explain how the degrees of freedom associated with SS_T, SS_W, and SS_B are derived.

3. Explain how an ANOVA problem can be viewed as a regression problem.

4. What are the two types of estimates of the population variance used in ANOVA?

5. Explain in your own words how the base-line prediction error is partitioned into two components in ANOVA.

6. Which statistic is being compared in the Kruskal–Wallis test?

7. Explain why the t test should not be used to compare each pair of means among several samples.

8. Explain what the F distribution is and how it is used in analysis of variance.

9. State the assumptions required of the Kruskal–Wallis test.

10. How is the central limit theorem utilized in ANOVA?

11. Which statistical test is appropriate for the following comparative analyses? Also state the null and alternative hypotheses.

    a. Comparison of the number of sick leave days among five racial groups.
    b. Comparison of the intensity of sickness experienced by four age groups.
    c. Comparison of the types of illnesses among four social classes.

12. In a study to determine if region of birth (four categories) is related to marital status (six categories), what is the number of degrees of freedom?

References

1. Scheffé, H. (1959). *The Analysis of Variance.* New York: Wiley.
2. Neter, J., and Wasserman, W. (1974). *Applied Linear Statistical Models.* Homewood, Ill.: Richard D. Irwin.
3. Siegel, Sidney (1956). *Nonparametric Statistics.* New York: McGraw-Hill.

C h a p t e r 13

Testing Relationships

New Statistical Topics

Test for concordance
F and t tests for correlation and regression coefficients

13.1 Overview

This chapter examines various procedures for testing bivariate relationships. In testing, the researcher questions whether sample findings portray patterns of association in the population at large or whether they merely reflect sampling variation. For example, Anne wonders whether her descriptions in Chapters 4 and 5 of how various factors are related in social interaction are generalizable to U.S. society as a whole. To complete her analysis, Anne should test those descriptive measures that yield a nonzero value to determine the extent to which the sample findings are indicative of actual relationships in the population.

This chapter retraces Anne's research activities in Chapters 4 and 5 and introduces techniques for statistical inference appropriate to each situation. As such, it can be considered a continuation of those chapters. Thus, although the descriptive and inferential procedures are presented in separate chapters, their division is primarily for pedagogical purposes. In practice, statistical inference is carried out immediately after the descriptive measures are calculated.

13.2 Chi-square Test of Independence for Nominal Data

Chapter 4 presented two classes of measures of association for nominal data: chi-square-based measures as represented by phi and PRE measures as represented by lambda. The chi-square test is obviously the appropriate test of association for chi-square-based measures. As noted in Chapters 11 and 12, this test, used to determine whether two or more samples are drawn from identical populations, is a test of association as well. The sampling distribution for lambda is too complex for an introductory text and will not be presented here. Where lambdas were calculated for descriptive purposes, chi squares could be substituted for inference. Those interested in the lambda sampling distribution may wish to consult Upton's [1] text.

This section introduces a chi-square statistic modified to test relations in a 2×2 table. Recall from Chapter 9 that the continuous chi-square distribution is used as a convenient approximation to a discrete sampling distribution. The approximation becomes problematic for a 2×2 table where df equals 1: $(2-1)(2-1)$. The computed values of the chi-square test statistic with 1 degree of freedom will not take on many different values, especially when N is small. Its sampling distribution retains many of the characteristics of a discrete distribution.

A method for improving the approximation for a 2×2 table is known as Yates's correction for continuity. The procedure consists of subtracting .5 from the absolute difference between each observed and expected value before proceeding with the rest of the calculation:

$$\chi^2 = \sum_{j=1}^{c} \sum_{i=1}^{r} \frac{(|O_{ij} - E_{ij}| - .5)^2}{E_{ij}}$$

This procedure in effect corrects for the discontinuity in the χ^2 values by bringing the expected values closer to the observed ones. The χ^2 value computed with this formula will be smaller than the χ^2 value using the formula without correction. In a 2×2 table, where $a, b, c,$ and d represent cell frequencies, as follows,

a	b	$a + b$
c	d	$c + d$
$a + c$	$b + d$	N

the preceding formula can be simplified as follows:

$$\chi^2 = \frac{N\left(|bc - ad| - \dfrac{N}{2}\right)^2}{(a + b)(c + d)(a + c)(b + d)} \tag{13.1}$$

We can apply Formula 13.1 to the problem in Chapter 4 where Anne calculated a phi statistic to find that race and attitude toward the police are associated in a sample of grade school children. The data from which the phi statistic was obtained is reproduced here as Table 13.1.

TABLE 13.1   Responses to the Role of a Police Officer by Race

		Race (X)		
Responses (Y)		Nonwhite	White	Total
Protector of community		22	19	41
Enforcer of law		13	3	16
	Total	35	22	57

Substituting the values from Table 13.1 into Formula 13.1, a χ^2 of 2.624 is obtained:

$$\chi^2 = \frac{57(\,|(19)(13) - (22)(3)\,| - 28.5)^2}{(41)(16)(35)(22)} = \frac{1,325,606.25}{505,120} = 2.624$$

The df pertaining to this χ^2 is 1. At an α of .01, the critical value is 6.635, while at an α of .05, it is 3.841. The obtained value of 2.62 is not significant at either the .01 or .05 level. Therefore, the association found at the sample level may reflect sampling variation, rather than a true relationship in the population. The observed cell frequencies do not depart radically enough from the expected cell frequencies for Anne to conclude that there is an association between race and attitude in the population of grade school children as a whole.

Exercises

1. Test whether the desired GPA level is related to generation (parents versus children) using data from Exercise 7, Chapter 4.

2. Test the relationship between the two variables in Exercise 16, Chapter 4.

3. Assume that there are 10 times as many cases in Exercise 1, Chapter 4 by multiplying each cell frequency by 10. Compute chi square to test the relation between the community size and auto deal:

   a. Among males.
   b. Among females.
   c. Among all the subjects.

4. Refer to Exercise 20, Chapter 4. Compute chi square to test the relation between social class and reference group comparison:

   a. Using only codings 1 and 2 for the variable reference group.
   b. Using only codings 3 and 4 for the variable reference group.
   c. Combining codings (1 and 2) and then (3 and 4) for the variable reference group.
   d. Using all four codings for reference group.
   e. Sum the chi squares obtained from steps a, b, and c. Does the sum equal the chi square obtained in step d?

13.3 Test of Concordance for Ordinal Data

Research Question and Data
In Chapter 4, Anne obtained the data in Table 13.2 through an experiment on the living arrangements in the university dormitories. She calculated the gamma to be .44. The data show that the clearer the boundaries are, the greater the ease of interaction in the sample. However, although the relationship characterizes the sample, it may not exist in the population. To determine whether she has obtained an atypical sample result, Anne decides to test the gamma statistic.

An Appropriate Test and Its Assumptions
The population parameter that G estimates is γ. The value of γ is best tested through a comparison of the number of concordant to discordant pairs, $(N_s - N_d)$. When γ is 0, the expected value of $(N_s - N_d)$ is 0. When γ is positive, $(N_s - N_d)$ is expected to be greater than 0; and when γ is negative, $(N_s - N_d)$ is expected to be less than 0. The test statistic for $(N_s - N_d)$ is given in the section on sampling distribution and is based on the following assumptions:

1. Variables X and Y are independently measured at the ordinal or higher level.
2. A random sample is drawn.

The Statistical Hypotheses
The null hypothesis states that there is no association between clarity of boundaries and ease of interaction:

$$H_0: \ \gamma = 0$$

From the literature, however, Anne suspects that the clearer the boundaries are, the easier the interaction. Therefore, a positive gamma is hypothesized and a one-tailed test is needed:

$$H_1: \ \gamma > 0$$

The Test Statistic and Its Sampling Distribution
The exact sampling distribution of gamma is difficult to specify. Fortunately, with $N \geq 50$, the sampling distribution can be approximated by the z distribution, and

TABLE 13.2   Ease of Interaction by Clarity of Boundaries

	Clarity of Boundary (X)			
Ease of Interaction (Y)	Low	Medium	High	Total
High	62	55	146	263
Medium	42	210	71	323
Low	196	35	83	314
Total	300	300	300	900

gamma can be tested with a z-test statistic. Other than gamma, the z-test statistic presented here can also be used for testing any ordinal measure discussed in Chapter 4 whose numerator is based on the difference between concordant and discordant pairs.

This z-test statistic is similar to that of a difference in means test. It is obtained by (1) subtracting the difference between the concordant and discordant pairs from 0, the value of γ hypothesized under H_0, and then (2) dividing the numerator by the estimated standard error of $(N_s - N_d)$, as follows:

$$z = \frac{(N_s - N_d) - 0}{\hat{\sigma}_{Ns-Nd}} = \frac{N_s - N_d}{\hat{\sigma}_{Ns-Nd}} \tag{13.2}$$

The variance of the sampling distribution, in turn, is calculated as follows:

$$\hat{\sigma}^2_{Ns-Nd} = \frac{N^3}{9}\left(1 - \frac{\sum_{i=1}^{r} R_i^3}{N^3}\right)\left(1 - \frac{\sum_{j=1}^{c} C_j^3}{N^3}\right) \tag{13.3}$$

where R_i refers to the row marginal totals
C_j refers to the column marginal totals
r refers to the number of rows and
c refers to the number of columns

In a one-tailed test of Anne's hypotheses at the .05 level, the critical z value is 1.65. Thus, if the test statistic z is computed to be larger than 1.65, the null hypothesis can be rejected in favor of the alternative hypothesis.

Calculation of the Test Statistic

The formula for the estimated variance calls for summing the cubes of row and column totals:

$$\sum R_i^3 = 263^3 + 323^3 + 314^3 = 82,848,858$$
$$\sum C_j^3 = 300^3 + 300^3 + 300^3 = 81,000,000$$

Based on these sums, the estimated variance is computed as

$$\hat{\sigma}^2_{Ns-Nd} = \frac{N^3}{9}\left(1 - \frac{\sum R_i^3}{N^3}\right)\left(1 - \frac{\sum C_j^3}{N^3}\right)$$

$$= \frac{900^3}{9}\left(1 - \frac{82,848,858}{900^3}\right)\left(1 - \frac{81,000,000}{900^3}\right) = 63,825,374$$

From the estimated variance, the estimated standard error is obtained:

$$\hat{\sigma}_{Ns-Nd} = \sqrt{63,825,374} = 7,989.078$$

From Chapter 4, the values of N_s and N_d are calculated to be 141,169 and 55,594, respectively. Substituting these values into the z formula, we have

$$z = \frac{N_s - N_d}{\hat{\sigma}_{Ns-Nd}} = \frac{141,169 - 55,594}{7,989.078} = 10.711$$

The Decision
The value of z is so large that the null hypothesis is rejected beyond the .0001 significance level. If there is no association between the variables, the chances of obtaining a G of .44 is less than 1 time out of 10,000 times of repeated sampling. The positive relationship between clarity of boundaries and ease of interaction found in the sample reflects an association in the population of students who live in the dormitory.

Exercises

5. Test the association between social class and reference group among blacks in Los Angeles in Exercise 20, Chapter 4.

6. Test the association between personality compatibility and professional competence in Exercise 19, Chapter 4.

7. Test the association between sex and title in Exercise 2, Chapter 4.

8. Test the association between proximity and reaction in Exercise 24, Chapter 4.

9. Test the association between community size and auto deal in Exercise 1, Chapter 4.

SPSS Session

Recall from Chapter 4 that to obtain a gamma statistic the data must be crosstabulated first with the CROSSTABS command. Within this command, the STATISTICS subcommand can be used to request the calculation of a gamma. The output associated with the STATISTICS subcommand in which a gamma is requested is shown in SPSS Figure 13.1. In addition to the gamma value, a t value is included for testing the significance of gamma. The T value is obtained by dividing the gamma value by the standard error under the hypothesis of independence (ASE0). SPSS, however, calculates the standard error differently from the text, resulting in a t value that is slightly different from the z value obtained in the text. These t values are not in general distributed as a Student's t, but as a normal distribution under the null hypothesis in large samples. The conclusion reached

Statistic	Value	ASE1	T-value	Approximate Significance
Gamma	.43491	.04244	9.66364	

SPSS FIGURE 13.1   Gamma and Its Test of Significance

using the *t* value in SPSS Figure 13.1 is the same as that using the *z* value in the text.

13.4 Tests of Linear Relationship for Interval Data

Recall that Anne regressed income on education for a sample of U.S. residents in Chapter 5 and found the two to be highly correlated. In fact, the slope, *b*, is 5.952, and Pearson's correlation coefficient is .782. Can Anne assume that a linear relationship exists between education and income in the U.S. population as a whole?

13.4.1 F Test

The population parameters that correspond to the sample statistics of *r* and *b* are ρ and β. When there is a linear relationship between education and income, both ρ and β should be greater than 0. Therefore, only one null hypothesis is necessary to test both parameters: $\rho = 0$ or $\beta = 0$.

Chapter 5 pointed out that the regression line predicts the conditional means of the dependent variable *Y* for every value of the independent variable *X*. When $\beta = 0$, however, the regression line is flat, yielding the same conditional mean of *Y* for every *X*. In hypothesizing that β or $\rho = 0$, Anne is testing then that $\mu_{y1} = \mu_{y2} = \mu_{y3}$, and so on, where μ_{y1}, μ_{y2}, and μ_{y3} refer to the conditional means of *Y* for different values of *X*. Note the equivalence of this null hypothesis to that of the analysis of variance. In fact, to test β or ρ, ANOVA can be performed on the regression data for which the independent variable, unlike that of Chapter 12, is not a nominal but an interval scale variable.

The following assumptions are made in performing ANOVA on the regression data. In addition to random sampling, the *Y* distributions within each category or value of *X* are assumed to be normally distributed, and their variances are assumed to be equal.

The Statistical Hypotheses
The null hypothesis states that there is no linear relationship between education and income:

$$H_0: \quad \rho = \beta = 0$$

Although Anne suspects that the two variables are positively correlated, ANOVA would permit only a nondirectional alternative hypothesis:

$$H_1: \quad \rho \neq \beta \neq 0$$

The Test Statistic and Its Sampling Distribution

The sampling distribution used in ANOVA is the F distribution. As defined in Chapter 12, the test statistic F for a one-way ANOVA is

$$F = \frac{MSS_B}{MSS_W} = \frac{SS_B/df_B}{SS_W/df_W}$$

where SS_B refers to the between sum of squares and SS_W refers to the within sum of squares. In applying ANOVA to regression data, these terms are converted to regression terms as follows:

$$F = \frac{SSR/df_R}{SSE/df_E}$$

where SSR refers to the explained sum of squares and df_R is its associated degrees of freedom, and SSE refers to the unexplained sum of squares and df_E is its associated degrees of freedom. Thus the appropriate F test statistic for a bivariate regression analysis is the ratio of the sums of squares, each divided by its degrees of freedom. See Box 13.1 for a summary of equivalent terms between ANOVA and regression procedures.

The F ratio can be computed directly from these terms of SSR and SSE, or it can be calculated from the Pearson's r. In Chapter 5, r^2 was presented as the ratio of the explained sum of squares to the total sum of squares:

$$r^2 = \frac{\sum (Y' - \overline{Y})^2}{\sum (Y - \overline{Y})^2} = \frac{\text{explained SS}}{\text{total SS}} = \frac{SSR}{SST}$$

Box 13.1   Equivalent Terms for Various Sums of Squares

Terms	ANOVA	Regression	Symbols in Regression
Total sum of squares	SS_T	TSS	$\sum (Y - \overline{Y})^2$
Explained sum of squares	SS_B	SSR	$\sum (Y' - \overline{Y})^2$
Unexplained sum of squares	SS_W	SSE	$\sum (Y - Y')^2$

In addition, k^2, the coefficient of alienation, equals $(1 - r^2)$ and is the ratio of the unexplained sum of squares to the total sum of squares:

$$(1 - r^2) = \frac{\sum (Y - Y')^2}{\sum (Y - \overline{Y})^2} = \frac{\text{unexplained SS}}{\text{total SS}} = \frac{\text{SSE}}{\text{SST}}$$

Therefore, SSR, or the explained sum of squares, equals

$$\text{SSR} = r^2 \left[\sum (Y - \overline{Y})^2 \right]$$

and the SSE, or unexplained sum of squares, equals

$$\text{SSE} = [1 - r^2] \left[\sum (Y - \overline{Y})^2 \right]$$

The degrees of freedom for SSR and SSE are obtained as follows. The unexplained sum of squares, SSE, is calculated about the regression line, with two regression coefficients, a and b, which must be estimated. Thus 2 degrees of freedom are lost for df_E, resulting in $(N - 2)$ degrees of freedom. The degrees of freedom for the total sum of squares, df_T, equals $(N - 1)$, because TSS is estimated about the mean of Y, for which 1 degree of freedom is lost. The remaining degrees of freedom, df_R, associated with SSR, the explained sum of squares, can be calculated from the difference between the two previous df's: $(N - 1) - (N - 2) = 1$.

When reformulating the F ratio in terms of r, the common term $\Sigma(Y - \overline{Y})^2$ cancels out and the following is obtained for a bivariate regression analysis, which has df_R of 1 and df_E of $(N - 2)$ degrees of freedom:

$$\begin{aligned} F_{(1, N-2)} &= \frac{\text{SSR} / \text{df}_R}{\text{SSE} / \text{df}_E} \\ &= \frac{r^2}{1 - r^2} \frac{N - 2}{1} = \frac{r^2}{1 - r^2} (N - 2) \end{aligned} \tag{13.4}$$

Calculation and Interpretation of the Test Statistic

Anne calculates the F statistic with df_1 of 1 and df_2 of 6 as follows:

$$F_{(1, 6)} = \frac{(.782)^2 (6)}{1 - (.782)^2} = \frac{3.669}{.388} = 9.456$$

Since the critical value at the .05 level of significance for $F_{(1,6)}$ is 5.99, there is evidence to suggest that education and income are correlated in the U.S. population as a whole.

13.4.2 An Alternative: The t Test

An alternative to the F test is the t test for linear relationships. The advantage of the latter is that it can test either a directional or nondirectional alternative hypothesis. Since Anne has the alternative hypothesis that income and education are positively related and therefore (ρ or β) > 0, she should use the t test. As discussed in Chapter 12, the t and F distributions are related. The square of the t score with v degrees of freedom is equivalent to an F ratio with $df_R = 1$ and $df_E = v$:

$$t^2_{(v)} = F_{(1,v)}$$

For example, for a two-tailed test with df = 10, a t value of $|2.228|$ is required to reject the null hypothesis at the .05 level of significance. Now square 2.228 to obtain a t^2 of 4.9639. This value of 4.9639 also represents the F value for 1 and 10 degrees of freedom at an α of .05.

Thus, if the square root of the F statistic in Formula 13.4 is taken, the result is a t-test statistic with df of $(N - 2)$ for testing a linear relationship:

$$t_{(N-2)} = \frac{r}{\sqrt{\frac{(1 - r^2)}{(N - 2)}}} \tag{13.5}$$

An inspection of Formula 13.5 shows that the t value can be positive or negative, since the r within the formula is either positive or negative. This is why a directional alternative hypothesis can be tested with the t test.

Using the r value from the preceding section, a t value of 3.08 is obtained:

$$t = \frac{.782}{\sqrt{\frac{1 - .612}{8 - 2}}} = 3.076$$

Since the critical value for a one-tailed t test is 1.943 at an α of .05 for df of 6, the t test leads to the same conclusion as did the F test. To check on the equivalence of the t to the F test, square the *obtained* t value and, except for rounding errors, it will yield the same value as the obtained F ratio in the preceding section. Square the *critical* t value of 2.447 for *a two-tailed test*, and it will also yield the same value as the critical F ratio in the preceding section. Note that the SPSS regression analysis calculates both the F and t test as its standard output.

More on the Interpretation of the F and t Test
The results of the t and F tests should be interpreted with caution. Both tests evaluate whether or not the linear regression equation $Y' = a + bX$ provides any

improvement in the prediction of Y values over using the mean of Y. When these tests are significant, at least some improvement in prediction with the linear rule is noted. The existence of a *linear* relationship in the population is also indicated. However, these tests do not evaluate whether additional improvement in prediction is possible if other nonlinear rules or models are employed. Nor do they reveal the existence of other types of relationship. Thus, when nonsignificant results are obtained, they may simply mean that data can be predicted with a nonlinear rather than a linear prediction rule.

Summary

Tests of Relations

Nominal data: 2×2 table only

$$\chi^2 = \frac{N\left(|bc - ad| - \dfrac{N}{2}\right)^2}{(a + b)(c + d)(a + c)(b + d)}, \qquad \text{where df} = 1$$

Ordinal data: For $N \geq 50$

$$z = \frac{(N_s - N_d) - 0}{\hat{\sigma}_{Ns-Nd}}$$

$$\hat{\sigma}^2_{Ns-Nd} = \frac{N^3}{9}\left(1 - \frac{\displaystyle\sum_{i=1}^{r} R_i^3}{N^3}\right)\left(1 - \frac{\displaystyle\sum_{j=1}^{c} C_j^3}{N^3}\right)$$

where R_i = row marginal totals
$\quad C_j$ = column marginal totals
$\quad r\ $ = number of rows
$\quad c\ $ = number of columns

Interval data:

$$F_{(1, N-2)} = \frac{r^2}{1 - r^2}(N - 2), \qquad \text{where df}_R = 1 \text{ and df}_E = (N - 2)$$

$$t_{(N-2)} = \frac{r}{\sqrt{(1 - r^2)/(N - 2)}}, \qquad \text{where df} = (N - 2)$$

Exercises

10. Test a nondirectional alternative hypothesis with the data in Exercise 1, Chapter 5.

    a. Compute SSR and SSE.
    b. Compute MSSR and MSSE.
    c. Compute F as a ratio of the preceding two MSSs.
    d. Compute F using r.
    e. Can H_0 be rejected? What is the conclusion?

11. Using the same set of data, test a directional alternative hypothesis.

12. Using the data in Exercise 11, Chapter 5:

    a. Test the relationship between unemployment and crime.
    b. Test the relationship between suicide and unemployment.
    c. Test the relationship between education and unemployment.

SPSS Notes

The testing of Pearson's r is automatically conducted with the CORRELATION command. By default the printout provides a one-tailed test of significance. The r values that are significant at the .01 and .001 levels are preceded with a single asterisk (*) and double asterisks (**), respectively. To replace the one-tailed with a two-tailed test, use the OPTIONS subcommand in SPSS/PC+. Specify a 3 after the subcommand, and the values that are significant at the .01 and .001 levels for a two-tailed test will be indicated similarly by asterisks. For an exact significance level, specify 5 after OPTIONS. In SPSS, the PRINT subcommand performs the same functions as the OPTIONS in SPSS/PC+. The following "PRINT=TWOTAIL SIG" in SPSS is equivalent to "OPTIONS=3 5" in SPSS/PC+.

The REGRESSION command is also used to test both the slope and the r. This command is used for both bivariate and multivariate regression analysis. Because the procedure and the interpretation of the printout is the same whether the command is used for bivariate or multivariate testing, the discussion of this command is postponed to Chapter 15 where multivariate analysis is discussed.

SPSS Exercises

Using the City data, test if the following sets of variables are significantly related.

1. Educational expenditure (EDUC) and per capita income (INCOME).

2. The unemployment rate (UNEMPLOY) and the crime rate (CRIME).

3. Population density (POPDENSE) and the crime rate (CRIME).

4. The infant mortality rate (INFANT) and the number of hospital beds (NUMBEDS).

General Conceptual Problems

1. Explain the relationship between ϕ^2 *and* χ^2.

2. Explain how the t and F distributions are related.

3. What type of test is available for examining the association between two ordinal-level variables?

4. Are the assumptions met when a two-sample test is converted into a two-variable test of independence in χ^2 ?

5. Explain how ANOVA and a test for linear regression coefficients are related.

6. Under what condition is a t or F test appropriate for the correlation coefficient?

7. If r is as high as .8 between education and income in a sample of adult males, can it be concluded that education and income are significantly related?

8. If r_1 is significant at the .01 level and r_2 is significant at the .05 level, which relationship is stronger?

9. Decompose r^2 into explained and unexplained SS. Explain what they mean in your own words.

References

1. Upton, Graham J. G. (1978). *The Analysis of Cross-Tabulated Data*. New York: Wiley.

P a r t **III**

Multivariate Analysis

$$C \quad h \quad a \quad p \quad t \quad e \quad r \quad \mathit{14}$$

Multivariate Analysis of Nominal or Categorical Variables

New Statistical Topics

Marginal and partial tables   Statistical control
Interaction effect   Modeling
Loglinear analysis   Odds ratio
Maximum likelihood ratio chi square

14.1 Overview

Bivariate analysis serves to establish whether or not an association exists between two variables, facilitating, in the process, a search for causal relationship. As a starting point, this type of analysis certainly suffices. Social phenomena, however, are often too complex to be accounted for by a single factor. Even something relatively simple such as an individual's level of education may have to be explained by an array of independent variables, from social class to aspirational level. Therefore, to supplement the bivariate analysis, the researcher often analyzes the interrelations of three or more variables at a time. We call this process **multivariate analysis**.

One primary focus of multivariate analysis is **modeling**. Here, the aim is to construct and then select among various versions of social reality called **models**. These models reflect the complexity of a social phenomenon by employing multiple independent variables for its explanation. The researcher tests these models against empirical data, selecting the one that has the most explanatory power.

Often the selected independent variables in a model are interrelated, generating overlapping effects on the dependent variable. A second concern of multivariate analysis, then, is to isolate the unique contribution of each independent variable. This could be accomplished through statistically controlling the effects of other variables while examining that of a particular independent variable. **Statistical control** can also be applied to determine whether the observed relationship between an independent and a dependent variable is indeed genuine and cannot be accounted for by a third variable. Thus, multivariate analysis furthers the goal of explanatory research by extending the search for causal relations that is begun in bivariate analysis. This chapter presents a multivariate technique for analyzing nominal or categorical data called **loglinear analysis**.

14.1.1 Statistical Topics

Causation is not a concrete entity whose "existence" can be uncovered by any special statistical technique. Therefore, causal inference between two variables is, at best, indirect, based on agreed-upon criteria that, when satisfied, presumably indicate the existence of a causal relationship. Traditionally, three criteria are applied to establish causal relationships:

1. *Association:* It must be shown that as one variable, X, changes, the other variable, Y, changes with it in some systematic way.
2. *Time order:* If X is the cause of Y, then X must precede or occur at the same time as Y.
3. *Elimination of alternative hypotheses:* If X is the cause of Y, the original association found between X and Y should remain unchanged when the effects of all other relevant variables are controlled.

Bivariate analysis that provides evidence that an association exists in both the sample and the population can be used to satisfy criterion 1. Some methods for measuring and testing bivariate relationships have been presented in previous chapters. As for criterion 2, no statistical analysis would reveal the direction of influence between two variables. Instead, this criterion may be satisfied through a logical analysis of the time order between two variables. For example, with two variables such as race and social isolation, the former could not possibly be the effect of the latter. Alternatively, a particular research design may provide clear indication of chronology. Examples of such designs are the experiment and the longitudinal study. Finally, in studies for which the chronological order is not clear-cut, its determination relies heavily on a hypothesis derived from a theory.

To satisfy criterion 3, the researcher must determine that the relationship between two variables is not **spurious.** That is, other variables are not responsible for the observed relationship between the independent and dependent variables. This may be accomplished in some experimental designs by holding other variables constant while manipulating the independent variable to observe corresponding changes in the dependent variable. Where actual control is not attainable during the study, statistical control is exercised during the analysis through multivariate procedures such as loglinear analysis. It is in this sense that multivariate procedures further the search for causal relationships.

In addition to this function, multivariate analysis is also applied to modeling complex social phenomena and processes. Modeling may entail choosing, from various sets of independent variables, the set that best explains a dependent variable. In the selection, two criteria apply: **goodness of fit** and **substantive meaning**. According to the first principle, the selected model should be the one that most closely reflects social reality. Statistically, this translates to a model that gives the best prediction possible for a dependent variable. The second requirement refers to the fact that the chosen model should lend itself best to a substantive or theoretical interpretation.

Modeling may also proceed with the selection from one set of independent variables of those variables that have the most significant contribution to the explanation of the dependent variable. Sometimes the researcher starts with a full set, paring down the number necessary to give an adequate explanation. Or the reverse procedure may be used, by adding explanatory variables until the point of diminishing returns is reached. In such cases, a third criterion of **parsimony** applies. This criterion states that the best model is the simplest, requiring the least number of variables for the explanation. These three principles should be kept in mind while loglinear modeling is discussed.

14.1.2 Social Applications

Anne realizes that the United States she comes to know in the decade of the 1990s is very much a product of the changes brought about by the social and civil rights movement of the 1960s. Social movements, riots, indeed, fads and crazes all fall under the rubric of collective behavior. The study of collective behavior is challenging not only because such behavior is, by its very nature, unpredictable, but because it is the product of a complex convergence of structural, social, and personal factors as well.

Not only is past collective behavior a partial determinant of the present social conditions. Recent social unrest such as the Rodney King riot in 1992, which so captured the nation's attention, often echoes past occurrences such as the Watts riots some 30 years ago. Therefore, to gain a better understanding of the present, Anne decides to examine the L.A. riots of the 1960s. In search of causes for these riots, she finds a study of attitudes toward participation in the Watts riots. The researcher, Ransford [1], sent out black interviewers to survey a sample of 312 black males from three areas of Los Angeles shortly after the violence in Watts. Because few respondents admitted to actual participation in the riots, Ransford focused on examining "the willingness to use violence" to gain black rights. He brought in a number of explanatory variables for this purpose. In the following sections, Anne examines some of the hypotheses in this study, applying statistical techniques and reasoning similar to Ransford's. Then she reanalyzes the multivariate data using loglinear procedures.

14.2 Marginal and Partial Tables

Ransford's major hypothesis states that blacks who are structurally isolated and disengaged from society are more likely to consider violence as a necessary means for redressing racial injustice. The dependent variable was measured through the following question: "Would you be willing to use violence to get Negro rights?" The independent variable, social isolation, was operationally defined as the amount of social contact a black man had with whites on the job, in the neighborhood, on the streets, and through organizations and social activities. Ransford's data on racial contact and willingness to use violence are presented in Table 14.1. One way to assess the existence and strength of association is to compute a percentage difference. From the computed percentage difference of |27|, Anne gathers that the isolates are indeed more prone to violence: 44% of blacks who have low racial contact, as compared with 17% of those who have high contact, are willing to use violence.

Once Ransford established the bivariate relationship between the variables, he proceeded to examine if it could be affected or explained away by other variables. For this purpose, he selected a number of theoretically relevant variables that might have an effect on the original relationship between isolation and willingness to use violence. Powerlessness was one of these explanatory variables; in this context, the explanatory variables are often called **test** or **control variables**. Ransford speculated that the powerless are more likely to resort to violence.

To determine whether this is the case, Anne first crosstabulates the dependent and independent variables with the test variable to obtain the **marginal tables** shown in Table 14.2(a) and (b). Note that four individuals in the sample were apparently not measured or coded on powerlessness; the sample size is reduced to 298 at this point. Using marginal tables, Anne next determines if there are any **marginal associations** between the independent or the dependent variable and the test variable. An inspection of Table 14.2(a) and (b) reveals that powerlessness is associated not only with willingness to use violence, but also with isolation, as Ransford hypothesized.

Ransford further expected the isolates to be more willing to use violence when they perceive that they are powerless within the institutional framework.

TABLE 14.1 Original Relationship: Willingness to Use Violence by Racial Isolation

Willingness to Use Violence		Racial Contact		
		Low	High	Total
Willing		44% (48)	17% (33)	81
Not willing		56% (62)	83% (159)	221
	Total	100% (110)	100% (192)	302

% Diff = 27

TABLE 14.2 Marginal Tables and Relations

(a)

Willingness to Use Violence	Powerlessness	
	Low	High
Willing	15% (23)	40% (58)
Not willing	85 (131)	60 (86)
Total	100% (154)	100% (144)

% Diff = 25

(b)

Powerlessness	Racial Contact	
	Low	High
High	72% (78)	35% (66)
Low	28 (31)	65 (123)
Total	100% (109)	100% (189)

% Diff = 37

In other words, he speculated that isolation has differential effects depending on whether the individual is powerless or not. Statistically, this is known as an **interaction effect** between powerlessness and isolation. To explore the possible existence of an interaction effect, Ransford next controlled the effect of the test variable and reexamined the relationship between the independent and dependent variables.

Anne decides to establish statistical control by first dividing the original sample into subgroups based on the attributes of powerlessness. Then, within each subgroup, she crosstabulates the independent variable again with the dependent variable as in Table 14.3. The crosstabulations in Table 14.3(a) and (b) are now referred to as **partial tables**. With the exception of the two missing cases, if the marginal frequencies of the partials are summed, they would equal those of the original table. Similarly, if the cell frequencies within the partials are summed, they would equal those of the original cell frequencies. Since each subgroup in Table 14.3(a) or (b) is homogeneous with respect to the test variable of powerlessness, this process *controls* or *eliminates* the variation in the original variables that is due to the test variable. Thus one way of achieving statistical control is through the use of partial tables.

TABLE 14.3 Willingness to Use Violence by Isolation Controlling for Powerlessness

(a)

Powerlessness Low

Willingness to Use Violence	Racial Contact	
	Low	High
Willing	23% (7)	13% (16)
Not willing	77 (24)	87 (107)
Total	100% (31)	100% (123)

% Diff = 10

(b)

Powerlessness High

Willingness to Use Violence	Racial Contact	
	Low	High
Willing	53% (41)	26% (17)
Not willing	47 (37)	74 (49)
Total	100% (78)	100% (66)

% Diff = 27

By controlling powerlessness, Anne can determine the unique effect of isolation. She next calculates a percentage difference within each partial to reexamine the relationship between isolation and willingness to use violence when powerlessness is controlled. Among blacks who feel highly powerless, 53% of the isolated versus 26% of the integrated are willing to resort to violence, yielding a percentage difference of |27|. In contrast, among blacks who do not feel powerless, the percentage difference is only |10|. Thus, although isolation has an impact, powerlessness specifies the conditions under which it is more or less likely to lead to a willingness to use violence. When the isolated individuals feel powerless, they are more willing to resort to violence. However, not all isolated blacks are ready to use violence; those who feel they are in control of their own destiny are less likely to do so. Anne's analysis reveals that an interaction exists between powerlessness and isolation, as Ransford hypothesized. Again, interaction is present when the effect of an independent variable such as isolation is not constant on the dependent variable, but depends on the particular level of another explanatory variable such as powerlessness.

14.3 Loglinear Analysis

Although the preceding analysis revealed the presence of interaction, it does not indicate the extent of its contribution to the explanation of the dependent variable. Nor does it determine the simultaneous impact of the two explanatory variables. This being the case, Anne decides to reanalyze the data using the loglinear procedure. **Loglinear analysis** is a modeling technique that is appropriate for univariate, bivariate, or multivariate problems involving nominal or categorical variables. Its unique contribution lies in its ability to handle complex interaction patterns among variables. Very generally, the technique proceeds by taking a set of observed cell frequencies as given and then attempts to account for the *variation in these observed cell frequencies*. The approach is contrasted with the more customary aim of explaining the *variation in the values of the dependent variable*. Depending on whether the data are univariate, bivariate, or multivariate, the cell frequencies are then considered as the possible function of one, two, or more categorical variables. As a result, the variables are not differentiated into independent and dependent variables. Instead, all variables may have **statistical effects** that produce changes in the cell frequencies of a table.

To account for the observed cell frequencies, the researcher builds hypothetical models of the effects of the variable(s). These models are used to generate *patterns of expected cell frequencies*. In testing a model, the expected cell frequencies are compared to the observed cell frequencies to determine the fit between the two. The goodness of fit is expressed by a chi-square statistic, or in terms of *residuals*, the deviation between the expected and observed cell frequencies. The model that produces expected frequencies with the smallest *weighted squared residuals* is selected as the one that best explains the observed data.

14.3.1 Odds Ratio

A statistical measure central to loglinear analysis is the **odds ratio**. In a univariate distribution, the odds ratio gives the probability of obtaining one versus another category of the variable. Take as an example the dichotomous variable of "willingness to use violence" in Table 14.1. The odds ratio of being in favor of violence is defined as

$$\text{odds of using violence} = \frac{f_i}{f_j}$$

where f_i refers to the frequency of individuals who are willing and f_j refers to the frequency of those who are unwilling to use violence. When an odds ratio is obtained from the distribution of a *single* variable, it is called a **first-order odds ratio**.

From Table 14.1, 81 respondents are willing and 221 are unwilling to use violence. Therefore, the first-order odds ratio is .37: 81/221. An odds ratio of .37 means that for every 37 individuals who favor the use of violence there are 100 individuals who do not favor its use. Odds ratios generally vary between the limits of 0 and ∞. When the two frequencies are equal, the odds ratio will be 1.00.

In a bivariate table, an odds ratio or odds ratios may be calculated for each conditional distribution that is defined by a category of the independent variable. These are called **conditional odds ratios**. In Table 14.1, the conditional odds ratios refer to the odds ratios for using violence under the two conditions of high and low racial contact. When racial contact is low, the conditional odds ratio is .77: 48/62, and when the contact is high, it is .21: 33/159. If the ratio of these two conditional odds ratios is taken, the resulting ratio of 3.67: .77/.21, is referred to as a **second-order odds ratio**.

The second-order odds ratio can be used as a measure of association between the two variables. In the preceding example, it indicates that the willingness to use violence is 3.67 times greater among those having little contact than among those having more contact. When two variables are independent of each other, their second-order odds ratio is 1.00. When they are related, their second-order odds ratio is either greater or smaller than 1.0. The greater the departure of the value from 1.0 is, the stronger the relationship that is indicated. Furthermore, the degree of association indicated by t, a value of a second-order odds ratio, and its reciprocal, $1/t$, is the same. For example, we could very well have said that the odds ratio for the use of violence is .273 (1/3.67 or .21/.77) among those having more contact than among those having little contact.

For multivariate problems involving more than two variables, an odds ratio higher than the second order can be used. In Table 14.3, among those who are high in powerlessness, the association between racial contact and willingness to use violence is higher (the second-order odds ratio = 3.19) than among those who are low in powerlessness (the second-order odds ratio = 1.95). A **third-order odds ratio,** based on the ratio of the second-order odds, can be calculated: 1.95/3.19 = .61. Third-order odds ratios are used to measure the *interaction* between the independent and control variables. When there is no interaction, the third-order odds ratio equals 1.00. This value of 1.0 is obtained only when all second-order odds ratios have the same value, regardless of the categories of the control variable under which they are calculated. A departure from 1.0 indicates the presence of interaction; therefore the odds ratio of .61 points to the interaction between powerlessness and racial contact.

Using an odds ratio, the researcher can summarize simple to complex effects, such as interaction, with a single value. A comparison of the different orders of odds ratios enables the researcher to sort out the extent of the statistical effect of each variable, their joint effects, and their interactive effects.

14.3.2 Modeling Variable Effects

At the start of a loglinear analysis, hypothetical models are built to represent the effects of one, two, or more variables. Consider the simplest case of a single variable. The model for a univariate distribution with no effect has equal cell frequencies. Thus, whereas models are conceptualized in terms of the effects of variables, these effects, in turn, give rise to distinctive patterns of expected cell frequencies. To summarize and describe these patterns, odds ratios are used. This model, for example, has first-order odds ratio(s) of 1.0.

With two variables, X and Y, a number of models can be built. In the simplest or **base-line model,** neither variable has an effect. The expected cell frequencies of this model are all equal, but they must sum to the observed sample size. Model 1 in Table 14.4(a) is recalculated from Table 14.1 to show the expected cell frequen-

TABLE 14.4 Models with Expected and Observed Cell Frequencies for Loglinear Analysis

(a) Model 1: {no effect}				(b) Model 2: {Y}				(c) Model 3: {X}		
	X_1	X_2			X_1	X_2			X_1	X_2
Y_1	75.5	75.5	151	Y_1	40.5	40.5	81	Y_1	55	96	151
	(48)	(33)			(48)	(33)			(48)	(33)	
Y_2	75.5	75.5	151	Y_2	110.5	110.5	221	Y_2	55	96	151
	(62)	(159)			(62)	(159)			(62)	(159)	
	151	151	302		151	151	302		110	192	302

(d) Model 4: {X, Y}				(e) Model 5: {X, Y, XY}			
	X_1	X_2			X_1	X_2	
Y_1	29.5	51.5	81	Y_1	48	33	81
	(48)	(33)			(48)	(33)	
Y_2	80.5	140.5	221	Y_2	62	159	221
	(62)	(159)			(62)	(159)	
	110	192	302		110	192	302

cies of the base-line model; the observed frequencies are given within parentheses. According to this model, all first- and higher-order odds ratios equal 1.0.

Model 2 in Table 14.4(b) illustrates the effect of a single variable, Y, the willingness to use violence. When such an effect exists, the cell frequencies within each column are distributed in the same manner as the row marginal distribution of the Y variable. In other words, because racial contact, X, does not have an effect at this point, the conditional distributions of the use of violence are the same, regardless of the level of contact.

Model 3 in Table 14.4(c) shows the cell frequencies being affected by racial contact, X, alone. The cell frequencies within each row are distributed in the same manner as the marginal distribution of racial contact, X. Thus models involving the effect of one variable show the influence of the marginal distribution of that variable on the cell frequencies. In models 2 and 3, the first-order and conditional odds ratios of either Y or X are allowed to depart from 1.00, but all other odds ratios are set to 1.00.

Model 4 in Table 14.4(d) reflects the independence of X and Y. The cell frequencies are identical to those obtained under the assumption of independence discussed in Chapter 4. In this model, the first-order and conditional odds ratios of *both variables* are allowed to depart from 1.00, but second- and all higher-order odds ratios are set to 1.00. Model 5 in Table 14.4(e) contains not only the separate effects of the two variables but also their joint effect, indicating that the two variables are associated. This is known as a **saturated model**, because it takes into account all possible effects of the variables involved in the analysis. Therefore, its expected cell frequencies are identical to the observed cell frequencies. In this model, all first- and second-order odds ratios are allowed to depart from 1.00, but all higher-order odds ratios are set to 1.00.

For a three-variable model, a third type of effect is possible: the three-variable interaction. Thus, statistical effects could refer to the effect of (1) the marginal distribution of a variable, (2) the association or independence of two variables, or (3) the interaction among three variables, and so on. Another method of labeling the effects is by the number of variables involved. A single-variable effect, due to X or Y, is referred to as a **one-way effect**. A two-variable joint or association effect is called a **two-way effect**. A three-variable or interactive effect is known as a **three-way effect**.

14.3.3 Hierarchical Models

As more variables are included in the analysis, the number of possible models increases rapidly. Obviously, not all the models make practical or theoretical sense. To simplify their task, many researchers focus on testing what are known as **hierarchical models**. In these models, the existence of a higher-order effect implies the existence of lower-order effects. In this text, discussion is confined to hierarchical models.

Table 14.5 presents some of the possible models in symbolic terms for a three-variable analysis of X, Y, and Z. Based on this system of representation, can the reader specify all possible models in a two-variable analysis?

TABLE 14.5   Various Three-variable Loglinear Models

{no effect}	Uniform distribution of cell frequencies; only the sample size is taken into account in calculating the expected frequencies.
{X, Y, Z}	All the variables are independent of each other and each has an independent effect.
{Y, XZ}	Two variables, *XZ*, are associated in the model. Consequently, the lower-order individual effects of *X* and *Z* need not be specified again. However, because *Y* is not included in the higher-order effect, the individual effect of *Y* is explicitly stated.
{XY, XZ}	Two pairs of variables are associated; the third pair is not. The individual effects of *X*, *Y*, and *Z* are included in the higher-order effects.
{XY, ZY, XZ}	Each of the three pairs is associated.
{XYZ}	All pairs are associated and there is interaction among the three. This is the saturated model, which includes all effects listed in the previous models.

14.3.4 Estimating the Cell Frequencies

After building a model and summarizing the hypothesized effects of the variables in this model with lower- and higher-order odds ratios, the researcher generates the expected cell frequencies. These expected frequencies must conform to the particular pattern of odds ratios for that model. More specifically, in place of actual counts, the natural logarithms of the expected cell frequencies are modeled. For, in expressing the cell frequencies in logarithms, interactive effects can be accounted for as easily as independent effects.

An equation is written to express the effects of the various variables on the logarithms of the expected cell frequencies. For a two-variable saturated model such as that in Table 14.4(e) of racial contact, *X*, and use of violence, *Y*, the equation for the *ij*th cell frequency is given as

$$\ln(f_{ij}) = \mu + \lambda_j^x + \lambda_i^y + \lambda_{ji}^{xy}$$

The term μ represents the mean of the logarithms of all the frequencies in a table. If neither powerlessness nor the use of violence has any effect on the cell frequencies, then the model of {no effect} has the expected logarithm in each cell of

$$\ln(f_{ij}) = \mu$$

When the variables do have an effect, their effects are represented by lambdas, λ. The λ_j^x indicates the effect of the *j*th category of variable *X*. Thus λ_2^x refers to the effect of having high racial contact. For example, the equation

$$\ln(f_{ij}) = \mu + \lambda_j^x + \lambda_i^y$$

describes the model {X, Y}, wherein both racial contact and the use of violence have an effect on the cell frequencies, but these variables are independent of each other.

The term λ_{ji}^{xy} measures the joint effect of racial contact and use of violence on the cell frequencies. In the saturated two-variable model with the hypothesized joint effect, model {XY}, the cell frequency count is a function of the row and column variables and their joint effect.

The lambdas are usually estimated in such a manner that they sum to zero across all categories of a variable. That is, the sum of the effects of all categories of a variable equals 0:

$$\sum \lambda_j^x = \sum \lambda_i^y = 0$$

In a three-variable analysis, with X = racial contact, Y = use of violence, and Z = powerlessness, the model {XY, YZ, XZ} indicates that each variable has an independent effect. Each pair of variables is associated and therefore has a joint effect as well. The equation for this model of one- and two-way effects is

$$\ln(f_{ijk}) = \mu + \lambda_j^x + \lambda_i^y + \lambda_k^z + \lambda_{ji}^{xy} + \lambda_{ik}^{yz} + \lambda_{jk}^{xz}$$

The saturated model of one-, two-, and three-way effects, model {XYZ}, which includes not only the impact of each variable, but their joint and interactive effects as well, is expressed by this equation:

$$\ln(f_{ijk}) = \mu + \lambda_j^x + \lambda_i^y + \lambda_k^z + \lambda_{ji}^{xy} + \lambda_{ik}^{yz} + \lambda_{jk}^{xz} + \lambda_{jik}^{xyz}$$

14.3.5 Maximum Likelihood Ratio Chi-square Test Statistic

In the next step of the analysis, the expected cell frequencies are compared to the observed cell frequencies to determine how well the expected frequencies generated by a specific model fit the actual data. If the squared residuals are small, the fit is good and the effects hypothesized in the model can be used to interpret the observed data. Otherwise, an alternative model that gives a better fit to the data is sought. At this point, it may appear that the analysis need go no further because the best model would be the *saturated* model, which fits the data perfectly. However, there are other criteria of selection in addition to that of goodness of fit. As pointed out in Section 14.1, a good model is one that is *parsimonious* as well, requiring the least number of variables and effects to explain the data. Therefore, if both a saturated model and a lower-order model give a good fit to the data, then, based on the criterion of parsimony, the lower-order model should be selected as the better model. Finally, a good model should make theoretical and substantive sense; otherwise, model fitting is nothing but an exercise in after-the-fact rationalization. Thus, before concluding that the saturated model is the best one possible, the analysis should continue along the following lines:

1. Determining the fit of a particular model
2. Determining the comparative fit between a simpler or lower-order model and a more complex or higher-order model

A measure that tests the goodness of fit between the expected and observed frequencies is Pearson's χ^2 discussed in Chapter 13. However, a more appropriate statistic is the **maximum likelihood ratio chi square.** It is defined as

$$L^2 = 2\sum_{j=1}^{c}\sum_{i=1}^{r} O_{ij} \ln\left(\frac{O_{ij}}{E_{ij}}\right)$$

where O_{ij} refers to the observed frequencies
E_{ij} refers to the expected frequencies
ln refers to the natural logarithms
r refers to the number of rows and
c refers to the number of columns

In general, the L^2 value can be interpreted in the same manner as χ^2. The larger the value is, the more the observed cell frequencies deviate from the expected cell frequencies and, therefore, the poorer the fit of the model to the data. Also, L^2 has some desirable characteristics that make it more appropriate for use in the comparative assessment of various models. Recall in regression analysis that there is a constant total sum of squares, TSS, for a particular set of data which can be partitioned. The L^2s too can be interpreted as various sums of squares. The maximum L^2, similar to TSS, is calculated from a comparison of the observed data to a base-line model of no effect like the one shown in Table 14.4(a). Once this L^2 value is obtained, it can be partitioned into component L^2's attributable to the effects of different variables. These component L^2 values are additive. They sum to the maximum L^2 value for a set of data, whereas the Pearson's chi-square components do not necessarily do so. With these component L^2 values, the *unique* and *independent* effect of each variable can be estimated. Thus, in estimating the independent effects, the L^2 test statistic provides statistical control similar to that obtained through holding test variables constant in partial tables.

More specifically, the L^2 of a model that contains an effect or effects gives a measure comparable to that of the sum of squared errors, SSE, in regression analysis. Therefore, in comparing hierarchical models, the L^2 values of higher-order models should be equal to or smaller than those of lower-order models. Also, to test whether a simpler or more complex model gives a better fit to the observed data, the difference in L^2 values of the two models yields another L^2 statistic. Because of the additive nature of the L^2 values, this latter L^2 statistic represents the improvement in fit given by the more complex model, and it can be tested to determine whether the gain is significant. The following sections will show how L^2 is used to test both individual and successive hierarchical models.

14.4 *Evaluating Individual Loglinear Models*

Research Question and Data

Anne reanalyzes Ransford's data in Section 14.2 using loglinear techniques. Since the analysis is too complex to do by hand, the following SPSS program is used to evaluate six different models. Each model is *substantively meaningful*, although only one will be chosen as the model that best describes the data.

```
DATA LIST FREE/POWERLES CONTACT VIOLENCE NUM.

BEGIN DATA.

1 1 1 7    1 2 1 16    1 1 0 24    1 2 0 107

2 1 1 41   2 2 1 17    2 1 0 37    2 2 0 49

END DATA.

WEIGHT BY NUM.

HILOGLINEAR VIOLENCE (0,1) CONTACT POWERLES (1,2)

  /DESIGN=VIOLENCE CONTACT POWERLES

  /DESIGN=VIOLENCE CONTACT BY POWERLES

  /DESIGN=VIOLENCE BY CONTACT POWERLES BY CONTACT

  /DESIGN=VIOLENCE BY POWERLES CONTACT BY POWERLES

  /DESIGN=VIOLENCE BY CONTACT CONTACT BY POWERLES VIOLENCE BY POWERLES

  /DESIGN=VIOLENCE BY CONTACT BY POWERLES.
```

The information on the partials from Table 14.3 is entered in this program with the following coding:

POWERLES	: 1	(low)	2	(high)
CONTACT	: 1	(low)	2	(high)
VIOLENCE	: 1	(willing)	0	(unwilling)

The command HILOGLINEAR stands for hierarchical loglinear analysis. After the command name HILOGLINEAR, a list of the variables to be included in the analysis is given. The minimum and maximum values for each variable are then entered in parentheses following the variable name. If the values are the same for a string of successive variables, their entry can be omitted except for the last variable in the string.

A number of DESIGN subcommands can be used with the command HILOG-LINEAR, each requesting the analysis of a different model. The model is specified in the same manner as discussed in Section 14.3.3. However, in place of letters such as X or Y, the names of the variables are used. In specifying higher-order terms, the variable names are separated by the keyword BY to differentiate them from a listing of simple effects.

Specifically, the program requests the analysis of these six models:

Model 1: $\{Y, X, Z\}$
Model 2: $\{Y, XZ\}$
Model 3: $\{YX, ZX\}$
Model 4: $\{YZ, XZ\}$
Model 5: $\{YX, XZ, YZ\}$
Model 6: $\{YXZ\}$

Model 1 hypothesizes the independence of all three variables, while model 2 postulates that isolation and powerlessness are associated with each other (joint effect of XZ), but not with the use of violence. In models 3 and 4, isolation or powerlessness, but not both, are associated with the use of violence (joint effect of YX or YZ); in addition, they are associated with each other (joint effect of XZ). All three variables are associated in model 5, while in model 6, the saturated model, the additional effect of interaction (three-way effect of YXZ) among these variables is examined.

With the specification of a saturated model, the HILOGLINEAR procedure automatically outputs the observed and expected frequencies, residuals, and standardized residuals, as well as the L^2 and χ^2 values. The test of k-way associations is also given.

The Statistical Hypotheses

Anne is testing the null hypothesis that the expected frequencies of a particular model coincide with the observed data:

$$H_0: \quad O_{ij} = E_{ij}, \quad \text{for a particular model}$$

She needs to test only five null hypotheses, each corresponding to one of the first five models specified in her SPSS program. The fit of the last and saturated model is predetermined to be perfect and requires no testing.

Test Statistics and Their Sampling Distributions

Two different test statistics, the Pearson's chi square, χ^2, and the likelihood ratio chi square, L^2, are used to determine the departure of the observed frequencies from the frequencies expected under the null hypothesis. Both the L^2 and the Pearson's χ^2 have approximate chi-square distributions when the model hypothesized under the null hypothesis holds true. Since the chi-square distributions vary according to their degrees of freedom, the latter must be determined. The degrees of freedom associated with a particular model with all dichotomous categorical variables equal the number of cells in the partial tables (or bivariate table when only two variables are considered) minus the number of effects to be estimated in the model including sample size.

For example, Anne has a total of eight cells from the two partial tables. Therefore, the df for the base-line model is 7, because 1 degree of freedom is lost when the cell frequencies must sum to N: (8 − 1). For the model {X, Y, Z}, df equals 4 because 3 additional degrees of freedom are lost, one for each effect specified in the model: (8 − 1 − 3).

For models with polytomous variables, the degrees of freedom equal the total number of cells minus the number of independent parameters to be estimated in the model. Consider the example of two variables, X and Z, when X has three categories and Z has four categories. The number of lambdas to be estimated for X is 2, since the third is determined, for all lambdas sum to 0 under the test model. On the other hand, the number of estimated lambdas for Z is 3, since the fourth is again fixed under the restriction of the zero sum. Thus, for the model {X, Z}, 5 degrees of freedom would be lost for the X and Z effects, in addition to one for sample size, resulting in df of 6: (12 − 5 − 1).

In interpreting the test results for *individual models*, Pearson's chi square is more appropriate for smaller samples, whereas the likelihood ratio chi square is often used with larger samples. For evaluating *several models* simultaneously, the maximum likelihood ratio chi square is definitely more useful because it can be partitioned.

Interpretation of SPSS Output

The HILOGLINEAR procedure calculates the expected frequencies generated by the odds ratios that satisfy the requirements of the model specified in the DESIGN subcommand. Residuals and standardized residuals are also computed. Standardized residuals are defined as $(O - E)/\sqrt{E}$. A detailed and descriptive assessment of how well the model fits the data can be gained by reading the display of the frequencies and residuals. The particular cell for which these values are displayed is identified by the codes of the variables in the second column. The column of particular importance is that of the standardized residuals. Any value over |2| in this column indicates that there is significant departure from the observed cell frequency.

Anne notes from an inspection of the standardized residuals (not reproduced here) of model {Y, X, Z} that all but two of them are over |2.0|, with the largest being 7.05. The second model {Y, XZ} gives a better fit according to the standardized residuals. The third model {YX, XZ} provides even better estimates with no standardized residuals over |2.0|. The fourth model {YZ, XZ} generates a fit no better than the third model. The standardized residuals of the fifth model {YX, YZ, ZX} show considerable improvement over all other models, with the highest standardized residual being −.45. Thus Anne concludes that as higher-level effects are assumed the models provide progressively better fit.

To evaluate the overall fit of a particular model, Anne examines the portion of the output that gives the chi squares. One such output is given for model {*Y, X, Z*}:

```
Likelihood ratio chi square = 75.32338 DF = 4 P = .000
        Pearson chi square = 90.71423 DF = 4 P = .000
```

The P refers to the probability of obtaining a chi square as large as or larger than the displayed (obtained) value with its associated degrees of freedom when the null hypothesis is true. With a P of .000, both chi squares are significant beyond the .0005 level. The model of independence of the three variables {*Y, X, Z*} does not give a good fit to the data, regardless of which chi square Anne interprets.

The second model {*Y, XZ*} has 3 degrees of freedom because there is one more effect to be estimated, *XZ*. Recall that the specification of {*Y, XZ*} is a hierarchical designation of the following effects of {*Y, X, Z, XZ*}. This model gives a better fit to the data because both chi-square values are lower:

```
Likelihood ratio chi square = 37.25196 DF = 3 P = .000
        Pearson chi square = 38.27225 DF = 3 P = .000
```

The third model {*YX* and *XZ*} provides even better estimates because the likelihood ratio chi square is 13.16818. However, with a P of .001, its fit could still be improved on. The fourth model {*YZ, XZ*} generates a fit no better than the third model {*YX, XZ*}. The fifth model {*YX, YZ, XZ*} represents a considerable improvement over all previous models because its goodness-of-fit statistics indicate that it is not unlikely to obtain the observed sample data when the model holds true. In fact, the discrepancies between the observed and the cell frequencies expected under this model are probably due to sampling error only:

```
Likelihood ratio chi square = .63990 DF = 1 P = .424
```

A similar Pearson chi-square value is obtained. Since the last model {*YXZ*} is saturated, the observed and expected frequencies are identical, resulting in residual values of 0. As the chi-square value of 0 shows, the fit is perfect for this model.

14.5 Comparing Hierarchical Loglinear Models

Research Question

After evaluating the individual models, Anne proceeds to assess whether the improvement given by each of her six models is significant. Then, based on this assessment, she can select the model that best meets all three criteria for a good model. She can also determine whether the interaction between powerlessness and racial contact found in Ransford's analysis is important to the explanation of the use of violence.

The Data

For her analysis, Anne first gathers the information pertaining to the various L^2 statistics from the SPSS output and displays them together in the first half of Table 14.6. Note that the information for the base-line model in the first row of the table

TABLE 14.6 Individual and Comparative Tests of the Models Submitted in the SPSS Program

Test of individual models: Model of

{no effect}	$L^2 = 161.825$	df = 7	$P = .000$
1. {Y, X, Z}	$L^2 = 75.323$	df = 4	$P = .000$
2. {Y, XZ}	$L^2 = 37.252$	df = 3	$P = .000$
3. {YX, XZ}	$L^2 = 13.168$	df = 2	$P = .001$
4. {YZ, XZ}	$L^2 = 12.554$	df = 2	$P = .002$
5. {YX, YZ, XZ}	$L^2 = .640$	df = 1	$P = .424$
6. {YXZ}	$L^2 = .000$	df = 0	$P = 1.000$

Comparative test of models:

1 compared to {no effect}	$L^2 = 86.502$	df = 3	$P \le .0005$
2 compared to 1	$L^2 = 38.071$	df = 1	$P \le .0005$
3 compared to 2	$L^2 = 24.084$	df = 1	$P \le .0005$
4 compared to 2	$L^2 = 24.698$	df = 1	$P \le .0005$
5 compared to 3	$L^2 = 12.528$	df = 1	$P \le .001$
5 compared to 4	$L^2 = 11.914$	df = 1	$P \le .001$
6 compared to 5	$L^2 = .640$	df = 1	$P \le .424$

comes from the portion of the SPSS output that gives the test of k-way effects, reproduced as SPSS Figure 14.1. The last line of this figure evaluates the base-line model in which one-way or higher-order effects are not present. It is the L^2 value, 161.825, of this model that is comparable to the total sum of squares in regression analysis and that is being partitioned in the analysis of various effects. The rest of the information in the first half of Table 14.6 comes from the SPSS output after each model is evaluated. The second half of Table 14.6 will be explained in the following section.

An Appropriate Method

In evaluating hierarchical models, usually two limiting models are employed for comparison:

1. The saturated model with all possible effects present, yielding expected frequencies that coincide exactly with observed frequencies
2. The base-line model of no effect, fitted to sample size, in which the expected frequencies are identical for all cells

```
Tests that K-way and higher-order effects are zero.


    K     DF    L.R. Chisq    Prob   Pearson Chisq    Prob    Iteration

    3     1          .640    .4237            .631    .4271            4
    2     4        75.323    .0000          90.714    .0000            2
    1     7       161.825    .0000         187.101    .0000            0
```

SPSS FIGURE 14.1   Tests of k-Way Effects from Hiloglinear

The comparative assessment begins with the computation of L^2 for both limiting models. The base-line model provides an L^2 value similar to the TSS, whereas the saturated model yields a L^2 value of 0. Because effects are hypothesized, the L^2 of the base-line model of no effect is partitioned, permitting an L^2 value to be assigned to the hypothesized effect(s) in each model.

A model of a higher order is tested against one of lower order by taking the difference in their L^2 values and degrees of freedom (df). The resulting difference is another L^2 value with its own df, which can be evaluated as to its significance. The L^2 and df values in the second half of Table 14.6 are obtained in this manner. For example, in comparing model 2 to model 1, Anne obtains the L^2 value of 38.071, which comes from subtracting 37.252 from 75.323, and a df of 1, which comes from subtracting 3 from 4. If this L^2 value is significant, it means that model 2 provides a significantly better fit to the data than model 1. Another way of looking at it is that the additional effect hypothesized in model 2, XZ, is significant. Again, the L^2 values can be subtracted in this manner because of their additivity.

The Sampling Distribution

The L^2 test statistic, which is derived from taking the difference between two L^2 values, has an approximate chi-square distribution with degrees of freedom equal to the difference of df's between the two models. It provides an index of the improvement in goodness of fit given by the higher-order model. The larger the difference in L^2 values is, the more improvement in goodness of fit there is and the better the fit between the higher-order model and the observed data.

The Statistical Hypotheses

When model 1 is compared to the model of {no effect}, the null hypothesis that the effects Y, X, and Z equal 0 is being tested against the alternative hypotheses that these effects are not 0:

$$H_0: \quad Y = X = Z = 0$$
$$H_1: \quad Y \neq 0, X \neq 0, \text{ or } Z \neq 0$$

When model 2 is compared to model 1, the null hypothesis that the XZ effect is equal to 0 is being tested. The comparison of the third to the second model tests the null hypothesis that the additional effect YX is equal to 0. The reader should try to derive the null hypotheses for the remainder of the comparisons.

Interpretation of Results

When model 1 is compared to the model of {no effect}, the resulting L^2 value is 86.502 (161.825 – 75.323) with a df of 3 (7 – 4). This L^2 value is significant at the .0005 level ($P = <.0005$). This means that model 1 provides a significant improvement over the base-line model. The same can be said of model 2 when it is compared to model 1: an L^2 of 38.071 is obtained, which is also significant at the .0005 level.

Note that models 3 and 4 are not hierarchical with respect to one another, since each includes an effect that is excluded in the other. Therefore, they cannot be compared to each other; instead, they are both evaluated against the lower-order model 2. For the same reason, model 5 is assessed against both models 3 and 4, since they both represent a lower-order model of 5. For example, in evaluating model 5 against model 3, the additional joint effect of YZ is shown to be significant, and, in evaluating model 5 against model 4, the additional joint effect of YX is also found to be significant. Therefore, model 5 provides a better fit to the data than either model 3 or 4.

As the models increase in complexity, they fit the data more and more closely. At the bottom of Table 14.6, the answer to Anne's question is found: the three-way interaction is not significant ($L^2 = .64$ with $P = .424$). Although interaction is present in the sample, it probably does not exist in the population, being more of an artifact of sampling. The last line of Table 14.6 also provides the information necessary for the selection of the best-fitting model. Since the addition of the interaction term to the model does not significantly improve its fit, based on the principle of *parsimony*, Anne selects model $\{YX, YZ, XZ\}$ as the model that best describes the data.

Summary

Loglinear Analysis

First-order odds ratio = f_i / f_j

Maximum likelihood ratio chi square:

$$L^2 = 2 \sum_{j=1}^{c} \sum_{i=1}^{r} O_{ij} \ln\left(\frac{O_{ij}}{E_{ij}}\right)$$

where O_{ij} = observed frequencies E_{ij} = expected frequencies
r = number of rows c = number of columns

Hierarchical loglinear models for variables X, Y, and Z:

{no effect}: Base-line model
$\{X\}$ $\{Y\}$ $\{Z\}$: One-way effect model
$\{XY, XZ, YZ\}$: Two-way effect model
$\{XYZ\}$: Three-way effect model (saturated model)

Test model:

1. Categorical dependent and independent variables
2. Random sampling

Exercises

1. Ransford [2] was also interested in the reactions of the white majority toward campus protests and black riots. Many whites were outraged by such incidents as student takeovers of buildings or by black power demands, but Ransford hypothesized that blue-collar workers were especially antagonistic toward the black and student movements. He researched his hypothesis using a sample of 477 white Los Angeles residents. The dependent variable, hostility toward student demonstrations, is trichotomized into high, medium, and low categories. The independent variable, occupation, is also trichotomized into blue collar (BC), business white collar (BWC), and professional white collar (Prof) workers. As test variables, gender and powerlessness, among others, are used. The original and partial relations are shown next. Note that N in these tables does not add to sample size because of the problem of no response or missing values.

Hostility	Occupation		
	Blue Collar	Business White Collar	Professional White Collar
Low	13%	26%	34%
Medium	37	44	41
High	50	30	25
Total	100%	100%	100%
	(163)	(159)	(137)

	Male			Female		
Hostility	BC	BWC	Prof.	BC	BWC	Prof.
High	57%	30%	23%	43.5%	29%	20%
Total	(70)	(79)	(61)	(85)	(80)	(76)

	Low Powerlessness			High Powerlessness		
Hostility	BC	BWC	Prof.	BC	BWC	Prof.
High	43%	30%	23%	60%	28%	30%
Total	(79)	(101)	(101)	(71)	(57)	(36)

Dichotomize hostility into high and low-medium levels and occupation into blue- and white-collar jobs.
   a. For the variable of hostility toward student demonstrations, develop a frequency table for a model indicating that the variable has no effect.
   b. Selecting two variables, hostility and occupation, generate a contingency table for a base-line model.
   c. Using the variables hostility and occupation, develop frequency tables expected under the various models discussed in Section 14.3.2.

2. Specify what lower-order models are included in the following hierarchical models: {X, YZ, WPQ}; {XY, ZWP, Q}; {X, YZWP, Q}; {XYZW, P}.

3. Compute the odds ratio for each of the following sets of data involving the same variables.

	Male	Female
Use violence	25	25
Not use violence	25	25

20	20		18	22		30	10		40	0
30	30		27	33		15	45		5	55

SPSS Exercise

1. Based on the data in Exercise 1, develop two models, one involving the effect of occupation and sex and the other involving the effect of occupation and powerlessness on hostility. Dichotomize all variables and run HILOGLINEAR to interpret the effects of each model and to select the better model.

General Conceptual Problems

1. Distinguish among the following concepts: association, concordance, covariation, correlation, and causal relation.

2. For what level of variables and what type of analysis is the loglinear method appropriate?

3. In a hierarchical loglinear analysis, what is the base-line model? What is the saturated model?

4. What is the relationship between proportion, odds ratio, and percentage?

5. What does a hierarchical model mean in loglinear analysis?

6. What does the first-order odds ratio measure? What is the range of its value?

7. What does the lambda measure in loglinear analysis?

8. What is the value of the second-order odds ratio if a 2×2 table contains an empty diagonal cell?

9. When there is no interaction between two variables, that is, when they are independent, how is it reflected in the value of higher-order odds ratios?

10. What is the maximum likelihood ratio chi-square statistic? What are the advantages of using it in loglinear analysis?

References

1. Ransford, H. E. (1968). Isolation, Powerlessness and Violence: A Study of Attitudes and Participation in the Watts Riots, *American Journal of Sociology* 73:581–591.

2. Ransford, H. E. (1972). Blue Collar Anger: Reactions to Student and Black Protest, *American Sociological Review* 37:333–346.

C h a p t e r **15**

Multivariate Analysis: Interval Data

New Statistical Topics

Partial correlation coefficient   Multiple correlation coefficient
Partial regression coefficient   Multiple regression equation
Standardized regression coefficient

15.1 Overview

When multivariate analysis involves interval variables, the **multiple regression** technique is used. A multiple regression equation is developed, very much like the bivariate equation, to predict the value of a dependent variable based on more than one independent variable. Its predictive power is then evaluated by the **multiple correlation coefficient**, and the unique impact of each independent variable is estimated by its **partial regression coefficients**. Thus multiple regression focuses on the analysis of both the simultaneous and total effects of several independent variables. As such, it is a useful technique for modeling. From the partial regression coefficients, the independent variables that have the most significant contributions can be identified to form a parsimonious model that gives the best explanation of the data. Furthermore, the procedure can be used to explore the interactive effects of the independent variables and the effects of categorical independent variables, although these topics are not addressed in this text. With its ability to deal with issues such as interactive effects and modeling, multiple regression is a powerful multivariate technique.

To this point, multivariate techniques appropriate for ordinal data have not been discussed. Although there are procedures designed specifically for ordinal data, one customary approach is to treat the ordinal variables as either categorical or interval. We will follow this approach here by recommending that when the data have few values they be considered as categorical, and loglinear analysis can be used. Otherwise, with a wider range of values and if further assumptions are met, the data can be treated as interval, and the multiple regression technique can be applied.

In this chapter, Anne searches for explanations that would help her understand the emergence of social unrest and riots. There are many theories of such collective behavior, some of which are couched in functionalist, others in conflict, and still others in symbolic interactionist terms. The one that appeals most to Anne is Smelser's [1] theory. Smelser views collective behavior from the functionalist perspective as a disturbance to the equilibrium of the social order, resulting from a convergence of preconditions and precipitating factors. Anne proposes to test selected aspects of Smelser's theory with secondary data that she has gathered from the data banks of the Research Institute.

15.2 Multiple Regression

In multiple regression the researcher develops an equation to describe the individual contribution of a number of independent variables toward predicting a dependent variable. The technique provides a much more realistic method for dealing with social phenomena that are too complex to be accounted for by one independent variable.

15.2.1 Multiple Regression Equation

The **multiple regression equation** that the researcher builds has the general form of

$$Y' = a + b_1 X_1 + b_2 X_2 + \cdots + b_k X_k$$

where k equals the number of independent variables. For illustration, let us take the case of two independent variables. The generalized equation is reduced to the following, representing the regression of Y, the dependent variable, on the two independent variables of X_1 and X_2:

$$Y' = a + b_{y1.2} X_1 + b_{y2.1} X_2 \tag{15.1}$$

15.2.2 Unstandardized Regression Coefficients

Equation 15.1 is an extension of bivariate regression in Equation 5.1. As in bivariate regression, the regression coefficient a in Equation 15.1 represents the predicted value of Y when $X_1 = X_2 = 0$. There is, however, a major difference between the b's in the equations. The b's in multiple regression refer to **partial slopes** or **partial regression coefficients**. The term partial indicates that these b's, unlike those in bivariate regression, are obtained by *controlling* some independent variables, not by *ignoring* all other independent variables as random effects. They represent the change in the dependent variable that is due solely to a unit change in *one* independent variable. The regression coefficient $b_{y1.2}$ (read as b sub $y1$ dot 2) indicates the amount of change in Y' when X_1 increases by 1 unit while controlling X_2. Similarly, $b_{y2.1}$ gives the change in Y' per unit change in X_2 while controlling X_1. In this manner, the regression model allows the researcher to determine the unique contribution of each independent variable. The sign of the partial slope indicates whether the dependent variable is changing in the same or opposite direction as the independent variable.

To calculate a partial slope such as $b_{y1.2}$, which isolates the effect of X_1, from the effect of X_2 on Y, the following steps are followed:

1. To eliminate the effect of the independent variable X_2 on the dependent variable Y, regress Y on X_2. Then calculate the Y residuals, the variation in Y that is unexplained by X_2. Since X_2 is allowed to explain as much of the variation in Y as possible, the unexplained variation, as represented by the residuals, embodies the effects of *chance* and of *other variables* on Y.
2. Regress the other independent variable X_1 on the independent variable X_2, and calculate the residuals, the amount of variation in X_1 left unexplained by X_2.
3. To determine the portion of the Y residuals that is due solely to the change in the independent variable X_1, calculate the bivariate regression slope of the residual Y on the residual X_1. The result is the partial slope $b_{y1.2}$. Since the variations in X_1 and Y that are associated with X_2 have been eliminated in steps 1 and 2, the slope of the residuals gives the change in Y due to X_1 alone.

The preceding steps are incorporated into the following computational formulas of the partial slopes:

$$b_{y1.2} = \frac{b_{y1} - (b_{y2})(b_{21})}{1 - b_{12}b_{21}} \tag{15.2}$$

$$b_{y2.1} = \frac{b_{y2} - (b_{y1})(b_{12})}{1 - b_{12}b_{21}} \tag{15.3}$$

Again, $b_{y1.2}$ gives the change in Y' due to X_1 while controlling for X_2, and $b_{y2.1}$ gives the change in Y' due to X_2 while controlling for X_1. The computational formula for the regression coefficient a is given by

$$a = \overline{Y} - b_{y1.2}\overline{X}_1 - b_{y2.1}\overline{X}_2 \tag{15.4}$$

Again the a represents the value of Y' when $X_1 = X_2 = 0$. Once the partial regression coefficients in an equation involving two independent variables are obtained, they can be used to compute the partial regression coefficients in an equation involving three independent variables, as follows:

$$b_{y1.23} = \frac{b_{y1.2} - (b_{y3.2})(b_{31.2})}{1 - b_{13.2}(b_{31.2})}$$

15.2.3 Graphic Interpretation of the Regression of Y on X_1 and X_2

A graphic representation of the regression model with $k = 2$ independent variables is displayed in Figure 15.1. The X_1 and X_2 variables are now represented as axes that are perpendicular to each other on a two-dimensional, horizontal plane. By adding the axis for the dependent variable Y, which is vertical as well as perpendicular to both the X_i axes, the figure is transformed into a three-dimensional graph. If data points were plotted on this graph, each would result from the convergence of a unique set of X_1, X_2, and Y values. To plot an observation that has values of $X_1 = 4$, $X_2 = 7$, and $Y = 4$, go 4 units along the X_1 axis. From this point on, move in a line parallel to the X_2 axis until $X_2 = 7$ is reached. Finally, extend upward from the intersection of $X_1 = 4$ and $X_2 = 7$ in a line parallel to the Y axis to the Y value of 4. This dot in the three-dimensional plane represents the observation.

The regression equation is represented by a two-dimensional plane within the three-dimensional space. The angle at which the regression plane intersects the plane perpendicular to the X_1 axis represents the partial slope of the regression of Y on X_1 with X_2 held constant. See arrow 1 in Figure 15.1. Similarly, the

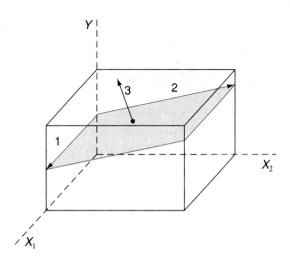

FIGURE 15.1   Regression Plane

angle at which the regression plane intersects the plane perpendicular to the X_2 axis is the partial slope of the regression of Y on X_2 with X_1 held constant. See arrow 2 in Figure 15.1. The tilt of the whole regression plane itself is then determined by the slopes of the two partials. See arrow 3 in the same diagram.

In determining the values of the a and b's, the least-squares method is used. This method involves estimating a, $b_{y1.2}$, and $b_{y2.1}$ in such a way that the total sum of squares of the distances from all the data points to the regression plane is minimized:

$$\sum_{i=1}^{N} (Y_i - Y')^2 = \sum_{i=1}^{N} (Y_i - a - b_{y1.2}X_1 - b_{y2.1}X_2)^2 = \text{a minimum}$$

Therefore, the closer the points lie to this regression plane, the better the fit of the regression equation. The farther the data points are from the regression plane, the worse the fit. With a better fit, the independent variables are able to account for more of the variance of the dependent variable.

15.2.4 Standardized Partial Regression Coefficient

The partial b's discussed previously are unstandardized partial regression coefficients. As pointed out in Chapter 5, their values are affected by the units with which the variables are measured. Therefore, they cannot be used to assess the extent to which an independent variable accounts for the variation in the dependent variable. A low value may indicate that *either* the unique contribution of the independent variable is small *and/or* the measurement unit of the independent variable is smaller in relation to that of the dependent variable.

For a better index of the contribution of the independent variables, the **standardized regression coefficients** can be used. Recall that standardized regression coefficients are called beta weights, and they are symbolized by b^* (Chapter 5). Beta weights do not depend on the raw measurement units. They are calculated from variables that have been standardized by the formula $z = (X - \overline{X})/s$, and whose measurements are expressed in standard deviation units from the mean. The **partial beta weight** measures the amount of change in standard deviation units of the dependent variable that is produced by a change in one standard deviation unit of the independent variable, with other variables controlled. A partial beta weight of .7 ($b^*_{y1.2} = .7$) means that as X_1 changes 1 standard deviation unit, Y changes by .7 standard deviation unit when X_2 is controlled.

Because the beta weights are standardized, they are indexes of the relative contribution of each independent variable to the prediction of the dependent variable. Therefore, unlike an unstandardized partial slope, the value of a beta weight can be used as an assessment of the relative effect of independent variables that are not measured in the same unit.

A simple computational formula can be obtained from the definition of the beta weight as a b adjusted for the difference in the standard deviations of Y and the particular X_i as follows:

$$b^*_{y1.2} = b_{y1.2}\frac{s_1}{s_y} \qquad (15.5)$$

$$b^*_{y2.1} = b_{y2.1}\frac{s_2}{s_y} \qquad (15.6)$$

where s_1, s_2 refer to the standard deviations of the variables X_1 and X_2, and s_y refers to the standard deviation of the variable Y. Since the value of a beta weight depends heavily on the standard deviation of a given sample, it should not be used to generalize beyond a sample.

Being slopes of standardized variables, beta weights can be used to predict the standardized score of a dependent variable. The regression equation for standard scores becomes

$$Z'_y = b^*_{y1.2}Z_1 + b^*_{y2.1}Z_2 \qquad (15.7)$$

As in the case of bivariate regression, the regression coefficient a reduces to 0 when predicting standard z scores.

15.3 Calculating a Multiple Regression Equation

Research Question and Data

In the data banks of the Research Institute, Anne finds information on cities concerning the actual incidents of racial unrest in the 1980s. She therefore decides to build a model based on Smelser's theory of collective behavior to predict these incidents. Smelser postulates that certain preconditions must exist for collective behavior to emerge: (1) structural conditions that facilitate collective behavior, (2) strain caused by existing social arrangements, and (3) a generalized belief that action must be taken to change the status quo. In addition, a chain of more immediate events must precede the outbreak. These are (4) a precipitating incident that leads to (5) the mobilization of participants and (6) a final breakdown of social control [1].

Of the six factors, information is not available on at least four. However, Anne does have the data on the percentage of blacks in the inner city and the income differential between blacks and whites in each city. These are given in Table 15.1. Income differential serves as an indicator of social strain. The higher the inequality in income is, the more likely it is to give rise to a feeling of relative deprivation, providing the undercurrent of discontent that facilitates the emergence of collective behavior. Percentage black is an indicator of structural conduciveness. The larger the percentage of the blacks in a city is, the easier it will be to mobilize them.

TABLE 15.1 Data on Income Inequality, Percent Black and Occurrence of Racial Unrest in 10 Cities

City	Income Inequality	Percent Black	Occurrence of Racial Unrest
A	4	47	2
B	5	39	5
C	12	74	8
D	7	44	4
E	3	28	1
F	2	32	0
G	6	51	3
H	6	52	2
I	11	48	5
J	9	43	5

In studies such as Spilerman [2] and Morgan and Clark [3], the size of the black population was found to be a powerful variable, which overshadows the contributions of most other variables in explaining the development of racial unrest. Given such empirical findings, Anne questions how much impact social strain has, independent of structural conduciveness. She would like to develop a model that describes the relationship of these two variables to racial unrest in the cities. The model should be sufficiently detailed so that she can specify the change in occurrence of racial unrest due to a change in (1) income inequality and (2) percentage black.

An Appropriate Method
Anne can construct a model by finding the multiple regression equation for these variables. Both the unstandardized and the standardized partial slopes can be obtained through the equation to interpret the asymmetric effect of income inequality and percentage black on racial unrest.

Calculation and Interpretation
Although complex procedures such as multiple regression equations are usually done by computer, to obtain a better sense of the logic behind the formulas, we will compute them by hand first. The components for computation can be produced either manually or with the help of SPSS. If SPSS is used, the bivariate regression coefficients in Table 15.2 can be obtained through the REGRESSION command first discussed in Chapter 5. A series of REGRESSION commands such as the following, specifying one independent variable, can be used to calculate the bivariate slopes:

```
REGRESSION VARIABLES=Y X /DESCRIPTIVES=MEAN STDDEV /DEPENDENT=Y
    /METHOD=ENTER.
```

TABLE 15.2 Regression Coefficients for Various Combinations of Racial Unrest, Income Inequality, and Percent Black

Dependent Variable	Independent Variable	Regression Coefficient
Racial unrest (Y)	Income inequality (X_1)	$b_{y1} = .63452$
Racial unrest (Y)	Percent black (X_2)	$b_{y2} = .13551$
Income inequality (X_1)	Percent black (X_2)	$b_{12} = .19768$
Percent black (X_2)	Income inequality (X_1)	$b_{21} = 2.87310$

The DESCRIPTIVES subcommand under the REGRESSION command can be used to generate the means and standard deviations of all the variables as well. Table 15.3 displays these statistics obtained from SPSS.

Using the preceding data, partial regression coefficients are calculated as follows:

$$b_{y1.2} = \frac{b_{y1} - (b_{y2})(b_{21})}{1 - b_{12}b_{21}} = \frac{.63452 - (.13551)(2.8731)}{1 - (.19768)(2.8731)} = .5675$$

$$b_{y2.1} = \frac{b_{y2} - (b_{y1})(b_{12})}{1 - b_{12}b_{21}} = \frac{.13551 - (.63452)(.19768)}{1 - (.19768)(2.8731)} = .0233$$

$$a = \overline{Y} - b_{y1.2}\overline{X}_1 - b_{y2.1}\overline{X}_2 = 3.50 - (.5675)(6.5) - (.0233)(45.8) = -1.25$$

The regression equation obtained from these regression coefficients is:

incident of racial unrest = −1.25 + .57 income inequality + .02 percent black

To illustrate how this equation is used, the observed values of percentage black and income differential for city A are inserted in the equation to obtain predicted incidents of racial unrest:

incidents of racial unrest = −1.25 + .57 (4) + .02 (47) = 1.97

The predicted value Y' of 1.97 is very close to the observed value Y of 2.00. The residual $(Y - Y')$ equals .03.

TABLE 15.3 Means and Standard Deviations of Racial Unrest, Income Inequality, and Percent Black from SPSS

	Mean	Standard Deviation
Racial unrest (Y)	3.50	2.369
Income inequality (X_1)	6.50	3.308
Percent black (X_2)	45.80	12.612

To compare the relative contribution of each variable, Anne computes the standardized regression coefficients from the partial regression coefficients as follows:

$$b^*_{y1.2} = b_{y1.2}\frac{s_1}{s_y} = .567\frac{3.308}{2.369} = .792$$

$$b^*_{y2.1} = b_{y2.1}\frac{s_2}{s_y} = .023\frac{12.612}{2.369} = .122$$

Interestingly, Anne finds the effect of income inequality between blacks and whites in the city is much more important than the percentage of blacks in the inner city in determining the occurrence of racial unrest. These results are not necessarily consistent with previous research.

Calculation of Regression Coefficients by SPSS
The preceding manual calculation could have been done much more easily by SPSS with the REGRESSION command. Because the REGRESSION command performs multivariate as well as bivariate regression, the three variables RIOT, UNEQUAL, and BLACK can be entered together under this command to obtain a multiple regression analysis, as follows:

```
REGRESSION VARIABLES=RIOT UNEQUAL BLACK /DEPENDENT=RIOT /METHOD=ENTER.
```

Only selected portions of the SPSS output from this command are displayed in SPSS Figure 15.1. Unstandardized partial regression coefficients are listed

```
Multiple R              .88992
R Square                .79196
Adjusted R Square       .73252
Standard Error         1.22509


Analysis of Variance

                    DF      Sum of Squares      Mean Square
Regression          2             39.99408         19.99704
Residual            7             10.50592          1.50085

F =     13.32385        Signif F =  .0041

Variable               B        SE B       Beta          T  Sig T  Partial
UNEQUAL            .56748     .18780     .79255      3.022  .0193  .75237
BLACK              .02333     .04926     .12423       .474  .6502  .17623
(Constant)       -1.25726    1.60599                 -.783  .4594
```

SPSS FIGURE 15.1   Regressing Racial Unrest on Income Inequality and Percent Black

under column B, and beta weights are shown under column Beta in the figure. For now, concentrate only on these columns; other portions of the output will be explained later. Note that these b and beta values confirm those obtained earlier.

Summary

Multiple Regression

Multiple regression equation:

$$Y' = a + b_{y1.2}X_1 + b_{y2.1}X_2$$

Regression coefficients:

$$b_{y1.2} = \frac{b_{y1} - (b_{y2})(b_{21})}{1 - b_{12}b_{21}}, \qquad b_{y2.1} = \frac{b_{y2} - (b_{y1})(b_{12})}{1 - b_{12}b_{21}}$$

$$a = \overline{Y} - b_{y1.2}\overline{X}_1 - b_{y2.1}\overline{X}_2$$

Beta weights:

$$b_{y1.2}^* = b_{y1.2}\frac{s_1}{s_y}, \qquad b_{y2.1}^* = b_{y2.1}\frac{s_2}{s_y}$$

Exercises

1. Based on the following data, compute $b_{y1.2}$ by:
   a. Using residuals obtained in the three steps as described in section 15.2.2.
   b. Computing the bivariate regression coefficients and using Formula 15.2.
   c. Using SPSS.

Y	1	9	5	2	4	4
X_1	3	4	6	7	8	10
X_2	7	6	3	5	9	10

2. The following are 1960s data (hypothetical) concerning white students' participation in demonstrations in favor of the civil rights movement. From the Research Institute's data banks, Anne has selected 10 schools and four variables:

   Percentage of white students participating in demonstrations (Demo)
   Size of the university (Size)
   Academic level of the institution (Academic)
   Percentage of black students (% black)

School	Demo	Academic	% Black	Size
A	10	10	4	10
B	6	5	4	7
C	3	4	2	5
D	3	7	2	2
E	2	4	2	3
F	8	9	6	8
G	3	5	2	6
H	2	8	2	6
I	9	9	6	9
J	3	9	3	9

With participation in demonstration as the dependent variable and two other variables as independent variables, use SPSS to compute the partial regression coefficients and the beta weights. Then interpret the results.

3. Using an appropriate system of subscript notation:
   a. Write the regression equation of Y on X_1, X_2, and X_3.
   b. Express each regression coefficient as a function of lower-order regression coefficients.

15.4 Partial Correlation

In addition to the beta weights, which give an asymmetric measure of impact, Anne would like to calculate a symmetric measure of association between each of the independent and dependent variables. The **partial correlation coefficient** is such a measure. It provides the researcher with information about the degree of association between two variables while controlling at least one other variable. In contrast, the bivariate correlation determines the total association, included in which may be the effects of variables other than the independent variable. Except for this difference, the partial correlation is much like the bivariate correlation, r. It varies between -1 and 1. As usual, the sign indicates the type of relationship that exists between the independent and dependent variables. The partial correlation is not a PRE measure, but like r, when squared, it yields another statistic that is interpreted as a measure of proportional reduction in error. Thus the $r^2_{y1.2}$ value gives the proportion of variance in Y that is explained by X_1 with X_2 controlled. Being a squared value, this measure varies between 0 and 1.

Like the partial slope, the partial correlation $r_{y1.2}$ is obtained from the residuals of the X_1 and Y variables, both regressed on a second independent variable, X_2. However, instead of calculating the bivariate slope on the residuals, Pearson's r is computed. Although this explanation clarifies the logic underlying the partial correlation, to compute it as such would be tedious. Therefore, when computing by hand, a simpler computational formula is available that uses only bivariate correlations among the three variables:

$$r_{y1.2} = \frac{r_{y1} - r_{y2}r_{12}}{\sqrt{(1 - r_{y2}^2)(1 - r_{12}^2)}} \tag{15.8}$$

$$r_{y2.1} = \frac{r_{y2} - r_{y1}r_{12}}{\sqrt{(1 - r_{y1}^2)(1 - r_{12}^2)}} \tag{15.9}$$

Calculation of the Partial Correlations

The bivariate correlations among the three variables needed to calculate the partial correlations can be computed by hand or by SPSS. By specifying CORR with the DESCRIPTIVES subcommand in REGRESSION, these correlations can be obtained. Alternatively, the correlation matrix in Table 15.4 can be produced by using the CORRELATION command (Chapter 5):

```
CORRELATION VARIABLES=RIOT UNEQUAL BLACK.
```

From the table, $r_{y1} = .886$, $r_{y2} = .722$, and $r_{12} = .754$. Inserting these numbers into Formula 15.8, Anne obtains a value of .753 for the partial correlation between income inequality and racial unrest, controlling for percentage of blacks.

$$r_{y1.2} = \frac{r_{y1} - (r_{y2})(r_{12})}{\sqrt{(1 - r_{y2}^2)(1 - r_{12}^2)}} = \frac{.886 - (.722)(.754)}{\sqrt{(1 - .722^2)(1 - .754^2)}} = .753$$

The partial correlation can also be calculated easily for percent black (X_2) and racial unrest (Y), with income inequality (X_1) held constant:

$$r_{y2.1} = \frac{r_{y2} - r_{y1}r_{12}}{\sqrt{(1 - r_{y1}^2)(1 - r_{12}^2)}} = \frac{.722 - (.886)(.754)}{\sqrt{(1 - .886^2)(1 - .754^2)}} = .176$$

The partial correlations can now be squared to obtain a measure of proportional reduction in error: $r_{y1.2}^2 = .753^2 = .567$, and $r_{y2.1}^2 = .176^2 = .031$.

TABLE 15.4 Correlation Matrix of Racial Unrest, Income Inequality, and Percent Black

		Racial Unrest Y	Income Inequality X_1	Percent Black X_2
Racial unrest	(Y)			
Income inequality	(X_1)	.886		
Percent black	(X_2)	.722	.754	

```
----- Variables in the Equation -----

Variable        Correl  Part Cor  Partial

BLACK           .721515  .081656   .176225
UNEQUAL         .886168  .520940   .752370
```

**SPSS FIGURE 15.2   Partial Correlations Produced
by the Statistics Subcommand**

Calculation of the Partial Correlations by SPSS

Partial correlations can be obtained through the optional subcommand STATIS-
TICS ZPP in the REGRESSION command as follows:

```
REGRESSION VARIABLE=RIOT UNEQUAL BLACK /STATISTICS=ZPP
          /DEPENDENT=RIOT /METHOD=ENTER.
```

When the STATISTICS subcommand is used, only those statistics specifically
requested are displayed. The statistical output from this command is given in
SPSS Figure 15.2. The partial correlations are found under the "Partial" column.

Interpretation

First, Anne notes that, in contrast to other research findings, income inequality is
a much more powerful explanatory variable than percent black because it alone
accounts for 57% of the variance in the occurrence of racial unrest, while percent
black alone is responsible for only 3% of the variance. A comparison of the
bivariate correlation of racial unrest and income inequality to their partial correlation controlling for percent black shows that the effect of income inequality on
racial unrest remains almost as strong as the original relationship, .753 as compared to .886. On the other hand, the effect of percent black on racial unrest is
considerably reduced when income inequality is held constant, a comparison of
.176 to .722. Consequently, Anne speculates that income inequality is a function
of percent black in the inner city, rather than vice versa. The effect of percent black
is probably interpreted through income inequality; that is, racial unrest is more
probable when there is a high concentration of *poor* blacks in the inner city.

Summary

Partial Correlation

Partial correlation coefficients:

$$r_{y1.2} = \frac{r_{y1} - r_{y2}r_{12}}{\sqrt{(1 - r_{y2}^2)(1 - r_{12}^2)}}, \qquad r_{y2.1} = \frac{r_{y2} - r_{y1}r_{12}}{\sqrt{(1 - r_{y1}^2)(1 - r_{12}^2)}}$$

Exercises

4. Using the residuals computed earlier in Exercise 1, calculate $r_{y1.2}$.

5. For the following data:

$$
\begin{array}{lll}
r_{12} = .9 & r_{y2} = .8 & r_{y1} = .8 \\
r_{12} = .9 & r_{y2} = -.8 & r_{y1} = -.8 \\
r_{12} = .05 & r_{y2} = .09 & r_{y1} = .8 \\
r_{12} = .4 & r_{y2} = .5 & r_{y1} = .05
\end{array}
$$

   a. Compute $r_{y1.2}$.
   b. Is there any set of inconsistent data that makes the calculation of the partial correlation impossible?
   c. Discuss the extent of correlation as shown by the original bivariate correlations and the partial correlations in each case.

6. Refer to the calculations in Exercise 5. Is it possible to have (1) a higher value and (2) a different sign for the partial than for the bivariate correlation?

7. If $r_{y1.2} = 0$, prove that

$$ r_{12.y} = r_{12} \sqrt{\frac{1 - r_{y2}^2}{1 - r_{y1}^2}} $$

15.5 Multiple Correlation Coefficients

As in the case of bivariate regression, a number of measures can be calculated to determine the fit of the multiple regression model to the actual data.

15.5.1 Coefficient of Multiple Determination

To measure the improvement in the prediction of Y using the regression equation, a PRE measure called the **coefficient of multiple determination**, or R^2 is used. To differentiate the statistic from r^2 to which it is analogous, the uppercase R is used. R^2 determines the proportion of variance in the dependent variable that is accounted for by two or more independent variables. It is defined as

$$ R^2 = \frac{SSR(\text{explained SS})}{TSS(\text{total SS})} $$

If the multiple regression equation fits all the data points perfectly, all the residuals will be 0 and $R^2 = 1$. When there is no improvement in prediction using this equation over using the mean of Y, then $R^2 = 0$.

Although illustrative, it would be extremely cumbersome to compute the coefficient of multiple determination from the preceding formula. It is much simpler to obtain it from a combination of the bivariate and partial correlations, as follows:

$$R^2_{y.12} = r^2_{y1} + r^2_{y2.1}(1 - r^2_{y1}) \tag{15.10}$$

Note that the subscripting for R^2 is slightly different than for the partials. The dependent variable is given to the left of the dot, while all the independent variables are listed to the right of the dot.

According to this formula, R^2 is obtained by first using one independent variable (X_1) to explain as much of the variance in Y as possible. Then the second independent variable X_2 is used to explain the proportion of variance in Y left unexplained by X_1. To avoid duplication of effects, the first variable is controlled when the effect of the second variable is being determined.

By manipulating the terms in Formula 15.10, a formula for $r^2_{y2.1}$ can be obtained that highlights its relation to R^2:

$$r^2_{y2.1} = \frac{R^2_{y.12} - r^2_{y1}}{1 - r^2_{y1}} \tag{15.11}$$

This formula shows $r^2_{y2.1}$ as the proportion of variance in Y that is unaccounted for by X_1 but is explained by X_2.

When the two independent variables are unrelated ($r_{12} = 0$), the coefficient of multiple determination is simply the sum of the squares of the correlations of the dependent variable with each independent variable:

$$R^2_{y.12} = r^2_{y1} + r^2_{y2}$$

From this equation, it can be seen that R^2 cannot be less in magnitude than any of the bivariate correlations. How much of an increment is made in R^2 by the addition of a new variable depends on whether this variable is related to other independent variables in the equation. If it is uncorrelated, its contribution is unique and will increase the value of R^2. On the other hand, if it is highly correlated, its contribution will overlap with the contributions made by other variables, and R^2 will not be greatly affected.

As with bivariate regression, by subtracting R^2 from 1, the proportion of unexplained variance in Y is obtained as

$$1 - R^2_{y.12} = \frac{\text{SSE(unexplained SS)}}{\text{TSS (total SS)}} \tag{15.12}$$

15.5.2 Adjusted R²

An inspection of SPSS Figure 15.1 from Section 15.3 shows a statistic called the **adjusted R square** displayed directly below the R^2. Adjusted R^2 is calculated as a companion measure of R^2 when sample data are used to estimate the regression equation. The value of R^2 is often inflated by factors such as sampling fluctuation, which is larger in smaller samples, and the inclusion of a large number of independent variables. Therefore, the following correction is often made so that the adjusted R^2 reflects the actual goodness of fit in the population more closely.

$$\hat{R}^2 = R^2 - \frac{k}{N - k - 1}(1 - R^2) \tag{15.13}$$

where k refers to the number of independent variables.

15.5.3 Multiple Correlation Coefficient

Recall that by taking the square root of r^2 we obtain another measure of association in bivariate analysis. In the same manner, the *positive root* of R^2 yields the **multiple correlation coefficient, R:**

$$R = +\sqrt{R^2} \tag{15.14}$$

The value of R indicates the strength of the linear relationship between Y and the independent variables, X_1 to X_k. The concept of the type of relationship, however, is not meaningful for R, because some independent variables may be positively correlated, while others may be negatively correlated with the dependent variable. By convention, a plus sign is adopted, but it is not meant as an indication of the type of relationship. Thus, unlike r, which varies between −1 and 1, R has limits of 0 and 1.

15.5.4 Calculating and Interpreting the Multiple Correlation Coefficients

After studying the unique effect of each independent variable, Anne now plans to ascertain their total contribution to the prediction of racial unrest. This is accomplished by calculating R^2, which determines the explanatory power of the model as a whole. The bivariate and partial correlation coefficients necessary for the computation of R were obtained in previous sections. Substituting these values into Formula 15.10, we have

$$R^2_{y.12} = r^2_{y1} + r^2_{y2.1}(1 - r^2_{y1}) = .886^2 + .176^2(1 - .886^2) = .792$$
$$R = +\sqrt{R^2} = +\sqrt{.792} = .889$$

These values are the same as those obtained from SPSS and displayed in SPSS Figure 15.1.

The adjusted R^2 of .73 is computed as follows:

$$\hat{R}^2 = R^2 - \frac{k}{N - k - 1}(1 - R^2) = .792 - \frac{2}{10 - 2 - 1}(1 - .792) = .733$$

In conclusion, the regression model with percent black and income inequality accounts for 79% of the variance in the occurrence of racial unrest in cities. Even with an adjusted R^2, the equation accounts for almost three-quarters of the variance in racial unrest. Therefore, the model appears to have a great deal of explanatory power. The amount of variance left unexplained by the two independent variables is

$$(1 - R^2_{y.12}) = 1 - .792 = .208$$

However, since the two independent variables are highly correlated ($r_{12} = .754$), the coefficient of multiple determination is *not* the sum of the squares of the bivariate correlations of the dependent variable with each independent variable:

$$r^2_{y1} + r^2_{y2} = .886^2 + .722^2 = 1.306 \neq .792$$

Summary

Multiple Correlation Coefficients

Coefficient of multiple determination:

$$R^2_{y.12} = r^2_{y1} + r^2_{y2.1}(1 - r^2_{y1})$$

Adjusted R^2:

$$\hat{R}^2 = R^2 - \frac{k}{N - k - 1}(1 - R^2)$$

Multiple correlation coefficient:

$$R = +\sqrt{R^2}$$

Exercises

---

8. Compute R^2 for the data in Exercise 1.

9. Compute $(1 - R^2)$ and $(1 - r^2_{y2.1})$ for the data in Exercise 1.

10. Compute R^2's for the data in Exercise 5.

11. Show that Formula 15.11 reduces to $R_{y.12}^2 = r_{y1}^2 + r_{y2}^2$ when $r_{12} = 0$.

12. For the following sets of data:

r_{y1}	r_{y2}	r_{12}
.7	.6	.6
.7	.6	.1
.2	.2	.6
.7	−.7	.1
.2	.6	.6
.2	−.6	.6

a. Compute $R_{y.12}^2$ for each set of data, if possible.
b. Discuss the relationship between $R_{y.12}^2$ and the bivariate correlations.

13. a. Compute adjusted R^2 for the data in Exercise 1.
b. Using the R^2 in Exercise 1, compute the adjusted R^2 for N of 20, 50, and 100. What happens to the adjusted R^2 values as sample size increases?

14. A college admission policy is based on the scores of four tests:

X_1: SAT score (standard admission test)
X_2: ELM score (elementary algebra test)
X_3: English test
X_4: General test

To study the relations among these tests, the following data were obtained from 100 students:

| Variables | Mean | Standard Deviation | Correlation | | | |
			X_1	X_2	X_3	X_4
X_1	60	10				
X_2	20	5	.5			
X_3	35	8	.4	.3		
X_4	74	12	.6	.2	.6	

a. Compute the regression equation of X_1 on X_2 and X_3.
b. Compute the regression equation of X_1 on X_3 and X_4.
c. Try formulating the equation for $R_{1.234}^2$.

15.6 Problem of Multicollinearity in Regression Problems

In reaching her conclusions, Anne is acutely aware of their tentative nature. Since the bivariate correlation between percent black and income inequality is very high, .754, she is concerned that including both variables in the regression equation may create a problem known as **multicollinearity**. Multicollinearity occurs when highly correlated independent variables are introduced into the multivariate regression equation, rendering the regression results difficult to interpret, as can be seen from the following.

1. If two or more independent variables are highly correlated, they may not be conceptually distinct. Such *conceptual redundancy* makes it meaningless to consider the unique contribution of each variable. The whole procedure of controlling the second independent variable while examining the effect of the first becomes methodologically questionable. For when the two are highly correlated, they will change together in such a way as to make it artificial or impossible to separate their effects.

2. More specifically, the standard errors of the partial regression and partial correlation coefficients become extremely large when independent variables are highly correlated. A slight change in sampling or measurement procedure or the introduction of a new independent variable into the equation may cause a radical change in the values of these coefficients [4]. The problem may be ameliorated somewhat by using a large sample.

3. The problem of multicollinearity is especially serious when there are *different blocks* of highly correlated independent variables [5]. As redundant variables are entered into a regression equation, their common predictive power is averaged out, resulting in a reduction of the values of the coefficients within blocks of intercorrelated variables. Suppose that Anne uses three indicators to measure social class and two to measure intelligence. Indicators of the same concepts are highly correlated and, when entered into the same regression equation, the predictive power of each would be averaged out among other indicators of the same concepts. In such cases, it would be erroneous to interpret the partial correlation of any of the three indicators as an index of the effect of social class. Nor would it make sense to compare the effect of social class to that of intelligence by taking any one indicator from each block.

4. Any increase in the value of the multiple correlation coefficient becomes minimal with the addition of a new but redundant variable since it provides little new information. In addition, with high intercorrelations among the independent variables, R will not be much larger than the largest bivariate correlation with the dependent variable.

In short, multicollinearity makes it difficult to assess the unique contributions of the independent variables, although it has no impact on their total effects or on the goodness of fit of the equation to the observed data.

15.7 Tests of Multiple and Partial Correlations

Anne's prediction model accounts for 79% of the variance in racial unrest in the 10 cities, while the multiple correlation coefficient equals .89. As high as these values are, the question still remains as to whether Anne can infer that the model has predictive power for U.S. cities as a whole. Anne decides to resolve this issue by testing the significance of the multiple correlation coefficient.

15.7.1 F *Test of the Multiple Correlation*

The ANOVA procedure can be extended and applied directly to multiple regression problems. Its test model requires interval-level measurements and random sampling. An assumption is also made that each variable is distributed normally about all the other variables in the multiple regression equation.

The Statistical Hypotheses

The null hypothesis states that none of the k independent variables in the model is correlated with the dependent variable, in which case the value of R equals 0 in the population:

$$H_0: \ \beta_1 = \beta_2 = \cdots = \beta_k = 0 \ \text{ or } \ R = 0$$

where β_j refers to the partial slopes of the k independent variables in the population. The alternative is that at least one independent variable is truly correlated with the dependent variable, in which case the value of R is significantly greater than 0:

$$H_1: \ \text{at least one } \beta_j \neq 0 \ \text{ or } \ R > 0$$

The Test Statistic and Its Sampling Distribution

The R^2 represents the ratio of SSR to TSS in a multivariate analysis, just as the r^2 refers to the same ratio in a bivariate analysis. Therefore, the sums of squares can be used in a multivariate analysis as in a bivariate analysis (Chapter 13). The explained sum of squares equals

$$\text{SSR} = \sum (Y' - \overline{Y})^2 = R^2 \left[\sum (Y - \overline{Y})^2 \right]$$

and the unexplained sum of squares equals

$$\text{SSE} = \sum (Y - Y')^2 = [1 - R^2] \left[\sum (Y - \overline{Y})^2 \right]$$

The degrees of freedom associated with the total sum of squares (TSS) equals $(N - 1)$. With SSE being calculated about the regression line, there is, in addition to the regression coefficient a, a partial slope for each of the k independent variables to be estimated. Therefore, the degrees of freedom associated with SSE are $[N - (k + 1)]$, where $(k + 1)$ represents the degrees of freedom lost for the k independent variables and the a coefficient. The remaining degrees of freedom associated with SSR are $(N - 1) - (N - k - 1) = k$.

When SSE and SSR are each divided by its df, the mean sums of squares are obtained. The F-test statistic is formed from the ratio of MSSR to MSSE, in which their common term $\sum(Y - \overline{Y})^2$ is canceled:

$$F_{(k,N-k-1)} = \frac{R^2}{1 - R^2} \frac{N - k - 1}{k} \tag{15.15}$$

This test statistic has an F sampling distribution, with df_1 of k and df_2 of $(N - k - 1)$. Table 15.5 summarizes all the components for computing the F ratio.

Calculation and Interpretation

Using the R^2 value computed in Section 15.5, Anne obtains the following F ratio:

$$F_{(2,7)} = \frac{.792}{1 - .792} \frac{10 - 2 - 1}{2} = \frac{.792}{.208} \frac{7}{2} = 13.327$$

To test her model at the .05 significance level, Anne compares the obtained F ratio to a critical $F_{(2,7)}$ of 4.74. Since the obtained value of 13.33 is far greater than the critical value of 4.74, Anne rejects the null hypothesis in favor of the alternative hypothesis. The model using percent black and income inequality to predict racial unrest does have explanatory power.

When the multiple regression equation is computed by SPSS with the REGRESSION command, ANOVA is carried out at the same time. The portion of SPSS Figure 15.1 for ANOVA is reproduced in SPSS Figure 15.3. As can be seen, the same F value is obtained, with the exact significance level calculated to be .0041 in the SPSS output.

TABLE 15.5 ANOVA Table for Testing the Null Hypothesis That $R = 0$

	Sum of Squares	df	Mean Sum of Squares
Total	$\sum(Y - \overline{Y})^2$	$N - 1$	
Explained	$\sum(Y' - \overline{Y})^2 = R^2\left[\sum(Y - \overline{Y})^2\right]$	k	$\dfrac{R^2\left[\sum(Y - \overline{Y})^2\right]}{k}$
Unexplained	$\sum(Y - Y')^2 = [1 - R^2]\left[\sum(Y - \overline{Y})^2\right]$	$N - k - 1$	$\dfrac{[1 - R^2]\left[\sum(Y - \overline{Y})^2\right]}{N - k - 1}$

```
Analysis of Variance

                        DF        Sum of Squares        Mean Square

Regression              2              39.99408           19.99704
Residual                7              10.50592            1.50085

F  =       13.32385       Signif F  =   .0041
```

SPSS FIGURE 15.3 ANOVA Table Produced by the Regression Command

15.7.2 t *Test of the Partial Correlation*

The test of R gives an overall evaluation, but not a detailed assessment, of the significance of the regression model. All that Anne can conclude from the result is that at least one independent variable, and therefore the whole model, has explanatory power in the population as well. To obtain a more specific analysis of the effect of each independent variable, the partial correlations should be tested individually.

An Appropriate Test and Assumptions

The ANOVA procedure can again be extended to test the partial correlations. In testing for the partial correlation, the partial slope is also tested. In addition, a t test is available that, unlike the ANOVA, permits directional hypotheses to be tested. Being able to test the direction is important because the partial r's range from -1 to 1, although R ranges from 0 to 1. A two-tailed t test, in this case, is equivalent to the F test. Only the t procedure will be considered here.

The Statistical Hypotheses

Anne's null hypothesis states that income inequality has no effect on racial unrest when percent black is controlled:

$$H_0: \ \beta_{y1.2} = 0 \ \text{ or } \ \rho_{y1.2} = 0$$

where $\beta_{y1.2}$ and $\rho_{y1.2}$ refer to the partial slope and correlation in the population. The alternative hypothesis states that income inequality does contribute to the explanation of the dependent variable:

$$H_1: \ \beta_{y1.2} \neq 0 \ \text{ or } \ \rho_{y1.2} \neq 0$$

The Test Statistic and Its Sampling Distribution
The formula for the *t*-test statistic is

$$t = \frac{r_{y1.2} - \rho_{y1.2}}{\sqrt{\dfrac{1 - r_{y1.2}^2}{N - k - 1}}}$$

Since $\rho_{y1.2}$ equals 0 under the null hypothesis, the formula reduces to

$$t = \frac{r_{y1.2}}{\sqrt{\dfrac{1 - r_{y1.2}^2}{N - k - 1}}} \tag{15.16}$$

This test statistic has a *t* sampling distribution with $(N - k - 1)$ degrees of freedom, where $(k + 1)$ represents degrees of freedom lost through estimating the regression coefficients of *a* and *k* independent variables.

Calculation and Interpretation
The partial correlation between income inequality and racial unrest yields the following *t* score:

$$t = \frac{.753}{\sqrt{\dfrac{1 - .567}{10 - 2 - 1}}} = \frac{.753}{.249} = 3.028$$

This *t* value with df of 7 is greater than the critical value of 2.365 for a two-tailed test at the .05 level.

The test of the partial for percent black and racial unrest can be calculated similarly. Alternatively, Anne can examine the output of the REGRESSION procedure in SPSS Figure 15.1 under the columns of T and Sig T for an answer. According to the SPSS output, the *t* value for BLACK of .474 is not significant at the .05 significance level; instead, its probability of occurrence is .65. This means that the variable percent black is probably not related to racial unrest when income inequality is controlled. Thus the significance of the regression model depends on income inequality alone. The second independent variable, percent black, can be eliminated without reducing by much the predictive power of the model.

Note from the SPSS output that the T values can also be obtained directly through dividing the partial slope value under column B by the standard error of the partial slope given under column SE B:

$$t = \frac{B}{SE\ B} = \frac{b_{y1.2}}{\hat{\sigma}_{b_{y1.2}}} \tag{15.17}$$

Thus testing the partial correlation is equivalent to testing the partial slopes. Using either Formula 15.16 or 15.17 will yield the same value (except for rounding errors) and the same conclusion.

Summary

Tests of Relationships

Null hypothesis for multiple correlation: $\beta_1 = \beta_2 = \cdots = \beta_k = 0$ or $R = 0$

$$F_{(k,N-k-1)} = \frac{R^2}{1 - R^2} \frac{N - k - 1}{k} \quad \text{with df}_1 = k \text{ and df}_2 = (N - k - 1)$$

where k = the number of independent variables

Null hypothesis for partial correlation: $\beta_{y1.2} = 0$ or $\rho_{y1.2} = 0$

$$t = \frac{r_{y1.2}}{\sqrt{\dfrac{1 - r_{y1.2}^2}{N - k - 1}}} \quad \text{or} \quad t = \frac{b_{y1.2}}{\hat{\sigma}_{b_{y1.2}}} \quad \text{with df} = (N - k - 1)$$

Test model:

1. Interval-level measurement
2. Random sampling
3. Each variable distributed normally about all others

15.8 Model Building Using Tests of Significance

Using the t (or F) test for the partial, the researcher can proceed to build a model of a social phenomenon by including in it only those explanatory variables that have a significant impact on the dependent variable. The model can be built through either a process of elimination or addition. In elimination, the researcher enters all the potential explanatory variables into the regression equation. Then the variable with the least explanatory power is removed from the equation, after which the reduced model is reevaluated. For example, Anne decides she would eliminate the variable percent black since it does not appear to have great impact on the occurrence of racial unrest. She recalculates the regression equation with only income differential as the independent variable and obtains an r^2 of .785, a value only slightly lower than the R^2 of .792 for the model with two independent variables. The F or t test performed on the Pearson's r shows a significance beyond the .01 level.

With more than two explanatory variables, the deletion can proceed until only those independent variables are left that have been tested to be significant. When this happens, each independent variable in the model makes a contribution to the prediction of the dependent variable. Elimination of any of these variables may significantly decrease the value of R^2.

In the method of stepwise addition, the researcher begins with the most powerful of the explanatory variables and then adds independent variables, one at a time, until the value of R^2 is not significantly increased by the inclusion. Again, this means including independent variables whose effect on the dependent variable is significant according to the t test. The underlying logic of the two procedures is essentially the same. With either method, the researcher attempts to build the most powerful model with the least number of variables or terms in the regression equation.

Exercises

15. Based on the data in Exercise 2, test the partial correlation coefficient between Demo and % Black controlling Academic.

16. For the data in Exercise 2, use SPSS to compute a multiple regression equation using all the independent variables. Also compute bivariate correlations, partial beta weights, R, and R^2.

    a. Compare significance levels of:

       r between Demo and % Black
       r between Demo and % Black controlling Academic
       r between Demo and % Black controlling Academic and Size
       R between Demo and (Academic, % Black, and Size)

    b. Examine the significance of different models by comparing:

       Model with (% Black) versus model with (% Black and Academic)
       Model with (% Black, Academic) versus (% Black, Academic, Size)

    c. Interpret the results in terms of the significance of the contribution of each variable.

SPSS Exercises

To explain the variation in the crime rates in cities of 25,000 or more inhabitants, select independent and control variables as follows, and perform correlation and regression analyses together with significance tests.

1. Dependent variable: Serious crime rate (CRIME)
   Independent variable: Unemployment rate (UNEMPLOY)
   Control variable: City size (POPLATON)

2. Dependent variable: Serious crime rate (CRIME)
   Independent variable: Percent below poverty level (POORMAN)(POORFAM)
   Control variable: Population density (POPDENSE)

3. Dependent variable: Serious crime rate (CRIME)
   Independent variable: Population change (POPCHNGE)
   Control variable: Number of policemen per 1,000 residents (POLICE)

The quality of city life can be measured by the infant mortality rate. Consider it a dependent variable and examine the effects of other variables on it.

4. Independent variable: Percent of health expenditure in general budget (HEALTH)
   Control variable: Number of hospital beds per 1,000 residents (NUMBEDS)

5. Independent variable: Per capita income (INCOME)
   Control variable: Health care expenditure (HEALTH)

6. Independent variable: Percent completing 16 years of schooling (COLLEGE)
   Control variable: Percent professional, technical workers (PROF)

7. Finally, examine the combined effects of these various independent variables and interpret the findings.

General Conceptual Problems

1. What does the coefficient of multiple determination measure? How is it different from r^2?

2. Explain what is meant by the multiple regression plane. How is it drawn?

3. Does the addition of an independent variable always increase the amount of R^2?

4. Can R^2 be less in magnitude than any of the bivariate correlations between the dependent and independent variables? Explain.

5. Explain in your own words what partial correlation is and how it is calculated.

6. Does having a negative value for the multiple correlation coefficient make sense? Explain.

7. Explain what is meant by the asymmetry of the beta weight.

8. What is multicollinearity? How is it produced? What effects does it have on regression analysis?

References

1. Smelser, N. (1962). *Theory of Collective Behavior*. New York: Free Press.
2. Spilerman, S. (1970). The Causes of Racial Disturbances: A Comparison of Alternative Explanations, *American Sociological Review* 35:627–649.
3. Morgan, W. R., and Clark, T. N. (1973). The Causes of Racial Disorders: A Grievance-level Explanation, *American Sociological Review* 38:611–624.
4. Blalock, H. M. (1964). *Causal Inferences in Nonexperimental Research Design*. Chapel Hill: University of North Carolina Press.
5. Gordon, R. (1968). Issues in Multiple Regression, *American Journal of Sociology* 73:592–616.

Chapter *16*

An Overview of Statistical Analysis

This book has described Anne's venture into the United States, a world of which she knows little but desires to know more. In the process of delving into this country, she has asked questions that constitute some of the traditional concerns of social scientists. The answers she has arrived at may or may not have been familiar to the reader; they, however, do not form the focus of the text. The important consideration is the manner in which Anne, as a researcher, inquires and then obtains answers to these questions.

We have assumed that the reader is also venturing into a new world, the world of statistics, in an undertaking that parallels Anne's to a certain extent. In describing Anne's explorations, we have demonstrated not only how social scientists conduct research, but how statistics is an integral part of this endeavor. Anne began her undertaking by deriving research questions from her observations and past research and, most importantly, from the theories that form the core of the social science disciplines. As new research questions were raised, she searched for appropriate statistical procedures that could help to provide answers to them. She realized that statistics may not have a solution to every research problem. However, when it did, the answers came in the form of numbers that were meaningless until they were interpreted within the framework of the initial questions and/or theoretical perspectives.

Thus, through emphasizing these logical processes that underlie any statistical analysis, we attempt to reinforce the notion that blind utilization of formulas would not yield meaningful results. Nor would numbers alone explain social reality. Furthermore, by covering the major and most commonly used statistical procedures, we have provided a basic tool kit for the task of data analysis. In grasping these essentials of "doing" statistics, the reader is well on the road to becoming a competent data analyst.

Such an analyst knows what statistical procedures are available, how to compute them, and how to interpret the findings. But, more importantly, this individual knows how to match the appropriate techniques to the research questions posed. The skill of choosing the appropriate type of analysis can be developed by acquiring an overview and an appreciation of the entire research process. It can be sharpened further through an awareness of the considerations that enter into the selection of an appropriate technique.

Under this heading of considerations, there are the macro concerns. These are issues that must be considered in any selection, discussions of which are scattered throughout the text. In this chapter, they are gathered and summarized under three headings: (1) univariate and multivariate analysis, (2) description and inference, and (3) level of measurement. As each is considered, the researcher is moved farther along in the decision-making process.

16.1 From Univariate to Multivariate Analysis

Social scientists seek to establish patterns and regularity in the occurrence of events around them. In their attempt to do so, they ask questions and then develop tentative answers. Since Anne knew very little of the United States, her inquiries have proceeded from the simple to the complex; her later questions built on the answers obtained from earlier ones. On a parallel plane, with statistical procedures matching her research goals, her data analysis began with the examination of one variable at a time and culminated in model building and the simultaneous analysis of multiple variables. Anne's progress illustrates that a researcher must first determine the complexity of the statistical analysis that is needed to answer the research question posed at the beginning of a project.

In statistics the level of complexity is often correlated with the number of variables included in the analysis. Even very complex issues can usually be resolved by proceeding step by step, from univariate to multivariate analysis. At the simplest level of univariate analysis, only one variable is examined at a time. An analysis of the variables at this level essentially entails a summary of their patterns of variation or nonvariation. The researcher examines how the variable is distributed and typically considers the following issues: What is the overall shape of the distribution? What is the central tendency and how well does it summarize the distribution? Is there much variation and what is the range of the variation?

Bivariate analysis represents a more sophisticated approach. Here the main concern is with finding an explanation for the variation of a variable, identified as the dependent variable. Statistical explanation is achieved when the dependent variable is shown to change systematically with the independent variable. To substantiate the covariation, the researcher calculates a measure of association between the two variables. These measures indicate the strength and, when applicable, the nature of the relationships.

The statistical explanation of the dependent variable remains the aim of multivariate analysis. However, by taking into account several independent variables, multivariate analysis provides more of an approximation to what happens in the complex real world. Clearly, most social processes involve multiple factors acting on the same dependent variable. Consequently, the term *modeling* is often applied to multivariate analysis. The effects of the independent variables become the primary focus of the analysis, the issues being statistical control and the possibility of spurious relationships, and the interaction among these variables. Statistical control is exercised to determine the unique contribution of each variable to the explanation of the dependent variable. In the process of specifying these unique contributions, the researcher may find some relationships to be spurious. The possibility and form of interaction among independent variables are also topics of major concern in multivariate analysis, although we have only dealt very superficially with these topics in the text.

Table 16.1 summarizes the specific tasks of each level of analysis. However, regardless of the number of variables involved, the overall aim of the analysis remains the same. It is the search for regularity, whether it be the pattern of variation of one variable or the pattern of covariation between two or among more variables. In deciding whether one or more variables should be analyzed, the researcher makes a first step toward selecting the appropriate statistical technique. The decision locates the researcher in one of the cells in Table 16.1. Note, however, that the use of one level of analysis does not preclude the use of others in the same project. Although the final analysis may involve a number of variables, the researcher usually begins with the individual variables that are to be included. Therefore, before the multivariate analysis the researcher may conduct a univariate and perhaps even a bivariate analysis.

There is also a certain parallel between the level of complexity of the statistical analyses and research goals. In Chapter 1, empirical studies were classified into three types according to their purposes: exploratory, descriptive, and explanatory. In turn, the purpose depends on the state of knowledge regarding the particular topic. With little accumulated information, the study is likely to be exploratory or descriptive. Explanatory research, on the other hand, is built on the foundation of earlier studies in which accurate description of the phenomenon of interest has already been achieved. Thus, in terms of research goals, an approximate progression toward the complexity of finding cause and effect rela-

TABLE 16.1 Statistical Procedures Classified According to the Number of Variables Included in the Analysis

1. **Univariate**: Describing a sample by its characteristics one at a time

2. **Bivariate**: Searching for and specifying the relationship between two variables

3. **Multivariate**: Modeling or specifying multicauses; elimination of spurious relationships

tionships is also discernible. Very generally, then, exploratory and descriptive research requires less complex statistical analysis than explanatory research.

16.2 *From Description to Inference*

The second decision to be made in selecting an appropriate statistical technique revolves around the distinction between a sample and the population from which it is drawn. Information pertaining to the sample is factual, while conclusions about the population are estimations and therefore probabilistic. The researcher is said to describe the sample and to infer the population parameters from sample statistics. Indeed, the division of the field into descriptive and inferential statistics has provided a basis for the organization of this text and can be sustained on both theoretical and pedagogical grounds.

In practice, however, the separation tends to be artificial. The two are not mutually exclusive. The researcher frequently checks the significance levels of statistical measures while describing the characteristics of a sample. The descriptive information provides the basis for the researcher to make the inferential leap to the population.

Although descriptive and inferential analyses are not mutually exclusive tasks, when the researcher intends to make an inference, she or he should draw a random or probability sample. There is nothing inherent in the inferential procedures themselves that would prevent the researcher from extending whatever patterns are found in the sample to the population itself, however inappropriately. Therefore, if a probability sample is not selected at the outset, the researcher may derive grossly inaccurate conclusions and generalizations about the population based on a biased sample.

Not only does the sampling design determine whether inferential statistics should be used, but it is also related to the purpose of the research. For exploratory research, it is unlikely that the researcher draws a probability sample. In descriptive and explanatory research, however, usually some efforts are made to select a probability sample. Often, then, the analysis is limited to the use of descriptive statistics in exploratory studies, whereas both descriptive and inferential statistics are likely to be employed in the other types of studies.

In certain situations, probability sampling may have taken place, but the resulting sample may be inadequate. For example, a very sophisticated sampling design may have been developed for a survey research. But if the response rate is only 50%, the sample is still suspect for the information it provides. Given such cases, the researcher should approach the *interpretation* of the results with caution.

At any rate, in making the *additional* decision as to whether descriptive or inferential statistics is required, the researcher locates himself or herself in one of the six possible cells of Table 16.2. This brings the researcher one step closer to the goal of selecting an appropriate statistical technique for the analysis.

★**TABLE 16.2 Statistical Procedures Classified According to the Function and the Number of Variables Included in the Analysis**

Descriptive Statistics	Inferential Statistics
Examining sample data	Inferring population parameters from sample statistics
Univariate	
1a. Describe the sample by its characteristics, one at a time	**1b.** Test if the sample statistic differs from the population parameter significantly Test if the difference between or among sample statistics is significant
Bivariate	
2a. Search for and specify relationships	**2b.** Test if the relationship is significant
Multivariate	
3a. Modeling or specify multicauses Eliminate spurious relationship	**3b.** Test if the effect of one or more variables is significant

The reader should be cautioned that the classification of some inferential procedures in Table 16.2 as univariate is somewhat artificial. These are the "difference" tests listed in 1b, which are differentiated further according to the number of samples involved. Although listed as univariate procedures, these techniques are used, in effect, to examine the implied relationship between an independent nominal or categorical variable and a dependent interval variable. The independent variable supplies the categories that define the populations under study. This usually means that the two or more samples are not drawn individually, but are differentiated from the initial random sample. Furthermore, the independent variable is not explicitly taken into account again in the actual computation of the test statistic. Instead, the distributions of the dependent variable in the samples defined by the independent variable are then examined, and a test statistic is calculated to summarize their difference. Because the various samples represent conditional distributions, the difference, if any, in these distributions implies that a relationship exists between the independent and dependent variable. From this perspective, the label of "two" or "three" or more samples can be considered a misnomer. And only in the restricted sense that the independent variable is not included in the calculation can the procedures be called univariate.

16.3 From Nominal to Interval Measurement

The final major consideration is the measurement level of the data. By identifying the appropriate level, the researcher arrives at a tentative decision on the statistical procedure needed for the analysis. A related concern is whether the variable is continuous or discrete. For some inferential procedures, this, rather than the measurement level, is the paramount issue. Thus the number of variables included in the analysis, the level of measurement (or the continuous/discrete nature) of these variables, and whether the researcher aims to make a statement about the sample only or the population as well constitute the three overall considerations common to choosing an appropriate statistical technique. Table 16.3 gives a classification of all the procedures covered in this text according to the three criteria. In this table, the six cells of Table 16.2, labeled as 1a, 1b, 2a, 2b, 3a, and 3b, are now expanded to include specific techniques, subdivided according to the different levels of measurement. The chapter numbers appear in parentheses to facilitate locating the techniques within the text.

Keep in mind that techniques that are appropriate for a lower level can always be used on a higher level of measurement. Thus, as the level of measurement increases, the choice of available techniques also increases. As a rule, the researcher would not want to ignore information by choosing a technique that is appropriate for a lower level. However, depending on the occasion, this may be the correct decision to make.

For descriptive statistics, if the information can best be communicated by using a lower-level technique, the researcher should not hesitate to do so. Thus, if the median describes a skewed interval distribution better than the mean, the median should be used. Or if the researcher is more interested in examining the bivariate relationship in detail while controlling for other variables, partial tables rather than a more complex multivariate procedure should be used.

For inferential statistics, whether the assumptions contained in a test model are appropriate for the occasion should be considered carefully in the selection process. For example, parametric statistics usually require that explicit assumptions be made about the normality of the population distribution and about population parameters. Less stringent assumptions are required by nonparametric statistics. The choice lies between making assumptions that may not be valid or using a less powerful technique.

16.4 Other Issues in the Selection of a Statistical Procedure

Once the level of the technique is decided on, other considerations that are micro in nature and specific to the technique govern the choice. For example, if the purpose is to describe the sample one characteristic at a time (analysis 1a), the researcher must decide whether it is the shape, the central tendency, or the dispersion of the distribution, or all three that are required. If the aim is to compute a test of difference (analysis 1b), the number of samples is an additional consideration. When there are two samples, the question of whether these are independent or related samples must be addressed. Also, in bivariate descriptive analysis (analysis 2a), the decision to use a symmetric or an asymmetric measure must be made. Other factors not given in the table are the data arrangement and size of the table. Finally, in building multivariate models (analysis 3a), the treat-

TABLE 16.3 Statistical Procedures Classified According to the Levels of Measurement, the Functions, and the Number of Variables Included in the Analysis

	Nominal	Ordinal	Interval/Ratio
1a. Describing the sample by its characteristics, one at a time			
Overall shape	—— Frequency distribution and graphic representation (2) ——		
Central tendency	Mode (3)	Median (3)	Mean (3)
Dispersion	Variation ratio (3)	Range (3)	Average deviation (3)
		Interquartile range(3)	Standard deviation (3)
			Variance (3)
			CRV (3)
			z Scores (3)
1b. Testing the significance of the difference between statistic(s) and parameter(s) or between/among statistics			
One sample	Chi-square test (9)	K–S test (9)	z Test (8)
			t Test (9)
			Chi-square test of a variance (9)
			Point and interval estimation (10)
Two samples	Chi-square test (11)	Mann–Whitney (11)	z Test (11)
			t Test (11)
More than two samples	Chi-square test (12)	Kruskal–Wallis (12)	ANOVA (12)
2a. Searching for or specifying relationships			
Symmetric	Phi (4)	Spearman's rho (5)	Pearson's r (5)
	Cramer's V (4)	Gamma, Yule's Q (4)	Eta squared (5)
	Contingency coefficient C (4)	Tau-b (4)	
	Lambda (4)		
Asymmetric	Lambda (4)	Somer's d (4)	Bivariate regression (5)
2b. Testing for significance of relationships			
	Chi-square test (13)	Test of concordance (13)	F test (13)
			t Test (13)
3a. Building multivariate models			
	Loglinear analysis (14)		Multiple regression and correlation (15)
			Partial correlation (15)
3b. Testing multivariate model			
	Likelihood ratio Chi-square test (14)		F test (15)
			t Test (15)

ment of interaction may affect the selection from among available techniques for each level of measurement.

All these additional micro considerations are handled within each chapter as the procedure itself is discussed, under the headings of Characteristics and Properties and An Appropriate Technique. Since their discussions are confined to easily identifiable sections and since they are too numerous to be summarized within a table, they are not presented again in Table 16.3. The reader should use Table 16.3 as a summary chart to help select a cell with its range of techniques appropriate for particular research goals and the data. Then, if necessary, the additional assumptions for each listed procedure should be reviewed before making a final selection.

An Introduction to SPSS

SECTION 1: GENERAL ORIENTATION

1.1 Computers and Research

Today, doing social research without computers is like learning astronomy without telescopes. We can hand-tabulate interview responses, but the process is as inefficient as trying to decipher the constellations with our naked eyes. Computers perform sophisticated statistical analysis on a vast volume of data in an infinitesimal amount of time. The importance of computers in social research is not limited to quantitative data analysis. Computers play a vital role at various stages of the research process: they are used for telephone interviewing, sampling, coding for content analysis, cleaning a data file, and so on.

Learning to use the computer for statistical analysis has now become easier than ever before. There are packages of prewritten computer programs for practically any analysis that the researcher decides to perform. Without much prior computer experience, students can learn to use these softwares easily. Among the most powerful packages, such as SAS, MINITAB, and BMDP, there is one used most frequently by social scientists. It is SPSS, Statistical Packages for Social Sciences. SPSS targets social science researchers by providing the statistical procedures most applicable to social data.

There are two versions of SPSS: one for the mainframe and the other for microcomputers. The mainframe version is now referred to as SPSS, although many users still call it by its old name, SPSSX. The PC version is called SPSS/PC+. Although the mainframe SPSS is more powerful than SPSS/PC+, the latter has the advantage of easy-to-follow menu-driven operation. The mainframe SPSS also has a menu mode, but it is an optional feature that requires the installation of an interface for most computers and operating systems. SPSS/PC+ comes in different modules; users can purchase and install only those modules they need.

Furthermore, microcomputers are less expensive and more accessible than main-frames; their memory capacity has expanded while their prices have lowered. Therefore, we place more emphasis on the use of SPSS/PC+ than on the main-frame SPSS, although we discuss both in the text. The rest of this appendix is organized as follows: Sections 1 and 4 discuss preparatory work for analysis, SPSS language, and concepts common to both the mainframe and microcomput-ers. All students should read these sections. In addition, students planning to use SPSS/PC+ should read Section 2, while those planning to use SPSS can skip this section and go on to read Section 3.

1.2 Data Preparation and Coding

Before SPSS can be used for statistical analysis, the data set must be prepared in such a way that SPSS can understand and process it. Consider a hypothetical survey of a statistics course for the social sciences. Suppose the following ques-tions were asked of each student in the class:

1. Year at school: Freshman (Fr) _____
               Sophomore (So) _____
               Junior (Ju) _____
               Senior (Sen) _____
2. Major: 1. Social science _____
          2. Humanities _____
          3. Natural science _____
          4. Other _____
3. Number of units carried: _____
4. Grade point average: _____
5. Primary reason for taking the course:
    1. It is required for the major.
    2. I am interested in statistics.
    3. The instructor has a good reputation.
    4. It is given at a convenient time.
    5. Other reasons.

The data thus collected can be conceptualized in terms of cases, variables, and categories or values. Each student who responds to the questionnaire is a **case** or unit of analysis. Alternatively, a student's answers, taken collectively, also repre-sent a case. Each question measures a **variable**, a characteristic of the respondent. The variable is identified by a **variable name** that begins with a letter, A through Z, and should contain no more than eight characters. The five variables in the preceding questionnaire are assigned the names of LEVEL, MAJOR, UNITS, GPA, and REASON. A variable assumes different **categories** or **values** in different cases. For example, LEVEL has four categories to describe a respondent, whereas GPA takes on a value specific to each student.

Coding refers to assigning numbers or letters to represent the attributes of a variable. In the above survey the Fr stands for freshman, So for sophomore, and so on. UNITS and GPA are coded with actual values given by respondents. Variables coded with numbers are called **numeric** variables, whereas variables coded with letters are called **string** variables.

In Figure 1, the data for each case are coded on a line that runs 80 columns long and is called a **record**. If the data require more than 80 columns, two or more records may be used per case. The data are coded in **fixed format**, that is, the codes of a variable are entered in the same column(s) of a line for each respondent. Thus LEVEL appears in columns 1 through 3, MAJOR in column 6, UNITS in columns 10 and 11, and so on.

The alternative to the fixed is the **free format**. Here the codes of a variable are entered in any column(s), provided that they appear in the same order, separated by a blank(s) and/or comma. In addition, data pertaining to different cases may be entered on the same record. Figure 2 exhibits the same data in free format.

Thus data preparation begins with assigning a name to each variable and then coding the variables of each case in either fixed or free format.

1.3 Components of an SPSS Program

For SPSS to perform a statistical analysis, a set of instructions, given in the form of **commands**, must be entered into the computer. These commands, taken collec-

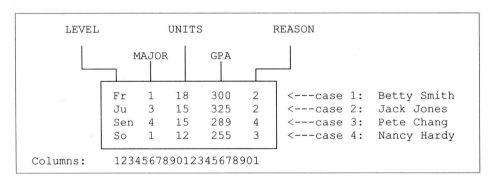

FIGURE 1

```
Fr   1   18   300   2   Ju   3   15   325   2
Sen      4    15    289   4   So
1    12    255   3
```

FIGURE 2

tively, comprise a **program**. An SPSS program typically consists of commands that perform three basic functions: (1) data definition and entry, (2) data modification, and (3) data analysis. The program first informs SPSS how the data should be interpreted and then enters the data in fixed or free format. If the data need to be transformed, the program modifies them either permanently or temporarily. Finally, the program invokes the specified SPSS procedure(s) to perform a desired analysis. All three components are found in the program in Figure 3, written to produce a frequency distribution for the class survey described previously.

1. *Data definition:* The DATA LIST command defines the variables in a data set, indicating the names assigned to variables and their locations and formats. The BEGIN DATA and END DATA commands signal the beginning and end of the data lines. In between these two commands, the prepared data lines are entered.
2. *Data modification:* The IF command changes the original data on UNITS into a new variable, called LOAD, with two categories.
3. *Procedure:* The procedural command FREQUENCIES generates frequency distributions and bar charts for two variables, MAJOR and LOAD.

1.4 Components of the SPSS Command Language

Most SPSS commands have three components:

1. *Command keyword:* The command keyword instructs the computer to perform a selected task. For example, DATA LIST and FREQUENCIES are command keywords for two different tasks.
2. *Subcommand keyword:* Subcommands are parts of a command; they cannot stand alone but must be used with a command. They provide more precise instructions or request additional data output or analysis. An example of a subcommand is the VARIABLE subcommand in FREQUENCIES.

```
Data definition ----->   DATA LIST FIXED/LEVEL 1-3 (A)   MAJOR 6 UNITS 10-11
                            GPA 15-17 (2) REASON 21.
                         BEGIN DATA.
                         Fr    1    18    300    2
Data entry ---------->   Ju    3    15    325    2
                         Sen   4    15    289    4
                         So    1    12    255    3
                         END DATA.
Data modification---->   IF  (UNITS LE 18)  LOAD = 1.
                         IF  (UNITS GT 18)  LOAD = 2.
Procedure ----------->   FREQUENCIES   VARIABLES=MAJOR LOAD /BARCHART.
```

FIGURE 3

3. *User specification:* Many subcommands require additional information that must be supplied by the user. They provide the details of the subcommand and are tailored to the demands of the user. In the FREQUENCIES command the words MAJOR and LOAD are user specifications, telling SPSS the variables for which frequency tables and bar charts are to be constructed. Some user specifications are also coded in keywords. Examples are BARCHART in the FREQUENCIES command and the LE in the IF command. These keywords have standard meanings across different programs.

SECTION 2: SPSS/PC+

2.1 Syntax

All SPSS/PC+ commands begin with a **keyword** (or keywords), which is a specifically defined word having a particular meaning in SPSS/PC+. A command may continue for as many lines as is necessary, each line being 80 columns long. Each command must end with a **command terminator**, a period. Commands, except for BEGIN and END DATA, may begin in any column of a line.

2.2 SPSS/PC+ Operating Modes

SPSS/PC+ provides three environments in which to enter the commands: the MENU environment, the REVIEW editor environment, and the COMMAND PROMPT interactive environment. SPSS/PC+ can operate in each of these environments or combination of environments, resulting in several **operating modes**.

Only the MENU environment, which is recommended for beginners, will be presented here. This environment requires the least knowledge of the command language syntax from the user. With its system of menus, the user can build a command by browsing through the items of different menus and the related explanations of syntax and functions.

2.3 An Overview of the Menu Environment

To obtain an overview of the MENU environment, turn on the computer and move to the proper subdirectory. Load SPSS/PC+ by typing "SPSSPC" and pressing the ENTER key. Upon loading SPSS/PC+, the default MENU environment is in effect. SPSS/PC+ can operate in two modes in this environment: the **MENU mode** and the **REVIEW mode**.

2.3.1 The Three Windows in the Screen Display

The menu shown in Figure 4 appears on the screen after pressing the ENTER key. The screen is divided into three parts or *windows*: the **MENU** and **HELP** windows on the upper half and the **SCRATCH.PAD** window on the lower half.

The MENU Window

The upper-left quadrant of the screen is called the MENU window because it contains a number of items from which to choose. Generally, the menu items are parts of SPSS/PC+ commands or components of the SPSS/PC+ language. Note that the window currently contains the MAIN MENU, and a highlighting bar, the **menu bar**, sits on the top item, "orientation." The menu bar can be moved up or down the list of items by using the **up** and **down arrow keys**.

The HELP Window

The HELP window in the upper-right quadrant explains the item highlighted in the menu window. For the moment, with "orientation" highlighted, the HELP window describes what this item entails. Now use the down arrow key to move the menu bar to "read or write data." Note how the label and the description in the HELP window change to those of "read or write data." Move the bar farther down and again the HELP window changes its contents to explain the highlighted item.

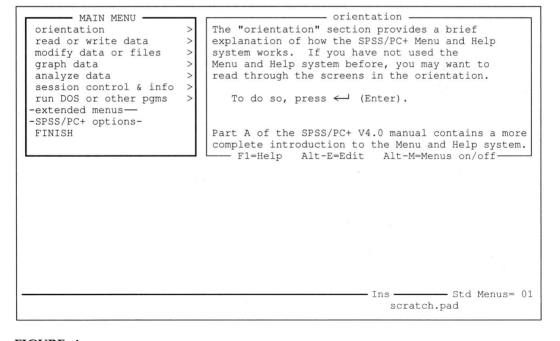

FIGURE 4

The SCRATCH.PAD Window

When appropriate items are selected from the menu, they are stored in the lower half of the screen, called SCRATCH.PAD. At present this area of the screen is blank. However, as soon as a menu item is selected, it will be copied from the menu and **pasted** onto SCRATCH.PAD.

2.3.2 *The Structure of the Menu System*

Because of the complexity of the SPSS/PC+ language, the components of the commands are grouped in a series of menus organized in a hierarchical structure. Figure 5 shows the hierarchical organization up to the point of the

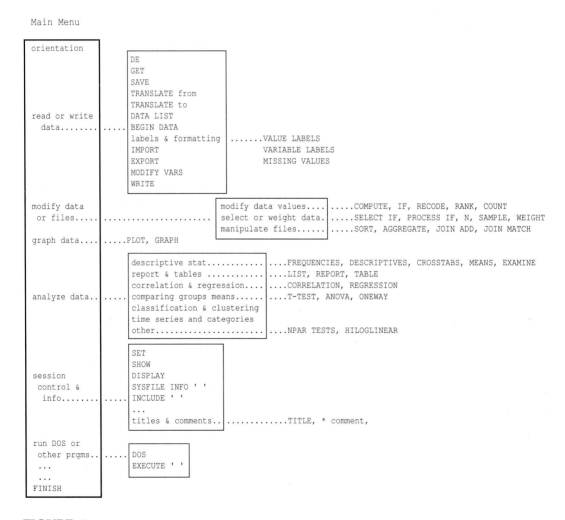

FIGURE 5

command keywords. As can be seen from this figure, the MAIN MENU contains the major categories of tasks performed by SPSS/PC+. The first item on the MAIN MENU is "orientation," providing a brief sketch of the MENU environment. The second item, "read or write data," refers to the tasks of data entry and definition as well as data output. The third item, "modify data or files," refers to the task of data manipulation. The various statistical analyses and graphic representations are subsumed under the fourth and fifth items of "graph data" and "analyze data." The tasks of controlling and changing standard SPSS/PC+ modes of operation are grouped under the sixth item "session control and info." The seventh item permits the user to execute DOS or other programs while within the SPSS/PC+ program. Finally, the last line, "FINISH," is an actual command to terminate an SPSS/PC+ session.

From this MAIN MENU, the user can move down the hierarchy of menus; branching off from any specific task item on the menu is another menu of commands that pertains to the performance of this task. For example, in moving to the next menu from the item of "analyze data," an item called "descriptive statistics" will be found. Then further branching off from this item of "descriptive statistics" is a third menu that lists by their keywords all the commands that calculate descriptive statistics. See Figure 5. From the item FREQUENCIES, the user can move down another menu containing the subcommands of FREQUENCIES. Generally, then, moving down the menus means moving from the general to the specifics of writing a command. The menus begin with type of tasks to be performed, followed by the commands available for its performance, and finally end with the menus specific to a command. Because of this system of branching off from an item in a menu to another menu with more items, the structure is called hierarchical. To illustrate the structure of the menu system, the three main parts of the procedural command FREQUENCIES in Figure 3 are shown in Figure 6, together with the menus under which the components are found.

2.3.3 *Operating within the Menu Mode*

When using the menus to build a command, use the following keys to move within a menu and from menu to menu and to select a command or subcommand. To indicate specific keys on the keyboard, their names are bracketed and capitalized. A + sign linking the names of two keys means to press the keys simultaneously.

Main Menu Task Group	Menu Task Subgroup	Menu Command	Menu Subcommand	Menu User Specification
Analyze data	Descriptive statistics	FREQUENCIES	/VARIABLES /BARCHART.	MAJOR LOAD

FIGURE 6

Moving within a Menu

1. Up and down arrow keys move the menu bar up and down the menus.
2. <ALT+PGDN> and <ALT+PGUP> keys scroll the text in the HELP window.

Moving from Menu to Menu

1. The right arrow key moves *one level down* to a lower-layer menu of the highlighted item.
2. The left arrow key moves *one level up* to the preceding layer of the menu.
3. The <ALT+ESC> keys allow a return to the MAIN MENU in one step from any point in the hierarchy of menus.

Pasting Items

To build a command, select the appropriate parts of the command from the menus by highlighting the items and pressing <ENTER>. The ENTER key performs the same function as the right arrow key in moving one level down the layers of menus. In addition, it pastes the highlighted items onto SCRATCH.PAD in the lower half of the screen.

2.4 REVIEW: The Text Editor

REVIEW is a full screen editor that can be used in conjunction with the MENU system. REVIEW permits the user to edit mistypings and incorrect entries and also to enter entire programs of commands and data sets without the help of the menus. After gaining more experience with SPSS/PC+, the user will appreciate the efficiency of entering the program through the REVIEW mode.

Switching between the MENU and REVIEW operating modes is done in two ways:

1. To change from MENU to REVIEW mode, press <ALT+E>.
2. To change from REVIEW to MENU mode, press <ALT+E> or <ESC>.

To determine which mode SPSS/PC+ is currently operating under, try selecting menu items or moving the cursor around in SCRATCH.PAD. If SPSS/PC+ is in REVIEW mode, the menu items cannot be selected, and if it is in MENU mode, the cursor cannot be moved around in SCRATCH.PAD.

2.4.1 The REVIEW Windows

REVIEW works with two windows separated by a line in the middle of the screen. Each window is an on-screen display area of a file: the **SPSS.LIS** file in the upper window and the **SCRATCH.PAD** file in the lower window. In SCRATCH.PAD, programs and data sets are created. The results and messages produced upon execution of a program are saved in the SPSS.LIS window. When none has been executed, the window is blank. SPSS/PC+ automatically saves the contents of SCRATCH.PAD and SPSS.LIS at the end of a session. The user can retrieve these files as long as another session has not begun.

The SPSS.LIS window is hidden behind the MENU and HELP windows. To view SPSS.LIS, the user must clear the MENU and HELP windows from the screen by pressing <ALT+M> while in MENU mode. Pressing these keys also causes a switch to REVIEW mode. To work in this window, move the cursor that normally rests in the lower window by pressing <F2>. A mini-menu appears at the bottom of the screen with three items. Place the menu bar on the item "Switch" and press <ENTER>. The cursor is moved to the upper window. Note how the label at the lower-right corner of the screen changes from SCRATCH.PAD to SPSS.LIS. To return to the lower window, press <F2> and select "Switch" again. The label at the lower-right corner of the screen changes back to SCRATCH.PAD. To return to MENU mode and restore the menu, press <ALT+M>.

Figure 7 summarizes the transfer keys from one window to another and from one operating mode to another. <ALT+E> shifts between the MENU and REVIEW operating modes and therefore working with the MENU or the SCRATCH.PAD window. <ALT+M> serves the same functions, at the same time clearing or restoring the menu window. The key <F2> moves the cursor between SPSS.LIS and SCRATCH.PAD.

2.4.2 Function Keys

REVIEW works primarily through function keys, F1 through F10. Each function key calls forth its own mini-menu at the bottom of the screen when the key is pressed. The mini-menu contains a number of items or commands associated with a specific editing or related task. In REVIEW mode the selection of a command on a mini-menu leads to its immediate execution.

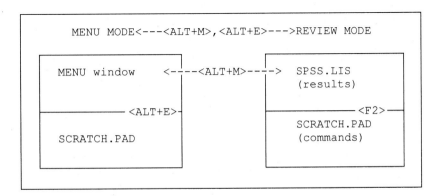

FIGURE 7

For a quick reference for the function keys, press <F1>, select "Review Help," and then press <ENTER>. The screen will display a guide to these keys. To cancel any function key command, press <ESC>.

A summary of the function and other command keys used in REVIEW is given in the accompanying table.

Function Keys	Task Areas	Items in Mini-menu
F1	Information	Review help and menus, variable and file lists, glossary
F2	Windows	Switch windows, change window size, zoom
F3	Input files	Insert file, edit different file
F4	Lines	Insert, delete, undelete
F5	Find and replace	Find text, replace text
F6	Go to	Area, output page, line in error, after last line executed
F7	Define area	Mark/unmark lines, rectangle, command
F8	Area actions	Copy, move, delete, round numbers, copy glossary entry
F9	Output file	Write area or file, delete file
F10	Execute	Run commands from cursor or marked area, exit to prompt

Motion Keys	Command
HOME	Go to the top of the screen
END	Go to the bottom of the screen
CTRL+HOME	Go to the top of the file
CTRL+END	Go to the bottom of the file
Arrow keys	Move the cursor one space left or right, one line up or down
DEL	Delete the character under the cursor
BACKSPACE	Delete the character to the left of the cursor
ENTER	Start a new line

2.5 An SPSS/PC+ Session

The reader's knowledge of the principal components of a program, the SPSS/PC+ operating modes, and the organization of SPSS/PC+ language in menu form is put to use in writing and executing a program in this section. The following are instructions for a complete SPSS/PC+ session, which consists of pasting and executing the commands in Figure 8.

2.5.1 Selecting and Pasting Commands from the Menu

Data Definition Command

1. In MENU mode with the MAIN MENU window displayed, press the down arrow key to highlight the second item on the menu, "read or write data." Then press <ENTER>.

```
DATA LIST FREE /LEVEL (A3) MAJOR UNITS GPA REASON.
BEGIN DATA.
Fr    1    18    300    2
Ju    3    15    325    2
Sen   4    15    289    4
So    1    12    255    3
END DATA.
FREQUENCIES /VARIABLES MAJOR.
```

FIGURE 8

2. The MAIN MENU disappears, and the menu "read or write data" replaces it in the menu window. Press the down arrow key to move the menu bar until it highlights "DATA LIST"; then press <ENTER>. The command "DATA LIST" is pasted onto the SCRATCH.PAD window. At the same time, the menu window changes to that of the DATA LIST.

3. Within the DATA LIST MENU, move the menu bar to "FREE/"; then press <ENTER>. "FREE/" is also pasted onto SCRATCH.PAD.

4. When the FREE MENU appears, place the menu bar at "variables"; then press <ENTER>. A *typing window* appears beneath the menu and the cursor is now located in this window. Type the information, in this case, LEVEL; then press <ENTER>.

5. Within the same FREE MENU, move the menu bar down to "(A)"; then press <ENTER>. Note the pasting of "(A)" onto SCRATCH.PAD and the reappearance of the typing window for specifying the maximum number of columns the coding will take. Type 3; then press <ENTER>. The number "3" is pasted after "A" within the parentheses.

6. Within the same FREE MENU, move the menu bar up to "variables" again; then press <ENTER>. Type the following in the typing window that appears: MAJOR UNITS GPA REASON, and press <ENTER>. The numerical variables are pasted onto SCRATCH.PAD. If an attempt is made to move the cursor, it would fail, since SPSS/PC+ is in MENU mode. Suppose a mistake is made and RESON rather than REASON is entered. To edit the error, change to REVIEW mode by pressing <ALT+E>. Now move the cursor so that it sits on top of the letter "S." Then press the letter "A" and note its addition to complete the variable name REASON. Other additions and deletions can be made while in REVIEW mode. After editing, move the cursor back to where it was before entering the REVIEW mode and press <ALT+E> to reenter MENU mode.

Begin and End Data Command

7. Since BEGIN DATA is a command and not a subcommand subsumed under the DATA LIST command, it is necessary to go back up the hierarchy of menus. Press the left arrow key until the READ OR WRITE DATA MENU is reached.

8. With the menu bar highlighting "BEGIN DATA," press <ENTER>. The commands "BEGIN DATA" as well as "END DATA" are now pasted onto SCRATCH.PAD, with a blank line in between.

9. Type a data line, then press <ENTER>. Note that data are typed directly onto the blank line between the BEGIN DATA and END DATA commands. Pressing <ENTER> provides a new blank data line and at the same time moves the cursor to that line. Type the second line, the third, and so on, until the last line of data is entered in the same way. After the last data line is entered, press <ESC>, which retrieves the MAIN MENU.

Frequencies Command

10. Within the MAIN MENU, move the menu bar to the item "analyze data"; then press <ENTER>.

11. When the ANALYZE DATA MENU appears, the menu bar is resting on "descriptive statistics." Press <ENTER>. Nothing is pasted onto SCRATCH.PAD because this is not a command keyword.

12. When the DESCRIPTIVE STATISTICS MENU appears, the menu bar is resting on "FREQUENCIES." Press <ENTER>. The command keyword is pasted onto SCRATCH.PAD.

13. When the FREQUENCIES MENU appears, move the menu bar to "~/VARIABLES"; then press <ENTER>. The symbol ~ indicates that this item must be included to complete the command.

14. With the menu bar still resting on "~/VARIABLES," press <ALT+T> to get the typing window. Type MAJOR in the typing window; then press <ENTER>. MAJOR is pasted after VARIABLES in SCRATCH.PAD.

2.5.2 Correcting Mistakes

If at any point a typing error is pasted onto SCRATCH.PAD, the mistake can be corrected by activating REVIEW as described previously. Press <ALT+E> to enter the REVIEW mode, and move the cursor around with the arrow keys to edit the errors in the SCRATCH.PAD window. A common source of error is pasting unnecessary commands or subcommands by incorrectly pressing <ENTER> instead of the right or left arrow.

2.5.3 Executing Commands

To execute a program:

1. Press <ALT+E> in MENU mode to enter REVIEW.

2. Move the cursor to the DATA LIST command by pressing the up arrow key repeatedly or by pressing <CTRL+HOME> to move the cursor in one step to the beginning of the commands in SCRATCH.PAD.

3. Press <F10>, and a mini-menu appears at the bottom of the screen. Select "Run from cursor" from this menu; then press <ENTER>. This command

submits for execution all the SPSS/PC+ commands from the line onward on which the cursor is placed.

2.5.4 Displaying the Output

Upon execution of commands, the screen clears. First the commands and then the results of the procedure FREQUENCIES appear on screen. If the results are too long to be presented in one screen, a message **MORE** will appear in the upper-right corner of the screen. Press <SPACEBAR> and the computer will display the next screen of results.

After displaying all the results, the computer returns to the MAIN MENU with the MENU mode operative. The SPSS/PC+ commands pasted in SCRATCH.PAD remain as before. The results that have been displayed are now stored in SPSS.LIS.

If there are errors in the program, the computer will give error messages. Correct the mistakes and resubmit the program.

2.5.5 Exiting SPSS/PC+

1. Return to the MAIN MENU, if necessary, by pressing <ESC> or the left arrow key.
2. Select the command "FINISH" from the menu and paste it onto SCRATCH.PAD.
3. Press <F10> to display its mini-menu at the bottom of the screen.
4. Select the command "Run from cursor" from the mini-menu, and press <ENTER>.
5. The computer exits SPSS/PC+ into the DOS, the operating system.

2.5.6 Printing the Output

The output can be printed while in SPSS/PC+ or in DOS. If the latter method is used, exit SPSS/PC+ first. Then use the DOS command PRINT to print the SPSS.LIS file, which contains the output of the procedural commands. Since the contents of the SPSS.LIS file will be replaced by new results when SPSS/PC+ is invoked again, it is necessary to copy SPSS.LIS to another file to keep it permanently. Use the DOS command, COPY, to do this.

Within the SPSS/PC+ environment the SET command allows the output to be printed. Insert the **SET** command at the beginning of the program after all errors have been removed from the program as follows: SET /PRINTER ON. SET is an operation control command and is found under the SESSION CONTROL & INFO MENU. After selecting the command keyword "SET," highlight "output" on the SET MENU and press <ENTER>. Within the OUTPUT MENU, select the "PRINTER" subcommand. The PRINTER MENU consists of two items only, "ON" and "OFF." Select "ON."

SECTION 3: THE MAINFRAME SPSS

3.1 Syntax

Compared to SPSS/PC+, the mainframe SPSS offers more statistical procedures and data transformation facilities and can handle more complex file structures, such as a nested file. However, the basic language and syntax are the same for the two versions. Every SPSS command begins in column 1. Subcommands and keywords can continue for as many lines as necessary. All continuation lines are indented one or more columns. An input line is usually less than 80 characters long, although the length may vary by type of computer and operating system.

3.2 Operating Modes

Like SPSS/PC+, SPSS also has three operating modes: the menu, the interactive, and the editor modes. The menu-driven mode for writing and executing commands is available under the SPSS manager interface. The interactive mode is provided when the user executes the system command, SPSS. Upon execution of this command, a prompt "SPSS>" appears on the screen so that the user can enter a command.

The third mode is most often used by practitioners of SPSS. It involves using an editor specific to the operating system, such as EDIT/EDT or FSE, to write a series of SPSS commands. These commands are saved as a command file under a name with the suffix "SPS." Data lines are entered and saved along with the commands or are written and saved separately as an external file using the editor. The command file with the data or with an external data file is submitted for a batch execution as follows:

```
SPSS command file.SPS /OUTPUT = output file.LIS
```

The subcommand OUTPUT after the slash indicates the name of the file, which contains the output. This file can be printed or displayed by using the editor. Without this subcommand, the output will be displayed on the monitor directly.

3.3 Commands and Subcommands

Some major differences between SPSS and SPSS/PC+ are summarized next. The command delimiter, a period, is necessary after each command in SPSS/PC+, but is optional in SPSS. File names are enclosed in apostrophes or quotation marks in SPSS/PC+, but in SPSS they may appear without any delimiter. SPSS/PC+ uses the OPTIONS subcommand to control the operation and output of some procedures; SPSS does not have this subcommand, but has equivalent ones. For example, for the DESCRIPTIVES command, the following table shows (1) some of the corresponding subcommands in SPSS of the OPTIONS subcommand in SPSS/PC+, (2) a subcommand in SPSS that does not have an equivalent in SPSS/PC+, and (3) vice versa:

SPSS/PC+	SPSS
OPTION 1	MISSING INCLUDE
OPTION 3	SAVE
(none)	FORMAT INDEX
OPTION 8	(none)

Another difference is that SPSS uses keywords to identify the statistic requested under the STATISTICS subcommand, whereas SPSS/PC+ usually uses a number. For example, under the DESCRIPTIVES command:

SPSS/PC+	SPSS
STATISTICS=1 5	STATISTICS=MEAN STDDEV

SECTION 4: CONCLUSION

4.1 SPSS SESSIONS within the Text

Within the text, the students will find sections in most chapters devoted to the use of SPSS; these are labeled SPSS Sessions. A model program is usually given in the section for the performance of a specific analysis. These programs are based on SPSS/PC+. In cases where there is a difference between the microcomputer and the mainframe version, we specifically denote how the SPSS command differs from the SPSS/PC+ command. Unless there is a need to differentiate between the two versions, we use the term SPSS to refer to both versions. To learn SPSS, it is important to enter and execute these model programs. Although the program in Section 2 is built through the MENU mode, the model programs in the SPSS Sessions could be entered in either the MENU or REVIEW mode when using SPSS/PC+. When using SPSS, we suggest using an editor and submitting the commands in a batch.

4.2 Data Sets and Codebooks Stored in the Diskette

The diskette, which comes with the text, contains two data files named GSS.DAT and CITY.DAT. They are to be used for the SPSS Exercises in various chapters. Codebooks, GSS.COD and CITY.COD, also included in the diskette, provide the names, locations, and descriptions of the variables in the data set. Finally, there is an explanatory file, stored under READ.ME, on how to set up these files for use in SPSS/PC+. Students learning SPSS will have to ask their instructor to help them import and set up these files in the mainframe before they can be used.

Tables

TABLE A Areas under the Normal Curve

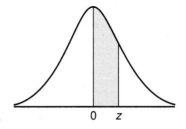

z	.00	.01	.02	.03	.04	.05	.06	.07	.08	.09
0.0	.0000	.0040	.0080	.0120	.0159	.0199	.0239	.0279	.0319	.0359
0.1	.0398	.0438	.0478	.0517	.0557	.0596	.0636	.0675	.0714	.0753
0.2	.0793	.0832	.0871	.0910	.0948	.0987	.1026	.1064	.1103	.1141
0.3	.1179	.1217	.1255	.1293	.1331	.1368	.1406	.1443	.1480	.1517
0.4	.1554	.1591	.1628	.1664	.1700	.1736	.1772	.1808	.1844	.1879
0.5	.1915	.1950	.1985	.2019	.2054	.2088	.2123	.2157	.2190	.2224
0.6	.2257	.2291	.2324	.2357	.2389	.2422	.2454	.2486	.2518	.2549
0.7	.2580	.2612	.2642	.2673	.2704	.2734	.2764	.2794	.2823	.2852
0.8	.2881	.2910	.2939	.2967	.2995	.3023	.3051	.3078	.3106	.3133
0.9	.3159	.3186	.3212	.3238	.3264	.3289	.3315	.3340	.3365	.3389
1.0	.3413	.3438	.3461	.3485	.3508	.3531	.3554	.3577	.3599	.3621
1.1	.3643	.3665	.3686	.3718	.3729	.3749	.3770	.3790	.3810	.3830
1.2	.3849	.3869	.3888	.3907	.3925	.3944	.3962	.3980	.3997	.4015
1.3	.4032	.4049	.4066	.4083	.4099	.4115	.4131	.4147	.4162	.4177
1.4	.4192	.4207	.4222	.4236	.4251	.4265	.4279	.4292	.4306	.4319
1.5	.4332	.4345	.4357	.4370	.4382	.4394	.4406	.4418	.4430	.4441
1.6	.4452	.4463	.4474	.4485	.4495	.4505	.4515	.4525	.4535	.4545
1.7	.4554	.4564	.4573	.4582	.4591	.4599	.4608	.4616	.4625	.4633
1.8	.4641	.4649	.4656	.4664	.4671	.4678	.4686	.4693	.4699	.4706
1.9	.4713	.4719	.4726	.4732	.4738	.4744	.4750	.4758	.4762	.4767

Continued

TABLE A *Continued*

z	.00	.01	.02	.03	.04	.05	.06	.07	.08	.09
2.0	.4772	.4778	.4783	.4788	.4793	.4798	.4803	.4808	.4812	.4817
2.1	.4821	.4826	.4830	.4834	.4838	.4842	.4846	.4850	.4854	.4857
2.2	.4861	.4865	.4868	.4871	.4875	.4878	.4881	.4884	.4887	.4890
2.3	.4893	.4896	.4898	.4901	.4904	.4906	.4909	.4911	.4913	.4916
2.4	.4918	.4920	.4922	.4925	.4927	.4929	.4931	.4932	.4934	.4936
2.5	.4938	.4940	.4941	.4943	.4945	.4946	.4948	.4949	.4951	.4952
2.6	.4953	.4955	.4956	.4957	.4959	.4960	.4961	.4962	.4963	.4964
2.7	.4965	.4966	.4967	.4968	.4969	.4970	.4971	.4972	.4973	.4974
2.8	.4974	.4975	.4976	.4977	.4977	.4978	.4979	.4980	.4980	.4981
2.9	.4981	.4982	.4983	.4984	.4984	.4984	.4985	.4985	.4986	.4986
3.0	.49865	.4987	.4987	.4988	.4988	.4988	.4989	.4989	.4989	.4990
3.1	.49900	.4991	.4991	.4991	.4992	.4992	.4992	.4992	.4993	.4993
3.2	.4993129									
3.3	.4995166									
3.4	.4996631									
3.5	.4997674									

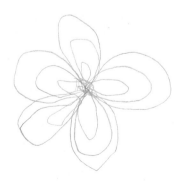

TABLE B Critical Values of *t*

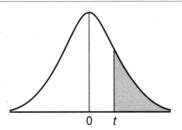

	Level of Significance for Two-tailed Test					
	.10	.05	.025	.01	.005	.0005
	Level of Significance for One-tailed Test					
df	.20	.10	.05	.02	.01	.001
1	3.078	6.314	12.706	31.821	63.657	636.619
2	1.886	2.920	4.303	6.965	9.925	31.598
3	1.638	2.353	3.182	4.541	5.841	12.941
4	1.533	2.132	2.776	3.747	4.604	8.610
5	1.476	2.015	2.571	3.365	4.032	6.859
6	1.440	1.943	2.447	3.143	3.707	5.959
7	1.415	1.895	2.365	2.998	3.499	5.405
8	1.397	1.860	2.306	2.896	3.355	5.041
9	1.383	1.833	2.262	2.821	3.250	4.781
10	1.372	1.812	2.228	2.764	3.169	4.587
11	1.363	1.796	2.201	2.718	3.106	4.437
12	1.356	1.782	2.179	2.681	3.055	4.318
13	1.350	1.771	2.160	2.650	3.012	4.221
14	1.345	1.761	2.145	2.624	2.977	4.140
15	1.341	1.753	2.131	2.602	2.947	4.073
16	1.337	1.746	2.120	2.583	2.921	4.015
17	1.333	1.740	2.110	2.567	2.898	3.965
18	1.330	1.734	2.101	2.552	2.878	3.922
19	1.328	1.729	2.093	2.539	2.861	3.883
20	1.325	1.725	2.086	2.528	2.845	3.850
21	1.323	1.721	2.080	2.518	2.831	3.819
22	1.321	1.717	2.074	2.508	2.819	3.792
23	1.319	1.714	2.069	2.500	2.807	3.767
24	1.318	1.711	2.064	2.492	2.797	3.745
25	1.316	1.708	2.060	2.485	2.787	3.725
26	1.315	1.706	2.056	2.479	2.779	3.707
27	1.314	1.703	2.052	2.473	2.771	3.690
28	1.313	1.701	2.048	2.467	2.763	3.674
29	1.311	1.699	2.045	2.462	2.756	3.659
30	1.310	1.697	2.042	2.457	2.750	3.646
40	1.303	1.684	2.021	2.423	2.704	3.551
60	1.296	1.671	2.000	2.390	2.660	3.460
120	1.289	1.658	1.980	2.358	2.617	3.373
∞	1.282	1.645	1.960	2.326	2.576	3.291

Source: Abridged Table 3 of R. A. Fisher and F. Yates, *Statistical Tables for Biological, Agricultural and Medical Research* published by Longman Group UK Ltd., London (1974), 6th ed. (previously published by Oliver & Boyd Ltd., Edinburgh), and by permission of the authors and publishers.

TABLE C Critical Values of Chi Square

Sismifiganue

p df	0.995	0.990	0.975	0.950	0.900	0.750	0.500
1	$392,704.10^{-10}$	$157,088.10^{-9}$	$982,069.10^{-9}$	$393,214.10^{-8}$	0.0157908	0.1015308	0.454936
2	0.0100251	0.0201007	0.0506356	0.102587	0.210721	0.575364	1.38629
3	0.0717218	0.114832	0.215795	0.351846	0.584374	1.212534	2.36597
4	0.206989	0.297109	0.484419	0.710723	1.063623	1.92256	3.35669
5	0.411742	0.554298	0.831212	1.145476	1.61031	2.67460	4.35146
6	0.675727	0.872090	1.23734	1.63538	2.20413	3.45460	5.34812
7	0.989256	1.239043	1.68987	2.16735	2.83311	4.25485	6.34581
8	1.34441	1.64650	2.17973	2.73264	3.48954	5.07064	7.34412
9	1.73493	2.08790	2.70039	3.32511	4.16816	5.89883	8.34283
10	2.15586	2.55821	3.24697	3.94030	4.86518	6.73720	9.34182
11	2.60322	3.05348	3.81575	4.57481	5.57778	7.58414	10.3410
12	3.07382	3.57057	4.40379	5.22603	6.30380	8.43842	11.3403
13	3.56503	4.10692	5.00875	5.89186	7.04150	9.29907	12.3398
14	4.07467	4.66043	5.62873	6.57063	7.78953	10.1653	13.3393
15	4.60092	5.22935	6.26214	7.26094	8.54676	11.0365	14.3389
16	5.14221	5.81221	6.90766	7.96165	9.31224	11.9122	15.3385
17	5.69722	6.40776	7.56419	8.67176	10.0852	12.7919	16.3382
18	6.26480	7.01491	8.23075	9.39046	10.8649	13.6753	17.3379
19	6.84397	7.63273	8.90652	10.1170	11.6509	14.5620	18.3377
20	7.43384	8.26040	9.59078	10.8508	12.4426	15.4518	19.3374
21	8.03365	8.89720	10.28293	11.5913	13.2396	16.3444	20.3372
22	8.64272	9.54249	10.9823	12.3380	14.0415	17.2396	21.3370
23	9.26043	10.19567	11.6886	13.0905	14.8480	18.1373	22.3369
24	9.88623	10.8564	12.4012	13.8484	15.6587	19.0373	23.3367
25	10.5197	11.5240	13.1197	14.6114	16.4734	19.9393	24.3366
26	11.1602	12.1981	13.8439	15.3702	17.2919	20.8434	25.3365
27	11.8076	12.8785	14.5734	16.1514	18.1139	21.7494	26.3363
28	12.4613	13.5647	15.3079	16.9279	18.9392	22.6572	27.3362
29	13.1211	14.2565	16.0471	17.7084	19.7677	23.5666	28.3361
30	13.7867	14.9535	16.7908	18.4927	20.5992	24.4776	29.3360
40	20.7065	22.1643	24.4330	26.5093	29.0505	33.6603	39.3353
50	27.9907	29.7067	32.3574	34.7643	37.6886	42.9421	49.3349
60	35.5345	37.4849	40.4817	43.1880	46.4589	52.2938	59.3347
70	43.2752	45.4417	48.7576	51.7393	55.3289	61.6983	69.3345
80	51.1719	53.5401	57.1532	60.3915	64.2778	71.1445	79.3343
90	59.1963	61.7541	65.6466	69.1260	73.2911	80.6247	89.3342
100	67.3276	70.0649	74.2219	77.9295	82.3581	90.1332	99.3341
X	−2.5758	−2.3263	−1.9600	−1.6449	−1.2816	−0.6745	0.0000

TABLE C *(Continued)*

df \ p	0.250	0.100	0.050	0.025	0.010	0.005	0.001
1	1.32330	2.70554	3.84146	5.02389	6.63490	7.87944	10.828
2	2.77259	4.60517	5.99146	7.37776	9.21034	10.5966	13.816
3	4.10834	6.25139	7.81473	9.34840	11.3449	12.8382	16.266
4	5.38527	7.77944	9.48773	11.1433	13.2767	14.8603	18.467
5	6.62568	9.23636	11.0705	12.8325	15.0863	16.7496	20.515
6	7.84080	10.6446	12.5916	14.4494	16.8119	18.5476	22.458
7	9.03715	12.0170	14.0671	16.0128	18.4753	20.2777	24.322
8	10.2189	13.3616	15.5073	17.5345	20.0902	21.9550	26.125
9	11.3888	14.6837	16.9190	19.0228	21.6660	23.5894	27.877
10	12.5489	15.9872	18.3070	20.4832	23.2093	25.1882	29.588
11	13.7007	17.2750	19.6761	21.9200	24.7250	26.7568	31.264
12	14.8454	18.5493	21.0261	23.3367	26.2170	28.2995	32.909
13	15.9839	19.8119	22.3620	24.7356	27.6882	29.8195	34.528
14	17.1169	21.0641	23.6848	26.1189	29.1412	31.3194	36.123
15	18.2451	22.3071	24.9958	27.4884	30.5779	32.8013	37.697
16	19.3689	23.5418	26.2962	28.8454	31.9999	34.2672	39.252
17	20.4887	24.7690	27.5871	30.1910	33.4087	35.7185	40.790
18	21.6049	25.9894	28.8693	31.5264	34.8053	37.1565	42.312
19	22.7178	27.2036	30.1435	32.8523	36.1909	38.5823	43.820
20	23.8277	28.4120	31.4104	34.1696	37.5662	39.9968	45.315
21	24.9348	29.6151	32.6706	35.4789	38.9322	41.4011	46.797
22	26.0393	30.8133	33.9244	36.7807	40.2894	42.7957	48.268
23	27.1413	32.0069	35.1725	38.0756	41.6384	44.1813	49.728
24	28.2412	33.1962	36.4150	39.3641	42.9798	45.5585	51.179
25	29.3389	34.3816	37.6525	40.6465	44.3141	46.9279	52.618
26	30.4346	35.5632	38.8851	41.9232	45.6417	48.2899	54.052
27	31.5284	36.7412	40.1133	43.1945	46.9629	49.5449	55.476
28	32.6205	37.9159	41.3371	44.4608	48.2782	50.9934	56.892
29	33.7109	39.0875	42.5570	45.7223	49.5879	52.3356	58.301
30	34.7997	40.2560	43.7730	46.9792	50.8922	53.6720	59.703
40	45.6160	51.8051	55.7585	59.3417	63.6907	66.7660	73.402
50	56.3336	63.1671	67.5048	71.4202	76.1539	79.4900	86.661
60	66.9815	74.3970	79.0819	83.2977	88.3794	91.9517	99.607
70	77.5767	85.5270	90.5312	95.0232	100.425	104.215	112.317
80	88.1303	96.5782	101.879	106.629	112.329	116.321	124.839
90	98.6499	107.565	113.145	118.136	124.116	128.299	137.208
100	109.141	118.498	124.342	129.561	135.807	140.169	149.449
X	+0.6745	+1.2816	+1.6449	+1.9600	+2.3263	+2.5758	+3.0902

Source: Table 8 of E. S. Pearson and H. O. Hartley (eds.), *Biometrika Tables for Statisticians*, Vol. 1 (ed. 3), London (1966), with the kind permission of the Trustees of Biometrika.

TABLE D   Critical Values of *D* in the Kolmogorov–Smirnov One-sample Test

Sample Size (N)	Level of Significance for *D*				
	.20	.15	.10	.05	.01
1	.900	.925	.950	.975	.995
2	.684	.726	.776	.842	.929
3	.565	.597	.642	.708	.828
4	.494	.525	.564	.624	.733
5	.446	.474	.510	.565	.669
6	.410	.436	.470	.521	.618
7	.381	.405	.438	.486	.577
8	.358	.381	.411	.457	.543
9	.339	.360	.388	.432	.514
10	.322	.342	.368	.410	.400
11	.307	.326	.352	.391	.408
12	.295	.313	.338	.375	.450
13	.284	.302	.325	.361	.433
14	.274	.292	.314	.349	.418
15	.266	.283	.304	.338	.404
16	.258	.274	.295	.328	.392
17	.250	.266	.286	.318	.381
18	.244	.259	.278	.309	.371
19	.237	.252	.272	.301	.363
20	.231	.246	.264	.294	.356
25	.21	.22	.24	.27	.32
30	.19	.20	.22	.24	.29
35	.18	.19	.21	.23	.27
Over 35	$\dfrac{1.07}{\sqrt{N}}$	$\dfrac{1.14}{\sqrt{N}}$	$\dfrac{1.22}{\sqrt{N}}$	$\dfrac{1.36}{\sqrt{N}}$	$\dfrac{1.63}{\sqrt{N}}$

Source: Table 1 of F. J. Massey, Jr., "The Kolmogorov–Smirnov Test for Goodness of Fit," *Journal of the American Statistical Association* vol. 46, 1951. Reprinted with permission from the *Journal of the American Statistical Association*. Copyright 1951 by American Statistical Association. All rights reserved.

TABLE E Probabilities of U in the Mann–Whitney Test, N_2 of 3 to 8

$N_2 = 3$

U \ N_1	1	2	3
0	.250	.100	.050
1	.500	.200	.100
2	.750	.400	.200
3		.600	.350
4			.500
5			.650

$N_2 = 4$

U \ N_1	1	2	3	4
0	.200	.067	.028	0.14
1	.400	.133	.057	.029
2	.600	.267	.114	.057
3		.400	.200	.100
4		.600	.314	.171
5			.429	.243
6			.571	.343
7				.443
8				.557

$N_2 = 5$

U \ N_1	1	2	3	4	5
0	.167	.047	.018	.008	.004
1	.333	.095	.036	.016	.008
2	.500	.190	.071	.032	.016
3	.667	.286	.125	.056	.028
4		.429	.196	.095	.048
5		.571	.286	.143	.075
6			.393	.206	.111
7			.500	.278	.155
8			.607	.365	.210
9				.452	.274
10				.548	.345
11					.421
12					.500
13					.579

$N_2 = 6$

U \ N_1	1	2	3	4	5	6
0	.143	.036	.012	.005	.002	.001
1	.286	.071	.024	.010	.004	.002
2	.428	.143	.048	.019	.009	.004
3	.571	.214	.083	.033	.015	.008
4		.321	.131	.057	.026	.013
5		.429	.190	.086	.041	.021
6		.571	.274	.129	.063	.032
7			.357	.176	.089	.047
8			.452	.238	.123	.066
9			.548	.305	.165	.090
10				.381	.214	.120
11				.457	.268	.155
12				.545	.331	.197
13					.396	.242
14					.465	.294
15					.535	.350
16						.409
17						.469
18						.531

Source: Table I of H. B. Mann and D. B. Whitney, "On a Test of Whether One of Two Random Variables Is Stochastically Larger Than the Other," *Annals of Mathematical Statistics* 18 (1947): 52–54, with the kind permission of the authors and the Institute of Mathematical Statistics.

Continued

TABLE E *(Continued)*

				$N_2 = 7$			
N_1 $\backslash$ U	1	2	3	4	5	6	7
0	.125	.028	.008	.003	.001	.001	.000
1	.250	.056	.017	.006	.003	.001	.001
2	.375	.111	.033	.012	.005	.002	.001
3	.500	.167	.058	.021	.009	.004	.002
4	.625	.250	.092	.036	.015	.007	.003
5		.333	.133	.055	.024	.011	.006
6		.444	.192	.082	.037	.017	.009
7		.556	.258	.115	.053	.026	.013
8			.333	.158	.074	.037	.019
9			.417	.206	.101	.051	.027
10			.500	.264	.134	.069	.036
11			.583	.324	.172	.090	.049
12				.394	.216	.117	.064
13				.464	.265	.147	.082
14				.538	.319	.183	.104
15					.378	.223	.130
16					.438	.267	.159
17					.500	.314	.191
18					.562	.365	.228
19						.418	.267
20						.473	.310
21						.527	.355
22							.402
23							.451
24							.500
25							.549

Continued

TABLE E *(Continued)*

<table>
<tr><td colspan="9" align="center">$N_2 = 8$</td></tr>
<tr><td>N_1
U</td><td>1</td><td>2</td><td>3</td><td>4</td><td>5</td><td>6</td><td>7</td><td>8</td></tr>
<tr><td>0</td><td>.111</td><td>.022</td><td>.006</td><td>.002</td><td>.001</td><td>.000</td><td>.000</td><td>.000</td></tr>
<tr><td>1</td><td>.222</td><td>.044</td><td>.012</td><td>.004</td><td>.002</td><td>.001</td><td>.000</td><td>.000</td></tr>
<tr><td>2</td><td>.333</td><td>.089</td><td>.024</td><td>.008</td><td>.003</td><td>.001</td><td>.001</td><td>.000</td></tr>
<tr><td>3</td><td>.444</td><td>.133</td><td>.042</td><td>.014</td><td>.005</td><td>.002</td><td>.001</td><td>.001</td></tr>
<tr><td>4</td><td>.556</td><td>.200</td><td>.067</td><td>.024</td><td>.009</td><td>.004</td><td>.002</td><td>.001</td></tr>
<tr><td>5</td><td></td><td>.267</td><td>.097</td><td>.036</td><td>.015</td><td>.006</td><td>.003</td><td>.001</td></tr>
<tr><td>6</td><td></td><td>.356</td><td>.139</td><td>.055</td><td>.023</td><td>.010</td><td>.005</td><td>.002</td></tr>
<tr><td>7</td><td></td><td>.444</td><td>.188</td><td>.077</td><td>.033</td><td>.015</td><td>.007</td><td>.003</td></tr>
<tr><td>8</td><td></td><td>.556</td><td>.248</td><td>.107</td><td>.047</td><td>.021</td><td>.010</td><td>.005</td></tr>
<tr><td>9</td><td></td><td></td><td>.315</td><td>.141</td><td>.064</td><td>.030</td><td>.014</td><td>.007</td></tr>
<tr><td>10</td><td></td><td></td><td>.387</td><td>.184</td><td>.085</td><td>.041</td><td>.020</td><td>.010</td></tr>
<tr><td>11</td><td></td><td></td><td>.461</td><td>.230</td><td>.111</td><td>.054</td><td>.027</td><td>.014</td></tr>
<tr><td>12</td><td></td><td></td><td>.539</td><td>.285</td><td>.142</td><td>.071</td><td>.036</td><td>.019</td></tr>
<tr><td>13</td><td></td><td></td><td></td><td>.341</td><td>.177</td><td>.091</td><td>.047</td><td>.025</td></tr>
<tr><td>14</td><td></td><td></td><td></td><td>.404</td><td>.217</td><td>.114</td><td>.060</td><td>.032</td></tr>
<tr><td>15</td><td></td><td></td><td></td><td>.467</td><td>.262</td><td>.141</td><td>.076</td><td>.041</td></tr>
<tr><td>16</td><td></td><td></td><td></td><td>.533</td><td>.311</td><td>.172</td><td>.095</td><td>.052</td></tr>
<tr><td>17</td><td></td><td></td><td></td><td></td><td>.362</td><td>.207</td><td>.116</td><td>.065</td></tr>
<tr><td>18</td><td></td><td></td><td></td><td></td><td>.416</td><td>.245</td><td>.140</td><td>.080</td></tr>
<tr><td>19</td><td></td><td></td><td></td><td></td><td>.472</td><td>.286</td><td>.168</td><td>.097</td></tr>
<tr><td>20</td><td></td><td></td><td></td><td></td><td>.528</td><td>.331</td><td>.198</td><td>.117</td></tr>
<tr><td>21</td><td></td><td></td><td></td><td></td><td></td><td>.377</td><td>.232</td><td>.139</td></tr>
<tr><td>22</td><td></td><td></td><td></td><td></td><td></td><td>.426</td><td>.268</td><td>.164</td></tr>
<tr><td>23</td><td></td><td></td><td></td><td></td><td></td><td>.475</td><td>.306</td><td>.191</td></tr>
<tr><td>24</td><td></td><td></td><td></td><td></td><td></td><td>.525</td><td>.347</td><td>.221</td></tr>
<tr><td>25</td><td></td><td></td><td></td><td></td><td></td><td></td><td>.389</td><td>.253</td></tr>
<tr><td>26</td><td></td><td></td><td></td><td></td><td></td><td></td><td>.433</td><td>.287</td></tr>
<tr><td>27</td><td></td><td></td><td></td><td></td><td></td><td></td><td>.478</td><td>.323</td></tr>
<tr><td>28</td><td></td><td></td><td></td><td></td><td></td><td></td><td>.522</td><td>.360</td></tr>
<tr><td>29</td><td></td><td></td><td></td><td></td><td></td><td></td><td></td><td>.399</td></tr>
<tr><td>30</td><td></td><td></td><td></td><td></td><td></td><td></td><td></td><td>.439</td></tr>
<tr><td>31</td><td></td><td></td><td></td><td></td><td></td><td></td><td></td><td>.480</td></tr>
<tr><td>32</td><td></td><td></td><td></td><td></td><td></td><td></td><td></td><td>.520</td></tr>
</table>

TABLE F Critical Values of U in the Mann–Whitney Test, N_2 of 9 to 20

Critical values of U at $\alpha = .001$ with direction predicted or at $\alpha = .002$ with direction not predicted

N_1 \ N_2	9	10	11	12	13	14	15	16	17	18	19	20
1												
2												
3									0	0	0	0
4		0	0	0	1	1	1	2	2	3	3	3
5	1	1	2	2	3	3	4	5	5	6	7	7
6	2	3	4	4	5	6	7	8	9	10	11	12
7	3	5	6	7	8	9	10	11	13	14	15	16
8	5	6	8	9	11	12	14	15	17	18	20	21
9	7	8	10	12	14	15	17	19	21	23	25	26
10	8	10	12	14	17	19	21	23	25	27	29	32
11	10	12	15	17	20	22	24	27	29	32	34	37
12	12	14	17	20	23	25	28	31	34	37	40	42
13	14	17	20	23	26	29	32	35	38	42	45	48
14	15	19	22	25	29	32	36	39	43	46	50	54
15	17	21	24	28	32	36	40	43	47	51	55	59
16	19	23	27	31	35	39	43	48	52	56	60	65
17	21	25	29	34	38	43	47	52	57	61	66	70
18	23	27	32	37	42	46	51	56	61	66	71	76
19	25	29	34	40	45	50	55	50	66	71	77	82
20	26	32	37	42	48	54	59	65	70	76	82	88

Critical values of U at $\alpha = .01$ with direction predicted or at $\alpha = .02$ with direction not predicted

N_1 \ N_2	9	10	11	12	13	14	15	16	17	18	19	20
1												
2					0	0	0	0	0	0	1	1
3	1	1	1	2	2	2	3	3	4	4	4	5
4	3	3	4	5	5	6	7	7	8	9	9	10
5	5	6	7	8	9	10	11	12	13	14	15	16
6	7	8	9	11	12	13	15	16	18	19	20	22
7	9	11	12	14	16	17	19	21	23	24	26	28
8	11	13	15	17	20	22	24	26	28	30	32	34
9	14	16	18	21	23	26	28	31	33	36	38	40
10	16	19	22	24	27	30	33	36	38	41	44	47
11	18	22	25	28	31	34	37	41	44	47	50	53
12	21	24	28	31	35	38	42	46	49	53	56	60
13	23	27	31	35	39	43	47	51	55	59	63	67
14	26	30	34	38	43	47	51	56	60	65	69	73
15	28	33	37	42	47	51	56	61	66	70	75	80
16	31	36	41	46	51	56	61	66	71	76	82	87
17	33	38	44	49	55	60	66	71	77	82	88	93
18	36	41	47	53	59	65	70	76	82	88	94	100
19	38	44	50	56	63	69	75	82	88	94	101	107
20	40	47	53	60	67	73	80	87	93	100	107	114

Source: Tables 1, 3, 5, and 7 of D. Auble, "Extended Tables for the Mann–Whitney Statistic," *Bulletin of the Institute of Educational Research* at Indiana University (1953), with the kind permission of the author and publisher.

TABLE F *(Continued)*

Critical values of U at $\alpha = .025$ with direction predicted or at $\alpha = .05$ with direction not predicted

N_1 \ N_2	9	10	11	12	13	14	15	16	17	18	19	20
1												
2	0	0	0	1	1	1	1	1	2	2	2	2
3	2	3	3	4	4	5	5	6	6	7	7	8
4	4	5	6	7	8	9	10	11	11	12	13	13
5	7	8	9	11	12	13	14	15	17	18	19	20
6	10	11	13	14	16	17	19	21	22	24	25	27
7	12	14	16	18	20	22	24	26	28	30	32	34
8	15	17	19	22	24	26	29	31	34	36	38	41
9	17	20	23	26	28	31	34	37	39	42	45	48
10	20	23	26	29	33	36	39	42	45	48	52	55
11	23	26	30	33	37	40	44	47	51	55	58	62
12	26	29	33	37	41	45	49	53	57	61	65	69
13	28	33	37	41	45	50	54	59	63	67	72	76
14	31	36	40	45	50	55	59	64	67	74	78	83
15	34	39	44	49	54	59	64	70	75	80	85	90
16	37	42	47	53	59	64	70	75	81	86	92	98
17	39	45	51	57	63	67	75	81	87	93	99	105
18	42	48	55	61	67	74	80	86	93	99	106	112
19	45	52	58	65	72	78	85	92	99	106	113	119
20	48	55	62	69	76	83	90	98	105	112	119	127

Critical values of U at $\alpha = .05$ with direction predicted or at $\alpha = .10$ with direction not predicted

N_1 \ N_2	9	10	11	12	13	14	15	16	17	18	19	20
1											0	0
2	1	1	1	2	2	2	3	3	3	4	4	4
3	3	4	5	5	6	7	7	8	9	9	10	11
4	6	7	8	9	10	11	12	14	15	16	17	18
5	9	11	12	13	15	16	18	19	20	22	23	25
6	12	14	16	17	19	21	23	25	26	28	30	32
7	15	17	19	21	24	26	28	30	33	35	37	39
8	18	20	23	26	28	31	33	36	39	41	44	47
9	21	24	27	30	33	36	39	42	45	48	51	54
10	24	27	31	34	37	41	44	48	51	55	58	62
11	27	31	34	38	42	46	50	54	57	61	65	69
12	30	34	38	42	47	51	55	60	64	68	72	77
13	33	37	42	47	51	56	61	65	70	75	80	84
14	36	41	46	51	56	61	66	71	77	82	87	92
15	39	44	50	55	61	66	72	77	83	88	94	100
16	42	48	54	60	65	71	77	83	89	95	101	107
17	45	51	57	64	70	77	83	89	96	102	109	115
18	48	55	61	68	75	82	88	95	102	109	116	123
19	51	58	65	72	80	87	94	101	109	116	123	130
20	54	62	60	77	84	92	100	107	115	123	130	138

TABLE G   Critical Values of *F*

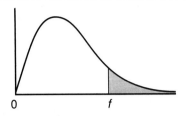

$p = .001$

df₁ df₂	1	2	3	4	5	6	8	12	24	∞
1	405,284	500,000	540,379	562,500	576,405	585,937	598,144	610,667	623,497	636,619
2	998.5	999.0	999.2	999.2	999.3	999.3	999.4	999.4	999.5	999.5
3	167.5	148.5	141.1	137.1	134.6	132.8	130.6	128.3	125.9	123.5
4	74.14	61.25	56.18	53.44	51.71	50.53	49.00	47.41	45.77	44.05
5	47.04	36.61	33.20	31.09	29.75	28.84	27.64	26.42	25.14	23.78
6	35.51	27.00	23.70	21.90	20.81	20.03	19.03	17.99	16.89	15.75
7	29.22	21.69	18.77	17.19	16.21	15.52	14.63	13.71	12.73	11.69
8	25.42	18.49	15.83	14.39	13.49	12.86	12.04	11.19	10.30	9.34
9	22.86	16.39	13.90	12.56	11.71	11.13	10.37	9.57	8.72	7.81
10	21.04	14.91	12.55	11.28	10.48	9.92	9.20	8.45	7.64	6.76
11	19.69	13.81	11.56	10.35	9.58	9.05	8.35	7.63	6.85	6.00
12	18.64	12.97	10.80	9.63	8.89	8.38	7.71	7.00	6.25	5.42
13	17.81	12.31	10.21	9.07	8.35	7.86	7.21	6.52	5.78	4.97
14	17.14	11.78	9.73	8.62	7.92	7.43	6.80	6.13	5.41	4.60
15	16.59	11.34	9.34	8.25	7.57	7.09	6.47	5.81	5.10	4.31
16	16.12	10.97	9.00	7.94	7.27	6.81	6.19	5.55	4.85	4.06
17	15.72	10.66	8.73	7.68	7.02	6.56	5.96	5.32	4.63	3.85
18	15.38	10.39	8.49	7.46	6.81	6.35	5.76	5.13	4.45	3.67
19	15.08	10.16	8.28	7.26	6.61	6.18	5.59	4.97	4.29	3.52
20	14.82	9.95	8.10	7.10	6.46	6.02	5.44	4.82	4.15	3.38
21	14.59	9.77	7.94	6.95	6.32	5.88	5.31	4.70	4.03	3.26
22	14.38	9.61	7.80	6.81	6.19	5.76	5.19	4.58	3.92	3.15
23	14.19	9.47	7.67	6.69	6.08	5.65	5.09	4.48	3.82	3.05
24	14.03	9.34	7.55	6.59	5.98	5.55	4.99	4.39	3.74	2.97
25	13.88	9.22	7.45	6.49	5.88	5.46	4.91	4.31	3.66	2.89
26	13.74	9.12	7.36	6.41	5.80	5.38	4.83	4.24	3.59	2.82
27	13.61	9.02	7.27	6.33	5.73	5.31	4.76	4.17	3.52	2.75
28	13.50	8.93	7.19	6.25	5.66	5.24	4.69	4.11	3.46	2.70
29	13.39	8.85	7.12	6.19	5.59	5.18	4.64	4.05	3.41	2.64
30	13.29	8.77	7.05	6.12	5.53	5.12	4.58	4.00	3.36	2.59
40	12.61	8.25	6.60	5.70	5.13	4.73	4.21	3.64	3.01	2.23
60	11.97	7.76	6.17	5.31	4.76	4.37	3.87	3.31	2.69	1.90
120	11.38	7.31	5.79	4.95	4.42	4.04	3.55	3.02	2.40	1.56
∞	10.83	6.91	5.42	4.62	4.10	3.74	3.27	2.71	2.13	1.00

df₁ and df₂ represent the degrees of freedom associated with the larger and smaller estimates of variance, respectively.

TABLE G (*Continued*)

df₁ df₂	1	2	3	4	5	6	8	12	24	∞
1	4,052	4,999	5,403	5,625	5,764	5,859	5,981	6,106	6,234	6,366
2	98.49	99.01	99.17	99.25	99.30	99.33	99.36	99.42	99.46	99.50
3	34.12	30.81	29.46	28.71	28.24	27.91	27.49	27.05	26.60	26.12
4	21.20	18.00	16.69	15.98	15.52	15.21	14.80	14.37	13.93	13.46
5	16.26	13.27	12.06	11.39	10.97	10.67	10.27	9.89	9.47	9.02
6	13.74	10.92	9.78	9.15	8.75	8.47	8.10	7.72	7.31	6.88
7	12.25	9.55	8.45	7.85	7.46	7.19	6.84	6.47	6.07	5.65
8	11.26	8.65	7.59	7.01	6.63	6.37	6.03	5.67	5.28	4.86
9	10.56	8.02	6.99	6.42	6.06	5.80	5.47	5.11	4.73	4.31
10	10.04	7.56	6.55	5.99	5.64	5.39	5.06	4.71	4.33	3.91
11	9.65	7.20	6.22	5.67	5.32	5.07	4.74	4.40	4.02	3.60
12	9.33	6.93	5.95	5.41	5.06	4.82	4.50	4.16	3.78	3.36
13	9.07	6.70	5.74	5.20	4.86	4.62	4.30	3.96	3.59	3.16
14	8.86	6.51	5.56	5.03	4.69	4.46	4.14	3.80	3.43	3.00
15	8.68	6.36	5.42	4.89	4.56	4.32	4.00	3.67	3.29	2.87
16	8.53	6.23	5.29	4.77	4.44	4.20	3.89	3.55	3.18	2.75
17	8.40	6.11	5.18	4.67	4.34	4.10	3.79	3.45	3.08	2.65
18	8.28	6.01	5.09	4.58	4.25	4.01	3.71	3.37	3.00	2.57
19	8.18	5.93	5.01	4.50	4.17	3.94	3.63	3.30	2.92	2.49
20	8.10	5.85	4.94	4.43	4.10	3.87	3.56	3.23	2.86	2.42
21	8.02	5.78	4.87	4.37	4.04	3.81	3.51	3.17	2.80	2.36
22	7.94	5.72	4.82	4.31	3.99	3.76	3.45	3.12	2.75	2.31
23	7.88	5.66	4.76	4.26	3.94	3.71	3.41	3.07	2.70	2.26
24	7.82	5.61	4.72	4.22	3.90	3.67	3.36	3.03	2.66	2.21
25	7.77	5.57	4.68	4.18	3.86	3.63	3.32	2.99	2.62	2.17
26	7.72	5.53	4.64	4.14	3.82	3.59	3.29	2.96	2.58	2.13
27	7.68	5.49	4.60	4.11	3.78	3.56	3.26	2.93	2.55	2.10
28	7.64	5.45	4.57	4.07	3.75	3.53	3.23	2.90	2.52	2.06
29	7.60	5.42	4.54	4.04	3.73	3.50	3.20	2.87	2.49	2.03
30	7.56	5.39	4.51	4.02	3.70	3.47	3.17	2.84	2.47	2.01
40	7.31	5.18	4.31	3.83	3.51	3.29	2.99	2.66	2.29	1.80
60	7.08	4.98	4.13	3.65	3.34	3.12	2.82	2.50	2.12	1.60
120	6.85	4.79	3.95	3.48	3.17	2.96	2.66	2.34	1.95	1.38
∞	6.64	4.60	3.78	3.32	3.02	2.80	2.51	2.18	1.79	1.00

p = .01

Continued

TABLE G   *Continued*

$p = .05$

df_1 / df_2	1	2	3	4	5	6	8	12	24	∞
1	161.4	199.5	215.7	224.6	230.2	234.0	238.9	243.9	249.0	254.3
2	18.51	19.00	19.16	19.25	19.30	19.33	19.37	19.41	19.45	19.50
3	10.13	9.55	9.28	9.12	9.01	8.94	8.84	8.74	8.64	8.53
4	7.71	6.94	6.59	6.39	6.26	6.16	6.04	5.91	5.77	5.63
5	6.61	5.79	5.41	5.19	5.05	4.95	4.82	4.68	4.53	4.36
6	5.99	5.14	4.76	4.53	4.39	4.28	4.15	4.00	3.84	3.67
7	5.59	4.74	4.35	4.12	3.97	3.87	3.73	3.57	3.41	3.23
8	5.32	4.46	4.07	3.84	3.69	3.58	3.44	3.28	3.12	2.93
9	5.12	4.26	3.86	3.63	3.48	3.37	3.23	3.07	2.90	2.71
10	4.96	4.10	3.71	3.48	3.33	3.22	3.07	2.91	2.74	2.54
11	4.84	3.98	3.59	3.36	3.20	3.09	2.95	2.79	2.61	2.40
12	4.75	3.88	3.49	3.26	3.11	3.00	2.85	2.69	2.50	2.30
13	4.67	3.80	3.41	3.18	3.02	2.92	2.77	2.60	2.42	2.21
14	4.60	3.74	3.34	3.11	2.96	2.85	2.70	2.53	2.35	2.13
15	4.54	3.68	3.29	3.06	2.90	2.79	2.64	2.48	2.29	2.07
16	4.49	3.63	3.24	3.01	2.85	2.74	2.59	2.42	2.24	2.01
17	4.45	3.59	3.20	2.96	2.81	2.70	2.55	2.38	2.19	1.96
18	4.41	3.55	3.16	2.93	2.77	2.66	2.51	2.34	2.15	1.92
19	4.38	3.52	3.13	2.90	2.74	2.63	2.48	2.31	2.11	1.88
20	4.35	3.49	3.10	2.87	2.71	2.60	2.45	2.28	2.08	1.84
21	4.32	3.47	3.07	2.84	2.68	2.57	2.42	2.25	2.05	1.81
22	4.30	3.44	3.05	2.82	2.66	2.55	2.40	2.23	2.03	1.78
23	4.28	3.42	3.03	2.80	2.64	2.53	2.38	2.20	2.00	1.76
24	4.26	3.40	3.01	2.78	2.62	2.51	2.36	2.18	1.98	1.73
25	4.24	3.38	2.99	2.76	2.60	2.49	2.34	2.16	1.96	1.71
26	4.22	3.37	2.98	2.74	2.59	2.47	2.32	2.15	1.95	1.69
27	4.21	3.35	2.96	2.73	2.57	2.46	2.30	2.13	1.93	1.67
28	4.20	3.34	2.95	2.71	2.56	2.44	2.29	2.12	1.91	1.65
29	4.18	3.33	2.93	2.70	2.54	2.43	2.28	2.10	1.90	1.64
30	4.17	3.32	2.92	2.69	2.53	2.42	2.27	2.09	1.89	1.62
40	4.08	3.23	2.84	2.61	2.45	2.34	2.18	2.00	1.79	1.51
60	4.00	3.15	2.76	2.52	2.37	2.25	2.10	1.92	1.70	1.39
120	3.92	3.07	2.68	2.45	2.29	2.17	2.02	1.83	1.61	1.25
∞	3.84	2.99	2.60	2.37	2.21	2.09	1.94	1.75	1.52	1.00

Source: Abridged from Table 5 of R. A. Fisher and F. Yates, *Statistical Tables for Biological, Agricultural and Medical Research* (1974 ed.), published by Longman Group UK Ltd., London (previously published by Oliver and Boyd Ltd., Edinburgh), and by permission of the authors and publishers.

TABLE H   Table of Random Numbers

Line/Column	(1)	(2)	(3)	(4)	(5)	(6)	(7)	(8)	(9)	(10)	(11)	(12)	(13)	(14)
1	10480	15011	01536	02011	81647	91646	69179	14194	62590	36207	20969	99570	91291	90700
2	22368	46573	25595	85393	30995	89198	27982	53402	93965	34095	52666	19174	39615	99506
3	24130	48360	22527	97265	76393	64809	15179	24830	49340	32081	30680	19655	63348	58629
4	42167	93093	06243	61680	07856	16376	39440	53537	71341	57004	00849	74917	97758	16379
5	37570	39975	81837	16656	06121	91782	60468	81305	49684	60672	14110	06927	01263	54613
6	77921	06907	11008	42751	27756	53498	18602	70659	90655	15053	21916	81825	44394	42880
7	99562	72905	56420	69994	98872	31016	71194	18738	44013	48840	63213	21069	10634	12982
8	96301	91977	05463	07972	18876	20922	94595	56869	69014	60045	18425	84903	42508	32307
9	89579	14342	63661	10281	17453	18103	57740	84378	25331	12566	58678	44947	05585	56941
10	85475	36857	43342	53988	53060	59533	38867	62300	08158	17983	16439	11458	18593	64952
11	28918	69578	88231	33276	70997	79936	56865	05859	90106	31595	01547	85590	91610	78188
12	63553	40961	48235	03427	49626	69445	18663	72695	52180	20847	12234	90511	33703	90322
13	09429	93969	52636	92737	88974	33488	36320	17617	30015	08272	84115	27156	30613	74952
14	10365	61129	87529	85689	48237	52267	67689	93394	01511	26358	85104	20285	29975	89808
15	07119	97336	71048	08178	77233	13916	47564	81056	97735	85977	29372	74461	28551	90707
16	51085	12765	51821	51259	77452	16308	60756	92144	49442	53900	70960	63990	75601	40719
17	02368	21382	52404	60268	89368	19885	55322	44819	01188	65255	64835	44919	05944	55157
18	01011	54092	33362	94904	31273	04146	18594	29852	71585	85030	51132	01915	92747	64951
19	52162	53916	46369	58586	23216	14513	83149	98736	23495	64350	94738	17752	35156	35749
20	07056	97628	33787	09998	42698	06691	76988	13602	51851	46104	88916	19509	25625	58104
21	48663	91245	85828	14346	09172	30168	90229	04734	59193	22178	30421	61666	99904	32812
22	54164	58492	22421	74103	47070	25306	76468	26384	58151	06646	21524	15227	96909	44592
23	32639	32363	05597	24200	13363	38005	94342	28728	35806	06912	17012	64161	18296	22851
24	29334	27001	87637	87308	58731	00256	45834	15398	46557	41135	10367	07684	36188	18510
25	02488	33062	28834	07351	19731	92420	60952	61280	50001	67658	32586	86679	50720	94953
26	81525	72295	04839	96423	24878	82651	66566	14778	76797	14780	13300	87074	79666	95725
27	29676	20591	68086	26432	46901	20849	89768	81536	86645	12659	92259	57102	80428	25280
28	00742	57392	39064	66432	84673	40027	32832	61362	98947	96067	64760	64584	96096	98253
29	05366	04213	25669	26422	44407	44048	37937	63904	45766	66134	75470	66520	34693	90449
30	91921	26418	64117	94305	26766	25940	39972	22209	71500	64568	91402	42416	07844	69618
31	00582	04711	87917	77341	42206	35126	74087	99547	81817	42607	43808	76655	62028	76630
32	00725	69884	62797	56170	86324	88072	76222	36086	84637	93161	76038	65855	77919	88006
33	69011	65797	95876	55293	18988	27354	26575	08625	40801	59920	29841	80150	12777	48501
34	25976	57948	29888	88604	69717	48708	18912	82271	65424	69774	33611	54262	85963	03547
35	09763	83473	73577	12908	30883	18317	28290	35797	05998	41688	34952	37888	39817	88050

Source: Table XII.4 of *CRC Handbook of Tables for Probability and Statistics* (Boca Raton, Fla.: CRC Press, 1966), p. 480, with the kind permission of the publisher. Copyright CRC Press.

Continued

TABLE H *Continued*

Line/Column	(1)	(2)	(3)	(4)	(5)	(6)	(7)	(8)	(9)	(10)	(11)	(12)	(13)	(14)
36	91567	42595	27958	30134	04024	86385	29880	99730	55536	84855	29080	09250	79656	73211
37	17955	56349	90999	49127	20044	59931	06115	20542	18059	02008	73708	83517	36103	42791
38	46503	18584	18845	49618	02304	51038	20655	58727	28168	15475	56942	53389	20562	87338
39	92157	89634	94824	78171	84610	82834	09922	25417	44137	48413	25555	21246	35509	20468
40	14577	62765	35605	81263	39667	47358	56873	56307	61607	49518	89656	20103	77490	18062
41	98427	07523	33362	64270	01638	92477	66969	98420	04880	45585	46565	04102	46880	45709
42	34914	63976	88720	82765	34476	17032	87589	40836	32427	70002	70663	88863	77775	69348
43	70060	28777	39475	46473	23219	53416	94970	25832	69975	94884	19661	72828	00102	66794
44	53976	54914	06990	67245	68350	82948	11398	42878	80287	88267	47363	46634	06541	97809
45	76072	29515	40980	07391	58745	25774	22987	80059	39911	96189	41151	14222	60697	59583
46	90725	52210	83974	29992	65831	38857	50490	83765	55657	14361	31720	57375	56228	41546
47	64364	67412	33339	31926	14883	24413	59744	92351	97473	89286	35931	04110	23726	51900
48	08962	00358	31662	25388	61642	34072	81249	35648	56891	69352	48373	45578	78547	81788
49	95012	68379	93526	70765	10593	04542	76463	54328	02349	17247	28865	14777	62730	92277
50	15664	10493	20492	38391	91132	21999	59516	81652	27195	48223	46751	22923	32261	85653

Answers to Selected Exercises

Chapter 1

1. a. *Functionalist:* There is a value consensus among the administrators, faculty members, and students. They all agree on the importance of the quality of education and for this goal they view tuition raise as necessary.

Conflict theorist: Administrators, faculty members, and students have different vested interests and disagree on the necessity of tuition raise. Students would view it as the result of mismanagement of the budget and a protest movement may arise, especially among students from poor financial background.

Symbolic interactionist: Face-to-face interaction between professors and students is more likely to be intimate at a small private college than at a large public university. The quality of interaction in turn will affect students' attitudes toward tuition raise. Those in close communication with professors are likely to identify with the university goals and support tuition raise, whether they are rich or poor.

1. b. *Functionalist:* The researcher's job is to explain the different components of the university system in terms of their functions and to show how they are interrelated. Key questions raised will be what function each part performs for the university as a social system and how it is related to other parts of the system.

Conflict theorist: The researcher's job is to identify competing interests and those in power and show how the latter maintain their position. Key questions will be who have exerted the power to create existing social arrangements and who benefits from them.

Symbolic interactionist: The researcher's job is to observe in detail symbolic interaction carried on among individual actors. Key questions will be what the unspoken understandings among them are, how actors interpret the situation they are placed in, and the roles played by others.

2. *Functionalist:* Students are likely to share the same values as professors and administrators and support tuition raise regardless of their own financial conditions.

Conflict theorist: Students with meager financial resources are likely to be active in a protest movement against tuition raise on any campus, whether large or small.

Symbolic interactionist: Students in small private colleges are less likely to oppose tuition raise than those in large public universities whether they are financially well-to-do or not.

3. *Functionalist:*

Dependent: attitude toward tuition raise

Independent: role (administrator, professor, student)

Extraneous: financial status

Conflict theorist:

Dependent: attitude toward tuition raise

Independent: financial status of the student

Extraneous: size of the university

Symbolic interactionist:

Dependent: attitude toward tuition raise

Independent: type of school

Extraneous: student's financial status

9. a. Prejudice: Preconceived judgment or opinion
Indicators (narrowed to racial prejudice): Would you vote for a black president? Would you marry a black (or white)?

c. Mental health: Psychological well-being
Indicator: Seeing a psychiatrist, psychologist, or counsellor
Indicator: Self-reported symptoms

f. Alcoholism: Habitual overdrinking of alcohol
Indicator: Frequency and amount of alcohol consumption

11. a. ordinal   **b.** ordinal   **c.** ratio   **d.** ordinal

13. Not necessarily, for reasons such as the following. If the phenomenon being studied is rapidly changing and if surveying the entire population takes a long time, the researcher will be faced with the possibility of having a population that is essentially different at the end of the project than at the beginning. If many interviewers are hired, it is difficult to train them to administer the questionnaire in a uniform way, resulting in low reliability.

15. Sampling error refers to the variability in sample outcomes when samples of the same size are drawn repeatedly from the same population.

17. No, they are different. Descriptive statistics refers to statistical procedures that analyze the characteristics of sample(s), whereas inferential statistics refers to procedures for making inferences about population characteristics based on sample data. On the other hand, the distinction between descriptive and explanatory analysis is one of research goal. In descriptive analysis, characteristics of sample(s) or population(s) are described; in explanatory analysis, causes are sought to account for the characteristics described.

19. If the research findings are based on probability sampling, the probability of the sampling error is known and an estimation of the population characteristics can be made with a known margin of error.

21. Poverty; unemployment; natural hazards such as earthquake and fire.

Chapter 2

1. a.

Single	88	21.10%
Cohabitation	42	10.07
Married	190	45.56
Divorced	56	13.43
Widowed	23	5.52
Other	18	4.32
Total	417	100.00%

b. Married: f = 190; 45.56%

Nonmarried: f = 227; 54.44%

c. Separated, domestic partners, no answer

4. 279

6. a. Aspiration

	N	cf
High school diploma	40	40
Some college	32	72
College or above	28	100
Total	100	

b. Actual

	%	Cum %
0–4	2.7	2.7
5–7	4.8	7.5
Grade school grad	6.4	13.9
9–11	12.2	26.1
High school grad	38.2	64.3
Some college	16.3	80.6
College grad	19.4	100.0

c. As many as 64.3% attained only high school education, while only 40% had such a low aspiration. 80.6% attained some college education, while fewer people (72%) aspire to have only that much education. 28% aspire to have college education or more, as compared to 19.4% who have actually accomplished that level. In short, the aspiration level is higher than the actual attainment.

8. Number of middle class: 2,200; number of working class: 1,650.

11.

	f	%
20.0–29.9	1	8.33
30.0–39.9	1	8.33
40.0–49.9	2	16.67
50.0–59.9	3	25.00
60.0–69.9	4	33.34
70.0–79.9	1	8.33
Total	12	100.00%

13. Hourly wage rate

Original	Improved
0–5.00	0.00–4.99
	5.00–9.99 avoid an overlap
0–5.50	0.51–5.50
	5.51–10.50
0–under 5.00	0.00–4.99

15. A pie chart is preferable to a bar chart when:
Immediate impression of relative size of each category is desired.
Not too many categories exist.
The concept of the total makes sense.
Nominal variable with no order and no time sequence is involved.

17.

	P%, 1970	Degree	*P*%, 1989	Degree
Two parents	88.9	320.04	79.9	287.64
Mother only	9.9	35.64	16.2	58.32
Father only	1.2	4.32	3.9	14.04

19. Both are equally effective.

21. When there are too many leaves.

Chapter 3

1. a. Mode: to acquire occupational skill; variation ratio = .44

   b. There is a high concentration in the mode; less than half of the sample falls outside the mode. The next highest concentration is in the category of "to enhance knowledge": 18.2%.

   Note that the bases for calculating percentages are different in Questions 1 and 2, although the data come from the same sample, the reason being that the numbers of missing values are different for the two questions.

4. Median = 5; IQR = 6

6. For health care: median = 3 or no opinion; range = 5; IQR = 1
For immigration: median = 3; range $\doteq$ 7; IQR = 2

8. Mean = 87.4; s = 9.95; AD = 7.92

10. For students: mean = 23.89; s = 3.84; AD = 3.40; CRV = .16
For parents: mean = 22.3; s = 1.36; AD = 1.22; CRV = .06

11. For euthanasia: P(guilty) = .28; s = .45
For public slander and child support: P = .68; s = .47

13. X = 2.037

15. a. Median = 71; Q_1 = 62; Q_3 = 85.5   **b.** IQR (box length) = 14.5

  c. Boundaries for whiskers: 40.25 and 107.25; actual whiskers: 43 and 100. Boundaries for outliers: from 18.5 to 40.25 and from 107.25 to 129.

General Conceptual Problems

1. Proportion: frequency of a category standardized by sample size.
Percentage: a proportion multiplied by 100.
Rate: a proportion per a selected base.
Mean: the proportion of the category coded as 1 in a dichotomous variable, where categories are coded either as 0 or 1.

3. The balance point of a distribution is the point where a fulcrum could be placed so that weights on one side of the fulcrum are balanced against weights on the other side.

5. A dichotomous nominal variable can be considered as an interval variable by assigning 1 to one category and 0 to the other. The standard deviation can be calculated for such dichotomous variables.

7. The whiskers are the outermost scores on either end of the distribution that are not outliers. An outlier is 1.5 to 3.0 times the box length away from the border of the box.

9. The box plot displays the median and the dispersion in terms of the IQR, as well as outliers and extreme values. With a holistic approach accompanied by numerical precision and visual effectiveness, box plot is also good for the comparison of groups. The histogram and polygon display the frequency distribution, its central tendency, but do not summarize its dispersion as the box plot does. They are also less effective for the comparison of groups.

11. Religious denominations: mode; annual income: mean, median, or mode; degree of patriotism: median or mode; gender: mode.

13. The squared deviations about the mean sum to a minimum value. If any other value is chosen instead of the mean, the sum of squared deviations about this value will be larger.

15. Average deviation: The absolute values of the deviations from the median or mean are taken. An average is then obtained of these absolute values.
Standard deviation: The squared deviations from the mean are computed, summed, and then averaged; the square root of the averaged squared deviation is then taken to undo partially the effect of the initial squaring.

Chapter 4

1. **a.** IV = sex; DV = type of deal
   b. Sex   **c.** By column
   d. In a small town, the %diff = |25|; in a large city, %diff = |6|
   e. Combine bad and medium or split medium equally between bad and good.
   f. Yes, the effect of sex is more pronounced in a small town.

3. **a.** % of rich women = 24
   c. %diff = |20|; men more likely to be rich.

5.

	Males	Females	Total
Dr./Prof.	58 (39.34)	15 (33.66)	73
Mixed	10 (10.78)	10 (9.22)	20
Mr./Ms.	15 (32.88)	46 (28.12)	61
Total	83	71	154

7. **a.** Phi = .30
   b. No, unless there are 30 A's and 30 C+ to B's

9. Phi = .258; %diff = |25|. The values are very close.

11.

	Young			Old			
	M	F	T	M	F	T	
Dr./Prof.	28	5	33	30	10	40	For the young, phi = .623
Other	10	36	46	15	20	35	For the old, phi = .327
Total	38	41	79	45	30	75	

13. For base line: predict medium-bad, the number of correct predictions = 37; errors = 24
    Knowing male: correct predictions = 17; errors = 15
    Knowing female: correct predictions = 20; errors = 9
    Total errors, same as base line = 24; therefore PRE = 0

15. Small town: $\lambda_{yx} = 0$; large city: $\lambda_{yx} = 0$; total: $\lambda_{yx} = 0$

17. **a.** λ_{yx} = .833   **b.** phi = .866; %diff = |85.71|

19. Between compatibility and professional competence
    a. $N_s = 7$; $N_d = 1$; $T_x = 3$; $T_y = 3$; $T_{xy} = 1$
    b. Predict N_s
    c. 1 Error

21. Combining middle and upper class and calculating Q: $Q = .04$

    a. %diff for the $2 \times 2 = |2|$

23. $G = .75$

25. For the first table: $\phi = .58$; %diff $= |50|$; Yule's $Q = -1$; $\lambda_{yx} = 0$
For the second table: Cramer's $V = 1$; G and the d's $= .2$; $\lambda_{yx} = 1$

General Conceptual Problems

3. PRE $= 0$ does not necessarily mean statistical independence, although statistical independence means PRE $= 0$.
When a PRE measure such as lambda $= 0$, phi based on statistical independence may or may not be zero.

5. a.

$\lambda = 1$				$\lambda = 0$			
10	0	0		15	20	10	45
0	10	0		3	5	5	13
0	0	10		1	10	5	16
				19	35	20	74

    c.

$\phi = 1$			$\phi = 0$	
10	0		10	2
0	10		15	3

7. The base-line prediction is the criterion prediction rule against which other prediction models are compared. The base line is usually set as the prediction based on the central tendency (mean, mode).

10. The coefficients should have absolute values that range from 0 to 1, with sign to indicate positive or negative relationship whenever applicable. They should also have standardized and meaningful interpretation of these upper and lower limits and values that can be interpreted precisely as in the case of PRE measures whose values indicate proportionate reduction in errors with reference to the base-line model.

12. Yule's $Q = \dfrac{Ns - Nd}{Ns + Nd}$

$$= \dfrac{Ns + Nd - 2\min(Ns, Nd)}{Ns + Nd} = \dfrac{.5(Ns + Nd) - \min(Ns, Nd)}{.5(Ns + Nd)}$$

$$= \dfrac{E_1 - E_2}{E_1}$$

Chapter 5

4. Regressing GNP (Y) on educational expenditure (X): $Y' = -2.82 + 2.76X$
Regressing educational expenditure (X) on GNP (Y): $X' = 2.78 + 0.18Y$

5. a. $Y = a + bX$ an equation of a straight line (1)
 $Y_1 = a + bX_1$ since (X_1, Y_1) lies on the line (2)
 $Y_2 = a + bX_2$ (3)
 $Y_2 - Y_1 = b(X_2 - X_1)$ subtract (2) from (3)
 $b = \dfrac{Y_2 - Y_1}{X_2 - X_1}$

b. $b_{yx} = .5; b_{xy} = 2$

7. In case of twins, the conditions are not the same as those under which the regression equation was calculated.

9. a. $Y' = -.3 + 1.9X$

 c. Yes; sum of squared residuals equals 1.1 when using regression equation calculated in 9a, whereas using the other equations the squared residuals sum to 8.75 in both cases.

11. a. For crime (Y) and income (X): $r = b^* = .853$, while $b_{yx} = 5.832$

 c. r and b^* are regression coefficients calculated on standardized scores, while b_{yx} is a regression coefficient calculated on raw data.

 e. The second highest positive correlation is between income and welfare: .753; the third highest is between education and unemployment: .733. The highest negative correlation is found between income and suicide: −.665.

13. a. $r = .21$ **c.** $b_{yx} = -.7$ and $s_{xy} = -1750$

15. To calculate r, standardized scores are used; hence no difference.

17. $\sum(Y - Y') = 0$ because the least-squares line is a running mean. Therefore, the whole term equals 0.

19. $r_s = .85$

21. Eta squared = .1966

23. When the relationship between the variables is in fact linear.

General Conceptual Problems

 1. a. Visual representation of the relationship, positive or negative

 b. Checking of the assumption of linearity

 c. Checking of other conditions such as degree of clusteredness, outliers

 3. Pearson's r measures the change in the Y (or X) standard score per unit change in the X (or Y) standard score.

 5. Nonlinear relationship; small variance in Y for each unit change in X

 7. The ratio of the explained SS to the total SS, where the explained SS represents the improvement in prediction using the regression line, while the total SS refers to the original squared errors in predicting Y from its mean.

 9. For Pearson's r: conditional mean for an interval of values of X
 For correlation ratio: conditional mean for a discrete value of X

11. The Spearman's rho is a Pearson's r calculated on ranks. Since r^2 is a PRE measure, so is r_s^2. The latter measures the reduction in error variance when predicting the ranks of Y with knowledge of the ranks of X.

13. Yes, the standardized regression coefficient gives a better idea of the strength of association.

Chapter 6

1. $0 \leq p(X) \leq 1$

3. A probability is a number that is assigned to an event to indicate the likelihood or the chance that the event will occur. Probabilities are determined based on the interpretation the researcher places on the concept. Three such interpretations are identified in the text. When the classic *a priori* interpretation (f/N) is used as an estimate of a probability, an assumption is made that every element in the sample space has an equal probability of occurrence. This equiprobability assumption is reasonable for a simple game of tossing a coin or drawing a card. However, in social research on human behavior, the equiprobable event assumption may or may not be tenable depending on actual sampling procedures.

5. a. Not mutually exclusive, not exhaustive categories

   b. Valid sample space: events are exhaustive and mutually exclusive, width of the interval need not be equal

7. {H1} {H2} {H3} {H4} {H5} {H6}
   {T1} {T2} {T3} {T4} {T5} {T6}

9. {minority1,sanction1} {minority1,sanction2} . . .
   {minority2,sanction1} {minority2,sanction2} . . .
   {dominant1,sanction1} {dominant1,sanction2} . . .
   {dominant2,sanction1} {dominant2,sanction2} . . .
   (4)(4) = 16 events

11. a. {HHH} {HHT} {HTH} {HTT}
      {THH} {THT} {TTH} {TTT}

13.

Game 1	Game 2	Game 3	Game 4	Game 5
	win +3		*win +3*	
win +2	lose +1	win +2	lose +1	win +2
lose 0		*lose 0*		*lose 0*

15. a. 7! **b.** $\dfrac{9!}{(9-7)!} = \dfrac{9!}{2!}$

17. $\dfrac{10!}{(10-3)!} = (10)(9)(8)$

19. $\dbinom{7}{3} = \dfrac{7!}{3!(7-3)!} = 35$

21. 4 whites can be chosen from 8 whites in $\binom{8}{4}$ ways.

3 blacks can be chosen from 5 blacks in $\binom{5}{3}$ ways.

Thus the committee can be chosen in $\binom{8}{4}\binom{5}{3}$ ways.

23. a. $\left(\dfrac{4}{52}\right)^3$ **b.** $\left(\dfrac{4}{52}\right)\left(\dfrac{3}{51}\right)\left(\dfrac{2}{50}\right) = \dfrac{\binom{4}{3}}{\binom{52}{3}}$ **c.** $1 - \left(\dfrac{48}{52}\right)^3$

25. a. $AB'C'$ or $A'BC'$ or $A'B'C$ **c.** $A'B'C'$

27. a. $\dfrac{\binom{542}{1}\binom{112}{3}}{\binom{654}{4}}$ **c.** $\dfrac{\binom{34}{2}\binom{7}{2}\binom{508}{2}\binom{105}{2}}{\binom{654}{8}}$

29. a. $\dfrac{\binom{4}{2}\binom{48}{1}}{\binom{52}{3}}$ **c.** $3!\left(\dfrac{13}{52}\right)^3$ **e.** $\dfrac{\binom{13}{1}\binom{13}{1}\binom{13}{1}\binom{13}{0}}{\binom{52}{3}}$

31. a. $\binom{8}{1}(.1)^1(.9)^7 = .3826$ **c.** $(.1)(.03) = .003$

e. With independent selection: $\left[\binom{8}{3}(.1)^3(.9)^5\right]\left[\binom{8}{3}(.03)^3(.97)^5\right] = .0000429$

General Conceptual Problems

1. Probability theory provides the foundation for inferential statistics. The use of inferential statistics permits the researcher to conclude whether she or he has found something of significance that could be used as a basis for constructing a theory. This point will be discussed in detail in Chapter 10.

3. a $p(A \text{ or } B) = p(A) + p(B)$
$p(A \text{ and } B) = 0$

b. $p(A \text{ and } B) = p(A)p(B)$
$p(A \text{ or } B) = p(A) + p(B) - p(A)p(B)$

5. Because elementary events are mutually exclusive: $p(A) = p(E_1) + p(E_2) + p(E_3)$

7. Permutation: an arrangement of all or part of a set of objects with regard to order. Combination: the number of ways of selecting r objects from N without regard to order.

9. $\binom{5}{1} + \binom{5}{2} + \binom{5}{3} + \binom{5}{4} + \binom{5}{5} = 31$ or $2^5 - 1 = 31$

Chapter 7

1. **a.** $\left(\frac{1}{2}\right)^3$ **c.** $\binom{3}{1}\left(\frac{1}{2}\right)^1\left(\frac{1}{2}\right)^2$

3. **a.** $\displaystyle\sum_{K=2}^{7}\binom{7}{K}\left(\frac{1}{4}\right)^K\left(\frac{3}{4}\right)^{7-K} = 1 - P_0 - P_1 = 1 - \left(\frac{3}{4}\right)^7 - \binom{7}{1}\left(\frac{1}{4}\right)^1\left(\frac{3}{4}\right)^6$

5. $E(X) = 4.95$; $V(X) = 4.50$

7. IQ score, height, mistakes, etc.

9. **a.** $z = \dfrac{12 - 10}{5} = .4$; $z = \dfrac{15 - 10}{5} = 1.0$; $p(.4 \le z \le 1.0) = .3413 - .1554 = .1859$

  c. $z = \dfrac{7 - 10}{5} = -.6$; $p(z \ge -.6) = .2257 + .5000 = .7257$

11. **a.** $z = .84$; $X = 80$; $\overline{X} = 72.3$; $s = 9.17$

  c. $z = .25$; $X = 82.3$; $\overline{X} = 72.3$; $s = 40$

13. Standardize to a distribution with a mean of 0 and an s of 1 first; then convert this standard distribution to a new distribution with a mean of 500 and an s of 100 as follows:
$$\frac{X - 447.45}{100.92} = (z)(100) + 500$$

16. Jury verdict: $p(X \le 2) = .9716$; judge verdict: $p(X \le 2) = .0419$

21. $p(X \le 65) = .4681$; $z = -.08$

General Conceptual Problems

1. If a normal distribution can be assumed, the probability of an interval of values occurring can be computed, given its mean and standard deviation, since the normal distribution is defined as a function of these two parameters.

3. A binomial experiment
   a. The experiment consists of N identical trials.
   b. Each trial results in one of two outcomes: success or failure.
   c. The success on a single trial is equal to p and remains the same from trial to trial. The probability of a failure is equal to $(1 - p) = q$.
   d. The trials are independent.
   e. The experimenter is interested in the number of successes in the N trials.

5. Answer is d.

7. The sampling distribution of a statistic gives the probabilities of the occurrence of different values of the statistic when samples are drawn repeatedly from a population with a hypothesized parameter. Therefore, the distribution provides the link between sampled statistics and a population parameter, permitting the researcher to make inferences about a parameter based on sample results.

9. No, only normal distribution can be standardized to the standard normal.

11. As the sample size increases, the standard error of sample means decreases.

Chapter 8

1. Functionalism: Rape represents a serious disturbance to the equilibrium of the social system. Catching, convicting, and sentencing the offender restores the equilibrium. Through his or her ability to convict and sentence the offender, the judge plays a key role in affirming the central values of society and restoring social balance. Therefore, a judge is more likely to convict than a jury.

3. Proposition: Compared to a jury, the judge has more responsibility for maintaining consensus and social equilibrium.

   Assumptions: Rape is dysfunctional; once equilibrium is disturbed, it must be restored; conviction represents restoration and affirmation.

   If *P*, then *E*: If judge's central role is to maintain social consensus and equilibrium and if rape is a disturbance to society, then a judge is more likely to convict an alleged rapist than a jury.

   E or not *E*

   P confirmed or disconfirmed

5. **a.** Research hypothesis: $\pi \geq .4$, where π = proportion of cheating

   b. H_0: $\pi = .39$ specific statement

   H_0: $\pi > .39$ diffuse statement

7. Type I error: reject $\pi = .4$ when true. If Type I error is not reduced, the instructor may conclude that there is more widespread cheating when there is not. The instructor may become overly suspicious, which may have the effect of a self-fulfilling prophecy on the students.

   Type II error: Not reject H_0 when false. If Type II error is not reduced, the instructor may conclude that cheating is not a problem when it is. The instructor may become too trusting, which may also induce more cheating.

9. At α of .01: when $N = 50$, power = .7054

   when $N = 100$, power = .9582

   when $N = 200$, power = .9997

   As *N* increases, so does the power.

11. At α of .05, power = .3228

13. Based on data in Section 8.11, H_0: $\mu = 2.1$; H_1: $\mu \neq 2.1$. At α of .01, two-tailed, c.v. of ± 2.58, the z value remains the same at 3.539. Reject H_0.

15. Type II error = .281; power = .719 at α of .05

General Conceptual Problems

1. Statistical inference is based on the knowledge of exact (or approximate) probabilities of events occurring given certain assumptions. It is tested hypothetico-deductively through setting up and eliminating one of two alternative hypotheses, thus following logically valid procedures. Apart from random error, other biases have been controlled. It is an objective and standardized procedure based on empirical evidence.

3. a. Summarizes, gives meaning to, and interprets data

   b. Links discrete events into a coherent body of explanation

   c. Provides guidelines for developing hypotheses and selection of phenomena to observe

5. At the conclusion of testing, a researcher may be subject to making a Type I or II error, but not both. These errors are inversely related and cannot be reduced simultaneously without increasing sample size. (Type I + Type II) does not equal unity. Type I error is determined from the H_0 sampling distribution and set by the α level. Type II error is determined from the H_1 sampling distribution and cannot be measured precisely unless the alternative hypothesis is stated in a specific rather than diffuse form.

7. As the sample size increases, Type I error decreases, power increases, and Type II error decreases for a given significance level.

9. Region of rejection is the area where the probability of a sample outcome occurring is so small under the null hypothesis that, if the outcome does fall into this region, we can reject H_0 with minimal risk of being wrong.

11. Power of the test discriminates between a pair of hypotheses, H_0 and H_1. The power refers to the probability of rejecting H_0 when it is false.

Chapter 9

1. $t = -17.46$; reject H_0 at beyond .0001.

3. As sample size increases from 100 to 150, the t value increases also from .765 to .939. Therefore, a higher significance level is obtained for the same difference by increasing sample size.

5. a. H_0: $\mu = 27,900$; H_1: $\mu \neq 27,900$; $\alpha = .01$;   c.v. $= \pm 2.617$

   b. $t = 5.679$

7. $\chi^2 = 29.758$; two-tailed, .05 level, c.v. of 24.4330 and 59.3417; fail to reject H_0 as chi-square value falls in between these two critical values

9. $\chi^2 = 17.60$; one-tailed, .05 level, c.v. of 10.117; since obtained chi-square value is not smaller than c.v., do not reject H_0

11. At α of .01, critical $D = .238$, obtained $D = .145$; fail to reject H_0

13. At α of .05, critical D = .375, obtained D = .268; fail to reject H_0

15. At α of .05, critical D = .375, obtained D = .25; fail to reject H_0; combining the categories reduces significance level.

17. χ^2 = 25.146, one-third of its original value. Multiply the chi square based on percentages by $N/100$ to obtain the correct chi-square value.

19. a. χ^2 = 11.468; critical value = 9.488 at α of .05; reject H_0

    c. For the same obtained chi-square value, the fewer the categories, the more significant the value.

General Conceptual Problems

1. Yes, the chi-square value is affected by the sample size. If proportions in the categories remain the same, the chi-square value varies according to the number of cases. If each cell frequency is doubled, the chi-square value is doubled. Thus the significance level increases with sample size if the proportionate sample distribution remains unchanged.

3. The chi-square distribution approaches a normal distribution as the degrees of freedom approach infinity. The chi-square and normal distributions are related in the sense that the sum of the k squared standard normal scores equals the chi square with df = k.

5. The K–S test compares the sample and a theoretical population distribution by comparing their cumulative frequency distributions. For various intervals, the proportions of cases are computed; then cumulative proportions are obtained. The greatest divergence between the two cumulative distributions for corresponding points is used as a test statistic. The test involves determining the probability that such a divergence could have occurred by chance if the sample were drawn from the theoretical distribution.

7. Examples of families of distributions: t distribution by df, chi-square distribution by df, and K–S distribution by N.

9. Yes, the K–S test assumes a continuous population distribution, although the sample data are usually discrete. With a large number of ties, the K–S test can still be used with appropriate grouping of data into ordered categories. Since cumulative frequencies are being compared within predetermined intervals, the effect of ties is not important.

Chapter 10

1. $E(\overline{X}) = \mu$; $E(s^2) \neq \sigma^2$

4. $E(\overline{X}_i - \mu)^2 < E(mdn_i - mdn)^2$

5. 95% CI = [1.015 to 1.025]

7. [1.009, 1.031]; [1.013, 1.027]; [1.016, 1.024]. As N increases, the width of the interval decreases. In other words, with the larger sample size, the same precision in estimation is attained with smaller margins of error.

9. $N = 384.16$

11. $k = .196$

13. a. 95% CI = [.288, .508], using conservative approach
95% CI = [.291, .505], using sample data

    b. $N = 384.16$

15. a. 99% CI = [.495, .725]   **b.** $N = 665.64$

17. $P = .39$ or 39%

General Conceptual Problems

1. Point estimate from sample, confidence level with which to estimate, and precision, the degree of accuracy with which to estimate

3. One-tailed test cannot be conceptualized as a part of interval estimation. Interval estimation is comparable to two-tailed tests only.

5. $\overline{X} \pm 1.96 \dfrac{s}{\sqrt{N-1}}$ refers to the interval between 1.96 standard error units above and below the sample mean. Since the sampling distribution of the sample mean is approximately normal when the sample size is sufficiently large, 95% of these intervals will contain the population mean when calculated from samples drawn repeatedly from the same population.

Chapter 11

1. $t = 14.963$; using the conservative value of df = 60, one-tailed, reject H_0 at α of .01

3. $t = 5.011$; two-tailed test; reject H_0 at α of .01

6. $t = 6.017$; df = 79; two-tailed; reject H_0 at .01

8. Data set 1: $t = -.978$; fail to reject H_0

    Data set 2: $t = -3.150$; reject H_0 at .01

10. $t = .360$; two-tailed; fail to reject H_0 at .05

12. $z = -2.43$; two-tailed; reject H_0 at .05

14. $z = -3.77$; two-tailed; reject H_0 at .01

16. $p(z < .82) = .79 =$ Type II error

18. $U' = 115.5$; $U = 16.5$; critical value = 28; reject H_0 at .01

General Conceptual Problems

1. If independent random samples of sizes N_1 and N_2 are drawn from populations with finite means of μ_1 and μ_2 and finite variances of σ_1^2 and σ_2^2, respectively, then the sampling distribution of the difference between the two sample means $(\overline{X}_1 - \overline{X}_2)$ will be approximately normal with a mean of $(\mu_1 - \mu_2)$ and a variance of $(\sigma_1^2/N_1 + \sigma_2^2/N_2)$, provided that N_1 and N_2 are sufficiently large.

3. Paired difference analysis is applied when the selection of a case in one sample implies the selection of a case in the second sample. The following are situations where it is applied: matched pairs of experimental and control groups, the same individuals in before-and-after experimental designs, and pairs of parent and child, husband and wife.

5. If an independent random sample is drawn, every random combination of sample elements is independent of every other combination. Thus the subgroups generated by categories of an independent variable will constitute independent subsamples.

7. $(N_1 - 1) + (N_2 - 1) = N_1 + N_2 - 2$

   Loss of 1 df in computing s_1^2 from $\overline{X}_1$

   Loss of 1 df in computing s_2^2 from $\overline{X}_2$

9. Yes, it implies a relationship, but a significant difference can be found when N is large even if the association is minimal.

Chapter 12

1. **a.** $\hat{\sigma}_W^2 = 3.0$ **b.** $\hat{\sigma}_B^2 = 5.0$ **c.** $F = 1.67$, fail to reject H_0

3. **a.** critical $F = 3.02$ **c.** critical $F = 9.95$

5. $F = 1.67$; fail to reject H_0 at the .05 level

7. $H = 15.59$; corrected for ties $H = 15.93$; reject H_0 at beyond .01 level

9. **a.** $\chi^2 = 20.733$; df $= 3$; $p = .0001$
   b. $\chi^2 = 22.004$; df $= 6$; $p = .0012$
   c. $\chi^2 = 6.212$; df $= 3$; $p = .1017$
   d. $\chi^2 = 49.557$; df $= 12$; $p = .0000$

   $\Sigma(\chi^2) = 22.004 + 6.212 + 20.733 = 48.949 \neq 49.557$

   The sum the of three chi squares does not equal the original chi square exactly. However, if we used the likelihood ratio chi square, discussed in Chapter 14, additivity would be exact.

   The distinction between professional and nonprofessional is large; also the distinction within the professional occupations is large. However, the distinction between businessmen and truck drivers is small and insignificant.

General Conceptual Problems

1. ANOVA tests the difference of means of several populations through analyzing variances. In ANOVA, two estimates of the common population variance are compared. Under H_0 of equal population means, the ratio of these two estimates will be 1. The departure from the ratio of 1 indicates that the population means are not equal.

3. ANOVA problems can be approached as problems of improvement in prediction. In regression analysis, if no information is given about the independent variable, the

prediction of the dependent variable would be its mean (the grand mean). In regression analysis the deviation of each score from this grand mean, the total variation in ANOVA, is subdivided into two components: within-group variation and between-group variation. The between-group variation, which is the sum of squared deviations of the group means from the grand mean, is the explained SS in regression analysis. The within-group variation, which is the sum of squared deviations of the individual scores from its group mean, is the unexplained SS in regression analysis.

In ANOVA, group means are the predicted values for each category of the independent variable; in regression, the predicted values represent running means for the continuous independent variable.

5. $SS_T = SS_B + SS_W$

$$\sum\sum(X - \overline{X})^2 = \sum\sum(\overline{X}_j - \overline{X})^2 + \sum\sum(X - \overline{X}_j)^2$$

SS_B: the sum of squared deviations of group means from the grand mean.

SS_W: the sum of squared deviations of each score from its group mean.

7. A sample mean, in such cases, is being compared repeatedly to other sample means. These repeated comparisons cannot be considered independent, while the α level is determined on the assumption of independent tests. Therefore, the α does not yield a true estimate of the probability of Type I error in repeated testing.

9. Dependent variable: ordinal, continuous

Independent variable: nominal

Random sampling

Independent samples (mutual independence among various samples)

11. **a.** One-way ANOVA

   b. K–W test

   c. Chi-square test

Chapter 13

1. $\chi^2 = 4.31$; reject H_0 at α of .05

3. **a.** $\chi^2 = 1.1126$ **b.** $\chi^2 = 18.2025$ **c.** $\chi^2 = 4.2524$

   The df = 2 for all test statistics; only the chi-square value of 18.20 is significant at the .05 level.

5. $z = 1.27$; fail to reject H_0 at α of .05

7. Chi square based on table given in answer to Question 2b, Chapter 4:

   $\chi^2 = 34.55$; df = 1; reject H_0 at beyond .001 level

9. $z = .16$; fail to reject H_0 at α of .05

11. $t = 4.317$; reject H_0 at beyond the .01 level

General Conceptual Problems

1. Chi square is used as a test of significance because the chi-square test statistic approximates the chi-square distribution for a given df. Phi is a measure of association based on chi square. Since chi square varies by N, phi is adjusted for N as follows:

$$\phi = \sqrt{\chi^2/N}.$$

3. For $N \geq 50$, $z = \dfrac{(Ns - Nd) - 0}{\hat{\sigma}_{Ns - Nd}}$. The test is based on the fact that the difference between the numbers of concordant and discordant pairs distributes normally.

5. In a regression problem, the null hypothesis tests that the conditional means of Y for every value of an interval variable X are equal. In an analysis of variance, the null hypothesis tests that the conditional means of Y for each category of a nominal or categorical variable X are equal. Using the same assumptions, the test statistic is the same in each case.

7. $r = .8$ in a sample alone does not tell whether or not the relationship is significant, that is, also found in the population. A test of significance must be performed to determine the probability that the $r = .8$ is not due to sampling error.

9. Total SS $= \Sigma(Y - \overline{Y})^2$

Explained SS $= \Sigma(Y' - \overline{Y})^2 = r^2\big[\Sigma(Y - \overline{Y})^2\big]$

Unexplained SS $= (1 - r^2)\big[\Sigma(Y - \overline{Y})^2\big]$

The total SS is the sum of squared deviations of the observed Y values from the mean of Y, the dependent variable. What is explained by the regression equation is measured by the sum of squared differences between the predicted value and the base-line prediction of the mean of the dependent variable. The unexplained component is the sum of squared deviations of the observed value of the dependent variable from the value predicted by the regression equation.

Chapter 14

1. $Y =$ hostility; $X =$ occupation

a.
Y_1	229.5
Y_2	229.5

b.
	X_1	X_2
Y_1	114.75	114.75
Y_2	114.75	114.75

c. Model: {Y}

	X_1	X_2
Y_1	147.5	147.5
Y_2	82.0	82.0

Model: {X}

	X_1	X_2
Y_1	81.5	148.0
Y_2	81.5	148.0

Model: {X, Y}

	X_1	X_2
Y_1	105.0	190.0
Y_2	58.0	106.0

Model: {XY}

	X_1	X_2
Y_1	81.0	214.0
Y_2	82.0	82.0

2. {*X, Y, Z, W, P, Q, YZ, WP, WQ, PQ, QPW*}

  {*X, Y, Z, W, P, Q, XY, ZW, ZP, WP, ZWP*}

  {*X, Y, Z, W, P, Q, YZ, YW, YP, ZW, ZP, WP, YZW, YZP, ZWP, WPY, YZWP*}

  {*X, Y, Z, W, P, XY, XZ, XW, YZ, YW, ZW, XYZ, XYW, XZW, YZW, XYZW*}

3. First-order odds for use of violence: 50/50
   Conditional odds for males: 25/25; same for females
   Second-order odds: (25/25)/(25/25) = 1

   First-order odds: 40/60
   Conditional odds for males: 20/30; same for females
   Second-order odds: (20/30)/(20/30) = 1

   First-order odds: 40/60
   Conditional odds for males: 18/27; for females: 22/33
   Second-order odds: (18/27)/(22/33) = .667/.667 = 1

   Second-order odds: (30/15)/(10/45) = 2/.222 = 9.091 for the fourth table

   Second-order odds: (40/5)/(0/55) = undefined for the fifth table

General Conceptual Problems

1. Association: the distribution of *Y* is not the same for each value (category) of *X*.
   Concordance: the rank order within a pair of subjects on variable *X* is the same as the rank order within the same pair on variable *Y*.
   Correlation: the association between two interval variables.
   Covariation: a unit change in a quantitative variable is accompanied by a systematic amount of change in another quantitative variable.
   Causal relation: nonspurious association between the antecedent variable and the succeeding variable.

2. Base-line model: model of no effect when all expected cell frequencies are equal and they sum to *N*.

   Saturated model: model that includes all possible effects when the expected cell frequencies are identical to the raw data.

5. Hierarchical model: the existence of a higher-order effect implies the existence of lower-order effects. For example, {*XYZ*} = {*X, Y, Z, XY, ZY, ZX, XYZ*}.

7. The strength of the effect of a category of a variable or interaction of categories of variables. Lambdas sum to zero across all categories of a variable in a loglinear analysis.

9. The second-order odds ratio = 1.

Chapter 15

1. **a.** $b_{y1.2} = -.04$ **b.** Same value

3. $Y' = a + b_{y1.23}X_1 + b_{y2.13}X_2 + b_{y3.12}X_3$

$$b_{y1.23} = \frac{b_{y1.2} - (b_{y3.2})(b_{31.2})}{1 - b_{13.2}(b_{31.2})}$$

$$a = \overline{Y} - b_{y1.23}\overline{X}_1 - b_{y2.13}\overline{X}_2 - b_{y3.12}\overline{X}_3$$

5. **a.** .3058; −.3058; .8; -.1890

   b. No inconsistent data

7. $r_{1y.2} = \dfrac{r_{1y} - r_{12}r_{y2}}{\sqrt{(1 - r_{12}^2)(1 - r_{y2}^2)}} = 0$

   $r_{1y} = r_{12}r_{y2}$

   $$r_{12.y} = \frac{r_{12} - r_{1y}r_{2y}}{\sqrt{(1 - r_{1y}^2)(1 - r_{2y}^2)}} = \frac{r_{12} - (r_{12}r_{y2})r_{2y}}{\sqrt{(1 - r_{1y}^2)(1 - r_{2y}^2)}}$$

   $$= \frac{r_{12}(1 - r_{y2}^2)}{\sqrt{(1 - r_{1y}^2)(1 - r_{2y}^2)}} = r_{12}\sqrt{\frac{1 - r_{y2}^2}{1 - r_{1y}^2}}$$

9. $1 - R_{y.12}^2 = .982$

   $1 - r_{y2.1}^2 = .991$

11. $R_{y.12}^2 = r_{y1}^2 + r_{y2.1}^2(1 - r_{y1}^2)$

    When $r_{12} = 0$:

    $$r_{y2.1}^2 = \frac{[r_{y2} - (r_{y1})(r_{21})]^2}{(1 - r_{y1}^2)(1 - r_{21}^2)} = \frac{r_{y2}^2}{1 - r_{y1}^2}$$

    $$R_{y.12}^2 = r_{y1}^2 + \frac{r_{y2}^2}{1 - r_{y1}^2}(1 - r_{y1}^2)$$

13. **a.** Adjusted $R^2 = -.64$

15. **a.** $t = 3.477$; reject H_0 at α of .01

    b. $t = 2.623$; reject H_0 at α of .05

General Conceptual Problems

1. The coefficient of multiple determination measures the proportion of variance in the dependent variable that is accounted for simultaneously by two or more independent variables. The coefficient of determination measures the proportion of variance in the dependent variable accounted for by only one independent variable.

3. The addition of an independent variable does not increase R^2 if (a) it is highly correlated with independent variables already included, or (b) it is not correlated with the dependent variable.

5. Partial correlation is the correlation between two variables while controlling for other variable(s). It is calculated as the correlation between the residuals of the two variables, both regressed on the same control variable(s).

7. The beta weight is asymmetric in that it determines either the extent to which X affects Y or the extent to which Y affects X, but not their mutual effect on each other.

Index

V.J.
Sony Latin Amer. Prog.
Hernando de Aguirre 61,
                        Offici
    Santiago.
            CHILE